THE
MOODY
HANDBOOK
OF
THEOLOGY

THE
MOODY
HANDBOOK
OF
THEOLOGY

PAUL ENNS

MOODY PRESS
CHICAGO

Library of Congress Cataloging in Publication Data

Enns, Paul P., 1937-
 The Moody handbook of theology / by Paul P. Enns.
  p.   cm.
 Includes indexes.
 ISBN 0-8024-3428-2
 1. Theology—Handbooks, manuals, etc.   I. Title.
BR118.E67   1989
230—dc20   89-3380
                                                              CIP

9 10 8

Printed in the United States of America

This book is dedicated to
the members of "Kitchen Table Theology 101"
Helen, my wife, and
Terry and Jeremy, my sons,
with whom I have shared many of these doctrines

CONTENTS

INDEX OF CHARTS

FOREWORD

There is no higher activity in which the mind may be engaged than the pursuit of a knowledge of God. Since man through the exercise of his mind alone can never come to a knowledge of God (1 Cor. 1:19-20; 2:14) he is dependent upon the revelation of Himself which God has given to him (1 Cor. 2:9-10). Since God has revealed Himself through creation (Rom. 1:19-20), some seek Him through a study of the natural sciences, only to find that what can be learned through this area is limited and incomplete. God has revealed Himself at various times and in various ways (Heb. 1:1) and has caused that revelation to be accurately recorded by inspiration of the Holy Spirit in an inerrant Scripture. If mortals really want to know God they must give themselves to a study of the written Word of God.

People may pursue this knowledge by different approaches to the Bible. Some will develop a biblical theology, in which the theologian will synthesize the teachings of the Bible, deriving these truths, stage by stage, within the time boundaries of particular biblical eras or authors' lifetimes. Others will develop a systematic theology, in which Bible doctrines may be considered comprehensively and organized in a philosophical or logical format. Others will study doctrines according to their historical development throughout time from the close of the canon of Scripture until the present day. This study considers both the erroneous interpretations which were rejected by the church as well as the true conclusions approved by it. One may be safeguarded from error by considering the history of the interpretation of any doctrine, rejecting the false and accepting the true. Others may concentrate on contemporary theology. This study is important in order to present the truth of the Bible in the context of current ideologies. Still others may pursue the study of Scripture by comparing various systems of theology which have arisen through the course of church history. There is certainly merit and benefit in all these approaches. Volumes on any one of these methods have been written and are readily available for in-depth consultation.

In this present work Dr. Paul P. Enns brings together in one volume a compendium including all these theological methods. Whatever the interest of the student he will find pertinent material at hand without having to go from volume to volume or from author to author to bring this material together. The author begins with a treatment of biblical theology, and follows this with sequential studies of systematic theology, historical theology, dogmatic theology, and contemporary theology. Thus, within a common analysis, these various approaches to the knowledge of God in the Word are assembled, explained, and demonstrated in this *Moody Handbook of Theology*.

This work is written out of an unshakable committment to the integrity, authority, and inerrancy of the Word of God. It is written from an evangelical viewpoint, although many divergent interpretations and systems are presented and evaluated in the light of the Word of God. The author seeks to fulfill the injunction of Titus 2:1, "Speak the things which are fitting for sound doctrine."

This work may be used by any serious student who desires to understand God's revelation, whether it is considered biblically, systematically, or historically. As a result the attentive reader will be able to fit biblical truth into current theological thinking or into various systems that have arisen to organize God's truth.

May the God who has revealed Himself be pleased to use this work to lead many into a knowledge of Himself.

J. Dwight Pentecost
Distinguished Professor Emeritus
Dallas Theological Seminary
Dallas, Texas

PREFACE

On several occasions students have greeted me after a seminary lecture with "What's an amil?" or "What is the difference between systematic theology and biblical theology?" or "What is liberation theology?" These questions made me aware that there is a need for a general introductory work in the entire area of theology that can provide answers to simple, basic questions. It is with that in mind that the *Moody Handbook of Theology* has been written. It's intended audience is not only Bible institute, college, and seminary students, but also Sunday school teachers and other lay people who are interested in learning more about theology.

Many theological works are entirely too advanced for the average reader or beginning student of theology. Often the student must consult numerous works to find simple answers to basic questions. This *Handbook of Theology* is not intended to be definitive or exhaustive; rather, it is an *introductory* work that will provide basic answers for questions in biblical theology, systematic theology, historical theology, dogmatic theology, and contemporary theology. Although there are many helpful books in each of these areas, there is a need for a basic work that overviews the entire spectrum of theology. It is that purpose this *Handbook of Theology* is intended to fulfill.

Because of the magnitude of the subjects covered, it is, of course, impossible to deal with all the sources and all the theologians in each of the areas. New theologies are emerging constantly! In some categories such as contemporary theology, only representative works and theologians have been cited.

Although the discussion in the five major areas is intended to provide a basic introduction, additional information can be obtained through the section at the end of each chapter designated "For Further Study." Under this area a number of sources have been listed to facilitate research on the given topic. Beginning study should pursue the sources cited by a single asterisk

(*). These are generally brief books, single chapters in books, articles in dictionaries, or, on some occasions, a more advanced title so cited because of its major importance. More demanding studies are normally designated by two asterisks (**) for those who want to expand their research.

It should be understood that the selections for the source lists were made from the standpoint of what would be most helpful to the general reader; as a result, the lists are not exhaustive. Therefore, some worthy works have been omitted.

In addition to the book lists, indexes are also provided at the end of the book for the reader to look up a subject by topic, author, and Scripture.

Careful documentation in the form of endnotes is present throughout the book. At times the number of these notes may seem alternately deficient or excessive. However, every deliberate effort has been made to include or omit documentation according to the estimated needs of the readers. These endnotes not only locate the sources and verification for quotations or ideas, but they also provide the reader with additional avenues for study.

Objectivity, fairness, and accuracy in presenting various viewpoints has been a serious goal in the production of this book. Recognized authorities within each theological category or viewpoint, such as Calvinism, Arminianism, and Catholicism, have been selected as representatives of those positions. Any oversight in proper documentation of ideas has been entirely unintentional.

Recognition must also be given to certain people who have been influential in this work. I wish to thank Moody Press for its support and willingness to undertake the project. My appreciation is extended to Dana Gould, Executive Editor of Moody Press, for his helpfulness, encouragement, and availability to discuss the project. And thanks to Bob Ramey, editor at Moody Press, for his graciousness and for his many useful suggestions in the editing process.

Four individuals have been particularly influential in shaping my theological thinking and that debt must be acknowledged. I wish to thank Dr. William R. Eichhorst, President and Professor of Systematic Theology, Winnipeg Bible College and Winnipeg Theological Seminary. He gave me my initial love for the doctrinal truths of Scripture. His commitment to the authority and doctrines of Scripture helped shape my theological thinking and my confidence in the Word of God. I am also indebted to the professors at Dallas Theological Seminary who through their writings and lectures have been influential in my theological awareness. In particular I honor Drs. John F. Walvoord, J. Dwight Pentecost, and Charles C. Ryrie. Their abilities to communicate God's truth with expertise and insight in speaking and in writing have been an inspiration to me.

I wish to thank my wife and sons (to whom this book is dedicated) for their support, encouragement, and sacrifice during my writing. Through their commitment to this ministry, an arduous task has been lightened. Each of us is committed to the historic doctrines of the Christian faith and many a dinner hour has been spent discussing the wonderful truths of Scripture.

Above all I thank my Lord, who has energized me in this project. It has been a lengthy, time-consuming project, yet the Lord has been faithful in strengthening me over the long hours at the computer. It is my prayer that the reader will come to a greater love for our great God and Savior Jesus Christ through the study of these doctrines. Knowledge is important, but it must issue in response. Jesus said, "You shall love the Lord your God with all your heart, and with all your soul, and with all your mind" (Matt. 22:37). It is my great hope that this *Handbook of Theology* will contribute to the fulfillment of this great and foremost commandment in the life of the reader.

PART 1:
BIBLICAL THEOLOGY

1

INTRODUCTION TO BIBLICAL THEOLOGY

DEFINITION

The term *biblical theology* can be used in different ways. Although the usage adopted in this volume focuses on a special *method* of theological study, it should be understood that the term is widely used to refer to a *movement* that is basically antagonistic to evangelical faith. This negative usage is here considered and discarded before the legitimate meaning of biblical theology is discussed.

First of all, then, this expression is used to describe the biblical theology *movement*. This was an outgrowth of liberalism and neo-orthodoxy. It began with the publication of Walther Eichrodt's first volume of Old Testament theology in 1933 and ended with the publication of von Rad's second volume of Old Testament theology in 1960.[1] Brevard Childs suggests the movement experienced its demise in May 1963 with the publication of John A. T. Robinson's *Honest To God*.

The movement initially was a reaction to liberalism and sought a return to an exegetical study of the Scriptures, particularly emphasizing a study of biblical words. Kittel's monumental ten-volume *Theological Dictionary of the New Testament* is an outgrowth of that. As a movement, however, it never separated itself from its liberal underpinnings; it retained the historical-critical methodology. For example, in studying the gospels, adherents of the biblical theology movement applied the historical-critical methodology in attempting to discover which of the words attributed to Christ were actually spoken by Him.

While the movement recognized the weak message of liberalism of the eighteenth and nineteenth centuries, it retained the liberal presuppositions concerning the Bible. Adherents held to the neo-orthodox view of revelation, taught evolution as a theory of origins, and emphasized the human aspect of the Bible rather than the divine. As a result, the movement was self-defeating. It was impossible to do a serious, exegetical study of the Scriptures while at the same time denying the authority of the Scriptures.[2]

A second way in which the term *biblical theology* is used is for that *methodology* that takes its material in an historically oriented manner from the Old and New Testaments and arrives at a theology. It is exegetical in nature, drawing its material from the Bible as opposed to a philosophical understanding of theology; it stresses the historical circumstances in which doctrines were propounded; it examines the theology within a given period of history (as in Noahic or Abrahamic eras) or of an individual writer (as Pauline or Johannine writings).

Biblical theology in the above-defined sense may be called "that branch of theological science which deals systematically with the historically conditioned progress of the self-revelation of God as deposited in the Bible."[3]

Several elements are important to observe in this definition:[4]

SYSTEMATIZATION

Biblical theology investigates the periods of history in which God has revealed Himself or the doctrinal emphases of the different biblical writers are set forth in a systematic fashion. Biblical theology, while presented in a systematized form, is distinct from systematic theology that assimilates truth from the entire Bible and from outside the Scriptures in systematizing biblical doctrine. Biblical theology is narrower. It concentrates on the emphasis of a given period of history as in the Old Testament or on the explicit teaching of a particular writer as in the New Testament.

HISTORY

Biblical theology pays attention to the important historical circumstances in which the biblical doctrines were given. What can be learned from the Old Testament era of revelation? What were the circumstances in the writing of Matthew or John? What were the circumstances of the addressees of the letter to the Hebrews? These are important questions that help resolve the doctrinal emphasis of a particular period or of a specific writer.

PROGRESS OF REVELATION

An orthodox doctrine that evangelicals have long held is the belief in progressive revelation; God did not reveal all truth about Himself at one time but revealed Himself "piecemeal," portion by portion to different people throughout history (cf. Heb. 1:1). Biblical theology traces that progress of revelation, noting the revelation concerning Himself that God has given in a particular era or through a particular writer. Hence, God's self-disclosure was not as advanced to Noah and Abraham as it was to Isaiah. An earlier book of the New Testament, such as James, reflects a more primitive view of the church than books written later, such as the pastoral epistles.

BIBLICAL IN NATURE

In contrast to systematic theology, which draws its information about God from any and every source, biblical theology has a narrower focus, drawing its information from the Bible (and from historical information that expands or clarifies the historical events of the Bible). Biblical theology thus is exegetical in nature, examining the doctrines in the various periods of history or examining the words and statements of a particular writer. This enables the student to determine the self-disclosure of God at a given period of history.

RELATION TO OTHER DISCIPLINES[5]

EXEGETICAL STUDIES

Biblical theology has a direct relationship to exegesis ("to explain; to interpret"), inasmuch as biblical theology is the result of exegesis. Exegesis lies at the foundation of biblical theology. Exegesis calls for an analysis of the biblical text according to the literal-grammatical-historical methodology. (1) The passage under consideration should be studied according to the normal meaning of language. How is the word or statement normally understood? (2) The passage should be studied according to the rules of grammar; exegesis demands an examination of the nouns, verbs, prepositions, etc., for a proper understanding of the passage. (3) The passage should be studied in its historical context. What were the political, social, and particularly the cultural circumstances surrounding it? Biblical theology does not end with exegesis, but it must begin there. The theologian must be hermeneutically exacting in analyzing the text to properly understand what Matthew, Paul, or John wrote.

INTRODUCTORY STUDIES

Although it is not the purpose of biblical theology to provide a detailed discussion of introductory matters, some discussion is essential since interpretive solutions are sometimes directly related to introductory studies. Introduction determines issues like authorship, date, addressees, and occasion and purpose for writing. For example, the dating of the book of Hebrews is significant in that it relates to the extent of the suffering of the audience to whom the book is written. Persecution became severe after the burning of Rome in A.D. 64. Even more critical is the issue of the addressees in Hebrews. If the audience is understood to be unbelievers, the book will be studied in one fashion; if the audience is understood to be Hebrew Christians the book will be understood differently. By way of other examples, the audience of Matthew, Mark, and Luke also determines how these writers are evaluated. For example, Matthew's theological viewpoint ought to be understood from the standpoint of having been written to a Jewish audience. The theological viewpoint of the writer is clearly related to introductory issues.

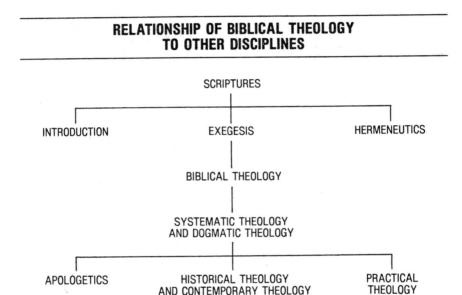

RELATIONSHIP OF BIBLICAL THEOLOGY TO OTHER DISCIPLINES

SYSTEMATIC THEOLOGY STUDIES

There are both similarities and differences between biblical and systematic theology. Both are rooted in the analysis of Scripture, although systematic theology also seeks truth from sources outside the Bible. In noting the

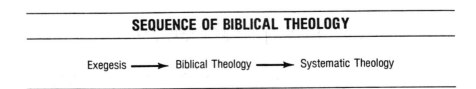

SEQUENCE OF BIBLICAL THEOLOGY

Exegesis ⟶ Biblical Theology ⟶ Systematic Theology

relationship of these two theologies, numerous distinctions can be observed. (1) Biblical theology is preliminary to systematic theology; exegesis leads to biblical theology which in turn leads to systematic theology. (2) Biblical theology seeks to determine what the biblical writers said concerning a theological issue, whereas systematic theology also explains why something is true, adding a philosophical viewpoint. (3) While biblical theology provides the viewpoint of the biblical writer, systematic theology gives a doctrinal discussion from a contemporary viewpoint. (4) Biblical theology analyzes the material of a particular writer or period of history, whereas systematic theology investigates all materials both biblical and extra-biblical that relate to a particular doctrinal matter.

Contrasts between biblical and systematic theology can be portrayed.

CONTRASTS BETWEEN
BIBLICAL AND SYSTEMATIC THEOLOGIES

BIBLICAL THEOLOGY	SYSTEMATIC THEOLOGY
Restricts its study to the *Scripture*.	Seeks truth from *Scripture and* from *any source* outside the Bible.
Examines the *parts* of Scripture.	Examines the *whole* of Scripture.
Compiles information on a doctrine from *a specific writer* (e.g., John or Paul) or a *particular era* (e.g., Abrahamic, Mosaic, prophetic).	Compiles information on a doctrine by correlating *all the Scriptures*.
Seeks to understand *why* or *how* a doctrine developed.	Seeks to understand *what* was ultimately written.
Seeks to understand the *process* as well as the result—the product.	Seeks to understand the result—the *product*.
Views the *progress* of revelation in different eras (as in Edenic, Noahic).	Views the *culmination* of God's revelation.

METHODOLOGY

Biblical theology of the Old Testament is best understood when examining the Old Testament for a "center" or unifying principle. Many different proposals have been suggested concerning a unifying theme of the Old Testament. Walter Kaiser has suggested "promise" as the unifying theme; Elmer Martens suggests "God's design" as the focal point; whereas Eugene Merrill suggests "kingdom" as the underlying theme of the Old Testament.

Whatever theme is emphasized, biblical theology of the Old Testament should be able to see the unfolding of that theme in the different periods of the Old Testament (progressive revelation). (See further discussion of methodology under "Introduction to Old Testament Theology," chap. 2.)

Since the writing of the New Testament books probably encompassed less than fifty years,[6] biblical theology of the New Testament must concern itself with the viewpoint of the different New Testament authors. Thus, the biblical theology of the New Testament is studied according to Pauline theology, Petrine theology, Johannine theology, and so forth. This study evaluates what particular doctrines the writers of the New Testament emphasized and how they developed those doctrines. (See further discussion of methodology under "Introduction to New Testament Theology," chap. 9.)

IMPORTANCE[7]

SHOWS HISTORICAL DEVELOPMENT OF DOCTRINE

Biblical theology is important in that it prevents the study of doctrine apart from its historical context. In the study of systematic theology it is entirely possible to ignore the historical context of doctrinal truth; biblical theology serves to avert that problem by paying attention to the historical milieu in which the doctrine was given.

SHOWS EMPHASIS OF THE WRITER

Biblical theology reveals the doctrinal teaching of a particular writer or during an entire period. In that sense, biblical theology systematizes the Scriptures pertinent to a writer or period and determines the major teaching or doctrinal focus of the writer or period of time. It enables the student to determine what was emphasized during the Abrahamic era or what was emphasized by the apostle John, providing a different perspective from that normally attained through the study of systematic theology.

SHOWS HUMAN ELEMENT IN INSPIRATION

While it is true that the Bible is verbally inspired and inerrant, it is also true that the writers of Scripture each wrote according to their distinctive style. Biblical theology emphasizes the human factor in the writing of Scripture (but not to the exclusion of inspiration). Thus biblical theology is intent on discovering what John or Paul taught or what was emphasized during a period of Old Testament history. Biblical theology "points up the individual backgrounds, interest, and style of the authors. Biblical Theology emphasizes the part that the writers had in the composition of the Word of God, while, of course, building on the divine superintendence of the writings."[8]

NOTES ON BIBLICAL THEOLOGY

1. J. Goldingay, "The Study of Old Testament Theology: It's Aims and Purpose," *Tyndale Bulletin* 26 (1975), p. 34.
2. For a conservative discussion, evaluation, and critique see G. F. Hasel, "Biblical Theology Movement" in Walter A. Elwell, ed., *Evangelical Dictionary of Theology* (Grand Rapids: Baker, 1984), pp. 149-52; and Geoffrey W. Bromiley, "Biblical Theology" in Everett F. Harrison, ed., *Baker's Dictionary of Theology* (Grand Rapids: Baker, 1960), pp. 95-97. For a non-conservative evaluation see Brevard S. Childs, *Biblical Theology in Crisis* (Philadelphia: Westminster, 1970) and James Barr, "Trends and Prospects in Biblical Theology," *Journal of Theological Studies* 25 (1974):265-82.
3. Charles C. Ryrie, *Biblical Theology of the New Testament* (Chicago: Moody, 1959), p. 12. See also the helpful brief discussion in Charles C. Ryrie, *Basic Theology* (Wheaton: Victor, 1986), p. 14.
4. Ryrie, *Biblical Theology of the New Testament*, pp. 12-14.
5. See discussion by Ryrie, *Biblical Theology of the New Testament*, pp. 14-19; and Geerhardus Vos, *Biblical Theology: Old and New Testaments* (Grand Rapids: Eerdmans, 1948), pp. 14-16.
6. Less than thirty years according to John A. T. Robinson, *Redating the New Testament* (Philadelphia: Westminster, 1976), p. 352.
7. See Ryrie, *Biblical Theology of the New Testament*, pp. 20-24; and Vos, *Biblical Theology*, pp. 17-18.
8. Ryrie, *Biblical Theology of the New Testament*, p. 23.

FOR FURTHER STUDY ON BIBLICAL THEOLOGY

* Geoffrey W. Bromiley. "Biblical Theology." In Everett F. Harrison, ed., *Baker's Dictionary of Theology*. Grand Rapids: Baker, 1960. Pp. 95-97.
** Brevard S. Childs. *Biblical Theology in Crisis*. Philadelphia: Westminster, 1970.
** Donald Guthrie. *New Testament Theology*. Downers Grove, Ill.: InterVarsity, 1981. Pp. 21-74.
** Gerhard Hasel. *Old Testament Theology: Basic Issues in the Current Debate*, rev. ed. Grand Rapids: Eerdmans, 1982. This is an important work in discussing the methodology of Old Testament theology.
* _____. "Biblical Theology Movement." In Walter A. Elwell, ed., *Evangelical Dictionary of Theology*. Grand Rapids: Baker, 1984. Pp. 149-52.
** Walter C. Kaiser, Jr. *Toward an Old Testament Theology*. Grand Rapids: Zondervan, 1978. Pp. 1-19.
** Elmer A. Martens. *God's Design: A Focus on Old Testament Theology*. Grand Rapids: Baker, 1981.
* J. Barton Payne. *The Theology of the Older Testament*. Grand Rapids: Zondervan, 1962. Pp. 15-24.
* Charles C. Ryrie. *Biblical Theology of the New Testament*. Chicago: Moody, 1959. Pp. 11-24.
* Geerhardus Vos. *Biblical Theology: Old and New Testaments*. Grand Rapids: Eerdmans, 1948. Pp. 3-18.

2

INTRODUCTION
TO OLD TESTAMENT THEOLOGY

The study of Old Testament theology is a complex task. There is no unanimity among Old Testament scholars on which approach to take. The discussion under "Methodology of Old Testament Theology" will introduce the reader to the varying approaches that are taken. It is possible to study the Old Testament under the topics of God, sin, salvation, and so forth, but that is limiting inasmuch as it is little more than a systematic theology of the Old Testament. Because of the span of time involved it is profitable to study the Old Testament dealing with the differing eras it records in which God has revealed Himself. Within that framework it is possible to study the major doctrines within each era (as Chester Lehman does)—which is helpful, but it fails to tie the study together. It is also possible to see a common theme in the different eras as does Kaiser in his helpful work. This is important in seeing a unity in Old Testament theology.

It seems best to see the unity of the Old Testament as developed around the theme of "kingdom." The theme is emphasized throughout the Old Testament—in the Law, the Prophets, and the Writings. Throughout the Old Testament God dispensed His theocratic kingdom through mediators. God appointed human leaders through whom He revealed His will and made Himself known. The final, ultimate form of God's theocratic kingdom is the millennial kingdom governed by Jesus Christ. It is ultimately that kingdom to which the Old Testament looks forward.

By way of introduction, then, Old Testament theology should see the unfolding of God's revelation; it should be based on a study of the Old Testament text; and it should draw the study together around the developing focus of the theocratic "kingdom."

HISTORY OF OLD TESTAMENT THEOLOGY[1]

EARLY DEVELOPMENTS

There is no evidence of an organized study of biblical theology in the Old Testament or New Testament. The earliest evidence is found with Irenaeus (c. A.D. 130-200) who recognized the progressive revelation of God. Later, Augustine (A.D. 354-430) suggested five historical periods of divine revelation. During the Reformation the issues were basically soteriological, and thus biblical theology as a science did not develop during that time.

NINETEENTH CENTURY

The modern beginnings of biblical theology can be traced to John Philip Gabler who described biblical theology as "the religious ideas of Scripture as an historical fact, so as to distinguish the different times and subjects. and so also the different stages in the development of these ideas."[2] Gabler denied the supernatural, however, and the first conservative work did not appear until E. W. Hengstenberg's *Christology of the Old Testament* (1829-1835). Earlier, Georg Lorenz Bauer (1755-1806) published the first Old Testament theology, dividing it into theology, anthropology, and Christology. Many Old Testament theology works followed, including Gustave Friedrich Oehler's monumental work in 1873-74.[3]

HISTORY OF RELIGIONS

The history of religions school followed the temper of the nineteenth century. It built upon Darwin's evolutionary theory, applying the theory to religion. The Hebrew faith was not seen as a unique religion but as having a relationship with other religions, because they all evolved from a common source. Similarities between Christianity, Judaism, Buddhism, and Hinduism could readily be seen. Thus, the Old Testament was evaluated, not as divine revelation, but in its historical development.

Old Testament theology, according to the history of religions school, accepted the theories of Wellhausen, which denied the unity of the Old Testament by relegating the writings of individual books to several authors over a period of time.[4] Thus, the Old Testament "was reduced to a collection of materials from detached periods and consisted simply of Israelite reflections of as many different pagan religions."[5]

SALVATION-HISTORY SCHOOL

Reacting to the humanistic approach to the Bible was the Heilsgeschichte (Salvation History) school that sought to emphasize God's activity in history. J. C. K. von Hoffman and other theologians examined the Old Testament and noted the progressive development of salvation. The emphasis of this school was on the ministry of Christ at His first advent and also the consummating ministry at His second advent. This school had both strengths and weaknesses. Its strength was its return to divine revelation; its weakness was its rejection of the inspiration of Scripture (they accepted some of higher criticism's views of the Bible). This school had considerable influence into the twentieth century.

NEO-ORTHODOXY

A shift in Old Testament theology occurred following World War I. The reasons for this were: "(1) a general loss of faith in evolutionary naturalism; (2) a reaction against the conviction that historical truth can be attained by pure scientific 'objectivity' or that such objectivity is indeed attainable; and (3) the trend of a return to the idea of revelation in dialectical (neo-orthodox) theology."[6] The Old Testament theologies that were written in the beginning of the twentieth century reflected the reaction against scientific humanism as well as the acceptance of the subjectivity of neo-orthodoxy. Konig's Old Testament theology rejected the Wellhausen theory but had other defects; Eissfeldt followed the thinking of the historicists in denying the activity of God, yet he emphasized the subjective nature of the theologian's faith in encountering God. Eichrodt rejected Eissfeldt's theory, held to the historical theory of Gabler, but also emphasized the subjective nature of the study.

While neo-orthodoxy led to a generally more serious attitude toward the Scriptures, it still acknowledged many aspects of higher criticism, including a denial of verbal plenary inspiration. In addition, the Old Testament theologies written under the influence of neo-orthodoxy emphasized the subjective element (to the neglect of objectivity) in their approach to the Scriptures.

CONSERVATISM

At the beginning of the twentieth century, Princeton Seminary was providing leadership in conservative theology. From this school came some of the important Old Testament works, principally *Biblical Theology* by Geerhardus Vos. Other Princeton men, such as William Henry Green, Robert Dick Wilson, and B. B. Warfield, also made strong contributions. More recently, works by O. T. Allis and E. J. Young of Westminster Seminary have provided important Old Testament theological studies. Charles C. Ryrie, of Dallas Theological Seminary, has also written an important Old Testament theology, *The Basis of the Premillennial Faith*, seeing the unity of the Old Testament based on the unconditional covenants of God with Israel.

METHODOLOGY OF OLD TESTAMENT THEOLOGY[7]

There is no consensus concerning the methodology of Old Testament theology. Over the past two centuries there has been considerable diversity in the development of an Old Testament theology. The following are some of the approaches that have been used.

THE DOGMATIC-DIDACTIC METHOD

The term *dogmatic* relates this to dogmatic or systematic theology. It follows the God-man-salvation structure as first employed by Georg Lorenz Bauer in 1796 and more recently by R. C. Denton. Denton states that "the most basic affirmation of Old Testament religion is that Yahweh is the God of Israel, and Israel is the people of Yahweh."[8]

THE GENETIC-PROGRESSIVE METHOD

This approach traces the revelation of God in the significant eras of Old Testament history, particularly centered on the covenants God made with Noah, Abraham, and Moses. This method is employed by Chester K. Lehman who derived the method from his teacher, Geerhardus Vos. Lehman states, "We discover that the most fundamental line of cleavage in divine revelation centers in the several covenants which God made with man. . . . It will be my plan to consider individually and in order the covenants made by God with Noah, Abraham, Moses, and through Christ. All the teaching centering in these covenants will be considered in relation to these several covenants."[9] Eichrodt also follows this basic principle (although he is listed in the following category). Lehman also acknowledges insights from Gustave Oehler. R. E. Clements of Cambridge University could also be considered in this category.[10]

THE CROSS-SECTION METHOD

This method was developed by Walther Eichrodt in the 1930s by suggesting that the covenant was the center of Old Testament study. He relies on the historical nature of the Old Testament and develops his theology by "making a cross-section through the historical process, laying bare the inner structure of religion."[11] Out of the covenant principle Eichrodt develops three major categories: God and the people, God and the world, and God and man to show the development of thought and institution. The Dutch theologian C. Vriezen follows a similar thesis establishing the "communion" as the center of Old Testament study. The emphasis is on the unity of the Old Testament. Walter Kaiser, Jr. also sees a unity of the Old Testament centered on the "promise" of the Old Testament, to which every writer of the Old Testament consciously contributed.[12]

THE TOPICAL METHOD

John L. McKenzie develops an Old Testament theology without consideration of the New Testament. In contrast to other Old Testament theologies that attempt to see a relationship between the testaments, McKenzie writes as if the New Testament did not exist. He agrees with Harnack or Bultmann, who apparently stated that the Old Testament is not a Christian book.[13] McKenzie develops his Old Testament theology around Israel's experience of Yahweh. Recognizing that not every experience is of equal value, he is selective in determining what is included in his study but emphasizes that "the totality of the experience" is the important thing.[14] other works that fit this category are Georg Fohrer, *Basic Theological Structures of the Old Testament* and W. Zimmerli, *Old Testament Theology in Outline.*

DIACHRONIC METHOD

G. von Rad, who wrote a two volume *Old Testament Theology,* says that an Old Testament theology must "re-tell" Israel's kerygma or confession of the Old Testament, which the nation Israel stated in historical context. He did not mean factual history, however, but "interpretive" history. The "re-telling" was not in statements of faith; "they were acts by which the people expressed their awareness of their relation to God."[15] Von Rad did not find a central theme in his Old Testament theology but contented himself to "narrating what the Old Testament says about its own contents."[16]

FORMATION-OF-TRADITION METHOD

Hartmut Gese developed an Old Testament theology that "must be understood essentially as an historical process of development. . . . there is neither a Christian nor a Jewish theology of the OT, but *one* theology of the OT realized by means of the OT formation of tradition."[17] He saw a relationship and unity between the New Testament and the Old Testament so that the New Testament "brings about the OT . . . brings the so-called OT to an end." The unity of the two testaments was to be found in the "tradition process" that was common in both. The New Testament was to be seen as the goal of the Old Testament. In this approach Gese, like von Rad, did not see a common theme or central point of Old Testament study. Peter Stuhlmacher, also of the Formation-of-Tradition school, argued for a central point that was "the gospel of the justification in Christ."

THE THEMATIC-DIALECTICAL METHOD

Since W. Brueggemann sees a stalemate in Old Testament theology methodology, he has proposed a thematic and dialectical relationship, citing the works of Terrien, Westermann, and Hanson, each one using a dialectical system (reasoning process that seeks to resolve conflict between opposing ideas). For example, Terrien argues for the reality of God's pre^c ence as being at the center of biblical faith, everything else being dependent on it. This also provides the continuity between the Old Testament and the New Testament. The dialectic employed by Terrien is ethical/aesthetic. "The 'ethical' aspect of the dialectic is presented in the historical-covenantal materials and the 'aesthetic' in the wisdom and psalmic materials."[18]

NEW BIBLICAL THEOLOGY METHOD

Brevard Childs has called for a "new biblical theology" that moves beyond the historical-critical method (which exalted human reason as the ultimate authority and treated the Bible like any other book) that underlies most Old Testament theologies. He suggests the abandonment of the historical-critical method (rejecting the history of religions school) and proposes as his thesis the canon of the New Testament church. He suggests dealing with the biblical text in its final form as the normal method of doing Old Testament theology.

MULTIPLEX CANONICAL OLD TESTAMENT THEOLOGY

Hasel proposes some essentials that should be included in the study of an Old Testament theology. (1) An Old Testament theology should be a theology of the canonical Old Testament; it is distinct from the history of Israel or the history of religions concept. (2) Hasel argues against a center or key concept of Old Testament theology, but rather "providing summary explanations and interpretations of the final form of the individual OT writings or blocks of writings that let their various themes, motifs, and concepts emerge and reveal their relatedness to each other."[19] (3) Follow a multiplex approach, which allows individual books and blocks of books to exist side by side with their varying emphases. (4) Follow the historical sequence of the date of origin of the Old Testament books. (5) Present the longitudinal themes of the Old Testament as they emerge from the theologies of the book or groups of books. (6) Examine the various longitudinal themes to discover a relationship between them. (7) An Old Testament theology should be seen as part of a larger whole, standing in relationship to the New Testament.

"PROMISE" AS THE THEME

A popular evangelical Old Testament theology is Walter Kaiser's approach in seeing the unity of the Old Testament around the theme of promise. Kaiser develops an Old Testament theology based on the exegesis of Scripture, using the promise of the Abrahamic Covenant in Genesis 12:1-3 in which God set apart a special people to Himself. This is seen in the phrase

"I am the Lord your God who brought you up out of the land of Egypt"–a formula mentioned in whole or part 125 times in the Old Testament.[20] This theme is developed in the establishment of Israel as the people of God in the Mosaic era, the promise of the Messiah in the Davidic era, and the promise of the future kingdom in the prophetic era.

"GOD'S DESIGN" AS THE THEME

Another evangelical approach is to recognize "that God's design is the key to the content of the Old Testament."[21] Martens builds his thesis on an exegesis of Exodus 5:22–6:8 and draws four basic conclusions reflecting his Old Testament: (1) "Yahweh's initial design for his people is deliverance"; (2) "Yahweh's design is to form a godly community"; (3) "Yahweh's intention is that there be an on-going relationship with his people"; (4) "Yahweh's intention for his people is that they enjoy the good life."[22]

IDENTIFICATION OF AN OLD TESTAMENT THEOLOGY

Several elements should be evident in an Old Testament theology. (1) The doctrine of the inspiration of Scripture is necessary if justice is to be done to the biblical text. There can be no true examination of the biblical text if man sits in judgment upon that text with the criterion of human reason. (2) Old Testament theology should involve exegesis of the biblical text, applying proper hermeneutical principles, thereby allowing the biblical text to speak for itself. This results in an inductive rather than a deductive study. (3) Old Testament theology is built on the premise of progressive revelation and, through exegesis, discovering the progress of the revelation of God in history. (4) Old Testament theology examines the different eras, particularly as noted through the covenants God made with His mediators, to discover how God has revealed Himself in biblical history. (5) An Old Testament theology should discern a unity of the Scriptures; the revelation that God has given concerning Himself should reflect an ultimate consummating purpose whereby the God of the Old and New testaments brings glory to Himself. That unity is found in the kingdom concept.

It is best to see the unity and the center or thematic principle of the Old Testament in the concept of the kingdom of God.[23] This theme can be seen from the very beginning of Genesis to the concluding words of the prophets. Scripture indicates that God mediates His will on earth through mediators.[24]

At any point in history, beginning in Genesis, God rules His mediatorial kingdom on earth through appointed agents. Adam was the first mediator of God's kingdom on earth; Messiah will be the final mediator.

God's purpose for man from the very beginning was that man was destined to rule over creation. Man was to be king of the earth.[25] With the fall of man God has been working to restore man as king of the earth. The ultimate form of man's rule over the earth will be Messiah's kingdom.

THE KINGDOM: UNIFYING THEME OF OLD TESTAMENT THEOLOGY
(Some Important Highlights)

Mediator	Mediatorial Rule
ADAM	Mediated the theocratic kingdom rule over creation. Man was to obey God and subdue nature and animal life.
NOAH	Mediated the theocratic kingdom through the administration of justice. Noah instituted capital punishment as a recognition of the sanctity of life.
ABRAHAM	1. Father of a nation through whom God would one day administer His rule over the world. 2. Received the Abrahamic covenant which promised: (a) Land, (b) Posterity, (c) Blessing.
MOSES AND ISRAEL	1. God's will was revealed through the Mosaic law. God was king; Israel the subjects; the Mosaic law the constitution of the theocratic kingdom. 2. Israel mediates God's truth to the nations through the Mosaic law.
DAVID	1. David mediated God's rule on earth in the Davidic era (c. 1010-970 B.C.). 2. Received the Davidic Covenant which, in anticipating Messiah's kingdom promised: (a) A Dynasty, (b) A Kingdom, (c) A Throne, (d) An Everlasting Rule.
PROPHETS	1. When the kings apostatized, God raised up prophets as mediators of His theocratic kingdom. 2. The prophets had a twofold message: (a) They exhorted the people to obey the Mosaic Law in the theocratic kingdom; (b) They prophesied concerning the final form of the kingdom: Messiah's millennial rule. 3. Isaiah saw a suffering Messiah as foundational to the future kingdom reign of Messiah. 4. Jeremiah announced the New Covenant—it is the basis whereby God will bless Israel in the future. The New Covenant anticipates Israel as a regenerated people in the future kingdom. 5. Ezekiel envisioned a restored worship in the future kingdom. 6. Daniel saw Messiah destroying all earthly kingdoms and establishing the millennial kingdom.

The unconditional covenants of the Old Testament are important and also point to the kingdom as the center or theme of Old Testament theology.

In the Abrahamic Covenant (Gen. 12:1-3) God called a man through whom He would provide redemption and blessing. Under the Palestinian Covenant (Deut. 30) Israel, the offspring of Abraham, was promised a land wherein God would bless them. However, that blessing will ultimately come through Messiah, a descendant of both Abraham and King David (2 Sam 7:12-16; Matt. 1:1). Moreover, the blessing will be made possible through regenerated people as promised in the New Covenant (Jer. 31:31-34).

These four covenants form the foundation of an Old Testament theology in which God will redeem and bless His people. The relationship and emphasis of these covenants can be seen in the following diagram:

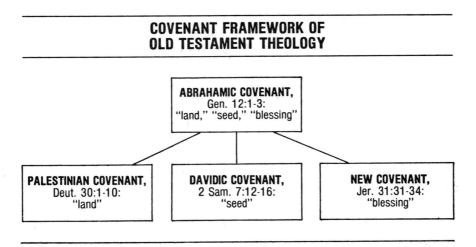

COVENANT FRAMEWORK OF OLD TESTAMENT THEOLOGY

EMPHASIS OF OLD TESTAMENT THEOLOGY

Old Testament theology can be summarized under the central theme of *kingdom*. From the beginning of history God has worked through appointed mediators in administrating the mediatorial kingdom throughout Old Testament history. All of those administrations, however, anticipated the culminating mediatorial kingdom: the Millennium under the rule of Messiah. The unconditional covenants of the Old Testament in particular define the nature of the future millennial kingdom. With the Abrahamic Covenant God began to deal with a special people, Israel. God promised them a land, a posterity that would issue in Messiah and a people over whom He would rule, and spiritual blessing that would involve forgiveness. Throughout the remainder of the Old Testament writings, God deals with Israel to bring her to a place of spiritual blessing in which she will be the agent for God to bless the nations of the world.

Israel was given the conditional Mosaic Covenant as the demonstration of God's holiness, which was His standard. Those who would enter into fellowship with a holy God would also have to have His holy standard. That would be accomplished through forgiveness—promised in the New Covenant (Jer. 31:31-34). The prophetic books add further detail regarding how that will be achieved. Isaiah and Zechariah picture not only a reigning Messiah, but also a suffering Messiah through whom God provides forgiveness. Many of the prophetic books detail the climactic age when, at Messiah's return, the nation Israel is repentant, forgiven, and restored to the land that was promised to her (Deut. 30:1-10). The nations of the world will also enter into blessing. In God's program of dealing with Israel and the Gentiles to bring them to a place of blessing, a repetitious theme of the Old Testament is the continuing sin of the human race and the grace of God to restore an errant humanity.

It is God's promise to David, however, that indicates David's greater Son will be the One through whom this future kingdom will be inaugurated (2 Sam. 7:12-16). In this magnificent statement God promises David that His dynasty, issuing in Messiah, will never be terminated and Messiah's kingdom rule will be forever.

But what is the purpose of it all? The book of Zechariah concludes with an appropriate emphasis: the holiness of God. God's purpose in wooing sinful people back to fellowship with Himself is to bring glory to His name. God is holy and all that will enter into fellowship with Him must be holy. The day when God is worshiped in His holiness by a regenerated people in a restored world will be the millennial kingdom.

NOTES ON OLD TESTAMENT THEOLOGY

1. See the helpful summaries by J. Barton Payne, *The Theology of the Older Testament* (Grand Rapids: Zondervan, 1962), pp. 25-43; and Gerhard Hasel, *Old Testament Theology: Basic Issues in the Current Debate*, rev. ed. (Grand Rapids: Eerdmans, 1982), pp. 15-34.

2. Payne, *Theology of the Older Testament*, p. 27.

3. See his concept of Old Testament theology in Gustave Friedrich Oehler, *Theology of the Old Testament* (Reprint. Grand Rapids: Zondervan, n.d.), pp. 5-47.

4. See Gleason L. Archer, Jr., *A Survey of Old Testament Introduction* (Chicago: Moody, 1964), pp. 73-165, for an excellent discussion and refutation of this theory.

5. Hasel, *Old Testament Theology*, p. 30.

6. Ibid., p. 31.

7. Ibid., pp. 41-96.

8. Ibid., p. 43.

9. Chester K. Lehman, *Biblical Theology*, 2 vols. (Scottdale, Pa.: Herald, 1971), 1:38.

10. Ronald E. Clements, *Old Testament Theology* (Atlanta: Knox, 1978).

11. Hasel, *Old Testament Theology*, p. 52.

12. Walter C. Kaiser, Jr., *Toward an Old Testament Theology* (Grand Rapids: Zondervan, 1978), p. 11.

13. John L. McKenzie, *A Theology of the Old Testament* (Garden City, N.Y.: Doubleday, 1974), p. 319.

14. Ibid., pp. 31-35.

15. Kaiser, *Toward an Old Testament Theology*, p. 3.

16. Hasel, *Old Testament Theology*, pp. 72-73.

17. Ibid., pp. 75-76.

18. Ibid., pp. 82-83.

19. Ibid., p. 93.

20. Kaiser, *Toward an Old Testament Theology*, pp. 12-13.

21. Elmer A. Martens, *God's Design: A Focus on Old Testament Theology* (Grand Rapids: Baker, 1981), p. 12.

22. Ibid., pp. 18-19.

23. Eugene H. Merrill, "Daniel as a Contribution to Kingdom Theology" in *Essays in Honor of J. Dwight Pentecost*, edited by Stanley D. Toussaint and Charles H. Dyer (Chicago: Moody, 1986), p. 211.

24. Alva J. MacClain, *The Greatness of the Kingdom* (Chicago: Moody, 1968), pp. 7, 197. This is a most important work on the subject of the mediatorial kingdom and ought to be studied carefully.

25. See Erich Sauer, *The King of the Earth* (Grand Rapids: Eerdmans, 1962).

FOR FURTHER STUDY ON OLD TESTAMENT THEOLOGY

** Gerhard Hasel. *Old Testament Theology: Basic Issues in the Current Debate*. 3d rev. ed. Grand Rapids: Eerdmans, 1982. Pp. 15-96.

** Walter C. Kaiser, Jr. *Toward an Old Testament Theology*. Grand Rapids: Zondervan, 1978. Pp. 1-40.

* _____. "Old Testament Theology." In *New Dictionary of Theology*, edited by Sinclair B. Ferguson, David F. Wright, and J. I. Packer. Downers Grove, Ill: InterVarsity, 1988. Pp. 477-79.

* Eugene H. Merrill. "Daniel as a Contribution to Kingdom Theology." In *Essays in Honor of J. Dwight Pentecost*, edited by Stanley D. Toussaint and Charles H. Dyer. Chicago: Moody, 1986. Pp. 211-25.

* J. Barton Payne. *The Theology of the Older Testament*. Grand Rapids: Zondervan, 1962. Pp. 25-43.

3

THEOLOGY OF THE EDENIC ERA

CREATION AND ITS PURPOSE

THE CREATOR

No defense is given concerning the existence of God. The record concerning Him is simply, "In the beginning God." The existence of God is assumed. He reveals Himself as *Elohim*, which is related to the name *El*, having a root meaning of "power" or "fear." It suggests "God's greatness or superiority over all other gods."[1] The name Elohim identifies God as "the subject of all divine activity revealed to man and as the object of all true reverence and fear for men."[2] It emphasizes His sovereignty (Gen. 24:3; Isa. 37:16; 54:5); His role as Judge (Ps. 50:6; 58:11; 75:7); His majesty or glory (Isa. 40:28; 65:16); His role as the Savior God (Gen. 17:8; 26:24; 28:13); and His intimacy with His people (Gen. 48:15; Ps. 4:1; Jer. 23:23).

While God presents Himself as a transcendent God, He is also immanent, seeking fellowship with man. He recognizes the creation of man as very good (Gen. 1:31); He creates man in His own image and likeness that He may have a relationship with man and that man may rule over the earth (Gen. 1:26); He speaks with man (Gen. 1:28-30); He creates an environment especially for man (Gen. 1:3-25, 29-30); He tests man's loyalty (Gen. 2:16-17); He seeks man (Gen. 3:9).

THE CREATION OF THE WORLD

"In the beginning" describes the time of God's creation. This is not myth; it is an historical event. Genesis 1:1 gives the principal statement with three circumstantial clauses following in v. 2, suggesting there is no gap between 1:1 and 1:2. The word *created* (Heb. *bara*) suggests God created *ex nihilo*, "out of nothing." It was not a refashioning of previous materials (cf. Rom. 4:17; Heb. 11:3). The days of creation are referred to as "it was evening and it was morning," suggesting twenty-four hour days. The statements "second day," "third day," also demand twenty-four hour days.[3] The creation account is a denial of any form of evolution—atheistic, theistic, or threshhold. If man is the product of an evolutionary process then man is not morally accountable to God; if, however, God directly created man, then man is accountable to God and was also created that he might walk in holiness for fellowship with God.

But what was the purpose of creation? Without question the greatness, the immensity, the magnitude of creation was to bring glory to God.[4]

CREATION OF MAN

Man's creation was special and unique. Man was created on the last day, the climax of God's creation; at the conclusion of man's creation, God noted, "it was *very* good" (Gen. 1:31). Man is not the product of evolution but the direct creation of God (Gen. 1:27; 2:7; 5:1; Deut. 4:32). Genesis 1:27 gives the general statement; Genesis 2:7 provides additional details of the same account. It is also important to note that Christ acknowledged that God directly created man (Matt. 19:4). God also created the individual species (Gen. 1:27). What is particularly significant, however, is that God created man in His own image and likeness. This does not refer to bodily form, since God is spirit (John 4:24), but a spiritual, natural, and moral likeness. In his spiritual likeness, man as a regenerated being may have fellowship with God (Eph. 2:1, 5); in his natural likeness, man has intellect, emotions, and will to know and commune with God; in his moral likeness, man may know and obey the precepts of God.

RESPONSIBILITY OF MAN

God's purpose in creating man is stated in Genesis 1:26, "let them rule." God placed man in the garden to rule over His creation. Adam was God's mediator, placed on earth to dispense His will on earth. Man's destiny as God's mediator is further seen in Psalm 8:6-7, "Thou dost make him to rule over the works of thy hands; Thou has put all things under his feet, All sheep and oxen, And also the beasts of the field, the birds of the heavens, and the fish of the sea, whatever passes through the paths of the seas." As God's mediator, Adam was to exercise authority over all creation—plant and animal life. Adam was to rule over God's creation.

God placed man in a perfect environment and gave him a test. Man was permitted to eat of any tree of the garden but not from the tree of the knowledge of good and evil (Gen. 2:17). Should he do so, death would result. The tree of the knowledge of good and evil was to develop man spiritually; not to have knowledge is a sign of immaturity (Deut. 1:39). God's purpose was that man should attain to a knowledge of good and evil through *not* eating of the fruit. In this way man would glorify God—and man would rule over

God's kingdom on earth in its unfallen estate. But man disobeyed God and attained to the knowledge of good and evil—the wrong way.[5]

FALL AND JUDGMENT

THE TEMPTATION AND SIN

God placed man in the garden and gave man the opportunity to obey Him and lead the human race into eternal blessing (he could have been confirmed in righteousness by eating from the tree of life). It was a test concerning Adam's loyalty and obedience to God.

The solicitation to sin came to Eve through the serpent. The fact that the serpent could tempt Eve suggests evil was present (although man had not yet sinned). It must forever remain a riddle as to where sin came from; it is one of the mysteries of life. Although it was the serpent speaking, it was Satan who engineered the temptation. It was possible because he was "crafty" ("clever," Matt. 10:16). The serpent opposed the glory of God and sought to disrupt man's fellowship with God and man's rule over God's creation. Satan, through the serpent, raised doubt about God's word (Gen. 3:1); he lied by saying that man would not die (Gen. 3:4), expressing it in strongest terms, "You surely shall not die!"[6] Eve submitted to the temptation, sinning in the manner common to the human race: through the lust of the flesh, lust of the eyes, and the boastful pride of life (cf. 1 John 2:16). Adam also participated in the sin; although Eve was deceived (1 Tim. 2:14), Adam realized what he was doing, hence, the greater judgment. For this reason Adam is constituted the first sinner (Rom. 5:12-21).

JUDGMENT

Adam and Eve now came to a knowledge of good and evil but not in the manner they should have. Immediately the world around them looked different; they recognized their nakedness, something they had not previously considered (Gen. 3:7). Their minds had become defiled, hindering fellowship with God.

God called for Adam, the mediator of His truth, to accountability (Gen. 3:9). Adam as head of the human race was being held responsible. God first pronounced judgment upon the serpent and Satan who was the power behind the serpent (Gen. 3:14-15). Because the serpent sought to exalt himself he would be abased, crawling on his belly, eating the dust in his path. Genesis 3:15 should be understood as referring to Satan. Although he would have a minor victory, the seed of the woman (Christ) would deal Satan a death blow. God also judged the woman; she would have pain in childbirth (Gen. 3:16) and desire for her husband[7] who would rule over her. The judgment on Adam meant he would work hard; the ground would resist him.[8]

The tragic news awaited Adam: death would occur. Adam and Eve died both physically and spiritually.

PROMISE OF REDEMPTION

In Genesis 3:15 God announced the enmity that would come between Satan and mankind. This is the *protevangelium*, the first announcement of the gospel in Scripture. Satan would be dealt a destructive, head crushing blow. This is a reference to Christ's victory over Satan at the cross (Col. 2:14-15; Heb. 2:14) when Christ would render Satan powerless, enabling man to be forever restored to fellowship with God, making possible man's ultimate rule. Satan would have a minor victory ("you shall bruise him on the heel"), suggesting the death of Christ; however, that very death would spell Satan's defeat.

Although Adam and Eve had sinned, incurring death, God moved to resolve man's dilemma by pointing to a future Savior who would eliminate death, restore believing man to fellowship with God, and consummate history with Messiah's reign on earth to restore all that Adam had lost.

Even though Adam lost considerable authority in his kingdom rule as God's mediator, Genesis 3:15 looks to the future when the Messianic kingdom will be inaugurated, restoring all that Adam lost.

SUMMARY

Several things should be noted regarding God's revelation in the Edenic era. (1) God revealed Himself as omnipotent and sovereign in the creation of the universe and world. (2) God is holy, demanding obedience for fellowship with Himself. (3) God is a God of grace, as manifest through the promise of a Savior. (4) Man is the apex of God's creation, created in the image and likeness of God for fellowship with God and for rule over God's creation. (5) Man is a responsible creature, answerable to a holy God. Man is constituted a sinner through the sin of Adam. (6) God initiates His redemptive program by promising a Savior to Adam and Eve. The promise anticipates Messiah's ultimate triumph over Satan, providing the basis for the restored kingdom.

NOTES ON THE EDENIC ERA

1. Jack B. Scott, "El" in *Theological Wordbook of the Old Testament*, 2 vols., edited by R. Laird Harris et al. (Chicago: Moody, 1980), 1:42.
2. Ibid., 1:44.

3. Whenever the numeral appears with the Hebrew word *yom* (day) it demands a twenty-four hour day. See also the excellent study by Weston W. Fields, *Unformed and Unfilled* (Nutley, N.J.: Presbyterian & Reformed, 1976).

4. Erich Sauer, *The Dawn of World Redemption* (Exeter: Paternoster, 1964), pp. 25-29.

5. C. F. Keil and F. Delitzsch, *Biblical Commentary on the Old Testament*, 25 vols. (Reprint. Grand Rapids: Eerdmans, 1968), 1:84-86.

6. The Hebrew construction is an infinitive absolute which expresses emphasis when it immediately precedes the verb.

7. The meaning of *desire* (Heb. *shuq*, "violent craving") is difficult to determine since it is only used three times in the Old Testament (Gen. 3:16; 4:7; Song 7:10). It may have reference to sexual desire as in Song of Solomon 7:10 or desire to be under his rule or perhaps desire to rule over him.

8. The word describing Adam's toil (Heb. *yizabon*, Gen. 3:17) also describes Eve's pain in childbirth (Gen. 3:16).

FOR FURTHER STUDY ON THE EDENIC ERA

* William Dyrness. *Themes in Old Testament Theology*. Exeter: Paternoster, 1979.

** E. W. Hengstenberg. *Christology of the Old Testament*. Reprint. Grand Rapids; Kregel, 1970. Pp. 13-24.

** Walter C. Kaiser, Jr. *Toward an Old Testament Theology*. Grand Rapids: Zondervan, 1978. Pp. 71-79.

* Geerhardus Vos. *Biblical Theology: Old and New Testaments*. Grand Rapids: Eerdmans, 1948. Pp. 27-44.

4

THEOLOGY OF THE NOAHIC ERA

CAINITES AND SETHITES

The Noahic period sees the degradation and deterioration of the human race. This age marks the cleavage between the godly line of Seth and the ungodly line of Cain; two distinct branches of humanity are being worked out. The period could be characterized as describing the "natural development of the human race . . . (while) revelation here bears on the whole a negative rather than positive character. It contents itself with bestowing a *minimum* of grace."[1]

The downward trend of sin during the period begins with Cain murdering Abel (Gen. 4:1-8). Cain became angry when God acknowledged the offering of Abel who had brought a better offering because he brought it by faith (Heb.11:4). The Lord warned Cain of sin "crouching at the door" (Gen. 4:7). Keil and Delitzsch picture sin "as a wild beast, lurking at the door of the human heart, and eagerly desiring to devour his soul (1 Pet. 5:8)."[2] In a premeditated act, Cain killed his brother, Abel, and was banished by the Lord (Gen. 4:8-11). The ground that had received the innocent blood of Abel would now resist Cain; in toil and hardship he would draw the produce from the ground (Gen. 4:12).

With Cain's murderous act, a new civilization develops. City life emerges (4:16-17), polygamy occurs (4:19), the arts develop (4:21), metallurgy advances man's cause (4:22), but violence is also evident (4:23). It appears that in the development of civilization, man attempted to mitigate the effects of the curse apart from God.[3]

Genesis 5 traces the descent of the Sethite line as distinct from the Cainite line. The Sethites represent the godly line, while the Cainites represent the ungodly line. The contrast is seen: the fifth descendant from Cain was Lamech, the first polygamist; the fifth descendant from Seth was Enoch, the first to walk with God. Moreover, it was the Sethite line that began to worship God (Gen. 4:26).

THE FLOOD

Genesis 6 describes the further deterioration of the human race result-ing in God's judgment through the Noahic flood. Why does Noah stand out alone as a righteous man when the Sethite line was established as a godly line? While there is considerable controversy over the identification of the "sons of God" (Gen. 6:2), it seems best to the overall context to suggest that the sons of God refers to the godly line of Seth while the daughters of men refers to the ungodly line of Cain.[4] With the intermarriage of the godly Seth-ites and the ungodly Cainites, the human race became entirely corrupted, sinking to the level of "flesh," suggestive of weakness, sinful stock, and abandonment to a life of sin.[5] The sinfulness of man covered the inhabited earth, and the sinfulness was intense and deeply rooted (Gen. 6:5). This period marks man's overt rebellion against God's kingdom and constituted authority.

Noah, as the mediator of God's kingdom rule, stood out alone as a righteous man in a sinful world (Gen. 6:9-11). Noah was upright toward man and God: he was righteous (Heb. *zedek*), which is viewed manward, and he was blameless (Heb. *tamim*), which is viewed godward (6:9).[6] The contrast between Noah and the world is observable: Noah was righteous while the earth was corrupt; Noah walked with God but the earth was filled with vio-lence.

Sin demands judgment, and the Lord announced His righteous judg-ment upon sin (Gen. 6:7, 13); His Spirit would no longer strive with man. The twofold concept of judgment and blessing, which is so frequent in the Old Testament, is seen again in Genesis 6:7-8. While God promised to judge sinful humanity He also announced His blessing upon Noah. God's media-torial kingdom would be established through the Noahic line.

NOAHIC COVENANT

The first act of Noah following the Flood was to build an altar and worship the Lord (Gen. 8:20). This is the first account in the Old Testament of worshiping the Lord through a blood sacrifice on an altar. The burnt of-ferings would later be revealed as dedicatory offerings (Lev. 1:1-7).

Having earlier announced His covenant (Gen. 6:18), following the Flood God established it with Noah (Gen. 9:9). The Noahic Covenant estab-lishes principles whereby man is to rule over God's kingdom on earth. (1) God made provision for the transmission of the human race (9:1). Man was commanded to fill the earth because the population was down to eight per-sons. The command to subdue the earth (cf. Gen. 1:28; 9:1) is no longer present; that was forfeited through sin. (2) Fear of man was placed in the animals (9:2). Animals had voluntarily subjected to man previously but be-cause man would now become carnivorous, God placed the fear of man in animals for their protection and preservation. (3) Provision for sustaining human life (Gen. 9:3-4). Man no longer must be a vegetarian; he was now given meat to eat. Blood, however, was not to be eaten because it represented life (cf. Lev. 17:14). (4) Provision for protecting human life (Gen. 9:5-6). As the administrator of God's kingdom, Noah was to guard the sanctity of human life. God placed a value on human life to the extent that whoever killed another man would have to forfeit his own life. God viewed murder as an assault on *His* person because man is made in the image of God. This is a consistent teaching of both the Old Testament and the New Testament (Ex. 21:12-24; Lev. 24:17, 21; Num. 35:29-34; 2 Sam. 4:9-12; Rom. 13:4). Vengeance was not to be taken personally as a blood avenger, but it was to be taken through constituted governmental authority.[7] (5) God promised never again to send a flood that would destroy all humanity (Gen. 9:11).

Noah mediated God's covenant to all humanity. It is also an unconditional covenant inasmuch as no conditions are attached to the covenant. God indicated it was something He would do (Gen. 6:18; 9:9, 11).

BLESSING OF SHEM

Although humanity was down to eight members, God once more indicates He will bless the human race. As He had earlier announced the blessing through the seed of the woman (Gen. 3:15), now He announces future blessing through the line of Shem (Gen. 9:26), indicating a narrowing of the mediatorial line. The statement, "Blessed be the Lord," suggests the true faith would be preserved among the descendants of Shem.[8] Further, the statement identifies the descendants of Shem in fellowship with the Lord. The translation "Lord," printed in all capital letters in many English versions of the Old Testament, renders the tetragramaton, YHWH. It was previously pronounced Jehovah, but probably should be pronounced Yahweh. The name is significant, for it later comes to denote the Lord in His covenant relationship with Israel. This is anticipated in Exodus 6:3. The statement also suggests that Messiah, the Promised One who will establish the kingdom, would come through the line of Shem.

The descendants of Shem can be traced to Israel's history. Arpachshad (Gen. 10:22) "is the ancestor of the Hebrews."[9] Eber (Gen. 10:24) apparently is the source for the name Hebrew and identifies Abraham as a descendant (Gen. 14:13).[10] The descendents of Japheth were also promised blessing (Gen. 9:27). The name Japheth means "to be wide," suggesting an expansion over a wide area. The name Elohim is used in the blessing of Japheth, suggesting "God as Creator and Governor of the world; for it had respect primarily to the blessings of the earth, not to spiritual blessings; although Japheth would participate in these as well."[11]

Although God had judged a depraved world with the Flood, the future blessing of all people is announced. That blessing will originate through the covenant God, Yahweh, to His covenant people, the descendants of Shem. God now reveals that He will administer His kingdom program through the line of Shem eventuating in the Hebrew people.

TOWER OF BABEL

In the land of Shinar the people found a plain and settled down (Gen. 11:2). Here they decided to build a city "and a tower whose top will reach into heaven" (v. 4). Some think this was a ziggurat, an elevated platform on which worship was conducted.[12] When the Lord saw what the people were doing, He confused their speech to prevent them from proceeding with their construction. The terminology describing God's action is illuminating. The Lord's transcendence and immanence is evident (Gen. 11:7). He who is distant "came down" to see what the people were doing. The Trinity is also implied in the statement, "Let *Us* go down."

The sin of the people was: (1) they were rebelling against the explicit command of God (Gen. 9:1); (2) they were seeking their own glory instead of the Lord's glory. They declared, "let *us* make . . . let *us* build for *ourselves* . . . let *us* make for *ourselves*" (Gen. 11:3-4); (3) they wanted to make a name for themselves (Gen. 11:4). They wanted to build a tower that would bring them honor; (4) they wanted to avoid dispersion so they built a tower that would become a rallying point.[13] They wanted to build their own kingdom instead of God's kingdom.

Through the confusion of the language, God accomplished His purpose. The people were scattered and fulfilled His command (Gen. 9:1) by filling the earth.

SUMMARY

During the Noahic period God revealed Himself to the people. (1) He is a righteous God, demanding obedience to His command. (2) God does not overlook sin; He judges sin. (3) God is both transcendent and immanent. The God who is "wholly other" is also the God who communes with mankind. (4) God receives the worship of His people. The first mention of worship with a blood sacrifice is mentioned during this era. (5) God is sovereign; His will shall come to pass. (6) God will bless the Hebrew people and ultimately the nations of the world through Shem, the Messianic line. The kingdom is anticipated through Shem.

Notes on the Noahic Era

1. Geerhardus Vos, *Biblical Theology: Old and New Testaments* (Grand Rapids: Eerdmans, 1948), p. 45.

2. C. F. Keil and F. Delitzsch, *Biblical Commentary on the Old Testament*, 25 vols. (Reprint. Grand Rapids: Eerdmans, 1968), 1:112.

3. Howard F. Vos, *Genesis* (Chicago: Moody, 1982), pp. 32-33.

4. Considerable evidence can be garnered for both views. See Vos, *Genesis*, pp. 36-37; and Gleason L. Archer, Jr., *Encyclopedia of Bible Difficulties* (Grand Rapids: Zondervan, 1982), pp. 77-78. Keil and Delitzsch make the important point that the phrase "took wives for themselves" is a common Old Testament statement referring to marriage. It does not refer to fornication. Hence, it cannot refer to angels. If angels were in view it would have been a fornicatious act, not marriage (cf. Keil & Delitzsch, *Biblical Commentary*, 1:131).

5. H. C. Leupold, *Exposition of Genesis* (Grand Rapids: Baker, 1942), 1:255-56.

6. Derek Kidner, *Genesis* (Downers Grove, Ill.: InterVarsity, 1967), p. 87.

7. It is so understood by prominent Old Testament scholars: Keil and Delitzsch, *Biblical Commentary*, 1:153; Vos, *Genesis*, p. 50; Leupold, *Genesis*, p. 333; and John Davis, *Paradise to Prison* (Grand Rapids: Baker, 1975), pp. 127-28.

8. E. W. Hengstenberg, *Christology of the Old Testament* (Grand Rapids: Kregel, 1970), p. 24. This is a classic work, tracing the prophecies of Christ in the Old Testament, and ought to be studied by the serious student.

9. Allen P. Ross, "The Table of Nations in Genesis 10—Its Content," *Bibliotheca Sacra* 138 (January-March 1981):28.

10. Vos, *Genesis*, p. 54.

11. Keil and Delitzsch, *Biblical Commentary*, 1:159.

12. William White and E. M. Blaiklock suggest the dating precedes the time of the ziggurats. Compare "Babel, Tower of" in *The New International Dictionary of Biblical Archaeology*, edited by Edward M. Blaiklock and R. K. Harrison (Grand Rapids: Zondervan, 1983), p. 85.

13. Vos, *Genesis*, p. 56.

For Further Study on the Noahic Era

* William Dyrness. *Themes in Old Testament Theology*. Exeter: Paternoster, 1979.

* Walter C. Kaiser, Jr. *Toward an Old Testament Theology*. Grand Rapids: Zondervan, 1978. Pp. 80-83.

** J. Barton Payne. *The Theology of the Older Testament*. Grand Rapids: Zondervan, 1962.

** Geerhardus Vos. *Biblical Theology: Old and New Testaments*. Grand Rapids: Eerdmans, 1948. Pp. 45-65.

5

THEOLOGY OF THE PATRIARCHAL ERA

The kingdom concept becomes more evident in Genesis 12. This chapter marks a change in God's dealing with humanity. In the early chapters of Genesis God dealt with mankind in general. With the sinfulness of the human race established, God now moves to bless and redeem a fallen humanity by working through a special people. Abraham becomes the central figure through whom God will work. He promises a blessing to Abraham and His posterity that will result in Messiah's advent with blessing to the Hebrew people and the nations of the world in the millennial kingdom.

ABRAHAMIC COVENANT[1]

NATURE OF THE COVENANT

God determined to call out a special people for Himself through whom He would bring blessing to all the nations. The Abrahamic Covenant is paramount to a proper understanding of the kingdom concept and is foundational to Old Testament theology. (1) The Abrahamic Covenant is described in Genesis 12:1-3 and is an *unconditional* covenant. There are no conditions attached to it (no "if" clauses, suggesting its fulfillment is dependent on man). (2) It is also a *literal* covenant in which the promises should be understood literally. The land that is promised should be understood in its literal or normal interpretation—it is not a figure of heaven. (3) It is also an *everlasting* covenant. The promises that God made to Israel are eternal.

FEATURES OF THE COVENANT

There are three main features to the Abrahamic Covenant.

The promise of land (Gen. 12:1). God called Abraham from Ur of the Chaldees to a land that He would give him (Gen. 12:1). This promise is reiterated in Genesis 13:14-18 where it is confirmed by a shoe covenant; its dimensions are given in Genesis 15:18-21 (precluding any notion of this being fulfilled in heaven). The land aspect of the Abrahamic Covenant is also expanded in Deuteronomy 30:1-10, which is the Palestinian Covenant.

The promise of descendants (Gen. 12:2). God promised Abraham that He would make a great nation out of him. Abraham, who was 75 years old and fatherless (Gen. 12:4), was promised many descendants. This promise is amplified in Genesis 17:6 where God promised that nations and kings would descend from the aged patriarch. This promise (which is expanded in the Davidic Covenant of 2 Sam. 7:12-16) would eventuate in the Davidic throne with Messiah's kingdom rule over the Hebrew people.

The promise of blessing and redemption (Gen. 12:3). God promised to bless Abraham and the families of the earth through him. This promise is amplified in the New Covenant (Jer. 31:31-34; cf. Heb. 8:6-13) and has to do with "Israel's spiritual blessing and redemption."[2] Jeremiah 31:34 antici-pates the forgiveness of sin.

The unconditional and eternal nature of the covenant is seen in that the covenant is reaffirmed to Isaac (Gen. 21:12; 26:3-4). The "I will" promises suggest the unconditional aspect of the covenant. The covenant is further confirmed to Jacob (Gen. 28:14-15). It is noteworthy that God reaffirmed these promises amid the sins of the patriarchs, which fact further empha-sizes the unconditional nature of the Abrahamic Covenant.

FULFILLMENT OF THE COVENANT

God's method of fulfilling the Abrahamic Covenant is literal, inasmuch as God partially fulfilled the covenant in history:[3] God blessed Abraham by giving him the land (Gen. 13:14-17); God blessed him spiritually (Gen. 13:8, 18; 14:22, 23; 21:22); God gave him numerous descendants (Gen. 22:17; 49:3-28).

The important element of the Abrahamic Covenant, however, demands a future fulfillment with Messiah's kingdom rule. (1) Israel as a nation will possess the land in the future. Numerous Old Testament passages antici-pate the future blessing of Israel and her possession of the land as promised to Abraham. Ezekiel envisions a future day when Israel is restored to the *land* (Ezek. 20:33-37, 40-42; 36:1-37:28). (2) Israel as a *nation* will be con-verted, forgiven, and restored (Rom. 11:25-27). (3) Israel will repent and receive the *forgiveness* of God in the future (Zech. 12:10-14). The Abraham-ic Covenant finds its ultimate fulfillment in connection with the return of Messiah to rescue and bless His people Israel. It is through the nation Israel that God promised in Genesis 12:1-3 to bless the nations of the world. That ultimate blessing will issue in the forgiveness of sins and Messiah's glorious kingdom reign on earth.

SUMMARY

The progressive revelation of God is seen during the Abrahamic era. God moves to resolve the dilemma of sin that has entered the human race. Instead of dealing with mankind in general as previously, God begins to work with an individual, Abraham, through whom He will call out a special people. Through these people God will bless the nations of the earth. The descendants of Abraham will be the mediators of God's will on earth, and it is through these people, Israel, that Messiah will come and establish His kingdom. Thus God promised blessing through the descendants of Abraham—a blessing that later would include forgiveness of sins (Jer. 31:34).

NOTES ON THE PATRIARCHAL ERA

1. See the following discussions on the Abrahamic Covenant: J. Dwight Pentecost, *Things to Come* (Grand Rapids: Zondervan, 1958), pp. 65-94; Charles C. Ryrie, *The Basis of the Premillennial Faith* (Neptune, N.J.: Loizeaux, 1953), pp. 48-75; and John F. Walvoord, *The Millennial Kingdom* (Grand Rapids: Zondervan, 1959), pp. 139-58.
2. Pentecost, *Things to Come*, p. 71.
3. Ryrie, *The Basis of the Premillennial Faith*, pp. 50-52.

FOR FURTHER STUDY ON THE PATRIARCHAL ERA

* William Dyrness. *Themes in Old Testament Theology*. Exeter: Paternoster, 1979.
** Walter C. Kaiser, Jr. *Toward an Old Testament Theology*. Grand Rapids: Zondervan, 1978. Pp. 84-99.
* Elmer A. Martens. *God's Design: A Focus on Old Testament Theology*. Grand Rapids: Baker, 1981. Pp. 31-36.
* Charles C. Ryrie. *The Basis of the Premillennial Faith*. Neptune, N.J.: Loizeaux, 1953. Pp. 48-75.
** Geerhardus Vos. *Biblical Theology: Old and New Testaments*. Grand Rapids: Eerdmans, 1948. Pp. 66-99.

6

THEOLOGY OF THE MOSAIC ERA

When Jacob, his sons, and their families descended into Egypt, it was a large family that was migrating to Egypt; however, as the book of Exodus opens, the family of Jacob has grown into a nation. This nation will be the key instrument of God's revelation to humanity. When the Hyksos people and later the Egyptians oppressed Israel, God determined to bring the Israelites out of bondage. In Exodus 12, at the climax of the plagues, God sent the death angel through Egypt. Whoever had applied lamb's blood to the doorposts and above the doorways of their houses was redeemed—it took an act of faith to apply the blood to the house. This great act of delivering Israel from Egypt foreshadowed a greater act of redemption that God would accomplish through a descendant of Jacob—the Messiah. God led redeemed Israel down to Sinai where He entered into a covenant with the nation. He was setting the Israelites apart as a special people for Himself. Israel became the mediator of God's theocratic kingdom on earth through the Mosaic Covenant.

ISRAEL: THE PEOPLE OF GOD

In Exodus 19 God entered into a conditional treaty, the Mosaic Covenant, with Israel. The pattern of the covenant follows the form of the ancient suzerainty-vassal treaty.[1] The conditional nature of the covenant states what the suzerain (king) has done for his subjects (vassals). The conditions of the covenant are then set forth to the people; they are obligated to obey the king. The suzerain, meanwhile, promises to protect and provide for His subjects. His blessing of protection and provision is contingent on the subjects' obedience. If they obey Him, they can expect His blessing; if they disobey Him, they can expect chastisement.

THE SUZERAINTY-VASSAL TREATY FORMAT
OF THE MOSAIC COVENANT IN EXODUS 19

Treaty Elements	Exodus 19	Mosaic Elements
Traditional Preamble	V. 3*b*	Recognition of the king
Historical Prologue	V. 4	Reminder of God's past provision
General Stipulations	V. 5*a*	Conditions for Israel to keep
Promised Blessings	Vv. 5*b*-6*a*	Promise of blessing

This treaty known as the Mosaic Covenant was entered into by the Lord and the nation Israel. The Lord reminded the people of their obligation: obedience (Ex. 19:5). The people agreed to the covenant when they said, "All that the Lord has spoken we will do!" (Ex. 19:8). With the ratification of the covenant, the nation Israel—the mediator of God's theocratic kingdom upon earth—was born.

MEDIATOR TO THE NATIONS

God promised to make Israel "a kingdom of priests and a holy nation" (Ex. 19:6). She was set apart to the Lord to mediate His truth to other nations. This was a missionary injunction. A priest was a mediator, representing the people to God; in that sense the entire nation Israel was to be a mediator of the kingdom of God to the nations of the world. Israel's was a universal priesthood. "They were to be mediators of God's grace to the nations of the earth even as in Abraham 'all the nations of the earth were to be blessed.' "[2]

The course of Israel's history was failure upon failure, hence, she never attained to her divine purpose as a mediator of God's truth. Isaiah looks to the future when the true Israelite, Messiah, will fulfill the Lord's destiny for the nation. Israel as a nation was to be a spiritual light to the nations of the world. She failed, but Messiah will ultimately herald the light of God to the nations through the establishment of the millennial kingdom (Isa. 42:6; 49:6; 51:4; 60:1, 3).

These statements of Isaiah are in the Servant passages, describing how God's light will go forth to the nations. It will be through His Servant, the Messiah, upon whom God has put His Spirit (Isa. 42:1); He will bring the light of God to the Gentiles (Isa. 42:6; 49:6). The result will be the blessing of God to the ends of the earth, promised to the patriarch, Abraham (Gen.

12:2-3). But Messiah will also restore the fallen nation (Isa. 49:6), restoring all that Adam lost. The pre-Fall conditions of Eden will once again exist through the glorious kingdom reign of Messiah when the earth will know His truth (Isa. 51:3-4). In that day God will honor Abraham's descendants once more as Jerusalem becomes the center of truth, and the nations of the world will stream to Israel for a knowledge of that truth (Isa. 60:1-3).

CONSTITUTION OF THE NATION

Having entered into a covenant with the nation Israel, God gave Israel her constitution, comprising much of Exodus, Leviticus, and Deuteronomy. These were the stipulations of the covenant in the mediatorial kingdom that Israel was to obey if the nation was to enjoy the blessing of God.

The Law can be divided into three categories: the civil, ceremonial, and the moral laws.[3]

THE MORAL LAW

The moral law is found principally in the Ten Commandments (Ex. 20:2-17; Deut. 5:6-21), although not restricted to them. The Ten Commandments are listed in two categories: man's relationship to God, covering the first four comandments (Ex. 20:2-11), and man's relationship to man, covering the last six commandments (Ex. 20:12-17). The moral law begins with the statement, "I am the Lord your God, who brought you out of the land of Egypt" (Ex. 20:2), hence, "the standard of moral measurement in deciding what was right or wrong, good or evil, was fixed in the unwavering and impeccably holy character of Yahweh, Israel's God. His nature, attributes, character, and qualities provided the measuring stick for all ethical decision."[4]

THE CIVIL LAW

The civil law involves many of the laws appearing in Exodus 21:1–24:18, as well as in Leviticus and Deuteronomy. These laws reflect social concerns whereby the Israelites would live with proper concern for their neighbors in the mediatorial kingdom. The laws have reference to slaves, injury to others, property rights, oppression of widows and orphans, money lending, and many other concerns.

THE CEREMONIAL LAW

The ceremonial law, described mainly in Exodus 25:1–40:38 (as well as in Leviticus and Deuteronomy), involves the tablernacle, the clothing and function of the priests, and the sacrifices and offerings.

It should be noted that these categories are intermingled in the text of Exodus-Deuteronomy; within a given context, all three aspects of the law may be described. Nor is it always a simple matter to distinguish between the three aspects of the law. In any case, the law was Israel's constitution with the Lord, the King. Israel was to obey this law to enjoy the blessing of the Lord, her suzerain in the mediatorial kingdom. When Israel disobeyed the law it was the function of the prophet to call the nation back in obedience to the law.

WORSHIP OF THE NATION

In calling out a special people for Himself, God also made provision whereby the fledgling nation could meet with the Lord; thus He prescribed the tabernacle worship whereby Israel could approach the infinite holy God. There the Lord would meet with Israel (Ex. 25:22; 29:42, 43; 30:6, 36).

The Lord called for Israel to build a tabernacle. (1) It provided a way for God to dwell in the midst of the nation (Ex. 25:8). (2) It provided a way for God to reveal His glory (Ex. 40:34, 35). (3) It provided a way for sinful people to approach a holy God because it was the center of sacrificial worship (Lev. 17:11). (4) It was a reminder of the separation of a holy God from a sinful people. (5) It anticipated the redemption in Christ (Heb. 8:5).

The tabernacle was divided into two rooms, the Holy Place and the Holy of Holies. God instructed Israel to place a wooden chest, called the ark, in the Holy of Holies, and covering the ark, a mercy seat. Here God dwelt with the nation (Ex. 25: 22). At the entrance to the court of the tabernacle was the altar of burnt offering where the priest daily offered burnt offerings to the Lord (Ex. 29:38). It was a reminder to the nation that it required blood to approach God. The priests, which were of the tribe of Levi, were set apart as mediators between the nation and a holy God. They served in the tabernacle worship. The entire tabernacle worship system was a reminder of the infinite holiness of God; it reminded the nation that a mediator was necessary for approach to God.

PALESTINIAN COVENANT

The Book of Deuteronomy anticipates the possession of the land by Israel. The people journeyed through the wilderness and came up on the east side of the Dead Sea in anticipation of possessing the land. This is an important emphasis of the book since "Sixty-nine times the writer of Deuteronomy repeated the pledge that Israel would one day 'possess' and 'inherit' the land promised to her."[5] The Lord reiterated the conditional nature of the covenant by citing the necessity of obedience for blessing (Deut. 28:1-14) while citing the judgments for disobedience (Deut. 28:15-68). The judgments anticipated the dispersions by Assyria (722 B.C.), Babylon (586 B.C.), and Rome (A.D. 70) (Deut. 28:64). However, when all those calamities were over, God revealed that Israel would once again possess the land (Deut. 30:1-10). This would ultimately be fulfilled in the millennial kingdom.

NATURE OF THE COVENANT

The nature of the Palestinian Covenant is as follows: "(1) The nation will be plucked off the land for its unfaithfulness (Deut. 30:1-3); (2) there will be a future repentance of Israel (Deut. 28:63-68); (3) their Messiah will return (Deut. 30:3-6); (4) Israel will be restored to the land (Deut. 30:5); (5) Israel will be converted as a nation (Deut. 30:4-8; cf. Rom. 11:26-27); (6) Israel's enemies will be judged (Deut. 30:7); (7) the nation will then receive her full blessing (Deut. 30:9)."[6]

The Palestinian Covenant is important inasmuch as it reaffirmed Israel's title deed to the land. The promise of the Palestinian Covenant is not abrogated because of the conditional Mosaic Covenant.[7] The Palestinian Covenant is termed an eternal covenant (Ezek. 16:60) because it is a part of the unconditional Abrahamic Covenant and an amplification of it.

FULFILLMENT OF THE COVENANT

A study of Deuteronomy 28-30 shows that God foretold Israel's apostasy and dispersion under Assyria, Babylon, and Rome prior to her occupation of the land. Before the Palestinian Covenant will be fulfilled Israel must first come to a place of repentance and knowledge of Messiah (Zech. 12:10-14) and be regathered to the land from the nations where the people have settled over the millennia. The Palestinian Covenant, then, is a future, eschatological event finding fulfillment in Israel's appropriation of the land in the millennial kingdom.

SUMMARY

The Mosaic worship brought additional revelation concerning God. (1) God is holy; He cannot be approached without a mediator. God's holiness is also seen in that He demands moral uprightness by His people, hence He gave them a moral code by which to live. (2) God is immanent in that He cares for His people and dwells with them. (3) Blood is important in the worship of a holy God. Blood is necessary as an expiation of sin, and without blood it is impossible to approach God. (4) The mediatorial work of the Levitical priesthood points ahead to the Mediator who will once for all reconcile sinful man to a holy God. (5) God has covenanted Himself to a special people, Israel. In the Old Testament era God rules over Israel in the mediatorial kingdom through established mediators.

NOTES ON THE MOSAIC ERA

1. See George E. Mendenhall, *Law and Covenant in Israel and the Near East* (Pittsburgh: Biblical Colloquium, 1955); and Meredith G. Kline, *Treaty of the Great King* (Grand Rapids: Eerdmans, 1963).
2. Walter C. Kaiser, Jr., *Toward an Old Testament Theology* (Grand Rapids: Zondervan, 1978), p. 109.
3. Ibid., pp. 114-18; and Leon Wood, *A Survey of Israel's History* (Grand Rapids: Zondervan, 1970), pp. 148-50.
4. Kaiser, *Toward an Old Testament Theology*, p. 114.
5. Ibid., p. 124.
6. J. Dwight Pentecost, *Things to Come* (Grand Rapids: Zondervan, 1958), p. 97.
7. Ibid., p. 97.

FOR FURTHER STUDY ON THE MOSAIC ERA

* William Dyrness. *Themes in Old Testament Theology*. Exeter: Paternoster, 1979.
** Walter C. Kaiser, Jr. *Toward an Old Testament Theology*. Grand Rapids: Zondervan, 1978. Pp. 100-121.
* Elmer A. Martens. *God's Design: A Focus on Old Testament Theology*. Grand Rapids: Baker, 1981. Pp. 37-115.
** Geerhardus Vos. *Biblical Theology: Old and New Testaments*. Grand Rapids: Eerdmans, 1948. Pp. 100-182.

7

THEOLOGY OF THE MONARCHICAL ERA

In God's original promise to Abraham, He promised to bless the patriarch, giving him an innumerable posterity. God promised to give Abraham a great name and make him a blessing through his posterity. It is the promise regarding these promised descendants in Genesis 12:2 that is amplified in the Davidic Covenant of 2 Samuel 7:12-16. God promised David that he would have a son, Solomon, who would establish his throne; moreover, David's lineage would be perpetuated, ultimately issuing in the kingdom rule of Messiah, who would have a political kingdom, an earthly rule that would endure forever.

DAVIDIC COVENANT

The kingdom concept reaches its zenith in the Davidic Covenant, which predicts the future millennial reign of David's greater Son, the Messiah.

NATURE OF THE COVENANT

In 2 Samuel 7 God promised David the following: "(1) David is to have a child, yet to be born, who shall succeed him and establish his kingdom. (2) This son (Solomon) shall build the temple instead of David. (3) The throne of his kingdom shall be established forever. (4) The throne will not be taken away from him (Solomon) even though his sins justify chastisement. (5) David's house, throne, and kingdom shall be established forever."[1]

Solomon, the son of David, would be established on the throne of Israel, and God promised the blessings of the Davidic Covenant would be continued through Solomon. The essence of the Davidic Covenant is given in 2 Samuel 7:16 and contains four important elements. (1) *House.* This refers to the royal dynasty of David; God promised David a continuing posterity that would be of the royal line of David. This promise verified that the lineage of David would not be destroyed but would issue in Messiah who would reign over the earth. (2) *Kingdom.* The word *kingdom* involves a people and a dominion over whom the king will rule; it is the sphere of the king's rulership. It is a political kingdom. (3) *Throne.* The throne suggests the authority and the power of the king in his rule. (4) *Forever.* Forever emphasizes that the right to rule will never be taken from the family of David; moreover, the posterity of David will never cease to rule over the house of Israel.

FULFILLMENT OF THE COVENANT

The nature of the ultimate fulfillment of the covenant can be understood in examining the initial fulfillment of the promises to David. Solomon's throne was a literal, political throne; therefore, the ultimate fulfillment through Messiah will also be literal and political (as well as spiritual). God reiterated the future fulfillment of the Davidic Covenant to David in Psalm 89. God swore in an oath to David that his lineage would continue forever and that David would have a descendant ruling above the kings of the earth (Ps. 89:3-4, 27-29, 33-37).

Other psalms anticipate the establishment of the Messianic kingdom. Psalm 110, referred to as a "purely Messianic Psalm," anticipates Messiah subjugating the nations of the earth to Himself. The psalm anticipates His judgment of the earthly kings (110:5-6) and His subsequent rule (110:2). It reflects a conquering enemy (110:1). Psalm 2 has a similar emphasis. Despite the rebellion of unbelieving nations, Yahweh installs Messiah on Zion, the holy mountain of Jerusalem, from where He will rule the earth.

The Old Testament prophets also expected a literal fulfillment of the Davidic Covenant through Messiah. They reiterated the promises of the future fulfillment amid Israel's sin and apostasy (suggesting the unconditional nature of the covenant).[2] Isaiah prophesied of the Son who would be given, exercising a governmental rule on the throne of David (Isa. 9:6-7); he spoke of the justice of Messiah's kingdom rule (Isa. 11:4-5). Jeremiah envisioned a day of tranquility in which a "righteous Branch of David" would "execute justice and righteousness on the earth" (Jer. 33:15). Jeremiah promised the continuation of the Davidic line enabling Messiah, a descendant of David, to fulfill this promise (Jer. 33:15-17; cf. also 23:5-6; 30:8-9). Ezekiel also anticipated the fulfillment of the Davidic Covenant in which David (a title of Messiah) would rule over them (Ezek. 37:24-28). It is important to notice that the prophecy of Ezekiel was given to a nation that had apostatized continually and was now in captivity in Babylon for her sins. Hosea also reaffirmed the covenant (Hos. 3:4-5), as did Amos (Amos 9:11) and Zechariah (Zech. 14:4, 9).

"Thus the Old Testament proclaims a kingdom to be established on the earth by the Messiah, the Son of David, as heir of the Davidic Covenant. The

Jews expected such a kingdom for they took God literally at His word, which strongly and repeatedly confirmed the hopes and promises of the covenant with David."[3]

SUMMARY

Although the Old Testament thus far has emphasized considerably man's alienation from God through sin, the monarchical era has revealed that God will ultimately move to restore man from his subservience to sin. He will do it through Messiah, a descendant of David. God will eventually give Messiah an earthly political and spiritual kingdom over Israel and over the nations in which Messiah will rule in righteousness.

NOTES ON THE MONARCHICAL ERA

1. John F. Walvoord, *The Millennial Kingdom* (Grand Rapids: Zondervan, 1959), p. 195; and Walter Kaiser, *Toward an Old Testament Theology* (Grand Rapids: Zondervan, 1978), pp. 143-64 (a discussion of the promise of 2 Sam. 7).

2. Walvoord, *The Millennial Kingdom*, pp. 196-97; and Charles C. Ryrie, *The Basis of the Premillennial Faith* (Neptune, N.J.: Loizeaux, 1953), p. 80.

3. Ryrie, *Basis of the Premillennial Faith*, pp. 88-89.

FOR FURTHER STUDY ON THE MONARCHICAL ERA

* William Dyrness. *Themes in Old Testament Theology*. Exeter: Paternoster, 1979.

** Walter C. Kaiser, Jr. *Toward an Old Testament Theology*. Grand Rapids: Zondervan, 1978. Pp. 143-64.

** Elmer A. Martens. *God's Design: A Focus on Old Testament Theology*. Grand Rapids: Baker, 1981. Pp. 117-89.

* Charles C. Ryrie. *The Basis of the Premillennial Faith*. Neptune, N.J.: Loizeaux, 1953. Pp. 76-104.

8

THEOLOGY OF THE PROPHETIC ERA

FUNCTION OF THE PROPHET

The prophets of Israel played an important role in declaring Israel's future kingdom blessings regarding the original promise given to Abraham in Genesis 12:1-3 and amplified under the Palestinian Covenant (Deut. 30:1-10) and the Davidic Covenant (2 Sam. 7:12-16).

The prophetic office was instituted in Deuteronomy 18:15-18 and immediately anticipated the greater prophet, Messiah, to whom the people would listen (Deut. 18:18). Several different terms are used to describe a prophet. The Hebrew term *nabhi* means a spokesman or a speaker and denotes "one who has been called or appointed to proclaim as a herald the message of God himself."[1] A second Hebrew term describing the prophet is *roeh*, which means "to see" (1 Sam. 9:9); it is the older word for prophet and is basically synonymous with *nabhi*.[2] *Roeh* was the popular designation, whereas *nabhi* was the technical term.[3] A third term, *seer*, means "to see or behold," and is also synonymous with *roeh*. All three terms are used in 1 Chronicles 29:29, suggesting they are synonymous.[4]

A major function of the Old Testament prophet as administrator of the theocratic kingdom was to call Israel back to the Mosaic law to which the Israelites were bound to the Lord in the suzerainty-vassal treaty.[5] The Mosaic law was a conditional covenant whereby God promised to bless the Israelites if they would obey Him; if they disobeyed Him, He would chastise them. Another function (among others) of the prophets was to proclaim predictive messages. The culmination of these predictive messages pertained to Israel's future under Messiah's kingdom rule.

ANTICIPATION OF THE SERVANT: ISAIAH

The book of Isaiah has been referred to as the Romans of the Old Testament. The prophet Isaiah provides a majestic picture of Messiah through whom God will bring light to the nations, redeem Israel, provide forgiveness, and bring universal blessing to the earth in the millennial kingdom.

Isaiah's prophecies are mingled with announcements of impending judgments and future blessings. These future blessings depict a day when Israel will repent of her sins and enjoy the blessing of restoration to the land in Messiah's kingdom. Foundational to Isaiah's theology is the call of the prophet described in Isaiah 6.[6] In this theophany Isaiah saw the glory of the Lord enthroned and surrounded by cherubim. Isaiah was also reminded of the holiness of God (Isa. 6:3). The nation Israel was to recognize the holiness of God and itself walk in holiness (Lev. 11:44). The prophet goes on to describe a future day when Israel will be holy to the Lord and God's glory will fill the earth.

Isaiah is unusually descriptive in depicting Messiah's future kingdom blessing to Israel and the nations. The prophet refers to Messiah as the "Branch of the Lord" (Isa. 4:2); Messiah will sprout out of the Davidic line and bring blessing to the entire earth. Messiah will also be Immanuel, "God with us," in His life and ministry (Isa. 7:14). It is clear from Matthew 1:23 that the prophecy finds fulfillment in the birth of Christ. Christ's presence through His words and works demonstrates "God with us," for He performed the works of God and spoke the words of God.

Isaiah describes Him both as "a child born" and "a son given," the former suggesting His humanity and the latter His deity (Isa. 9:6). Isaiah's titles of Messiah also emphasize His deity: "Wonderful Counselor" (cf. 28:29), "Mighty God," and "Eternal Father" (Isa. 9:6).

Isaiah emphasizes that Messiah will not only bring blessing to Israel, but to the nations of the world. The despised area of Galilee, known as "Galilee of the Gentiles," would become glorious because of Messiah's presence (Isa. 9:1-2; cf. 42:6; 49:6). But Messiah is also destined to rule. As a descendant of the lineage of David, He will exercise governmental rule over the earth in the future kingdom (Isa. 9:7). His government will be just and equitable (Isa. 11:1-5). But His rule will be preceded by a judgment upon the nations of the world (Isa. 24:1-23). At that time Messiah will bless Israel (Isa. 14:1-2) and the nations (Isa. 25:6-12), restoring all that Adam lost. The curse of death will be removed through Messiah's rule (Isa. 25:8). During the kingdom the earth will know the truth because Messiah, the Teacher, will guide the people into His truth (Isa. 30:20-21). Messiah will bring His healing to the world (Isa. 35:5-6)—a healing that will be effective on those that walk in holiness (Isa. 35:8).

In developing His topic of the future glory of the Lord, Isaiah shows how God will bring blessing to Israel and the nations of the world. It will be on the basis of forgiveness of sin; hence, Isaiah deals not only with a reigning Messiah but also with a suffering Messiah—who is the same Person.

Messiah will suffer a violent death as a substitute for the sins of the world (Isa. 52:13–53:12).[7]

Isaiah's theology provides considerable insight into God's method of resolving the dilemma of sin in the human race. Through Messiah, sin will be atoned for and the glory of God manifest on the earth in the future millennial kingdom.

ANTICIPATION OF A REGENERATED PEOPLE: THE NEW COVENANT

The New Covenant, foretold by the prophet Jeremiah, explains how God's people Israel will enjoy the kingdom blessings. It is through a regenerated heart.

NATURE OF THE NEW COVENANT

The prophet Jeremiah announced the impending invasion by Nebuchadnezzar and the subsequent captivity in Babylon. But Jeremiah envisioned a future day when God would restore the fortunes of Israel and bring them back into the land (Jer. 30:3). This would be an eschatological restoration for it would follow the time of great tribulation for Israel (Jer. 30:7). Jeremiah prophesied the rebuilding of Jersualem in that future day (Jer. 30:18-24) and the resultant kingdom blessings (Jer. 31:1-12). The blessing of Israel in that future day would be based on the New Covenant that God would make with Israel (Jer. 31:31-34). That New Covenant is made with the nation Israel (Jer. 31:31) and will be in contrast with the Old Covenant, the Mosaic Covenant, which could not produce righteousness in the people.

Eleven provisions of the New Covenant are as follows:[8]

(1) The new covenant is an unconditional grace covenant resting on the 'I will' of God. . . . (2) The new covenant is an everlasting covenant. . . . (3) The new covenant also promises the impartation of a renewed mind and heart which we may call regeneration. . . . (4) The new covenant provides for restoration to the favor and blessing of God. . . . (5) Forgiveness of sin is also included in the covenant, 'for I will remove their iniquity, and I will remember their sin no more' (Jer. 31:34b). (6) The indwelling of the Holy Spirit is also included. This is seen by comparing Jeremiah 31:33 with Ezekiel 36:27. (7) The teaching ministry of the Holy Spirit will be manifested, and the will of God will be known by obedient hearts. . . . (8) As is always the case when Israel is in the land, she will be blessed materially in accordance with the provisions of the new covenant. . . . (9) The sanctuary will be rebuilt in Jerusalem, for it is written 'I . . . will set my sanctuary in the midst of them for evermore. My tabernacle also shall be with them' (Ezek. 37:26-27a). (10) War shall cease and peace shall reign according to Hosea 2:18. . . . (11) The blood of the Lord Jesus Christ is the foundation of all the blessings of the new covenant, for 'by the blood of thy covenant I have sent forth thy prisoners out of the pit wherein is no water' (Zech. 9:11).

FULFILLMENT OF THE COVENANT

Although the New Covenant is quoted in Hebrews 8, it cannot be taken to mean the New Covenant is fulfilled in the church for in Jeremiah 31:31, as well as in Hebrews 8:8, it is stated that the covenant is made with "the house of Israel and with the house of Judah." The covenant will be fulfilled with the nation with which the covenant is made.[9] The time of the fulfillment of the New Covenant is eschatological as seen from the context of Jeremiah 31. In the section of Jeremiah 30-33 the setting is established in Jeremiah 30:3 where it states, "Behold, days are coming," suggesting an eschatological setting (cf. Jer. 31:27). Jeremiah 30:7 describes the future tribulation period, whereas the remainder of Jeremiah 30 is millennial. Other prophets also regard the New Covenant as eschatological and therefore future (Isa. 55:3; Ezek. 16:60, 62; 20:37; 34:25-26; Hos. 2:18-20).[10] Isaiah related the fulfillment of the New Covenant to the return of Messiah and the forgiveness of Israel (Isa. 59:20-21). Jeremiah related it to Israel's restoration to the land (Jer. 32:37, 40-41). "The sequence of events set up by the prophets is that Israel will first be regathered and restored to the land and then will experience the blessings of the new covenant *in the land.* . . . Fulfillment of the prophecies requires the regathering of all Israel, their spiritual rebirth, and the return of Christ."[11] The New Covenant is not fulfilled in the church but in the future kingdom.

ANTICIPATION OF A RENEWED WORSHIP: EZEKIEL

The prophet Ezekiel describes the restoration of Israel to the land, her regeneration, and Israel's renewed worship in the millennial kingdom.

Just before Nebuchadnezzar's destruction of the Temple in 586 B.C. the glory of God left the Temple (Ezek. 11:23). God's holiness had been offended by the idolatry and apostasy of the people Israel. They had violated the Mosaic Covenant, which had bound them to the Lord, and had prostituted their faith. Ezekiel, however, foresaw a future day, when Israel would be restored to the land (Ezek. 36:1–37:28), worshiping God in a new, future Temple in the millennial kingdom (Ezek. 40:5ff.). Ezekiel describes the return of God's glory to this new, future Temple as coming from the east where it had also departed (Ezek. 43:2-4).

In a detailed discussion Ezekiel describes a converted and restored people worshiping God in new surroundings in the millennial Temple. Ezekiel 33-48 is eschatological, describing how God will convert and restore the nation to the land. Messiah, under the title of David, will be their King and Shepherd (Ezek. 34:23-24). God will bring them back into the land where they will enjoy rest and peace in the kingdom (Ezek. 36:1–37:28). The Hebrew people will be converted as God gives them a new heart and puts His Holy Spirit within them (Ezek. 36:25-27). After the Lord destroys their northern enemy (Ezek. 38:1–39:6) the land is cleansed and prepared for millennial worship. Chapters 40-48 describe the millennial worship of the Lord in detail.[12]

There are at least five distinct purposes for the millennial Temple.

> (1) *To Demonstrate God's Holiness.* . . . (the) infinite holiness of Jehovah's nature and government . . . had been outraged and called into question by the idolatry and rebellion of His professed people. . . . This has necessitated the . . . judgment of sinful Israel . . . along with . . . the wicked surrounding nations. . . . This is followed by the display of divine grace in restoring the prodigal nation to Himself. . . . (2) *To Provide a Dwelling-Place for the Divine Glory.* . . . This is "the place of my throne, and the place of the soles of my feet, where I will dwell in the midst of the children of Israel forever" (43:7). . . . (3) *To Perpetuate the Memorial of Sacrifice.* It is not sacrifice, of course, rendered with a view of obtaining salvation, but sacrifice commemorative of an accomplished salvation maintained in the presence of the revealed glory of Jehovah. . . . (4) *To Provide the Center for the Divine Government.* When the divine Glory takes up its residence in the temple, the announcement is not only that the temple is God's dwelling-place and the seat of worship, but also that it is the radiating centre of the divine government. "This is the place of my throne" (43:7). . . . (5) *To Provide Victory over the Curse* (47:1-12). From under the threshold of the temple house the prophet sees a marvelous stream issuing and flowing eastward in ever increasing volumes of refreshment until it enters in copious fulness into the Dead Sea, whose poisonous waters are healed. . . . Traversing the course of this wondrous life-giving water, the seer finds both banks clothed with luxuriant growth of trees of fadeless leaf and never-failing fruit, furnishing both medicine and food.[13]

Ezekiel began his prophecy by describing the glory of God (Ezek. 1:4-28) and concluded his book by describing the return of God's glory to the millennial Temple (Ezek. 43:2). Ezekiel thus describes God's judgment and victory over sin whereby His glory can again be manifested to His people Israel and to the nations of the world.

ANTICIPATION OF THE FIFTH KINGDOM: DANIEL

Daniel provides considerable detail in describing the destruction of the false kingdoms and the establishment of Messiah's kingdom.

God enabled Daniel to interpret dreams and visions that foretold God's consummation of the age. Nebuchadnezzar, king of Babylon, had a dream that Daniel interpreted as spanning the course of Gentile domination over Israel. Daniel interpreted the four kingdoms to Nebuchadnezzar as being Babylon, Medo-Persia, Greece, and Rome (Dan. 2:36-43). Following the demise of the four kingdoms Daniel saw another kingdom that would never be destroyed: "It will crush and put an end to all these kingdoms, but it will itself endure forever" (Dan. 2:44). This was the fifth kingdom; it is Messiah's kingdom. This fifth kingdom crushed the four preceding kingdoms with a stone cut "without hands," suggesting Messiah's kingdom has no human origin (Dan. 2:45).

Chapter 7, a parallel passage, describes the same four Gentile powers, destroyed by the Son of Man (a title of Messiah), who delivers up the kingdom to the Ancient of Days (Dan. 7:13-14). The converted Hebrew people will flourish in this new kingdom (Dan. 7:27). Daniel further describes seventy weeks (490 years) allotted to the Hebrew people. The seventy weeks describe God's plan for making provision for sin ("to finish the transgression, to make an end of sin, to make atonement for iniquity," 9:24), and for establishing His righteous kingdom upon earth ("to bring in everlasting righteousness, to seal up vision and prophecy, and to anoint the most holy place" 9:24). Sixty-nine weeks (483 years) have been fulfilled in history, culminating with the death of Christ in A.D. 33 (Dan. 9:26). The seventieth week (7 years) remains future wherein Israel will suffer during the tribulation and under the "prince who is to come" (Dan. 9:26). However, the prince (popularly called Antichrist) who opposes Israel will himself be destroyed (Dan. 11:45). Israel will be rescued from oppression, and those who have died will be resurrected (Dan. 12:1-2). Daniel describes a resurrection to "everlasting life" and a resurrection to "everlasting contempt" (Dan. 12:2). These resurrections will undoubtedly be separated by the millennial age.

Daniel has given a detailed picture of the consummation of the age. God is sovereign who does as He will and will consummate this age according to His good pleasure (Dan. 2:21; 4:35). The Gentile world powers that have opposed God and His truth will be conquered and destroyed; Israel, the oppressed nation, will be rescued and established in the future millennial kingdom. God's glory will be manifested in the kingdom to come (Dan. 12:3).

ANTICIPATION OF THE DAY OF THE LORD: JOEL

The prophet Joel provides further insight into the kingdom concept through His description of the future judgment of Israel, the nations, and the millennial blessings.

Joel called the people of Judah to repentance in the light of the terrible locust plague that had devastated the nation (Joel 2:12-13). The locust plague prefigured the Day of the Lord (1:15), a concept that involves three features: (1) it may denote any judgment of God in history; (2) it may denote an eschatological judgment; (3) it may signify the blessings of the millennial age.[14] Thus the Day of the Lord is "that extended period of time beginning with God's dealing with Israel after the rapture at the beginning of the tribulation period and extending through the second advent and the millennial age unto the creation of the new heavens and new earth after the millennium."[15] Joel devotes 2:18–3:21 to describing this eschatological emphasis of the Day of the Lord, both in future judgment and blessing.

Having exhorted the people to repent, Joel pictures a future day when Israel has repented: "Then the LORD will be zealous for His land, and will have pity on His people" (2:18). Joel describes the future day when the Lord will move to bless Israel in the millennial kingdom: (1) the land will be productive (2:21-27); (2) Israel will live in peace (2:26); (3) the Lord will dwell in the midst of the people (2:27); (4) the Spirit will be poured out on the nation (2:28-32).[16]

The day of future blessing is also the day of destruction for Israel's enemies. At the time of Israel's repentance God will judge the nations based on their treatment of Israel (3:2-6). The Lord will be exalted as He renders judgment upon the nations (3:9-17), and the world will recognize that the Lord is Israel's God, dwelling in Jerusalem (3:17). Joel pictures the consummation of the age with God's blessing upon the land of Israel (3:18-21). As God had planned for His redeemed people to be holy, so it will be in that day. Jerusalem will be holy, and all that dwell in it will be holy to the Lord (3:17).

ANTICIPATION OF MESSIAH'S ADVENT: ZECHARIAH

God gave the prophet Zechariah eight night visions to emphasize the judgment upon the nations and the glorious future of His people Israel in the kingdom. The significance of the visions, which had both near and far implications, can be seen in the chart on the next page.

The visions survey Israel's suffering (1:7-17), which is terminated by Messiah destroying the oppressors (1:21). After Israel's enemies are destroyed, Jerusalem enjoys expansion and growth (2:1-13), which will only happen after the nation has been cleansed of sin's defilement (3:1-10). Then Israel will fulfill its function in being a light to the nations—which was God's original intention for the nation (Isa. 49:6; 60:1-3; Zech. 4:1-14). But before Israel can experience blessing, God will reveal His holiness, judging individual sin according His holy standard (5:1-4), as well as national sin (5:5-11). Judgment will issue from Jerusalem, the holy center of a holy God (6:1-8).

The kingdom blessings will be inaugurated by Messiah, who is called the Branch (6:12) and who will also rule as Priest and King (6:13). In the presentation of the two burdens (chaps. 9-14), Zechariah describes how this glorious kingdom age will come about. It is through the work of Messiah who comes in humility to Jerusalem (9:9) as the Good Shepherd but is rejected and sold for thirty pieces of silver in favor of the worthless shep-

ZECHARIAH'S VISIONS

Vision	Immediate Significance	Future Fulfillment
FIRST (1:7-17)	Encouragement because of Gentile domination—the Temple will be built.	Release from Gentile domination.
SECOND (1:18-21)	Nations now having dominion will be overthrown.	Messiah terminates "Times of the Gentiles"—Babylon, Medo-Persia, Greece, Rome.
THIRD (2:1-13)	Jerusalem will be restored and rebuilt in their day.	Prosperity and blessing of Jerusalem in Millennium.
FOURTH (3:1-10)	Joshua, representing nation, cleansed, enabling nation to serve God.	Messiah cleanses nation, enabling Israel to be a light to the nations.
FIFTH (4:1-14)	God's power enabling them to complete Temple (4:6-7)—power ministered through Joshua and Zerubbabel.	God's power enabling nation to be light to the world—power ministered through Messiah.
SIXTH (5:1-4)	God will quickly judge individual sin in the restored nation.	God will judge sin at the end of the "Times of the Gentiles."
SEVENTH (5:5-11)	God will judge the commercial exploiters during the restoration (Neh. 5:1-13).	Wicked commercial exploitation by the nations will be permanently judged and removed (Rev. 18).
EIGHTH (6:1-8)	God stands ready to judge Israel's enemies.	God will judge the nations: North—Assyria, Babylon, Rome; South—Egypt.

herd (11:12-17). The Good Shepherd is wounded (13:6) and killed by His own people (13:7). Yet at His second advent He will come in triumph, rescuing a repentant people (12:10-14), delivering them from their enemies (14:1-4), exalting Jerusalem as a bastion of truth (14:10), and ruling over the nations of the world in the kingdom (9:10).

Messiah has made provision for sin. In that day all that dwell in the Lord's presence will be cleansed of sin and will be holy for the Lord is holy (14:20-21).

SUMMARY

The prophetic books have provided a developing concept of God's future dealing with Israel and the world. The prophets provide an expanded picture of Messiah's work in His first and second advents, focusing on the ultimate establishment of the future kingdom. Isaiah details His substitutionary atonement (Isa. 52:13–53:12) while Zechariah also dwells on His sufferings (Zech. 11:12-13; 13:6-7). A great emphasis, however, is given to Messiah's second advent and His glorious reign on earth. Closely related to that event is Israel's repentance, forgiveness, and restoration. The two go hand in hand for it is through Israel that God will bless the nations of the world. Thus, it is these two intertwined concepts that the prophets describe. But the final focus does not rest with Israel; it rests with the glory of God. Isaiah's ministry focused on a holy God (Isa. 6) as did Ezekiel's (Ezek. 1). Isaiah spoke of a future kingdom age when only the holy one would fellowship with a holy God (Isa. 35:8); Ezekiel detailed the future worship of a holy God, glorious in His appearance with His people (Ezek. 43:2, 4, 5). Zechariah concludes with an emphasis on the holiness of God (Zech. 14:20-21). The recognition and adoration of the holiness of God will be achieved in the future kingdom age.

Notes on the Prophetic Era

1. Gleason L. Archer, Jr., *A Survey of Old Testament Introduction* (Chicago: Moody, 1964), p. 284

2. Francis Brown, S. R. Driver, and C. A. Briggs, *A Hebrew and English Lexicon of the Old Testament* (Oxford: Clarendon, 1968), pp. 611, 909.

3. E. J. Young, *My Servants The Prophets* (Grand Rapids: Eerdmans, 1952), pp. 63-64. This is a most important volume in discussing the meaning, nature, and function of the Old Testament prophet.

4. See also J. A. Motyer, "Prophecy, Prophets," in James D. Douglas, ed., *The New Bible Dictionary* (Grand Rapids: Eerdmans, 1962), p. 1037, suggesting that the three terms are synonymous.

5. Alva J. McClain, *The Greatness of the Kingdom* (Chicago: Moody, 1968), pp. 116-17.

6. See Walter Kaiser, *Toward an Old Testament Theology* (Grand Rapids: Zondervan, 1978), pp. 205-7.

7. The pronouns "*He* was pierced through for *our* transgressions, *He* was crushed for *our* iniquities; . . . And by *His* scouring *we* are healed" (Isa. 53:5) emphasize the concept of substitutionary atonement.

8. Ryrie, *The Basis of the Premillennial Faith* (Neptune, N.J.: Loizeaux, 1953), pp. 112-14.

9. J. Dwight Pentecost, *Things to Come* (Grand Rapids: Zondervan, 1958), pp. 119-20.

10. Ryrie, *Basis of the Premillennial Faith*, pp. 110-11.

11. Ibid., p. 111.

12. For a discussion of the interpretive views concerning a millennial Temple see Hobart E. Freeman, *An Introduction to the Old Testament Prophets* (Chicago: Moody, 1968), pp. 308-24; and Paul D. Feinberg, "A Study of Ezekiel's Temple Vision," unpublished B.D. thesis (Fullerton, Calif.: Talbot Seminary, 1963).

13. Merrill F. Unger, "The Temple Vision of Ezekiel," *Bibliotheca Sacra* 106 (January 1949):57-64.

14. James Orr, "Eschatology of the Old Testament," in James Orr, ed., *The International Standard Bible Encyclopaedia*, 5 vols. (Grand Rapids: Eerdmans, 1939), 2:977. Orr states: "The 'Day of Jehovah,' in the prophetic writings, is conceived of, sometimes more generally, as denoting any great manifestation of God's power in judgment or salvation (e.g. the locusts in Joel 2), sometimes more eschatologically, of the final crisis in the history of God's kingdom, involving the overthrow of all opposition, and the complete triumph of righteousness (e.g. Isa. 2:2-5; Joel 3; Amos 9:11ff; Zech. 14, etc.)."

15. Pentecost, *Things to Come*, pp. 230-31.

16. There are varying views on the fulfillment of Joel 2:28-32 prompted mainly because it is used by Peter at Pentecost (Acts 2:16-21). (1) *Fulfillment in Joel's day.* This is not a popular view. (2) *Fulfillment at Pentecost.* Amillennialists generally hold this view, equating the church age with the Messianic age. Compare E. J. Young, *An Introduction to the Old Testament* (Grand Rapids: Eerdmans, 1964), p. 255. A problem with this view is how the phenomenon of Joel 2:30-32 can be understood to have already been fulfilled. (3) *Eschatological View.* Some, such as Charles Feinberg, suggest no part of this is fulfilled at Pentecost; it is entirely eschatological, or future. Pentecost is an illustration of Joel 2. Compare Charles L. Feinberg, *The Minor Prophets* (Chicago: Moody, 1976), pp. 81-82. (4) *Continuous Fulfillment View.* Hobart Freeman suggests the entire church age is a continuous fulfillment of Joel 2. Compare Hobart Freeman, *Old Testament Prophets*, pp. 155-56. (5) *Partial Fulfillment View.* These adherents suggest the Spirit was given at Pentecost making available God's blessing upon Israel, but the eschatological aspects of the prophecy are yet unfulfilled. Compare John F. Walvoord, *The Holy Spirit* (Grand Rapids: Zondervan, 1965), p. 229. This final view has the least problems connected with it.

FOR FURTHER STUDY ON THE PROPHETIC ERA

** E. W. Hengstenberg. *Christology of the Old Testament.* Reprint. Grand Rapids: Kregel, 1970. Pp. 122-699.

** Walter C. Kaiser, Jr. *Toward an Old Testament Theology.* Grand Rapids: Zondervan, 1978. Pp. 182-261.

* Elmer A. Martens. *God's Design: A Focus on Old Testament Theology.* Grand Rapids: Baker, 1981. Pp. 191-248.

* Charles C. Ryrie. *The Basis of the Premillennial Faith.* Neptune, N.J.: Loizeaux, 1953. Pp. 105-25.

** Geerhardus Vos. *Biblical Theology: Old and New Testaments.* Grand Rapids: Eerdmans, 1948. Pp. 185-296.

9

INTRODUCTION TO
NEW TESTAMENT THEOLOGY

See the Introduction to Biblical Theology for a definition, relationship to other studies, methodology, and importance.

As in the study of Old Testament theology, there is little agreement on the approach to New Testament theology, particularly as seen in the history of the discipline. Those rejecting the inspiration of Scripture view the New Testament as any other piece of literature and approach the study of the New Testament from a critical standpoint. From that foundation, there is great diversity of opinion, some seeing the New Testament as a conflict between the different writers, as a history of salvation, as a synthesis of other ancient religions, as an existential encounter, or as an embellishment of the life of Christ by the New Testament writers. Conservatives, who affirm the inspiration of Scripture, usually approach the study of New Testament theology by arranging the material according to the divisions of systematic theology; others follow the theological emphases of the New Testament writers.

HISTORY

New Testament theology is a recent development of the last two centuries. Prior to that time theology was interested in dogmatics, the doctrinal formulations of the church, and systematics, which many times was philosophical speculation. In an address in 1787 J. P. Gabler leveled an attack against the methodology of dogmatic theology, criticizing its philosophical approach. A rationalistic approach to understanding the New Testament followed. The Bible was to be viewed as a human book in understanding how it was written and what the individual writers emphasized.

F. C. Baur of Tubingen (1792-1860) was a leader in the rationalist approach. He employed Hegel's philosophy of thesis—antithesis—synthesis

75

to the New Testament writings. Thus Baur saw contradiction between the Jewish emphasis of Peter's writings and the Gentile emphasis of Paul's writings. H. J. Holtzmann (1832-1910) furthered this thought, denying any idea of divine revelation and espousing the theory of conflicting theologies in the New Testament.

Wilhelm Wrede (1859-1906) influenced New Testament theology considerably in emphasizing the history-of-religions approach. Wrede denied that the New Testament was a document of theology: rather, it was to be viewed as history of first-century religion. Theology, in fact, was not to be considered the correct term: religion was a better term in identifying the New Testament writings because it expressed the writers "believing, hoping, loving" rather than being a "record of abstract theological reflections."[1]

Rudolf Bultmann (1884-1976) emphasized the form-critical approach to the New Testament in which he sought to uncover its underlying material.[2] Bultmann taught that the New Testament had been enshrouded with the opinions and reinterpretations of the writers. The task now involved a "demythologization" of the New Testament to strip away the writers' embellishments and arrive at the true words of Jesus. Bultmann saw no connection between the historical Jesus and the Christ represented in the New Testament.[3]

Oscar Cullmann (b. 1902) emphasized God's acts in history in accomplishing man's salvation. This was termed *Heilsgeschichte* or "salvation history." Cullmann rejected many of the radical features of form criticism, advocating instead the exegesis (explanation and interpretation) of the New Testament, with an emphasis on history. Like others of his persuasion, Cullmann emphasized the Christology of the New Testament.[4]

There has been no consensus or unanimity in what approach should be undertaken in the study of New Testament theology. The majority approach would be built on the presupposition that denies biblical inspiration, hence, viewing the New Testament as conflicting theologies. Conservative writers, however, have challenged this position and built a New Testament theology based on the inspiration and unity of Scripture.

METHODOLOGY

Since all the books of the New Testament were written within fifty years of each other, New Testament theology does not concern itself with periods of revelation as does Old Testament theology. Rather, "Biblical Theology of the New Testament systematizes the truth as it was progressively revealed through the various writers of the New Testament."[5] Thus New Testament theology examines the theology of the synoptics, Luke, Acts, Paul, Peter, John, Hebrews, and the writers of the general epistles.

In establishing a New Testament theology, some follow the general outline of systematic theology; however, that methodology would not sufficiently reveal the emphases of the individual writers. It seems best to set forth a New Testament theology by analyzing the writings of the individual New Testament writers that will reflect what the individual writer says about a subject.[6]

Several factors should be considered in the development of a methodology.[7] (1) Revelation is progressive, culminating in the revelation concerning Christ. New Testament theology should seek to delineate the culminating doctrines concerning Christ and redemption. (2) The emphasis of the New Testament climaxes in the belief in the death and resurrection of Christ and the hope of His return. New Testament theology should focus on these doctrines from the various statements of the New Testament writers. (3) New Testament theology should recognize that the teachings of Jesus and the teachings of the other New Testament writers are a unity and are complementary. (4) The diversity of the New Testament writings does not suggest contradiction, but stems from the divine origin of the New Testament. (5) New Testament theology should employ the analytic method (but not to the exclusion of the thematic method) because that method adequately reflects the diversity of the New Testament.

NOTES ON NEW TESTAMENT THEOLOGY

1. R. B. Gaffin, Jr., "New Testament Theology" in *New Dictionary of Theology*, edited by Sinclair B. Ferguson and David F. Wright (Downers Grove, Ill: InterVarsity, 1988), p. 462.
2. See Stephen H. Travis, "Form Criticism" in I. Howard Marshall, ed., *New Testament Interpretation: Essays on Principles and Methods* (Grand Rapids: Eerdmans, 1977), pp. 153-64.
3. Donald Guthrie, *New Testament Theology* (Downers Grove, Ill.: InterVarsity, 1981). p. 25.
4. Compare Oscar Cullmann, *The Christology of the New Testament*, rev. ed. (Philadelphia: Westminster, 1963).
5. Charles C. Ryrie, *Biblical Theology of the New Testament* (Chicago: Moody, 1959), p. 19.
6. Ryrie, *Biblical Theology*, pp. 19-20.
7. Compare Gaffin, "New Testament Theology," pp. 463-65.

FOR FURTHER STUDY ON NEW TESTAMENT THEOLOGY

* R. B. Gaffin, Jr. "New Testament Theology" in *New Dictionary of Theology* edited by Sinclair B. Ferguson and David F. Wright. Downers Grove, Ill.: InterVarsity, 1988. Pp. 461-66.

** Donald Guthrie. *New Testament Theology*. Downers Grove, Ill.: InterVarsity, 1981. Pp. 21-74.

** G. Hasel. *New Testament Theology: Basic Issues in the Current Debate*. Grand Rapids: Eerdmans, 1975.

** George E. Ladd. *A Theology of the New Testament*. Grand Rapids: Eerdmans, 1974.

* G. R. Osborne. "New Testament Theology" in Walter A. Elwell, ed., *Evangelical Dictionary of Theology*. Grand Rapids: Baker, 1984. Pp. 768-73.

* Charles C. Ryrie. *Biblical Theology of the New Testament*. Chicago: Moody, 1959. Pp. 11-24.

10

THEOLOGY OF THE SYNOPTICS

In developing the theology of the synoptic gospels, it is important to understand the viewpoint of the writer. To whom did Matthew, Mark, and Luke write? Why did they write? What is the particular emphasis of each writer? What themes do they stress? These are important questions in biblical theology that determine what theological emphases and concerns were developed by the individual writers. The nature of biblical theology rests particularly with the concerns of the human writer (without neglecting or ignoring the fact of divine inspiration).

Introductory matters of authorship, date, audience, and purpose are included to establish the particular emphasis of the individual writers.

The term *synoptic* comes from the Greek word *sunoptikos*, "to see things together," and characterizes the three gospels, Matthew, Mark, and Luke. They are studied together because their view of the life of Christ is considered sufficiently similar.

THE SYNOPTIC PROBLEM

A problem in studying the synoptic gospels is the relationship of the three to each other. Did the gospels make any use of each other's writings? Did they have a common source (called "Q" for the German word *quelle*, meaning "source") that they all drew on? There is considerable agreement among the three gospels, particularly with reference to Mark. B. F. Westcott has noted the percentages of differences and similarities in the gospels as the chart on the next page illustrates.[1]

The chart reveals that ninety-three percent of Mark is found in the other three gospels; in other words, there is little that is unique to Mark. Excluding the questionable ending of 16:9-20, there are about thirty verses that are unique to Mark.

COMPARING THE GOSPELS:
DIFFERENCES AND SIMILARITIES

Gospel	% Peculiarities	% Coincidences
MARK	7	93
MATTHEW	42	58
LUKE	59	41
JOHN	92	8

There are both agreements and dissimilarities.[2] There are agreements among the three gospels in the way they record their events (cf. Matt. 9:6; Mark 2:10; Luke 5:24). They also reveal a common use of rare words. But they also record dissimilarities, for example, the birth narratives and the genealogies are different in Matthew and Luke. Even parallel accounts are different, such as the order of the temptations (Matt. 4:1-11; Mark 1:12-13; Luke 4:1-13).

What then is the relationship of the three gospels to each other? Several theories have been suggested.[3]

ORAL TRADITION THEORY

It was believed that the preaching of the early church provided fixed forms to the life and ministry of Jesus, but there were no written forms behind the synoptic gospels.

INTERDEPENDENCE THEORY

In 1789 Griesbach taught that the first writer drew upon oral tradition, the second writer used the material from the first writer, while the third writer drew upon the other two.

PRIMITIVE GOSPEL THEORY

In 1778 Lessing taught that the gospel writers borrowed from a primitive source called *Urevangelium*, which no longer exists.

FRAGMENTARY THEORY

In 1817 Schleiermacher taught that the gospel writers compiled their accounts from many fragmentary writings about the life of Christ.

TWO-DOCUMENT THEORY

A more recent development, this theory suggests that since Matthew and Luke are usually found in agreement with Mark, and since so much material of Mark is found in Matthew and Luke, Mark must have been written first and used by Matthew and Luke. But since Matthew and Luke have considerable material in common not found in Mark, they must have drawn from a second common source, called "Q."

FOUR-DOCUMENT THEORY

Streeter suggested four original, independent sources behind the final written form of the gospels: Mark in Rome about A.D. 60, "Q" in Antioch about A.D. 50, "M" (private "saying" source of Matthew) in Jerusalem about A.D. 65, and "L" (private source of Luke) in Caesarea about A.D. 60.

MODERN DEVELOPMENTS[4]

Modern critical theories have arisen in which attempt is made to explain the human origin and production of the gospel writings. While this methodology can have some validity and some conservative scholars employ these critical studies to understand the biblical records, there are inherent dangers. The reader is specifically referred to the article in the *Talbot Review* for an evaluative study of redaction criticism. The explanations given below are a general explanation; they can be given a more liberal or a more conservative slant, depending on the writer.

Historical criticism.[5] When the text is obscure, scholars attempt to discover "what actually happened" to help clarify the narrative. This is done by noting discrepancies in parallel accounts, examining secular history material, noting whether some events actually happened, recognizing supernatural occurrences (attempt is made to final a natural explanation), "invented" stories by the church, and other methods. A basic problem in historical criticism is that it approaches the Bible like any other book and acknowledges the possibility of error; in this sense it is incompatible with the doctrine of biblical inspiration.[6]

Source criticism. Source criticism attempts to identify the sources used in writing the synoptic gospels and identify their relationship to the gospels. For example, where there are duplicate accounts of a story, an attempt is made to explain a literary connection or an underlying source. Mark 4:10-13 is cited in suggesting Mark used another source in which vv. 11-12 were not present.[7] Agreement in wording also suggests there is a common underlying source. Advocates of source criticism suggest the writers used a common source to which they adhered but felt the freedom to add detail and "were not worried about precision in historical details."[8] The problem with source criticism is twofold: it tends to ignore the divine element in inspiration and acknowledge error; it is built on conjecture without any demonstrable proof of underlying sources.

Form criticism.[9] Rudolf Bultmann was one of the pioneers of form criticism that regarded the synoptic gospels as "folk literature." The gospel writers, according to Bultmann, actually collected and edited material and wrote the way the church traditionally understood the events rather than writing historically accurate events. Form criticism thus builds on source criticism and attempts to explain how Mark and Q arose. Mark is a product of the early church, which embellished the life of Christ. Matthew and Luke used Mark with additional embellishments to form their gospels (they were not historical Matthew and Luke, but second century writers). Therefore, most of the gospels do not contain historical data but are embellishments of the early church. The embellishments occurred to encourage suffering Christians. These "inventions" became indistinguishable from historic fact.[10]

Redaction criticism.[11] "Redaction criticism is a method of biblical criticism which seeks to determine the evangelist's point of view by ascertaining the creative editorial work carried out by him on his sources." The writer is not merely a historian, but he becomes a theologian in the "modification, composition and creation of tradition." The writer may be creative, altering or embellishing the historical tradition, or even departing from historical events.[12] An example of this is Gundry's approach to interpreting Matthew in which he suggests the visit of the magi was not an historical event but based on the shepherd story that he changed to suit his theological purpose.[13] Redaction criticism seeks to distinguish between the writer's theological viewpoint and his source materials.

A major problem, obviously, in attempting to solve the manner in which the gospels were written is that the above-mentioned theories are mainly conjecture. There is, for example, no evidence of a Q source. Also, the more recent theories generally build on a thesis that Mark was written first—which is a serious problem because it militates against eighteen centuries of tradition and also the comments of the church Fathers. It does not militate against inspiration to suggest Mark was written first and Matthew and Luke borrowed from Mark; however, it appears highly unlikely. Several factors need to be considered in a solution:

(1) The above theories stress the human aspect in the writing of the gospels, which is a legitimate consideration, but it sometimes neglects the divine element. In John 14:26 Jesus promised the disciples the Holy Spirit would "bring to your remembrance all that I said to you." This is an important statement suggesting a supernatural element in the writing of Scripture. How could the gospel writers remember the details of the life of Christ? Or the conversations? Supernaturally. It was promised by the Lord in the Upper

Room. This aspect ought not to be neglected in considering a solution. This *is* a divine element in the writing of Scripture.

(2) The writers wrote from firsthand knowledge and frequently as eyewitnesses. Matthew and John were eyewitnesses who wrote what they had observed and experienced; Mark wrote through information from Peter; Luke probably gained his knowledge from Paul and others as well as through his own research (Luke 1:3).

(3) There were other eyewitnesses who saw and heard the Lord and who could provide information (Luke 1:2-3). Although it is generally suggested that Luke drew on written sources (and that is certainly possible), Luke 1:2-3 seems to suggest he investigated eyewitnesses and servants of the Lord who handed the information down to him.

(4) They wrote through divine revelation and inspiration. Some elements simply cannot be explained on human terms. Paul, for instance, wrote and taught as a result of divine revelation; he stresses that he did not receive his gospel from any man—not even the apostles. God revealed His truth to Paul directly (Gal. 1:11-12; Eph. 3:3).

INTRODUCTION TO SYNOPTIC THEOLOGY

MATTHEW

Author. There is early support sugggesting that Matthew, the tax collector, originally wrote in Aramaic, an important testimony for the priority of Matthew. Approximately A.D. 150, Papias, bishop of Hierapolis, testified: "So then Matthew composed the oracles in the Hebrew language, and each one interpreted them as he could."[14] Origen (c. 185-254) stated that Matthew was prepared for the "convert of Judaism, and published in the Hebrew language." Irenaeus stated that Matthew wrote while Peter and Paul were still alive; Mark wrote after they had died.[15]

Date. Recognizing that Matthew wrote to a Jewish audience, an early date for Matthew can be argued from the standpoint of *need.* It is reasonable to suggest that there were 20,000 Jews in Jerusalem who believed in Christ. These believers would need an explanation concerning the Messiahship of Jesus, encouraging their faith from a Jewish standpoint and also confuting their opponents.[16] The rapid growth of the number of Jewish believers constituted a primary and immediate need for a gospel written distinctively to Jewish believers.

The view of the early church was that "Matthew wrote his Gospel before the other Evangelists composed theirs. This testimony is so persistent and unanimous that it ought to have some weight in deciding this question."[17] Matthew was likely written about A.D. 50.[18]

Audience. The audience of Matthew's gospel is linked to the nature and growth of the early church. Because it had not separated from Judaism, it is clear that the early church was predominantly Jewish: shortly after Pentecost, 5,000 Jewish men[19] believed. There would have been an early need to explain why, if Jesus was indeed the Messiah, the kingdom had not come. Matthew wrote to explain this to his Jewish audience.

Theological Purposes. Matthew captures the Messianic hope and expectation of the Jews. He instructs his readers that the true Messiah, the Son of David, has indeed come. While the other gospel writers recognize Jesus as the promised Messiah, it is Matthew who presents Him as uniquely for the Jews.

The purposes of Matthew's gospel are twofold.[20] The *first* is to prove Jesus is the Messiah. *Messiah* is a Jewish title for Israel's king who will bring salvation to Israel at the end of the age. Matthew presents Jesus as Israel's Messiah (Anointed One) who fulfills the function of prophet, priest, and king in one Person. The *second* purpose is to present the kingdom program of God. Since Jesus is Israel's Messiah and since the nation rejected the Messiah, Matthew explains that while the kingdom has been offered to the Jews, it has been postponed because of Israel's rejection. Messiah's earthly kingdom will be established at His Second Advent.

MARK

Author. The early church gave strong witness to John Mark's authorship of the second gospel. Papias writing at about A.D. 150 stated: "Mark, having become the interpreter of Peter, wrote down accurately everything that he remembered."[21] Irenaeus writing about A.D. 185 stated: "Now after their decease (Peter and Paul) Mark, the disciple and interpreter of Peter, also handed down to us in writing what Peter had preached."[22]

Date. Because Irenaeus testified that Mark wrote after the death of Peter and Paul,[23] and because Paul probably died in the summer or fall of A.D. 66, Mark likely wrote his gospel in A.D. 66 or 67. Because the destruction of Jerusalem is not mentioned, it is certain that Mark wrote before A.D. 70.

Audience. Writing about A.D. 195, Clement of Alexandria states that Roman people asked Peter to write an account of the life of Christ for them. It is likely that Mark helped Peter fulfil that request from the Romans. Internal evidence, through a translation of Aramaic terms, also indicates a non-Jewish audience.

Theological Purpose. Because the Romans were a people of action rather than thought, Mark presents Christ as "the mighty Worker rather than the profound Thinker, the Man who conquers by doing."[24] Mark's style, as well as his content, reflects that theological purpose. Because Mark presents Christ as a man of action, he omits the genealogy and birth narratives and begins with the baptism of Christ, moving swiftly into the public ministry of Christ.

The capstone of Mark's emphasis of Jesus is his portrayal of Christ as the Servant who came to minister and give His life as a ransom for many (Mark 10:45). Mark's goal was to present his Roman readers with the dynamic of the Son of Man as Servant, thereby elliciting faith in Him.

LUKE

Author. External evidence is strong in affirming Luke the physician as the author of the third gospel. The Muratorian Canon (A.D. 160-200) reports that Luke, a physician and traveling companion of Paul, traced the matters and compiled a gospel of Christ's life. Irenaeus (c. A.D. 185) also testified: "Then Luke, the follower of Paul, recorded in a book the gospel as it was preached by him."[25] Clement of Alexandria and Origen also ascribe authorship to Luke.

Date. The date of the writing of Luke is intertwined with the writing of Acts. Acts was probably written in A.D. 63 because the book closes abruptly, describing Paul's imprisonment, whereas his release, which occurred in A.D. 63, is not mentioned. The statement of Acts 1:1 indicates the gospel of Luke was written before Acts. Luke probably wrote near the end of his time in Palestine, perhaps between A.D. 58 and 60.

Audience. Although Luke addressed his gospel to Theophilus, this was probably a dedication; a Gentile audience is undoubtedly in view as Luke's audience. Because of Paul's three missionary journeys there was a great need for a gospel distinct from the others, aimed particularly for the Greek mind.[26] There is considerable evidence for a Greek audience.[27] (1) The genealogy of Jesus is traced to Adam, the father of the entire human race, rather than to a Jewish patriarch. (2) Fulfilled prophecies occur in the sayings of Christ addressed to the Jews, not as narrative apologetics as in Matthew. (3) Jewish terminology, such as "rabbi," is avoided. (4) Greek names are substituted for Hebrew names (cf. Luke 6:16; 23:33).

Theological Purpose. Luke has a cosmopolitan emphasis, stressing the universality of the gospel and that Jesus is the redeemer of the world. This is emphasized through linking the genealogy of Jesus with Adam, the common ancestor of all mankind.[28] This emphasis is particularly seen in Luke's use of parables. "Admission to the Kingdom is open to Samaritans (9:51-6, 10:30-7, 17:11-19) and pagans (2:32, 3:6, 38, 4:25-7, 7:9, 10:1, 24:47) as well as to Jews (1:33, 2:10); to publicans, sinners and outcasts (3:12, 5:27-32, 7:37-50, 19:2-10, 23:43) as well as to respectable people (7:36, 11:37, 14:1); to the poor (1:53, 2:7, 6:20, 7:22) as well as to the rich (19:2, 23:50); and to women as well as to men."[29] This stresses the purpose for Luke's writing: "For the Son of Man has come to seek and to save that which was lost" (Luke 19:10).

DISCUSSION OF SYNOPTIC THEOLOGY

DOCTRINE OF GOD

It is necessary to study systematic theology to arrive at a biblically comprehensive picture of the nature and attributes of God. (Even then the infinite God remains incomprehensible.) However, while the synoptic gospels provide just one portion in the study of God, "The writers of the NT all share the view of God which is seen in the OT."[30] Many of God's attributes are portrayed in the synoptics, as the following list makes clear.

The providence of God is seen in His provision for the birds (Matt. 6:26; 10:29). *The fatherhood of God* emphasizes His provision for His children (Matt. 6:32). *The grace of God* is given to believers and unbelievers alike (Matt. 5:45). *The kingship of God* is stressed: He has a throne (Matt. 5:34; 23:22); He is Lord (Matt. 4:7, 10; Luke 4:8, 12). *The judgment of God* is equitable to all (Matt. 3:7; 7:1, 2; Luke 3:7); greater privileges will call for greater judgment (Matt. 11:22-24); He will avenge His own (Luke 18:7). *The glory of God* was revealed to the three on the Mount of Transfiguration (Matt. 17:1-8; Mark 9:2-8; Luke 9:28-36). *The goodness of God* is incomparable (Matt. 19:17; Mark 10:17; Luke 18:18-19). *The power of God* is exhibited in His ability to raise the dead (Mark 12:24-27); with Him all things are possible (Mark 10:27; Luke 1:37; 18:27). *The Trinity of God* is revealed at the baptism of Christ (Mark 1:9-11) and at the commissioning of the apostles (Matt. 28:19).

DOCTRINE OF CHRIST

Virgin Birth. Matthew and Luke both emphasize that the Holy Spirit generated the humanity of Christ (Matt. 1:18; Luke 1:35). Matthew takes great pains to emphasize Mary had no involvement with a man prior to the birth of Jesus (Matt. 1:18-25). Mark, too, emphasizes that Jesus is "the son of Mary" rather than the son of Joseph (Jewish custom usually used the father's name).

Humanity. All three gospels emphasize the humanity of Jesus. Matthew emphasizes his human genealogy (1:1-17), his human birth (1:25), and his infancy (2:1-23). Luke similarly emphasizes his birth and lowly estate (2:1-20), his conformity to Jewish custom (2:21-24), and his growth as a young boy (2:41-52). Mark emphasizes the humanity of Jesus more than Matthew and Luke through his emphasis on the work, life, and activities of Jesus. All three stress His humanity in the temptations (Matt. 4:1-11; Mark 1:12-13; Luke 4:1-13). Things like maneuvering fishing boats, paying taxes, talking with different people, sweating blood, crying because of abandonment on the cross, all reflect the humanity of Jesus. Yet He was not an ordinary man; He forgives sin, has authority over nature, reveals the Shekinah of God— these things "place him in a class of his own."[31]

Sinlessness. Although the synoptic gospels present Jesus as a man, they also indicate He is not an ordinary man—He is virgin born and sinless. Because He was virgin born He did not have the sin nature nor the inclination to sin (note James 1:14-15). Jesus called men to repentance but there is no record that He ever confessed sin or repented. His baptism was "to fulfill all righteousness" (Matt. 3:15), not for confession (Matt. 3:6). The temptations also emphasize that while He was tested in all areas that we are, yet He was sinless (Matt. 4:1-11; Mark 1:12-13; Luke 4:1-13). In His rebuke of Peter He revealed His complete disassociation from sin (Matt. 16:23).

Deity. Matthew stresses Jesus as the *Son of David* (Matt. 9:27; 12:23; 15:22; 20:30, 31; 21:9, 15; 22:42). In Matthew 9:27 it is clear that the blind men understood the Son of David to be the Messiah who could do the work of Messiah—such as open the eyes of the blind (Isa. 35:5), which is a work of God (Ps. 146:8). The use of the name in Matthew 21:9 reveals its significance as the coming Redeemer who would bring salvation to the nation and rescue her, bringing in a time of blessing (Ps. 118:25-26).

Matthew continually presents Jesus as the *Messiah* inasmuch as He fulfills the Old Testament predictions concerning Messiah (1:22-23; 2:5-6; 3:3; 4:14-16; 8:16-17; 11:5; 12:17-21; 13:34-35; 21:4-6, 9, 16, 42; 23:39; 24:30; 26:31, 64). In Matthew 16:16 Jesus readily accepts Peter's confession of Him as the Christ, the Anointed One. In Mark 14:61-62 Jesus answered the high priest's question as to whether He is the Messiah by the affirmative "I am."

The origin of the term *Son of Man* is Daniel 7:13 where He is pictured as triumphantly delivering the kingdom to the Father. The position of the Son of Man at the right hand of the Father relates it to Psalm 110:1 and the One who is Lord. Matthew 26:63-64 indicates the term is basically synonymous with Son of God. The term emphasizes various themes: authority (Mark 2:10); glorification (Matt. 25:31); humiliation (Matt. 8:20); suffering and death (Mark 10:45); relationship with the Holy Spirit (Matt. 12:32); salvation (Luke 19:10).[32] "Jesus thought of himself in terms of a heavenly Messiah fulfilling on earth a ministry on men's behalf which would culminate in scenes of final glory."[33]

Jesus was the *Son of God* in an absolutely unique sense. "Jesus spoke of God as 'the Father', 'my Father', 'my heavenly Father', and 'your heavenly Father'—fifty-one times in all."[34] Jesus indicated His awareness of the unique relationship (Matt. 11:27), as did the Father (Matt. 3:17; Mark 1:11). A son is of the same nature and essence as a father; in affirming Jesus as His Son, God the Father was saying that Jesus, His Son, is deity because He is of the same essence as the Father.

Atoning Work. Following His rejection by the nation Israel, Christ foretold His sufferings in Jerusalem (Matt. 16:21; 17:22; 20:18-29; 26:1-5; Mark 8:31; 9:31; 10:32-34; Luke 9:22, 44; 18:31-33). In these passages Jesus foretold who would initiate His death, who would kill Him, how He would be killed, that He would suffer additional things but that He would be raised after three days.

Christ taught the disciples that His death would be a substitutionary atonement (Matt. 20:28; Mark 10:45). The statement that He would give His life as a ransom *for* many implies substitution.[35] In this statement Jesus also used the word ransom (Gk. *lutron*), which meant the ransom money paid to free a slave; Christ paid the price—His death—to free many from the bondage of sin.[36] At the institution of the Lord's Supper, Christ indicated that the bread and cup depicted the body and blood of Christ; the blood would be shed on behalf of many for the forgiveness of sins (Matt. 26:26-29; Mark 14:22-25; Luke 22:15-20). The price of redemption is described as His blood; the scope of redemption is many; the result of redemption is forgiveness. Through His death Christ effected a New Covenant providing forgiveness that the Old Covenant (the Mosaic law) could not achieve.

Resurrection. Christ predicted His resurrection on several occasions (Matt. 16:21; 17:22-23; 20:19; Mark 8:31; 9:31; 10:34; Luke 9:22; 18:33). Moreover, He specified that He would rise on the third day (a clear example of His omniscience). All the gospels stress the *physical* resurrection of Christ (Matt. 28; Mark 16; Luke 24; John 20).

There were numerous witnesses of His resurrection: Mary Magdalene and the other women (Mark 16:2-8; John 20:1); Peter and John (John 20:2-10); Mary Magdalene (John 20:11-18); the other women (Matt. 28:9-10); two disciples traveling to Emmaus (Luke 24:13-32); the ten disciples gathered in the Upper Room (John 20:19-25); the eleven disciples gathered a week later (John 20:26-31); the disciples fishing at Galilee (John 21:1-25); the eleven in Galilee (Matt. 28:16-20); the disciples in Jerusalem (Luke 24:44-49).

John describes the face cloth still "rolled up" (John 20:7), retaining the circular shape as though the head were still in it but lying "in a place by itself." It is detached from the rest of the wrappings, but the shape of the headpiece and the wrappings tell John what has happened. The body of the Lord Jesus Christ has passed through the wrappings—He is risen.

DOCTRINE OF THE HOLY SPIRIT

Concerning the virgin birth of Christ. Matthew and Luke both relate the conception of Jesus in Mary's womb to the Holy Spirit coming upon her (Matt. 1:18; Luke 1:35).

Concerning the baptism of Christ. At Jesus' baptism the Holy Spirit came upon Him to endue Him with power for His public ministry. The Holy Spirit also revealed the origin of Christ's ministry (the Father) and Jesus' unity with the triune God. Jesus did not work independent of the Father.

Concerning the temptation of Christ. Mark 1:12 emphasizes that it was the Spirit who drove Christ into the wilderness to be tempted of the Devil.[37] The confrontation would prove the impeccability of the Son.

Concerning the ministry of Christ. Matthew 12:28 reveals that the ministry of Christ was done through the Holy Spirit—a public witness to all that His power came from heaven (cf. Luke 4:18-19).

Concerning the inspiration of Scripture. In citing Psalm 110:1, Mark 12:36 states, "David himself said in the Holy Spirit," implying that the Holy Spirit guided David to pen the correct words as he wrote Psalm 110. This example indicates the ministry of the Holy Spirit in the inspiration of Scripture.

DOCTRINE OF THE CHURCH

There is no developed doctrine of the church in the synoptic gospels. The word *church* (Gk. *ekklesia*) is used only three times in Matthew and not at all in Mark and Luke. Probably the only occurrence in Matthew where it is used in a technical sense is 16:18 where it is seen as still future.

DOCTRINE OF LAST THINGS

The synoptic gospels provide extensive material concerning last things. The word *kingdom* (Gk. *basileia*) is predominant in the synoptic gospels, occurring fifty-six times in Matthew, twenty-one times in Mark, and forty-six times in Luke (only five times in John).[38] Matthew also uses the term *king* more times (twenty-three) than any other New Testament book. The synoptic gospels stress that Jesus came to establish the millennial kingdom. The first occurrence of the term is in Matthew 3:2 where John the Baptist preached, "Repent, for the kingdom of heaven is at hand." Jesus preached the same message (Matt. 4:17), exhorting the people to repent in anticipation of Messiah's kingdom. He revealed His credentials through His words (Matt. 5-7) and through His works (Matt. 8-10). In the light of this evidence, the nation's leaders gave their evaluation: "This man casts out demons only by Beelzebul the ruler of demons" (Matt. 12:24). The King had been rejected by His subjects. As a result the kingdom would be held in abeyance. Jesus described the interim period between the rejection of Messiah at His first advent and His reception at His second advent in the parables of Matthew 13. Prior to the King's return to establish the millennial kingdom Jesus revealed the calamities that would befall Israel and the world. The Tribulation will occur (Matt. 24:4-28; Mark 13:5-23; Luke 21:8-23), followed by the Second Advent of Christ (Matt. 24:29-51; Mark 13:24-37; Luke 21:24-36); Israel will be held accountable for the privileges and knowledge the nation has had (Matt. 25:1-30); the Gentiles will also be judged according to their response to the message in the Tribulation (Matt. 25:31-46).

Notes on the Synoptic Gospels

1. Brooke Foss Westcott, *An Introduction to the Study of the Gospels*, 8th ed. (London: Macmillan, 1895), p. 195.

2. D. Edmond Hiebert, *An Introduction to the New Testament: The Gospels and Acts* (Chicago: Moody, 1975), 1:161-63.

3. For a discussion of the synoptic problem with proposed solutions, see Hiebert, *Introduction to the New Testament*, 1:160-90; Everett F. Harrison, *Introduction to the New Testament* (Grand Rapids: Eerdmans, 1964), pp. 136-45; and Robert G. Gromacki, *New Testament Survey* (Grand Rapids: Baker, 1974), pp. 54-59. These works provide an explanation as well as a useful critique of the different views.

4. This writer holds to the position described by Wendell G. Johnston et al., "The Evangelical and Redaction Criticism in the Synoptic Gospels," *Talbot Review*, vol. 1, no. 2 (Summer 1985), pp. 6-13. An excellent bibliography is provided for further study of redaction criticism.

5. See I. Howard Marshall, "Historical Criticism" in I. Howard Marshall, ed., *New Testament Interpretation* (Grand Rapids: Eerdmans, 1977), pp. 126-38.

6. Ibid., p. 137. "It is highly unlikely that Matthew's description of the healing of *two* Gadarene demoniacs (Matt. 8:28-34) is to be regarded as historical." In examining the resurrection narratives Marshall states, "There may be a stage at which the difficulties involved in explaining away an apparent historical error are greater than those caused by accepting the existence of the error" (p. 135). It is apparent that this view of Scripture cannot be reconciled with the biblical doctrine of inspiration and inerrancy.

7. Ibid., p. 148.

8. This is a further example of the damaging results of critical methodology. It is impossible to hold this view of David Wenham and still believe in biblical inerrancy. If there are errors in historical details then the Bible is not an inerrant book. In contrast to Wenham, E. J. Young explains the orthodox solution to the conflict. See E. J. Young, *Thy Word Is Truth* (Grand Rapids: Eerdmans, 1957), pp. 132-34.

9. See Stephen H. Travis, "Form Criticism" in *New Testament Interpretation*, pp. 153-64.

10. Johnston et al., "The Evangelical and Redaction Criticism," p. 6.

11. Ibid., pp. 7ff.

12. Thus in composition criticism, which some include in redaction criticism, the gospel writers invent new sayings by Jesus which He never spoke. See Stephen S. Smalley, "Redaction Criticism" in *New Testament Interpretation*, p. 181.

13. Robert H. Gundry, *Matthew: A Commentary on His Literary and Theological Art* (Grand Rapids: Eerdmans, 1982), pp. 26-27.

14. "The Fragments of Papias" in J. B. Lightfoot, ed., *The Apostolic Fathers* (Grand Rapids: Baker, 1956), p. 265.

15. Irenaeus, "Against Heresies" in Cyril C. Richardson, ed., *Early Christian Fathers* (New York: Macmillan, 1970), p. 370.

16. Henry C. Thiessen, *Introduction to the New Testament* (Grand Rapids: Eerdmans, 1943), p. 136.

17. J. H. Kerr, *An Introduction to the New Testament* (New York: Revell, 1931), p. 26.

18. It is noteworthy that the liberal John A. T. Robinson dates Matthew prior to A.D. 62, sometime between 40 and 60. Compare *Redating the New Testament* (Philadelphia: Westminster, 1976), pp. 107 and 86-117.

19. The Greek word for *men* is *andron*, meaning "men" as distinct from "women." The inference is that in addition to the 5,000 men, there were also women and children that believed.

20. Stanley D. Toussaint, *Behold the King* (Portland, Ore.: Multnomah, 1980), pp. 18-20.

21. "The Fragments of Papias," p. 265.

22. Irenaeus, "Against Heresies," p. 370.

23. Ibid., p. 370.

24. Ibid., p. 185.

25. Ibid., p. 370.

26. Thiessen, *Introduction to the New Testament*, pp. 156-57.

27. Scroggie, *Guide to the Gospels*, pp. 337-39.

28. G. H. Schodde, "Matthew, Gospel of" in James Orr, ed., *The International Standard Bible Encyclopaedia*, 5 vols. (Grand Rapids: Eerdmans, 1939), 3:2011.

29. Norval Geldenhuys, *Commentary on the Gospel of Luke* (Grand Rapids: Eerdmans, 1951), p. 43.

30. Donald Guthrie, *New Testament Theology* (Downers Grove, Ill.: Inter-Varsity, 1981), p. 75.

31. Ibid., p. 222.

32. Ibid., pp. 280-81.

33. Ibid., p. 281.

34. Ibid., pp. 303-4.

35. The Greek preposition *anti*, translated "for," demands the idea of *substitution*. The same preposition is used in Luke 11:11 illustrating a father giving a snake *instead of* a fish. The preposition clearly means "in place of," i.e., substitution.

36. See the helpful discussion in Lawrence O. Richards, *Expository Dictionary of Bible Words* (Grand Rapids: Zondervan, 1985), pp. 517-18.

37. The verb "impelled" is *ekballo*, a strong term, literally meaning "to throw out." Hence, the stress that the confrontation was initiated by the Holy Spirit who forced Christ into the wilderness meeting.

38. A most valuable work that discusses the nature of the kingdom in both the Old Testament and the New Testament, and that reveals God's purpose in establishing a millennial kingdom through Messiah, is Alva J. McClain, *The Greatness of the Kingdom* (Chicago: Moody, 1968).

FOR FURTHER STUDY ON THE SYNOPTIC GOSPELS

** Donald Guthrie. *New Testament Theology*. Downers Grove, Ill.: InterVarsity, 1981.

** George E. Ladd. *A Theology of the New Testament*. Grand Rapids: Eerdmans, 1974.

** Leon Morris. *New Testament Theology*. Grand Rapids: Zondervan, 1986.

* Charles C. Ryrie. *Biblical Theology of the New Testament*. Chicago: Moody, 1959. Pp. 27-95.

11

THEOLOGY OF ACTS

INTRODUCTION TO THEOLOGY OF ACTS

AUTHOR

The authorship of Acts is closely tied to the authorship of Luke. Both Luke and Acts are addressed to Theophilus (Luke 1:3; Acts 1:1); the authorship of one necessitates the same authorship for the other. See discussion under Luke in the Theology of the Synoptics.

DATE

There is strong evidence to suggest a date of A.D. 63 for the authorship of Acts. (1) It best explains the abrupt ending of Acts. Paul was brought to Rome in A.D. 61 where he remained in custody until A.D. 63. The book ends abruptly and optimistically, expecting Paul's release. (2) Following the burning of Rome in A.D. 64, Nero initiated a fierce persecution of the Christians in Rome. Had the book been written after A.D. 64, it is inconceivable that the book would have closed on an optimistic note. (3) Had Paul already been executed (which occurred about A.D. 67), some mention of it would undoubtedly have been made. (4) The impact of the destruction of Jerusalem in A.D. 70 was felt throughout the Roman world, yet no mention is made of that event, indicating it had not yet taken place.

PURPOSES

Luke purposed to provide an account of the *origin and development of the church* under the power and guidance of the Holy Spirit; that theme is carried forward in Acts 1:8 and throughout the book.[1]

Luke's account of the movement of Christianity can also be seen as an *apologetic for Christianity.* "The apologetic thrust seems to look in two directions, to meet the charges of the Jews against Christianity and to present

Christianity in a favorable light to the Roman world."[2] Christianity had been maligned by both Romans and Jews. Luke shows that Christianity follows in the historic pattern and upon the foundation of Judaism. In this sense the book can also be seen as a polemic toward the Jews who accused Christianity as a subversive movement (cf. Acts 18:14-15).

Acts also reveals that *Paul's apostolic authority* and power is equivalent to Peter's authority and power. For example, Paul duplicates the miracles of Peter.

SIMILAR APOSTOLIC MIRACLES

Miracles	Peter	Paul
Heal the lame	3:2	14:8
Shadow brought healing	5:15	19:12
Exorcism	5:16	16:18
Confronted sorcerer	8:18-20	13:6-10
Raised the dead	9:36-40	20:9-10

Luke also traces the *continued rejection of Messiah* by the Jewish nation, begun in the gospels and continuing in the book of Acts. The Sanhedrin arrested and jailed Peter and John (Acts 4:1-22) and prohibited them from preaching in Christ's name (Acts 4:17). The Sanhedrin arrested and jailed the apostles (Acts 5:17-18) and incited the people to stone Stephen (Acts 6:12–7:60). The unbelieving Jews persecuted Paul at Antioch of Pisidia (Acts 13:45, 50) and later stoned him, leaving him for dead (Acts 14:19). The Jews still rejected Paul's message at the conclusion of Acts (Acts 28:17-28).

DISCUSSION OF THEOLOGY OF ACTS

GOD

Sovereignty of God. Luke explains Christ's death resulting from the decree (Gk. *boule*) and foreknowledge of God (Acts 2:23). The decree of God means His "counsel is predetermined and inflexible. Both phrases emphasize the resolute and inviolable determinateness of the decree."[3] Amid persecution the apostles encouraged themselves in the sovereignty of God (Acts 4:24-31). God is referred to as Lord (Gk. *despota*), from which the English word *despot* is derived (Acts 4:24). God had previously decreed (*boule*) the events of the cross, having marked them out beforehand (Gk. *proorisen*).

God's sovereignty is also seen in election (Acts 13:48). The precise number that had been appointed to eternal life, believed.[4]

God's existence and common grace. At Lystra Paul declared the "living God" to his hearers, reminding them that He is Creator and has given them rain and fruitful seasons (Acts 14:15-18). Paul also reminded the Athenians that God had given them life and breath and had also marked out the times and boundaries (Acts 17:22-31).

CHRIST

Luke's emphasis concerning Christ is two-fold in Acts: he stresses His crucifixion and death, and also His resurrection.

Crucifixion and death of Christ. Many of the statements regarding the death of Christ reflect the apostles' indictment of the Jews in the crucifixion of Christ. Christ was nailed to a cross by godless men (Acts 2:23); Christ was shamefully put to death—by crucifixion (Acts 3:15; 5:30; 10:39; cf. 13:28-29). The Righteous One was murdered (Acts 7:52).

Resurrection of Christ. Several themes regarding the resurrection are emphasized: (1) Christ's resurrection was predicted in Psalm 16:8-11 and fulfilled in Psalm 2:7 (Acts 2:22-32; 13:33-37); (2) Christ's resurrection was proclaimed with great power (Acts 4:2, 10, 33); (3) God not only raised Christ but also exalted Him to a position of authority (Acts 5:31); (4) Christ's resurrection was attended by witnesses (Acts 10:40-41); (5) His resurrection is a harbinger of future judgment (Acts 17:31); (6) Christ's resurrection was to be proclaimed to Jews and Gentiles in fulfillment of prophecy (Acts 26:23).

Return of Christ. At the ascension of Christ the angels promised the gazing disciples that Christ would return "in just the same way" as they had seen Him go into heaven—visible, physical, and personal (Acts 1:9-11). Peter announced the millennial age when he spoke of the "period of restoration of all things" (Acts 3:21).

It is significant that the death and particularly the resurrection were central in the preaching of the New Testament church as recorded in Acts.

HOLY SPIRIT

His deity. Acts 5:3-5 records a principal statement concerning the deity of the Holy Spirit. In confronting Ananias, Peter reminded him that he had lied to the Holy Spirit (Acts 5:3), while in a parallel statement Peter exclaimed, "You have not lied to men but to God" (Acts 5:5), thereby equating the Holy Spirit with God.

His work. By His work of baptizing believers into the Body of Christ, the Holy Spirit is building the church (Acts 1:5; 11:15-16). The Spirit is also active in filling believers for witness (Acts 1:8; 2:4; 4:31; 5:32; 9:17) and in leading them in ministry (Acts 8:26-30; 10:19; 11:19; 16:7; 20:23; 21:4, 11).

SALVATION

Salvation is through faith in Christ. Faith is stressed in Acts 10:43. Gentiles do not need to first become Jews; they receive forgiveness and salvation simply through believing (cf. Acts 11:21; 14:23; 16:31).

Believing involves repentance. On numerous occasions the gospel heralds exhorted the people to believe in Christ; on other occasions they urged the people to repent (cf. Acts 2:38; 3:19; 5:31; 8:22; 11:18; 17:30; 20:21; 26:20). This indicates the terms should be understood synonymously.[5] Paul's statement, "repentance toward God and faith in our Lord Jesus Christ" (Acts 20:21), suggests repentance is bound up in faith. To have faith is to repent; without repentance faith is not possible.

Salvation is through the grace of God. When Paul came to Achaia he helped those who had believed "through grace" (Acts 18:27). In this way God in time manifested His grace to Lydia (Acts 16:14) and to others (Acts 13:48) what had been resolved before time began.

Salvation is apart from any works. The Jerusalem Council in Acts 15 resolved that Gentiles did not need to be circumcised nor observe the law of Moses to be saved. They were saved by faith alone.

CHURCH

As might be expected, Acts provides considerable material on the doctrine of the church because the book records the birth and growth of the church.

Formation of the church. The church is formed through the baptizing work of the Spirit, which introduces believers into the Body of Christ (1 Cor. 12:13). In Acts 1:5 the baptizing work is still future, indicating the church has not yet been born. In Acts 11:15-16 Peter rehearsed that the Spirit fell on the Gentiles just as He had upon them "at the beginning." The beginning— Acts 2—marks the beginning of the church and the Holy Spirit's activity of baptizing believers into the Body of Christ. This unique work of the Holy Spirit included not only Jews, but also Samaritans (Acts 8:14-17) and Gentiles (Acts 10:44-48; 19:6).

Organization of the church. The apostles were the foundation of the church (Acts 2:42), but elders were appointed[6] to lead the local churches (Acts 14:23; 15:4). The term elder (Gr. *presbuteros*) suggests the maturity and dignity of the office. Elders were a plurality in a local church (Acts

14:23; 15:2, 4) and were responsible for spiritual leadership in the assembly (Acts 11:30; 14:23). Deacons (although not specifically named in Acts) are probably referred to in Acts 6.

Functions of the church. Acts provides valuable insight concerning the New Testament functioning of the church. (1) Instruction was important in the early church (Acts 2:42; 4:2; 11:26; 12:24; 13:46; 15:35; 17:11; 18:5; 19:8, 10, 20; 20:3, 7, 17-35) and involved teaching propositional truth, such as the apostles' doctrine (Acts 2:42), the resurrection (4:2, 33; 24:15, 21; 26:8), and facts about Christ (5:20, 25, 28, 42; 7:52; 8:5; 9:20-22; 10:36; 11:20; 13:16-41; 28:23). It also included debate and arguing (9:29; 17:2-3, 17; 18:28; 19:8). (2) Fellowship included material things (4:32-35; 6:1-3; 16:15, 34), the Lord's Supper (2:42; 20:7), prayer (2:42; 4:24-31; 12:5, 12; 13:3; 20:36; 21:5), suffering (4:1-21; 5:17-42; 7:1-60; 8:1; 9:1-2; 11:19; 12:1-19), and was in Christ (13:52; 16:5, 25, 34, 40; 19:17). (3) Worship was reflected in the reverence the believers had for the Lord (2:46-47; 4:23-31; 5:11; 9:31). (4) Service most notably involved evangelism (4:33; 5:14, 42; 8:4, 12, 13, 26-40; 9:42; 10:34-48; 11:24; 13:12, 48; 14:21; 16:5, 14, 31; 17:2-3, 17, 34; 22; 26; 28:23-31).

Notes on Acts

1. In Luke 24:47 "proclaimed" (*keruchthenai*) is emphatic, standing first in the Greek text; "nations" or "Gentiles" (*ethne*) is also emphatic; hence, the stress is that forgiveness is to be *proclaimed* to *Gentiles*.

2. D. Edmond Hiebert, *An Introduction to the New Testament*, 3 vols. (Chicago: Moody, 1975), 1:256.

3. Gottlob Schrenk, *"Boulomai, boule, boulema"* in Gerhard Kittel, ed., *Theological Dictionary of the New Testament*, 10 vols. (Grand Rapids: Eerdmans, 1964), 1:635.

4. "Appointed" (*tetagmenoi*) is a perfect passive participle that describes action antecedent to the main verb "believed" (aorist participle). The grammatical inference is that the appointing by the Lord came first; belief by the very number that had been appointed to eternal life followed.

5. Charles C. Ryrie, *Biblical Theology of the New Testament* (Chicago: Moody, 1959), pp. 116-17.

6. The term "appoint" is *cheirotoneo*, meaning "to elect by show of hands."

For Further Study on Acts

** Donald Guthrie. *New Testament Theology*. Downers Grove, Ill.: InterVarsity, 1981.

** George E. Ladd. *A Theology of the New Testament*. Grand Rapids: Eerdmans, 1974.

* Walter L. Liefield. "Luke, Theology of" in Walter A. Elwell, ed. *Evangelical Dictionary of Theology*. Grand Rapids: Baker, 1984. Pp. 662-64.

** Leon Morris. *New Testament Theology*. Grand Rapids: Zondervan, 1986.

* Charles C. Ryrie. *Biblical Theology of the New Testament*. Chicago: Moody, 1959. Pp. 99-134.

12
THEOLOGY OF JAMES

INTRODUCTION TO THEOLOGY OF JAMES

AUTHOR

James, the half-brother of the Lord, is the best suggestion for the authorship because: (1) There is a similarity of language in the epistle and James' speech in Acts 15. (2) There is a similarity between the epistle and the teaching of Jesus (cf. Ja. 1:22 and Matt. 7:20, 24; Ja. 3:12 and Matt. 7:16; Ja. 2:5 and Matt. 5:3).

DATE AND PLACE OF WRITING

Recognition of James, the Lord's half-brother, as the author points to Jerusalem as the locality for the writing. Mention of the "'early and latter rain' (5:7), the effect of the hot winds on vegetation (1:11), the existence of salt and bitter springs (3:11), the cultivation of figs and olives (3:12), and the familiar imagery of the sea as near by (1:6; 3:4) all are reminiscent of conditions in Palestine."[1]

The date of the epistle must be prior to A.D. 63 because according to Josephus, James was martyred at that time.[2]

DESTINATION

The epistle is addressed to "the twelve tribes who are dispersed abroad" (1:1), suggesting Jewish believers. The phrase, "who are dispersed abroad," is the Greek word *diaspora*, normally used to denote the Jews scattered among the nations (cf. Deut. 28:25 in Septuagint). Additionally, they were meeting in a synagogue (2:2), were monotheistic (2:19), and were familiar with the Jewish formulae of oaths.[3]

THEOLOGICAL PURPOSE

The Hebrew believers were encountering trials, undoubtedly persecution from unbelieving Jews. Since the believers did not know how to understand or cope with the persecution, James wrote to give them insight. Within the assembly carnality prevailed. With the emphasis of James on the problems of the rich, there were undoubtedly divisions between rich and poor in the assembly. James, as Amos in the Old Testament, wrote to condemn wrong attitudes in the matter of money and oppression of the poor.

James's purpose in writing was to give the corrective to the carnal spirit that prevailed, showing faith as the antidote to the problems.

DISCUSSION OF THEOLOGY OF JAMES

SCRIPTURES

There is a strong emphasis on the Old Testament in the book of James. In his five chapters James refers or alludes to twenty-two books of the Old Testament. "By doing this James obviates the need for any formal statement of inspiration; he merely assumes it."[4] This reflects that James was steeped in the Old Testament and was writing to a Jewish audience equally familiar with the Old Testament. But since the epistle had a wide audience, it also suggests the importance of the Old Testament for the church.

There is an emphasis on the teaching of Jesus. James contains some fifteen allusions to the Sermon on the Mount (cf. 3:6 with Matt. 5:22; 3:12 with Matt. 7:16; 4:11 with Matt. 7:1). Since James was unconverted during the life of Christ, he must have gathered information about Jesus' teaching from those who heard Him.

There is an emphasis on the authority of Scripture. James refers to the "word of truth" that has power to save people (1:18). He refers to the "Scripture" (2:8, 23; 4:5-6) as the final point of appeal; Scripture is the final authority. James rebukes the quarreling of his addressees and bases the rebuke on the authority of Scripture (4:5-6).

There is an emphasis on the work of Scripture. The Scripture has power to save a soul (1:21); the Scripture reveals man's sin (1:23-25); the Scripture judges in the present and in the Last Day (2:12).[5]

GOD

James's view of God reflects concepts from Israel's conditional relationship with God under the Mosaic law: obedience brings blessing; disobedience brings chastisement (Deut. 28). Thus James presents the sinner as an enemy of God: friendship with the world makes one an enemy of God (4:4-5). When the rich oppress the poor they can only expect misery and judgment (5:1-8)—this also is a common theme of the Old Testament prophets (cf. Amos 2:6-8). Conversely, the obedient can expect blessing. The one who asks in faith receives wisdom (1:5); the one who has persevered under trial will appreciate "every perfect gift" coming down from the Father of lights (1:17).

MAN AND SIN

James connects the doctrinal and the applicational when he exhorts his hearers to control the tongue because man's tongue is leveled against his fellow man who is "made in the likeness of God" (3:9). With this statement James affirms the creation account of Genesis 1:26-27.

Although man is made in the likeness of God, through the fall man is constituted a sinner, possessing the sin nature which James describes as lust (1:14). It is this lust that is the inner response to the outer solicitation that results in sin (1:15). James's discussion on this issue is important inasmuch as it provides a clearer understanding of how sin take places than perhaps any other passage of Scripture.

James refers to sin (Gk. *hamartia*, "to miss the mark") six times: sin has its derivation in lust within a person (1:15); sin results in spiritual and eternal death (1:15); sin is showing partiality and failing to love (2:8-9); sin is failure to do good (4:17); sin can be forgiven (5:15, 20). James also refers to sin (Gk. *parabates*) as a transgression of God's standard (2:9, 11).

SALVATION

Although Luther understood James as a "strawy epistle" because he saw it in contrast to Paul's emphasis on justification by faith alone, James has a great deal to say about faith. Faith is the way man must approach God (1:6; 5:15); faith must be in Jesus Christ (2:1); and works will demonstrate the reality of the faith (2:18).[6] "The difference between James and Paul is not that of faith versus works, but a difference of relationship. James emphasizes the work of the believer in relation to faith and Paul the work of Christ in relation to faith."[7]

NOTES ON JAMES

1. D. Edmond Hiebert, *An Introduction to the New Testament*, 3 vols. (Chicago: Moody, 1962), 3:52-53.
2. Josephus, "The Antiquities of the Jews" in William Whiston, ed., *Josephus: Complete Works* (Grand Rapids: Kregel, 1960), 20.9.1.
3. Hiebert, *Introduction to New Testament*, 3:50-51.
4. Charles C. Ryrie, *Biblical Theology of the New Testament* (Chicago: Moody, 1959), p. 137.

5. "Judged" (*krinesthai*) is "signifying not just a future event but a deliberate choice of the law of liberty (and mercy) in preference to the old ruthless rigor of the 'Law.' " See Fritz Rienecker *A Linguistic Key to the Greek New Testament*, edited by Cleon Rogers, Jr. (Grand Rapids: Zondervan, 1982), p. 729.

6. The definite article with "faith" (*ten pistin*) emphasizes "*the* faith"; the reality of *the faith* is demonstrated by works (2:18). The definite article also appears in 2:14.

7. Ryrie, *Biblical Theology of the New Testament*, p. 140.

For Further Study on James

** Donald Guthrie. *New Testament Theology*. Downers Grove, Ill.: InterVarsity, 1981.

** George E. Ladd. *A Theology of the New Testament*. Grand Rapids: Eerdmans, 1974.

** Leon Morris. *New Testament Theology*. Grand Rapids: Zondervan, 1986.

 * Charles C. Ryrie. *Biblical Theology of the New Testament*. Chicago: Moody, 1959. Pp. 131-47.

13

THEOLOGY OF PAUL

INTRODUCTION TO PAULINE THEOLOGY

BACKGROUND AND TRAINING

Paul was born about A.D. 3 to a prestigious family whose members were Roman citizens (Acts 22:28) living in the city of Tarsus. Paul was raised in a strict Jewish home, circumcised the eighth day, and was of the tribe of Benjamin (Phil. 3:5). Paul was later trained in Jerusalem under Gamaliel, a Pharisee and respected member of the Sanhedrin (Acts 5:34). Gamaliel was only one of seven scholars in his nation's history to receive the title, "Rabban" (our master). Gamaliel was a grandson of Hillel, founder of the school of interpretation bearing his name. Hillel was less strict than the school of Shammai. Paul himself became a Pharisee, adhering strictly to Jewish law and customs (Phil. 3:5). It was this intense loyalty to Judaism and the traditions of the elders that caused him to persecute the Christians (Acts 9:1-2; Phil. 3:6). He did this with a pure conscience at first (Acts 23:1; 2 Tim. 1:3). Later, he interpreted his action as blasphemy (1 Tim. 1:13).

OUTLINE OF TRAVELS AND MINISTRY

Following his conversion in late A.D. 33 or early 34, Paul spent several months in Damascus (Acts 9:23; Gal. 1:17); when his opponents sought his death, he returned to Jerusalem (Acts 9:26). Shortly thereafter, he departed for his home town of Tarsus (Acts 9:30). He spent three years in Arabia (A.D. 34-36), probably in some form of ministry inasmuch as he began to serve immediately after his conversion. After the three years he returned to Jerusalem (Gal. 1:18) and then departed for Syria and Cilicia (Gal. 1:21). About A.D. 46 Paul again visited Jerusalem (Acts 11:30; 12:25; Gal. 2:1-21). It was there that the church set Paul and Barnabas apart for the first missionary journey (A.D. 46-48; Acts 13:1–14:28). During that journey the duo evangelized Asia Minor and the island of Cyprus. It was in Asia Minor that Paul

CHRONOLOGY OF PAUL'S LIFE

Date: A.D.	Event
3 (?)	Paul's birth
18-30	Training in Jerusalem
33/34	Conversion
34-36	In Arabia
46	In Jerusalem
46-48	First Missionary Journey: Asia Minor
48-49	Jerusalem Council
49-52	Second Missionary Journey: Asia Minor & Europe
53-57	Third Missionary Journey: Asia Minor & Europe
58-60	Imprisonment in Caesarea
60-61	Journey to Rome
61-63	Imprisonment in Rome
63-66	Ministry as far as Spain
66-67	Imprisonment in Rome and execution

began a ministry to Gentiles when the Jews repudiated the gospel (Acts 13:46). Paul's typical pattern was established: "an initial proclamation to Jews and Gentile adherents to Judaism, whether full proselytes or more loosely associated, and then, being refused further audience in the synagogue, a direct ministry among Gentiles."[1] The Jerusalem Council took place in A.D. 49 (Acts 15) and resolved an important issue: it enabled Paul (and others) to keep preaching the gospel to Gentiles without Jewish encumbrances; Gentiles were not required to be circumcised. The decision was important in maintaining the purity of the gospel and separating law from grace. The second missionary journey (A.D. 49-52; Acts 15:36–18:22) took Paul and Silas across Asia Minor, where they revisited the churches, and on to Europe (Acts 16:11ff.). The third missionary journey (A.D. 53-57; Acts 18:23–21:16) took Paul to Ephesus, where he spent nearly three years, and on to Macedonia and Achaia. He was arrested in Jerusalem upon his return and imprisoned in Caesarea (A.D. 58-66; Acts 24:1–26:32). Paul appealed to Caesar and eventually spent two years in prison in Rome (A.D. 61-63; Acts 28:30-31). Paul was released from his first Roman imprisonment, spent A.D. 63-66 in ministry, probably traveling as far as Spain, was again arrested and executed in Rome in A.D. 67 (2 Tim. 4:6-8).

	THE EPISTLES OF PAUL			
Class	**Name**	**Date: A.D.**	**Origin**	**Theology**
General	Galatians	48	Antioch in Syria	Soteriology and Eschatology
	1 Thessalonians	50	Corinth	
	2 Thessalonians	50	Corinth	
	1 Corinthians	55	Ephesus	
	2 Corinthians	55	Macedonia	
	Romans	57	Corinth	
Prison	Ephesians	62	Rome	Christology
	Philippians	63	Rome	
	Colossians	62	Rome	
	Philemon	62	Rome	
Pastoral	1 Timothy	63	Macedonia	Ecclesiology
	Titus	63	Corinth	
	2 Timothy	67	Rome	

DISCUSSION OF PAULINE THEOLOGY

GOD

Revelation. Paul's theology represents a high watermark in terms of a theology of God. Paul portrays God as sovereign, revealing Himself in grace through Jesus Christ (Rom. 1:16-17; 3:21; 1 Cor. 2:10; 2 Cor. 12:7). That which God purposed from all eternity has now been revealed in time. That revelation is a manifestation of "our Savior Christ Jesus, who abolished death and brought life and immortality to light through the gospel" (2 Tim. 1:10; cf. 1 Tim. 3:16). The gospel which Paul preached was not of human origin, but Paul received it directly from the Lord (Gal. 1:12; 2:2). Through the death of Christ, God remains just but is free to justify one who believes in Jesus.

God has revealed Himself in judgment to unbelievers (Rom. 1:18; 2:5; 2 Thess. 1:7). Wrath (*orge*) expresses "the deep-seated anger of God against sin. This anger arises from His holiness and righteousness."[2] Because of His holiness God cannot overlook sin.

God will reveal Himself in glorious blessing to believers (Rom. 8:18-19; 1 Cor. 1:7, 3:13, 4:5; 2 Cor. 5:10). "Glory" suggests the glorious radiance at the triumphant return of Jesus Christ, with all the attendant blessings for believers (Rom. 8:18).

God has revealed His program for the church which was previously a mystery (Rom. 16:25; Gal. 3:23; Eph. 3:3, 5). Satan attempts to hinder the revelation of God (2 Cor. 4:4) and the work of the church by blinding unbelievers so that the gospel cannot enlighten them.

Sovereignty. The concept of God's sovereignty dominates the writings of Paul. He employs a number of terms to emphasize this concept. (1) *Predestine* (Gk. *proorizo*) means "to mark out with a boundary beforehand" (Eph. 1:5, 11; Rom. 8:29, 30; 1 Cor. 2:7). Predestine is only used six times in the entire New Testament, and five occurrences are found in Paul's epistles. Paul indicates the believer's salvation is rooted in eternity past with the predestinating work of God. (2) *Foreknow* (Gk. *proginosko*) means "to know beforehand, to take note of, to fix the regard upon" (Rom. 8:29; 11:2).[3] Foreknow "emphasizes not mere foresight but an active relationship between the one who foreknows and those who are foreknown."[4] (3) *Elect* or *choose* (Gk. *eklegomai*) means "to call out" (Eph. 1:4; 1 Thess. 1:4). The blessings of Ephesians 1:3 are realized by the believer because God chose the believer in eternity past (Eph. 1:4). God's choice[5] emphasizes He chose the believers for Himself. (4) *Adoption* (Gk. *huiothesia*) means "to place as a son" (Eph. 1:5) and emphasizes the Roman ceremony of adoption of one's own son into the status of adulthood with all its privileges. Adoption was the result of God's predestination of believers in eternity past. (5) *Called* (Gk. *kletos*) refers to God's effectual call to salvation (cf. Rom. 1:1, 7; 8:28). It is the call of God that enables a person to believe. This term is related to unconditional election (God chose us without any merit on our part) and irresistible grace (the one called does not resist the call). (6) *Purpose* (Gk. *protithemi*) means "to place before" and suggests God purposes in Himself to sum up all things in Christ (Eph. 1:9-10). (7) *Will* (Gk. *boule*) refers to the sovereign counsel of God in which He acts. Ephesians 1:11 is a general summary; not only does God act sovereignly with regard to securing the believer's salvation, but God works all things—all history is consummated according to the sovereign will of God.

An important conclusion concerning Paul's teaching on sovereignty ought to be observed: "1. The ultimate source of predestination is the absolute sovereignty of God. 2. The purpose of predestination is salvation, and the issue of it is service. 3. Predestination does not override human responsibility."[6]

CHRIST

Humanity. While Paul provides some of the strongest statements of the deity of Christ he also emphasizes the humanity of Christ. Christ was born of a woman (Gal. 4:4).[7] He was no phantom; He had his humanity from his earthly mother. Christ was a physical descendant[8] of David (Rom. 1:3; 2 Tim. 2:8). Christ physically descended from David (Rom. 1:3).

Christ committed no sin (2 Cor. 5:21). Christ "knew no sin" refers to knowledge of sin gained by experience; He did not experience sin in His life because He had no sin nature (Rom. 8:3). Christ came in the "likeness of sinful flesh"—He came as a man but without the sinful nature. He did not come in the mere likeness of flesh—then He would not have been truly human; He did not come in the likeness of sin—then He would have had indwelling sin. God's grace came through the last Adam, to redeem what the first Adam lost (cf. Rom. 5:15; 1 Cor. 15:21, 45, 47).

Deity. A fully developed theology of the deity of Christ can be found in Paul's writings. Christ is the sphere in which all things have been created; moreover, "All the laws and purposes which guide the creation and government of the Universe reside in Him."[9] Paul's emphasis that Christ is "from heaven" (1 Cor. 15:47; cf. 2 Cor. 8:9) suggests His preexistence and eternality.

Paul states that the fulness of deity dwells in Christ (Col. 2:9). *Deity* (Gk. *theotes*) "emphasizes divine nature or essence. . . . He was and is absolute and perfect God."[10] Interestingly, Paul emphasizes that the deity was in "bodily form," suggesting the full humanity of Jesus. This verse is a strong Pauline affirmation of the *God-man* Jesus.

Christ exists in the form of God (Phil. 2:6). The word *form* (Gk. *morphe*) suggests the inherent character or essential substance of the person. Christ in His essential nature exists[11] as deity. Paul addresses Christ as God on several occasions. He is called "God blessed," a reference to deity (Rom. 9:5). A better rendering of this verse would be "Christ, who is God over all, blessed for ever."[12] In Titus 2:13 Paul refers to "our great God and Savior, Jesus Christ." Greek grammar demands that the two nouns, God and Savior, refer to the same person—Jesus Christ.[13] This is a clear Pauline statement of Christ's deity.

Lordship. Jesus' designation as Lord is an important study inasmuch as the "title *Lord* occurs at least 144 times plus 95 more times in connection with the proper name *Jesus Christ.*"[14]

Lord designates His deity (Rom. 10:9; 1 Cor. 12:3; Phil. 2:9). The name *Lord* was frequently used as a translation of the Hebrew name *Adonai* in the Septuagint; the divine character of God would be applied to Jesus through the title Lord. The name of God Himself is applied to Jesus.[15]

Lord designates power (Phil. 2:9). The lordship bestowed on Christ "who is now equal with God, manifests itself especially in the fact that also all the invisible powers of creation are subjected to him."[16]

Lord denotes divine sovereignty. To preach Jesus as Lord is to proclaim His sovereignty (2 Cor. 4:5); to bow before Jesus is to worship Him and thereby acknowledge Him as sovereign God. Christ's sovereignty over all Christians is especially emphasized in Romans 14:5-9 and in titles like "Our Lord Jesus Christ," "Our Lord Jesus," and "Jesus Christ Our Lord."[17]

Lord denotes Jesus' kingship and rule. Lord should also be understood as a variant of "king"; the two titles are actually interchangeable. In this sense, Lord emphasizes Jesus' kingship over Israel and the church as well as His lordship over the whole world (cf. 1 Tim. 6:15; 1 Cor. 15:25).[18]

HOLY SPIRIT

Pauline theology provides an extensive discussion of both the Person and work of the Holy Spirit.

His Person. The following attributes of the Holy Spirit's Person are dealt with in Paul's letters. (1) Intellect. The Holy Spirit investigates the deep things of God (1 Cor. 2:10) and then teaches them to believers (1 Cor. 2:13). (2) Will. The Holy Spirit has a will in that He distributes gifts "just as He wills" (1 Cor. 12:11). The Holy Spirit gives "not according to the merits or wishes of men, but according to his own will."[19] (3) Emotion. The Holy Spirit can be grieved (Eph. 4:30). (4) Deity. The deity of the Holy Spirit is evidenced in that He is an intercessor like Christ (cf. Rom. 8:26-27, 34) and He indwells the believer along with the Father and Son (Rom. 8:9-11). The benediction equates all three members of the godhead as equal (2 Cor. 13:14).

His Works. Paul's writings also affirm the many important works the Holy Spirit performs as a member of the Trinity. (1) He regenerates. The Holy Spirit brings new life to believers (Titus 3:5). (2) He baptizes. The Holy Spirit joins believers and their Lord by placing them into the Body of Christ (1 Cor. 12:13). (3) He indwells. The Holy Spirit lives in each believer; those that are not indwelt are not believers (Rom. 8:9; 1 Cor. 12:7). (4) He seals. The Holy Spirit puts God's mark of identity and ownership on believers; He is Himself the seal, thus verifying their salvation (Eph. 1:13; 4:30). (5) He gives gifts. The Holy Spirit sovereignly dispenses spiritual abilities to believers (1 Cor. 12:4, 7, 11). (6) He fills. The Holy Spirit controls believers when conditions are met (Eph. 5:18). (7) He empowers. The Holy Spirit enables believers to live by His power (Gal. 5:16).

SIN

Definition.[20] Paul uses a number of different Greek words to describe the nature of sin. *Hamartia* is a general word used to describe sinful acts (Rom. 4:7; 11:27). *Hamartia* links Christ's death with man's sin (1 Cor. 15:3). In the plural form it denotes the accumulation of sins (Gal. 1:4), whereas in the singular it denotes the state of sinfulness (Rom. 3:9, 20; 5:20; 6:16, 23). *Paraptoma* denotes a false step in contrast to a true one (Rom. 4:25; Gal. 6:1; Eph. 2:1). *Parabasis* means stepping aside, a deviation from a true faith (Rom. 2:23; 4:15; Gal. 3:19). *Anomia* means lawlessness or iniquity (2 Cor. 6:14; 2 Thess. 2:3).

Explanation.[21] Sin is a debt, suggesting man's obligation and inability to meet the debt (Eph. 1:7; Col. 1:14). It is deviation from a straight path; the Mosaic Law had established God's standard, but the people fell short of His standard (Rom. 2:14, 15, 23; 4:15).

Sin is lawlessness and becomes rebellion (Rom. 11:30; Eph. 2:2; 5:6; Col. 3:6), involving both external acts and internal attitudes. Romans 1:29-31 combines both acts and attitudes; acts are murder, immorality, drunkenness, and homosexuality while attitudes are envy, foolishness, and faithlessness. Paul also characterizes sin as a task-master, making slaves of unbelievers (Rom. 6:16-17), and a falsehood that suppresses the truth (Rom. 1:18) and exchanges it for a lie (Rom. 1:25).

SALVATION

Paul brings some of the great soteriological themes to their fullest development. Paul's doctrine of soteriology was centered in the grace of God; it was God who initiated salvation purely out of His grace, which satisfied His divine justice and brought release from sin's bondage and a legal declaration of righteousness to the believer.

Forgiveness. When God forgave us our trespasses, He did so out of His grace (Col. 2:13). *Forgiven* (Gk. *charizomai*) means "to grant as a favor, to give graciously, to forgive out of grace."[22] The word is closely linked with the word for grace, emphasizing that forgiveness is rooted in God's grace; no human merit is involved. Thus it also has the connotation of pardon, canceling a debt, or releasing a prisoner.[23] Another Pauline word for forgiveness (Gk. *aphesis*) has a basic meaning of "release" or "send away" but theologically means "to pardon" or "cancel an obligation or punishment" (Eph. 1:7; Col. 1:14).[24] The grace of God reaches a zenith in Paul's theology as he extols its grandeur—God has graciously canceled the debt of sin that man could not pay.

Redemption. The word *redemption* (Gk. *apolutrosis*) is a particularly Pauline term; it is used ten times in the New Testament, seven of them in Pauline writings. Redemption means to set free by the payment of a price. The background of the term relates to the Roman slave markets where a slave was put up for sale and the purchaser paid the necessary price to set the slave free. Paul employs the term to describe the believer's release from bondage and enslavement to sin. But Paul also establishes the payment for redemption—the blood of Christ. His death was necessary to accomplish deliverance from sin. Romans 3:24 emphasizes that Christ's death satisfied and turned aside the wrath of God, making redemption possible. The passage also links justification with redemption; because redemption was accomplished man can be declared righteous (cf. Rom. 8:23; 1 Cor. 1:30; Gal. 3:13; Eph. 1:7, 14; 4:30; Col. 1:14).

Propitiation. The noun *propitiation* occurs only four times in the New Testament, in Romans 3:25; Hebrews 2:17; and 1 John 2:2; 4:10. This word (from Gk. *hilasmos* and *hilasterion*) means to expiate, to appease, or atone for. It indicates that Christ fully met and satisfied the demands of a righteous and holy God. Through the shed blood of Jesus Christ, God's holiness has been satisfied and His wrath averted. Romans 3:26 explains that through the death of Jesus Christ, God can be just (His integrity is maintained) and yet He may still declare the believer in Christ righteous. God does not overlook sin, however. The death of Christ was sufficient in providing atonement for sin so that God's holiness and justice are fully satisfied. Propitiation, therefore, is important in showing how a sinful man might be reconciled to a holy God—it is through the atonement of Christ. God is propitiated (satisfied) with the death of Christ as making full payment for sin.[25] (See also the discussion under "Meaning of the death of Christ," in chap. 24.)

Justification. Justification is a peculiarly Pauline term. The verb is used forty times in the New Testament, but Paul uses the word twenty-nine times. Justification is a legal act whereby God declares the believing sinner righteous on the basis of the blood of Christ. The basic meaning of justification is "to declare righteous." Several other things can be learned about Paul's usage of justification: justification is a gift of God's grace (Rom. 3:24); it is appropriated through faith (Rom. 5:1; Gal. 3:24); it is possible through the blood of Christ (Rom. 5:9); and it is apart from the law (Rom. 3:20; Gal. 2:16; 3:11). This last point is a major emphasis of Paul and undoubtedly the thesis of the book of Galatians—man is not justified by the works of the law but by faith in Jesus Christ.[26]

CHURCH[27]

Definition. The word *church* (Gk. *ekklesia*) simply means "a called out group." It is most often used in a technical sense of believers whom God has called out of the world as a special group of His own. It is, however, occasionally used in a non-technical sense to refer, for example, to a mob (translated "assembly"), as in Acts 19:32. *Church* is used in two primary ways in the New Testament—the *"universal"* church and the *local* church. Paul uses the term to refer to the wide company of believers transcending a single congregation (Gal. 1:13; Eph. 3:10, 21; 5:23-25, 27, 29, 32). When the term is referring to the Body of Christ the universal sense is intended (Eph. 1:22; Col. 1:18, 24). *Church* refers to the local church when a particular assembly of believers in a given location at a given time is intended. Thus Paul refers to the individual churches at Corinth (1 Cor. 1:2; 4:17; 7:17; 2 Cor. 1:1; 8:1), Galatia (Gal. 1:2, 22), Philippi (Phil. 4:15), Colossae (Col. 4:15, 16), and Thessalonica (2 Thess. 1:1).

The church as a union of Jews and Gentiles on equal footing as fellow heirs in Christ (Eph. 3:6) is a distinctly New Testament entity. The church was unknown in the Old Testament (Eph. 3:5); the knowledge about the church was given to Paul through revelation (Eph. 3:3).

Explanation. Paul depicts the church as an organism making up the "complex structure of the Body of Christ which carries on living activities by meanings of the individual believers, who are distinct in function but mutually dependent on and governed by their relation to Christ, the Head."[28]

Entrance into the church is through the baptizing work of the Holy Spirit who places believers into union with Christ and with other believers (1 Cor. 12:13). The baptizing work of the Spirit occurs simultaneously with saving faith, is non-experiential, and includes all believers, regardless of class or social position. As a head gives direction to a human body, so Christ, as Head of the church, gives direction to the church, having authority over it (Eph. 1:22-23; Col. 2:10). It is through union with Christ that the church grows to maturity (Col. 2:19) as it subjects itself to the authority of Christ (Eph. 1:22-23).

Paul teaches that God has given spiritual gifts for the building up of the Body of Christ (Eph. 4:11-13). The doctrine of spiritual gifts is almost exclusively Pauline; the only reference apart from Paul is a brief statement in 1 Peter 4:10. *Spiritual gifts* is the translation of one Greek word *charisma*, literally, "grace gift." A concise definition is "a God-given ability for service."[29] Paul describes the gifts in Romans 12, 1 Corinthians 12, and Ephesians 4. (See "Gifts of the Holy Spirit" for an expanded discussion.)

Organization. While the church is a living organism, it is also an organization, involving offices and function. There are two designated offices in the New Testament church. The office of *elder* (Gk. *presbuteros*) emphasizes maturity and dignity and normally denotes an older person. Elders were appointed as leaders in the local churches (1 Tim. 5:17; Titus 1:5). The term *bishop* or *overseer* (Gk. *episkopos*) denotes the work of shepherding by the elder (1 Tim. 3:1). The terms are basically synonymous, although elder signifies the office whereas overseer emphasizes function. The work of the elders involved teaching (1 Tim. 5:17), ruling (1 Tim. 5:17), shepherding, nurturing, and caring for the flock (1 Tim. 3·1). Their qualifications are listed in 1 Timothy 3:1-7.

The other church office is that of *deacon* (Gk. *diakonos*), meaning "servant." From the qualifications cited in 1 Timothy 3:8-13 it is evident the deacons were also involved in spiritual ministry, albeit as subordinate to the elders. Along with the elders they had an authoritative position in the local church (cf. Phil. 1:1).

It is not entirely clear whether Paul was advocating a separate office of deaconness (1 Tim. 3:11). The word *gunaikas*, translated "women," may refer to the wives of the deacons or to a separate class of deaconesses.

Ordinances. Although the subject of baptism is prominent in the New Testament, it is not a major emphasis in Pauline theology. The verb *baptizo* is used eighty times in the New Testament, but Paul uses it only sixteen times and only eleven of those refer to water baptism (three of them in Acts). Furthermore, he uses the verb six times in his explanation that Christ did not send him to baptize (1 Cor. 1:13-17); thus, apart from that reference, Paul refers to water baptism only twice in the epistles (1 Cor. 15:29). In his explanation to the Corinthians Paul makes it clear that baptism is not a part of the gospel (1 Cor. 1:17-18). Paul seems to emphasize the baptism of the Spirit more than water baptism (cf. Rom. 6:3; 1 Cor. 10:2; 12:13; Gal. 3:27).

Paul provides a detailed explanation of the Lord's Supper (1 Cor. 11:23-34), which he received through direct revelation from the Lord (1 Cor. 15:3; Gal. 1:12). Paul presents the Lord's Supper as a memorial (1 Cor. 11:25) and admonishes the Corinthians not to partake in a casual manner; in so doing they would drink judgment to themselves. Paul's further rebuke relates to an accompanying meal, sometimes referred to as the *agape*, in which some would gorge themselves while others would have little to eat. It disrupted fellowship and resulted in eating and drinking the Lord's Supper in an unworthy manner; they were "eating without recognizing the symbolism which reminds of the Lord's body, without seeing Christ and His death in it all."[30]

LAST THINGS

Regarding the church. Since Paul has provided significant new teaching concerning the nature of the church, it is appropriate that Paul should bring that teaching to a consummation, describing the future of the church. Paul refers to the translation of the church in which some living believers will not die but be transformed more quickly than an eye can cast a glance (1 Cor. 15:51-57). At that time, departed church age believers will rise to receive resurrection bodies (1 Thess. 4:16) and the living, transformed believers will be suddenly snatched up to be with Christ (1 Thess. 4:13-18).

Paul emphasizes the practical nature of this doctrine: "comfort one another with these words" (1 Thess. 4:18). Following the rapture of the church believers will stand before the *bema*, the *judgment seat* of Christ, to be recompensed for deeds done in the body, whether good or worthless. Salvation is not the issue; rather, it is the works of the believer. One whose works were done in the flesh will be burned up; there will be no reward, but the believer will be saved—with no works to show for it (1 Cor. 3:15). One whose works are acceptable by the Lord will be rewarded—not in terms of salvation, for that has been established. Rewards are spoken of in terms of crowns (1 Thess. 2:19; 2 Tim. 4:8).

Regarding Israel. Paul deals with Israel's election in Romans 9-11, lamenting Israel's rejection of Messiah (Rom. 9:1-3; 10:1-5). Israel had great privileges but scorned them (Rom. 9:4-5), yet since God has sovereignly elected Israel, He will not fail in His purpose for the nation. The fact that God has not abandoned His people (Rom. 11:1) is evident by the fact that there is a remnant of believing Jews, of which Paul was one (Rom. 11:1, 5). However, while Israel has been blinded, it is temporary. Paul envisions a future day when Israel's blindness will be lifted and "all Israel will be saved" (Rom. 11:26). There will be a future national turning to Christ in faith. Paul relates that event to the return of Messiah: "The Deliverer will come from Zion, He will remove ungodliness from Jacob" (Rom. 11:26).

Regarding the world. While Paul has referred to future hope for the church and the future conversion of Israel, he deals extensively with the future judgment of God upon an unbelieving world. Paul uses the term *wrath* (Gk. *orgē*) to describe the judgment of God that will descend upon the world. This term is decidedly a Pauline term, being used twenty-one times in his writings while only fifteen times in the remainder of the New Testament. Paul frequently uses *orgē* to describe a future "day of wrath" (Rom. 2:5) that the stubborn and unrepentant people will face. Paul warns that the wrath of God will come upon those who are morally impure (Eph. 5:6; Col. 3:6). Paul, however, takes great pains to show that believers will not endure the wrath of God. They will be saved from that day (Rom. 5:9; 1 Thess. 1:10; 5:9).[31]

Paul also identifies the period as a time the "man of lawlessness," also called the "son of destruction" (2 Thess. 2:3), will appear and exalt himself as God (2 Thess. 2:4). He is unable to exalt himself in this present age because of a restrainer (2 Thess. 2:6)—whom many identify as the Holy Spirit in this church age. When the restrainer is removed, the "lawless one will be revealed" (2 Thess. 2:8), deceiving the people through his Satan-inspired miracles. But at the Second Advent of Christ, the lawless one (popularly known as the Antichrist) will be destroyed (2 Thess. 2:8).

Notes on Paul

1. Richard Longenecker, *The Ministry and Message of Paul* (Grand Rapids: Zondervan, 1971), p. 44.
2. Fritz Rienecker, *Linguistic Key to the Greek New Testament*, edited by Cleon Rogers (Grand Rapids: Zondervan, 1982), p. 349.
3. Ibid., p. 367.
4. Charles C. Ryrie, *Biblical Theology of the New Testament* (Chicago: Moody, 1959), p. 169.
5. *Exelexato* is in the middle voice, suggesting God chose us for Himself.
6. Ryrie, *Biblical Theology of the New Testament*, pp. 172-73.
7. The aorist participle *genomenon* emphasizes the event of Christ's birth. The preposition *ek* emphasizes His origin; He came from a human mother.
8. "Descendant" is *spermatos*, literally sperm or seed, emphasizing the human descent.
9. J. B. Lightfoot, *Saint Paul's Epistles to the Colossians and to Philemon* (Reprint. Grand Rapids: Zondervan, 1959), p. 150.
10. Rienecker, *Linguistic Key to the Greek New Testament*, p. 573.
11. The present participle *huparchon* emphasizes that Christ continues to exist as deity. Deity is His state of existence.
12. Donald Guthrie, *New Testament Theology* (Downers Grove, Ill.: InterVarsity, 1981), pp. 339-40, prefers this RSV marginal reading which is similar to the NIV.
13. The Granville Sharpe rule states that when there are two nouns joined by *kai*, with the first noun having the article and the second being anarthrous (without the article), then the two nouns refer to the same person or thing.
14. Ryrie, *Biblical Theology of the New Testament*, p. 176.
15. Oscar Cullmann, *The Christology of the New Testament* rev. ed., (Philadelphia: Westminster, 1963), p. 217; and Donald Guthrie, *New Testament Theology*, p. 291.
16. Ibid., p. 218.
17. Guthrie, *New Testament Theology*, p. 298.
18. Cullmann, *Christology of the New Testament*, pp. 220-21.
19. Charles Hodge, *The First Epistle to the Corinthians* (London: Banner of Truth, 1958), p. 253.
20. See Guthrie, *New Testament Theology*, pp. 200-201.
21. Ibid., pp. 201-4.
22. Rienecker, *Linguistic Key to the Greek New Testament*, p. 574.
23. Barclay M. Newman, Jr., *A Concise Greek-English Dictionary of the New Testament* (London: United Bible Societies, 1971), p. 197.
24. William F. Arndt and F. Wilbur Gingrich, *A Greek-English Lexicon of the New Testament and Other Early Christian Literature* 2d ed., edited by F. Wilbur Gingrich and Frederick W. Danker (Chicago: U. of Chicago, 1979), p. 125.
25. See the helpful discussion concerning the substitutionary blood atonement in which Herman Ridderbos also discusses the word *propitiation* in *Paul: An Outline of His Theology* (Grand Rapids: Eerdmans, 1975), pp. 186-93.
26. Ibid., pp. 159-81.

27. See the helpful material concerning Paul's doctrine of the church in Ryrie, *Biblical Theology of the New Testament*, pp. 188-202.
28. Ibid., p. 191.
29. Ibid., p. 193.
30. James L. Boyer, *For a World Like Ours* (Grand Rapids: Baker, 1971), p. 109.
31. In Romans 5:9 and 1 Thessalonians 1:10 Paul uses the definite article, *tes*, to indicate a specific kind of wrath. The expression refers to *the* wrath of God—the tribulation period from which, Paul teaches, believers will be spared. The wrath of God will be poured out upon stubborn, unrepentant and immoral people—not upon believers.

FOR FURTHER STUDY ON PAUL

** F. F. Bruce. *Paul: Apostle of the Heart Set Free*. Grand Rapids: Eerdmans, 1978.

** Donald Guthrie. *New Testament Theology*. Downers Grove, Ill.: InterVarsity, 1981.

** George E. Ladd. *A Theology of the New Testament*. Grand Rapids: Eerdmans, 1974.

* Richard Longenecker. *The Ministry and Message of Paul*. Grand Rapids: Zondervan, 1971.

** _____. *Paul, Apostle of Liberty*. Grand Rapids: Baker, 1976.

* _____. "Pauline Theology." In Merrill C. Tenney, ed., *Zondervan Pictorial Encyclopedia of the Bible*. Grand Rapids: Zondervan, 1975. 4:657-65.

** J. Gresham Machen. *The Origin of Paul's Religion*. Grand Rapids: Eerdmans, 1925. A classic work by a great theologian.

** Leon Morris. *New Testament Theology*. Grand Rapids: Zondervan, 1986.

* S. Motyer. "Paul, Theology of." In Walter A. Elwell, ed., *Evangelical Dictionary of Theology*. Grand Rapids: Baker, 1984. Pp. 829-31.

** Herman Ridderbos. *Paul: An Outline of His Theology*. Grand Rapids: Eerdmans, 1975. This is an important, extensive, and well-documented treatment of Paul's theology.

* Charles C. Ryrie. *Biblical Theology of the New Testament*. Chicago: Moody, 1959. Pp. 151-222.

* N. T. Wright. "Paul." In *New Dictionary of Theology*, edited by Sinclair B. Ferguson, J. I. Packer, and David F. Wright. Downers Grove, Ill.: InterVarsity, 1988. Pp. 496-99.

14
THEOLOGY OF HEBREWS

INTRODUCTION TO HEBREWS

The introductory questions concerning the addresses and occasion and purpose for writing are particularly important in discussing the theology of Hebrews. The view that is taken concerning these issues will determine the interpretation of the theology of Hebrews.

AUTHORSHIP

The authorship of Hebrews has posed a problem throughout the history of the Christian church and has been vigorously debated without resolve. The author nowhere identifies himself in the book, yet it seems he was known to the readers (5:11-12; 10:32-34; 12:4; 13:9, 18-19, 23). He understood their circumstances and wrote with regard to them.

DATE AND PLACE OF WRITING

The book was written early; Clement of Rome quoted from it in A.D. 96. The present tense regarding the sacrifices (7:8; 8:4, 13; 9:1-10) suggests the Temple was still standing; therefore, it was written prior to A.D. 70. Although the believers in the book were undergoing persecution, they had not experienced martyrdom (12:4). Because the fierce persecution began with the burning of Rome in A.D. 64, it is likely the book was written before that time.

The place of writing is difficult to determine. The reference "those from Italy greet you" could refer to Italy as a place of writing.

DESTINATION

The title "To The Hebrews" is a second-century addition to the manuscript that may merely reflect the second-century opinion concerning the destination. The intrinsic evidence points to an assembly of Hebrew believers as the destination. (1) The book follows an argument from a Jewish standpoint through comparing Christ to the Levitical system. (2) The book uses Old Testament quotations. (3) The book has extensive mention of the Levitical priesthood. (4) Terminology occurs that is exclusively Jewish: angels, miracles, high priest, Moses, Aaron, law, covenant, tabernacle, holy place, sacrifices, and blood. (5) It contains an elaborate resumé of Hebrew history. (6) There is a detailed discussion of the tabernacle.

The location of the readers is difficult to determine. Although it is not without problems, the suggestion that Jerusalem is the destination seems most reasonable.[1] The present tense concerning offering gifts in 8:4 suggests conditions under which the offerings were actually being carried out.

THEOLOGICAL PURPOSE

The purpose of the book is to demonstrate the superiority of Christ and Christianity over Judaism. The addressees were Hebrew Christians: they are termed "holy brethren" (3:1), "partakers of a heavenly calling" (3:1), and "partakers of Christ" (3:14). Although their present condition was dangerous, the writer nonetheless considered them saved (6:9) but in need of maturity (6:1) and progress in their walk with Christ. They were in danger of lapsing back into Judaism (5:11-6:3; 10:19-25).

These Hebrew Christians were suffering persecution and had become discouraged (10:32-34; 12:4). They had lost their property and had suffered public ridicule and ostracism for their faith in Christ. The writer addresses these circumstances, exhorting them to go on to maturity (4:14; 6:11ff.; 10:23, 36; 12:1). He also warns them about the seriousness of apostasy (6:4-8; 10:26-31; 12:14-29).

THEOLOGY OF HEBREWS

GOD

The writer of Hebrews emphasizes both the Person of the majestic God and the way He has revealed Himself to His people.

His Person. The writer pictures the Father as exalted in the heavens, enthroned on high (1:3). The phrase is a title of God referring to Psalm 110:1. A similar picture is given in 8:1 where the term "Majesty" is again used. Since the book is written to a Jewish audience, this undoubtedly refers to "the Glory which rested on the Mercy Seat in the Holy of Holies."[2]

The writer also discusses the approach to God by referring to His throne. Because Christ is the believer's intercessor, they may draw near to God (7:25; 10:22; cf. 9:24) and do so with confidence (12:22-24). Jesus has assumed an authoritative position at the right hand of the Father (12:2).

The Jewish believers are reminded that their God was living, in contrast to the idols that are dead (cf. Ps. 115:3-8; Isa. 46:6-7; Jer. 10:5-10). The writer exhorts them not to return to a dead system but to serve the living God (Heb. 9:14; cf. 10:31; 12:22).

The use of fire as a figure of God symbolizes the judgment of God (12:29). This relates to the theme of Hebrews in warning them of forsaking the living God. They will experience the disciplinary judgment of God should they return to Judaism.

The book concludes with a mention of God as peace (13:20). He is able to give peace to the Jewish believers amid their persecution.

His Revelation. The apex of God's revelation was through His Son (1:1-2). In the Old Testament God spoke piecemeal and in many different ways, but the climax of His revelation was in the Person of His Son. The statement suggests there is no need for any further revelation. What greater revelation about God can be given than that which has come through Christ?

As a witness to the revelation in Christ, God performed miracles through the hands of His witnesses, the apostles, testifying to the great salvation in Christ (2:4). It is noteworthy that the writer of Hebrews places himself outside the age of miracles, indicating it was the previous generation that witnessed the miracles.

The magnitude of God's grace is seen because through it Christ suffered death on behalf of all people.[3] Hence, it is important that they appropriate this grace of God that has been manifested through Christ (12:15).

The theme of judgment is stressed in Hebrews because of the danger of the Hebrew Christians reverting to Judaism. Hence, they are reminded not to trample under foot the Son of God through whom they were sanctified, for God will judge them for so repudiating the blood of Christ (10:30). However, should God judge them, it is a disciplinary action—an indication that He is dealing with them in a Father-child relationship (12:5-13). Since God will ultimately judge everyone (12:23), the Hebrew believers should not refuse the warnings (12:25). Those who have been faithful will be rewarded (6:10).

CHRIST

Christology is clearly the major theological emphasis of Hebrews. In the development of the book, the author shows the superiority of Christ to prophets (1:1-3), to angels (1:4-2:18), to Moses (3:1-4:13), and to Aaron (4:14-10:39). Christ is at the heart of the doctrinal section of the book (chaps. 1-10). The Christological emphasis is necessary when considering the addressees. The Hebrew Christians were being persecuted for their faith and were contemplating reverting to Judaism. The writer of Hebrews shows them the folly of this by reminding them that in so doing they would be reverting to an inferior system when, in fact, they had been given a superior revelation in Christ. The author of Hebrews shows differing facets of Christ to demonstrate His superiority.

Titles. The designation *Christ* (the Anointed One) is used throughout the epistle (3:6, 14; 5:5; 6:1; 9:11, 14, 24, 28; 11:26). It is a reminder that the Anointed One, the kingly Messiah, has come. In the chapter dealing with the better sanctuary (chap. 9), the author employs the name four times. Messiah as High Priest has entered heaven, not simply an earthly sanctuary that is a mere copy of the true in heaven (9:11, 24). Messiah has offered His own blood to provide complete cleansing (9:14). Messiah bore the sins once but will appear a second time for salvation (9:28).

The human name, *Jesus*, emphasizes that in His humanity as a human high priest He has achieved what the Levitical high priest failed to do (2:9; 3:1; 6:20; 7:22; 10:19; 12:2, 24; 13:12). Jesus took on humanity and suffered death on behalf of everyone (2:9). Jesus is the Apostle and High Priest who supplanted the Levitical priesthood (3:1). Jesus has entered heaven's Holy of Holies and remains forever our high priest according to the order of Melchizedek (6:20). He has also guaranteed and mediated a better covenant (7:22; 12:24), provided His blood whereby believers may enter the Holy of Holies (10:19), brought completion to faith (12:2), and fulfilled the Old Testament types in securing salvation (13:12).

The term *Son* is used to emphasize the greater relationship that Jesus has to the Father (1:2, 5, 8; 3:6; 5:5, 8; 7:28). The Son is greater than angels by being the heir, creator, sustainer, and exact representation of the Father (1:2). The son has a privileged relationship with the Father and will consummate the age as ruler (1:5,8; 5:5). The Son is greater than Moses, has authority over God's people (3:6), and is greater than the law, not having the weakness of Levitical priests (7:28).

Christ is also designated a permanent *High Priest*, who has made propitiation for sins (2:17). As High Priest He identifies with the people, yet is sinless (4:15); is in the presence of the Father (4:14); endures forever (6:20); is holy, innocent, undefiled, separate from sinners, and exalted to heaven (7:26; 9:11); and finally, as High Priest He has finished His work (8:1).

Deity. Jesus' deity is affirmed through the names ascribed to Him. In Hebrews 1:8-10 the author quotes from Psalm 45:6-8 and 102:25 but in the preface to the quotation he states: "But of the Son He says." The quotations that follow have reference to the Son. Thus the Son is referred to as "God" (1:8, 9) and "Lord" (1:10).

In 1:3 the deity of Jesus is seen through His intrinsic nature and being. He is the "radiance of His glory." "As the rays of light are related to the sun, and neither exists without the other, so Christ is the effulgence of the divine glory. They are essentially one; that is, both are God."[4] Jesus is the "exact representation" (Gk. *charakter*) of God's nature (1:3). The word means an engraving or mark left by an engraving tool; as a coin reflects the mint from which it came, so Jesus reflects the Father.

The author also depicts Jesus as deity through His works. He is the creator of the ages (Gk. *aion*), "the sum of the periods of time" (1:2). He is the sustainer (Gk. *pheron*) who "carries all things forward on their appointed course."[5]

Sinless humanity. The author of Hebrews stresses the true, unblemished humanity of Jesus that was brought about so He could make a full provision for sin. As a man Jesus partook of "flesh and blood" to show His true humanity (2:14). As a man Jesus was subject to the same temptations as all humanity (2:18; 4:15). As a man He experienced suffering amid "loud crying and tears" in anticipation of the cross (5:7). As a man He submitted to the Father (2:13; 5:7). But while Jesus was fully and genuinely a man, He was without sin—He was impeccable (4:15; 7:26).

Priesthood. Christ is superior because He is a priest according to the order of Melchizedek, not according to the Aaronic priesthood. The Melchizedekian priesthood of Christ is superior because:[6] (1) Christ's priesthood is new and better (7:15; cf. 7:7, 19, 22; 8:6); (2) Christ's priesthood is permanent (7:16); (3) Christ retains the priesthood permanently (7:24); (4) Christ's priesthood is based on a better covenant (8:6; 6:13).

Even though the writer of Hebrews deals with other doctrines, it is clear that the focus of His theology is Christological.

HOLY SPIRIT

Although the doctrine of the Holy Spirit is not discussed extensively, several things are noted in Hebrews. (1) The sign gifts were displayed through the sovereign will of the Holy Spirit (2:4). (2) The Holy Spirit is the author of Scripture (3:7; 9:8; 10:15). (3) Salvation involves becoming a partaker of the Holy Spirit (6:4). (4) Repudiating salvation through Christ is insulting to the Holy Spirit (10:29).

SIN

The doctrine of sin in Hebrews is fundamental to its theme of warning Hebrew Christians from lapsing into Judaism and thereby sinning against Christ. Thus in 6:4-6 a stern warning tells the Hebrew Christians that if they have once been enlightened and have become partakers of salvation and then fall away, it will be impossible for them to ever repent and be restored. God indicates He will confirm them in spiritual atrophy or babyhood if they return to Judaism; there will be no restoration for them. The same stern warning is given in 10:26-30. There is no further sacrifice than that of Christ; if they go on sinning willfully by returning to Judaism, they will find no sacrifice for their sins in the Levitical system. All they can expect is the severe judgment of God.

Thus the writer warns the Hebrews against hardening their hearts (3:7-11) and exhorts them to pursue sanctification and not come short of the grace of God (12:14-15). He reminds them of Moses who rejected the temporary pleasures of sin and sought instead to endure suffering and hardship (11:25). The Hebrew Christians needed similarly to reject the sin of regression and pursue sanctification, even if that would mean suffering. The sin of unbelief (lack of faith) was at the root of their problem; the writer challenges them to lay aside the sin of unbelief that entangled them and look instead to Jesus, the pioneer of their faith, who finished the course that was set before Him (12:1-2).

SALVATION

In contrasting Christ to angels, the writer explains that a function of angels is to render aid to those who inherit salvation (1:14). More to the theme of Hebrews, however, is the exhortation in 2:3, "How shall we escape if we neglect so great a salvation?" This statement implies Christ to be superior to the Old Testament sacrifices in that He provided a complete salvation through His atonement. The Hebrew Christians' intended regression to Judaism is the target of the warning. "So great" emphasizes the once-for-all death of Christ that secured salvation—something that was unattainable through the blood of bulls and goats (10:4).

Jesus' superior provision in salvation is seen in that He experienced death for every one (2:9), and through that death He brought "many sons to glory" (2:10). The fact that Jesus' salvation is able to bring many sons to glory emphasizes the finality and security of it. The Hebrew Christians had no such security under the Old Covenant. The writer further emphasizes Christ's complete submission and obedience to the will of the Father; through His perfect obedience Christ became "the source of eternal salvation" (5:9). The Hebrew believers needed to know these significant truths, but they were dull and needed to be taught the elementary doctrines of the faith.

NOTES ON HEBREWS

1. B. F. Westcott, *The Epistle to the Hebrews* (Reprint. Grand Rapids: Eerdmans, 1965), pp. xxxvii-xlii.
2. Ibid., p. 213.
3. The fact that Christ died is stressed in the Greek text. Death (*thanatou*) standing last in the sentence for emphasis.

4. Homer A. Kent, Jr., *The Epistle to the Hebrews: A Commentary* (Grand Rapids: Baker, 1972), p. 37.
5. Fritz Rienecker, *Linguistic Key to the Greek New Testament*, edited by Cleon Rogers (Grand Rapids: Zondervan, 1982), p. 664.
6. Charles C. Ryrie, *Biblical Theology of the New Testament* (Chicago: Moody, 1959), pp. 247-48.

FOR FURTHER STUDY ON HEBREWS

* F. F. Bruce. "Hebrews, Epistle to the." In Merrill C. Tenney, ed., *Zondervan Pictorial Encyclopedia of the Bible*. Grand Rapids: Zondervan, 1975. 3:87-93.

** Donald Guthrie. *New Testament Theology*. Downers Grove, Ill.: Inter-Varsity, 1981.

** George E. Ladd. *A Theology of the New Testament*. Grand Rapids: Eerdmans, 1974.

* Chester K. Lehman. *Biblical Theology: New Testament*. Scottdale, Pa.: Herald, 1974. 2:431-58.

** Leon Morris. *The Cross in the New Testament*. Grand Rapids: Eerdmans, 1965. Pp. 270-308.

* Charles C. Ryrie. *Biblical Theology of the New Testament*. Chicago: Moody, 1959. Pp. 225-61.

** George B. Stevens. *The Theology of the New Testament*, 2nd. rev. ed. Edinburgh: Clark, 1918. Pp. 483-522.

15

THEOLOGIES OF PETER AND JUDE

INTRODUCTION TO PETER'S THEOLOGY

This study of biblical theology will focus on the doctrinal teachings by Peter from his two epistles and his preaching in Acts.

THE EPISTLES

The First Epistle. This received early authentication by Eusebius, Irenaeus, Tertullian, and other church Fathers. The internal evidence also suggests the apostle Peter as the author: he is so named (1:1), and there is considerable agreement between 1 Peter and Peter's speeches in Acts. The book was probably written prior to A.D. 64 and addressed to Hebrew believers living among the Gentiles (1:1). Peter's purpose in writing is to encourage the believers who were suffering persecution. He describes them as being "distressed by various trials" (1:6). Charged with disloyalty to the state (2:13-15), they were being slandered, ridiculed, and maligned for failing to indulge in heathen practices (3:13-17; 4:4-5). Peter termed their suffering a "fiery ordeal" (4:12). The thesis of Peter's first epistle is hortatory and stated in 5:12—the believers were to stand firm in God's grace amid their suffering.

The Second Epistle. This has probably the weakest evidence of any New Testament book; it was, however, never rejected or regarded as a spurious book. Origen (c. A.D. 240) was the first to attribute the book to Peter. The internal evidence points to the apostle Peter as the author. He is so named (1:1) and indicates he was an eyewitness of the Lord (1:16), suggesting he was one of the three. There is also a similarity to Peter's speeches in Acts.[1] The letter was written about A.D. 65, probably to a broad readership. Peter's purpose in writing this letter can be stated twofold. (1) Negatively, he was warning the believers concerning the outbreak of antinomianism (flagrant disregard for God's commands) and heretical teachers who were infiltrating the assemblies. (2) Positively, Peter exhorted the believers to "grow in the grace and knowledge of our Lord and Savior Jesus Christ" (3:18).

THE AUTHOR

The apostle Peter was the son of Jonah (Matt. 16:17) or John (John 1:42), and was a brother of Andrew (John 1:40). He was originally from Bethsaida (John 1:44) but later moved to Capernaum (Mark 1:21, 29). Peter was a fisherman by trade (Luke 5:1-11).

At the beginning of His public ministry Jesus called Peter to salvation (John 1:42), and about a year later He called him as an apostle (Matt. 10:1-2). As one of the Twelve, Peter was given apostolic authority to perform miraculous signs, which vindicated the Messianic message (Matt. 10:1-15), and frequently he spoke for the group (Matt. 15:15; 16:16; 18:21; 19:27). Peter was also one of the select three, along with James and John. In that company he witnessed the transfiguration of Christ (Matt. 17:1), which he later wrote about (2 Pet. 1:16). As one of the three Peter was a "pillar of the church" (Gal. 2:9) and later became a leader in the church. He was a spokesman in selecting a successor to Judas (Acts 1:15-22), a spokesman at Pentecost (Acts 2:14-36), and also at the Jerusalem Council (Acts 15:7-11). Peter was the apostle to the Jews, which is also reflected in his speeches and in his first epistle (1 Pet. 1:1). One line of tradition suggests Peter ultimately went to Rome, but it is not certain.

DISCUSSION OF PETER'S THEOLOGY

Peter's theology is clearly Christ-centered and in that emphasis expounds on the important doctrines related to Christ's Person. He recounts Christ's sinlessness, His substitutionary atonement, His resurrection, and His glorification. Peter dwells considerably on the sufferings, humiliation, and rejection of Christ.

CHRIST

A study of Peter's use of the names of Christ is illuminating. In His sermons in Acts, Peter refers to Jesus or Jesus of Nazareth. In Acts 2:22 Peter identifies Him as "Jesus the Nazarene," perhaps to remind His hearers of Jesus as the rejected one, because the term *Nazarene* would have had a negative connotation. In Acts 2:36 he refers to Him as "Jesus" but reminds the people He is no mere man, for "God has made Him both Lord and Christ." Peter lays stress on this fact with his words, "know for certain."[2] In Acts 3:13 Peter refers to the glorification of Jesus, linking it with the titles, "Servant" (3:13), "Holy," "Righteous One" (3:14), and "Prince of Life"

(3:15). Therefore, while Peter again mentions Jesus in 3:16, he also emphasizes the authority and power connected with the name.

Peter preferred the designation *Christ* in his epistles, most often using the title *Messiah* to describe His sufferings. Peter writes that Christ shed His precious blood (1 Pet. 1:19), suffered as a substitute[3] (1 Pet. 2:21), suffered in the flesh (1 Pet. 4:1), suffered in front of witnesses (1 Pet. 5:1), and died for sin *once* (emphatic) for all (1 Pet. 3:18). In the light of this, Peter encourages the believers to set apart Christ as Lord in their hearts (1 Pet. 3:15), to keep a good conscience amid suffering for Christ (1 Pet. 3:16), to rejoice amid sufferings for Christ (1 Pet. 4:13-14), because in the end God will call them to eternal glory through their union with Christ (1 Pet. 5:10).

Peter also uses the compound name of Christ, but in so doing he emphasizes not the suffering of Christ, but the resurrection, glorification, and Second Coming. Through the Lord Jesus Christ the believer has been born again to a living hope (1 Pet. 1:3), having been saved through the resurrection of Jesus Christ (1 Pet. 3:21), presently being built up as a spiritual house (1 Pet. 2:5), glorifying Jesus Christ through the exercise of spiritual gifts (1 Pet. 4:11), and growing in the knowledge of Jesus Christ (2 Pet. 1:8; 3:18). Therefore, they can anticipate the glorious appearing of Jesus Christ (1 Pet. 1:13; 2 Pet. 1:16) when their trials will glorify Jesus Christ (1 Pet. 1:7).

SALVATION

As has been noted in the preceding discussion, Peter emphasizes Christ in His work of salvation: He was a perfect sacrifice, like a spotless, unblemished lamb (1 Pet. 1:19); He committed no acts of sin (1 Pet. 2:22); He died as a substitute once for all, the innocent for the guilty (1 Pet. 3:18). Peter emphasizes the act—He was killed for us.

The pronouns emphasize that Christ died in the place of sinners (1 Pet. 2:24). He ransomed[4] them from slavery to sin (1 Pet. 1:18).

Christ's salvation was planned in eternity past (1 Pet. 1:20) but revealed in history. He completed salvation through His resurrection, giving believers a living hope (1 Pet. 1:3).

SCRIPTURES

Aside from Paul, Peter may well provide the most extensive discussion concerning the doctrine of Scripture. Peter provides significant insight concerning the Holy Spirit's ministry in inspiration as well as affirming the inspiration of Paul's writings. He provides one of the most complete studies of the Scriptures: they are the product of the Holy Spirit; they produce regeneration and spiritual growth.

The following may be noted from Peter's doctrine of the Scriptures:

(1) The Scriptures are termed "the prophetic word" (2 Pet. 1:19), denoting the entire Old Testament. Peter indicates the Old Testament Scriptures are made certain through the appearing of Jesus Christ. (2) The Scriptures are living and remain forever[5] (1 Pet. 1:23). In contrast to corruptible human seed, God's word is incorruptible. (3) The Scriptures are uncontaminated and nourishing, enabling the believer to grow spiritually (1 Pet. 2:2). (4) The Scriptures are not of a purely human origin (2 Pet. 1:20). (5) The Scriptures are the product of men who spoke as they were carried along by the Holy Spirit, ensuring the accuracy of Scripture (2 Pet. 1:21). (6) The New Testament Scriptures are equally inspired with the Old Testament Scriptures (2 Pet. 3:16). Peter places the letters of Paul on par with the "rest of the Scriptures." (7) The Scriptures are the basis of theological truth (1 Pet. 2:6). Peter makes a theological point and bases it on a quotation from Isaiah 28:16.

CHRISTIAN LIFE

While Peter has remarks about other aspects of the Christian life, the major focus of his writing pertains to suffering. He was addressing Hebrew Christians who were suffering for their faith (1 Pet. 1:1). Peter wrote to encourage them and explain how believers ought to react to suffering, especially when the sufferings were undeserved (1 Pet. 1:6).

Peter wrote words of caution and encouragement regarding suffering. First, believers should expect trials and suffering and prepare their minds for it since Christ also suffered (1 Pet. 1:11; 4:12; 5:9). Second, believers should rejoice amid suffering because of the anticipation of Christ's return (1 Pet. 3:14; 4:13). Third, believers may suffer unjustly (1 Pet. 2:19, 20, 21, 23; 3:17). There is no credit if a Christian suffers for wrongdoing, but it is admirable before God if a believer bears up when suffering unjustly. Christ suffered and gave believers a pattern for following His example (1 Pet. 2:21-23; 3:17-18; 4:1). Finally, believers may suffer according to the will of God (1 Pet. 3:17; 4:19), but they will be strengthened by Him amid suffering (1 Pet. 5:10).

CHURCH

Although the word *church* does not appear in Peter's writings, he does discuss the doctrine of the church to some extent.

The universal church. Peter recognizes the unity of Jew and Gentile in one body (Acts 10:34-43). In a momentous declaration Peter announced that Gentiles were welcomed by God without first becoming Jewish proselytes through ritual (Acts 10:35).[6] Prior to that time Gentiles would first have to be baptized into Judaism, offer a sacrifice, and receive circumcision. This ritual would now be bypassed. Peter confirmed this truth in Acts 15:7-11.

The local church. In 1 Peter 5:1-4 Peter refers to the responsibilities of the elders in the local church. Their responsibility is to shepherd the flock of God. The task of shepherding would denote feeding (teaching), protecting, nurturing, and caring for the flock. This was not to be done in a domineering manner or for love of money, but with eagerness and as examples in godliness.

Peter also mentions baptism, using the analogy between baptism and Noah. As the waters of Noah symbolized the break with the old life, so water baptism symbolizes the break from the old sinful life (1 Pet. 3:21).[7]

LAST THINGS

The conditions. In 2 Peter, the apostle refers to the conditions that will preface the Lord's return; there will be false teachers who will enter the assembly. They will be known by their false teaching by which they deny the Master who bought them (2 Pet. 2:1). False teachers will also be characterized by their immorality (2 Pet. 2:14). They lead the unsuspecting astray but will be judged by Christ at His return (2 Pet. 2:9).

The coming of Christ. In his two epistles, Peter seems to distinguish between the rapture of the church and the Second Coming to judge the wicked.[8] The coming for believers at the rapture will be deliverance and blessing; hence, Peter indicates the present suffering of believers will culminate in praise and honor at the revelation of Christ (1 Pet. 1:7). Therefore, Peter encourages the believers to fix their hope at the revelation of Christ (the rapture would be implied) (1 Pet. 1:13). In 2 Peter, the apostle refers to Christ's coming in judgment upon those who mock His return (2 Pet. 3:1-7). This coming will be a "day of judgment and destruction of ungodly men" (v. 7).

Eternal state. Peter describes the suddenness of the coming of the Day of the Lord (2 Pet. 3:10). The Day of the Lord is used in several ways in Scripture, but as a general term it views the entire period beginning with the rapture and terminating at the end of the millennium; thus, the Day of the Lord involves judgment upon unbelievers but blessing for believers. From 2 Peter 3:10*b*-12 Peter describes the eternal state. At the end of the millennium the heavens will pass away with a great noise and the earth will be burned up. This is the sphere where sin took place; it is renovated in anticipation of eternity. Peter concludes his study on last things with a practical exhortation (2 Pet. 3:11).

INTRODUCTION TO JUDE'S THEOLOGY

The author of the small epistle of Jude is simply identified as the brother of James (v. 1). The identification with James suggests it was James, the head of the Jerusalem church. The author of Jude would then also be a half-brother of the Lord (cf. Matt. 13:55).[9] Jude was likely writing to an audience in or near Israel; the book suggests a Jewish audience. The occasion for writing this epistle is similar to 2 Peter—the presence of false teachers. The purpose for writing is stated in verse 3: "contend earnestly for the faith which was once for all delivered to the saints." Jude recognized the great need of warning the Christians concerning the libertines who would destroy their faith. In the light of this, the Christians were to stand firm in the faith and heed the words of the apostles.

DISCUSSION OF JUDE'S THEOLOGY

CHRIST

In a theme similar to 2 Peter, Jude warns against false teachers who deny "our only Master and Lord, Jesus Christ" (v. 4). The titles *Master* and *Lord* both refer to Christ.[10] This is a great Christological statement. *Master* (Gk. *despoten*) means Christ is "absolute ruler" (2 Pet. 2:1); the English word *despot* is derived from this Greek word. Jude also refers to Jesus as *Lord*, which is a title of deity (cf. v. 25). Lord is the New Testament equivalent of Yahweh (Jehovah) and is a clear statement of deity; Jude equates Jesus with Yahweh of the Old Testament (cf. v. 5). Jude further calls Jesus "Messiah," the Anointed One (cf. v. 25), who was the anticipated Redeemer and Ruler in the Old Testament. Although Jude is brief, he nonetheless gives a magnificent statement extolling the grandeur of Christ.

SALVATION

Jude addresses his letter "to those who are the called." In this statement Jude refers to the doctrine of election. The "called" are those who have been effectually called to salvation by God's efficacious grace. It is that grace of God which man does not resist. Jude further emphasizes the security of salvation in affirming that God will enable the believer to stand before His glorious presence (v. 24). To stand before God means to be able to maintain oneself, that is, to be accepted (contrast Ps. 1:5). Jude has affirmed the believer's security in salvation because of his election in the past and God's ability to keep the believer for future glorification.

ANGELS

Jude refers to angels who "abandoned their proper abode," probably a reference to Lucifer's fall from his exalted position wherein he took a host of angels with him (Isa. 14:12-17; Ezek. 28:12-19). Apparently some of those who fell were kept in bondage while others remained free and became demons. Jude also recognizes the hierarchy of angels in mentioning Michael, the archangel (v. 9), who was the defender of Israel (see further discussion under "Doctrine of Angels").

NOTES ON PETER AND JUDE

1. Everett F. Harrison, *Introduction to the New Testament* (Grand Rapids: Eerdmans, 1964), p. 399.
2. "Assuredly" (*asphalos*) is emphatic in the Greek text.
3. The Greek preposition *huper*, translated "for," suggests substitution.
4. The word "ransomed" is *elutrothete* from *lutroo*, meaning "to release, to procure a release by a ransom, to deliver by the payment of a price, to redeem." For the Jews, the picture of redemption would be God's deliverance from Egypt. For the Gentiles it would be the picture of a slave whose freedom was purchased with a price." Fritz Rienecker, *Linguistic Key to the Greek New Testament*, edited by Cleon Rogers (Grand Rapids: Zondervan, 1982), p. 748.
5. The two participles, *zontos* and *menontos*, emphasize that the word is *living* and is *remaining*.
6. Peter uses the word *ethnei* in Acts 10:35 to identify the Gentiles.
7. Roger M. Raymer, "1 Peter" in *The Bible Knowledge Commentary* 2 vols., edited by John F. Walvoord and Roy B. Zuck (Wheaton: Victor, 1983), 2:852.
8. Charles C. Ryrie, *Biblical Theology of the New Testament* (Chicago: Moody, 1959), p. 286.
9. Everett F. Harrison, *Introduction to the New Testament* (Grand Rapids: Eerdmans, 1964), p. 406.
10. This is an example of the Granville Sharpe Rule of Greek grammar that when two nouns are joined by *kai*, and the first noun has the article and the second does not, they refer to the same thing. Cf. A. T. Robertson, *Word Pictures in the New Testament* (Nashville: Broadman, 1933), 6:147-48.

FOR FURTHER STUDY ON PETER AND JUDE

SOURCES ON PETER

** Donald Guthrie. *New Testament Theology*. Downers Grove, Ill.: InterVarsity, 1981.

** George E. Ladd. *A Theology of the New Testament*. Grand Rapids: Eerdmans, 1974.

 * Chester K. Lehman. *Biblical Theology: New Testament*. Scottdale, Pa.: Herald, 1974. 2:267-77.

** Leon Morris. *The Cross in the New Testament*. Grand Rapids: Eerdmans, 1965. Pp. 316-38.

 * Charles C. Ryrie. *Biblical Theology of the New Testament*. Chicago: Moody, 1959. Pp. 265-89.

  * B. Van Elderen, "Peter, First Epistle"; and W. White, Jr., "Peter, Second Epistle." In Merrill C. Tenney, ed., *The Zondervan Pictorial Encyclopedia of the Bible*. Grand Rapids: Zondervan, 1975. 4:723-32. Both of these articles have a section dealing with the theology of Peter.

SOURCES ON JUDE

** Donald Guthrie. *New Testament Theology*. Downers Grove, Ill.: InterVarsity, 1981.

** George E. Ladd. *A Theology of the New Testament*. Grand Rapids: Eerdmans, 1974.

** Leon Morris. *New Testament Theology*. Grand Rapids: Zondervan, 1986.

  * Charles C. Ryrie. *Biblical Theology of the New Testament*. Chicago: Moody, 1959. Pp. 290-97.

16

THEOLOGY OF JOHN

INTRODUCTION TO JOHN'S THEOLOGY

THE APOSTLE JOHN

John, who was a brother of James and a son of Zebedee, was a fisherman in Galilee (Mark 1:19-20). He must have had a profitable venture for he had hired servants in the fishing business (Mark 1:20). His mother, Salome, was a sister of Mary, the mother of Jesus, making John a cousin of Jesus (cf. John 19:25 with Matt. 27:56, 61; Mark 15:40, 47). His mother was one of those who followed Jesus and contributed to His support (cf. Luke 8:3; Matt. 27:55-56; Mark 15:40-41). John was undoubtedly one of the two disciples who followed Jesus at the beginning of His ministry (John 1:35-37). About a year later, John was named one of the twelve apostles (Matt. 10:2). John, along with Peter and James, was one of the inner three who witnessed the transfiguration (Matt. 17:1-8), the raising of Jairus's daughter (Mark 5:37-43), and the Lord's agonizing in prayer at Gethsemane (Matt. 26:37-38). At the Last Supper, John, who was known as the disciple "whom Jesus loved," had a favored position beside Jesus (John 13:23). Jesus also committed Mary into John's care at His crucifixion (John 19:26-27). John saw the resurrected Lord at least twice before the ascension (in the upper room [John 20:19-29] and in Galilee [John 21:2]) and at least three times after (as Lord of the churches [Rev. 1:12-18], Judge of sinners [Rev. 5:4-7], and King of kings [Rev. 19:11-16]). In the Book of Acts John appears in a position of prominence along with Peter (Acts 3:1; 4:13; 8:14-17). John was known as one of the pillars of the church (Gal. 2:9). According to Irenaeus, John eventually moved to Ephesus and lived to be an old man, living into the reign of Trajan (A.D. 98-117).

JOHN'S THEOLOGY

The sources for the study of Johannine theology are the gospel of John, the three epistles of John, and the Book of Revelation. Although there are alternate approaches to the study of Johannine theology, this study will incorporate the teaching of Jesus as recorded in John's gospel as well as the specific writings of John himself. It is assumed that the Lord's teaching as recorded by John would also be considered John's theology simply because John recorded the statements of Jesus, suggesting they were a part of an important emphasis of John.

The theology of John centers on the Person of Christ and the revelation that God brought through the advent of Jesus Christ. The one who was God and was with God in eternity past now became flesh, and John beheld His glory. It is this revelation of light that John describes in his gospel, epistles, and Revelation. John provides a digest of his theology in the prologue of his gospel (John 1:1-18), wherein he describes the revelation of life and light through the Son but also describes a sin-darkened world rejecting that light.[1]

GOSPEL OF JOHN

External evidence, through the testimony of Ignatius, Polycarp, Tatian, Theophilus, and others attests to John's authorship of the gospel. The internal evidence is that he was a Palestinian Jew who was a witness of the events narrated. The evidence for John as the author is clear. Traditionally, the gospel of John has been dated late; Eusebius, for example, stated that John wrote "last of all," hence, the gospel of John has traditionally been dated A.D. 80-95. The liberal writer John A. T. Robinson, however, suggests a final composition date of about A.D. 65 for the gospel.[2] It is generally agreed, however, that John wrote his gospel last, and therefore, probably wrote to supplement the other gospels. For that reason John probably had in view the church and world in general as his audience. In contrast to the synoptists, John wrote to a general audience. His gospel's uniqueness is seen in that 92% of it is not found in the synoptics. John includes the great discourses and events of the life of Christ not found elsewhere (6:22-71; 7:11-52; 8:21-59; 9:1-41; 10:1-21; 11:1-44; 12:20-50; 13:1-20; 14:1–16:33; 17:1-26). John employs certain words more than other writers: light (21 times), life (35 times), love (31 times), as well as others such as Son of God, believe, world, witness, and truth. John's purpose in writing is stated in John 20:30-31—to incite belief in Jesus as the Christ. John therefore selected certain signs to demonstrate Jesus' authority over a particular realm.[3] By John's careful selection of signs he presented the authority of Jesus as the Messiah, encouraging faith in Him (20:30-31).

EPISTLES OF JOHN

1 John. First John has strong external evidence concerning John's authorship. Polycarp and Papias gave strong evidence of his authorship. Internally, the author is seen to be an eyewitness (1:1-4), with connections to the gospel of John (cf. 1:6 with 3:21, 3:8 with 8:44, 2:16 with 8:23, etc.). First John was probably written from Ephesus in A.D. 80, probably to the churches in the area surrounding Ephesus. There were two factors in the writing of 1 John: (1) John wrote concerning the presence of false teachers and the spiritual laxity of believers. He warned against the antichrists who deny the true humanity of Jesus. (2) John also wrote concerning the spiritual condition of the believers. Some were careless in their walk, involved with the world (2:15-17). John wrote to explain true fellowship with the Son.

2 John. There is not much external attestation to 2 John; internal evidence suggests a similarity of structure, style, and language with John's gospel. Second John has terminology that identifies it with 1 John: "truth," "walk," "new commandment," "love," and others. Second John was probably written about A.D. 80 from Ephesus. The destination of 2 John is "the chosen lady and her children." This could refer to: a) the universal church; b) a local church; or 3) an actual lady. By normal language usage, John was probably writing to a lady whom he knew but who is unknown to scholars today. John wrote to warn the lady (and the church that was probably meeting in her house) against the inroads of false teachers. The lady was hospitable, and John saw the distinct danger of the lady inviting the itinerant false teachers into her home. John warned her against showing hospitality to those false teachers (2 John 10).

3 John. The close association of 2 and 3 John relates both of these epistles to the first epistle and demands a common authorship. Third John was likely written from Ephesus about A.D. 80. Third John is addressed to "the beloved Gaius," unknown apart from this statement. John wrote to instruct Gaius concerning Diotrephes, an influential person in the church who desired to be in the prominent position. John wrote to encourage Gaius concerning the problem of Diotrephes and to denounce the sin of Diotrephes.

BOOK OF REVELATION

There is considerable external evidence for John's authorship of Revelation from such early writers as Justin Martyr, Irenaeus, and Tertullian. Internally the author reveals himself as John (1:1, 4, 9; 22:8). The Revelation also indicates a similarity with the gospel of John, employing words that are common to both: Logos, Lamb, Jesus, witness, true, overcome, dwell, fountain of living waters, and others.[4] Westcott, Lightfoot, and Hort suggest a date of A.D. 68 or 69 while traditionally a date of about A.D. 95 has been mentioned for the writing of Revelation. John addressed the Revelation to the seven churches of Asia (1:4). John wrote for several reasons: to encourage Christians amid persecution under Domitian (ascended A.D. 81) and remind them of the final triumph of Jesus Christ; to bring the Old Testament prophetic truths to their final consummation; and to provide a picture of the triumphant Christ in His judgments and in His millennial reign.

DISCUSSION OF JOHN'S THEOLOGY[5]

REVELATION

John describes revelation in two ways: it is through the Scriptures and through the Son.

The Scriptures. Jesus reminded the unbelieving Jews that the Scriptures bore witness of Him (John 5:39). Jesus was affirming that the Scriptures are propositional truth, revealing the light of God through Him. The present tense indicates the revelation in Scripture continues. Jesus further reminded His audience that Moses wrote of Him and they ought to have believed Moses' writings about Christ (John 5:45-47). Still later, Jesus declared that the "Scripture cannot be broken" (John 10:35). These statements are important to note. In His debate with unbelievers Jesus was resting His case upon the integrity and authority of the written revelation—the Scriptures.

The Son. In the prologue to his gospel, John declares that the revelation of God was manifest through the Son. The One who had been with the Father in all eternity (John 1:1) now tabernacled with humanity, and John exulted in seeing His glory. John no doubt refers to the transfiguration of Christ (Matt. 17:1-8) as well as the miracles of Christ (John 2:11). The revelation of Jesus was also a revelation of grace (John 1:16-17).

John sets the revelation through Christ apart from the revelation through Moses; the law came through Moses, but grace and truth came through Jesus Christ. John's intention is to emphasize the greater revelation that came through Christ. John concludes the prologue by stating the dilemma ("no man has seen God at any time") and the solution ("the only begotten God . . . He has explained Him"). John refers to Jesus as God[6] in saying Christ has explained the Father. The word *explained* (Gk. *exegesato*) compares to the English verb *exegetes* in suggesting Jesus has explained the Father.

THE WORLD

John used the word *world* a great deal; while it is only used fifteen times in the synoptic gospels, John used it seventy-eight times in his gospel and twenty-seven additional times in his other writings. John used the word *world* to describe the world in sin and darkness as well as under the domination of Satan.

The World in Darkness. John depicts the world in darkness and in opposition to Christ; the world is hostile to Christ and all that He stands for, but this is because the world is blind. The world did not recognize Messiah when He came into the world.[7] John describes two classes of people: those who come to the light and those who hate the light (John 1:12; 3:19-21). Persons of the world hate the light because the light exposes their sin; Jesus said that this was the reason the world hated Him (John 7:7). The world system leads people to sin even as Eve was first tempted in the garden: the lust of the flesh, the lust of the eyes, and the boastful pride of life (1 John 2:16). The basic issue of sin is the refusal to believe that Jesus is the light (John 3:19-20); the Holy Spirit continues to convict men concerning the same sin—refusal to believe in Christ (John 16:8-9). The tragic end result of sin is death (John 8:21, 24).

The World under Satan. Jesus explains why the unbelievers commit sin; it is because their origin is from the devil (John 8:44).[8] Because they are children of their father, the devil, it is natural that they commit the desires of their father. Because the devil is a liar from the beginning, it is natural that the devil's spiritual descendants should reject Christ who is the Truth. John continues this theme in 1 John 3:8 when he states, "the one who practices sin is of the devil." There is a spiritual relationship between the devil and the one who habitually practices sin. But Christ came to destroy the power of the devil so that the one believing in Christ need not live in spiritual bondage to the devil (1 John 3:9). Jesus rendered judgment upon the devil and broke his power (John 16:11).

THE INCARNATION

Light. Light is a popular term with John (John 1:4-5, 7-9; 3:19-21; 5:35; 8:12; 9:5; 11:9-10; 12:35-36, 46; 1 John 1:5, 7, 2:8-10; Rev. 18:23; 21:24; 22:5). In dealing with the incarnation, John refers to Jesus as the light that has come into a world darkened by sin. John declares, "In Him was life; and the life was the light of men" (John 1:4). Jesus does not show the way to the light; He is the light. Jesus equates Himself with God the Father in claiming to be the light. Just as the Father is the light (Ps. 27:1; 1 John 1:5), so the Son is the light of the world (John 8:12). It is a strong statement of deity. Because Jesus has come into the world as the light, it is imperative that men believe in Him (John 12:35, 36). Jesus, as the light of the world, can give physical light (John 9:7) and spiritual light (John 8:12).

Life. Life is also a popular term with John; he uses it thirty-six times in the gospel, thirteen times in 1 John, and fifteen times in the Revelation. The wonder of the incarnation is that Jesus is life (John 1:4). John equates Jesus with deity in that just as the Father is the fountain of life (Psalm 36:9; Jer. 2:13; John 5:26), so the Son has life in Himself (John 1:4). It is again a strong affirmation of the deity of Christ. Apart from God, everything else only has derived life, but Jesus has life in Himself. Everything and everyone else is dependent on Jesus for life and existence. "It is only because there is life in the Logos that there is life in anything on earth at all. Life does not exist in its own right. It is not even spoken of as made 'by' or 'through' the Word, but as existing 'in' Him."[9] As the life, Jesus gives eternal life to those who believe in Him (John 3:15, 16, 36; 4:14; 5:24; 20:31), He gives abundant life (John 10:10), and resurrection life (11:25); moreover, it is a present possession (1 John 5:11-13).

Son of God. John describes the incarnation of Christ by referring to Jesus as the "Son of God" or the "Son." Jesus used these terms of Himself; moreover, the unbelieving Jews caught the significance of the claim—they tried to stone Him for blasphemy because He was equating Himself with God (John 5:18). When Jesus claimed to be the Son of God He was claiming equality with God. Jesus clearly claimed to be the Son of God (John 10:36), and as such He has the prerogatives of deity: He is equal with the Father (John 5:18); He has life within Himself (John 5:26); He has the power to raise the dead (John 5:25); He gives life (John 5:21); He sets men free from slavery to sin (John 8:36); He receives honor equal with the Father (John 5:23); He is the object of faith (John 6:40); He is the object of prayer (John 14:13,14);[10] He has the power to answer prayer (John 14:13). Jesus indicated that His relationship to the Father was entirely unique. He always referred to God as "My Father," never "our Father" (cf. John 20:17). John has a decidedly strong emphasis on equating Jesus with God.

Son of Man. Jesus commonly used the title "Son of Man" to refer to His mission (John 1:51; 3:13-14; 5:27; 6:27, 53, 62; 8:28; 9:35; 12:23, 34; 13:31).[11] The origin of the term is undoubtedly Daniel 7:13 and reference to the heavenly being who receives the kingdoms of this world. The term is a complex one that seems to involve several ideas: the deity of the Son (note the equation of Son of Man with Son of God in John 5:25, 27); the royalty of the Son in that He receives dominion, glory, and a kingdom (Dan. 7:13); the humanity of the Son in that He suffers (John 3:14; 12:23, 34); the heavenly glory of the Son since He came down from heaven (John 1:51; 3:13; 6:32); and the salvation the Son came to bring (John 6:27, 53; 9:35). "The term, 'the Son of Man', then points us to Christ's conception of Himself as of heavenly origin and as the possessor of heavenly glory. At one and the same time it points us to His lowliness and His sufferings for men. The two are the same."[12]

ATONEMENT

In prophecy. The English word *atonement* comes from the two words "at" and "onement," suggesting reconciliation. Although the word *atone-*

ment is not a New Testament word, it designates what Christ accomplished on the cross through His suffering and death. When John the Baptist declared, "Behold, the Lamb of God who takes away the sin of the world!" John was bringing Old Testament sacrificial offerings to their consummation. Beginning with God's provision of a lamb in place of Isaac on Mount Moriah (Gen. 22:8), with the provision of the Passover lamb in Exodus 12 to the prophecy of Isaiah 53:7, where the prophet Isaiah indicated Messiah would go to His death, slaughtered like a lamb—the Old Testament sacrifices pointed to Messiah's atoning death. Undoubtedly, it is the consummation of that theme that John the Baptist describes in John 1:29. Jesus emphasized the same truth in John 6:52-59. He spoke of coming down from heaven and giving His life for the world (John 6:33, 51), the substitutionary atonement being suggested by the preposition "for" (Gk. *huper*). In this section Jesus taught that His death is vicarious (6:51), provides eternal life (6:53-55, 58), provides union with Christ (6:56, 57), and results in resurrection (6:54).

In history. The work which Christ came to do comes to a consummation in John 19:30. After six hours on the cross Jesus cried out, "It is finished!" (Gk. *tetelestai*). Jesus did not say, "I am finished," but rather "it is finished." He had completed the work that the Father had given Him to do; the work of salvation was accomplished. The perfect tense of the verb *tetelestai* could be translated, "it stands finished," meaning the work is forever finished and the finished results remain.[13]

In 1 John 2:1-2 John explains the provision that Christ has made for sin. Christ is an "advocate" (Gk. *parakletos*) for those who sin. In this context, advocate means a defense lawyer in a legal case. The believer has Christ as his defense attorney at the divine bar of justice. Moreover, John says Christ is the "propitiation" (Gk. *hilasmos*) for the sins of the world. The word is used only here, Romans 3:25, and in 1 John 4:10. Propitiation means Christ atoned for sin by paying the price and thereby assuaging the wrath of God. Propitiation is Godward and suggests that while sin had offended the holiness of God, through the death of Christ God the Father is satisfied and is free to show mercy and forgiveness to the believing sinner. John indicates the propitiation is "for our sins . . . but also for those of the whole world" (1 John 2:2). Christ's death was a substitutionary death that made provision for believers, but John emphasizes the sufficiency is "for the whole world." Although the whole world is not saved, because Christ is God His death is sufficient for the entire world; it is, however, effectual only in those who believe.

The resurrection. John describes the resurrection scene in John 20 to show that the atonement of Christ has come to a climax in the resurrection. The atonement of Christ does not end with His death but with His resurrection; the resurrection is necessary to vindicate the Son (Rom. 1:4). John vividly describes the race with Peter to the tomb. John arrived first, glanced into the tomb, and did not notice anything.[14] Peter entered, theorized what had happened, and then John also looked and understood. They saw the graveclothes lying in the grave and still retaining their shape as though the body were in them. The face-cloth was still wrapped in a circular shape (20:7), but the body was gone. John "saw and believed" because he understood only one thing could possibly have happened—the body had passed through the linen wrappings. Jesus had risen. John provides a clearer, more detailed description than the synoptic gospels of precisely what happened at the resurrection. John later describes how Christ passed through closed doors in His physical body and appeared to the apostles in His resurrected body (John 20:19, 26). John verifies the reality of the bodily resurrection of Christ, showing that Christ in His final work had overcome death and thereby brought hope and life to believers (John 11:25-26).

HOLY SPIRIT

In the Upper Room Discourse (John 14-16), John records Jesus' teaching concerning the Holy Spirit. These three chapters provide the most detailed information concerning the Person and work of the Holy Spirit.

His person. The personality of the Holy Spirit is seen in the personal pronouns that are used to describe Him. Even though the word *Spirit* (Gk. *pneuma*) is neuter, Jesus says *"He* will teach you all things" (John 14:26). "He" (Gk. *ekeinos*) is a masculine pronoun. Although one might have expected a neuter pronoun (it) to agree with the neuter noun (Spirit), it would have been wrong to refer to the Spirit as "it" since He is a person like the Father and Son. Jesus' reference to the Spirit as "He" confirms the personality of the Holy Spirit (cf. John 15:26; 16:13, 14).

His work. He convicts the world (John 16:8-11). The work of *convicting* (Gk. *elegxei*) is the work of a prosecuting attorney whereby He seeks to convince someone of something. The Holy Spirit acts as a divine prosecutor, convicting the world of sin because of its refusal to believe in Jesus; He also convinces the world of the righteousness of Christ because of His resurrection and ascension; and He convinces the world of judgment because Satan was judged at the cross.

He regenerates (John 3:6). In explaining the new birth to Nicodemus, Jesus indicates it is a birth by the Spirit.

He teaches the disciples (John 14:26). While the disciples were unable spiritually to assimilate all of the Lord's teaching, Jesus promised the Holy Spirit would remind them of Jesus' teaching. This statement also guarantees the accurate recording of the New Testament writings, inasmuch as the Holy Spirit would provide accurate recall as they would write the gospels.

He indwells (John 14:16-17). Jesus pointed to the new work of the Holy Spirit following Pentecost when the Spirit's presence with the believer would no longer be temporary as in the Old Testament, but His indwelling would be permanent. Jesus emphasized that following Pentecost the Holy Spirit would be "in them" (John 14:17) and that indwelling would be "forever" (John 14:16).

LAST THINGS

The rapture. Although John does not provide an explicit statement concerning the rapture as does Paul, John undoubtedly refers to the rapture in John 14:1-3. The rapture is related to the church, and Jesus was speaking to the nucleus of disciples that would compose the small beginnings of the church in Acts 2. Because the disciples were grieving at the imminent departure of Christ in John 14, He encouraged them by reminding them (as the infant church) that He was going to prepare dwelling places for them in His Father's home. His promise to return and take them to Himself (John 14:3) is understood as parallel to Paul's statement in 1 Thessalonians 4:13-18.

The Tribulation. John gives extensive coverage to the Tribulation, detailing the events in Revelation 6-19. The seven seals are unleashed upon the earth at the beginning of the Tribulation (Rev. 6:1–8:1), bringing the triumph of the Beast (6:1-2), war (6:3-4), famine (6:5-6), death (6:7-8), martyrdom (6:9-11), and celestial and earthly convulsions (6:12-17). The seals apparently continue through to the end of the Tribulation. The seventh seal initiates the seven trumpets (8:2–11:19). With the sounding of the trumpets the food and oxygen supply on earth is diminished (8:2-6), one-third of the sea life dies (8:7), the water source becomes polluted (8:10-11), the celestial bodies are darkened (8:12-13), people are tormented (9:1-12), and one-third of mankind is killed (9:13-21). The seventh trumpet inaugurated the bowl judgments (11:15-19; 15:1–16:21), resulting in painful sores (16:1-2), the death of sea life (16:3), rivers turning to blood (16:4-7), people scorched with heat (16:8-9), darkness (16:10-11), the unleashing of the mighty eastern army for the consummating battle (16:12-16), and a great earthquake, destroying the cities of the nations (16:17-21). Both religious Babylon (17:1-18) and commercial Babylon (18:1-24) are destroyed. The Tribulation culminates with Christ's return, whereupon He subjugates the nations of the world (19:11-21).

Antichrist. John uses the term *antichrist* to describe those of his day that held to false doctrine concerning Christ (1 John 2:18, 22; 4:3; 2 John 7). The nature of this heresy was a denial of the humanity of Jesus (2 John 7); Christ only appeared as a phantom; He did not really take on humanity. John declares that those who deny that Jesus came in the flesh are antichrist. John thus uses the term as referring to those who deny the true doctrine concerning Christ.

John refers to the culminating person who denies Christ as the Beast (Rev. 11:7; 13:1, 12, 14, 15). John describes this Beast as the "First Beast" (in contrast to the false prophet who supports the First Beast but is known as the Second Beast ["another beast," 13:11]). The First Beast is a political ruler (13:1-10) who emerges out of the final form of Gentile power and is empowered by Satan (13:2), receives worship and blasphemes the name of God for three and one-half years (13:4-6), persecutes believers (13:7), and dominates the world (13:8). The First Beast is supported by the Second Beast who is a false prophet and forces the people to worship the First Beast (13:11-12); he deceives the people through his ability to perform signs (13:14); he limits commerce to those who have received his mark (13:16-17).

At the Second Advent of Jesus Christ, both the First Beast and the Second Beast are thrown into the lake of fire (19:20).

Second Advent of Christ. At the end of the Tribulation John envisions the triumphant Christ returning with His bride, the church (Rev. 19:6-8).[15] The marriage of Christ and the church took place in heaven during the Tribulation period. Christ returns with His bride to inaugurate the wedding feast, the millennial kingdom that takes place on earth (19:9-10). John pictures Christ returning as a triumphant King—He has many crowns on His head (19:12)—who wages war against Satan, the Beast, and the unbelieving armies (19:11, 19). His weapon is the authority of His Word (19:13), with which He conquers and subjects the nations (19:15). He destroys the nations' rulers and casts the Beast, false prophet (Second Beast), and Satan into the lake of fire for one thousand years (19:19–20:3). With the conquest of His enemies, Christ establishes the millennial kingdom upon earth.

Millennial kingdom and eternal state. John describes the resurrection of Tribulation and Old Testament saints at the end of the Tribulation (Rev. 20:4-5); they are part of the "first resurrection." The term *resurrection* does not describe a general resurrection of believers, but a resurrection unto life (20:6). There are nonetheless several stages in the first resurrection: the church age saints are raised prior to the Tribulation (1 Thess. 4:13-18), whereas the Old Testament and Tribulation saints are raised after the Tribulation (Rev. 20:4). Unbelievers are raised at the end of the Millennium, whereupon they are cast into the lake of fire (Rev. 20:11-15).

In Revelation 21:1–22:21 John describes the eternal state. The new Jerusalem that John sees coming out of heaven (Rev. 21:1-8) is the abode of the church, the bride (21:9), but undoubtedly also the redeemed of all ages in eternity. The new Jerusalem is probably related both to the Millennium and the eternal state as this is the dwelling place Christ went to prepare (John 14:2). "In both periods eternal, not temporal, conditions obtain in the city and for its inhabitants. Therefore, the New Jerusalem is millennial and eternal as to time and position, and it is always eternal as to conditions inside it."[16] John describes the new Jerusalem as providing fellowship with

God (22:4), rest (14:13), fullness of blessing (22:2), joy (21:4), service (22:3), and worship (7:9-12; 19:1).[17]

NOTES ON JOHN

1. D. Edmond Hiebert, *An Introduction to the New Testament: The Gospels and Acts* (Chicago: Moody, 1975), 1:167-70.

2. John A. T. Robinson, *Redating the New Testament* (Philadelphia: Westminster, 1976), p. 307.

3. Merrill C. Tenney, *New Testament Survey* (Grand Rapids: Eerdmans, 1961), p. 190.

4. Everett F. Harrison, *Introduction to the New Testament* (Grand Rapids: Eerdmans, 1964), pp. 441-42.

5. For some of the outline and format of this section I am indebted to Dr. S. Lewis Johnson, *Johannine Theology*, unpublished class notes, Dallas Theological Seminary.

6. The 1975 edition of the United Bible Societies (UBS) *Greek New Testament* reads *monogenes theos*, "only begotten God," which has a "B" textual rating meaning there is "some degree of doubt." In this author's opinion, there is actually strong textual support for this reading. This being the case, it is a strong statement for the deity of Christ.

7. See the helpful discussion on *world* by Leon Morris, *The Gospel According to John* (Grand Rapids: Eerdmans, 1971), pp. 126-28.

8. "Of" (Gk. *ek*) in the phrase, "You are of your father the devil" means "out of." It denotes their origin—the evil one.

9. Morris, *The Gospel According to John*, pp. 82-83.

10. There is a textual variant in John 14:14. The *New American Standard Bible* reflects the reading of the UBS 1975 edition, which reads, "If you ask *Me* anything." To this writer, there is strong textual evidence to include "Me." The UBS text gives the reading a "B" rating, "there is some degree of doubt."

11. See the helpful discussion by Morris, *The Gospel According to John*, pp. 172-73.

12. Ibid., p. 173.

13. A beautiful explanation of this statement is provided in the sermon by Russell Bradley Jones, *Gold from Golgotha* (Chicago: Moody, 1945), pp. 100-105.

14. John uses three words to describe what he and Peter saw. From the entrance John *glanced in* (Gk. *blepei*) but did not see anything significant (John 20:5); Peter, however, entered the tomb and in seeing, *theorized* (Gk. *theorei*) what had happened (20:6). Then John also entered, *saw* (Gk. *eidon*), spiritually and physically, and believed (20:8).

15. The Greek word in the aorist tense, "came" (*elthen*), suggests that the marriage of Christ and His bride, the church, took place in heaven. Christ and His bride are now seen returning to earth for the marriage supper.

16. Charles C. Ryrie, *Biblical Theology of the New Testament* (Chicago: Moody, 1959), p. 362.

17. Ibid., pp. 362-63.

For Further Study on John

** W. Robert Cook. *The Theology of John.* Chicago: Moody, 1978.

** Donald Guthrie. *New Testament Theology.* Downers Grove, Ill.: InterVarsity, 1981.

 * Donald Guthrie. "Johannine Theology." In Merrill C. Tenney, ed., *The Zondervan Pictorial Encyclopedia of the Bible.* Grand Rapids: Zondervan, 1975. 3:623-36. Also see the articles on "John, The Apostle," "John, The Epistles of," and "John, Gospel of."

** Chester K. Lehman. *Biblical Theology: New Testament.* Scottdale, Pa.: Herald, 1974. 2:459-536.

 * Leon Morris. *The Cross in the New Testament.* Grand Rapids: Eerdmans, 1965. Pp. 144-79.

 * Charles C. Ryrie. *Biblical Theology of the New Testament.* Chicago: Moody, 1959. Pp. 301-63.

PART 2:
SYSTEMATIC THEOLOGY

17

INTRODUCTION TO SYSTEMATIC THEOLOGY

DEFINITION OF SYSTEMATIC THEOLOGY

The term *theology* is derived from the Greek *theos*, meaning "God," and *logos*, meaning "word" or "discourse"; hence, "discourse about God." The word *systematic* comes from the Greek verb *sunistano*, which means "to stand together" or "to organize"; hence, systematic theology emphasizes the systematization of theology. Chafer provides a suitable definition of systematic theology: "Systematic Theology may be defined as the collecting, scientifically arranging, comparing, exhibiting, and defending of all facts from any and every source concerning God and His works."[1]

In an alternate definition, Charles Hodge defines theology as "the science of the facts of divine revelation so far as those facts concern the nature of God and our relation to Him, as His creatures, as sinners, and as the subjects of redemption. All these facts, as just remarked, are in the Bible."[2]

It is apparent in these two contrasting definitions of systematic theology that Chafer holds to a wider view, emphasizing that systematic theology assimilates information about God from "any and every source"—including information outside of the Bible. Hodge restricts his definition about systematic theology to information gained from the Bible alone.

Millard Erickson provides a good comprehensive definition of theology as "that discipline which strives to give a coherent statement of the doctrines of the Christian faith, based primarily upon the Scriptures, placed in the context of culture in general, worded in a contemporary idiom, and related to issues of life."[3]

Erickson suggests five ingredients in a definition of theology.[4] (1) Theology is *biblical*, utilizing the tools and methods of biblical research (as well as employing insights from other areas of truth). (2) Theology is *systematic*, drawing on the entirety of Scripture and relating the various portions to each other. (3) Theology is *relevant* to culture and learning, drawing from cosmology, psychology, and philosophy of history. (4) Theology must be *contemporary*, relating God's truth to the questions and challenges of today. (5) Theology must be *practical*, not merely declaring objective doctrine, but relating to life itself.

DISTINCTION OF SYSTEMATIC THEOLOGY

Systematic theology is distinguished from other classifications of theology. The other classifications can be differentiated as follows.

BIBLICAL THEOLOGY

Biblical theology is a narrower focus of study, emphasizing the study of a particular era or writer (e.g., the prophetic era or Johannine [John's] theology).

HISTORICAL THEOLOGY

Historical theology is the study of the historical development and unfolding of theology. For example, historical theology observes the development of Christology in the early centuries of the Christian church, when the church councils formulated their position on a great many doctrines (such as the two natures of Jesus Christ).

DOGMATIC THEOLOGY

Dogmatic theology is sometimes confused with systematic theology, and some outstanding theology works have been entitled, "dogmatic theology" (cf. W. G. T. Shedd). Dogmatic theology is normally understood to denote the study of a creedal system as developed by a denomination or a theological movement.

CHRISTIAN THEOLOGY

Christian theology is another categorization that is sometimes used synonymously with systematic theology. The most recent work by Millard J. Erickson is so designated. Theological books by Emery H. Bancroft and H. Orton Wiley are other examples. While also systematizing theology, this designation emphasizes that it is written from a decidedly Christian perspective (but not suggesting that works designated systematic theology are not).

THEOLOGY PROPER

Theology proper is a category of study within systematic theology; it denotes the study of the nature and existence of God. To distinguish the study of God specifically (in contrast to the study of Jesus Christ, the Holy Spirit, the church, etc.), the term *proper* is used to distinguish the study of God from theology in general.

NECESSITY OF SYSTEMATIC THEOLOGY

AS AN EXPLANATION OF CHRISTIANITY

Systematic theology is necessary as a researched and studied explanation as well as a systematic organization of the doctrines that are foundational and necessary to Christianity. As a result of systematic theology, Christians are able to have a clear understanding about the fundamental beliefs of the Christian faith. The Bible was not written in a doctrinal outline; hence, it is important to systematize the parts of the Bible to understand the doctrinal emphasis of the entire Bible.

AS AN APOLOGETIC FOR CHRISTIANITY

Systematic theology enables Christians to defend their beliefs rationally against opponents and antagonists to the faith. Early in the Christian church believers used their systematized beliefs to address opponents and unbelievers. This is perhaps even more important today with the emergence of humanism, Communism, cults, and Eastern religions. The systemized doctrines of the Christian faith must be researched, delineated, and presented as a defense of historic Christianity.

AS A MEANS OF MATURITY FOR CHRISTIANS

Systematic theology is an assertion of Christian truth; these same truths are essential to the maturity of believers (2 Tim. 3:16-17). Paul's writings make it clear that doctrine (theology) is foundational to Christian maturity, inasmuch as Paul normally builds a doctrinal foundation in his epistles (e.g., Eph. 1-3) before he exhorts believers to live correctly (e.g. Eph. 4-6). Also many Christians have faithfully attended church services for decades and yet have little understanding of the major doctrines of the Christian faith. Yet a knowledge of correct doctrine is important in Christian maturity; moreover, it protects the believer from error (cf. 1 John 4:1, 6; Jude 4).

REQUIREMENTS OF SYSTEMATIC THEOLOGY

INSPIRATION AND INERRANCY OF SCRIPTURE

No adequate theology is possible without a belief in the inspiration and inerrancy of Scripture. If this doctrine is abandoned, reason becomes the source of authority and reason sits in judgment upon the text of Scripture.

APPLICATION OF PROPER HERMENEUTICAL PRINCIPLES

The application of hermeneutical principles will reinforce objectivity, forcing the interpreter to set aside biases and extremes.

SCIENTIFIC APPROACH

Theology should be scientific, in the sense of employing the general arts, culture, and biblical languages in drawing theological conclusions.[5]

OBJECTIVITY

Theology must be based on inductive research and conclusions, not deductive reasoning. The theologian must approach the Scripture with a *tabula rasa*, an open mind, allowing the Scripture to speak for itself without forming prejudicial opinions about what the Scripture should say.

PROGRESSIVE REVELATION

Although both the Old and New Testaments are inspired, it is a canon of interpretation that revelation is progressive. Therefore, in formulating truths about God and His dealing with man, the New Testament has priority over the Old Testament.

ILLUMINATION

Even while applying proper hermeneutics and methodology, there is a divine element to understanding God's truth. The believer is aided by the Holy Spirit's ministry of illumination in guiding the believer to an understanding of divine truth (1 Cor. 2:11-13).

RECOGNITION OF HUMAN LIMITATIONS

While employing a proper methodology, the student must nonetheless recognize the limitations of finite beings. Man will never be able totally to comprehend God. He must be satisfied with limited knowledge.

SOURCES OF SYSTEMATIC THEOLOGY

PRIMARY SOURCES

The Scriptures provide a primary source of theology in their revelation of God and man's relationship to Him. If God has revealed Himself (and He has), and if that self-revelation is accurately encoded in the sixty-six books of Scripture (and it is), then the Scriptures are the primary source of man's knowledge of God.

Nature is also a primary source of a knowledge of God (Ps. 19). Nature, in its harmonious revelation, is a constant witness concerning God's attributes, eternal power, and divine nature (Rom. 1:20).

SECONDARY SOURCES

The doctrinal confessions, such as the Nicene Creed, the Westminster Confessions, and many others, are important in understanding how other Christians over the centuries have understood theological concepts.

Tradition, in spite of its fallibility, is important in understanding affirmations about the Christian faith. What individuals, churches, and denominations have taught is a necessary consideration in formulating theological statements.

Reason, as guided by the Holy Spirit, is also a source of theology. Reason, however, must submit to the supernatural, rather than attempting to define it.

NOTES ON SYSTEMATIC THEOLOGY

1. Lewis Sperry Chafer, *Systematic Theology*, 8 vols. (Dallas: Dallas Seminary, 1947), 1:6.
2. Charles Hodge, *Systematic Theology*, 3 vols. (Reprint. London: Clarke, 1960), 1:21.
3. Millard J. Erickson, *Christian Theology*, 3 vols. (Grand Rapids: Baker, 1983), 1:21.
4. Ibid., 1:21-22.
5. William G. T. Shedd, *Dogmatic Theology*, 3 vols. (Reprint. Nashville: Nelson, 1980), 1:20ff.

FOR FURTHER STUDY ABOUT SYSTEMATIC THEOLOGY

* Emery H. Bancroft. *Christian Theology*, 2d rev. ed. Grand Rapids: Zondervan, 1976. Pp. 13-20.

** Bruce A. Demarest. *General Revelation: Historical Views and Contemporary Issues.* Grand Rapids: Zondervan, 1982.

** Millard J. Erickson. *Christian Theology*, 3 vols. Grand Rapids: Baker, 1983. 1:17-149.

* Charles C. Ryrie. *Basic Theology.* Wheaton: Victor, 1986. Pp. 13-22.

** A. H. Strong. *Systematic Theology.* Valley Forge, Pa.: Judson, 1907. Pp. 1-51.

* Henry C. Thiessen. *Lectures in Systematic Theology*, revised by Vernon D. Doerksen. Grand Rapids: Eerdmans, 1979. Pp. 1-20.

18

BIBLIOLOGY:
DOCTRINE OF THE BIBLE

INTRODUCTION TO BIBLIOLOGY

MEANING OF BIBLE

The English word *bible* is derived from the Greek word *biblion*, which means "book" or "roll." The name comes from *byblos*, which denoted the papyrus plant that grew in marshes or river banks, primarily along the Nile. Writing material was made from the papyrus plant by cutting the pith of the plant in one foot strips and setting it in the sun to dry. The strips were then laid in horizontal rows with rows of vertical strips glued to the horizontal rows in a criss-cross fashion similar to the way plywood is constructed today. The horizontal rows were smoother and became the writing surface. Sections of these strips were glued together to form a scroll up to thirty feet in length.

Eventually, the plural form *biblia* was used by Latin-speaking Christians to denote all the books of the Old and New Testaments.[1]

MEANING OF SCRIPTURE

The word translated "Scripture" comes from the Greek word *graphe*, which simply means "writing." In the Old Testament this writing was recognized as carrying great authority (e.g. 2 Kings 14:6; 2 Chron. 23:18; Ezra 3:2; Neh. 10:34). The "writings" of the Old Testament were eventually collected into three groups called the Law, Prophets, and Writings (or Psalms), and constituted the thirty-nine books of the Old Testament. These writings—the Scriptures—were formally combined into the Old Testament canon.

In the New Testament the Greek verb *grapho* is used about ninety times in reference to the Bible, while the noun form *graphe* is used fifty-one times in the New Testament, almost exclusively of the Holy Scriptures. In the New

Testament the designations vary: "the Scriptures," designating collectively all the parts of Scripture (e.g. Matt. 21:42; 22:29; 26:54; Luke 24:27, 32, 45: John 5:39; Rom. 15:4; 2 Peter 3:16) or individual parts of the Scriptures (Mark 12:10; 15:28; John 13:18; 19:24, 36; Acts 1:16; 8:35; Rom. 11:2; 2 Tim. 3:16); "the Scripture says," fairly synonymous with quoting God (e.g. Rom. 4:3; 9:17; 10:11; Gal. 4:30; 1 Tim. 5:18). They are also termed "Holy Scriptures" (Rom. 1:2) and "the Sacred Writings" (Gk. *hiera grammata*, 2 Tim. 3:15). The classic passage, 2 Timothy 3:16 stresses that these writings are not ordinary writings but are in fact "God-breathed," and as such they are authoritative and without error in all that they teach.[2]

DIVINE ORIGIN OF THE BIBLE

CLAIM OF THE BIBLE

There are many evidences that the Bible is an entirely unique book, quite unlike any other work. The unique claims within the Bible itself bear witness to its unusual character. Some thirty-eight hundred times the Bible declares, "God said," or "Thus says the Lord" (e.g. Ex. 14:1; 20:1; Lev. 4:1; Num. 4:1; Deut. 4:2; 32:48; Isa. 1:10, 24; Jer. 1:11; Ezek. 1:3; etc.). Paul also recognized that the things he was writing were the Lord's commandments (1 Cor. 14:37), and they were acknowledged as such by the believers (1 Thess. 2:13). Peter proclaimed the certainty of the Scriptures and the necessity of heeding the unalterable and certain Word of God (2 Pet. 1:16-21). John too recognized that his teaching was from God; to reject his teaching was to reject God (1 John 4:6).

In response to those who would reject the above-mentioned argument, it should be noted that the writers who made those claims for the Scripture were trustworthy men who defended the integrity of the Scripture at great personal sacrifice. Jeremiah received his message directly from the Lord (Jer. 11:1-3), yet because of his defense of the Scripture some attempted to kill him (Jer. 11:21); even his family rejected him (Jer. 12:6). Counterfeit prophets were readily recognized (Jer. 23:21, 32; 28:1-17). However, the Bible's claims should not be understood as arguing in a circle or by circular reasoning. The testimony of reliable witnesses—particularly of Jesus, but also of others such as Moses, Joshua, David, Daniel, and Nehemiah in the Old Testament, and John and Paul in the New Testament—affirmed the authority and verbal inspiration of the Holy Scriptures.[3]

CONTINUITY OF THE BIBLE

The divine origin of the Bible is further seen in considering the continuity of its teaching despite the unusual nature of its composition. It stands distinct from other religious writings. For example, the Islamic Koran was compiled by an individual, Zaid ibn Thabit, under the guidance of Mohammed's father-in-law, Abu-Bekr. Additionally, in A.D. 650, a group of Arab scholars produced a unified version and destroyed all variant copies to preserve the unity of the Koran. By contrast, the Bible came from some forty different authors from diverse vocations in life. For instance, among the writers of Scripture were Moses, a political leader; Joshua, a military leader; David, a shepherd; Solomon, a king; Amos, a herdsman and fruit pincher; Daniel, a prime minister; Matthew, a tax collector; Luke, a medical doctor; Paul, a rabbi; and Peter, a fisherman.

Moreover, the Bible was not only written by a diversity of authors, but also in different locations and under a variety of circumstances. In fact, it was written on three continents: Europe, Asia, and Africa. Paul wrote from a Roman prison as well as from the city of Corinth—both in Europe; Jeremiah (and perhaps Moses) wrote from Egypt in Africa; most of the other books were written in Asia. Moses probably wrote in the desert, David composed his Psalms in the countryside, Solomon contemplated the Proverbs in the royal courts, John wrote as a banished person on the island of Patmos, and Paul wrote five books from prison.

It is apparent that many of the writers did not know of the other writers of Scripture and were unfamiliar with the other writings, inasmuch as the writers wrote over a period of more than fifteen hundred years, yet the Bible is a marvelous, unified whole. There are no contradictions or inconsistencies within its pages. The Holy Spirit is the unifier of the sixty-six books, determining its harmonious consistency. In unity these books teach the triunity of God, the deity of Jesus Christ, the personality of the Holy Spirit, the fall and depravity of man, as well as salvation by grace. It quickly becomes apparent that no human being(s) could have orchestrated the harmony of the teachings of the Scripture. The divine authorship of the Bible is the only answer.

DIVINE REVELATION OF THE BIBLE

DEFINITION OF REVELATION

The word *revelation* is derived from the Greek word *apokalupsis*, which means "disclosure" or "unveiling." Hence, revelation signifies God unveiling Himself to mankind. The fact that revelation has occurred renders theology possible; had God not revealed Himself there could be no accurate or propositional statements about God. Romans 16:25 and Luke 2:32 indicate that God has unveiled Himself in the Person of Jesus Christ. That is the epitome of God's revelation.

Revelation may be defined as "that act of God whereby he discloses himself or communicates truth to the mind, whereby he makes manifest to his creatures that which could not be known in any other way. The revelation may occur in a single, instantaneous act, or it may extend over a long period of time; and this communication of himself and his truth may be perceived by the human mind in varying degrees of fullness."[4] The important emphasis here is that God discloses truth about Himself that man *would not otherwise know.*[5]

In the broader use of the term, *revelation* signifies "God's disclosure of Himself through creation, history, the conscience of man and Scripture. It is given in both event and word."[6] Revelation thus is both "general"—God revealing Himself in history and nature, and "special"—God revealing Himself in the Scriptures and in His Son.

This definition stands in contrast to the Barthian definition and those with a propensity toward existential theology. Karl Barth, the generally acknowledged father of neo-orthodoxy (see chap. 40), denied the validity of general revelation because of man's sin through the Fall. According to Barth, man could no longer attain to a knowledge of God through reason because of the Fall; God had to reveal Himself to the individual personally for the individual to attain a knowledge of God. Thus, for Barth, revelation consisted in the Word of God coming to man in an experiential encounter. The revelation could only be considered actual when an individual existential encounter with Christ had taken place.[7]

GENERAL REVELATION

General revelation, although not adequate to procure salvation, is nonetheless an important antecedent to salvation. General revelation is God revealing certain truths and aspects about His nature to all humanity, which revelation is essential and preliminary to God's special revelation.

God's revelation in nature is perhaps the most prominent demonstration of general revelation. Psalm 19:1-6 affirms His revelation to the human race in the heavens as well as on earth. The psalmist indicates that this revelation is continuous—it occurs "day to day" and "night to night" (v. 2). This revelation never ceases. Furthermore, it is a wordless revelation: "there is no speech, nor are there words" (v. 3). Finally, its scope is worldwide: "Their line [sound] has gone out through all the earth" (v. 4). No one is excluded from this revelation of God. Wherever man peers at the universe, there is orderliness. At a distance of ninety-three million miles from the earth, the sun provides exactly the right temperature environment for man to function on earth. Were the sun closer, it would be too hot to survive, and were it further away it would be too cold for man to function. If the moon were closer than two hundred forty thousand miles the gravitational pull of the tides would engulf the earth's surface with water from the oceans. Wherever man looks in the universe, there is harmony and order. Similarly, God has revealed Himself on earth (v. 1). The magnificence of the human body

TYPES OF DIVINE REVELATION

Type	Manifestation	Scripture	Significance
General Revelation	In Nature	Ps. 19:1-6	Reveals God exists. Reveals God's glory.
		Rom. 1:18-21	Reveals God is omnipotent. Reveals God will judge.
	In Providence	Matt. 5:45	Reveals God is benevolent to all people.
		Acts 14:15-17	Reveals God provides food for all people.
		Dan. 2:21	Reveals God raises up and removes rulers.
	In Conscience	Rom. 2:14-15	Reveals God has placed His law within the hearts of all people.
Special Revelation	In Christ	John 1:18	Reveals what the Father is like.
		John 5:36-37	Reveals the Father's compassion.
		John 6:63; 14:10	Reveals that the Father gives life to those who believe in the Son.
	In Scripture	2 Tim. 3:16, 17	Reveals all the doctrine, rebuke, correction, and guidance that the Christian needs for good living.
		2 Pet. 1:21	Reveals all that God has chosen to disclose through human authors directed by the Holy Spirit.

is perhaps the best evidence of general revelation on earth. The entire human body—its cardio-vascular system, the bone structure, the respiratory system, the muscles, the nervous system including its center in the brain—reveals an infinite God.

Romans 1:18-21 further develops the concept of general revelation. The "invisible attributes," "eternal power," and "divine nature" of God have been "clearly seen" (v. 20). The human race is rendered guilty and without excuse through God's revelation of Himself in nature. This revelation gives mankind an awareness of God but is of itself inadequate to provide salvation (cf. also Job 12:7-9; Psalm 8:1-3; Isa. 40:12-14, 26; Acts 14:15-17).

God has also revealed Himself to the human race through His providential control. It is through His providential goodness in supplying people with sunshine and rain that enables them to live and function (Matt. 5:45; Acts 14:15-17). Paul reminds the people at Lystra that God's providential goodness was a witness to them (Acts 14:17). God's providential control is also evident in His dealing with the nations. He disciplined His disobedient people Israel (Deut. 28:15-68) but will also restore them (Deut. 30:1-10); He judged Egypt for sinning against Israel (Ex. 7-11); He raised the nations to power and also caused their demise (Dan. 2:21*a*, 31-43).

Further, God has revealed Himself through conscience. Romans 2:14-15 indicates God has placed intuitional knowledge concerning Himself within the heart of man. "Man intuitively knows not only that God values goodness and abhors evil but also that he is ultimately accountable to such a righteous Power."[8] While the Jews will be judged according to the written law, Gentiles, who do not have the written Law, will be judged according to an unwritten law, the law of conscience written on their hearts. Moreover, Paul says the conscience acts as a legal prosecutor (v. 15). "Conscience may be regarded as an inner monitor, or the voice of God in the soul, that passes judgment on man's response to the moral law within."[9]

SPECIAL REVELATION

Special revelation involves a narrower focus than general revelation and is restricted to Jesus Christ and the Scriptures. Of course, all that is known of Christ is through the Scriptures; therefore, it can be said that special revelation is restricted to the Scriptures.

Special revelation as reflected in the Scriptures is given in propositional statements (something that neo-orthodoxy denies); in other words, it comes from outside of man, not from within man. Many examples reflect the propositional nature of special revelation: "Then God spoke all these words, saying," (Ex. 20:1); "These are the words of the covenant" (Deut. 29:1); "Moses finished writing the words of this law in a book until they were complete" (Deut. 31:24); "Then the word of the Lord came to Jeremiah after the king had burned the scroll and the words which Baruch had written at the dictation of Jeremiah, saying, 'Take again another scroll and write on it all the former words that were on the first scroll which Jehoiakim the king of Judah burned' " (Jer. 36:27-28; cf. v. 2); "the gospel which was preached by me is not according to man. For I neither received it from man, nor was I taught it, but I received it through a revelation of Jesus Christ" (Gal. 1:11-12).

Special revelation has been necessitated because of man's sinful estate through the Fall. In order to restore fallen humanity to fellowship with Himself it was essential that God reveal the way of salvation and reconciliation, hence, the essence of special revelation centers on the Person of Jesus Christ. He is displayed in Scripture as the One who has explained the Father (John 1:18). Although in the past people have not seen God, "Jesus has now given a full account of the Father."[10] Jesus declared that both His words (John 6:63) and His works (John 5:36) demonstrated that He revealed the Father—and both His words and His works are accurately recorded in Scripture. Hebrews 1:3 indicates Christ is the "radiance of (God's) glory and the exact representation of His nature." The first phrase indicates Christ radiates the Shekinah glory of God while the latter phrase reveals that Christ is the precise reproduction of the Father. Jesus Christ has fully revealed the Father to a sinful humanity and through His redemption has enabled mankind to be restored to fellowship with God.

Because the Bible is God-breathed (2 Tim. 3:16) and written by men carried along by the Holy Spirit (2 Pet. 1:21), the Bible is entirely reliable and accurate in its portrayal of Jesus Christ. There is, in fact, a correlation between the two aspects of special revelation: the Scripture may be termed the living, written Word (Heb. 4:12), while Jesus Christ may be designated the living, incarnate Word (John 1:1, 14). In the case of Christ there was *human* parentage but the Holy Spirit overshadowed the event (Luke 1:35), ensuring a sinless Christ; in the case of the Scriptures there was *human* authorship but the Holy Spirit superintended the writers (2 Pet. 1:21), ensuring an inerrant Word. The Bible accurately presents the special revelation of God in Christ.

INSPIRATION OF THE BIBLE

NECESSITY OF INSPIRATION

Inspiration is necessary to preserve the revelation of God. If God has revealed Himself but the record of that revelation is not accurately recorded, then the revelation of God is subject to question. Hence, inspiration guarantees the accuracy of the revelation.

DEFINITION OF INSPIRATION

Inspiration may be defined as the Holy Spirit's superintending over the writers so that while writing according to their own styles and personalities, the result was God's Word written—authoritative, trustworthy, and free from error in the original autographs. Some definitions by prominent evangelical theologians are as follows.

Benjamin B. Warfield: "Inspiration is, therefore, usually defined as a supernatural influence exerted on the sacred writers by the Spirit of God, by virtue of which their writings are given Divine trustworthiness."[11]

Edward J. Young: "Inspiration is a superintendence of God the Holy Spirit over the writers of the Scriptures, as a result of which these Scriptures possess Divine authority and trustworthiness and, possessing such Divine authority and trustworthiness, are free from error."[12]

Charles C. Ryrie: "Inspiration is . . . God's superintendence of the human authors so that, using their own individual personalities, they composed and recorded without error His revelation to man in the words of the original autographs."[13]

There are several important elements that belong in a proper definition of inspiration: (1) the divine element—God the Holy Spirit superintended the writers, ensuring the accuracy of the writing; (2) the human element—human authors wrote according to their individual styles and personalities; (3) the result of the divine-human authorship is the recording of God's truth without error; (4) inspiration extends to the selection of words by the writers; (5) inspiration relates to the original manuscripts.

The English word *inspiration* in its theological usage is derived from the Latin Vulgate Bible in which the verb *inspiro* appears in both 2 Timothy 3:16 and 2 Peter 1:21. The word *inspiration* is used to translate *theopneustos*, a hapax legomenon (meaning it appears only once in the Greek New Testament) found in 2 Timothy 3:16. *Theopneustos* means "God-breathed" and emphasizes the exhalation of God, hence, spiration would be more accurate since it emphasizes that Scripture is the product of the breath of God. The Scriptures are not something breathed into by God, rather, the Scriptures have been *breathed out* by God.

FALSE VIEWS OF INSPIRATION

Natural inspiration. This view teaches that there is nothing supernatural about biblical inspiration; the writers of Scripture were simply men of unusual ability who wrote the books of the Bible in the same way that an individual would write any other book.[14] The writers were men of unusual religious insight, writing on religious subjects in the same way men like Shakespeare or Schiller wrote literature.

Spiritual illumination. The illumination view suggests that some Christians may have spiritual insight that although similar to other Christians is greater in degree. In this view any devout Christian, illuminated by the Holy Spirit, can be the author of inspired Scripture. Adherents to this view suggest it is not the writings that are inspired, rather it is the *writers* who are inspired. Schleiermacher taught this view on the Continent while Coleridge propounded it in England.[15]

Partial or dynamic inspiration. The partial inspiration theory teaches that the parts of the Bible related to matters of faith and practice are inspired whereas matters related to history, science, chronology, or other non-faith matters may be in error. In this view God preserves the message of salvation amid other material that may be in error. The partial theory rejects both verbal inspiration (that inspiration extends to the words of Scripture) and plenary inspiration (that inspiration extends to the entirety of Scripture). Despite the presence of errors in Scripture, partial theorists teach that an imperfect medium is a sufficient guide to salvation. A. H. Strong was a proponent of this view.[16]

Problematic questions may be posed to adherents of this view: what parts of the Bible are inspired and what parts contain errors? Who determines what parts of the Bible are trustworthy and what parts contain errors? (Errantists differ with one another on their listings of errors.) How can doctrine be separated from history? (For example, the narratives about Jesus' virgin birth contain both history and doctrine.) How can the Bible be trustworthy in one area while in error in another area?

Conceptual inspiration. This view suggests that only the concepts or ideas of the writers are inspired but not the words. In this view God gave an idea or concept to the writer who then penned the idea in his own words. According to this view there can be errors in Scripture because the choice of words is left to the writer and is not superintended by God. In response, however, it is noted that Jesus (Matt. 5:18) and Paul (1 Thess. 2:13) both affirmed verbal inspiration. Pache rightly concludes, "ideas can be conceived of and transmitted only by means of words. If the thought communicated to man is divine and of the nature of a revelation, the form in which it is expressed is of prime significance. It is impossible to dissociate the one from the other."[17]

Divine dictation. The dictation view states that God dictated the words of Scripture and the men wrote them down in a passive manner, being mere amanuenses (secretaries) who wrote only the words they were told to write. This claim would render the Bible similar to the Koran which supposedly was dictated in Arabic from heaven. Although some parts of the Bible were given by dictation (cf. Ex. 20:1, "Then God spoke all these words"), the books of the Bible reveal a distinct contrast in style and vocabulary, suggesting the authors were not mere automatons. The beginning student in Greek will quickly discover the difference in style between the gospel of John and the gospel of Luke. John wrote in a simple style with a limited vocabulary, whereas Luke wrote with an expanded vocabulary and a more sophisticated style. If the dictation theory were true, the style of the books of the Bible should be uniform.

Neo-orthodox opinion. The neo-orthodox view emphasizes that the Bible is not to be exactly equated with the Word of God because God does not speak in mere propositions. God does not reveal mere *facts* about Himself; He reveals *Himself.* The Bible is not the *substance* of the Word of God, but rather the *witness* to the Word of God. It *becomes* the Word of God as the reader encounters Christ in his own subjective experience. Moreover, the Bible is enshrouded in myth necessitating a demythologizing of the Bible to discover what actually took place. The historicity of the events is unimportant. For example, whether or not Christ actually rose from the dead in time and space is unimportant to the neo-orthodox adherent. The important thing is the experiential encounter that is possible even though the Bible is tainted with factual errors. In this view the authority is the subjective experience of the individual rather than the Scriptures themselves.

To these views the evangelical Christian responds with contrasting points. The Bible is the objective and authoritative Word of God whether or not a person responds to it (John 8:47; 12:48). Furthermore, there are no objective criteria for evaluating what would constitute a "legitimate" encounter with God. Additionally, who would be capable of distinguishing myth from truth?

BIBLICAL VIEW OF INSPIRATION: VERBAL PLENARY

Christ's view of the Bible.[18] In determining the nature of biblical inspiration, nothing could be more significant than determining the view Christ held regarding the Scriptures. Certainly no one ought to hold a lower view of Scripture than He held; His view of the Scriptures ought to be the determinant and the norm for other persons' views. That is the foundational argument of R. Laird Harris. In defending the inspiration of the Scriptures he does not use 2 Timothy 3:16 or 2 Peter 1:21 as the primary argument (although he recognizes their validity); he instead argues from the standpoint of Christ's view of the Scriptures.[19]

(1) Inspiration of the whole. In His use of the Old Testament Christ gave credence to the inspiration of the entire Old Testament. In Matthew 5:17-18 Christ affirmed that not the smallest letter or stroke would pass from the law until it would be fulfilled. In v. 17 He referred to the law or the prophets, a common phrase designating the entire Old Testament. In this rather strong statement, Jesus affirmed the inviolability of the entire Old Testament and thereby affirmed the inspiration of the entire Old Testament.

In Luke 24:44 Jesus reminded the disciples that all the things written about Him in the law of Moses, the prophets, and the Psalms *must* be fulfilled. The disciples had failed to understand the teachings concerning the death and resurrection of Christ in the Old Testament, but because of the inspiration of the Old Testament, those prophesied events *had* to take place. By His threefold designation of the Old Testament, Christ was affirming the inspiration and authority of the entire Old Testament.

When Jesus debated with the unbelieving Jews concerning His right to be called the Son of God He referred them to Psalm 82:6 and reminded them "the Scripture cannot be broken" (John 10:35). "It means that Scripture cannnot be emptied of its force by being shown to be erroneous."[20] It is noteworthy that Jesus referred to a rather insignificant passage from the Old Testament and indicated that the Scripture could not be set aside or annulled.[21]

(2) Inspiration of the parts. Christ quoted from the Old Testament profusely and frequently. His arguments hinged on the integrity of the Old Testament passage He was quoting. By this method of argumentation, Christ was affirming the inspiration of the individual texts or books of the Old Testament. A few examples will suffice. In Jesus' encounter with Satan at the time of His temptation, He refuted the arguments of Satan by a reference to Deuteronomy. In Matthew 4:4, 7, 10 Jesus quoted from Deuteronomy 8:3; 6:13, 16, indicating Satan was wrong and emphasizing that these words written in Deuteronomy had to be fulfilled. In Matthew 21:42 Jesus quoted from Psalm 118:22, which teaches that the Messiah would be rejected. In Matthew 12:18-21 Jesus quoted from Isaiah 42:1-4, showing that His peaceable, gentle disposition and His inclusion of the Gentiles had all been foretold in the prophetic writings.

These are only selected examples, revealing that Christ quoted from various parts of the Old Testament, affirming their inspiration and authority.

(3) Inspiration of the words. In defending the doctrine of the resurrection to the Sadducees, Jesus quoted from Exodus 3:6 (significant because the Sadducees held only to the Pentateuch), *"I am* the God of Abraham."* In this response Jesus' entire argument hinged on the words "I am." Jesus was apparently supplying the verb which the Hebrew text only implies. Thus He supported the Septuagint (Greek) version which includes the verb. That version was so highly regarded by many of the Lord's contemporaries that it was practically equated with the original Scriptures.

In affirming the resurrection Jesus reminded the Sadducees that Exodus 3:6 said "I am." He elaborated: "God is not the God of the dead but of the living." If the words of the Old Testament were not inspired, His argument was useless; but if the very words of the Old Testament were actually inspired, then His argument carried enormous weight. In fact, Jesus' argument hinges on the *present tense* of the statement. Because it was written in

Exodus 3:6, "I am . . .", the doctrine of the resurrection could be affirmed; God is the God of the living patriarchs.

A similar example is found in Matthew 22:44 where Jesus, in debating the Pharisees, explained that their concept of Messiah was wrong. The Pharisees thought of Messiah as a political redeemer but Jesus shows them in His quotation from Psalm 110:1 that David, Israel's greatest king, saw Messiah as greater than himself, calling Him Lord. The entire argument of Christ rests on the phrase "my Lord." In quoting Psalm 110:1, Jesus rested His argument on the inspiration of the precise words "my Lord." If Psalm 110:1 did not read exactly "my Lord" then Christ's argument was in vain. An additional example is Christ's use of Psalm 82:6 in John 10:34 where His entire argument rests on the word "gods."

(4) Inspiration of the letters. In a number of His statements Christ reveals that He believed the letters of Scripture were inspired. In Matthew 5:18 Jesus declared, "not the smallest letter or stroke shall pass away from the Law, until all is accomplished." The term "smallest letter" refers to the Hebrew letter *yodh*, which looks like an apostrophe ('). The "stroke" refers to the minute distinction between two Hebrew letters. An equivalent would be the distinction between an O and a Q. Only the little "tail" distinguishes the Q from the O. Jesus emphasized that all the details of the Old Testament writings would be fulfilled down to the very letter.

(5) Inspiration of the New Testament. In the Upper Room discourse Christ made a significant statement that seems to point to the ultimate, accurate recording of the New Testament writings. In John 14:26 Jesus indicated that the Holy Spirit would provide accurate recall for the apostles as they penned the words of Scripture, thus guaranteeing their accuracy (cf. John 16:12-15). This may explain how an old man such as John, when penning the life of Christ, could accurately describe the details of the events that occurred years earlier. The Holy Spirit gave John and the other writers accurate recall of the events. Hence, Jesus affirmed not only the inspiration of the Old Testament but also the New Testament.[22]

An obvious conclusion is that Jesus Christ held a very high view of Scripture, affirming its inspiration in the entire Old Testament–the various books of the Old Testament, the precise words, the actual letters–and He pointed to the inspiration of the New Testament. Surely those who hold to only conceptual inspiration or other variants need to reconsider the attitude of Jesus to the Scriptures. Ought His view of the Bible not to be the standard? Is it legitimate to hold a *lower* view of Scripture than He held?

Paul's view of the Bible. (1) Inspiration of the Old and New Testaments. In 1 Timothy 5:18, Paul prefaced his remarks with "the Scripture says." Then he quoted from Deuteronomy 25:4 and Luke 10:7, thereby ascribing the status of Scripture to both the Old and New Testaments. Paul was saying that the New Testament is as much the inspired Word of God as the Old Testament.

(2) Inspiration of the words. In Paul's classic statement found in 2 Timothy 3:16, the apostle reminds the reader that all Scripture is "inspired by God." As indicated earlier, "inspired by God" is the Greek word *theopneustos*, meaning "God-breathed." This indeed is an important verse to consider in the entire subject of inspiration and inerrancy and, properly understood, resolves the problem.

Several things should be noted. First, since Scripture is God-breathed, it emphasizes that the origin of Scripture is God. This is consistent with the Old Testament prophets who received their messages from the mouth of God and so indicated by their frequent statements, "Thus says the Lord." Thus, the message spoken by the prophets was the message given to them by the Lord (cf. Ex. 4:15; 7:1-2; Jer. 1:9, etc.). Therefore, just as the word given to the prophets was trustworthy and reliable, so the Scriptures, which are God-breathed, are trustworthy and accurate because both communications come from the mouth of God. Paul's emphasis, then, is on the *origin* of the Scriptures: that which is God-breathed is "produced by the creative breath of the Almighty."[23] The fact that *theopneustos* occurs in the passive voice, and not the active, further emphasizes that God is the origin of the Scriptures, not man.[24]

(3) The entire Scriptures are God-breathed. Young clarifies: "If Paul means 'every Scripture,' he is looking at the various parts of the Bible, that is, he is considering Scripture distributively. He is then saying that whatever Scripture we consider, it is inspired of God. On the other hand, if he means 'all scripture,' it is clear that his reference is to the Scripture in its entirety. In either case he is saying that whatever may be called 'scripture' is inspired of God."[25]

In addition, all that is God-breathed is also designated Scripture. While the designation "Scripture" in v. 16 is sometimes understood to refer only to the Old Testament, it can be argued that Paul was using the designation "Scripture" not only for the Old Testament but also for the portions of the New Testament that had been written by that time (e.g., Paul must have considered the gospel of Luke canonical [1 Tim. 5:18]), and perhaps even the entire New Testament, some of which would be written in the future.[26]

Paul concludes that the Old and New Testaments are God-breathed, having their origin with God, not man. Paul thus affirms his belief in verbal inspiration.

Peter's view of the Bible. Peter's teaching concerning the Scriptures coincides with Paul's teaching. In 2 Peter 1:21 Peter emphasizes that no Scripture is produced as a result of human will; rather, it is the product of the superintending power of the Holy Spirit. Peter identifies the Scriptures as "the prophetic word" (v. 19), "prophecy of Scripture" (v. 20) and "prophecy" (v. 21); he declares that the Scripture is "something altogether reliable."[27] In verse 21 Peter explains why the Scripture is reliable. Like Paul, Peter affirms that Scripture has its origin with God. Although men penned the words of Scripture, they did so as they were carried along [Gk. *pheromenoi*] by the Holy Spirit.[28] Peter therefore acknowledges his belief in verbal inspiration inasmuch as it was the Holy Spirit who guided the writers of Scripture in their selection of words. This truth could be illustrated by a man who goes to the department store in a shopping center. Because he is in a hurry to get to the second floor he walks up the escalator. Although he is walking, the escalator is carrying him along, bringing him to the second floor. Similarly, although the writers of Scripture penned the words according to their educational abilities and their own distinctive styles, the Holy Spirit was carrying them along, ensuring the accuracy of all they were writing.

In 2 Peter 3:16 Peter refers to Paul's writings and indicates that the false teachers distort Paul's writings as they do *the rest of the Scriptures*. In this rather unique statement Peter places Paul's writings on a par with the Old Testament Scriptures.

Conclusion. The strongest defense for the verbal plenary inspiration of the Scriptures is the testimony of Jesus Christ. He testified to the inspiration of the entire Scriptures, the various books of the Old Testament and the actual words of Scripture as they had been originally recorded. The fact that He based His arguments on the precise wording of Scripture testifies to His exalted view of Scripture. In addition, Paul acknowledged that all Scripture was God-breathed; man was a passive instrument, being guided by God in the writing of Scripture. Peter's statement was similar in emphasizing that, in their passivity, men were carried along by the Holy Spirit in the writing of Scripture. The testimony of each of these witnesses draws attention to the verbal plenary inspiration of Scripture.

INERRANCY OF THE BIBLE

DEFINITION OF INERRANCY

In the past it was sufficient to state that the Bible was inspired; however, it has now become necessary to define the evangelical position more precisely. The result, as Charles Ryrie has shown, has necessitated the inclusion of additional verbiage. To state the orthodox view it is now necessary to include the terms "verbal, plenary, infallible, inerrant, unlimited inspiration!"[29] All this has been necessitated because of those who have retained words like *inspiration*, *infallible*, and even *inerrant* while denying that the Bible is free from error.

E. J. Young provides a suitable definition of inerrancy: "By this word we mean that the Scriptures possess the quality of freedom from error. They are exempt from the liability to mistake, incapable of error. In all their teachings they are in perfect accord with the truth"[30] Ryrie provides a syllogism for logically concluding the biblical teaching of inerrancy: "God is true (Rom. 3:4); the Scriptures were breathed out by God (2 Tim. 3:16); therefore, the Scriptures are true (since they came from the breath of God who is true)."[31]

In defining inerrancy it is also important to state what it does not mean. It does not demand rigidity of style and verbatim quotations from the Old Testament. "The inerrancy of the Bible means simply that the Bible tells the truth. Truth can and does include approximations, free quotations, language of appearances, and different accounts of the same event as long as those do not contradict."[32] At the Chicago meeting in October 1978, the International Council on Biblical Inerrancy issued the following statement on inerrancy: "Being wholly and verbally God-given, Scripture is without error or fault in all its teaching, no less in what it states about God's acts in creation, about the events of world history, and about its own literary origins under God, than in its witness to God's saving grace in individual lives."[33]

In a final definition it is noted that inerrancy extends to the original manuscripts: "Inerrancy means that when all the facts are known, the Scriptures in their original autographs and properly interpreted will be shown to be wholly true in everything they teach, whether that teaching has to do with doctrine, history, science, geography, geology, or other disciplines or knowledge."[34]

To suggest there are errors in the Bible is to impugn the character of God. If the Bible has errors it is the same as suggesting that God can fail, that He can make a mistake. "To assume that God could speak a Word that was contrary to fact is to assume that God Himself cannot operate without error. The very nature of God is at stake."[35]

EXPLANATION OF INERRANCY

Inerrancy allows for variety in style. The gospel of John was written in the simple style one might expect of an unlearned fisherman; Luke was written with a more sophisticated vocabulary of an educated person; Paul's epistles reflect the logic of a philospher. All of these variations are entirely compatible with inerrancy.

Inerrancy allows for variety in details in explaining the same event. This phenomenon is particularly observed in the synoptic gospels. It is important to remember that Jesus spoke in Aramaic and the writers of Scripture wrote their accounts in Greek, meaning they had to translate the original words into Greek. One writer would use slightly different words to describe the same incident, yet both would give the same meaning, albeit

THE WORD OF GOD:
TWO LIVING REVELATIONS

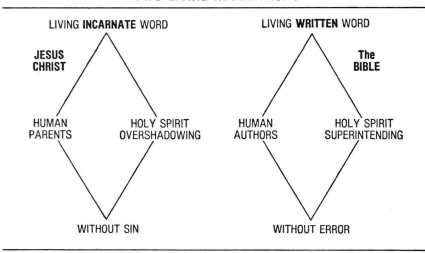

LIVING **INCARNATE** WORD

LIVING **WRITTEN** WORD

JESUS
CHRIST

The
BIBLE

HUMAN
PARENTS

HOLY SPIRIT
OVERSHADOWING

HUMAN
AUTHORS

HOLY SPIRIT
SUPERINTENDING

WITHOUT SIN

WITHOUT ERROR

with different words. There is an additional reason for variety in details. One writer might have viewed the event from one standpoint while the other gospel writer viewed it from another standpoint. This would make the details appear different, yet both would be accurate.

Inerrancy does not demand verbatim reporting of events. "In times of antiquity it was not the practice to give a verbatim repetition every time something was written out."[36] A verbatim quote could not be demanded for several reasons. First, as already mentioned, the writer had to translate from Aramaic to Greek in recording Jesus' words. Second, in making reference to Old Testament texts it would have been impossible to unroll the lengthy scrolls each time to produce a verbatim quote; furthermore, the scrolls were not readily available, hence, the freedom in Old Testament quotes.[37]

Inerrancy allows for departure from standard forms of grammar. Obviously it is wrong to force English rules of grammar upon the Scriptures. For example, in John 10:9 Jesus declares, "I am the door," whereas in verse 11 He states, "I am the Good Shepherd." In English this is considered mixing metaphors, but this is not a problem to Greek grammar or Hebrew language. In John 14:26 Jesus refers to the Spirit (*pneuma* = neuter) and then refers to the Spirit as "He" (*ekeinos* = masculine). This may raise an English grammarian's eyebrows, but it is not a problem of Greek grammar.

Inerrancy allows for problem passages. Even with so vast a work as the Holy Scriptures it is impossible to provide solutions to all the problems. In some cases the solution awaits the findings of the archaeologist's spade; in another case it awaits the linguist's research; in other cases the solution may never be discovered for other reasons. The solution to some problems must be held in abeyance. The answer, however, is never to suggest there are contradictions or errors in Scripture. If the Scriptures are God-breathed they are entirely without error.

Inerrancy demands the account does not teach error or contradiction. In the statements of Scripture, whatever is written is in accord with things as they are. Details may vary but it may still reflect things as they are. For example, in Matthew 8:5-13 it is noted that the centurion came to Jesus and said, "I am not qualified." In the parallel passage in Luke 7:1-10 it is noted that the elders came and said concerning the centurion, "He is worthy." It appears the elders first came and spoke to Jesus, and later the centurion himself came. Both accounts are in accord with things as they are.

PROBLEMS IN REJECTING INERRANCY[38]

Errantists conclude that errors can teach truth. They suggest it is unimportant to defend the Bible's accuracy concerning "minute details of chronology, geography, history, or cosmology or . . . alleged discrepancies."[39] However, matters of chronology, geography, history, and so forth, are not unimportant. Frequently, they are intertwined with significant theological truths. For instance, the historicity of Adam and Eve in Genesis 1 and 2 is important because Paul draws an analogy between Adam and Christ in Romans 5:12-21. If Adam is not historical the analogy breaks down. The chronology of Matthew 1 is important for it details the lineage of Jesus Christ. If His lineage is inaccurate, what can be said concerning the account of His life? The geography of Micah 5:2, announcing Christ's birth as being in Bethlehem, is important because the same verse also teaches the eternality of Christ. If the geography concerning Christ cannot be believed, can His eternality be believed?

The conclusion is obvious: if the Bible cannot be trusted in matters of chronology, history, and geography, it cannot be trusted in the message of salvation.

Errancy impugns the character of God. As has already been noted, Scripture is the result of the out-breathing of God (2 Tim. 3:16) and the superintending work of the Holy Spirit (2 Pet. 1:21). If the Scriptures contain errors then God erred.

Errantists disagree in listing errors. Errantists each have their own list of errors that differ from one another. "What are the criteria for determining areas in which errors are immaterial? . . . what or who decides the boundary lines between the territory of permissible errancy and the territory of necessary inerrancy?"[40]

CONCLUSION

Inerrancy is an important doctrine. When correctly understood, it means that the Bible speaks accurately in all its statements, whether theological matters, the creation account, history, geography, or geology. It does, however, allow for variety in details concerning the same account; it does not demand rigidity of style. In all the Bible's statements it is accurate and in accord with the truth.

CANONICITY OF THE BIBLE

DEFINITION OF CANONICITY

If the Scriptures are indeed inspired by God then a significant question arises: Which books are inspired? Historically, it was important for the people of God to determine which books God had inspired and which ones were recognized as authoritative.

The word *canon* is used to describe the inspired books. The word comes from the Greek *kanon* and probably also from the Hebrew *qaneh*, signifying a "measuring rod." The terms *canon* and *canonical* thus came to signify standards by which books were measured to determine whether or not they were inspired. It is important to note that religious councils at no time had any power to *cause* books to be inspired, rather they simply *recognized* that which God had inspired at the exact moment the books were written.

Jews and conservative Christians alike have recognized the thirty-nine books of the Old Testament as inspired. Evangelical Protestants have recognized the twenty-seven books of the New Testament as inspired. Roman Catholics have a total of eighty books because they recognize the Apocrypha as semicanonical.

CANONICITY OF THE OLD TESTAMENT

The Masoretic (Hebrew) text of the Old Testament divided the thirty-nine books into three categories: Law (Pentateuch); Prophets (Joshua, Judges, 1 and 2 Samuel, 1 and 2 Kings, major and minor prophets); and the Writings (sometimes called "The Psalms," including the poetry and wisdom books—Psalms, Proverbs, and Job; the Rolls—Song of Solomon, Ruth, Lamentations, Ecclesiastes, and Esther; the Historical Books—Daniel, Ezra, Nehemiah, and 1 and 2 Chronicles). Originally these thirty-nine books were counted as twenty-four by combining 1 and 2 Samuel, 1 and 2 Kings, 1 and 2 Chronicles, the minor prophets, and Ezra-Nehemiah. By the time of the New Testament this threefold division was recognized (Luke 24:44). Other designations such as "The Scripture" (John 10:35) and "The Sacred Writings" (2 Tim. 3:15) suggest a generally accepted Old Testament canon. This threefold division was also attested to by Josephus (A.D. 37-95), Bishop Melito of Sardis (ca. A.D. 170), Tertullian (A.D. 160-250), and others.[41] The Council of Jamnia in A.D. 90 is generally considered the occasion whereby the Old Testament canon was publicly recognized (while debating the canonicity of several books).

There is evidence of the manner in which the Old Testament books were recognized as canonical. Laird Harris[42] traces the continuity of recognition: Moses was recognized as writing under the authority of God (Ex. 17:14; 34:27; cf. Josh. 8:31; 23:6). The criterion for acknowledging the Pentateuch was whether it was from God's servant, Moses. Following Moses, God raised up the institution of prophecy to continue revealing Himself to His people (cf. Deut. 18:15-19; Jer. 26:8-15). The prophets to whom God spoke also recorded their revelation (cf. Josh. 24:26; 1 Sam. 10:25; Isa. 8:1; Ezek. 43:11). Harris concludes, "The law was accorded the respect of the author, and he was known as God's messenger. Similarly, succeeding prophets were received upon due authentication, and their written works were received with the same respect, being received therefore as the Word of God. As far as the witness contained in the books themselves is concerned, this reception was immediate."[43]

Specific tests to consider canonicity may be recognized. Did the book indicate Divine authorship? Did it reflect God speaking through a mediator? (e.g., Ex. 20:1; Josh. 1:1; Isa. 2:1). Was the human author a spokesman of God? Was he a prophet or did he have the prophetic gift? (e.g., Deut. 31:24-26; 1 Sam. 10:25; Neh. 8:3). Was the book historically accurate? Did it reflect a record of actual facts? How was the book received by the Jews?

In summary, the books of the Old Testament were divinely inspired and authoritative the moment they were written. There was human recognition of the writings; normally this was immediate as the people recognized the writers as spokesmen from God. Finally, there was a collection of the books into a canon.[44]

CANONICITY OF THE NEW TESTAMENT

There were several factors that caused the recognition of a New Testament canon. (1) Spurious writings as well as attacks on genuine writings were a factor. Marcion, for example, rejected the Old Testament and New Testament writings apart from the Pauline letters (he altered Luke's gospel to suit his doctrine). (2) The content of the New Testament writings testified to their authenticity and they naturally were collected, being recognized as canonical. (3) Apostolic writings were used in public worship, hence, it was necessary to determine which of those writings were canonical. (4) Ultimately, the edict by Emperor Diocletian in A.D. 303, demanding that all sacred books be burned, resulted in the New Testament collection.

The process of the recognition and collection took place in the first centuries of the Christian church.[45] Very early, the New Testament books were being recognized. Paul, for example, recognized Luke's writing on a par with the Old Testament (1 Tim. 5:18 quotes Deut. 25:4, and Luke 10:7 and refers to both texts as "the Scripture says"). Peter also recognized Paul's writings as Scripture (2 Peter 3:15-16). Letters were being read in the churches and even circulated among the church (cf. Col. 4:16; 1 Thess. 5:27).

In the post-apostolic era, Clement of Rome (c. A.D. 95) mentioned at least eight New Testament books in a letter; Ignatius of Antioch (c. A.D. 115) also acknowledged about seven books; Polycarp, a disciple of John, (c. A.D. 108), acknowledged fifteen letters. That is not to say these men did not recognize more letters as canonical, but these are ones they mentioned in their correspondence. Later Irenaeus wrote (c. A.D. 185), acknowledging twenty-one books. Hippolytus (A.D. 170-235) recognized twenty-two books. The problematic books at this time were Hebrews, James, 2 Peter, and 2 and 3 John.

Even more important was the witness of the Muratorian Canon (A.D. 170), which was a compilation of books recognized as canonical at that early date by the church. The Muratorian Canon included all the New Testament books except Hebrews, James, and one epistle of John.

In the fourth century there was also prominent recognition of a New Testament canon. When Athanasius wrote in A.D. 367 he cited the twenty-seven books of the New Testament as being the only true books. In A.D. 363 the Council of Laodicea stated that only the Old Testament and the twenty-seven books of the New Testament were to be read in the churches. The Council of Hippo (A.D. 393) recognized the twenty-seven books, and the Council of Carthage (A.D. 397) affirmed that only those canonical books were to be read in the churches.

How did the church recognize which books were canonical? There were certain tests applied to answer that question.[46]

(1) *Apostolicity.* Was the author an apostle or did he have a connection with an apostle? For example, Mark wrote under Peter's authority, and Luke wrote under Paul's authority.

(2) *Acceptance.* Was the book accepted by the church at large? The recognition given a particular book by the church was important. By this canon false books were rejected (but it also delayed recognition of some legitimate books).

(3) *Content.* Did the book reflect consistency of doctrine with what had been accepted as orthodox teaching? The spurious "gospel of Peter" was rejected as a result of this principle.

(4) *Inspiration.* Did the book reflect the quality of inspiration? The Apocrypha and Pseudepigrapha were rejected as a result of not meeting this

test. The book should bear evidence of high moral and spiritual values that would reflect a work of the Holy Spirit.

COMPOSITION OF THE BIBLE

RELIABILITY OF THE OLD TESTAMENT TEXT

Although we do not have the original manuscripts of either the Old or New Testaments, we nonetheless have a biblical text that is reliable. A history of the development of the Old Testament text will indicate this. The work of copying the ancient manuscripts was a tedious exercise, but the Jews very early developed strict rules for their work. Rules regulated the kind of parchment, the number of lines to be written, the color of the ink, and the manner of revision.[47] When parchments began to show wear, the Jew reverently buried the manuscripts. As a result, until the discovery of the Dead Sea Scrolls at Qumran, the oldest extant manuscripts were dated from A.D. 900.

Nonetheless, the reliability of the Old Testament text is seen in the careful transcription of the text in the days of Ezra and continuing later under the Masoretes, who developed a tradition of care and accuracy in copying the text. They ensured accuracy by counting the number of letters in a book, by noting the middle letter, and similar tedious procedures. For example, they noted that the Hebrew letter *aleph* occurred 42,377 times in the Old Testament. If the count in the new copy did not agree with the original copy the manuscript was recopied. When a word or statement appeared to be incorrect they left it in the text (called *kethib*) but made a marginal notation of their corrected suggestion (called *qere*). It was also the Masoretes who gave the Hebrew text its vowel pointing; prior to that time the Hebrew text was written only with consonants.

Several ancient sources indicate the reliability of the Old Testament text.

Dead Sea Scrolls. Prior to the discovery of the scrolls at Qumran the oldest extant manuscripts were dated from approximately A.D. 900. Some manuscripts of the Dead Sea Scrolls, which included copies of Isaiah, Habakkuk, and others, were dated back to 125 B.C., providing manuscripts one thousand years older than previously available. The major conclusion was that there was no significant difference between the Isaiah scroll at Qumran and the Masoretic Hebrew text dated one thousand years later. This confirmed the reliability of our present Hebrew text.

Septuagint. The Septuagint is a Greek translation of the Hebrew Old Testament to accommodate the dispersed Jews who had lost the Hebrew language. Tradition says that around seventy Hebrew scholars translated the Hebrew text into Greek (the name *Septuagint* means "seventy," hence, it is designated LXX). It was translated piecemeal in Alexandria, Egypt, between

250 and 150 B.C. As a translation it is uneven, but it is helpful in that it is based on a Hebrew text one thousand years older than our existing Hebrew manuscripts. Moreover, New Testament writers would at times quote from the Septuagint; this provides us with further insight concerning the Old Testament text.

Samaritan Pentateuch. This translation of the books of Moses was made to facilitate the worship of the Samaritans at Mount Gerizim (as a rival to Jerusalem). The translation is independent of the Masoretic text and, because it goes back to the fourth century B.C., it is a valuable witness to the text of the Old Testament. Although there are approximately six thousand differences with the Masoretic text, most of them are minor, related to matters of grammar and spelling.[48]

Aramaic Targums. Following Israel's return from captivity in Babylon, the Jews had generally abandoned Hebrew for Aramaic. It became necessary to provide the Scriptures for the Jews in their spoken language. The Targums was the result. Targums means "translations" or "paraphrases", and they are quite free in retelling the biblical accounts; nevertheless, they "provide a valuable background for the study of the NT besides witnessing to the text of the OT."[49]

RELIABILITY OF THE NEW TESTAMENT TEXT

While we do not have the autographs (original writings) of the New Testament, nonetheless, the witness to the New Testament books is formidable. For example, there are some five thousand extant manuscripts that contain either the complete New Testament or portions of it.

Papyrus manuscripts. These manuscripts are old and an important witness. For example, the Chester Beatty Papyrus dates from the third century.

Uncial manuscripts. Approximately two hundred forty manuscripts are called *uncial* manuscripts and are identified by *capital letters*. Codex (meaning "book") Sinaiticus contains all the New Testament and is dated A.D. 331. Codex Vaticanus contains most of the New Testament, is dated from the fourth century, and is considered one of the most important manuscripts. Alexandrinus, dated fifth century, contains all the New Testament except part of Matthew and is helpful in determining the text of Revelation. Others include Codex Ephraemi (5th century), Codex Bezae (5th-6th century), and Washington Codex (4th-5th century).

Minuscule manuscripts. There are some twenty-eight hundred *minuscule* manuscripts that are written in *small letters* usually in a flowing hand. They are normally not as old as uncial manuscripts. Some of the minuscules reveal a similarity of text-types and are referred to as a "family" relationship and are so categorized.

Versions. A number of early versions of the New Testament also help in understanding the correct text. Several *Syriac* versions exist, among them

Tatian's Diatessaron (A.D. 170), the Old Syriac (A.D. 200), the Peshitta (fifth century), and the Palestinian Syriac (fifth century). The Latin Vulgate, translated by Jerome (c. A.D. 400), influenced the Western church. The Coptic translations (translated in the third century), including the Sahidic Version and the Bohairic Version, influenced Egypt.

Through the study of the Greek manuscripts as well as the early versions, textual critics have been able to determine the text that is substantially that of the original writings. It is evident that the hand of God has preserved the various texts through the centuries to enable scholars to collate them and reconstruct the text as closely as possible to the original writings.

ILLUMINATION OF THE BIBLE

DEFINITION OF ILLUMINATION

Because the Bible is God-breathed and therefore in an entirely different dimension from other literature, it is necessary that man receives God-given help in understanding the Bible (1 Cor. 2:11). Additionally, the unregenerate man's sin-darkened mind cannot apprehend spiritual truths (1 Cor. 2:14). The work of illumination then is necessary to enable man to comprehend the Word of God (cf. Luke 24:44-45). *Illumination* can thus be defined as "the ministry of the Holy Spirit whereby He enlightens those who are in a right relationship with Him to comprehend the written Word of God."

EXPLANATION OF ILLUMINATION

There is a tendency to confuse illumination with revelation and inspiration. The distinction is noted: "In reference to the Bible, revelation relates to its content or material, inspiration to the method of recording that material, and illumination to the meaning of the record."[50] At the moment of salvation the believer is indwelt by the Holy Spirit who then takes the truths of God and reveals them (illumination) to the believer (1 Cor. 2:9-13). Since only God knows the things of God, therefore it is essential that the Spirit of God instructs the believer. This ministry of the Holy Spirit had been foretold by Jesus in the Upper Room Discourse. Jesus announced that the Spirit would teach them (John 14:26), guide them into all the truth (John 16:13), and disclose the truth of God to them (John 16:14, 15). This ministry of the Spirit, moreover, touches the mind (Rom. 12:2; Eph. 4:23; Col. 1:9-10) and heart, or volition (Acts 16:14; Eph. 1:18).[51]

INTERPRETATION OF THE BIBLE

Several important principles are basic in the interpretation of Scripture.

LITERAL INTERPRETATION

Literal interpretation means the words and sentences of Scripture are understood in their *normal* meaning—the ways that words are understood in normal communication. It is a literal or normal meaning of words that is the basis of communication. Biblically there is a precedence for interpreting the New Testament literally. Old Testament prophecies like Psalm 22, Isaiah 7:14; 53:1-12; Micah 5:2 have all been fulfilled literally.

GRAMMATICAL RELATIONSHIPS

Because we acknowledge the verbal (words) and plenary (full) inspiration of Scripture it is incumbent on us to pay attention to the words of Scripture. Grammatical relationships are important to study because words stand in relationship to each other; therefore, it is necessary to study verb tenses, pronouns, prepositions, conjunctions, and laws of structure.

HISTORICAL CONTEXT

The historical context is important as a framework from which to interpret the Scriptures. Every book of Scripture was written in a historical context that should be understood in order to help interpret the book accurately.

LITERARY CONTEXT

Interpreting in context involves three main steps.

Study the immediate context. The immediate context should be carefully studied; several paragraphs preceding and following the passage should be studied.

Study the more remote context. The major segment of the book (usually 2-3 chaps.) in which the passage occurs should be studied.

Consider the context of the entire book. The emphasis of the entire book should be studied.

The subject of interpretation is a major subject in itself and vitally important to the correct understanding of Scripture. The reader is encouraged to spend time in careful study of some of the valuable resources mentioned below.

NOTES ON BIBLIOLOGY

1. See F. F. Bruce, *The Books and the Parchments* (London: Pickering & Inglis, 1971) for helpful information on the languages of the Bible, the ancient manuscripts, the translations of the Bible, and how the Bible came down to us. For an up-to-date discus-

sion of the canon, history, and translations of the Bible see David Ewert, *From Ancient Tablets to Modern Translations* (Grand Rapids: Zondervan, 1983). A fascinating and detailed explanation of the preparation and use of papyrus is given by Pliny in *Natural History* and cited by C. K. Barrett, *The New Testament Background: Selected Documents* (New York: Harper, 1961), pp. 23-27.

2. For a thorough discussion see R. Mayer and C. Brown, "Scripture" in C. Brown, ed., *The New International Dictionary of New Testament Theology*, 4 vols. (Grand Rapids: Zondervan, 1978), 3:482-97.

3. See the excellent discussion by R. Laird Harris, *Inspiration and Canonicity of the Bible* (Grand Rapids: Zondervan, 1969), pp 45-71. Harris demonstrates that invoking the testimony of the aforementioned is not circular reasoning.

4. Henry C. Thiessen, *Lectures in Systematic Theology*, revised by Vernon D. Doerksen (Grand Rapids: Eerdmans, 1979), p. 7.

5. cf. Lewis Sperry Chafer, *Systematic Theology*, (Dallas: Dallas Seminary, 1947), 1:48.

6. C. M. Horne, "Revelation" in Merrill C. Tenney, ed., *Zondervan Pictorial Encyclopedia of the Bible* (Grand Rapids: Zondervan, 1975), 5:86.

7. Karl Barth, *Church Dogmatics*, translated and edited by G. W. Bromiley and T. F. Torrance (Edinburgh: Clark, 1956), 1:124-27, 333ff.; and Herbert Hartwell, *The Theology of Karl Barth, An Introduction* (Philadelphia: Westminster, 1964), pp,. 67-87. Bloesch appears to lean in this direction when he says, "one must not make the mistake of equating [biblical text and divine revelation]. . . . Scripture is more than a human witness to revelation: it is revelation itself mediated through human words. It is not in and of itself divine revelation, but when illuminated by the Spirit it *becomes* revelation to the believer" (italics mine), Donald G. Bloesch, *Essentials of Evangelical Theology* (San Francisco: Harper, 1982), 1:52. Thus, while acknowledging Scripture is a "veritable bearer of revelation," Bloesch nonetheless seems to make believer appropriation the criterion in defining revelation (pp. 51-56). Part of the problem is that Barth, Bloesch, and others confuse *revelation* with *illumination*. Illumination is the personal understanding and appropriation of revelation but distinct from it.

8. Bruce A. Demarest, *General Revelation: Historical Views and Contemporary Issues* (Grand Rapids: Zondervan, 1982), p. 231.

9. Ibid., pp. 232-33. See also the helpful article by A. M. Rehwinkel, "Conscience," in Walter A. Elwell, ed., *Evangelical Dictionary of Theology* (Grand Rapids: Baker, 1984), pp. 267-68. Rehwinkel says: "Conscience is an awareness restricted to the moral sphere. It is a moral awareness. . . . Conscience is that faculty by which one distinguishes between the morally right and wrong, which urges one to do that which he recognizes to be right, which passes judgment on his acts and executes that judgment within his soul. . . . conscience is innate and universal. It is not the product of environment, training, habit, or education, though it is influenced by all of these factors" (p. 267).

10. Leon Morris, *The Gospel According to John* (Grand Rapids: Eerdmans, 1971), p. 114.

11. B. B. Warfield, *The Inspiration and Authority of the Bible* (Philadelphia: Presbyterian and Reformed, 1948), p. 131.

12. Edward J. Young, *Thy Word Is Truth* (Grand Rapids: Eerdmans, 1957), p. 27.

13. Charles C. Ryrie, *A Survey of Bible Doctrine* (Chicago: Moody, 1972), p. 38.

14. Alan Richardson, *Christian Apologetics* (New York: Harper, 1948), p. 207. Richardson suggests there have been Christian books written from the second to the twentieth century that are inspired in precisely the same way as the Bible.

15. For an expanded discussion see A. H. Strong, *Systematic Theology* (Valley Forge, Pa.: Judson, 1907), pp. 204-8.

16. Ibid., pp. 211-22.

17. Rene Pache, *The Inspiration & Authority of Scripture* (Chicago: Moody, 1980), p. 58. Pache goes on to say that underlying the conceptual view is the refusal to "give credence to the authority of the sacred text" (p. 59).

18. See the excellent work of Jesus' view of the Bible by Robert P. Lightner, *The Saviour and the Scriptures* (Philadelphia: Presbyterian & Reformed, 1966), pp. 60-73.

19. R. Laird Harris, *Inspiration and Canonicity of the Bible* (Grand Rapids: Zondervan, 1969), p. 45ff.

20. Leon Morris, *The Gospel According to John* (Grand Rapids: Eerdmans, 1971), p. 527.

21. See the excellent discussion on John 10:35 in B. B. Warfield, *The Inspiration and Authority of the Bible* (Philadelphia: Presbyterian & Reformed, 1948), p. 138ff.

22. For additional discussions see Robert P. Lightner, *The Saviour and the Scriptures*, pp. 60-73; and Charles C. Ryrie, *What You Should Know About Inerrancy* (Chicago: Moody, 1981), pp. 57-78.

23. B. B. Warfield, *The Inspiration and Authority of the Bible* (Philadelphia: Presbyterian & Refomed, 1948), p. 296.

24. See E. J. Young, *Thy Word Is Truth*, pp. 20-21 as well as B. B. Warfield, *The Inspiration and Authority of the Bible*, p. 272.

25. Ibid., p. 19.

26. H. Wayne House, "Biblical Inspiration in 2 Timothy 3:16," *Bibliotheca Sacra*, 137 (January-March, 1980):56-57.

27. William F. Arndt and F. Wilbur Gingrich, *A Greek-English Lexicon of the New Testament and Other Early Christian Literature* 2nd ed., revised by F. Wilbur Gingrich and Frederick W. Danker (Chicago: U. of Chicago, 1979), p. 138.

28. Young states: "The men who spake from God are said to have been borne by the Holy Spirit. That is, the Spirit actually lifted them up and carried them along, and thus they spake. They were borne or carried along under the power of the Spirit and not by their own power. If a person picks up something and bears it, he does it by his own power. That which is picked up and borne, however, is absolutely passive. It was the Spirit of God who bore them. It was He who was active, and they who were passive. Thus He bore them to the goal of His own desiring," (E. J. Young, *Thy Word Is Truth*, p. 25).

29. Charles C. Ryrie, *What You Should Know About Inerrancy*, p. 16.

30. E. J. Young, *Thy Word Is Truth*, p. 113.

31. Charles C. Ryrie, "Some Important Aspects of Biblical Inerrancy" *Bibliotheca Sacra* 136 (January-March, 1979):17.

32. Charles C. Ryrie, *What You Should Know About Inerrancy,* p. 30. Note also the helpful illustrations Ryrie employs, pp. 31-32.

33. James Montgomery Boice, *Does Inerrancy Matter?* (Oakland: International Council on Biblical Inerrancy, 1979), p. 13.

34. Ibid.

35. E. J. Young, *Thy Word Is Truth*, p. 165.

36. Ibid., p. 119.

37. William R. Eichhorst, *The Issue of Biblical Inerrancy: In Definition and Defence* (Winnipeg, Man.: Winnipeg Bible College, n.d.), p. 9.

38. See the helpful literature by Charles C. Ryrie, "Some Important Aspects of Biblical Inerrancy," pp. 16-24; and *What You Should Know About Inerrancy* (Chicago: Moody, 1981), pp. 103-9.

39. David Hubbard, "The Current Tensions: Is There a Way Out?" in Jack Rogers, ed., *Biblical Authority* (Waco: Word, 1977), p. 168.

40. Ryrie, "Some Important Aspects of Biblical Inerrancy," p. 19.

41. Gleason L. Archer, Jr., *A Survey of Old Testament Introduction* (Chicago: Moody, 1964), pp. 62-65.

42. R. Laird Harris, *Inspiration and Canonicity of the Bible* (Grand Rapids: Zondervan, 1969), p. 156ff.

43. Ibid., p. 167.

44. "[Josephus] mentions that the boundary of the accepted books is marked by the time of Artaxerxes (465-425 B.C.), after which no authorized books were issued." D. Guthrie, "Bible" in Merrill C. Tenney, ed., *The Zondervan Pictorial Encyclopedia of the Bible*, 5 vols. (Grand Rapids: Zondervan, 1975), 1:560.

45. See R. Laird Harris, *Inspiration and Canonicity of the Bible*, pp. 199-218; and David Ewert, *From Ancient Tablets to Modern Translations* (Grand Rapids: Zondervan, 1983), pp. 125-34.

46. See Everett F. Harrison, *Introduction to the New Testament* (Grand Rapids: Eerdmans, 1964), pp. 103-6; Henry C. Thiessen, *Introduction to the New Testament* (Grand Rapids: Eerdmans, 1943), p. 10; and David Ewert, *From Ancient Tablets to Modern Translations*, pp. 130-32.

47. F. G. Kenyon, *Our Bible and the Ancient Manuscripts*, revised by A. W. Adams (New York: Harper, 1958), p. 79ff.

48. Ewert, *From Ancient Tablets to Modern Translations*, p. 100.

49. Ibid., p. 104.

50. Charles C. Ryrie, *A Survey of Bible Doctrine* (Chicago: Moody, 1972), pp. 47-48.

51. Pache, *The Inspiration and Authority of Scripture*, pp. 208-9.

FOR FURTHER STUDY ON BIBLIOLOGY

DIVINE ORIGIN

** David Baron. *Rays of Messiah's Glory: Christ in the Old Testament.* Winona Lake, Ind.: Alpha, n.d.

** Lewis Sperry Chafer. *Systematic Theology*, 8 vols. Dallas: Dallas Seminary, 1947. 1:30-31.

* Norman Geisler. *To Understand the Bible Look For Jesus.* Grand Rapids: Baker, 1979, pp. 32-36, 63-68, 98-101.

** E. W. Hengstenberg. *Christology of the Old Testament.* Reprint. Grand Rapids: Kregel, 1970.

* Josh McDowell. *Evidence That Demands a Verdict*, rev. ed., San Bernardino, Calif.: Here's Life, 1979. Pp. 15-24, 141-76.

* Ceil and Moishe Rosen. *Christ in the Passover.* Chicago: Moody, 1978.

* W. Graham Scroggie. *A Guide to the Gospels*. London: Pickering & Inglis, 1948. Pp. 479-86.

** Henry C. Thiessen, *Lectures in Systematic Theology*, revised by Vernon D. Doerksen. Grand Rapids: Eerdmans, 1977. Pp.47-48.

* John F. Walvoord. *Jesus Christ Our Lord.* Chicago: Moody, 1969. Pp. 79-95.

DIVINE REVELATION

** Louis Berkhof. *Systematic Theology*, 4th ed. Grand Rapids: Eerdmans, 1941. Pp. 36-40.

** Lewis Sperry Chafer. *Systematic Theology*, 8 vols. Dallas: Dallas Seminary, 1947. 1:48-60.

** Bruce A. Demarest. *General Revelation: Historical Views and Contemporary Issues*. Grand Rapids: Zondervan, 1982.

* Carl F. H. Henry. "Revelation, Special." In Walter A. Elwell, ed., *Evangelical Dictionary of Theology.* Grand Rapids: Baker, 1984. Pp. 945-48.

* C. M. Horne. "Revelation." In Merrill C. Tenney, ed., *Zondervan Pictorial Encyclopedia of the Bible*, 5 vols. Grand Rapids: Zondervan, 1975. 5:86-89.

* Robert P. Lightner. *The God of the Bible.* Grand Rapids: Baker, 1978. Pp. 50-63.

** Clark H. Pinnock. *Biblical Revelation.* Chicago: Moody, 1971.

* Henry C. Thiessen. *Lectures in Systematic Theology*, revised by Vernon D. Doerksen. Grand Rapids: Eerdmans, 1979. Pp. 7-17.

** B. B. Warfield. *The Inspiration and Authority of the Bible.* Philadelphia: Presbyterian and Reformed, 1948. Pp. 71-102. The same material appears in James Orr, ed., *The International Standard Bible Encyclopaedia*, 5 vols. Grand Rapids: Eerdmans, 1939. 4:2573-82.

DIVINE INSPIRATION

** J. Oliver Buswell, Jr. *A Systematic Theology of the Christian Religion*, 2 vols. Grand Rapids: Zondervan, 1962. 1:183-205.

** R. Laird Harris. *Inspiration and Canonicity of the Bible.* Grand Rapids: Zondervan, 1969. Pp. 17-128.

* Carl F. H. Henry. "Bible, Inspiration of." In Walter A. Elwell, ed., *Evangelical Dictionary of Theology*. Grand Rapids: Baker, 1984. Pp. 145-49.

** H. Wayne House. "Biblical Inspiration in 2 Timothy 3:16." *Bibliotheca Sacra* 137 (January-March, 1980):54-63.

* Robert P. Lightner. *The Saviour and the Scriptures.* Philadelphia: Presbyterian & Reformed, 1966. Pp. 11-103.

* Rene Pache. *The Inspiration & Authority of Scripture.* Chicago: Moody, 1980.

* Robert L. Saucy. *The Bible: Breathed from God.* Wheaton: Victor, 1978.

** John W. Wenham. *Christ and the Bible.* Downers Grove, Ill.: InterVarsity, 1972.

** B. B. Warfield. *The Inspiration and Authority of the Bible.* Philadelphia: Presbyterian & Reformed, 1948.

* Edward J. Young. *Thy Word Is Truth.* Grand Rapids: Eerdmans, 1957. Pp. 13-109.

BIBLICAL INERRANCY

* James M. Boice. *Does Inerrancy Matter?* Oakland, CA: International Council on Biblical Inerrancy, 1979.

* Paul D. Feinberg, "Bible, Inerrancy and Infallibility of." In Walter A. Elwell, ed., *Evangelical Dictionary of Theology*. Grand Rapids: Baker, 1984, Pp. 141-45.

** Norman L. Geisler, ed. *Inerrancy*. Grand Rapids: Zondervan, 1980. This is one of the finest works on the subject and deals with the major issues.

** _____. *Biblical Errancy: An Analysis of Its Philosophical Roots*. Grand Rapids: Zondervan, 1981.

** John Warwick Montgomery, ed. *God's Inerrant Word: An International Symposium on the Trustworthiness of Scripture*. Minneapolis: Bethany, 1974.

* Charles C. Ryrie. *What You Should Know About Inerrancy*. Chicago: Moody, 1981.

** John D. Woodbridge. *Biblical Authority*. Grand Rapids: Zondervan, 1982.

* E. J. Young. *Thy Word Is Truth*. Grand Rapids: Eerdmans, 1957. Pp. 113-85. These chapters are among the most helpful materials on the subject. They help explain many of the problems postulated by errantists.

BIBLICAL CANONICITY

** David Ewert. *From Ancient Tablets To Modern Translations*. Grand Rapids: Zondervan, 1983. Pp. 125-34.

* Donald Guthrie. "Bible." In Merrill Tenney, ed., *The Zondervan Pictorial Encyclopedia of the Bible*, 5 vols. Grand Rapids: Zondervan, 1975. 1:561-62.

** R. Laird Harris. *Inspiration and Canonicity of the Bible*. Grand Rapids: Zondervan, 1969. Pp. 199-245.

** Everett F. Harrison. *Introduction to the New Testament*. Grand Rapids: Eerdmans, 1964. Pp. 91-128.

* Rene Pache. *The Inspiration & Authority of Scripture*. Chicago: Moody, 1969. Pp. 173-85.

* Henry C. Thiessen. *Introduction to the New Testament*. Grand Rapids: Eerdmans, 1943. Pp. 3-30.

HUMAN COMPOSITION

** Gleason L. Archer, Jr. *A Survey of Old Testament Introduction*. Chicago: Moody, 1964. Pp. 31-58.

** F. F. Bruce. *The New Testament Documents: Are They Reliable?* London: InterVarsity, 1960.

* David Ewert. *From Ancient Tablets to Modern Translations*. Grand Rapids: Zondervan, 1983. Pp. 85-111, 135-82.

** Everett F. Harrison. *Introduction to the New Testament*. Grand Rapids: Eerdmans, 1964. Pp. 59-88.

* Josh McDowell. *Evidence That Demands a Verdict*. San Bernardino, CA: Campus Crusade, 1972. Pp. 43-79.

** Bruce M. Metzger. *The Text of the New Testament*, 2nd ed. New York: Oxford, 1968. This work is one of the most important in understanding the transmission of the New Testament text.

* Rene Pache. *The Inspiration & Authority of Scripture*. Chicago: Moody, 1969. Pp. 186-98.

* Merrill F. Unger. *Introductory Guide to the Old Testament*. Grand Rapids: Zondervan, 1951. Pp. 115-79.

DIVINE ILLUMINATION

** Lewis Sperry Chafer. *Systematic Theology*, 8 vols. Dallas: Dallas Seminary, 1947. 1:105-13.

* Rene Pache. *The Inspiration & Authority of Scripture*. Chicago: Moody, 1969. Pp. 199-212.

* Charles C. Ryrie. *A Survey of Bible Doctrine*. Chicago: Moody, 1972. Pp. 47-48.

* Robert L. Saucy. *The Bible: Breathed from God*. Wheaton: Victor, 1978. Pp. 103-12.

HUMAN INTERPRETATION

* Irving L. Jensen. *Independent Bible Study*. Chicago: Moody, 1963. Jensen has many helpful study books on individual books of the Bible. They are especially helpful in charting to gain an overview of the Bible book.

** Walter C. Kaiser, Jr. *Toward an Exegetical Theology*. Grand Rapids: Baker, 1981. While this book is intended for sermonic development, there is considerable material to help analyze and interpret the Scriptures.

* J. Robertson McQuilkin. *Understanding and Applying the Bible*. Chicago: Moody, 1983.

** A. Berkeley Mickelsen. *Interpreting the Bible*. Grand Rapids: Eerdmans, 1963.

** Bernard Ramm. *Protestant Biblical Interpretation*, 3rd ed. Grand Rapids: Baker, 1970.

* R. C. Sproul. *Knowing Scripture*. Downers Grove, Ill: InterVarsity, 1977.

* T. Norton Sterrett. *How to Understand Your Bible*. Downers Grove, Ill: Inter-Varsity, 1974. This is a particularly helpful volume; if the student has no background in interpretation this would be a good first acquisition.

* Robert A. Traina. *Methodical Bible Study*. Wilmore, KY: Robert Traina, Asbury Seminary, 1952.

** Henry A. Virkler. *Hermeneutics: Principles and Processes of Biblical Interpretation*. Grand Rapids: Baker, 1981.

* Oletta Wald. *The Joy of Discovery in Bible Study*, rev. ed. Minneapolis: Augsburg, 1975. This small volume (96 pp.) is particularly helpful for lay people.

19

THEOLOGY PROPER: DOCTRINE OF GOD

DEFINITION OF THEOLOGY PROPER

The word *theology* comes from the Greek word *theos*, meaning "God," and *logos*, meaning "word" or "discourse," hence, theology is a discourse about God. Theology is generally taken as a broad term covering the entire field of Christian belief (the study of Christ, the Holy Spirit, angels, etc.). Hence, the designation given to the study of God the Father is theology proper.

EXISTENCE OF GOD

COSMOLOGICAL ARGUMENT

Logically speaking the cosmological argument for the existence of God is inductive and a posteriori: the evidence is examined, and based on it a conclusion is drawn that God exists. The term *cosmological* comes from the Greek word *cosmos*, meaning "world." This argument is based on the fact that a cosmos, or world, exists. Because something cannot come from nothing, there must be an original cause that is the reason for the world's existence. A man wears a Bulova wristwatch. Although he has never seen a watchmaker, the fact of the existence of the wristwatch suggests there is a Swiss watchmaker who made the watch. The cosmological argument says that every effect must have a cause.[1]

TELEOLOGICAL ARGUMENT

As in the previous case, the teleological argument is inductive and a posteriori. *Teleological* comes from the Greek word *telos*, meaning "end." The teleological argument may be defined thus: "Order and useful arrangement in a system imply intelligence and purpose in the organizing cause.

The universe is characterized by order and useful arrangement; therefore, the universe has an intelligent and free cause."[2] The world everywhere evidences intelligence, purpose, and harmony; there must be a master architect behind all this evidence. The psalmist sees the magnificence of God's creation in the universe and recognizes that it testifies to His existence (Ps. 8:3-4; 19:1-4). God's harmony is observed throughout the universe and world: the sun being ninety-three million miles distant is precisely right for an adequate climate on earth; the moon's distance of two hundred forty thousand miles provides tides at a proper level; the earth's tilt provides the seasons. A conclusion is clear that God, the Master Designer, has created this magnificent universe. The alternative, that the world happened "by chance," is no more possible than a monkey's being able to create a work of Shakespeare on a typewriter by haphazard play on the keys.

ANTHROPOLOGICAL ARGUMENT

The anthropological argument, which is also inductive and a posteriori, is based on the Greek word *anthropos*, meaning "man." Contrary to the secular humanist who sees man simply as a biological being, the biblicist sees man as created in the image of God (Gen. 1:26-28). The image of God in man is spiritual, not physical (cf. Eph. 4:24; Col. 3:10). Man is not simply a physical being, but also a moral being with a conscience, intellect, emotion, and will. Chafer states: "There are philosophical and moral features in man's constitution which may be traced back to find their origin in God. . . . A blind force . . . could never produce a man with intellect, sensibility, will, conscience, and inherent belief in a Creator."[3]

MORAL ARGUMENT

The moral argument is related to the anthropological argument (some combine the two) and can be seen as a further consideration of that argument. The moral argument acknowledges that man has an awareness of right and wrong, a sense of morality. Where did this sense of moral justice come from? If man is only a biological creature why does he have a sense of moral obligation? Recognition of moral standards and concepts cannot be attributed to any evolutionary process. The biblicist recognizes that God has placed a sense of moral justice within the human race in contradistinction to all other creation. Romans 2:14-15 indicates that Gentiles who have had no revelation of the law have an inner, moral witness placed there by God.

ONTOLOGICAL ARGUMENT

The ontological argument, distinct from the preceding arguments, is deductive and a priori; it begins with an assumption and then attempts to prove that assumption. It is less significant than the preceding arguments.

The term *ontological* comes from the Greek present participle *ontos* (from the verb *eimi*) and means "being" or "existence." The ontological argument is philosophical rather than inductive. The argument reasons: "If man could conceive of a Perfect God who does not exist, then he could conceive of someone greater than God himself which is impossible. Therefore God exists." The argument rests on the fact that all men have an awareness of God. Because the concept of God is universal, God must have placed the idea within man. Anselm (1033?-1109) was the first proponent of this view. In the thinking of some, this argument has limited value, and few would affirm the usefulness of the ontological argument.

ANTI-THEISTIC THEORIES

ATHEISTIC VIEW

The term *atheist* comes from the Greek word *theos*, meaning "God," and the prefix *a* (Gk. *alpha*), which in Greek negates the preceding statement. Therefore, it means a nonbeliever in God. Ephesians 2:12 uses the term (translated "without God") to explain the status of unsaved Gentiles in their relationship toward God. Atheists can be classified into three categories:[4] (1) the *practical* atheist who lives as if there is no God; (2) the *dogmatic* atheist who openly repudiates God; (3) the *virtual* atheist who rejects God by his terminology (e.g. Paul Tillich: God is the "Ground of all being"). This classification would include those who deny a personal God.

AGNOSTIC VIEW

The term *agnostic* comes from the Greek *gnosis*, meaning "knowledge," accompanied by the *a* prefix. Therefore, an agnostic means one who lacks knowledge of God. Hence, an agnostic is one who says we cannot know that God even exists. The term, first coined by Thomas Huxley, covers varying degrees of skepticism. Agnostics are followers of pragmatism; their belief in something has to be scientifically verifiable, and because God is not scientifically verifiable, they leave Him out of their discussion.

EVOLUTION[5]

Evolution is an antisupernatural approach to life and its origin. It begins with the premise that there is no God and then seeks to explain life apart from any involvement by God. The implications are serious: if God created man, then man is a morally responsible being; if man is the product of evolution, then he is only biological and is not morally responsible to any god.

POLYTHEISM

The term *polytheism* comes from the Greek word *poly*, meaning "many," and *theos*, meaning "God"; hence, it involves a belief in many gods, or in a plurality of gods. History has noted many nations and societies that were polytheistic: early Romans were animistic; the people of India were pantheistic as well as polytheistic; Egyptians worshiped a multiplicity of gods, including the sun, the Nile, frogs, and even gnats.

PANTHEISM

Pantheism means that everything is God and God is everything. "God is all and all is God." Seneca said, "What is God? . . . He is all that you see and all that you do not see."[6] There are a number of different forms of pantheism:[7] *materialistic pantheism*, held by David Strauss, which believes in the eternity of matter and that matter is the cause of all life; *hylozoism*, the modern form held by Leibniz, which holds that all matter has a principle of life or psychical properties; *neutralism*, which says that life is neutral, neither mind nor matter; *idealism*, which suggests that ultimate reality is really mind, either individual mind or infinite mind; *philosophical mysticism*, which is absolute monism, teaching that all reality is a unit.

DEISM

Deists believe there is no personal God to whom man can relate. An impersonal God created the world and afterward divorced Himself from the human race and left man alone in his created world. Deists acknowledge only the transcendence of God; they deny His immanence.

REVELATION OF GOD

GENERAL REVELATION

The revelation of God in which He conveys truth about Himself to mankind is necessary to make theology possible. *Revelation* (Gk. *apokalupsis*) means "unveiling" or "disclosure." Revelation is thus God's disclosure to man, in which He reveals truth about Himself that man would not otherwise know.

General revelation, which is preliminary to salvation, reveals aspects about God and His nature to all mankind so that all humanity has an awareness of God's existence. Psalm 19:1-6 is a primary passage emphasizing the general revelation of God in the universe and in nature. The heavens speak of God's glory, for no one apart from a majestic God could bring the vast heavens into being. The earth, in all its beauty, harmony, and intricacy, reveals the handiwork of God. Romans 1:18-21 further stresses the general revelation of God and the fact that man is accountable to God. He has revealed "His invisible attributes, His eternal power and divine nature" so that mankind is without excuse (1:20).

God has also revealed Himself to all humanity through His providential provision and control (Matt. 5:45; Acts 14:15-17) so that mankind should respond to the gracious God. Furthermore, God has revealed Himself to all humanity through conscience, all mankind having an innate knowledge of Him (Rom. 2:14-15). (For further discussion of general revelation, see chapter 18, "Bibliology: Doctrine of the Bible.")

SPECIAL REVELATION

Special revelation is narrower than general revelation. While all mankind is the recipient of general revelation, not all are the recipients of special revelation.

There are many examples of special revelation. God revealed Himself through dreams and in visions to certain people. He spoke audibly to some and through theophanies to others. A *theophany* is a visible manifestation of God, usually thought of as an Old Testament occurrence. However, the greater emphasis of special revelation is twofold: God's revelation through Scriptures and through Jesus Christ. The biblical writers were carried along by the Holy Spirit in writing the Scriptures, assuring the accuracy of what was written. An inerrant record of God's disclosure is necessary for man to have a true understanding of God's Person and works.

This infallible record also reveals Jesus Christ, another aspect of special revelation. And Christ, in turn, has revealed the Father to mankind. The word *exegesis* ("to draw out; to explain") is derived from the Greek word translated "explained" (*exegesato*) in John 1:18. In that text the expression stresses that through His words (teachings) and works (miracles) Christ has explained the Father to mankind. A major emphasis of John's gospel is that Jesus came to reveal the Father. (For further discussion of special revelation, see chap. 18, "Bibliology: Doctrine of the Bible.")

ATTRIBUTES OF GOD

DEFINITION

The categorization and identification of God's attributes is somewhat arbitrary as can be seen by the variety in the following chart. Some identify a separate category (apart from attributes) for identifying the Person of God, listing features such as spirituality, personality, immensity, and eternity. A number of theologians such as Louis Berkhof, Charles Hodge, William Shedd, and Herman Bavinck follow with some variations the categories set forth in the Westminster Confession. Others such as J. Oliver Buswell, Jr., and Charles Ryrie refuse to categorize the attributes. It does seem helpful to assemble the characteristics of God systematically.

The attributes of God may be defined as "those distinguishing characteristics of the divine nature which are inseparable from the idea of God and which constitute the basis and ground for his various manifestations to his creatures."[8] God's attributes are to be distinguished from His works. God's attributes do not "add" anything to God; they reveal His nature. Gordon Lewis provides a comprehensive definition.

> God is an invisible, personal, and living Spirit, distinguished from all other spirits by several kinds of attributes: metaphysically God is self-existent, eternal, and unchanging; intellectually God is omniscient, faithful, and wise; ethically God is just, merciful, and loving; emotionally God detests evil, is longsuffering, and is compassionate; existentially God is free, authentic, and omnipotent; relationally God is transcendent in being, immanent universally in providential activity, and immanent with His people in redemptive activity.[9]

God's attributes are usually classified under two categories. The pairs of titles that are used depends on which of many contrasts the theologian wishes to emphasize. More frequent classifications include *absolute* and *relative, incommunicable* and *communicable (intransitive* and *transitive),* or *moral* and *non-moral.* In the study of God's attributes it is important not to exalt one attribute over another; when that is done it presents a caricature of God. It is all the attributes of God taken together that provide an understanding of the nature and Person of God. As already indicated, the following categorization, which follows the divisions of A. H. Strong, is somewhat arbitrary like any other listing.

ABSOLUTE ATTRIBUTES

Spirituality. God is spirit (not a spirit) who does not have corporeity or physical form (John 4:24). A body localizes, but God as spirit is everywhere; He cannot be limited. Although God does not have a body, He is nonetheless a substance but not material. Spirituality goes further than simply identifying God as not having a body; it also means He is the source of all life. The prohibition of Exodus 20:4 was given because God does not have a physical form, hence, it is wrong to make any likeness of Him. The many references to God's physical features (cf. Gen. 3:8; 1 Kings 8:29; Ps. 34:15; Isa. 65:2) are anthropomorphisms (figurative language giving God human characteristics used to attempt to make Him understandable).

Self-existence. God's self-existence means "He has the ground of His existence in Himself. . . . God is independent in His Being, but also . . . He is independent in everything else; in His virtues, decrees, works, and . . . causes everything to depend on Him."[10] Exodus 3:14 emphasizes His self-existence in His identification, "I AM WHO I AM." The verb *to be* emphasizes He has continual existence in Himself. John 5:26 further stresses that the Father has life in Himself. An unborn child is dependent on its mother for life; animals are dependent on their surroundings for life; trees and plants are dependent on sun and rain for life; every living thing is dependent on someone or something else but God is independent and existent in Himself (Dan. 5:23; Acts 17:28).

Immutability. Immutability "is that perfection of God by which He is devoid of all change, not only in His Being, but also in His perfections, and in His purposes and promises . . . and is free from all accession or diminution and from all growth or decay in His Being or perfections."[11] Change is always for better or for worse, but since God is absolute perfection, improvement or deterioration are impossible for Him. Malachi 3:6 teaches the doctrine of immutability: "I, the Lord, do not change." James 1:17 indicates there is no variation or shifting shadow with God. There is change throughout the world from year to year but God does not change in His Person nor in His response to His creatures. The value of this doctrine is enormous:

THE ATTRIBUTES OF GOD: VARIETIES OF CATEGORIZATION

Theologians	Categories	Attributes
Henry C. Thiessen Vernon D. Doerksen	Non-moral	Omnipresence Omniscience Omnipotence Immutability
	Moral	Holiness Righteousness and Justice Goodness and Mercy Truth
Augustus Hopkins Strong	Absolute/Immanent	Spirituality: life, personality Infinity: self-existence, immutability, unity Perfection: truth, love, holiness
	Relative/Transitive	Related to time and space: eternity, immensity Related to creation: omnipresence, omniscience, omnipotence Related to moral beings: truth and faithfulness mercy and goodness (transitive love), justice and righteousness (transitive holiness)

(continued next page)

The Attributes of God: Varieties of Categorization
(continued)

Theologians	Categories	Attributes
William G. T. Shedd Charles Hodge Louis Berkhof Herman Bavinck	Incommunicable	Shedd/Hodge: self-existence, simplicity, infinity, eternity, immutability Berkhof: self-existence, immutability, unity, infinity (perfection, eternity, immensity) Bavinck: independence, self-sufficiency, immutability, infinity: eternity, immensity (omniprescence); oneness (numerical, qualitative)
	Communicable	Shedd/Hodge: wisdom, benevolence, holiness, justice, compassion, truth Berkhof: spirituality intellectual knowledge wisdom veracity moral goodness (love, grace, mercy, longsuffering) holiness righteousness remunerative justice retributive justice sovereignty sovereign will sovereign power Bavinck: Life and Spirit spirituality invisibility Perfect in self-consciousness knowledge, omniscience wisdom veracity Ethical nature goodness righteousness holiness Lord, King, Sovereign will freedom omnipotence Absolute Blessedness perfection blessedness glory

The Attributes of God: Varieties of Categorization
(continued)

Theologians	Categories	Attributes
Millard J. Erickson	Greatness	Spirituality Personality Life Infinity Constancy

	Goodness	Moral Purity
		  holiness
		  righteousness
		  justice
		Integrity
		  genuineness
		  veracity
		  faithfulness
		Love
		  benevolence
		  grace
		  mercy
		  persistence

Gordon R. Lewis	Metaphysically	Self-existent Eternal Unchanging
	Intellectually	Omniscient Faithful Wise
	Ethically	Holy Righteous Loving
	Emotionally	Detests evil Long-suffering Compassionate
	Existentially	Free Authentic Omnipotent
	Relationally	Transcendent in being Immanent universally in providential activity Immanent with His people in redemptive activity

since God does not change, His love and His promises forever remain certain. For example, He will never change concerning His promise in John 3:16.

Unity. Two thoughts are expressed in the unity of God. First, it emphasizes that God is one numerically. It was this belief that set Israel apart from her polytheistic neighbors. Part of Israel's daily worship was the recitation of the Shema (Deut. 6:4) which affirmed, "Hear, O Israel! The Lord is our God, the Lord is one!" This statement was a declaration of monotheism, affirming that God is one in His essence and cannot be divided. It also affirmed Him as absolutely unique; there is none other that can be compared with Him (cf. Ex. 15:11).[12] The emphasis on God as numerically one is also stressed in 1 Timothy 2:5 and 1 Corinthians 8:6. Second, the unity of God stresses that God is not a composite and cannot be divided into parts. The statement stresses the "inner and qualitative unity" of God.[13] Because the Lord alone is God, none other is to share His glory, hence the prohibition, "Guard yourselves from idols" (1 John 5:21).

Truth. Truth means that the facts conform to reality; truth identifies things as they are. Properly defined in relation to God, truth is "that perfection of His being by virtue of which He fully answers to the idea of the Godhead, is perfectly reliable in His revelation, and sees things as they really are."[14] First, it means He is the true God in distinction to all others; there is none like Him (Isa. 44:8-10, 45:5); second, He is the truth in that His Word and His revelation are reliable (Num. 23:19; Rom. 3:3-4; John 14:1, 2, 6; Heb. 6:18; Titus 1:2). He can be trusted. Third, He knows things as they are; He is the beginning of all knowledge and makes it available to man in order that man may have fellowship with Him. He is the truth in a comprehensive sense: "He is the source of all truth, not only in the sphere of morals and religion, but also in every field of scientific endeavor."[15]

Love. First John 4:8 indicates "God is love" while verse 10 explains how that love is displayed: "In this is love, not that we loved God, but that He loved us and sent His Son to be the propitiation for our sins." Thus, God's love may be defined as "that perfection of the divine nature by which God is eternally moved to communicate himself. It is not a mere emotional impulse, but a rational and voluntary affection, having its ground in truth and holiness and its exercise in free choice."[16] The Greek term *agape*, translated "love," is frequently used to denote God and His response to humanity (cf. John 3:16; 5:42; Rom. 5:5, 8; 8:35, 39; 1 John 4:10, 11, 19; Rev. 1:5).[17] *Agape* denotes a reasoned-out love, rather than an emotionally-based love (but not devoid of emotion)—one that loves the object irrespective of the worth of the object and even though the love may not be reciprocated.

Holiness. The basic meaning of holiness is "set apart" or "separation" (Heb. *qedosh*; Gk. *hagiazo*). Many see holiness as the foremost attribute of all because holiness pervades all the other attributes of God and is consistent with all He is and does.

Several features are embraced in the holiness of God. It has a *transcendent* emphasis, indicating "He is absolutely distinct from all His creatures and is exalted above them in infinite majesty."[18] Exodus 15:11 explains that in His holiness God is without peer and awesome—revealed in the marvelous way He delivered Israel from the Egyptians. Isaiah 57:15 describes His transcendence: He is "high and exalted" living on a "high and holy place." It has an *ethical* emphasis, indicating "He is separate from moral evil or sin. 'Holiness' points to God's majestic purity, or ethical majesty."[19] The foundation of this emphasis is Leviticus 11:44, 45, "Be holy, for I am holy." Because God is morally pure, He cannot condone evil or have any relationship to it (Ps. 11:4-6). In His holiness God is the moral and ethical standard; He is the law. He sets the standard.[20]

RELATIVE ATTRIBUTES

Some attributes may be termed "relative" because they are related to time and space.

Eternity. The eternity of God is usually understood as related to time. By definition it means that God is not limited or bound by time; with God there is no succession of events; He is above all temporal limitations. "With Him there is no distinction between the present, past, and future; but all things are equally and always present to Him."[21] His eternity is expressed in Psalm 90:2, "from everlasting to everlasting, Thou art God." God's eternity extends backward to infinity and forward to infinity. Moreover, God's eternity is also related to His eternal rule in His universal kingdom (Ps. 102:12).[22] God's eternity is also related to His name. In Exodus 3:14 He informed Moses that His name is "I AM WHO I AM." Some scholars relate His name, Lord (v. 14), to "I AM WHO I AM" and to the present tense of the Hebrew verb *hayah*, meaning "to be." Hence, God's name reflects His eternity in that He is the "continually existing One." However, this is not to suggest that time is unreal or non-existent with God. While God sees everything as an eternal now, He nonetheless, in relation to man and creation, sees a succession of events in time.

Immensity. Immensity may be defined as "that perfection of the Divine Being by which He transcends all spatial limitations, and yet is present in every point of space with His whole Being."[23] First Kings 8:27 emphasizes this truth (cf. also Isa. 66:1; Jer. 23:23, 24; Acts 7:48, 49). Solomon declared, "heaven and highest heaven cannot contain Thee." Solomon had built a magnificent temple to the Lord but recognized that God could not be contained in a temple. Unlike human bodies that are bounded and limited to space, God in His immensity is not limited or localized. In His entire Being

He fills all places, but not to the same degree. "He does not dwell on earth as He does in heaven, in animals as He does in man, in the inorganic as He does in the organic creation, in the wicked as He does in the pious, nor in the Church as He does in Christ."[24] There are also relative attributes that are related to creation, that is, they reveal some aspects of God's person in His dealings with people and creation.

Omnipresence. In the next three attributes the prefix *omni* comes from the Latin word *omnis*, meaning "all." Thus, omnipresence means God is everywhere present (this is contrasted with pantheism, which states that God is *in* everything). More specifically, omnipresence may be defined as "God, in the totality of his essence, without diffusion or expansion, multiplication or division, penetrates and fills the universe in all its parts."[25] Psalm 139:7-12 explains the omnipresence of God. From the highest heaven to the depths of the earth and sea—God is everywhere present. There is no escaping God's presence. In the definition it is noted that God is present everywhere in the totality of His person. This definition militates against the idea that God is in heaven and only His power is on earth. A distinction should be recognized between the immensity of God and the omnipresence of God. Immensity emphasizes the transcendence of God and stresses that He is not bound by space, whereas omnipresence emphasizes His immanence, filling all space, including earth. The doctrine of omnipresence is a comfort to the believer who recognizes that no calamity can befall him that God is not present with Him; it is also a warning to the disobedient person that he cannot escape the presence of God.

Omniscience. The English word *omniscience* comes from the Latin words *omnis*, meaning "all," and *scientia*, meaning "knowledge"; thus it means that God has all knowledge. A more comprehensive definition will state that God knows all things actual and possible, past, present, and future, in one eternal act.[26] A number of things should be noted about God's omniscience.

(1) God knows all things that exist in actuality (Ps. 139:1-6; 147:4; Matt. 6:8; 10:28-30). The psalmist recognized the omniscience of God in that God knew his actions, his thoughts, his words before he even spoke them, and his entire life (Ps. 139:1-4).

(2) God knows all the variables concerning things that have not occurred. Jesus knew what Tyre and Sidon would have done had the gospel been preached to them (Matt. 11:21).

(3) God knows all future events. Because God is eternal and knows all things in one eternal act, events that are future to man are an "eternal now" to God. He knew the nations that would dominate Israel (Dan. 2:36-43; 7:4-8), and He knows the events that will yet transpire upon the earth (Matt. 24-25; Rev. 6-19).

(4) God's knowledge is intuitive. It is immediate, not coming through the senses; it is simultaneous, not acquired through observation or reason; it is actual, complete, and according to reality.

Omnipotence. The term *omnipotence* signifies that God is all powerful. However, it does not suggest that because God is all powerful He can and does do anything or everything at random. A proper definition states: "God is all-powerful and able to do whatever he wills. Since his will is limited by his nature, God can do everything that is in harmony with his perfections."[27] In other words, the question, "Can God create a stone so large that He could not lift it?" is not a legitimate question. God can do all things that are in harmony with His nature and Person.

The name *Almighty* means "the mighty one" and is probably derived from the verb meaning "to be strong" (cf. Gen. 17:1; 28:3; Isa. 13:6; Ezek. 1:24; Joel 1:15). Because God is Almighty, all things are possible (Matt. 19:26). The One who has formed the unborn child (Ps. 139:13-16) and created the heavens (Jer. 32:17) can do all things; nothing is too hard for Him. He does as He pleases (Ps. 115:3) and decrees all things in accordance with His will (Eph. 1:11).

God cannot do things that are not in harmony with His nature. He cannot go back on His word (2 Tim. 2:13); He cannot lie (Heb. 6:18); He has no relationship to sin (Hab. 1:13; James 1:13). Since God is able to do as He pleases, the doctrine of God's omnipotence becomes a source of great comfort for the believer (cf. Gen. 18:14; 1 Pet. 1:5). There are also relative attributes of God that relate to morality.

Truth. In speaking of God as truth it is implied that God is all that He as God should be and that His word and revelation are completely reliable.

(1) God is the truth in His person. He is perfectly complete and completely perfect as God; He is without peer (Isa. 45:5).

(2) God is the truth in His revelation (Ps. 110:5; 1 Pet. 1:25; Matt. 5:18). It means that He is completely true in His revelation to mankind. He is reliable. Unlike a mortal, God cannot lie (Tit. 1:2; Heb. 6:18); He speaks the truth and fulfills everything that He has promised to do (Num. 23:19). God is true in that He will never abrogate His promises (Rom. 3:3-4). In concert with the Father Jesus proclaimed, "I am the truth" (John 14:6). His word was reliable; His disciples could trust Him. The application of this doctrine is of significant value. Since God is truth it means His word to mankind is absolutely reliable and can be trusted implicitly. It means He will never renege on a promise He has made, such as in John 3:16.

Mercy. A general definition of mercy is "the goodness or love of God shown to those who are in misery or distress, irrespective of their deserts."[28] The Hebrew word *chesed* in the Old Testament emphasizes "help or kindness as the grace of a superior." It stresses the faithfulness of God despite man's unfaithfulness and therefore emphasizes pity, sympathy, and love. The New Testament Greek word *eleos* also includes the idea of pity and sympathy and may be translated "loving-kindness" in a general sense.[29] God's mercy seeks both the temporal need of mankind (Ruth 1:8; Heb. 4:16) as well as the eternal salvation of people (Rom. 9:23; Eph. 2:4; Titus 3:5; 1 Pet. 1:3; Isa. 55:7); however, the latter is the stress in the New Testament. His mercy extends to Israel (Ps. 102:13) as well as to Gentiles (Rom. 11:30-32; 15:9). His mercy is free of obligation and given according to His sovereign choice (Rom. 9:15-16, 18). A concordance study of *mercy* (use a concordance that lists the usage of the Hebrew word *chesed*) reveals that God is indeed "rich in mercy," which is particularly reflected in the Psalms (cf. 5:7; 6:4; 13:5; 17:7; 18:50; 21:7; 23:6, etc.; note: the word is frequently translated "loving-kindness").

Grace. Grace may be defined as the unmerited or undeserving favor of God to those who are under condemnation. A prominent Old Testament word describing God's grace is also *chesed.*[30] This word denotes deliverance from enemies, affliction, or adversity (Ps. 6:4; 31:7, 16; 57:3; 69:13-16); enablement (Ps. 85:7); daily guidance (Ps. 143:8); forgiveness (Num. 14:19; Ps. 51:1); and preservation (Ps. 23:6; 33:18; 42:8; 94:18; 119:75, 76). The New Testament word *charis* particularly focuses on the provision of salvation in Christ.[31] Grace is reflected in God providing salvation (Rom. 3:24; Eph. 1:7; 2:8); Christ brought grace and truth (John 1:18; Rom. 1:5); the grace of Christ enabled believers to have a positional standing before God (Rom. 5:2); Christ brought life instead of death through grace (Rom. 5:17); the grace of Christ exceeded the sin of Adam (Rom. 5:15, 20); the grace of Christ dispensed spiritual gifts to all believers (Rom. 12:6; Eph. 4:7); Jews and Gentiles alike are accepted through grace (Eph. 3:2).

Justice. Justice is sometimes taken together with the righteousness of God. The justice of God means that God is entirely correct and just in all His dealings with humanity; moreover, this justice acts in accordance with His law. The justice of God, therefore, is related to man's sin. Since God's law reflects God's standard, then God is righteous and just when He judges man for His violation of God's revealed law.

The justice of God is sometimes divided into several categories. The *rectoral justice* of God recognizes God as moral ruler who, in imposing His moral law in the world, promises reward for the obedient and punishment for the disobedient (Ps. 99:4; Rom. 1:32). The *distributive justice* of God relates to the execution of the law in terms of both reward and punishment (Isa. 3:10, 11; Rom. 2:6; 1 Pet. 1:17). Distributive justice is both positive and negative. On the positive side it is termed *remunerative justice* (a reflection of divine love), which dispenses reward to the obedient (Deut. 7:9; Ps. 58:11; Rom. 2:7). On the negative side it is termed *retributive justice*, an expression of divine wrath in which God punishes the wicked (Gen. 2:17; Deut. 27:26; Gal. 3:10; Rom. 6:23). Since God is just and righteous, the punishment of evildoers is fair because they receive the just penalty due them for their sin.[32]

NAMES OF GOD

ELOHIM

Elohim is a Hebrew plural form used more than two thousand times in the Old Testament and usually termed a "plural of majesty" of the general name for God. It comes from the abbreviated name, *El*, which probably has a root meaning "to be strong" (cf. Gen. 17:1; 28:3; 35:11; Josh. 3:10) or "to be preeminent."[33] It is usually translated "God" in the English translations. Elohim emphasizes God's transcendence: He is above all others who are called God. Some understand the relationship between El and Elohim in that Elohim is simply the plural form of El; the terms seem to be interchangeable (cf. Ex. 34:14; Ps. 18:31; Deut. 32:17, 21). In some passages, such as Isaiah 31:3, El draws the distinction between God and man so that El signifies the "power and strength of God and the defenselessness of human enemies" (cf. Hos. 11:9).[34]

ADONAI

The designation *Adonai* (Heb. *Adhon* or *Adhonay*) in its root means "lord" or "master" and is usually translated "Lord" in English Bibles. *Adonai* occurs 449 times in the Old Testament and 315 times in conjunction with Yahweh. *Adhon* emphasizes the servant-master relationship (cf. Gen. 24:9) and thus suggests God's authority as Master; One who is sovereign in His rule and has absolute authority (cf. Ps. 8:1; Hos. 12:14). Adonai should probably be understood as meaning "Lord of all" or "Lord par excellence" (cf. Deut. 10:17; Josh. 3:11). It is also possible to understand Adonai as a personal address meaning "my Lord."[35]

YAHWEH

The name *Yahweh* translates the Hebrew tetragrammaton (four lettered expression) YHWH. Because the name was originally written without vowels, it is uncertain how it should be pronounced. Hence, the American Standard Version translates it "Jehovah," whereas most modern translations render it "LORD" (to distinguish it from *Adonai*, "Lord"). Jewish scholars have generally pronounced it "Adonai" instead of actually pronouncing YHWH, out of respect for the sacredness of the covenant name.

Although there is considerable discussion concerning the origin and meaning of the name, this common designation (used 6,828 times in the

Old Testament) is likely related to the verb "to be." Thus in Exodus 3:14-15 the Lord declares, "I AM WHO I AM . . . The LORD . . . has sent me to you. This is My name forever." This has particular significance to the "I AM" claims of Christ (cf. John 6:35; 8:12; 10:9, 11; 11:25; 14:6; 15:1), who in His statements claimed equality with Yahweh.

By the name *Yahweh*, God identified Himself in His personal relationship with His people, Israel, and it was to this name that Abram responded in acknowledging the Abrahamic Covenant (Gen. 12:8). By this name God brought Israel out of Egypt, delivered them from bondage, and redeemed them (Ex. 6:6; 20:2). Whereas *Elohim* and *Adonai* were designations known to other cultures, the revelation of *Yahweh* was unique to Israel.

COMPOUND NAMES

There are a number of compound forms of the name of God involving the names El (or Elohim) and Yahweh.

El Shaddai. Translated "God Almighty," it probably relates to the word *mountain* and suggests the power or strength of God. By this name God is also seen as a covenant-keeping God (Gen. 17:1; cf. vv. 1-8 where the covenant is reiterated).

El Elyon. Translated "God Most High," it emphasizes the supremacy of God. He is above all so-called gods (cf. Gen. 14:18-22). Melchizedek recognized Him as "God Most High" inasmuch as He is possessor of heaven and earth (v. 19).

El Olam. Translated the "Everlasting God," it stresses the unchanging character of God (Gen. 21:33; Isa. 40:28).

Others. There are other compound terms that are sometimes mentioned as names of God, but they may simply be descriptions of God: *Yahweh-jireh*, "The LORD Will Provide" (Gen. 22:14); *Yahweh-Nissi*, "The LORD Our Banner" (Ex. 17:15); *Yahweh-Shalom*, "The LORD is Peace" (Judg. 6:24); *Yahweh-Sabbaoth*, "The LORD of Hosts" (1 Sam. 1:3); *Yahweh-Maccaddeshcem*, "The LORD Thy Sanctifier" (Ex. 31:13); *Yahweh-Tsidkenu*, "The LORD Our Righteousness" (Jer. 23:6).

THE TRINITY OF GOD

DEFINITION OF THE TRINITY

The Trinity of God is a doctrine that is fundamental to the Christian faith; belief or disbelief in the Trinity marks orthodoxy from unorthodoxy. Human reason, however, cannot fathom the Trinity, nor can logic explain it, and, although the word itself is not found in the Scriptures, the doctrine is plainly taught in the Scriptures. The early church was forced to study the subject and affirm its truth because of the heretical teachings that arose opposing the Trinity.

The term *Trinity* is not the best one because it emphasizes only the three persons but not the unity within the Trinity. The German word *Dreiein-igkeit* ("three-oneness") better expresses the concept. A proper definition then must include the distinctness and equality of the three persons within the Trinity as well as the unity within the Trinity. The word *Triunity* may better express the doctrine.[36] A proper definition of the Trinity states: "the Trinity is composed of three united Persons without separate existence—so completely united as to form one God. The divine nature subsists in three distinctions—Father, Son, and Holy Spirit."[37]

MISINTERPRETATIONS OF THE TRINITY

Tri-theism. In early church history men such as John Ascunages and John Philoponus taught that there were three who were God but they were only related in a loose association as, for example, Peter, James, and John were as disciples. The error of this teaching was that its proponents abandoned the unity within the Trinity with the result that they taught there were three Gods rather than three Persons within one Godhead.

Sabellianism or Modalism. This teaching, originated by Sabellius (c. A.D. 200), erred in the opposite from that of Tri-theism. Although Sabellius spoke of Father, Son, and Holy Spirit, he understood all three as simply three modes of existence or three manifestations of one God. The teaching is thus also known as *modalism* because it views one God who variously manifests Himself in three modes of existence: Father, Son, and Holy Spirit.

Arianism. Arian doctrine had its roots in Tertullian, who subordinated the Son to the Father. Origen carried Tertullian's concept further by teaching that the Son was subordinate to the Father "in respect to essence." This ultimately led to Arianism, which denied the deity of Christ. Arius taught that only God was the uncreated One; because Christ was begotten of the Father it meant Christ was created by the Father. According to Arius there was a time when Christ did not exist. Arius and his teaching were condemned at the Council of Nicea in A.D. 325.

EXPLANATION OF THE TRINITY

God is one in regard to essence. Early in church history the question developed whether Christ was the same as the Father in substance or in essence. Arius taught that Christ was like the Father in substance, yet the Father was greater than Christ; hence, although some equated the terms substance and essence, the proper way to designate the Trinity became "one in essence." The essential oneness of God is linked to Deuteronomy 6:4, "Hear, O Israel! The Lord is our God, the Lord is one (Heb. *echad*, "compound unity; united one"). This statement stresses not only the uniqueness of God but also the unity of God (cf. also James 2:19). It means all three Persons possess the summation of the divine attributes but yet the essence of God is undivided. Oneness in essence also emphasizes that the three Persons of the Trinity do not act independently of one another. This was a constant theme of Jesus in rebuffing the charges of the Jews (cf. John 5:19; 8:28; 12:49; 14:10).

God is three with respect to Persons. The word *persons* tends to detract from the unity of the Trinity, and it is readily recognized that persons is an inadequate term to describe the relationship within the Trinity. Some theologians have opted for the term *subsistence*, hence, "God has three subsistences." Other words used to describe the distinctiveness of the Three are: distinction, relation, and mode. The term *persons* is nonetheless helpful inasmuch as it emphasizes not only a manifestation but also an individual personality. In suggesting God is three with respect to His Persons it is emphasized that (1) each has the same essence as God and (2) each possess the fullness of God. "In God there are no three individuals alongside of, and separate from, one another, but only personal self-distinctions within the Divine essence."[38] This is an important deviation from modalism (or Sabellianism), which teaches that one God merely manifests Himself in three various ways. This unity within three Persons is seen in Old Testament passages such as Isaiah 48:16 where the Father has sent the Messiah and the Spirit to speak to the restored nation. In Isaiah 61:1 the Father has anointed the Messiah with the Spirit for His mission. These references emphasize both the equality and the unity of the three Persons.

The three Persons have distinct relationships. Within the Trinity exists a relationship that is expressed in terms of subsistence. The Father is not begotten nor does He proceed from any person; the Son is eternally begotten from the Father (John 1:18; 3:16, 18; 1 John 4:9). The term *generation* suggests the Trinitarian relationship in that the Son is eternally begotten of the Father. The Holy Spirit eternally proceeds from the Father and the Son (John 14:26; 16:7). The word *procession* suggests the Trinitarian relationship of the Father and the Son sending the Spirit.[39] It is important to note, however, that these terms denote a *relationship* within the Trinity and do not suggest inferiority in any way. Because the terms can tend to suggest inferiority some theologians deny their usefulness.[40]

The three Persons are equal in authority. Although terms like *generation* and *procession* may be used in referring to the functioning within the Trinity, it is important to realize that the three Persons are equal in authority. The Father is recognized as authoritative and supreme (1 Cor. 8:6); the Son is also recognized as equal to the Father in every respect (John 5:21-23); the Spirit is likewise recognized as equal to the Father and the Son (cf. Matt. 12:31). (This topic will be developed further under the discussion of the deity of Christ and the deity of the Holy Spirit.)

ANCIENT DIAGRAM OF THE HOLY TRINITY

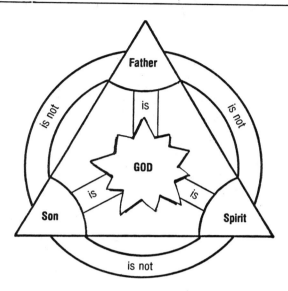

OLD TESTAMENT TEACHING

While there is no definitive or explicit statement in the Old Testament affirming the Trinity, it is fair to say that the Old Testament allows for the Trinity and implies that God is a triune being in a number of passages. In the creation account of Genesis 1 both God the Father and the Holy Spirit are seen in the work of creation. It is stated that God created heaven and earth (Gen. 1:1) while the Holy Spirit hovered over the earth to infuse it with vitality (Gen. 1:2). The term *God* in Genesis 1:1 is *Elohim*, which is a plural form for God. Even though this does not explicitly teach the Trinity, it certainly allows for it as seen in the plural pronouns "us" and "our" in Genesis 1:26. In Psalm 110:1 David recognized a distinction of persons between "LORD" and "my Lord." David implies that Messiah is One greater than an ordinary human king because he refers to Messiah with an ascription of deity, "my Lord." In the prophecy concerning Christ in Isaiah 7:14 the Lord makes it clear that the One born of a virgin will also be Immanuel, "God with us." It is an attestation to Messiah's deity. Two additional passages previously mentioned that imply the Trinity are Isaiah 48:16 and 61:1. In both of these passages all three Persons of the Godhead are mentioned and seen as distinct from one another.

NEW TESTAMENT TEACHING

Ultimately, to demonstrate that the Scriptures teach the Trinity, two things must be affirmed: that there is only one God, and that all three Persons are called God. While a fuller demonstration of the deity of each member of the Godhead is discussed under the respective categories, the teaching can be concisely stated here. The *Father* is called God (1 Cor. 8:6); the *Son* is called God (Heb. 1:8-10); the *Holy Spirit* is called God (Acts 5:3-4); God is *one God* (Deut. 6:4). Combining these four statements affirms the Trinity. There are additional New Testament passages in which the Father, Son, and Holy Spirit are seen in such a relationship as to affirm both their unity and equality.

In the act of making disciples Jesus commanded that the apostles were to baptize the new disciples "in the name of the Father and the Son and the Holy Spirit" (Matt. 28:18). It seems clear that the equality as well as the unity of the three Persons is intended. In Mary's conception the Trinity is involved: the Holy Spirit came upon Mary, the power of God overshadowed her, and the resultant offspring was called the Son of God (Luke 1:35). All three are also seen as distinct at the baptism of Jesus (a denial of modalism; cf. Luke 3:21-22). In John 14:16 the unity of the three is again mentioned: the Son asks[41] the Father who sends the Spirit to indwell believers forever. The unity of the three is clear. In Romans 8:9-11 all three are mentioned as indwelling the believer. The benediction of 2 Corinthians 13:14 surely is a strong affirmation of both the equality and unity of Father, Son, and Holy Spirit (cf. also 1 Cor. 2:4-8; Rev. 1:4-5).

DIFFICULTIES WITH THE DOCTRINE

Those who deny the Trinity sometimes object to the use of certain terms that seem to imply that Christ is inferior to the Father, which if true, would deny the Trinity. Several of these problematic terms are noted here.

Meaning of begotten. The term *begotten* is used in several senses with respect to Christ. First, it is evident from Matthew 1:20 that Christ was begotten in His humanity but not in His deity. Christ was God from all eternity (Mic. 5:2), but at Bethlehem He took to Himself an additional nature, namely, a human nature. The Holy Spirit superintended Mary's conception to assure the sinlessness of the humanity of Christ. It is with reference to the humanity of Christ that the term *begotten* is used; it could never be used with reference to His deity. Begotten does not relate to Jesus' being the Son of God. In time and space Jesus was declared to be the Son of God (Ps. 2:7; Acts 13:32-33; Rom. 1:4). These verses all emphasize that Jesus' Sonship is vindicated or verified as a result of the resurrection, but the resurrection did not make Him the Son of God. Jesus has been the son of God from eternity. Thus, Psalm 2:7 and Acts 13:33 emphasize that begotten refers to the public declaration of the Sonship of Christ (but not the origination of the Sonship).[42]

Meaning of first-born. Those who deny the deity of Christ frequently do so by referring to the term *first-born*, suggesting that if the term relates to Christ it must imply He had a beginning in time. However, both a lexical study of the word as well as a contextual study of the usages provides a different solution to the meaning for first-born. In its Old Testament culture the predominant emphasis was on the status of the oldest son. He enjoyed the double portion of the inheritance (Deut. 21:17), privileges over other family members (Gen. 27:1-4, 35-37), preferential treatment (Gen. 43:33), and the respect of others (Gen. 37:22). Figuratively, the word denotes priority or supremacy (Ex. 4:22; Jer. 31:9)[43] and is so used of Christ. In Colossians 1:18 where Christ is referred to as first-born the meaning is clear: as first-born, Christ is Head of the church and preeminent in everything.[44] In Hebrews 1:6 the supremacy of Christ as the first-born is seen in that angels worship Him. Only God is worshiped. Psalm 89:27 is perhaps one of the clearest explanations of the term *first-born.* This is an example of synthetic poetry in Hebrew in which the second line explains the first. In this Messianic Psalm God affirms that Messiah will be the first-born, that is, the highest of the kings of the earth. *First-born* is explained as ruling over the kings of the entire earth. From both a linguistic and exegetical study it is clear that *first-born* draws attention to the preeminent status of Jesus as Messiah.

Meaning of only-begotten. The term *only-begotten* (Gk. *monogenes*) (cf. John 1:14, 18; 3:16; 1 John 4:9) does not suggest a beginning point in time but rather means that Jesus as the only-begotten Son of God is "unique," "the only one of its kind," "the only example of its category."[45] Only-begotten "is used to mark out Jesus uniquely above all earthly and heavenly beings."[46] In Genesis 22:2, 12, 16 it reflects the concept of "only, precious" as Isaac was viewed by his father, Abraham.[47] John the apostle describes the glory radiated by the unique Son of God—no one else radiated the glory of the Father (John 1:14); moreover, the Son "explained" the Father—no one but the unique Son could explain the Father. It was the unique Son whom God sent into the world; eternal life was provided only through the unique Son of God (John 3:16). In examining the passages it is evident that *only-begotten* does not suggest a coming into existence, but rather it expresses the *uniqueness* of the person. Christ was unique as the Son of God, sent by the Father from heaven.

DECREES OF GOD

DEFINITION OF GOD'S DECREE

The decrees of God have been established in eternity past and have reference to God's sovereign control over every realm and over all events.

The decrees are reflected in Ephesians 1:11 in that He "works all things after the counsel of His will." Question 7 of the Westminster Shorter Confession states: "The decrees of God are his eternal purpose, according to the counsel of his will, whereby, for his own glory, he hath foreordained whatsoever comes to pass." Ultimately, there are only two options. Either God is sovereign and has absolute control over the world and universe *or* God does not have sovereign control, and the world and universe carry on in defiance of His holy will. Of course, the former is true; the world does not operate by chance. God has absolute control. Yet it must also be affirmed that man is responsible for sinful actions. God is never the author of sin nor does His sovereignty eliminate man's responsibility.

CHARACTERISTICS OF GOD'S DECREE

The decree is a single plan encompassing all things. Nothing is outside the scope of God's sovereign rule. Ephesians 1:11 emphasizes "all things" are brought to pass by His decree. Because everything is encompassed in God's sovereign plan it is sometimes spoken of in the singular—it is one decree.

The decree covering all things was formed in eternity past but is manifested in time. The believer was chosen by God in eternity past (Eph. 1:4; the phrase "before the foundation of the world" = "from all eternity").[48] The believer's salvation and calling is once more related to God's determination from eternity past (2 Tim. 1:9). In this passage it is emphasized that it is according to "His own purpose." Purpose (Gk. *prothesin*) emphasizes the resolve or decision of God in His calling and saving the believer. The decision for Christ to take on humanity and shed His blood for humanity was also made "before the foundation of the world" (1 Pet. 1:20).

The decree is a wise plan because God Who is wise has planned what is best. In Romans 9-11 Paul discusses the sovereignty of God and His election of Israel and concludes this "difficult to comprehend" section with a doxology extolling the wisdom of God in His sovereign acts (Rom. 11:33-36). God's wisdom and knowledge cannot be comprehended, and His decisions cannot be tracked as footprints in the sand. God has consulted no one and no one has advised Him. But because God knows all things He controls and guides all events *for His glory and for our good* (cf. Ps. 104:24; Prov. 3:19).

The decree is according to God's sovereign will—He does as He pleases. God does not adjust His plan according to the events of human history; instead, His decree governs human history. Daniel 4:35 is all encompassing: God "does according to His will" in the angelic realm as well as with the inhabitants of earth. In the context of the book of Daniel God determines the course of human history and the rulers of the kingdoms of earth (Dan. 2:21, 31-45). God has established His decrees in freedom and in independence of everything and everyone else.

The decree has two aspects. (1) The directive will of God. There are some things in which God is the author; He actively brings about the events. He creates (Isa. 45:18); He controls the universe (Dan. 4:35); He establishes kings and governments (Dan. 2:21); He elects people to be saved (Eph. 1:4).

(2) The permissive will of God. Even though God has determined all things, He may actively bring them about Himself, or He may bring them about through secondary causes. Sinful acts, for example, do not frustrate the plan of God, but neither is God the author of them. They are within the scope of God's decree and are part of His eternal plan and purpose, but man is nonetheless responsible for sinful acts. Hence, "a distinction must be made between the decree and its execution."[49] All acts—including sinful acts—conform to the eternal plan of God, but He is not directly the author of all acts. For example, when the people of Israel demanded a king to rule over them, they sinned against the Lord (1 Sam. 8:5-9, 19-22). But the Lord had foreordained that kings would come from Abraham's lineage (Gen. 17:6; 35:11), culminating in Messiah. The people sinned, but God's plan was being executed.

The purpose of the decree is the glory of God. The creation of the world is designed to reveal God's glory (Ps. 19:1). The vastness of the heavens and the beauty of the flora and fauna of earth reflect the glory of God. God's sovereign act whereby He predestined believers to salvation (Eph. 1:4-5) is "to the praise of the glory of His grace" (Eph. 1:6, 11-12). God is glorified in the display of His unconditional grace (cf. Rom. 9:23; Rev. 4:11).

Although all things are encompassed in the decree, man is responsible for sinful actions. This is known as an antinomy and is important in understanding the concept that although God is sovereign and has decreed all things, nonetheless man is responsible for sinful acts. *Antinomy* comes from the Greek word *anti*, meaning "against," and *nomos*, meaning "law," hence, an antinomy is something that is contrary to law or contrary to human understanding. An antinomy, of course, is such only in the mind of man; with God there is no antinomy.

In Acts 2:23 Peter explained that Jesus died because of the "predetermined plan and foreknowledge of God." "Plan" (Gk. *boule*) stresses the predetermined will or decision of God. Foreknowledge is a rough equivalent and suggests not merely previous knowledge but action. Hence, Christ died because of the decision of God in eternity; nevertheless, Peter held the people responsible for killing Christ saying, "you nailed to a cross by the hands of godless men and put Him to death." Although Christ's death was a result of the decree and plan of God, wicked men were responsible for His death.

Similarly, in Habakkuk 1:6 God explained to the prophet that He was raising up the Chaldeans to chastise His disobedient people in Judah. But when the Chaldeans concluded their work, God would hold them responsible (Hab. 1:11). Although God has decreed all things, man is responsible for his sins.

Some aspects of the decree are carried out by people. This distinguishes the decree of God from fatalism. The decree cannot be fatalism because the decree also involves the means, not only the end. For example, the decree of God involves electing certain ones to salvation, yet no one is saved apart from evangelism. On the one hand, the decree says the believer is chosen in Christ before the foundation of the world (Eph. 1:4), yet someone must present the gospel to the person to enable him to believe and be saved (Acts 16:31). In the matter of salvation, God uses people in evangelism to carry out His decree.

MANIFESTATION OF THE DECREE[50]

In the material realm. The creation of the world and universe in all its aspects comes under the divine decree of God (Ps. 33:6-11). Verse 6 emphasizes that heaven and earth were both created by the decree of God and He governs them from generation to generation (v. 11). Moreover, God has also appointed the nations and their boundaries (Deut. 32:8; Acts 17:26). The length of human life has also been decreed (Job 14:5), as well as the manner of our departure (John 21:19; 2 Tim. 4:6-8).

In the social realm. God has decreed the family (Gen. 2:18) and ordained that marriage be indissoluble (Matt. 19:1-9); the decree of marriage also involved children (Gen. 1:28; 9:1, 7). God also established government (Rom. 13:1-7); moreover, He is the One who establishes and removes kings (Dan. 2:21; 4:35). God sovereignly chose Israel and established her as a nation (Gen. 12:1-3; Ex. 19:5-6). Despite Israel's failure God has decreed her future restoration under Messiah (Joel 3:1-21; Zech. 14:1-11), and all nations will come under Messiah's rule (Psalm 2; Zech. 14:12-21). Although the church was decreed from eternity, it was not revealed until the New Testament that God would unite Jew and Gentile into one in the Body of Christ (Eph. 2:15; 3:1-13).

In the spiritual realm. (1) The order of the decrees. Debate has gone on for centuries in attempting to relate the sovereignty of God and man's freedom of choice in salvation. This difference is reflected in how different people have viewed the order of the decrees. The accompanying chart reflects the range of belief concerning election, the Fall, and the application of grace for eternal life.[51]

(2) Sin and the decrees. Additional issues related to sin may be summarized as follows. God may permit men to manifest evil (Rom. 1:24-28).

ORDER OF THE DECREES*

Supralapsarian (Limited Atonement)	Infralapsarian (Limited Atonement)	Amyraldian (Unlimited Atonement)	Lutheran	Wesleyan	Roman Catholic
Election of some to eternal life.	Permission of fall of man equals guilt, corruption, total inability.	Permission of fall of man equals corruption, guilt, moral inability.	Permission of fall of man equals guilt, corruption, total inability.	Permission of fall of man equals guilt, corruption, total inability.	Permission of fall of man equals loss of supernatural righteousness.
Permission of fall of man equals guilt, corruption and total inability.	Election of some to life in Christ.	Gift of Christ to render salvation possible to all.	Gift of Christ to render satisfaction for sins of world.	Gift of Christ to render satisfaction for sins of world.	Gift of Christ to offer satisfaction for all human sins.
Gift of Christ to redeem the elect and ground offer to all.	Gift of Christ to redeem his elect and ground offer to all.	Election of some for gift of moral ability.	Gift of means of grace to communicate saving grace.	Remission of original sin to all and gift to all of sufficient grace.	Institution of church, the sacraments, to apply satisfaction of Christ
Gift of the Holy Spirit to save the redeemed.	Gift of the Holy Spirit to save the redeemed.	Gift of the Holy Spirit to work moral ability in the elect.	Predestination to life of those who do not resist the means of grace.	Predestination of life of those who improve sufficient grace.	Application of satisfaction of Christ through sacraments, under operation of second causes.
Satisfaction of all the redeemed and regenerated.	Satisfaction of all the redeemed and regenerated.	Sanctification by the Spirit.	Sanctification through the means of grace.	Sanctification of all who cooperate with sufficient grace.	Building up in holy life of all to whom the sacraments are continued.

*Benjamin B. Warfield, **The Plan of Salvation** (Reprint. Grand Rapids: Eerdmans, 1977), p. 31.

God is never, however, the author of evil, nor does He solicit people to sin (James 1:13). God may directly prevent evil (2 Thess. 2:7). God may direct evil acts of men to accomplish His purpose (Acts 4:27-28). God does not make men sin, yet all things are within the scope of God's sovereign plan. God determines the boundary of evil and overrules evil (Job 1:6-12). God limited Satan in testing Job.

(3) Salvation and the decrees. God chose and predestined believers to salvation from before the foundation of the world (Eph. 1:4-5; 2 Tim. 1:9). He chose Jews and Gentiles united as one body in Christ (Eph. 3:11). God chose believers for individual blessing (Rom. 8:28).

OBJECTIONS ANSWERED

Objection: The decree does not allow for man's free will. The decree allows for man's responsible action, and man is held responsible for sinful choices. The concept of God's sovereignty and man's responsibility is an antinomy but is such only in the mind of man. With God there is no inconsistency in this; moreover, the biblical writers do not view it as an inconsistency (cf. Acts 2:23—Peter saw no contradiction in this). It should also be noted that God does not bring about all aspects of His decree through His directive will but rather through secondary causes, hence, sinful man acts according to his sinful nature. Man acts in harmony with his nature, and all these acts are within the scope of God's decree and man is held responsible for them. Additionally, there is a difference between an unbeliever and a believer. An unbeliever is compelled by his sinful nature to make decisions on the basis of his fallen nature; he is incapable of making righteous choices. The believer has greater latitude in making decisions because he is capable of making righteous choices.

Objection: The decree makes it unnecessary to preach the gospel. The objection relates once more to the antinomy in the mind of man. Paul taught that God had predestined people to salvation (Eph. 1:5-11) and taught the doctrine of election (Rom. 1:1; 8:30; 9:11), but with equal fervency Paul taught the necessity of preaching the gospel in order that people might be saved (Acts 16:31; Rom. 10:14-15; 1 Cor. 9:16). People are lost not because it has not been decreed for them to be saved but because they have refused to believe the gospel.

CONCLUSIONS

The decrees of God have very practical ramifications. (1) We should stand in awe of a great God who is wise, powerful, and loving. (2) We can entrust our entire lives to an Almighty God. (3) We should rejoice in the wonder of our salvation—that we were the choice of God in eternity past. (4) We should rest in peace as we observe the tumultuous world events, knowing that God is sovereignly controlling all things (this does not imply indifference). (5) God holds people responsible for sin. Although sin does not frustrate the plan of God, neither is He the author of it. (6) This teaching militates against the pride of man. Man, in his pride, desires to run his own life; the recognition that God is sovereign is humbling.

Notes on Theology Proper

1. J. Oliver Buswell, Jr., *A Systematic Theology of the Christian Religion* (Grand Rapids: Zondervan, 1962), pp. 82-84. Buswell discusses the necessity for the cosmological argument. The only other option is the eternality of the universe which can be refuted through the second law of thermodynamics.

2. Henry C. Thiessen, *Lectures in Systematic Theology*, revised by Vernon D. Doerksen (Grand Rapids: Eerdmans, 1977), p. 28.

3. Lewis Sperry Chafer, *Systematic Theology*, 8 vols. (Dallas: Dallas Seminary, 1947) 1:155, 157.

4. Thiessen, *Lectures in Systematic Theology*, pp. 32-33. See this work for a response to the anti-theistic theories. For a further refutation also see Lewis Sperry Chafer, *Systematic Theology*, 1:162-78.

5. Many excellent works have been written refuting the false teachings of evolution, particularly through the writing of biblicists like Bolten Davidheiser, Henry Morris, and others. Some works that ought to be consulted are John C. Whitcomb, Jr., *The Early Earth* (Grand Rapids: Baker, 1972); Henry M. Morris, *The Twilight of Evolution* (Grand Rapids: Baker, 1963); S. Maxwell Coder and George F. Howe, *The Bible, Science, and Creation* (Chicago: Moody, 1965); and Henry M. Morris, *The Biblical Basis for Modern Science* (Grand Rapids: Baker, 1984). The student researching this subject should consult the material provided by the Creation Research Society of San Diego.

6. Chafer, *Systematic Theology*, 1:174.

7. Thiessen, *Lectures in Systematic Theology*, pp. 34-38. See this work for a refutation of the various forms of pantheism as well as the other anti-theistic theories.

8. A. H. Strong, *Systematic Theology* (Valley Forge, Pa.: Judson, 1907), p. 244.

9. Gordon R. Lewis, "God, Attributes of," in Walter A. Elwell, ed., *Evangelical Dictionary of Theology* (Grand Rapids: Baker, 1984), p. 451.

10. Louis Berkhof, *Systematic Theology* (Grand Rapids: Eerdmans, 1941), p. 58.

11. Ibid.

12. S. R. Driver, *A Critical and Exegetical Commentary on Deuteronomy in The International Critical Commentary* 3rd ed., (Edinburgh: Clark, 1978), p. 90.

13. Berkhof, *Systematic Theology*, p. 62.

14. Ibid., p. 69.

15. Ibid.

16. Thiessen, *Lectures in Systematic Theology*, p. 86.

17. See Leon Morris, *Testaments of Love* (Grand Rapids: Eerdmans, 1981) for a definitive discussion of the biblical nature and meaning of love.

18. Berkhof, *Systematic Theology*, p. 73.

19. Ibid.

20. Wm. G. T. Shedd, *Dogmatic Theology*, 3 vols. (Reprint. Nashville: Nelson, 1980) 1:362-63.

21. Charles Hodge, *Systematic Theology*, 3 vols. (Reprint. London: Clarke, 1960), 1:385.

22. See Alva J. McClain, *The Greatness of the Kingdom* (Chicago: Moody, 1968), pp. 22-36, for a discussion tracing God's universal kingdom throughout eternity.

23. Berkhof, *Systematic Theology*, p. 60.

24. Ibid., p. 61.

25. Strong, *Systematic Theology*, p. 279.

26. It is important to recognize that in speaking of God's knowledge or foreknowledge it does not imply a passive awareness of what will happen, but in connection with His knowledge or foreknowledge He has decreed all events. Compare Shedd, *Dogmatic Theology*, 1:353-58, 396-99.

27. Thiessen, *Lectures in Systematic Theology*, p. 82.

28. Buswell, *A Systematic Theology of the Christian Religion*, p. 72.

29. Rudolph Bultmann, *"Eleos,"* in Gerhard Kittel, ed., *Theological Dictionary of the New Testament*, 10 vols. (Grand Rapids: Eerdmans, 1964), 2:479-85.

30. The Hebrew word *chesed* really denotes "loving-kindness," and the concept overlaps into both mercy and grace.

31. Charles C. Ryrie, *The Grace of God* (Chicago: Moody, 1963), pp. 9-26. This is a most helpful book on the entire subject of grace and is highly recommended for a proper understanding of this most important doctrine.

32. See Wm. G. T. Shedd, *Dogmatic Theology*, 1:365-85, for an excellent, extensive discussion of the subject.

33. Frank M. Cross, *"El,"* in *Theological Dictionary of the Old Testament*, 6 vols., revised, edited by G. Johannes Botterweck and Helmer Ringgren (Grand Rapids: Eerdmans, 1977), 1:244.

34. Helmer Ringgren, *"Elohim,"* in *Theological Dictionary of the Old Testament*, 1:273-74.

35. Merrill F. Unger and William White, Jr., eds., *Nelson's Expository Dictionary of the Old Testament* (Nashville: Nelson, 1980), pp. 228-29; and Otto Eissfeldt, *"Adhon,"* in *Theological Dictionary of the Old Testament*, 1:59-72.

36. Ryrie, *A Survey of Bible Doctrine*, p. 30.

37. Chafer, *Systematic Theology*, 1:276.

38. Berkhof, *Systematic Theology*, p. 87.

39. Ibid., pp. 88-89.

40. Buswell, *Systematic Theology*, 1:111-12, 119-20.

41. It is noteworthy that Jesus used *eroteso* from *erotao*, a term used by one on equal footing or familiarity. Jesus never used *aiteo*, an inferior requesting something of one who is superior. Compare W. E. Vine, *An Expository Dictionary of New Testament Words* (Westwood, N.J.: Revell, 1940), 1:79; H. Schonweiss, *"Aiteo,"* in Colin Brown, ed., *The New International Dictionary of New Testament Theology*, 4 vols. (Grand Rapids: Zondervan, 1976), 2:856-57.

42. See Buswell's helpful discussion, *Systematic Theology*, 1:106-9.

43. J. E. Rosscup, "First-born," in Merrill C. Tenney, ed., *Zondervan Pictorial Encyclopedia of the Bible*, 5 vols. (Grand Rapids: Zondervan, 1975), 2:540-41.

44. The participle *proteuon* emphasizes kind of action and draws attention to Christ in His preeminent status. The emphatic position of *proteuon* intensifies the emphasis.

45. William F. Arndt and F. Wilbur Gingrich, *A Greek-English Lexicon of the New Testament and Other Early Christian Literature*, revised by F. Wilbur Gingrich and Frederick W. Danker (Chicago: University of Chicago, 1979), p. 527; see also D. Moody, "God's Only Son: The Translation of John 3:16 in the Revised Standard Version," *Journal of Biblical Literature* 72 (1953), pp. 213-19.

46. Karl-Heinz Bartels, *"Monos,"* in *New International Dictionary of New Testament Theology*, 2:725.

47. Raymond E. Brown, "The Gospel According to John I-XII" in *The Anchor Bible*, 34 vols., 2d ed. (Garden City, N.Y.: Doubleday, 1966), 1:13-14.

48. Fritz Rienecker, *Linguistic Key to Greek New Testament*, translated and edited by Cleon Rogers (Grand Rapids: Zondervan, 1982), p. 521.

49. Berkhof, *Systematic Theology*, pp. 102-3 gives a clarifying discussion of the distinction between God enacting His decree or God determining His decree through secondary causes.

50. I am indebted to Thiessen, *Lectures in Systematic Theology*, pp. 104-10, for this section. This carefully organized and discussed section is most helpful in understanding this teaching.

51. See Benjamin B. Warfield, *The Plan of Salvation*, Revised (Grand Rapids: Eerdmans, 1977); Walter A Elwell, ed., *Evangelical Dictionary of Theology*, pp. 560-61, 1059-60; Herman Bavinck, *The Doctrine of God* (Grand Rapids: Baker, 1979), pp. 382-94; and Buswell, *Systematic Theology*, 2:134-36.

For Further Study on Theology Proper

THE EXISTENCE OF GOD

** Lewis Sperry Chafer. *Systematic Theology.* Dallas: Dallas Seminary, 1947. Pp. 162-78.

* Walter Elwell. ed. *Evangelical Dictionary of Theology.* Grand Rapids: Baker, 1984.

** Augustus Hopkins Strong. *Systematic Theology.* Valley Forge, Pa.: Judson, 1907. Pp. 90-110.

* Henry C. Thiessen. *Lectures in Systematic Theology.* Revised by Vernon D. Doerksen. Grand Rapids: Eerdmans, 1979. Pp. 32-40.

THE ATTRIBUTES OF GOD

** Herman Bavinck. *The Doctrine of God.* Grand Rapids: Baker, 1979. Pp. 113-251. This is a comprehensive and valuable study for the serious student.

** Lewis Sperry Chafer. *Systematic Theology*, 8 vols. Dallas: Dallas Seminary, 1947. 1:187-224.

** Stephen Charnock, *The Existence and Attributes of God,* 2 vols. Reprint. Grand Rapids: Baker, 1979. This is a classic and the most important work on the attributes of God.

** Millard J. Erickson. *Christian Theology.* Grand Rapids: Baker, 1983. 1:263-319.

* William Evans. *The Great Doctrines of the Bible*. Chicago: Moody, 1949. Pp. 28-48.
** Charles Hodge. *Systematic Theology*, 3 vols. Reprint. London: Clarke, 1960. 1:368-441.
* Robert P. Lightner. *The God of the Bible*. Grand Rapids: Baker, 1978. Pp. 88-106.
* J. I. Packer. *Knowing God*. Downers Grove, Ill.: InterVarsity, 1973. Pp. 67-158. A most helpful work, popularly written.
* Charles C. Ryrie. *A Survey of Bible Doctrine*. Chicago: Moody, 1972. Pp. 17-25.
** Wm. G. T. Shedd. *Dogmatic Theology*, 3 vols. Reprint. Nashville: Nelson, 1980. 1:334-92. A superlative treatment by an outstanding theologian. The serious student should interact with Shedd.
* Henry C. Thiessen. *Lectures in Systematic Theology*. Revised by Vernon D. Doerksen. Grand Rapids: Eerdmans, 1977. Pp. 75-88.
* A. W. Tozer. *The Knowledge of the Holy*. New York: Harper, 1961. One of the finest, popularly written treatments on the subject. This ought to be read first.

THE NAMES OF GOD

** Herman Bavinck. *The Doctrine of God*. Grand Rapids: Baker, 1979. Pp. 83-110.
** Louis Berkhof. *Systematic Theology*. Grand Rapids: Eerdmans, 1941. Pp. 47-51.
* Robert P. Lightner. *The God of the Bible*. Grand Rapids: Baker, 1978. Pp. 107-23.
* T. E. McComiskey. "God, Names of." In Walter A. Elwell, ed., *Evangelical Dictionary of Theology*. Grand Rapids: Baker, 1985. Pp. 464-68.
* Charles C. Ryrie. *A Survey of Bible Doctrine*. Chicago: Moody, 1972. Pp. 25-29.
** Ethelbert Stauffer. *"El* and *Elohim* in the Old Testament." In *Theological Dictionary of the New Testament*, 10 vols., edited by Gerhard Kittel and Gerhard Friedrich. Grand Rapids: Eerdmans, 1965. 3:79-92.
* Nathan J. Stone. *Names of God*. Chicago: Moody, 1944.

THE TRINITY OF GOD

* Emery H. Bancroft. *Christian Theology*. Grand Rapids: Zondervan, 1976. Pp. 85-89.
** Louis Berkhof. *Systematic Theology*. Grand Rapids: Eerdmans, 1941. Pp. 82-99.
** J. Oliver Buswell, Jr. *A Systematic Theology of the Christian Religion*. Grand Rapids: Zondervan, 1962. 1:102-29.
* Walter A. Elwell, ed. *Evangelical Dictionary of Theology*. Grand Rapids: Baker, 1984. Pp. 1112-13. Also see other individual articles related to the study.
** Millard J. Erickson. *Christian Theology*. Grand Rapids: Baker, 1983. 1:321-42.
* Charles C. Ryrie. *A Survey of Bible Doctrine*. Chicago: Moody, 1972. Pp. 29-35.
* Henry C. Thiessen. *Lectures in Systematic Theology*. Revised by Vernon D. Doerksen. Grand Rapids: Eerdmans, 1979. Pp. 89-99.
** Wm. G. T. Shedd. *Dogmatic Theology*, 3 vols., 2d ed. Reprint. Nashville: Nelson, 1980. 1:249-333.

THE DECREES OF GOD

** Herman Bavinck. *The Doctrine of God*. Grand Rapids: Baker, 1979. Pp. 337-407.
** Louis Berkhof. *Systematic Theology*. Grand Rapids: Eerdmans, 1941. Pp. 100-108.
* Walter A. Elwell. ed. *Evangelical Dictionary of Theology*. Grand Rapids: Baker, 1984. Pp. 302-4.

** Millard J. Erickson. *Christian Theology*, 3 vols. Grand Rapids: Baker, 1983. 1:345-63.

 * A. A. Hodge. *Outlines of Theology.* Reprint. Grand Rapids: Zondervan, 1973. Pp. 200-213.

** Charles Hodge. *Systematic Theology*, 3 vols. Reprint. London: Clarke, 1960. 1:535-49.

 * Robert P. Lightner. *The God of the Bible.* Grand Rapids: Baker, 1978. Pp. 76-87.

** Wm. G. T. Shedd. *Dogmatic Theology*, 3 vols. Reprint. Nashville: Nelson, 1980. 1:393-462. This is an extensive discussion in a superlative theology and ought to be consulted by the serious student.

 * Henry C. Thiessen. *Lectures in Systematic Theology.* Revised by Vernon Doerksen. Grand Rapids: Eerdmans, 1979. Pp. 100-110.

** Benjamin B. Warfield. *The Plan of Salvation.* Reprint. Grand Rapids: Eerdmans, 1977.

20

CHRISTOLOGY: DOCTRINE OF CHRIST

PRE-EXISTENCE AND ETERNALITY OF CHRIST

The eternality and deity of Christ are inseparably linked together. Those who deny His eternality also deny His deity. If the deity of Christ is established, there is no problem in accepting His eternality.

DIRECT PROOF

New Testament. There are numerous passages in the New Testament which explicitly affirm the eternality of Jesus Christ.

(1) John 1:1. The word "was" in the phrase, "In the beginning was the Word," is the Greek *hen*, the imperfect tense that stresses continual existence in past time. The phrase could thus be translated, "In the beginning the Word was continually existing." John's beginning probably goes back to the origin of the universe; John indicates that however far back one goes, the Word was continuously existing.[1]

(2) John 8:58. Although Abraham lived two thousand years before Christ, He could say, "before Abraham was born, I am." Although Jesus was born in Bethlehem, He claimed to have existed before Abraham. The tense is again important to notice. Before Abraham was born, Christ *was continuously existing.* The statement "I am," of course, is also a reference to His deity and a claim of equality with Yahweh. "I am" is a reference to Exodus 3:14, in which God identifies Himself as "I AM WHO I AM."[2]

(3) Hebrews 1:8. In verse 8 the writer of Hebrews begins a series of Old Testament quotations. The preface to those statements is, "But of the Son He says," hence, the statements that follow refer to Christ. Therefore, the statement, "Thy throne, O God, *is forever and ever,*" is a reference to the eternality of Christ.

(4) Colossians 1:17. Paul states, *"He is* before all things," stressing once more eternality and pre-existence of Christ through the use of the present tense.

Old Testament. (1) Micah 5:2. This statement emphasizes that "His goings forth are from long ago, From the days of eternity." Although Jesus was born in Bethlehem (prophesied in this verse), that was not His beginning; He has existed "from the days of eternity."

(2) Isaiah 9:6. Christ is called the "Eternal Father." This does not mean Christ *is* the Father, because they are two distinct Persons within the Trinity. It does mean that Christ also possesses the title of Father. The designation suggests both His pre-existence and eternality.

Indirect proof. (1) Christ's heavenly origin proves His eternal existence. John 3:13 stresses that Christ "descended from heaven." If Christ came down from heaven then Bethlehem cannot have been His beginning. This verse indicates He dwelt in heaven before coming to earth, therefore, He is eternal (cf. John 6:38).

(2) Christ's preincarnate work proves His eternal existence. John 1:3 says that Christ created all things ("all" is emphatic). If He created all things then He must be eternal (cf. 1 Cor. 8:6).

(3) Christ's titles prove His eternal existence. (a) *Yahweh.* In John 12:41 the apostle says that Isaiah saw "His glory," a reference to Christ in the context. John, however, quoted from Isaiah 6:10 where He is clearly referring to Yahweh (cf. Isa. 6:3, 5). John thus equates Jesus with Yahweh, the Lord of the Old Testament; because Yahweh is eternal then Jesus is eternal. (b) *Adonai.* In Matthew 22:44 Christ quotes Psalm 110:1, "The Lord said to My Lord," and applies it to Himself. The term "Lord" is *Adonai*, one of the Old Testament names of God. If Christ is designated Adonai, then He is eternal, for God is eternal.

(4) The theophanies prove His eternal existence. A theophany may be defined thus: "It is the Second Person of the Trinity who appears thus in human form. . . . The One of the three who is called LORD, or Jahweh, in the incident recorded in Genesis 18, is to be taken to be the Second Person of the Trinity."[3] The identification of Christ with the appearances of the angel of the Lord (the theophany) can be demonstrated in the following manner. The angel of the Lord is recognized as deity. He is referred to as God (Judg. 6:11, 14; note in verse 11 He is called "angel of the Lord," while in v. 14 He is called "Lord"). The angel of the Lord in other instances is distinct from Yahweh because He talks to Yahweh (Zech. 1:11; 3:1-2; cf. Gen. 24:7). The angel of the Lord could not have been the Spirit or the Father, because neither the Spirit nor the Father are ever revealed in physical form (cf. John 1:18). The angel of the Lord no longer appears after the incarnation of Christ. There is no mention of the angel of the Lord in the New Testament; He ceases to appear after the birth of Christ.

OLD TESTAMENT PROPHECIES OF CHRIST

PROPHECIES CONCERNING CHRIST'S LINEAGE[4]

Virgin birth. Genesis 3:15 is known as the *protevangelium* because it is the first prophecy (good news) about Christ. There will be enmity between Satan and Messiah, here identified by the phrase, "her seed." The phrase "her seed" concerns Mary alone and points to the virgin birth; Messiah is born of Mary alone. Matthew 1:16 also emphasizes this in the phrase "By whom" (Gk. *hes*), a feminine relative pronoun, emphasizing Jesus was born without Joseph's participation.

Line of Shem. In mentioning the specific name "Lord, The God of Shem" Genesis 9:26 "intimates the preservation of the true religion among the descendants of Shem."[5] The line of Shem will ultimately bring blessing to the lineage of the other two sons of Noah. Moreover, the more specific name "Lord" (Yahweh) is used "which refers to his revelation and to his institutions for man's redemption."[6] The designation "God of Shem" also suggests "that God would sustain to the posterity of Shem a relation entirely peculiar, favoring them with revelations of His will."

Line of Abraham. In Genesis 12:2 God promised Abraham, "I will . . . make your name great," suggesting Messiah would come from the posterity of Abraham and that "in you all the families of the *earth* shall be blessed." Matthew 1:1 and Galatians 3:16 interpret this promise (cf. Gen. 13:15) as being fulfilled in Christ.

Line of Isaac. It was through the descendants of Isaac that God would establish His covenant and institute His blessings (Gen. 17:19).

Line of Jacob. The line of Messianic blessing narrows further in that the blessing will not flow through Ishmael, but rather through Jacob (Gen. 25:23; 28:13). Numbers 24:17 stresses a ruler ("scepter") will come through the descent of Jacob who will crush the enemy and "have dominion" (v. 19; cf. Rom. 9:10-13).

Line of Judah. Genesis 49:10 affirms Messiah (as king) will come from the tribe of Judah. Messiah, of the tribe of Judah, will possess the "scepter." "The king held (the scepter) in his hand when speaking in public assemblies; and when he sat upon his throne he rested it between his feet, inclining towards himself."[7] This verse also explains that Judah will sustain a lineage "Until Shiloh comes." Shiloh is variously interpreted: as a title of Messiah meaning "Man of rest;"[8] of Messiah as "pacifier, peacemaker."[9] Messiah will be a man of peace (cf. Ps. 72:7; 122:7; Jer. 23:6; Zech. 9:10); the phrase "Until Shiloh comes" may be translated "Until He comes to whom it belongs." "And to Him shall be the obedience of the peoples" stresses Messiah's rule over the nations of the world in the millennial kingdom.

Line of David. Messiah will be a descendant of David (2 Sam. 7:12-16). In this promise to David (cf. v. 16), the Lord indicated his descendant (the

Messiah) would have an everlasting dynasty ("house"); He would rule ("throne") over people ("kingdom"), and His rule would be "eternal." Psalm 89 expands this promise.

OLD TESTAMENT PROPHECIES OF CHRIST

Topic	Prophecy	Passage
Christ's Lineage	Virgin birth	Genesis 3:15
	Lineage of Shem	Genesis 9:26
	Lineage of Abraham	Genesis 12:2
	Lineage of Isaac	Genesis 17:19
	Lineage of Jacob	Genesis 25:23; 28:13
	Lineage of Judah	Genesis 49:10
	Lineage of David	2 Samuel 7:12-16
Christ's Birth	Manner of birth	Isaiah 7:14
	Place of birth	Micah 5:2
Christ's Life	His forerunner	Isaiah 40:3
	His mission	Isaiah 61:1
	His ministry	Isaiah 53:4
	His teaching	Psalm 78:2
	His presentation	Zechariah 9:9
	His rejection	Psalm 118:22
Christ's Death	A painful death	Psalm 22
	A violent death	Isaiah 52-53
Christ's Victory	His resurrection	Psalm 16:10
	His ascension	Psalm 68:18
Christ's Reign	As sovereign king	Psalm 2
	From exalted Jerusalem	Psalm 24
	With governmental authority	Isaiah 9:6-7
	In peaceful justice	Isaiah 11
	For joyful restoration	Isaiah 35:1-10

PROPHECIES CONCERNING CHRIST'S BIRTH

The manner. Isaiah 7:14 promised a sign to the unbelieving King Ahaz. The prophecy was that a virgin would bear a son who would be called Immanuel—God with us. In all seven occurrences in the Old Testament, the term "virgin" (Heb. *almah*) "never refers to a maiden who has lost her virginity . . ."[10] The passage has both a near and a far fulfillment: in the immediate future it was fulfilled in the birth of Maher-shalal-hash-baz (Isa. 8:3), and in the distant future it was fulfilled in the virgin birth of Jesus Christ. Matthew 1:23 provides a commentary on this verse.

The place. Micah 5:2 identifies the birthplace of Christ as Bethlehem, a small town, too insignificant to be listed among the towns of Judah (cf. Josh.15:60), distinguished from Bethlehem of Zebulun (Josh. 19:15). Matthew 2:6 provides a commentary on this verse.

PROPHECIES CONCERNING CHRIST'S LIFE

His forerunner. Isaiah 40:3 identifies John the Baptist, the forerunner, calling the people to repentance and spiritual preparation because the kingdom of heaven was at hand (Matt. 3:3; John 1:23). Malachi 3:1 identifies the forerunner of Messiah as a *messenger* who will prepare the way for Messiah. Malachi 3:1 parallels Isaiah 40:3 in thought (cf. Matt. 11:10; Mark 1:2-3).

His mission. Isaiah 61:1 promises that Christ will be anointed by the Holy Spirit in ministry, empowering Him to preaching the gospel to the poor, releasing those in spiritual bondage, and giving sight to the blind (Luke 4:18-19). Isaiah 9:1-2 predicts that Christ will be identified with the despised of society and with the Gentiles. This was fulfilled when Christ settled in Nazareth (where a Roman garrison was stationed) and later in Capernaum (Matt. 4:15-16).

His ministry. Isaiah 53:4 describes Christ bearing the sicknesses of the people, which Matthew states is fulfilled in the earthly ministry of Christ as He heals those who are ill (Matt. 8:17). Isaiah 35:5-6 and Isaiah 61:1-2 are combined in Jesus' response to John's question, indicating that Christ's earthly ministry of giving sight to the blind, healing the lame, cleansing the lepers, raising the dead, and preaching the good news to the poor was fulfilling the prophecies of Isaiah (Matt. 11:5-6). Isaiah 42:2-4 describes Christ as being unlike the Pharisees. He is not quarrelsome or contentious; He is kind and compassionate; He will not crush the weak and feeble—He will comfort them. For this reason many Gentiles will believe in Him (Matt. 12:19-21).

His teaching. Psalm 78:2 predicted that Christ would teach in parables, revealing previously hidden truths (Matt. 13:35).

His presentation. Zechariah 9:9 predicts the triumphal entry of Christ, riding as king into Jerusalem on a previously unbroken animal (Matt. 21:5). Psalm 118:26 depicts Christ coming to the nation as the Deliverer with the people crying to Him for help and deliverance (Matt. 21:9). Psalm 110:1 describes Christ as greater than David; He is one whom David recognized as Lord and who would eventually subdue His enemies (Matt. 22:44).

His rejection. Psalm 118:22 declares that Christ will be rejected. Christ, being likened to the all-important cornerstone that ties a building together, will be rejected by the Jewish people (Matt. 21:42). Isaiah 29:13 says that the people will give Christ lip service but not genuine obedience (Matt. 15:8-9).

Zechariah 13:7 declares that Christ will be forsaken by all His friends at the crucial moment (Matt. 26:31). In combining Jer. 18:1-2; 19:1-15; 32:6-9 and Zechariah 11:12, 13, the Old Testament prophets predicted Christ's being sold for thirty pieces of silver (Matt. 27:9-10).

PROPHECIES CONCERNING CHRIST'S DEATH

A painful death. Psalm 22 depicts the sufferings of Christ. Here David uses many poetic expressions to vividly portray the intensity of the Lord's agonies. These figures of speech became literally true when Jesus suffered at His enemies' hands.[11] Psalm 22:1 prophesies Christ's cry on the cross wherein He judicially bore the sins of the world (Matt. 27:46; Mark 15:34). Verse 7 describes the passers-by who ridiculed Him (Matt. 27:39). Verse 8 prophesies the actual words of those hurling insults at Him (Matt. 27:43). Verse 16 prophesies the piercing of Christ's hands and feet (John 20:25). Verse 17 indicates that none of Christ's bones would be broken (John 19:33-36). Psalm 22:18 prophesies the soldiers gambling for Christ's clothes (John 19:24). Psalm 22:24 prophesies Christ's prayer to the Father concerning His impending death (Matt. 26:39; Heb. 5:7).

A violent death. Isaiah 52 and 53 also portray the future sufferings of Christ. Isaiah 52:14 describes the disfigurement of Christ as a result of His scourging (John 19:1).[12] Isaiah 53:5 prophesies the scourging and violent death of Christ (John 19:1, 18). Isaiah 53:7 prophesies the Messiah as a lamb—silent and obedient on the way to death (John 1:29).

PROPHECIES CONCERNING CHRIST'S VICTORY

His resurrection. Peter applies David's hope of Psalm 16:10 to Christ in Acts 2:27-28, indicating that these verses prophesied that Christ would be resurrected (Acts 2:24ff.). This was not fulfilled by David because David died and was buried (Acts 2:29); instead, this passage spoke of the resurrection of Christ (Acts 2:31; cf. Acts 13:35). Psalm 22:22 is applied to Christ typologically in Hebrews 2:12 where, following the resurrection, Christ expresses praise for His resurrection.

His ascension. Psalm 68:18 anticipates the God-ordained end of our Lord's earthly life (cf. Eph. 4:8).

PROPHECIES CONCERNING CHRIST'S REIGN

Numerous Old Testament passages refer to Christ's future millennial reign on earth. Psalm 2 describes the installation of Christ as king in Jerusalem, ruling over the nations of the world (Ps. 2:6-9). Psalm 24:7-10 depicts the victorious, returning king triumphantly entering Jerusalem to rule. Isaiah 9:6-7 describes Christ as the Son in His governmental rule. Isaiah 11:1-16 indicates Christ's reign will be a reign of justice (vv. 1-5), a peaceful reign

(vv. 6-9), and a rule over restored Israel and the nations of the world (vv. 10-16). Isaiah 24:23 prophesies Christ's reign will be in Jerusalem. Isaiah 35:1-10 emphasizes the blessings of the restored land and nation in Messiah's kingdom. Daniel 7:13-14 emphasizes Christ's rule will be over all people and nations. Zechariah 14:9-21 prophesies the destruction of Israel's enemies and Christ's rule over the nations of the world.

FULFILLED PROPHECIES CONCERNING CHRIST

Topic	Old Testament Prophecy	New Testament Fulfillment
Line of Abraham	Genesis 12:2	Matthew 1:1; Galatians 3:16
Line of Judah	Genesis 49:10	Matthew 1:2
Line of David	2 Samuel 7:12-16	Matthew 1:1
Virgin birth	Isaiah 7:14	Matthew 1:23
Birthplace: Bethlehem	Micah 5:2	Matthew 2:6
Forerunner: John	Isaiah 40:3; Malachi 3:1	Matthew 3:3
King	Numbers 24:17; Psalm 2:6	Matthew 21:5
Prophet	Deuteronomy 18:15-18	Acts 3:22-23
Priest	Psalm 110:4	Hebrews 5:6-10
Bore world's sins	Psalm 22:1	Matthew 27:46
Ridiculed	Psalm 22:7, 8	Matthew 27:39, 43
Hands and feet pierced	Psalm 22:16	John 20:25
No bones broken	Psalm 22:17	John 19:33-36
Soldiers gambled	Psalm 22:18	John 19:24
Christ's prayer	Psalm 22:24	Matthew 26:39; Hebrews 5:7
Disfigured	Isaiah 52:14	John 19:1
Scourging and death	Isaiah 53:5	John 19:1, 18
Resurrection	Psalm 16:10; 22:22	Matthew 28:6; Acts 2:27-28
Ascension	Psalm 68:18	Luke 24:50-53; Acts 1:9-11

INCARNATION OF CHRIST

MEANING OF THE INCARNATION

The word *incarnation* means "in flesh" and denotes the act whereby the eternal Son of God took to Himself an additional nature, humanity, through the virgin birth. The result is that Christ remains forever unblemished deity, which He has had from eternity past; but He also possesses true, sinless humanity in one Person forever (cf. John 1:14; Phil. 2:7-8; 1 Tim. 3:6).

EXPLANATION OF THE INCARNATION

Genealogies. There are two genealogies that describe the incarnation of Christ: Matthew 1:1-16 and Luke 3:23-38. There is considerable discussion and controversy concerning the relationship of these two genealogies. One thing is noteworthy: both genealogies trace Jesus to David (Matt. 1:1; Luke 3:31) and thereby emphasize His rightful claim as heir to the throne of David (cf. Luke 1:32-33). It appears that Matthew describes Joseph's lineage (cf. v. 16), and because an heir made his claim through the father, Jesus' right to the Davidic throne comes through Joseph, His adoptive father.[13] Luke cites Jesus' descent through Mary to Adam, "connecting Christ with the predicted seed of the woman."[14]

Virgin birth. The virgin birth was the *means* whereby the incarnation took place and guaranteed the sinlessness of the Son of God. For this reason the virgin birth was essential. Isaiah 7:14 predicted the virgin birth and Matthew 1:23 provides the commentary, indicating its fulfillment in the birth of Christ. Matthew 1:23 identifies Mary as a "virgin" (Gk. *parthenos*, clearly denoting a virgin).[15] The texts of Matthew and Luke are both clear on the teaching of the virgin birth. Matthew 1:18 emphasizes Mary was pregnant before she and Joseph lived together; moreover, the same verse indicates her pregnancy was due to the Holy Spirit. Matthew 1:22-23 stresses that the birth of Christ was in fulfillment of the prophecy of the virgin birth in Isaiah 7:14. Matthew 1:25 emphasizes that Mary remained a virgin *until* the birth of Christ. Luke 1:34 states that Mary had not had contact with a man, while in Luke 1:35 the angel explains to Mary that her pregnancy was due to the overshadowing of the Holy Spirit.[16]

HUMANITY OF CHRIST

MEANING OF CHRIST'S HUMANITY

The doctrine of the humanity of Christ is equally important as the doctrine of the deity of Christ. Jesus had to be a man if He was to represent fallen humanity. First John was written to dispel the doctrinal error that denies the true humanity of Christ (cf. 1 John 4:2). If Jesus was not a real man, then the death on the cross was an illusion; He had to be a real man to die for humanity. The Scriptures teach the true humanity of Jesus. However, they also show that He did not possess man's sinful, fallen nature (1 John 3:5).

HE WAS VIRGIN BORN

The virgin birth is an essential (and biblical) doctrine; it is necessary if Christ was to be sinless. If He had been born of Joseph He would have possessed the sin nature. There is considerable evidence in the gospels affirming the virgin birth of Christ. In Matthew 1:2-15 the active form of the verbs is used (this is not reflected in the New American Standard Bible): "Abraham begot Isaac" (v. 2, King James Version). In v. 16, however, there is a deliberate change to the passive form in describing the birth of Jesus. The verb in the phrase "by whom *was born* Jesus" is passive and emphasizes that in contrast to all the preceding men who sired their sons, Joseph did not beget Jesus.[17] (See preceding discussion for additional information.)

HE HAD A TRUE BODY OF FLESH AND BLOOD

The body of Jesus "was like the bodies of other men except for those qualities which have resulted from human sin and failure."[18] Luke 1-2 describes Mary's pregnancy and her giving birth to the child Jesus, affirming the Savior's true humanity. Jesus was not a phantom as the Docetists taught. Later in life He was recognizable as a Jew (John 4:9) and as the carpenter who had brothers and sisters (Matt. 13:55). Ultimately, He suffered greatly in His human body: He experienced the pain of the scourging (John 19:1), the horror of crucifixion (John 19:18), and on the cross He thirsted as a man (John 19:28). These elements emphasize His true humanity.

HE HAD A NORMAL DEVELOPMENT

Luke 2:52 describes Jesus' development in four areas: mental, physical, spiritual, and social. He continued to develop in His knowledge of things; He grew in His physical body; He developed in His spiritual awareness (there was no interaction with sin, of course, since He was sinless from birth until death); He developed in His social relationships. His development in these four areas was *perfect*; "at each stage he was perfect for that stage."[19]

HE HAD A HUMAN SOUL AND SPIRIT

Jesus was a complete human being, having a body, soul, and spirit. Prior to the cross, Jesus was troubled in His soul at the anticipation of the cross (John 12:27). There was a self-consciousness that He was to bear the sins of the world, and Jesus was overwhelmed at the prospect. John 11:33 describes in strongest terms the emotion that Jesus felt in His human spirit at the death of His friend Lazarus.[20] At the prospect of His impending crucifixion Jesus was troubled in His human spirit (John 13:21); when He ultimately died He gave up His spirit (John 19:30).

HE HAD THE CHARACTERISTICS OF A HUMAN BEING

When Jesus had fasted in the wilderness He became hungry (Matt. 4:2); when He and the disciples walked through Samaria He became tired and stopped at the well to rest (John 4:6); He was thirsty from the day's journey in the heat (John 4:7). Jesus also experienced human emotions: He wept over the death of His friend Lazarus (John 11:34-35); He felt compassion for the people because they were without capable leaders (Matt. 9:36); He experienced grief and wept over the city of Jerusalem (Matt. 23:37; Luke 19:41).

HE HAD HUMAN NAMES

He was called the "son of David," indicating He was a descendant of King David (Matt. 1:1). He was also called Jesus (Matt. 1:21), the equivalent of the Old Testament name Joshua (meaning, "Yahweh saves"). He was referred to as a "Man." Paul indicated a future day when the world would be judged by a "Man" (Acts 17:31). As a man Jesus is also mediator between God and men (1 Tim. 2:5).

DEITY OF CHRIST

MEANING OF CHRIST'S DEITY

During the early centuries of the church there were groups that denied the true humanity of Christ. But the reverse is the emphasis today. In the past two hundred years liberal theology has vigorously expressed a denial of Christ's deity. Yet C. S. Lewis was correct when he said that the only options available concerning the Person of Christ were: He was a liar, a lunatic, or Lord. Considering the enormous claims that Christ made, it would be impossible simply to designate Him a "good teacher." He claimed to be much more than a teacher.

To affirm that Christ is God is not simply to suggest He is "God-like." Christ is absolutely equal with the Father in His Person and His work. Christ is *undiminished deity.* In commenting on the phrase "(Christ) existed in the *form* of God" in Philippians 2:6, B. B. Warfield says, "He is declared, in the most express manner possible, to be all that God is, to possess the whole fulness of attributes which make God God."[21]

IMPORTANCE OF CHRIST'S DEITY

An attack on the deity of Jesus Christ is an attack on the bedrock of Christianity. At the heart of orthodox belief is the recognition that Christ died a substitutionary death to provide salvation for a lost humanity. If Jesus were only a man He could not have died to save the world, but because of His deity, His death had infinite value whereby He could die for the entire world.

TEACHING OF CHRIST'S DEITY

The Scriptures are replete with the personal claims of Christ as well as the testimony of others concerning His deity. The gospel of John is particularly rich in its emphasis on Christ's deity.

His names. (1) God. In Hebrews 1:8ff. the writer states the superiority of Christ to angels and ascribes Psalm 45:6-7 to Christ. The superscription to the quotation from Psalm 45:6-7 is, "But of the Son He says"; then He quotes the psalm saying, "Thy throne, *O God* is forever" and "therefore *God.*" Both designations "God" have reference to the Son (Heb. 1:8). Upon seeing the resurrected Christ with His wounds displayed, Thomas confessed, "My Lord and My *God*" (John 20:28). (Some who reject Christ's deity amazingly suggest that Thomas' statement was an outburst of profanity.) Titus 2:13 refers to Jesus as "our great God and Savior, Jesus Christ."[22] The Granville Sharpe rule of Greek grammar states that when two nouns are joined by *kai* (and) and the first noun has the article and the second does not, then the two nouns refer to the same thing. Hence, "great God" and "Savior" both refer to "Christ Jesus." John 1:18 declares that "the only begotten God"—a reference to Christ—has explained the Father.[23]

(2) Lord. In Christ's debate with the Pharisees He demonstrated that Messiah was greater than simply a descendant of David. He reminded them that David himself called Messiah "my Lord" (Matt. 22:44). In Romans 10:9, 13 Paul refers to Jesus as Lord. In verse 9 he emphasizes that it is recognition of Jesus as Lord (deity) that results in salvation. In verse 13 Paul quotes from Joel 2:32, where the reference concerns the Lord; but Paul applies it to Jesus, affirming Christ's equality with Yahweh of the Old Testament. In Hebrews 1:10 the writer applies Psalm 102:25 to Christ, calling Him "Lord."

(3) Son of God. Jesus claimed to be the *Son of God* on a number of occasions (cf. John 5:25). This name for Christ is frequently misunderstood; some suggest it means the Son is inferior to the Father. The Jews, however, understood the claim Christ was making; but saying He was the Son of God the Jews said He was "making Himself equal with God" (John 5:19).

His attributes. (1) Eternal. John 1:1 affirms the eternality of Christ. The verb "was" (Gk. imperfect *hen*) suggests His continuous existence in time past. In Hebrews 1:11-12 the writer applies Psalm 102:25-27, expressing the eternality of God, to Christ.

(2) Omnipresent. In Matthew 28:20 Christ promised the disciples, "I am with you always." Recognizing that Christ has a human nature as well as a divine nature, it should be stated that in His humanity He is localized in heaven, but in His deity He is omnipresent.[24] Christ's indwelling of every believer demands that He is omnipresent (cf. John 14:23; Eph. 3:17; Col. 1:27; Rev. 3:20).

(3) Omniscient. Jesus knew what was in the heart of man and therefore did not entrust Himself to man (John 2:25). He told the Samaritan woman her past history even though He had not met her previously (John 4:18). His disciples recognized His omniscience (John 16:30). His numerous predictions of His death demonstrate His omniscience (cf. Matt. 16:21; 17:22; 20:18-19; 26:1-2).

(4) Omnipotent. Jesus had all authority of heaven and earth (Matt. 28:18). He had the power to forgive sins—something only God can do (cf. Mark 2:5, 7, 10; Isa. 43:25; 55:7).

(5) Immutable. Christ does not change; He is forever the same (Heb. 13:8). This is an attribute of deity (Mal. 3:6; James 1:17).

(6) Life. All creation—humanity, animals, plants—are alive because they have been infused with life. Christ is different. He has life in Himself; it is not a derived life, but He *is* life (John 1:4; 14:6; cf. Ps. 36:9; Jer. 2:13).

His works. (1) Creator. John states that there is nothing that has come into being apart from Christ's creating it (John 1:3). Colossians 1:16 teaches that Christ created not only the earth but also the heavens and the angelic realm.

(2) Sustainer. Colossians 1:17 teaches that Christ is the cohesive force of the universe. Hebrews 1:3 suggests Christ "carries all things forward on their appointed course."[25] This is the force of the Greek participle *pheron.*

(3) Forgiver of sin. Only God can forgive sin; the fact that Jesus forgave sin demonstrates His deity (cf. Mark 2:1-12; Isa. 43:25).

(4) Miracle worker. The miracles of Christ were an attestation of His deity. It is a valuable study to note the miracles of Christ and see the claim of deity underlying the miracle. For example, when Jesus gave sight to the blind man, the people would have been reminded of Psalm 146:8, "The Lord opens the eyes of the blind."

He receives worship. It is a fundamental truth of Scripture that only God is to be worshiped (Deut. 6:13; 10:20; Matt. 4:10; Acts 10:25-26). The fact that Jesus receives the worship of people is a strong attestation to His deity. In John 5:23 Jesus said that He was to be accorded honor and reverence *just as* people honor the Father. If Jesus were not God, this statement would be utterly blasphemous. In the benediction of 2 Corinthians 13:14, the blessing of the triune God is accorded the believer. The manner of the benediction suggests the equality of the persons. At the triumphal entry Jesus applied the chanting of the young people to Himself by quoting Psalm 8:2, "Out of the mouth of infants and nursing babes Thou hast prepared praise for Thyself" (Matt. 21:16). Psalm 8 is addressed to Yahweh and describes the worship rendered to Him; Jesus applies that same worship to Himself. When the blind man who had been healed by Jesus met Him and discovered who Jesus was, the healed man worshiped Him (John 9:38). That Jesus did not reject the man's worship indicates He is God. In 2 Timothy 4:18 Paul refers to Jesus as Lord and ascribes glory to Him. Glory refers to the Shekinah of God and pertains only to deity. In Philippians 2:10 Paul envisions a future day wherein all in earth and heaven will worship Christ.

HYPOSTATIC UNION

MEANING OF HYPOSTATIC UNION

The hypostatic union may be defined as "the second person, the preincarnate Christ came and took to Himself a human nature and remains forever undiminished Deity and true humanity united in one person forever." When Christ came, a Person came, not just a nature; He took on an additional nature, a human nature—He did not simply dwell in a human person. The result of the union of the two natures is the theanthropic Person (the God-man).

EXPLANATION OF HYPOSTATIC UNION

The two natures of Christ are inseparably united without mixture or loss of separate identity. He remains forever the God-man, fully God and fully man, two distinct natures in one Person forever. "Though Christ sometimes operated in the sphere of His humanity and in other cases in the sphere of His deity, in all cases what He did and what He was could be attributed to His one Person. Even though it is evident that there were two natures in Christ, He is never considered a dual personality."[26] In summarizing the hypostatic union, three facts are noted: (1) Christ has two distinct natures: humanity and deity; (2) there is no mixture or intermingling of the two natures; (3) although He has two natures, Christ is one Person.

PROBLEM OF HYPOSTATIC UNION

The major difficulty in this doctrine involves the relationship of the two natures in the Lord Jesus. Several opinions on this point have developed.

Calvinistic view. John Calvin taught that the two natures are united without any transfer of attributes. An attribute could not be taken away from a nature without changing the essence of that nature. Walvoord states, "The two natures are united without loss of any essential attributes and that the two natures maintain their separate identity."[27] There can be no mixture of the two natures; "infinity cannot be transferred to finity; mind cannot be transferred to matter; God cannot be transferred to man, or vice versa. To rob the divine nature of God of a single attribute would destroy His deity, and to rob man of a single human attribute would result in destruction of a true humanity. It is for this reason that the two natures of Christ cannot lose or transfer a single attribute."[28]

Lutheran view. The Lutheran view of the two natures teaches that attributes of the divine nature are extended to the human nature with some important results. One important doctrinal result is the ubiquity of the human body of Christ, that is, the omnipresence of the divine nature of Christ is transferred to the human body of Christ. Consequently, the human nature of Christ passed into a ubiquitous state at the ascension and is physically present in the elements of holy communion. Although the elements do not change, the person partakes of Christ who is "in, with, under and by" the bread and cup.

RESULTS OF HYPOSTATIC UNION[29]

Both natures are necessary for redemption. As a man, Christ could represent man and die as a man; as God the death of Christ could have infinite value "sufficient to provide redemption for the sins of the world."

The eternal priesthood of Christ is based on the hypostatic union. "By incarnation He became Man and hence could act as a human Priest. As God, His priesthood could be everlasting after the order of Melchizedek, and He properly could be a Mediator between God and man."

KENOSIS AND HYPOSTATIC UNION

The kenosis problem involves the interpretation of Philippians 2:7, "(He) emptied [Gk. *ekenosen*] Himself." The critical question is: Of what did Christ empty Himself? Liberal theologians suggest Christ emptied Himself of His deity, but it is evident from His life and ministry that He did not, for His deity was displayed on numerous occasions. Two main points may be made. (1) "Christ merely surrendered the independent exercise of some of his relative or transitive attributes. He did not surrender the absolute or immanent attributes in any sense; He was always perfectly holy, just, merciful, truthful, and faithful."[30] This statement has merit and provides a solution to problem passages such as Matthew 24:36. The key word in this definition would be "independent" because Jesus did on many occasions reveal His relative attributes. (2) Christ took to Himself an additional nature. The context of Philippians 2:7 provides the best solution to the kenosis problem. The emptying was not a subtraction but an *addition*. The four following phrases (Phil. 2:7-8) explain the emptying: "(a) taking the form of a bond-servant, and (b) being made in the likeness of men. And (c) being found in appearance as a man, (d) He humbled Himself by becoming obedient to the point of death." The "emptying" of Christ was taking on an additional nature, a human nature with its limitations. His deity was never surrendered.

EARTHLY LIFE OF CHRIST

INTRODUCTION

The earthly life of Christ is important in the study of Christology inasmuch as it authenticates Jesus of Nazareth as the promised Messiah. The gospel writers demonstrate that Jesus fulfilled the Old Testament prophecies throughout His life. Matthew, for example, has 129 references to the Old Testament. Many of these are quoted with an introductory formula such as, "that it might be fulfilled, saying" (cf. Matt. 1:22; 2:5, 15, 17, 23, etc.). Each of the gospel writers wrote for a different audience, but all wrote as an apologetic concerning Christ and His claims. All the gospel writers emphasize the authenticity of His claims as Messiah.

WORDS OF CHRIST

The teaching of Christ was important in authenticating His claims of Messiahship, hence, the gospel writers give considerable space to the actual words or teachings of Christ. The following chart illustrates that emphasis in terms of space devoted to the actual words of Christ.[31]

WORDS OF CHRIST IN THE GOSPELS

Gospel	Verses (KJV)	Number of Words	Percent of Gospel
Matthew	1,071	644	Three-fifths
Mark	678	285	Three-sevenths
Luke	1,151	586	Nearly half
John	879	419	Not quite half
Totals	3,779	1,934	Almost half

This chart reveals that in their combined writings the actual words of Christ make up more than half the material in the gospels. Clearly, the gospel writers have a decided emphasis on the actual spoken words of Christ. Matthew emphasizes the words of Christ more than the other writers. In his gospel, Matthew records several major discourses of Christ. Matthew 5-7 records the Sermon on the Mount, which reveals the authority of Christ in His teaching. Throughout the discourse statements such as, "you have heard . . . but I say to you" occur and reflect Christ's authority. He taught contrary to tradition and the rabbis; moreover, He quoted no other teachers (as Israel's teachers customarily did); He was the authority within Himself. When the discourse ended the people were amazed at the authority in His teaching; He was most unlike their scribes.

Christ's omniscience was also reflected in His teaching, as in the parables of the kingdom (Matt. 13), in which He traced the course of this age, and in the Olivet Discourse (Matt. 24-25), as He revealed the cataclysmic events that would occur in the Tribulation. In the upper room discourse (John 14-16) Jesus instructed His disciples, teaching them important new truth concerning the Holy Spirit's ministry. In so doing, Jesus was preparing the disciples for His departure.

Additionally, the four gospels contain many discourses and parables reflecting the authority of Christ in His teaching. The teaching of Christ authenticated His claims as Messiah; He indicated the words He taught were from the Father who had sent Him (John 12:49) and that He had come forth from the Father (John 17:8). The words that Christ spoke were words of eternal life (John 6:63, 68); they reflected the wisdom of God (Matt. 13:54); even unbelievers were astonished at the wisdom and power in His teaching (Mark 6:2; Luke 4:22). The words of Christ were important in verifying the claims He made.

WORKS OF CHRIST

Isaiah prophesied that Messiah would give sight to the blind, hearing to the deaf, speech to the dumb, and healing to the lame (Isa. 29:18; 32:3; 35:5-6; cf. also Zeph. 3:19). When John's disciples came to inquire of Jesus, He reminded them of these prophecies and applied them to Himself (Matt. 11:4-5). The miracles that Jesus performed were attestations to His deity

JESUS' WORKS OF GOD

Work of Jesus	Work of God
Stilling the storm (Matthew 8:23-27)	Psalm 107:29
Healing the blind (John 9:1-7)	Psalm 146:8
Forgiving sin (Matthew 9:2)	Isaiah 43:25; 44:22
Raising the dead (Matthew 9:25)	Psalm 49:15
Feeding the 5,000 (Matthew 14:15-21)	Joel 2:22-24

and Messiahship; He performed the works of God in their midst. When the miracles are studied this truth becomes evident.

Many of the miracles that Christ performed anticipated His messianic, millennial kingdom.[32]

MILLENNIAL SIGNIFICANCE OF CHRIST'S MIRACLES

Miracle	Millennial Significance	Prophecy
Water to wine (John 2:1-11)	Joy, gladness	Isaiah 9:3, 4; 12:3-6
The 5,000 fed (Matthew 14:15-21)	Prosperity, abundance	Isaiah 30:23-24; 35:1-7
Walks on water (Matthew 14:26)	Environment change	Isaiah 30; 41
Catch of fish (Luke 5:1-11)	Abundance; authority over animal world	Isaiah 11:6-8
Storm stilled (Matthew 8:23-27)	Control of elements	Isaiah 11:9; 65:25
The blind healed (Matthew 9:27-31)	No physical or spiritual blindness	Isaiah 35:5
Raising the dead (Matthew 9:18-26)	Longevity; no death for believer	Isaiah 65:20

SELECTED MIRACLES IN JOHN'S GOSPEL[33]

Sign	Significance
Water changed to wine (2:1-11)	Quality
Healing the nobleman's son (4:46-54)	Space
Healing man at pool (5:1-18)	Time
Feeding the five thousand (6:1-14)	Quantity
Walking on the water (6:16-21)	Nature
Healing the blind man (9:1-41)	Misfortune
Raising Lazarus (11:1-44)	Death

When John wrote his gospel he selected seven pre-resurrection miracles that demonstrated Christ's authority in different realms. Christ performed many more miracles but those seven were representative in reflecting Christ's authority over every realm of mankind.

Jesus' witness to the nation concerned His words and His works—His teaching and His miracles. Both were attestations of His deity and Messiahship, hence, Jesus reminded John's disciples, "Go and report to John the things which you *hear* and *see*" (Matt. 11:4).

REJECTION OF CHRIST

Jesus came as Israel's Messiah and bore witness to His Messiahship through His words and His works. The gospel writers wrote their accounts of the life of Christ from a thematic viewpoint. This is particularly reflected in Matthew's gospel. In chapters 5-7 Matthew relates the teaching of Christ in the Sermon on the Mount and demonstrates His Messiahship through His teaching (Matt. 7:28-29); in chapters 8-10 Christ performed miracles over various realms as an authentication through His works. As a result, the nation was given the witness by Messiah through His words and His works. It was now incumbent on the nation to respond to the Messiah, and the religious leaders were the ones to lead the people in acknowledging the Messiah. In Matthew 12 the issue came to a climax as the religious leaders drew their conclusion: "This man casts out demons only by Beelzebul the ruler of the demons" (Matt. 12:24). They acknowledged that Christ performed miracles but concluded that He performed them through the power of Satan. The nation rejected her Messiah. As a result the kingdom that Christ offered would not be inaugurated at His first coming but would be held in abeyance until His Second Advent. Jesus then instructed His disciples concerning the interim age that would take place between His first and second comings (Matt. 13:1-52).

DEATH OF CHRIST[34]

Substitution. There are a number of theories concerning the significance of Christ's death. The emphasis of the New Testament, however, is that Christ died a substitutionary death on behalf of sinners. His death is also called *vicarious*, meaning, "one in place of another." The pronouns in Isaiah 53 stress the substitutionary nature of Christ's death: "But *He* was pierced through for *our* transgressions. *He* was crushed for *our* iniquities; The chastening for *our* well-being fell upon *Him*, And by *His* scourging *we* are healed." The tenor of 1 Peter 2:24 is similar: "and *He Himself* bore *our* sins in *His* body on the cross, that *we* might die to sin and live to righteousness; for by *His* wounds *you* were healed."

Two Greek prepositions teach the *substitutionary* aspect of Christ's death. The preposition *anti*, translated "for" and meaning "instead of," teaches substitution. Matthew 20:28 states, "the Son of man did not come to be served, but to serve, and to give His life a ransom for (*anti*) many" (cf. Mark 10:45). The usage of *anti* in Luke 11:11 indicates that "instead of" (substitution) is the basic meaning of this preposition. A second preposition, *huper*, meaning "in place of" also emphasizes substitution. First Timothy 2:6 states that Christ "gave Himself as a ransom for (*huper*) all." Galatians 3:13 also teaches this truth: "Christ redeemed us from the curse of the Law, having become a curse for (*huper*) us." By dying on the Roman cross Christ died as a substitute for all humanity (cf. 2 Cor. 5:21; 1 Pet. 3:18). This doctrine is important inasmuch as the righteous demands of a holy God were met completely through Christ's complete payment for sin. It is on this basis that God may declare believing sinners righteous and accept them into fellowship without any compromise on His part. All the believer's sins are placed on Christ, who completely atoned for them and paid for them through His death.

Redemption. A related truth is that Christ's death provided *redemption.* First Corinthians 6:20 states that believers "have been bought with a price." Bought is the Greek word *agorazo*, which pictures a slave being purchased in the ancient public slave market. Christ purchased believers out of the slave market of sin and set them free (cf. 1 Cor. 7:23; Gal. 3:13; 4:5; Rev. 5:9; 14:3, 4).

A further result of Christ's death is that man is reconciled to God, meaning that man, who was estranged and alienated from God, is now at peace with Him. The enmity and hostility has been removed (Rom. 5:10). Through his rebellion in the garden, man moved out of fellowship with God and needed to return to fellowship. Reconciliation is God providing peace where previously there was enmity, and God restoring man to fellowship with Himself (cf. 2 Cor. 5:18-20).

Propitiation. The death of Christ also provided *propitiation*, meaning that the righteous demands of a holy God were fully satisfied. Romans 3:25 explains that "God displayed (Christ) publicly as a propitiation [Gk. *hilasterion*] in His blood through faith." Christ provided a satisfactory payment for sin through His death. God was satisfied, His holiness was upheld, and His divine wrath was averted.

Forgiveness. Christ's death resulted in forgiveness for sinners. God could not forgive sin without a proper payment; Christ's death provided the legal means whereby God could forgive sin. Colossians 2:13 declares that God has "forgiven [Gk. *charisamenos*] us all our transgressions." The word *forgiveness* comes from the root word for grace; thus, forgiveness means "to forgive out of grace." The common word for forgiveness (Gk. *aphiemi*) means "to send away" (cf. Matt. 6:12; 9:6; James 5:15; 1 John 1:9).

Justification. A further result of Christ's death is *justification* for the believing sinner. Justification is also a legal act in which God the Judge declares the believing sinner righteous. Romans 5:1 explains: "Therefore having been justified [Gk. *dikaiothentes*] by faith, we have peace with God through our Lord Jesus Christ." The word *justified* (Gk. *dikaioo*) has both a negative and positive aspect. Negatively, it means the removal of the believer's sins; positively, it means the bestowal of Christ's righteousness upon the believer (cf. Rom. 3:24, 28; 5:9; Gal. 2:16). See the Doctrine of Salvation for a further discussion of the significance of the death of Christ.

RESURRECTION OF CHRIST

Importance. (1) The resurrection determines the validity of the Christian faith. Paul exclaimed, "If Christ has not been raised, your faith is worthless; you are still in your sins" (1 Cor. 15:17).

(2) It was the guarantee of the Father's acceptance of the Son's work. The resurrection indicated that the work of the cross was completed. Christ prayed that the cup would pass from Him (Matt. 26:39); it was a prayer not for the avoidance of the cross but for death to issue in life through the resurrection (Ps. 16:10). The Father heard the prayer (Heb. 5:7) and raised the Son from the dead, indicating His acceptance of Christ's work.

(3) It was essential in the program of God. Christ promised to send the Holy Spirit as a Helper for the disciples (John 16:7), but the Holy Spirit could only come to them if Christ would depart (necessitating the resurrection).

(4) It fulfilled the prophecies concerning His resurrection. David prophesied of Christ's resurrection (Psalm 16:10); Peter indicated the resurrection of Christ fulfilled the prophecy of Psalm 16:10. Christ Himself predicted not only His death but also His resurrection (Matt. 16:21; Mark 14:28).

Proofs. (1) The empty tomb. Either Christ was resurrected or someone stole the body. If opponents took the body why did they not simply produce it later? The disciples could not have stolen the body because Roman soldiers were guarding the tomb and had placed the Roman seal on the tomb. The empty tomb was an obvious proof of the resurrection.

(2) The shape of the linen wrappings. When John entered the tomb "he saw and believed" (John 20:8). John saw the linen wrappings that still retained the shape of the body and the headpiece "rolled up in a place by itself" (John 20:7; cf. 11:44). John knew no one could have taken the body out of the wrappings and replaced the wrappings to retain the shape of a body. There was only one explanation: the body of Jesus had passed through the linen wrappings.[35]

(3) The resurrection appearances. The resurrected Lord was seen by many people in the forty days that followed. Among them were the faithful women at the tomb, the two on the Emmaus road, Peter, the Twelve, five

hundred believers at one time, James, the apostles, and Paul (Matt. 28:1-10; Luke 24:13-35; 1 Cor. 15:5-8). Those witnesses were an important testimony to the veracity of the resurrection. Post-ascension appearances of the Lord Jesus to Paul and John are recorded in Acts and Revelation.

(4) The transformed disciples. The disciples knew Christ had died and were skeptical at first concerning His resurrection, but when they saw Him they were completely changed. The Peter of Acts 2 is quite different from the Peter of John 19. Knowledge of the resurrection made the difference.

(5) Observance of the first day of the week. The disciples immediately began to meet together in commemoration of Jesus' resurrection (John 20:26; Acts 20:7; 1 Cor. 16:2; Rev. 1:10).

(6) Existence of the church. The existence of the church is dependent on the fact of the resurrection. The early church grew through the preaching of the doctrine (Acts 2:24-32; 3:15; 4:2).

ASCENSION OF CHRIST

Facts of the ascension. The ascension of Christ is described in Mark 16:19, Luke 24:51, and Acts 1:9. It is also mentioned in Acts 2:33, where Peter indicates the evidence of Christ's ascension is the fact that He sent forth the Holy Spirit, who was witnessed by so many on the day of Pentecost. Peter further emphasizes that Christ's ascension was in fulfillment of Psalm 110:1 where the Lord said, "Sit at My right hand." Paul emphasizes the same truth in Ephesians 4:8, where he indicates Christ "ascended on high . . . and He gave gifts to men." The book of Hebrews encourages believers to draw near to the throne of grace with confidence because "we have a great high priest who has passed through the heavens, Jesus the Son of God" (Heb. 4:14). Peter indicates the believer is saved through an appeal to the risen, ascended Lord (1 Pet. 3:22).

Significance of the ascension.[36] (1) It ended the earthly ministry of Christ. It marked the end of the period of self-limitation during the days of His sojourn on earth.

(2) It ended the period of His humiliation. His glory was no longer veiled following the ascension (John 17:5; Acts 9:3, 5). Christ is now exalted and enthroned in heaven.

(3) It marks the first entrance of resurrected humanity into heaven and the beginning of a new work in heaven (Heb. 4:14-16; 6:20). A representative of the human race in a resurrected, glorified body is the Christian's intercessor.

(4) It made the descent of the Holy Spirit possible (John 16:7). It was necessary for Christ to ascend to heaven in order that He could send the Holy Spirit.

TEMPTATION OF CHRIST

DEFINITION

Although Christ was repeatedly "tempted" during His ministry (cf. Luke 4:13, 22:28; Mark 8:11), His great temptation (Matt. 4:1 and parallels) is the focus of this study unit. His temptation was a testing for demonstration of His purity and sinlessness (Heb. 4:15) without any possibility of enticement to evil (James 1:13).

PECCABILITY

The view that Christ could have sinned is termed *peccability* (Lat. *potuit non peccare*, "able not to sin,") while the view that Christ could not have sinned is designated *impeccability* (Lat. *non potuit peccare*, "not able to sin"). Among evangelicals the issue is not whether or not Christ sinned; all evangelicals would deny that Christ actually sinned. The question in the debate is whether or not Christ *could* have sinned. Generally (not always), Calvinists believe that Christ could not have sinned, whereas Arminians generally believe that Christ could have sinned but did not.

Those who hold to the peccability of Christ do so on the basis of Hebrews 4:15: He "has been tempted in all things as we are, yet without sin." If the temptation was genuine then Christ had to be able to sin, otherwise the temptation was not a genuine temptation. Charles Hodge, a Reformed theologian, is perhaps the best representative of this view. He states:

> If He was a true man He must have been capable of sinning. That He did not sin under the greatest provocation; that when He was reviled He blessed; when He suffered He threatened not; that He was dumb, as a sheep before its shearers, is held up to us as an example. Temptation implies the possibility of sin. If from the constitution of his person it was impossible for Christ to sin, then his temptation was unreal and without effect, and He cannot sympathize with his people.[37]

The radio and written ministries of M. R. DeHaan and Richard DeHaan also teach the peccability of Christ.

The supposed strength of this view is that it alone identifies Christ with humanity in His temptations—they were real temptations. The weaknesses of this view are that it does not sufficiently consider Christ in His Person as *God* as well as man. Additionally, the word *temptation* (Gk. *peirazo*) is also used of God the Father (Acts 15:10; 1 Cor. 10:9; Heb. 3:9) and the Holy Spirit (Acts 5:9).[38] It is unlikely that anyone would say the Father or the Holy Spirit could have sinned. The conclusion is that temptation does not demand the ability to sin. The people genuinely tempted God the Father and the Holy Spirit, but there was no likelihood of those Persons of the Trinity sinning.

IMPECCABILITY

Those who hold to impeccability suggest Christ's temptation by Satan was genuine, but it was impossible for Christ to sin.[39] Several introductory observations should be noted.

Observations. The purpose of the temptation was not to see if Christ could sin, but to show that He could not sin. The temptation came at a critical time: the beginning of Christ's public ministry. The temptation was designed to show the nation what a unique Savior she had: the impeccable Son of God. It is also noteworthy that it was not Satan who initiated the temptation but the Holy Spirit (Matt. 4:1). If Christ could have sinned, then the Holy Spirit solicited Christ to sin, but that is something God does not do (James 1:13).

Christ's peccability could relate only to His human nature; His divine nature was impeccable. Although Christ had two natures, He was nonetheless one Person and could not divorce Himself of His deity. Wherever He went, the divine nature was present. If the two natures could be separated then it could be said that He could sin in His humanity, but because the human and divine natures cannot be separated from the Person of Christ, and since the divine nature cannot sin, it must be affirmed that Christ could not have sinned.

Evidence. The evidence for the impeccability of Christ is set forth by William Shedd and others in the following way.

(1) The immutability of Christ (Heb. 13:8). Christ is unchangeable and therefore could not sin. If Christ could have sinned while on earth, then He could sin now because of His immutability. If He could have sinned on earth, what assurance is there that He will not sin now?

(2) The omnipotence of Christ (Matt. 28:18). Christ was omnipotent and therefore could not sin. Weakness is implied where sin is possible, yet there was no weakness of any kind in Christ. How could He be omnipotent and still be able to sin?

(3) The omniscience of Christ (John 2:25). Christ was omniscient and therefore could not sin. Sin depends on ignorance in order that the sinner may be deceived, but Christ could not be deceived because He knows all things, including the hypothetical (Matt. 11:21). If Christ could have sinned then He really did not know what would happen if He would sin.

(4) The deity of Christ. Christ is not only man but also God. If He were only a man then He could have sinned, but God cannot sin and in a union of the two natures, the human nature submits to the divine nature (otherwise the finite is stronger than the infinite). United in the one Person of Christ are the two natures, humanity and deity; because Christ is also deity He could not sin.

(5) The nature of temptation (James 1:14-15). The temptation that came to Christ was *from without.* However, for sin to take place, there must

be an *inner* response to the outward temptation. Since Jesus did not possess a sin nature, there was nothing within Him to respond to the temptation. People sin because there is an inner response to the outer temptation.

(6) The will of Christ. In moral decisions, Christ could have only one will: to do the will of His Father; in moral decisions the human will was subservient to the divine will.[40] If Christ could have sinned then His human will would have been stronger than the divine will.

(7) The authority of Christ (John 10:18). In His deity, Christ had complete authority over His humanity. For example, no one could take the life of Christ except He would lay it down willingly (John 10:18). If Christ had authority over life and death, He certainly had authority over sin; if He could withhold death at will, He could also withhold sin at will.

THE OFFICES OF CHRIST

HE IS A PROPHET

God spoke through the prophets to mankind. The office of prophet was established in Deuteronomy 18:15-18 and also looked forward to its ultimate fulfillment in Christ (cf. Acts 3:22-23). No singular prophet completely revealed the will of the Father except Jesus Christ. When Christ came He completely revealed the Father to the people; He explained the Father to the people (John 1:18).

HE IS A PRIEST

Whereas the prophet revealed God to man, the priest represented man to God. Psalm 110:4 establishes Christ's priesthood according to the order of Melchizedek (cf. Heb. 5:6-10; 6:20; 7:11, 17). As a priest: (1) Christ continually represents the believer because He lives forever (Heb. 7:24); (2) Christ completely saves the believer because His intercession never ceases (Heb. 7:25); (3) Christ has no personal sins to impede His work as priest (Heb. 7:27); (4) Christ finished His priestly work by *one* offering (Heb. 10:12).

HE IS A KING

Genesis 49:10 (see earlier discussion) prophesied that Messiah would come from the tribe of Judah and reign as king. Second Samuel 7:16 indicated Messiah would have a dynasty, a people over whom He would rule, and an eternal throne. In Psalm 2:6 God the Father announced the installation of His Son as King in Jerusalem. Psalm 110 indicates that Messiah would subjugate His enemies and rule over them (cf. Isa. 9:6-7; Dan. 7:13-14; Micah 5:2; Zech. 9:9; Matt. 22:41-46; 25:31; Luke 1:31-33; Rev. 1:5; 19:16).

These three offices of Christ as Prophet, Priest, and King are the key to the purpose of the incarnation. His prophetic office was involved with the revealing of God's message; the priestly office was related to His saving and intercessory work; His kingly office gave Him the right to reign over Israel and the entire earth. All the divine intention of these three historic offices was perfectly culminated in the Lord Jesus Christ.

PRESENT MINISTRY OF CHRIST

CHRIST IS BUILDING HIS CHURCH

Formation of the Body. First Corinthians 12:13 indicates the Holy Spirit is forming the church, the Body of Christ; however, Christ as head of the church is guiding and controlling it. Acts 2:47 indicates Christ is the One who is producing the increase in the church. This is consistent with Acts 1:1 where Luke indicates that the gospel he wrote describes the work Jesus *began* to do, suggesting that His work continues today in building the church.

Direction of the Body. Christ is not only head of the Body, but also head over it (Col. 1:18) in giving direction and sovereign rule (Eph. 5:23, 24). As the human head gives direction to the entire physical body, so Christ, as head of the church, gives direction to the church through the Word of God (Eph. 5:26).

Nurture of the Body. As an individual nourishes the human body, so Jesus Christ is the source of nourishment to the church; He is the means to nourish it to maturity (Eph. 5:29, 30).[41] Christ in His present work is bringing the Body to maturity.

Cleansing of the Body. Christ is involved in the cleansing of the Body. He is producing sanctification in the believer (Eph. 5:25-27). This denotes the progressive sanctification in which Christ is cleansing the church.

Giving gifts to the Body. Christ is the source of the spiritual gifts; the Holy Spirit administers them (Eph. 4:8, 11-13). Gifts are given with the purpose that the whole church might be built up and increased in this manner. Ephesians 4:11-13 indicates the gifts are given that the Body of Christ, the church, might grow to maturity.

CHRIST IS PRAYING FOR BELIEVERS

Christ's intercession assures the security of our salvation. The believer could lose his salvation only if Christ would be ineffective in His role as mediator (Rom. 8:34; Heb. 7:25). The intercession of Christ involves (1) His presence before the Father; (2) His spoken word (Luke 22:32; John 17:6-26); and (3) His continual intercession (note the present tense in the verbs).

Christ's intercession restores us to fellowship when that fellowship is broken through sin. Christ is termed the believers' "Advocate" (Gk. *parakletos*), meaning "defense attorney"(1 John 2:1). "In rabbinical literature the word could indicate one who offers legal aid or one who intercedes on behalf of someone else. . . . the word undoubtedly signified an 'advocate' or 'counsel for the defense' in a legal context."[42]

Christ is preparing a heavenly abode for us (John 14:1-3). In glory Christ is preparing many dwelling places in the Father's house. The picture is that of a wealthy oriental father who adds additional rooms to his large home in order to accommodate his married children. There is room for them all.

Christ is producing fruit in the lives of believers (John 15:1-7). As a vine is rooted to the branch and draws life and nourishment from the branch to sustain life and produce fruit, so the believer is grafted into spiritual union with Christ to draw spiritual nourishment from Christ. Spiritual fruit will be the result.

FUTURE WORK OF CHRIST

The hope exhibited in the Scriptures is the ultimate restoration of all things under Messiah. In one phase His coming will fulfill the glorious hope for the church, an event of resurrection and reunion (1 Cor. 15:51-58; 1 Thess. 4:13-18; Titus 2:13); in another phase His coming will be a judgment on the unbelieving nations and Satan (Rev. 19:11-21), and will be a rescue of His people, Israel, and the inauguration of the millennial reign (Mic. 5:4; Zech. 9:10). (See an extended discussion in chap. 26, "Eschatology: Doctrine of Last Things.")

NOTES ON CHRISTOLOGY

1. "There never was a time when the Word was not. There never was a thing which did not depend on Him for its very existence. The verb 'was' is most naturally understood of the eternal existence of the Word: 'the Word continually was.' " (Leon Morris, *The Gospel According to John* [Grand Rapids: Eerdmans, 1971], p. 73.) This commentary on John is one of the finest.

2. Ibid., p. 473. See Morris's helpful comments on this verse which he sees as stressing the deity and eternality of Christ.

3. J. Oliver Buswell, Jr., *A Systematic Theology of the Christian Religion* (Grand Rapids: Zondervan, 1962), 1:33.

4. The reader should consult E. W. Hengstenberg, *Christology of the Old Testament* (Reprint. Grand Rapids: Kregel, 1970). This masterful work, originally published in 1847, is a complete study of the Messianic prophecies from Genesis through Zechariah.

5. Hengstenberg, *Christology of the Old Testament*, p. 24.
6. Ibid.
7. C. F. Keil and F. Delitzsch, *Biblical Commentary on the Old Testament*, 25 vols. (Reprint. Grand Rapids: Eerdmans, 1968), 1:393.
8. Keil & Delitzsch, *Biblical Commentary*, 1:397.
9. Hengstenberg, *Christology of the Old Testament*, p. 30.
10. Gleason L. Archer, Jr., *Encyclopedia of Bible Difficulties* (Grand Rapids: Zondervan, 1982), pp. 266-68.
11. Allen P. Ross, "Psalms," in John F. Walvoord and Roy B. Zuck, eds., *The Bible Knowledge Commentary: Old Testament* (Wheaton, Ill.: Victor, 1985), p. 809.
12. Herbert M. Wolf, *Interpreting Isaiah* (Grand Rapids: Zondervan, 1985), p. 215. This is a most helpful book on the premillennial interpretation and theology of Isaiah.
13. A most important work in this study is W. W. Barndollar, *Jesus' Title to the Throne of David: A Study in Biblical Eschatology* (Findlay, Ohio: Dunham, 1963).
14. Walvoord, *Jesus Christ Our Lord*, p. 104.
15. William F. Arndt and F. Wilbur Gingrich, *A Greek-English Lexicon of the New Testament and Other Early Christian Literature*, 2d ed., revised by F. Wilbur Gingrich and Frederick W. Danker (Chicago: U. of Chicago, 1979), p. 627.
16. See Donald Grey Barnhouse: *Exposition of Bible Doctrine Taking the Epistle to the Romans as the Point of Departure*, 10 vols. (Grand Rapids: Eerdmans, 1963), 1:43-48. Barnhouse demonstrates the logical and scriptural necessity of the virgin birth.
17. The use of the passive form *egennethe*, instead of the active form *gennao*, stresses that Jesus was born of Mary without any participation by Joseph.
18. Walvoord, *Jesus Christ Our Lord*, p. 110.
19. A. T. Robertson, *Word Pictures in the New Testament*, 6 vols. (Nashville: Broadman, 1930), 2:36.
20. The verb translated "deeply moved" is *enebrimesato.* "It signifies a loud, inarticulate noise, and its proper use appears to be for the snorting of horses. When used of men it usually denotes anger. . .His feeling was no light emotion. Many feel that the word must be taken to mean anger, and if so it is probably anger against death that it meant" (Leon Morris, *The Gospel According to John*, p. 556).
21. B. B. Warfield, *The Person and Work of Christ* (Philadephia: Presbyterian and Reformed, 1950), p. 39.
22. As a point of Greek grammar it can be affirmed that both terms, *God* and *Savior*, refer to Christ.
23. There is a textual problem concerning this phrase, some manuscipts reading "the only begotten Son," others reading "only begotten God." The latter reading has strong manuscript support and is given a "B" rating in the United Bible Society text, suggesting only "some degree of doubt."
24. Walvoord, *Jesus Christ Our Lord*, p. 116.
25. Fritz Rienecker, *Linguistic Key to the Greek New Testament*, edited by Cleon Rogers (Grand Rapids: Zondervan, 1980), p. 664.
26. Walvoord, *Jesus Christ Our Lord*, p. 112.
27. Ibid., p. 114.
28. Ibid.

29. Walvoord delineates important results of the hypostatic union in *Jesus Christ Our Lord*, pp. 120-22.

30. Henry C. Thiessen, *Lectures in Systematic Theology*, revised by Vernon D. Doerksen (Grand Rapids: Eerdmans, 1979), pp. 216-17.

31. W. Graham Scroggie, *A Guide to the Gospels* (London: Pickering & Inglis, 1948), p. 193. This is a most helpful work in studying the life of Christ. Scroggie provides a great deal of helpful material such as the Old Testament citations in each of the Gospels, the parables, miracles, and words in each of the Gospels, and many additional features. The student of the Life of Christ will find this a very helpful tool.

32. R. W. McCarthy, "The Millennial Significance of Miracles of Christ," unpublished Th.M. thesis, Dallas Seminary.

33. This chart is an adaptation from Merrill C. Tenney, *John: The Gospel of Belief* (Grand Rapids: Eerdmans, 1949), p. 312.

34. See also the discussion under "Soteriology: Doctrine of Salvation."

35. Artists are notoriously poor theologians and all too often beautifully paint pictures depicting biblical scenes erroneously. A common resurrection painting shows neatly folded cloths lying on the edge of a slab. That illustration tells nothing of the resurrection and certainly does not reflect the emotion in the tomb when both Peter and John saw and believed. The verbs *theorei* (v. 6) and *eidon* (v. 8) stress that the disciples saw something extraordinary that caused them to believe. Barnabas Lindars acknowledges, "It could be argued that John means here that the napkin was still wrapped round, as it had been when it was bound round Jesus' face. This would lead to the conclusion that John means that the grave clothes were undisturbed by the resurrection. Jesus has passed through them, and not even the face cloth had been moved." (Barnabas Lindars, *The Gospel of John* in *The New Century Bible Commentary* [Grand Rapids: Eerdmans, 1972], p. 602.) Raymond Brown cites several sources that support this theory in *The Gospel According to John XIII-XXI* in *The Anchor Bible*, 34 vols. (Garden City, N.Y.: Doubleday, 1970), 2:985. See also Homer A. Kent, Jr., *Light in the Darkness: Studies in the Gospel of John* (Grand Rapids: Baker, 1974), pp. 217-18.

36. Walvoord, *Jesus Christ Our Lord*, pp. 223-24.

37. Charles Hodge, *Systematic Theology*, 3 vols. (Reprint. London: Clarke, 1960), 2:457.

38. Arndt and Gingrich, *A Greek-English Lexicon*, p. 640.

39. Perhaps the most capable and thorough discussion of this view is by Wm. G. T. Shedd, *Dogmatic Theology*, 3 vols. (Reprint. Nashville: Nelson, 1980), 2:330-49. Shedd's precision and thoroughness are seen here as elsewhere.

40. Walvoord, *Jesus Christ Our Lord*, pp. 119-20; cf. Shedd, *Dogmatic Theology*, 2:332.

41. "Nourish," *ektrephei*, means "to nourish children to maturity. . .(the) pres. tense denotes the whole process leading up to an attained goal." (Fritz Rienecker, *Linguistic Key to the Greek New Testament*, p. 539.)

42. Ibid., p. 786.

For Further Study on Christology

THE VIRGIN BIRTH

There are two primary sources that ought to be considered in a study of the virgin birth of Christ.

* Robert G. Gromacki. *The Virgin Birth: Doctrine of Deity.* Grand Rapids: Baker, 1974.

** J. Gresham Machen. *The Virgin Birth of Christ.* Reprint. Grand Rapids: Baker, 1967. This is the classic study of the doctrine by one of America's great theologians at the beginning of the twentieth century.

PROPHECIES OF CHRIST

** David Baron. *Rays of Messiah's Glory: Christ in the Old Testament.* Reprint. Winona Lake, Ind.: Alpha, 1979.

** Lewis Sperry Chafer. *Systematic Theology,* 8 vols. Dallas: Dallas Seminary, 1947. 5:181-87, 236-38.

* Norman Geisler. *To Understand the Bible Look for Jesus.* Reprint. Grand Rapids: Baker, 1979.

** E. W. Hengstenberg. *Christology of the Old Testament.* Reprint. Grand Rapids: Kregel, 1970.

* Ceil and Moishe Rosen. *Christ in the Passover.* Chicago: Moody, 1979.

* John F. Walvoord. *Jesus Christ Our Lord.* Chicago: Moody, 1969. Pp. 79-95.

THE PERSON OF CHRIST

* Emery H. Bancroft. *Christian Theology.* Grand Rapids: Zondervan, 1976. Pp. 103-5.

** Donald G. Bloesch. *Essentials of Evangelical Theology,* 2 vols. San Francisco: Harper, 1978. 1:120-47.

** Charles Hodge. *Systematic Theology,* 3 vols. Reprint. London: Clarke, 1960. 1:483-521.

* Charles C. Ryrie. *A Survey of Bible Doctrine.* Chicago: Moody, 1972. Pp. 52-55.

** Wm. G. T. Shedd. *Dogmatic Theology,* 3 vols. Reprint. Nashville: Nelson, 1980. 1:312-28.

** A. H. Strong. *Systematic Theology.* Valley Forge, Pa: Judson, 1907. Pp. 305-15.

* John F. Walvoord. *Jesus Christ Our Lord.* Chicago: Moody, 1969. Pp. 107-9.

** B. B. Warfield. *The Person and Work of Christ.* Philadelphia: Presbyterian and Reformed, 1950. Pp. 37-70.

THE MINISTRY OF CHRIST

** Alfred Edersheim. *The Life and Times of Jesus the Messiah,* 2 vols. Reprint. Grand Rapids: Eerdmans, 1969. Although written 100 years ago this work is extremely valuable in providing background material on Jewish social life and rabbinic writings.

* Donald Guthrie. *A Shorter Life of Christ.* Grand Rapids: Zondervan, 1970.

* Everett F. Harrison. *A Short Life of Christ.* Grand Rapids: Eerdmans, 1968.

** D. Martyn Lloyd-Jones. *Studies in the Sermon on the Mount,* 2 vols. Grand Rapids: Eerdmans, 1959. An outstanding exposition reflecting the authority and power of Jesus' teaching.

** J. Dwight Pentecost. *The Words and Works of Jesus Christ.* Grand Rapids: Zondervan, 1981. This is a valuable, thematic treatment by one who has taught the life of Christ for over thirty years.

* _____. *The Sermon on the Mount.* Portland: Multnomah, 1980.

21

PNEUMATOLOGY: DOCTRINE OF THE HOLY SPIRIT

Because the Holy Spirit is a member of the triune Godhead the special study of His person and work could not be more important. As might be expected wherever God and His truth are involved, false teaching has developed to distort or deny orthodox doctrine.[1] The Bible is rich with data about the Spirit from which a major theological segment can be readily constructed.

PERSONALITY OF THE HOLY SPIRIT

HIS IDENTITY CONFIRMS HIS PERSONALITY

The problem in the minds of many people is that personality can exist only in human beings, as though personality can relate only to finite beings but not to the infinite.[2] Since man is made in the image of God it is reasonable to expect similar characteristics between God and man. Hence, "It is possible to form some conception of divine personality by a study of the human, because man is made in the likeness of God."[3] Personality may simply be defined as possessing intellect, emotions, and will; then, by demonstrating that the Holy Spirit has intellect, emotions, and will it will be shown that He is a person and has personality.[4] The Holy Spirit is sometimes referred to as "it" or a "thing" or simply an influence. This study will demonstrate that the Holy Spirit is not simply an influence but a Person, having the characteristics of personality. Early in church history Arius denied the personality of the Holy Spirit. He said the Holy Spirit was only an influence emanating from the Father. He was condemned at the Council of Nicea, A.D. 325. His teaching has continued to the present time in Unitarianism and in the cults, such as the Jehovah's Witnesses.

HIS ATTRIBUTES CONFIRM HIS PERSONALITY

Intellect. The Holy Spirit has intellect inasmuch as "the Spirit searches all things" (1 Cor. 2:10). The word "search" means to examine or investigate a matter. The Holy Spirit examines the depths of God and reveals them to believers. The same word is used by Christ in John 5:39 where He states, "You search the Scriptures."

Knowledge. No human being has an awareness or knowledge of the thoughts of God, but the Holy Spirit understands the mind of God (1 Cor. 2:11).

Mind. Even as the Holy Spirit knows the Father, so the Father knows the mind of the Spirit (Rom. 8:27). The word mind (Gk. *phronema*) means "way of thinking, mind-(set); aim, aspiration, striving"[5] and clearly indicates that the Holy Spirit has intellect (cf. Eph. 1:17).

Emotions. Emotions or sensibility means to have feelings, to have an awareness and an ability to respond to something. Ephesians 4:30 commands, "do not grieve the Holy Spirit of God." The context emphasizes that the Holy Spirit is grieved when a believer sins by lying (v. 25), being angry (v. 26), by stealing or being lazy (v. 28), or speaking unkind words (v. 29). The noun form of the same word is used in describing the Corinthians' sorrow after Paul wrote them a stern letter (2 Cor. 2:2, 5). It is a *Person* who is grieved; a mere influence cannot be grieved.

Will. The Holy Spirit has a will, indicating He has the power of sovereign choice and decision. The Holy Spirit distributes spiritual gifts just as He wills.[6] The phrase "He wills" (Gk. *bouletai*) refers to "decisions of the will after previous deliberation."[7] The idea of sovereign choice is evident in this statement. By way of analogy, the same word "will" is used to describe the will of God the Father (James 1:18). Just as the Father has a will, so the Holy Spirit has a will. In Acts 16:6 the Holy Spirit exercised His will in forbidding Paul to preach in Asia and redirecting Paul to ministry in Europe. These Scripture passages clearly teach that the Holy Spirit has intellect, emotion, and will as part of a genuine personality.

HIS WORKS CONFIRM HIS PERSONALITY

The Holy Spirit performs works that are similar to the works of the Father and the Son. These works confirm the personality of the Holy Spirit.

The Spirit teaches. Before Jesus departed from the disciples He encouraged them by telling them He would send them "another Helper" (John 14:16). "Another" stresses that the Holy Spirit will be a Helper of the same kind as Christ.[8] Just as Jesus had taught the disciples (Matt. 5:2; John 8:2), so the Holy Spirit would teach them (John 14:26). The Holy Spirit would perform and carry on the same kind of teaching ministry as Christ did. The

Holy Spirit would cause them to remember the things Christ had taught them earlier; the Spirit would confirm Christ's teaching.

The Spirit testifies. Jesus promised the disciples that the Holy Spirit "will bear witness of Me" (John 15:26). The word "bear witness" means to testify concerning someone. The Holy Spirit would testify concerning the teaching of Christ that He had come forth from the Father and had spoken the truth of God. The same word is used of the disciples' testifying concerning Christ in John 15:27. As the disciples would bear witness concerning Christ so also would the Holy Spirit bear witness of Christ.

The Spirit guides. Jesus declared that when the Holy Spirit would come He would guide them into all the truth (John 16:13). The picture is that of a guide or escort leading a traveler into territory unfamiliar to the traveler, but familiar to the guide.

The Spirit convicts. John 16:8 declares the future ministry of the Spirit would be to "convict the world." "Convict" (Gk. *elegcho*) means to "convince someone of something; point something out to someone."[9] The Holy Spirit acts as a divine prosecutor in convicting the world concerning sin, righteousness, and judgment.

The Spirit regenerates. The one who experiences the new birth has been born of the Holy Spirit; He has been regenerated by the Spirit. Just as the Son of God gives life to believers (John 5:21), so the Holy Spirit regenerates people (cf. Ezek. 36:25-27; Titus 3:5).

The Spirit intercedes. In the time of a believer's weakness, the Holy Spirit takes the believer's groanings and intercedes on his behalf (Rom. 8:26). The Father understands the intercession of the Spirit and answers the prayer and works all things together for good in the believer's life because the Spirit has interceded for the child of God (Rom. 8:28). The same word regarding intercession is used of Christ in His intercessory work (Rom. 8:34; Heb. 7:25). Just as Christ intercedes on behalf of believers, so the Spirit also intercedes for them. One is again reminded: an inanimate entity could not intercede for others; a person intercedes.

The Spirit commands. In Acts 13:2 the Holy Spirit commanded that Paul and Barnabas be set apart for missionary work; Acts 13:4 adds that the two men were sent out by the Holy Spirit. In Acts 16:6 the Holy Spirit prohibited Paul and Silas from preaching in Asia; in Acts 8:29 the Holy Spirit directed Philip to speak to the Ethiopian eunuch.

HIS POSITION CONFIRMS HIS PERSONALITY

"Certain acts are performed toward the Holy Spirit which would be most incongruous if He did not possess true personality."[10]

The Spirit can be grieved. The Holy Spirit can be grieved when a believer sins (see earlier discussion; cf. Isa. 63:10).

The Spirit can be blasphemed. Blasphemy is normally thought of as being rendered against God the Father (cf. Rev. 13:6; 16:9). Christ was also blasphemed (Matt. 27:39; Luke 23:39); similarly, the Holy Spirit was also blasphemed (Matt. 12:32; Mark 3:29-30). The blasphemy against the Holy Spirit consisted of attributing the works of Christ to Satan when the Holy Spirit had borne witness to Christ's work as being from the Father.

The Spirit can be resisted. In his speech against the unbelieving Jews who ultimately stoned him to death, Stephen accused them of being "stiff-necked and uncircumcised in heart and ears . . . always resisting the Holy Spirit" (Acts 7:51). They stood in a long tradition of rejecting the work of God and resisting the admonitions of the Holy Spirit.

The Spirit can be lied to. When Peter confronted Ananias and Sapphira concerning their deceit, he accused them of having lied to the Holy Spirit (Acts 5:3). Ananias and Sapphira were both judged with death for their sin of having lied to the Spirit.

The Spirit can be obeyed. In Acts 10 the Lord revealed most graphically to Peter that He was also including Gentiles in the realm of His blessings. In this connection the Holy Spirit told Peter to accompany the two men to the house of Cornelius where this truth would become evident to the Gentiles. Peter obeyed the command of the Holy Spirit and went to the home of Cornelius in Caesarea. Peter obeyed the Holy Spirit.

These examples give evidence of the personality of the Holy Spirit in that He can be grieved, blasphemed, resisted, lied to, and obeyed. This could only be said with reference to a personality.

HIS DESIGNATIONS CONFIRM HIS PERSONALITY

The Greek word for Spirit is *pneuma* which is a neuter gender word. Any pronoun used to substitute for pneuma would normally also be neuter. However, the biblical writers did not follow this grammatical pattern; instead, they substituted masculine pronouns to designate the Holy Spirit.

SOME MASCULINE PRONOUNS FOR THE HOLY SPIRIT

Scripture	Neuter Noun	Masculine Pronoun
John 15:26	*pneuma* (Spirit)	*ekeinos* (He)
John 16:13	*pneuma* (Spirit)	*ekeinos* (He)
John 16:14	*pneuma* (Spirit)	*ekeinos* (He)

The purposeful change in grammar emphasizes the personality of the Holy Spirit. There would have been no reason to change from the neuter to the masculine unless the Spirit was understood to be a person.

DEITY OF THE HOLY SPIRIT

The deity of the Holy Spirit is inextricably bound up with the doctrine of the Trinity. A denial of one is a denial of the other. Conversely, belief in the Trinity necessitates a belief in the deity of the Holy Spirit.

DIVINE TITLES OF THE SPIRIT

The title *Spirit of God* evidences His relationship to the Father and the Son and also affirms His deity. "When He is called 'the Spirit of God' that means that He is the very Person of God. 1 Corinthians 2:11 clearly shows that as man and his spirit make one and the same being, so God and His Spirit are only one . . ."[11]

Probably in most instances when the term *Spirit of God* is used, it is a reference to the Holy Spirit rather than the Father, similarly, when the term *Spirit of Christ* is used it is usually a reference to the Holy Spirit. The reason for this is that if the Father were intended, it would be most normal to use God, LORD, and so forth; if Christ were intended, it would be most normal to use the name Jesus Christ. For example, in Romans 8:9-11 all members of the Trinity are mentioned: "Spirit of God dwells in you" (v. 9); "Christ is in you" (v. 10); "Spirit of Him (Father) who raised Jesus from the dead dwells in you" (v. 11). It seems fairly clear that "Spirit of God" is a reference to the Holy Spirit rather than to Christ or the Father. From Romans 8:9 and 8:13-14 it is further seen that "Spirit" and "Spirit of God" are synonyms and a reference to the third person of the Trinity.[12] A similar example can be seen in Acts 16:6-7 where "Holy Spirit" (v. 6) and "Spirit of Jesus" (v. 7) are synonyms. Ephesians 4:4 states there is only one Spirit, indicating the above proposition is true.

DIVINE ATTRIBUTES OF THE SPIRIT

Life (Rom. 8:2). Life is an attribute of deity (Josh. 3:10; John 1:4; 14:6; 1 Tim. 3:15). As the Father and the Son have life in themselves, so the Holy Spirit has life in Himself.

Omniscience (1 Cor. 2:10-12). Someone other than man must know about God. The spirit of man (the human spirit) knows the things pertaining to humanity; the Holy Spirit knows about God. The Holy Spirit searches the depths of God (1 Cor. 2:10); the same term *depth* (Gk. *bathos*) is used of the knowledge of God. It is unfathomable to man, but God the Holy Spirit knows the otherwise unsearchable and unfathomable (Rom. 11:33).

TITLES OF THE HOLY SPIRIT[13]

Title	Emphasis	Citation
One Spirit	His Unity	Ephesians 4:4
Seven Spirits	His perfection, omnipresence, and completeness	Revelation 1:4; 3:1
The Lord the Spirit	His sovereignty	2 Corinthians 3:18
Eternal Spirit	His eternity	Hebrews 9:14
Spirit of Glory	His glory	1 Peter 4:14
Spirit of Life	His vitality	Romans 8:2
Spirit of Holiness Holy Spirit Holy One	His holiness	Romans 1:4 Matthew 1:20 1 John 2:20
Spirit of Wisdom Spirit of Understanding Spirit of Counsel Spirit of Knowledge	His omniscience, wisdom, and counsel	Exodus 28:3 Isaiah 11:2
Spirit of Might	His omnipotence	Isaiah 11:2
Spirit of Fear of the Lord	His reverence	Isaiah 11:2
Spirit of Truth	His truthfulness	John 14:17
Free Spirit	His sovereign freedom	Psalm 51:12
Spirit of Grace	His grace	Hebrews 10:29
Spirit of Grace and Supplication	His grace and prayerfulness	Zechariah 12:10

Omnipotence (Job 33:4). The omnipotence of the Holy Spirit is seen in creation. In Genesis 1:2 the Holy Spirit is seen hovering over creation as a hen over its young; the Holy Spirit gave life to creation.[14]

Omnipresence (Ps. 139:7-10; John 14:17). In Psalm 139 David exclaims that He cannot flee from the presence of the Holy Spirit; if he ascends to heaven, He is there, if he descends into the depths of the earth, the Spirit is there also. Even if he could fly away swiftly, he could not escape the presence of the Spirit. The omnipresence of the Spirit is also taught in John 14:17 where Christ taught the disciples that the Spirit would indwell them all, an affirmation of the Spirit's omnipresence.

Eternity (Heb. 9:14). The Holy Spirit is called the Eternal Spirit in this passage. Through the Eternal Spirit Christ offered Himself without blemish to God. Just as the Holy Spirit had a part in the birth of Christ (Luke 1:35), in the same way He also had a part in the death of Christ.[15]

Holiness (cf. Matt. 12:32). One important aspect of deity is that God is holy, entirely set apart and separated from sin and sinners. The most common name for the Spirit is Holy Spirit, indicating the third person of the Trinity also possesses this transcendent attribute of deity.

Love (Gal. 5:22). The Holy Spirit is love and produces love in the child of God. If He did not possess love as a primary attribute He could not produce love in the believer.

Truth (John 14:17). The Holy Spirit is termed the "Spirit of truth" in John 14:17 and 15:26. Just as Christ was the truth (John 14:6) so the Spirit is the truth and leads people into the truth through the Scriptures.[16]

ATTRIBUTES OF THE TRIUNE GOD

Attribute	Father	Son	Holy Spirit
Life	Joshua 3:10	John 1:4	Romans 8:2
Omniscience	Psalm 139:1-6	John 4:17-18	1 Corinthians 2:10-12
Omnipotence	Genesis 1:1	John 1:3	Job 33:4
Omnipresence	Jeremiah 23:23-24	Matthew 28:20	Psalm 139:7-10
Eternity	Psalm 90:2	John 1:1	Hebrews 9:14
Holiness	Leviticus 11:44	Acts 3:14	Matthew 12:32
Love	1 John 4:8	Romans 8:37-39	Galatians 5:22
Truth	John 3:33	John 14:6	John 14:17

This chart reflects the unity and the equality of the Godhead. The Holy Spirit exhibits the same attributes of deity as the Father and the Son.

DIVINE WORKS OF THE SPIRIT

The works of the Holy Spirit give evidence of His deity.

Creation (Gen. 1:2). Several Scripture passages affirm that the Holy Spirit was involved in the work of creation. Genesis 1:2 indicates that the Spirit brooded over creation, bringing it to life. In Psalm 104:24-26 the psalmist describes the creation, and in v. 30 he indicates how God created:

"Thou dost send forth Thy Spirit, they are created." Job 26:13 expands the creation of God to the heavens; the Holy Spirit created not only the earth but also the heavens.[17] (See also previous discussion.)

Generating Christ (Matt. 1:20). The overshadowing of Mary by the Holy Spirit assured a sinless humanity of Christ. Christ in His deity is eternal, but the Holy Spirit begat the sinless human nature of Christ.

> He brought the humanity of Christ into being. It is too often assumed that Mary the mother of Christ contributed His humanity and that the Holy Spirit contributed His deity; but a moment's reflection would disclose that the deity of Christ was His own from all eternity and therefore was not originated at the time of His birth. He became incarnate when His eternal Person took on the human form. . . . The Spirit caused the humanity of Christ to originate and that is His act of generation.[18]

Inspiration of Scripture (2 Peter 1:21). There is an analogy between the Holy Spirit's generating Christ's humanity and the Spirit's superintending the writers of Scripture; just as the Holy Spirit overshadowed Mary, guaranteeing the sinlessness of Christ's humanity, so the Holy Spirit superintended the human writers to guarantee an inerrant Scripture. By analogy, a denial of one necessitates a denial of the other.

The writers of Scripture were carried along by the Holy Spirit, guaranteeing the inspiration of the books of Scripture. The Spirit's work in inspiration is analogous to the Father's work (cf. 2 Tim. 3:16).

Regeneration (Titus 3:5). To regenerate means to give life. The Holy Spirit causes the new birth; He is its author. Regeneration by the Holy Spirit is the spiritual counterpart of human reproduction in the physical realm. Human generation produces human life; spiritual regeneration produces spiritual life. The Holy Spirit produces the new birth, but He does it through the instrumentality of the Word of God (1 Peter 1:23). The same truth is taught in John 3:6 where Jesus indicates the Holy Spirit produces the new birth in that He regenerates the person.

Intercession (Rom. 8:26). Christ is an intercessor for believers, but so is the Holy Spirit. (See previous discussion on this verse.)

Sanctification (2 Thess. 2:13). There are three aspects of sanctification, the first being positional: "the setting apart which occurs when by the Holy Spirit the one who believes is joined unto Christ and thus comes to be in Christ."[19] (Cf. 1 Cor. 1:30; Heb. 10:14-15; 1 Pet. 1:2.)

Helping saints (John 14:16). In this text Jesus promised the disciples "another Helper." Helper is the Greek word *parakleton* which comes from two words, "along side" and "called," hence, "one called along side to help." In 1 John 2:1 the Lord Jesus is called the sinning saint's Paraclete ("Advocate" in most versions). The Holy Spirit is "another of the same kind" as Christ, a Helper who is called alongside to help the believer. The Holy

Spirit's work as the believer's Paraclete (Helper) demands His deity since His work is the same as Christ's in His role as Paraclete.

It becomes apparent that the works of the Holy Spirit indicate His deity —His oneness within the Godhead, together with the Father and the Son.

DIVINE PROCESSION OF THE SPIRIT

The relationship of the Holy Spirit to the other members of the Trinity is expressed by the term *procession*, indicating the Holy Spirit came forth from both the Father and the Son.

The Constantinople creed affirmed this doctrine in A.D. 381. The *filioque* ("and from the Son") phrase was added at the synod of Toledo in A.D. 589 to affirm the equality of the Son, based on John 15:26 which affirmed that both Christ and the Father sent the Spirit. This statement combated the heresy that depreciated the Person of Christ.

There are several indicators suggesting the doctrine of the procession of the Spirit. All designations such as "Spirit of God" affirm the procession of the Spirit in that He is the Spirit from God. The present tense of John 15:26 ("proceeds") is used to understand the eternality of the relationship. Hence, the Holy Spirit is spoken of as eternally proceeding from the Father and the Son. The eternal procession of the Spirit seems to be affirmed by Psalm 104:30, which indicates the Holy Spirit came forth from the Father in the Old Testament economy. The Greek Orthodox church understood the "eternal procession" as beginning with the incarnation of Christ (both occurred at the same time).[20]

A word of caution should be issued. The procession of the Holy Spirit does *not* indicate the subordination of the Spirit to the other members of the Trinity. J. Oliver Buswell discusses the problem and notes that this very term was understood by some in the ancient church that the Holy Spirit was a "quasi-dependent being." Buswell rejects the term, considering it a hindrance.[21]

REPRESENTATIONS OF THE HOLY SPIRIT

There are descriptions and depictions of the Holy Spirit in Scripture that vividly portray His Person and His work. These could variously be identified as type, illustration, emblem, or symbol and are thus categorized as representations of the Holy Spirit.

CLOTHING

Following His resurrection Jesus commanded the disciples to wait in Jerusalem, "until you are clothed with power from on high" (Luke 24:49). "Clothed" (Gk. *enduo*) is the normal word for "dress," or "clothe someone." The word is passive, indicating the individual does not clothe himself;

someone else (God) does it for him. The meaning of clothing is explained in the text by the phrase, "with power." The apostles were to stay in Jerusalem until they were clothed with the Holy Spirit's power.

DOVE

At the baptism of Christ the Holy Spirit descended "like a dove." Was it an actual dove? A study of the passages is helpful: "as a dove," (Matt. 3:16); "like a dove," (Mark 1:10); "in bodily form like a dove," (Luke 3:22); "beheld the Spirit descending," (John 1:32). According to Luke 3:22 and John 1:32 there must have been a physical representation of a dove. However, the dove only represented the Holy Spirit. Something in the quality and characteristics of the dove served as a vehicle to portray the Holy Spirit.

Each of the gospels emphasizes the descent of the Spirit as a dove "out of heaven," which stresses that the Holy Spirit has come from the presence of God in heaven. It is significant, of course, in emphasizing the Father's blessing and anointing of His Son for His public ministry. This was an important witness to the people, particularly those who opposed Christ.

The dove portrayed the Holy Spirit coming upon Christ at beginning of His public ministry and therefore emphasizes the power of the Holy Spirit on Christ for His work.

The dove is also a symbol of purity (cf. Matt. 10:16) and a representation of peace.

PLEDGE

In 2 Corinthians 1:22 Paul says God "gave us the Spirit in our hearts as a pledge." The word pledge (Gk. *arrabon*) means a "first installment, deposit, down payment, pledge, that pays a part of the purchase price in advance, and so secures a legal claim to the article in question, or makes a contract valid . . . (arrabon) is a payment which obligates the contracting party to make further payments."[22] Ephesians 1:14 reveals the nature of the Holy Spirit as the down payment of our ultimate and complete glorification in heaven. "Redemption" in Ephesians 1:14 looks forward to the final stage of the believer's redemption, that is, his ultimate glorification. The Holy Spirit as a pledge is a symbol of the believer's security in Christ.

FIRE

At Pentecost "tongues of fire" distributed themselves and rested on the Apostles (Acts 2:3). God's revelation of Himself by fire was not unusual and would have been understood by the Jews. It would have denoted the *presence of God.* This unusual occurrence, with the descent of the Holy Spirit, would signify that God was in this event (cf. Exod. 3:2). The occurrence also indicated the *approval of God.* When Peter proclaimed the resurrected Jesus moments later, the fire would symbolize the approval of God upon Peter's message (cf. Lev. 9:24; 1 Kings 18:38-39). The fire also symbolized the *judgment of God* (cf. Lev. 10:2). The unbelievers at Pentecost were ultimately judged for their unbelief at the destruction of the Temple in A.D. 70.

OIL

Oil is a type of the Holy Spirit inasmuch as the Old Testament practice of anointing priests and kings served as a type of the ministry of the Holy Spirit. Zechariah 4:1-14 illustrates the significance of oil as a type; oil depicted the Holy Spirit's power in strengthening Joshua and Zerubbabel to lead the people in completing the construction of the temple in 515 B.C. The constant flow of oil from the lampstand (v. 2) to the two leaders (vv. 3, 14) is interpreted in v. 6, "Not by might nor by power, but by My Spirit." In 1 Samuel 10:1 Samuel anointed Saul as king of Israel, the anointing representing the Spirit of the Lord coming upon him to lead the people (1 Sam. 10:6, 10). The Old Testament events, however, were only types for the ministry of the Holy Spirit in the New Testament.

OIL AS A TYPE OF THE SPIRIT

Significance	Scriptures
Spirit given for ministry.	Exodus 40:9-16 and Acts 1:8
Spirit illuminates.	Exodus 27:20-21 and 1 John 2:20
Spirit cleanses and sanctifies.	Leviticus 8:30; 14:17 and Romans 8:2-3

SEAL

The Holy Spirit is identified as the seal of the believer (2 Cor. 1:22; Eph. 1:13; 4:30). A seal means securing or fastening a stone with a seal as in Matthew 27:66 by the Roman authorities. Figuratively, sealing means to "mark (with a seal) as a means of identification . . . In papyrii, of all kinds of animals, so that the mark which denotes ownership also carries with it the protection of the owner."[23] Cattle branding would be a modern parallel of ancient sealing (cf. Isa. 44:5; Ezek. 9:4).

Several important truths emerge from the sealing of the Spirit. (1) It signified *ownership by God.* The Spirit's seal upon the believer indicates the believer belongs to God. (2) It suggests *security.* The seal is permanent, "for the day of redemption" (Eph. 4:30). (3) It also suggests *authority.* Just as the Roman authority existed over the area where the Roman seal was placed, so the authority of God is over the believer to whom He has given His Spirit.

WATER

During the final ritual at the Feast of Tabernacles the priest brought water from the pool of Siloam and poured it in the funnel beside the altar, amid the singing of worshipers. The event was a joyous one, in anticipation of Messiah's glorious reign (Zech. 14:16-21). During that event Jesus proclaimed, "If any man is thirsty, let him come to Me and drink. He who believes in Me, as the Scripture said, 'From his innermost being shall flow rivers of living water'" (John 7:37-38). The next verse gives the explanation: "But this He spoke of the Spirit" (John 7:39). Several points are noteworthy. Water as an emblem of the Holy Spirit signifies eternal life (cf. John 4:14; 7:37-39). Water signifies a reception of the Holy Spirit (Ezek. 36:25-27; John 7:39). It anticipates millennial blessings (study the background of John 7:37-39; cf. Isa. 12:3; Joel 2:28-32).

WIND

Wind is a most natural representation of the Holy Spirit since the word *spirit* (Gk. *pneuma*) may be translated *wind* as well as *spirit*. English words like *pneumatic* derive their meaning from the word *pneuma*. In explaining the new birth to Nicodemus, Jesus compared the birth by the Holy Spirit to the wind (John 3:8). The new birth was an inexplicable sovereign work of God; just as the wind blowing through the trees is inexplicable and sovereign, so is the new birth by the Holy Spirit. The Spirit does "as He wills;" no one dictates to Him just as no one dictates to the wind (cf. 1 Cor. 12:11).

THE SPIRIT IN REVELATION AND INSPIRATION

DEFINITIONS

Revelation. Revelation (Gk. *apokalupsis*) means "disclosure" or "unveiling" and is used to describe the unveiling of a statue upon completion by a great sculptor. In biblical truth revelation means God revealing to man something that man would not otherwise know (cf. Ezek. 2:2; 8:3).

Inspiration. Biblical inspiration can be defined as "God's superintending human authors so that, using their own individual personalities, they composed and recorded without error His revelation to man in the words of the original autographs."[24] In contrasting revelation with inspiration it may be stated that revelation refers to the *material* whereas inspiration refers to the *method*.[25] The word *inspiration* is taken from the Greek word *theopneustos* (meaning "God-breathed") in 2 Timothy 3:16. Scripture is that which is "breathed-out by God." The Scriptures are the product of the creative breath of God. "The 'breath of God' is in Scripture just the symbol of His almighty power, the bearer of His creative word."[26] A parallel can be observed:

GOD-BREATHED CREATIONS

God, by His breath	Formed the heavens, Psalm 33:6
	Revealed the Scriptures, 2 Timothy 3:16

CHANNELS OF REVELATION

Old Testament prophet. The Old Testament prophet's message did not originate with himself. He was merely the vehicle through whom God spoke to the people; he was guided by the Holy Spirit in giving forth his message (cf. Jer. 1:2, 4, 9, 11, 17).

The Holy Spirit. While the Old Testament prophet was usually the vehicle through whom God revealed Himself, it was the Holy Spirit who guided the writers of Scripture. Second Peter 1:21 indicates the Holy Spirit was the one who carried along the Old Testament prophets, safeguarding their words from error. Specific examples may be cited. The Holy Spirit controlled David. David exclaims, "The Spirit of the LORD spoke by me, and His word was on my tongue (2 Sam. 23:2). Acts 1:16 emphasizes the same truth in explaining David's prophecy concerning Judas, which had to be fulfilled because "the Holy Spirit foretold by the mouth of David" (cf. Acts 4:25; Matt. 22:43). The Holy Spirit controlled Ezekiel. Ezekiel's numerous prophecies were given through the control of the Holy Spirit who enabled the prophet to receive visions from God (Ezek. 2:2; 3:24; 8:3; 11:24). The Holy Spirit controlled Micah. The Holy Spirit filled the prophet to enable him to speak to the nation (Mic. 3:8).

METHODS OF REVELATION

God revealed Himself in various ways in the Old Testament.

Spoken Word. There are numerous examples in which God spoke audibly to people in the Old Testament. God spoke audibly to Abraham (Gen. 18:13, 17); He spoke to Moses that the people might hear (Exod. 19:9; 20:1ff.); He spoke to Isaiah (Isa. 6:8).

Dreams. Revelation through dreams seems to be an inferior mode of revelation. It was a privilege to communicate with God face-to-face, hence, the normal way God communicated to the heathen was through dreams. It was a method that rendered the unbelievers teachable. "A revelation by a dream found the recipient in a passive, nonconscious state, with the reality of what was dreamed found only in noncorporeal mental images. . . . The dream was more suitable for people of little or no spiritual discernment. . . . The recipient was neutralized in his personality, and existed only as an inert instrument to whom information might be imparted without hindrance by an improper, paganistic response."[27] Examples of God speaking in dreams are Abimelech (Gen. 20:3); Jacob (Gen. 31:10-13); Joseph (Gen. 37:5-9); Nebuchadnezzar (Dan. 2).

Visions. Visions seem to have been a higher category of revelation, reserved for spiritually mature people.[28] Prophets frequently received visions. One of the words for prophet is *seer*, which comes from the Hebrew word meaning "to see"; hence, the prophet (seer) is "one who sees." Examples of God's spokesmen receiving visions are: Abraham (Gen. 15:1); Nathan (1 Chron. 17:15); Ezekiel (Ezek. 1:1); Daniel (Dan. 8:1).

Theophanies. An Old Testament theophany was a manifestation of God in a physical sense. Theophany comes from the Greek words *theos* (God) and *phanein* (to appear); hence, a theophany is an appearance of God. It was a privilege to be visited by God in this fashion, and it "was normally reserved only for persons of high spiritual maturity."[29] Examples of Old Testament theophanies are to Abraham (Gen. 18); to Joshua (Josh. 5:14); to Gideon (Judg. 6:22); to Daniel (Dan. 6:22).

INSPIRATION OF THE OLD TESTAMENT

The Holy Spirit Himself was the means of all biblical inspiration. His superintending work assured the infallibility of the communication. In connection with the Old Testament this is observable on a number of occasions.

Old Testament writers were conscious that the Holy Spirit was guiding their writing (2 Sam. 23:2-3). It is emphasized four times in this passage that God spoke to David.

Christ taught that the Old Testament writers were guided by the Holy Spirit (Mark 12:36). In quoting Psalm 110 Jesus exclaimed that David spoke the words "in the Holy Spirit." Jesus based His argument on David's words as inspired by the Holy Spirit.

Apostles taught that the Old Testament writers were guided by the Holy Spirit (Acts 1:16; 4:24-25; 28:25). In explaining Judas's death Peter remarked that it had to come about this way because it had been foretold by the Holy Spirit through David (Acts 1:16).

INSPIRATION OF THE NEW TESTAMENT

While an important passage on inspiration such as 2 Timothy 3:16 has basically the Old Testament in view, there are nonetheless many passages which point to the inspiration of the New Testament.

Christ affirmed the inspiration of the New Testament. Christ predicted the apostles would be safeguarded in their writing, which enabled them to write without error as they remembered all He had spoken to them (John

14:26; 16:14). This explains how John could still remember all the details of the life of Christ when he wrote his gospel years later. At the time Jesus taught the disciples, they were unable to comprehend His teaching, but later the Holy Spirit would enable them to understand (John 16:12-15).

The Holy Spirit guided the New Testament writers in the following ways. (1) He helped the writers remember the facts of Christ's teaching. (2) He enabled them to understand theologically what they were writing. At the time Jesus spoke to them they did not grasp the significance of His impending death and resurrection. (3) He guaranteed the completion of the entire New Testament. The "all things" of John 14:26 has reference to all spiritual truth necessary for man and would of necessity imply the completion of the New Testament canon.

The New Testament writers recognized they were writing Scripture. In 1 Corinthians Paul had rebuked the Corinthians for a number of errors in the assembly and he gave them the correctives to their errors. He concluded by reminding the Corinthians, "the things which I write to you are the Lord's commandment" (1 Cor. 14:37). Paul recognized he was writing the Word of God to the Corinthians. Several conclusions can be drawn through Paul's writing: Paul's teaching had been given him through direct revelation (Gal. 1:12). Paul's teaching was taught to him by the Holy Spirit (1 Cor. 2:13). Paul's teaching was God's commandment and therefore free from error (1 Cor. 14:37; 1 Thess. 4:2, 15). Paul's teaching was recognized as God's word by the early church (1 Thess. 2:13).

The New Testament writers recognized each others' writings as inspired. In 1 Timothy 5:18 Paul prefaced his statement with "the Scripture says," and then quoted from Deuteronomy 25:4 and Luke 10:7. In quoting from both the Old and New Testaments Paul regarded them as equal in authority. The words Luke wrote were Scripture in the very same sense as Moses' recording of Deuteronomy. In 2 Peter 3:16 Peter equated Paul's writing with "the rest of the Scriptures." Paul's writing was put on a par with the Old Testament Scriptures. A similar parallel is given in 2 Peter 3:2.

DUAL SECTIONS OF
BIBLICAL AUTHORITY (2 PETER 3:2)

Authority	Sections
"You should remember . . ."	"words spoken beforehand by the holy prophets" (Old Testament)
	"the commandment of the Lord and Savior spoken by your apostles" (New Testament)

THE SPIRIT'S MINISTRY IN THE OLD TESTAMENT

REGENERATION

Did the Holy Spirit regenerate people in the Old Testament? In John 3 Jesus explained the new birth (which involved regeneration) to Nicodemus, reminding him that these things were taught in the Old Testament and therefore he ought to have known them (John 3:10). In all likelihood Jesus was referring to Ezekiel 36, because both passages involve a discussion of water and Spirit. In Ezekiel 11:19 and 36:25-27 God promises Israel a regeneration experience in the Millennium. God will give them a new heart and a new spirit—He will put His Spirit within them; He will regenerate them. Although these passages pertain to the future, the Old Testament believers would have also experienced regeneration. In Ezekiel 18:31 the people were commanded to "make yourselves a new heart and a new spirit." The two phrases parallel those of Ezekiel 36:25-27 as well as John 3:5 and suggest the Old Testament believer was regenerated by the Holy Spirit (cf. also Ps. 51:10).

SELECTIVE INDWELLING

In John 14:16-17 Jesus indicated that following Pentecost the Holy Spirit would begin a new ministry to believers that was unlike that of the Old Testament. The emphasis of this passage is that the new ministry would be an *indwelling* (in contrast to the Spirit simply being with them) and it would be *permanent*. While the promise of John 14 pertains to *all* believers and the indwelling is *permanent*, there was indwelling in the Old Testament, however, it was *selective* and it was *temporary*. (1) The Holy Spirit indwelt some people in the Old Testament. The Spirit indwelt Joshua (Num. 27:18) and David (1 Sam. 16:12-13).[30] (2) The Holy Spirit came upon some people in the Old Testament. Charles C. Ryrie suggests there is no great distinction between "indwelling" and "coming upon," "except that the idea of coming upon seems to imply the temporary and transitory character of the Spirit's relationship to Old Testament saints."[31] The temporary coming upon is seen in that the Spirit came upon an individual for a specific task. It is reasonable to assume that when the task had been carried out, the Spirit was no longer upon the individual. The Spirit came upon Othniel to conquer Cushan-ri-shathaim (Judg. 3:10); He came upon Gideon to defeat the Midianites (Judg. 6:34); He came upon Jephthah to defeat the Ammonites (Judg. 11:29); He came upon Samson to defeat the Philistines (Judg. 14:6); He came upon Balaam to prophecy blessing concerning Israel (Num. 24:2). "An evaluation of these texts shows that all involved empowerment for a physical activity. None of them had to do with salvation from sin in any sense."[32] Nor did the empowering have anything to do with the spiritual condition of the person. Jephthah was the son of a harlot, living in an idolatrous environment. Samson was a carnal man, living to satisfy his carnal desires. Balaam was an unbeliever. (3) The Holy Spirit filled some people in the Old Testament. God filled Bezalel with the Spirit, giving him wisdom for craftsmanship "to make artistic designs for work in gold, in silver " (Exod. 31:2-5) to beautify the tabernacle.

John Walvoord makes three observations concerning Old Testament indwelling. He points out that first, the Spirit's indwelling in the life of a person had no evident relationship to the person's spiritual condition. Second, the Spirit's indwelling was a sovereign working of God in the person to perform a specific task, for example, delivering Israel in warfare or building the tabernacle. Third, the Spirit's indwelling was temporary. The Spirit of the Lord came upon Saul but also departed from him (1 Sam. 10:10; 16:14). David was fearful that the Holy Spirit would leave him (Ps. 51:11).[33]

RESTRAINING SIN

Genesis 6:3 indicates the Spirit's striving or restraining sin would be limited because man refused to heed the Spirit's convicting ministry. In the context, God judged the people with the Noahic flood.[34] To those holding to a pretribulation rapture a parallel may be seen between the Old Testament and the New Testament.

PARALLEL JUDGMENTS: THE FLOOD AND THE TRIBULATION

Scripture	Spirit's Restraint Effected	Spirit's Restraint Lifted	God's Parallel Judgments
Genesis 6:3	Noah ministering	Noah removed	Flood
2 Thessalonians 2:7-8	Church ministering	Church removed	Tribulation

ABILITY FOR SERVICE

The Holy Spirit was given in the Old Testament to select individuals to perform specific tasks. Such enablings included: ability in artistic work for the Tabernacle and Temple, given to Bezalel (Exod. 31:2-5; 35:30-35) and Hiram (1 Kings 7:14); ability to lead the nation, given to Joshua (Num. 27:16-18), Saul (1 Sam. 10:10), and David (1 Sam. 16:13); ability in warfare, given to Othniel (Judg. 3:10), Gideon (Judg. 6:34), and Jephthah (Judg. 11:29); and unusual physical strength, given to Samson (Judg. 14:19).

THE SPIRIT IN RELATION TO CHRIST

Isaiah had prophesied that the Spirit would rest upon Messiah (42:1), giving Him wisdom, strength, and knowledge in His ministry (11:2-3). The gospel narratives continually reflect the power of the Holy Spirit upon Christ in His ministry in fulfillment of Isaiah's prophecies. That is not to say, however, that Christ did not have power within Himself; he did (John 10:18). The fact that He ministered in the power of the Holy Spirit stresses the unity of the Trinity (cf. John 5:31-44; 6:29; 8:18; 10:37-38, etc.).

THE VIRGIN BIRTH

The agent. Both Matthew and Luke emphasize the ministry of the Holy Spirit in causing Mary's conception. Matthew 1:20 stresses, "that which has been conceived in her is of [Gk. *ek*] the Holy Spirit," stressing origin. The origin of Jesus' birth was not through Joseph but through the agency of the Holy Spirit. Luke 1:35 uses the terms "come upon" and "overshadow" to describe the Holy Spirit's ministry with regard to Mary in causing the conception. The same term "come upon" (Gk. *eperchomai*) is used of the Holy Spirit's coming upon the apostles at Pentecost (Acts 1:8). It is unlikely the word is intended as a euphemism for sexual intercourse.[35] "Overshadow" suggests "God's powerful presence will rest upon Mary, so that she will bear a child who will be the Son of God. Nothing is said regarding how this will happen, and in particular there is no suggestion of divine begetting."[36] The significant point of emphasis in both gospels is that Jesus had no human father; Joseph did not beget Jesus. (See also the discussion under "Christology: Doctrine of Christ," chap. 20.)

The results. (1) The human nature of Christ came into existence. It was not a person who came into existence, for Christ as a Person existed from all eternity in His deity; however, the human nature of Christ had a beginning in Mary's womb.

(2) The human nature of Christ was sinless. Although Christ had a fully human nature, it was not stained by sin. Although He was born of a human mother, the conception by the Holy Spirit guaranteed the sinlessness of Christ. This fact reveals why the doctrine of the virgin birth is so important; had Jesus had a human father He would have been no different from anyone else. The testimony to the sinlessness of Christ is evident as Christ claimed for Himself: "there is no unrighteousness in Him" (John 7:18). John the apostle declared, "in Him there is no sin" (1 John 3:5).

(3) The human nature of Christ brought human limitations. Although Christ was sinless, the virgin birth resulted in a truly human nature. Christ

was tired (John 4:6); He became thirsty (John 4:7); He slept (Matt. 8:24); He wept (John 11:35). He submitted to the voluntary limitations of humanity.

THE LIFE AND MINISTRY OF CHRIST

The Holy Spirit anointed Christ. Luke 4:18 indicates Christ was anointed by the Holy Spirit, which probably occurred at His baptism when the Holy Spirit visibly came upon Christ. The Spirit's coming upon Jesus fulfilled the prophecy of Isaiah 61:1. Just as kings were anointed (2 Sam. 2:4) and priests were anointed (Exod. 28:41), so the Messiah would be anointed. The act of anointing conferred power; in this case the Holy Spirit would Himself be the anointing, empowering Christ for ministry.[37]

Several points may be made summarizing the anointing of Christ: (1) The anointing designated Jesus as Israel's Messiah and King. John 1:31 indicates John the Baptist "manifested" Jesus to the nation at His baptism. This was done in the manner of Old Testament kings (cf. 1 Sam. 16:6-13). (2) The anointing introduced Jesus to His public ministry (Acts 10:38). Following His baptism, Jesus began His public ministry of teaching and performing miracles. The anointing of the Holy Spirit set Jesus apart to His ministry as Israel's Messiah. The anointing was necessary because of Jesus' humanity and also to demonstrate the unity of the Trinity. (3) The anointing empowered Jesus for His public ministry (Luke 4:18). Although Jesus had power in Himself to perform miracles, He revealed the unity within the Triune Godhead and His dependence upon Another in the Trinity by receiving the Holy Spirit's empowering for ministry. (4) The anointing was a divine authentication of Jesus. At the baptism of Christ, the Father audibly confirmed Jesus as Messiah to the nation; the people heard the Father's authenticating statement, "This is My beloved Son in whom I am well pleased" (Matt. 3:17).

The Holy Spirit filled Christ. Luke 1:15 indicates John the Baptist, the forerunner, was filled with the Spirit while still in his mother's womb. The Messiah would certainly be filled with the Spirit to at least the same extent as the forerunner of Messiah. In Luke 4:1 it says, "Jesus, full of the Holy Spirit . . . was led about by the Spirit." The verb is in the imperfect tense, suggesting continuous action. "Jesus was now continuously under the guidance of the Holy Spirit."[38] Mark 1:12 states, "And immediately the Spirit impelled Him to go out into the wilderness." The present tense "impelled" stresses that "The entire earthly life of Jesus was bound up with the Holy Spirit from his birth to his death and resurrection."[39] The New Testament record of the life of Christ reveals a fulfillment of the predictions in Isaiah 11:2 and 42:1. Christ was continuously filled with the Holy Spirit.

THE DEATH OF CHRIST

Not only was the Holy Spirit responsible for bringing the humanity of Christ into existence and for empowering Christ in His earthly ministry, but the Holy Spirit also played a part in the death of Christ (Heb. 9:14).[40] The concept of the suffering Servant of Isaiah may be prominent in the mind of the writer of Hebrews. If this is the case, then the Spirit who comes upon the Servant in Isaiah 42:1 is also the Spirit who leads the Servant to bear the sins of many in Isaiah 52:13–53:12.[41]

THE RESURRECTION OF CHRIST

The biblical accounts indicate "each member of the godhead had a particular part in this great act of resurrection."[42] Christ was raised by the power of God the Father (Eph. 1:19-20; Ps. 16:10), but Christ also had the power to raise Himself (John 10:18). The Holy Spirit also was involved in effecting the resurrection of Christ. Romans 1:4 declares Christ to be "the Son of God with power by the resurrection from the dead, according to the Spirit of holiness." This is a possible reference to the Holy Spirit.[43] Romans 8:11 refers to "the Spirit of Him who raised Jesus from the dead." This is either a reference to the Holy Spirit or the Father. In 1 Peter 3:18 it declares that Christ was "made alive in the spirit." The phrase could refer to the instrumentality of the Holy Spirit in quickening Christ; most probably, however, it refers to His human spirit. A conclusion can be drawn, however, concerning the ministry of the Holy Spirit in the life of Jesus Christ. Pentecost states, "I would question whether there is any great work of God revealed in the Word of God in which all of the members of the Godhead do not work together to accomplish God's purpose."[44]

THE SIN AGAINST THE HOLY SPIRIT

HISTORICAL BACKGROUND

Although the Scriptures speak of sins against the Holy Spirit called *quenching* (1 Thess. 5:19) and *grieving* (Eph. 4:30), it is the *blaspheming* of the Holy Spirit that is usually in mind when "the sin" against the Spirit is mentioned.

In discussing the sin against the Holy Spirit (Matt. 12:31-32) it is important to consider the historical background against which the sin was committed. Jesus had manifested Himself to the nation Israel through His teachings (Matt. 5-7) and His miracles (Matt. 8-10). The Messianic signs had been performed in the midst of the nation. Now the religious leaders came to investigate Christ for themselves (cf. Luke 5:14 with 5:17). Who was Christ? Was He the Messiah? How would they explain His miracles? The conclusion of the Jewish leaders is reached in Matthew 12 and culminates in the sin against the Holy Spirit. In Matthew 12:22 they brought a demon-possessed man to Jesus and He healed the man. The response of the people in 12:23 reflects the influence of the religious leaders. The people exclaimed, "This man cannot be the Son of David, can he?"[45] The wording of their question anticipates a "no" answer. In 12:24 the Pharisees dogmatically asserted: "This man casts out demons only by Beelzebul the ruler of the demons." The One of whom the Father said, "I will put My Spirit upon Him" (12:18) was referred to as doing His work through the power of the Devil by the Pharisees. It was in this context that Jesus declared that blasphemy against the Holy Spirit would never be forgiven. This background is important to consider in discussing the sin of 12:31-32.

EXPLANATION

The sin is against Christ. The sin against the Holy Spirit also involved a sin against Christ. The crux of the matter is stated in Matthew 12:24. The religious leaders had heard Christ teach and had seen His miracles, but their evaluation of Christ was that He performed His miracles by the power of Satan. That was their sin against Christ. Instead of recognizing Him to be the Messiah, they said He performed miracles through Satan's power. They did not deny the miracles, but they rejected the source as being from God. They said He worked through the power of Satan. The One who was destined to be Israel's deliverer both spiritually and nationally was rejected and charged with being in league with Satan. That rejection was the foundation of the sin against the Holy Spirit.

The sin is against the Holy Spirit. The One upon whom God put His Spirit (12:18) was the One termed working through Satan by the Pharisees. God had said, "I will put My Spirit upon Him" (12:18), but the leaders said, "This man casts out demons only by Beelzebul the ruler of the demons" (12:24). The sin was committed in a historical context. The Pharisees had observed first-hand the public ministry of Christ. They had seen His miracles with their own eyes, yet they ascribed Christ's work to Satan. The sin against the Spirit was final and unforgivable because they had the witness of the words and works of Christ. Moreover, they could have been forgiven had they only rejected the witness of Christ (Matt. 12:32a), but they rejected the final witness, the testimony of the Holy Spirit. There was no further witness to be given them.[46] It should be noted that the sin against the Spirit was eternal (Matt. 12:31-32). There was no opportunity for repentance; it was unpardonable and would never be forgiven.

QUESTION

The question that may be asked is, Can the sin against the Holy Spirit be committed today? To commit the sin of blasphemy against the Holy Spirit would require the physical presence of Jesus Christ in which He would teach and perform miracles while the hearers and onlookers would reject His ministry saying He is working by the power of Satan. The sin of blasphemy against the Spirit is not the same as unbelief. There is no indication in Scripture that if a person has once refused the gospel that he will never again have an opportunity to believe nor is there a particular sin today that cannot be forgiven. Who has not refused the gospel the first time they heard it but later came to believe in Christ? Of course unbelief will not be forgiven if a person permanently persists in unbelief.

BAPTIZING WORK OF THE HOLY SPIRIT

INTRODUCTION

The subject of the baptizing work of the Holy Spirit has become a point of considerable controversy and diverse opinion. There is confusion on one hand with water baptism. Although there are many passages that refer to Spirit baptism, some people see these passages as referring to water baptism (cf. Rom. 6:4; Gal. 3:27). Others understand the baptizing work of the Spirit as a "second blessing," which may be empowerment for service and/ or may manifest itself through speaking in tongues.[47] Part of the confusion lies in a failure to understand the distinctive nature of the church. It was at Pentecost that the church was born and that the Holy Spirit began His work of building the church by baptizing believers into the Body of Christ.

DEFINITION

The baptizing work of the Holy Spirit may be defined as that work whereby the Spirit places the believer into union with Christ and into union with other believers in the Body of Christ (1 Cor. 12:13).

EXPLANATION

The baptism of the Holy Spirit is unique to the church age. The basic reference is 1 Corinthians 12:13, which states, "For by one Spirit we were all baptized into one body, whether Jews or Greeks, whether slaves or free, and we were all made to drink of one Spirit." That this ministry of the Spirit began at Pentecost can be seen by comparing Acts 1:5, which indicates the baptizing work is still future, with Acts 11:15, which indicates the "beginning" of this work was at Pentecost in Acts 2. The baptizing work did not occur in the Old Testament; it is unique to the church age which began at Pentecost.

The baptism of the Holy Spirit includes all believers in this age. The emphasis that "all" are baptized by the Holy Spirit is stated in several passages. In 1 Corinthians 12:13 it indicates "we were *all* baptized." In Romans

6 all who were baptized (v. 3) are those who have been united to Christ (v. 5), hence, all believers. In Galatians 3:27-28 it indicates "all of you" were baptized into Christ and became "one in Christ," no matter whether they were Jew or Greek, slave or free, male or female.

The baptism of the Holy Spirit brings believers into union with other believers in the Body of Christ. There is absolutely no distinction concerning those coming into union with one another: Jews, Gentiles, slaves, free people, men, women—all come into union with one another (1 Cor. 12:13). It is also noteworthy that the spiritual condition of the believer is not a factor —the Corinthians were noted for their carnality, yet all were included.

The baptism of the Holy Spirit brings believers into union with Christ. The very ones that were "baptized into Christ" (Rom. 6:3) were also "united with Him" (Rom. 6:5). This truth prohibits the baptism of the Spirit from being a work subsequent to salvation.

The baptism of the Holy Spirit is not experiential. Since this is a work done to the believer and not by the believer, and since the baptism occurs simultaneous to salvation, it is not experiential.

The baptism of the Holy Spirit is performed by the Holy Spirit. There are not two baptisms by the Spirit. Some groups distinguish between 1 Corinthians 12:13, *"by* one Spirit," suggesting the placing into the Body and Acts 1:5, *"with* the Holy Spirit," suggesting a subsequent act of empowering for service. However, the same Greek preposition *en* is used in both phrases, and it is precarious at best to attempt a distinction where the same Greek phrase is used in both passages. The Holy Spirit is the agent of the baptism (Acts 1:5; 1 Cor. 12:13).[48]

INDWELLING OF THE HOLY SPIRIT

FACT OF THE INDWELLING

A key verse that indicates the unique ministry of the Holy Spirit in this age is John 14:16 where Jesus promised the Spirit would indwell believers and that the indwelling would be permanent. This permanent indwelling would not be for a select few but for all believers. There are a number of indicators that affirm these facts.

The Holy Spirit is a gift. The Holy Spirit is a gift given to all believers in Jesus without exception; no conditions are attached to the gift of the Spirit except faith in Christ (John 7:37-39). Many Scriptures speak of the Holy Spirit as being "given" to believers. The word *give* in these instances means "to bestow a gift" (cf. 2 Cor. 1:22; 1 Thess. 4:8; 1 John 4:13).[49] Because the Holy Spirit is given as a gift, there is nothing the person can do to receive the gift apart from accepting it.

The Holy Spirit is given at salvation. This is the positive statement of which the negative is that the unbeliever does not possess the Spirit. Ephesians 1:13 indicates the Holy Spirit is given at the moment of salvation.[50] The sealing (and indwelling) with the Spirit took place at the time of believing. Galatians 3:2 also emphasizes this same truth.

A person not possessing the Holy Spirit is an unbeliever. Romans 8:9 emphasizes, "if anyone does not have the Spirit of Christ, he does not belong to Him." Jude 19 refers to unbelievers as "devoid of the Spirit."

The Holy Spirit indwells carnal believers. The carnal Corinthian Christians, who were guilty of incest, lawsuits against fellow believers, and other sins, were nonetheless indwelt by the Holy Spirit (1 Cor. 6:19). If only a select group is indwelt by the Spirit then the Corinthians would not all have been indwelt. Romans 8:9 and 2 Corinthians 1:22 demand a conclusion that all believers, regardless of their spiritual condition, are indwelt by the Holy Spirit.

Holy Spirit indwells believers permanently. Not only does the Holy Spirit indwell all believers, but it is a permanent indwelling (John 14:16). The Holy Spirit is given to believers as a "down payment," a verification of their future glorification (2 Cor. 1:22; Eph. 4:30).

PROBLEMS RELATED TO INDWELLING

There are a number of biblical texts that raise problems with the New Testament teaching on the permanent indwelling of the Holy Spirit. Some of these deserve special note.

Psalm 51:11. David's prayer, "Do not take Thy Holy Spirit from me," relates to the temporary indwelling of the Holy Spirit in the Old Testament economy. Following Pentecost the indwelling of the Spirit was permanent (John 14:16).

Acts 5:32. Peter is not establishing obedience as a condition for the indwelling of the Spirit, but rather Peter uses "obey" as a synonym for believe. The similar expression is used in Acts 6:7, where it is clear that the meaning is faith (cf. John 3:36).

Acts 8:14-17. This was a unique situation during the transition from law to grace and from Israel to the church. There had to be a clear evidence that the Samaritans were also receiving the Spirit just as the Jews. This is not normative to this age. If it were normative, then no one could receive the Spirit because it would take the apostles to confirm the indwelling, just as they did with the Samaritans.

SEALING OF THE HOLY SPIRIT

DEFINITION

The sealing of the Holy Spirit is one of many works God performs on behalf of the believer to secure his salvation (cf. 2 Cor. 1:22; Eph. 1:13;

4:30). Second Corinthians 1:22 says God "sealed us and gave us the Spirit in our hearts as a pledge." In Old Testament times a seal was used in various ways: a seal authenticated a document (e.g., a marriage contract); it authenticated a transfer of power from one ruler to another; it served as a lock to secure something, more by the authority it signified than by its intrinsic strength; it was used to verify a document such as a bill of divorce.[51] The Holy Spirit is given to the person who believes in Christ as a seal, identifying the believer as belonging to God.

EXPLANATION

The principal idea of sealing is that of *ownership.* The believer is sealed with the Spirit to identify the believer as belonging to God. Branding cattle would be a parallel; the rancher puts his brand on the steer as a sign that the steer belongs to him. God has put His seal, the Holy Spirit, within the believer to verify that the believer belongs to Him. Second Corinthians 1:22 indicates that the Holy Spirit Himself is the seal. The phrase "gave us the Spirit" explains the sealing, which is done to a believer; it is not something the believer does himself.[52] Moreover, the sealing is permanent—with a view to the believer's ultimate glorification (Eph. 4:30). Hence, the sealing not only emphasizes ownership but also *security.* The Holy Spirit verifies that the believer permanently belongs to God. The emphasis of all three of these passages is also that all believers are sealed. Despite their carnality, all the Corinthian Christians were sealed (2 Cor. 1:22); even those who were capable of grieving the Spirit were nonetheless sealed (Eph. 4:30). Furthermore, because there is no command to be sealed further indicates that all believers are sealed at the moment of conversion.

GIFTS OF THE HOLY SPIRIT

DEFINITION OF THE GIFTS

There are two Greek words generally used to describe spiritual gifts. The first is *pneumatikos,* meaning "spiritual things" or "things pertaining to the spirit." This word emphasizes the spiritual nature and origin of spiritual gifts; they are not natural talents but rather have their origin with the Holy Spirit. They are supernaturally given to a believer by the Holy Spirit (1 Cor. 12:11).

The other word often used to identify spiritual gifts is *charisma,* meaning "grace gift." The word charisma emphasizes that a spiritual gift is a gift of God's grace; it is not a naturally developed ability but rather a gift bestowed on a believer (1 Cor. 12:4). This emphasis is seen in Romans 12 where Paul discusses spiritual gifts. He stresses that spiritual gifts are received through the "grace given" to believers (Rom. 12:3, 6).

A concise definition of spiritual gifts is simply a "grace gift." A more complete definition is "a divine endowment of a special ability for service upon a member of the body of Christ."[53]

EXPLANATION OF THE GIFTS

Two concepts are involved in spiritual gifts. First, a spiritual gift *to an individual* is God's enablement for personal spiritual service (1 Cor. 12:11). Second, a spiritual gift *to the church* is a person uniquely equipped for the church's edification and maturation (Eph. 4:11-13).

It should also be noted what is *not* meant by spiritual gifts.[54] It does not mean *a place of service.* Some may suggest "he has a real gift for working in the slums." This, of course, is a wrong concept of spiritual gifts. Nor is a spiritual gift an age group ministry. Or some might say that "he has a real gift for working with senior highs." A spiritual gift is not the same as *a natural talent*; there may be a relationship, but a natural talent is an ability that a person may have from birth and develop, whereas a spiritual gift is given supernaturally by God at the moment of conversion. Natural talents and gifts may be contrasted thus:[55]

COMPARISON OF NATURAL AND SPIRITUAL ABILITIES

Comparisons	Natural Talents	Spiritual Gifts
Source:	From God Through parents	From God Independent of parents
Possessed:	From birth	Probably from conversion
Purpose:	To benefit mankind on the natural level	To benefit mankind on the spiritual level
Process:	Must be recognized, developed, exercised	Must be recognized, developed, exercised
Function:	Ought to be dedicated by believers to God for His use and glory	Ought to be used to God's glory

DESCRIPTION OF THE GIFTS

Apostle (Eph. 4:11). An important distinction must be made between the gift and the office of the apostle. The office of apostle was limited to the Twelve and to Paul. In Luke 6:13 Jesus called the disciples to Himself and chose twelve of them "whom He also named as apostles." To those twelve Jesus gave a unique authority that was limited to those holding the office of apostle (cf. Luke 9:1; Matt. 10:1). Later, in defending his own apostleship, Paul emphasized that the signs of a true apostle were performed by him (2 Cor. 12:12). The qualifications for the office of apostle are set forth in Acts 1:21-22; those holding the office had to have walked with the Lord from the baptism of John until the ascension of Christ. Paul's situation was unique; he referred to himself as an apostle but one "untimely born" (1 Cor. 15:8-9).

The gift of apostle is mentioned in 1 Corinthians 12:28 and also Ephesians 4:11. The word *apostle* comes from *apo,* meaning "from," and *stello,* meaning "to send." Hence, an apostle is one that is "sent from." It appears the word was used in a technical sense as well as a general sense. In a technical sense it was limited to the Twelve who had the office of apostle as well as the gift.[56] In that sense it was a foundational gift limited to the formation of the church (Eph. 2:20). When the foundation of the church was laid, the need for the gift ceased. Just as the office of apostle has ceased (because no one can meet the qualifications of Acts 1:21-22), so the gift of apostle in the strict sense has ceased. The word *apostle* is also used in a general sense of a "messenger" or a "sent one" in the cause of Christ. These are referred to as apostles but do not have either office or gift. The word is used in a non-technical sense of one who is a messenger (cf. Acts 14:14; 2 Cor. 8:23; Phil. 2:25).

Prophet (Rom. 12:6). The gift of prophecy is mentioned in Romans 12:6, 1 Corinthians 12:10, and Ephesians 4:11. The apostle received his information through direct revelation from God, hence Agabus announced the famine that would come over the world (Acts 11:28) and Paul's captivity in Jerusalem (Acts 21:10-11). Through direct revelation the prophet received knowledge of divine "mysteries" (1 Cor. 13:2) that man would not otherwise know. Prior to the completion of the canon the gift of prophecy was important for the edification of the church (1 Cor. 14:3). The prophet received direct revelation from God and taught the people for their edification, exhortation, and consolation (1 Cor. 14:3). Since the revelation came from God, it was true; the genuineness of the prophet was exhibited in the accuracy of the prophecy (cf. Deut. 18:20,22). Prophecy thus involved both foretelling future events but also forthtelling God's truth in terms of exhortation and instruction. The gift of prophecy is also related to the foundation of the church (Eph. 2:20). Because the foundation of the church has been laid and the canon of Scripture is complete there is no need for the gift of prophecy.

Miracles (1 Cor. 12:10). The nature of biblical miracles is a large subject, and the student is encouraged to study this as a separate topic.[57] Miracles did not happen at random throughout Scripture but occurred in three major periods: in the days of Moses and Joshua, Elijah and Elisha, and Christ and the apostles. There were select miracles outside that scope of time, but not many. Miracles were given to authenticate a message, and in each of the above mentioned periods, God enabled His messengers to perform unusual miracles to substantiate the new message they were giving. Miracles occurred in the New Testament era to validate the new message the apostles preached. With the completion of the canon of Scripture the need for miracles as a validating sign disappeared; the authority of the Word of God was sufficient to validate the messenger's word.

The gift of miracles (1 Cor. 12:10, 28) is a broader gift than the gift of healing. The word *miracles* means "power" or "a work of power." Examples of the exercise of miracles are Peter's judging of Ananias and Sapphira (Acts 5:9-11) and Paul judging Elymas the magician with blindness (Acts 13:8-11).[58] The word is also used to describe the miracles of Christ (Matt. 11:20, 21, 23; 13:54).

A distinction should be made between miracles and the gift of miracles. Although the gift of miracles—the ability of an individual to perform miraculous acts—ceased with the apostolic age, that is not to say miracles cannot and do not occur today. God may directly answer the prayer of a believer and perform a miracle in his life. God may heal a terminally ill person in answer to prayer, but He does not do it through the medium of another person.

Healing (1 Cor. 12:9). A narrower aspect of the gift of miracles is the gift of healing (1 Cor. 12:9, 28, 30). The word is used in the plural (Gk. *iamaton,* "healings") in 1 Corinthians 12:9, suggesting "the different classes of sicknesses to be healed."[59] The gift of healing involved the ability of a person to cure other persons of all forms of sicknesses. An examination of New Testament healings by Christ and the apostles is noteworthy. These healings were:[60] *instantaneous* (Mark 1:42); *complete* (Matt. 14:36); *permanent* (Matt. 14:36); *limited* (constitutional diseases [eg., leprosy, Mark 1:40], not psychological illnesses); *unconditional* (including unbelievers who exercised no faith and did not even know who Jesus was [John 9:25]); *purposeful* (not just for the purpose of relieving people from their suffering and sickness. If this were so, it would have been cruel and immoral for our Lord to leave the cities, where the sick sought healing, for the solitude of the country [Luke 5:15, 16]); *subordinate* (secondary to preaching the Word of God [Luke 9:6]); *significant* (intended to confirm Him and the apostles as the messengers of God and their message as a Word from God [John 3:2; Acts 2:22; Heb. 2:3, 4]); *successful* (except in the one case where the *disciples'* lack of faith was the cause of failure [Matt. 17:20]); and *inclusive* (the supreme demonstration of this gift was in raising the dead [Mark 5:39-43; Luke 7:14; John 11:44; Acts 9:40]).

A distinction should be made between the gift of healing and healing itself. As in the case of the other sign gifts, the gift of healing terminated with the completion of the canon of Scripture; there was no further need for the gift of healing. However, God may still respond to the prayers of His children and heal a person of illness; this is, however, without the agency of another person. God may heal a person directly. A distinction between these two forms of healing appears to be the case in Acts 9, where Peter heals Aeneas through the gift (Acts 9:34) but God heals Tabitha in response to the prayer of Peter (Acts 9:40).[61]

It should also be noted that there are a number of examples where God chose *not* to heal people (2 Cor. 12:8-9; 1 Tim. 5:23).

Tongues (1 Cor. 12:28). A number of observations help to clarify the meaning of this gift. (1) The book of Acts establishes that biblical tongues were languages (Acts 2:6, 8, 11). When the foreign Jews visited Jerusalem at Pentecost they heard the apostles proclaim the gospel in their native languages (cf. vv. 8-11).

(2) Tongues of Acts and Corinthians were the same. There is no evidence that the tongues of Corinthians were different from the ones in Acts or that they were angelic languages (1 Cor. 13:1).[62]

(3) Tongues were a lesser gift (1 Cor. 12:28). The foundational gifts that were given for the upbuilding of the church were apostle, prophet, evangelist, pastor-teacher, and teacher (1 Cor. 12:28; Eph. 4:11). Tongues were mentioned last to indicate they were not a primary or foundational gift (1 Cor. 12:28).

(4) Tongues were a temporary sign gift (1 Cor. 13:8). The phrase "they will cease" is in the *middle* voice, emphasizing "they will stop themselves." The implication is that tongues would not continue until "the perfect comes" —the time when knowledge and prophecy gifts would be terminated—but would cease of their own accord when their usefulness terminated. If tongues were to continue until "the perfect comes" the verb would likely be *passive* in form.

Tongues were a part of the miraculous era of Christ and the apostles and were necessary, along with the gift of miracles, as an authenticating sign of the apostles (2 Cor. 12:12). With the completion of the Scriptures there was no longer any need for an authenticating sign; the Bible was now the authority in verifying the message that God's servants proclaimed. Tongues were a sign gift belonging to the infancy stage of the church (1 Cor. 13:10-11; 14:20).

Tongues were used as a sign to unbelieving Jews and in this sense were used in evangelism (1 Cor. 14:21-22). When unbelieving Jews would enter the assembly and hear people speaking in foreign languages it was a sign to them that God was doing a work in their midst, reminiscent of Isaiah's day (Isa. 28:11-12). This sign should lead them to faith in Jesus as their Messiah.

Interpretation of tongues (1 Cor. 12:10). The gift of interpretation of tongues involved the supernatural ability of someone in the assembly to interpret the foreign language spoken by one who had the gift of tongues. The language would be translated into the venacular for the people who were present.

Evangelism (Eph. 4:11). The word *euanggelistas,* written in English as *evangelists,* means "one who proclaims the good news." One definition of the gift of evangelism is "the gift of proclaiming the Good News of salvation effectively so that people respond to the claims of Christ in conversion and in discipleship."[63]

Several things are involved in the gift of evangelism:[64] (1) It involves a burden for the lost. The one having this gift has a great desire to see people saved. (2) It involves proclaiming the good news. The evangelist is one who proclaims the good news. While men such as Billy Graham undoubtedly have the gift of evangelism, it is not necessary to limit the gift to mass evangelism. An evangelist will also share the good news with unbelievers on a one-to-one basis. (3) It involves a clear presentation of the gospel. The evangelist has the ability to present the gospel in a simple and lucid fashion; he proclaims the basic needs of salvation: sin, the substitutionary death of Christ, faith, forgiveness, reconciliation—in a way that unbelievers without a biblical background can understand the gospel. (4) It involves a response to the proclamation of the gospel. The one having the gift of evangelism sees a response to the presentation of the gospel; that is an indication he has the gift. (5) It involves a delight in seeing people come to Christ. Because it is his burden and passion, the evangelist rejoices as men and women come to faith in Christ.

Although only some people have the gift of evangelism, other believers are not exempt from proclaiming the good news. *All* believers are to do the work of evangelism (2 Tim. 4:5).

Pastor-Teacher (Eph. 4:11). One gift is in view in the statement of Ephesians 4:11, not two gifts. The word *pastor* (Gk. *poimenas*) literally means "shepherd" and is used only here of a gift. It is, however, used also of Christ who is the Good Shepherd (John 10:11, 14, 16; Heb. 13:20; 1 Pet. 2:25) and designates the spiritual shepherding work of one who is a pastor-teacher. The work of a pastor has a clear analogy to the work of the shepherd in caring for his sheep. "As a pastor, he cares for the flock. He guides, guards, protects, and provides for those under his oversight."[65] An example is found in Acts 20:28 where Paul exhorts the elders from Ephesus "to shepherd the church of God." It is to be done voluntarily, not for material gain nor by lording it over believers but rather by being examples of humility (1 Pet. 5:2-5).

There is a second aspect to this gift; it involves the ability to teach. It is sometimes said of a church pastor: "He can't teach very well but he is a fine pastor." That, of course, is impossible. If a person has this gift he is *both* a shepherd and a teacher. "As a teacher, the emphasis is on the method by which the shepherd does his work. He guides, he guards, he protects by teaching."[66] This is an important emphasis for the maturation of believers in a local church. Paul strongly exhorted Timothy to faithfulness in teaching the Word (1 Tim. 1:3, 5; 4:11; 6:2, 17).

There are several related terms. *Elder* (Titus 1:5) denotes the dignity of the office; *overseer* designates the function or the work of the elder (1 Tim. 3:2)—it is the work of shepherding; *pastor* denotes the gift and also emphasizes the work as a shepherd and teacher.

Teacher (Rom. 12:7; 1 Cor. 12:28). A pastor is also a teacher, but a teacher is not necessarily also a pastor. A number of factors would show that a person has the gift of teacher. He would have a great interest in the Word of God and would commit himself to disciplined study of the Word. He would have an ability to communicate the Word of God clearly and apply the Word to the lives of the people. This gift is clearly evidenced in a man who has the ability to take profound biblical and theological truths and communicate them in a lucid way so ordinary people can readily grasp them. That is the gift of teaching. This gift was emphasized considerably in the local churches in the New Testament because of its importance in bringing believers to maturity (cf. Acts 2:42; 4:2; 5:42; 11:26; 13:1; 15:35; 18:11, etc.).

Two things should be noted concerning the gift of teaching. First, it requires development. A person may have the gift of teaching, but for the effective use of the gift it would demand serious study and the faithful exercise of the gift. Second, teaching is not the same as a natural talent. Frequently public school teachers are given positions of teaching in a local church. It does not necessarily follow that their natural ability to teach means they have the spiritual gift of teaching. The natural ability and the spiritual gift of teaching are not the same.

Service (Rom. 12:7). The word *service* (Gk. *diakonia*) is a general word for ministering or serving others. The word is used in a broad sense and refers to ministry and service to others in a general way. A sampling of the usages of this word indicates that: Timothy and Erastus served Paul in Ephesus (Acts 19:22); Paul served the Jerusalem believers by bringing them a monetary gift (Rom. 15:25); Onesiphorus served at Ephesus (2 Tim. 1:18); Onesimus was helpful to Paul while he was in prison (Philem. 13); the Hebrew believers displayed acts of kindness (Heb. 6:10). From these and other examples, it appears an important aspect of serving is helping other believers who are in physical need. This gift would be less conspicuous, with the believer serving others in the privacy of a one-to-one relationship.

Helps (1 Cor. 12:28). The word *helps* (Gk. *antilempsis*) denotes "helpful deeds, assistance. The basic meaning of the word is an undertaking on behalf of another."[67] The word is similar to serving and some see these gifts as identical. Certainly they are quite similar if not the same. The word occurs only here in the New Testament, but the related Greek word, *antilambanesthai,* occurs in Luke 1:54; Acts 20:35; 1 Timothy 6:2. The gift of helps means "to take firm hold of some one, in order to help. These 'helpings' therefore probably refer to the succoring of those in need, whether poor, sick, widows, orphans, strangers, travellers, or what not."[68]

Faith (1 Cor. 12:9). While all Christians have saving faith (Eph. 2:8) and should exhibit faith to sustain them in their spiritual walk (Heb. 11), the gift of faith is possessed by only some believers. "The gift of faith is the faith which manifests itself in unusual deeds of trust. . . . This person has the capacity to see something that needs to be done and to believe God will do it through him even though it looks impossible."[69] Stephen exhibited this gift as he was a man "full of faith" (Acts 6:5). Men such as George Mueller and Hudson Taylor are outstanding examples of those possessing the gift of faith.[70]

Exhortation (Rom. 12:8). The word *exhortation* (Gk. *parakalon*) means "called alongside to help." The noun form is used of the Holy Spirit as the believer's helper (John 14:16, 26). "The exhorter is one who has the ability to appeal to the will of the individual to get him to act."[71] The gift of exhortation is "often coupled with teaching (cf. 1 Tim. 4:13; 6:2), and is addressed to the conscience and to the heart."[72]

The gift of exhortation may be either *exhortation,* urging someone to pursue a particular course of conduct (cf. Jude 3), or it may be *consolation* or *comfort* in view of someone's trial or tragedy (Acts 4:36; 9:27; 15:39).[73]

Discerning spirits (1 Cor. 12:10). In the early church, before the canon of Scripture was complete, God gave direct revelation to individuals who would communicate that revelation to the church. But how did the early believers know whether or not the revelation was true? How could they tell if it was from God, from a false spirit, or from the human spirit? To authenticate the validity of the revelation, God gave the gift of "distinguishing of spirits." Those having this gift were given the supernatural ability to determine if the revelation was from God or if it was false. John's exhortation to "test the spirits" has reference to this (1 John 4:1). Similarly, when two or three spoke the revelation of God in the assembly those having the gift of discerning of spirits were to determine if it was from God (1 Cor. 14:29; cf. 1 Thess. 5:20-21). Because direct revelation has terminated with the completion of the Scriptures, and because the gift of discerning spirits was dependent upon revelation being given, the gift of discerning spirits has ceased.

Showing mercy (Rom. 12:8). To show mercy (Gk. *eleon*) means to "feel compassion, show mercy or pity."[74] In the life of Christ, showing mercy was healing the blind (Matt. 9:27), aiding the Canaanite woman's daughter (Matt. 15:22), healing an epileptic (Matt. 17:15), and healing the lepers (Luke 17:13). The gift of showing mercy would thus involve showing compassion and help toward the poor, sick, troubled, and suffering people. Moreover, this compassion is to be performed with cheerfulness. The one possessing this gift should perform acts of mercy with gladness, not out of drudgery.

Giving (Rom. 12:8). The word *giving* (Gk. *metadidous*) means "to share with someone," hence, the gift of giving is the unusual ability and willingness to share one's material goods with others. The one who has the gift of giving shares his goods eagerly and liberally. The exhortation of Paul is to give "with liberality." "It refers to open-handed and open-hearted giving out of compassion and a singleness of purpose, not from ambition."[75] This gift is not reserved for the rich but for ordinary Christians as well. The Philippians apparently exercised this gift in their giving to Paul (Phil. 4:10-16).

Administration (Rom. 12:8; 1 Cor. 12:28). In Romans 12:8 Paul refers to the one who leads. This is from the Greek word *prohistimi*, which means "to stand before," hence, to lead, rule, or preside. It is used of elders in 1 Thessalonians 5:12 and 1 Timothy 5:17. First Corinthians 12:28 refers to the gift of "administrations" (Gk. *kubernesis*), literally, "to steer a ship." Although the above references refer to elders leading the people, the term would probably go beyond that, suggesting also leading in terms of Sunday school superintendent and beyond the local church in ministries such as president or dean of a Christian college or seminary.

Wisdom (1 Cor. 12:8). The gift of wisdom was important in that it stands first in this list of gifts. Paul explains the gift of wisdom in greater detail in 1 Corinthians 2:6-12 where it is seen to be divinely imparted revelation that Paul could communicate to the believers. Because this gift involved receiving direct revelation, it was a characteristic gift of the apostles who received direct revelation from God.[76] The gift of wisdom thus "is the whole system of revealed truth. One with the gift of wisdom had the capacity to receive this revealed truth from God and present it to the people of God."[77] Because this gift is related to receiving and transmitting direct revelation from God the gift has ceased with the completion of the canon of Scripture.

Knowledge (1 Cor. 12:8). The gift of knowledge appears to be closely related to the gift of wisdom and refers to the ability properly to understand the truths revealed to the apostles and prophets.[78] This gift relates to the foundational gifts of prophesying and teaching, which would have involved communication of God's direct revelation to the apostles and prophets (cf. 1 Cor. 12:28). Therefore, this gift too would have ceased with the completion of the Scriptures. First Corinthians 13:8 indicates the cessation of this gift.

The relationship of these gifts is seen in the following diagram:[79]

RELATIONSHIPS OF FOUNDATIONAL GIFTS

1 Corinthians 12:6-10	1 Corinthians 12:28	1 Corinthians 12:29-30
Word of wisdom	Apostleship	Apostleship
Word of knowledge	Prophesying Teaching	Prophesying Teaching

FILLING OF THE SPIRIT

The filling of the Holy Spirit is distinct from the other ministries of the Spirit inasmuch as it is conditional. Whereas ministries such as the indwelling, baptism, regenerating, and sealing are non-experiential and occur but once at the moment of conversion, the filling of the Spirit is experiential and also repeated.

DEFINITION

The basis for the filling of the Spirit is Ephesians 5:18, "be filled with the Spirit." The command to be filled with the Spirit is given in contrast to the warning "do not get drunk with wine." Drunkenness exhibits the inability of the person to control himself. The nature of the Christian's life is to be in contrast to the nature of the uncontrolled drunkard. The meaning of "filled" (Gk. *plerousthe*) is "control." "The indwelling Spirit of God is the One who should continually control and dominate the life of the believer."[80]

A further contrast can be noted between the spiritual believer and the carnal believer (1 Cor. 2:9-3:4). "The carnal man is the man who lives by the power of the flesh, according to the dictates of the flesh, and the spiritual man is the man who lives by the power of the Spirit."[81]

EXPLANATION

The filling of the Spirit is necessary for two reasons. (1) It is essential for the believer's maturity (1 Cor. 3:1-3). Paul admonished the Corinthian believers as being "fleshly" (Gk. *sarkikos*), "controlled by the flesh." The solution to carnality and walking according to the old nature was to be controlled or filled by the Spirit. (2) It is essential for the believer's service (Acts 4:31; 9:17, 20). Acts 4:31 illustrates the relationship between filling and service; it was the filling of the Spirit that enabled the believers to "speak the word of God with boldness." When Paul was filled with the Spirit he immediately began to proclaim Jesus as the Son of God (Acts 9:17, 20).

Ephesians 5:18 teaches three factors concerning the concept of being filled with the Spirit. (1) It is a command. Nowhere is the believer commanded to be indwelt or sealed with the Spirit; however, the believer is commanded to be filled with the Spirit. It is a command to "be continually being filled with the Spirit" for maturity and service. (2) It is conditional. Whereas there are no conditions related to the indwelling, baptism, sealing, and many other ministries of the Spirit, the filling of the Spirit is conditional. Obedience to other commands of Scripture are necessary in order to be filled with the Spirit. (3) It is repeated. Ephesians 5:18 is a present imperative, commanding to be "continually being filled." This indicates it is not a one-time experience but rather a repeated event.

CONDITIONS

Even though Ephesians 5:18 is a command to be filled with the Spirit and there are inferences about conditions necessary for being filled, it is surprising that there is no command in Scripture to pray for the filling of the Spirit. Since the command relates to a right relationship to the Holy Spirit, the conditions governing that relationship must have to do with the filling of the Spirit. There are several commands that relate to a believer's being filled with the Spirit.[82]

Do not grieve the Holy Spirit (Eph. 4:30). The context of Ephesians 4:30 relates to exhortations concerning sin. Believers are warned not to lie (4:25), not to prolong anger (4:26), and not to be bitter or unforgiving (4:31-32). When a believer does these things he grieves the Holy Spirit. Sin grieves the Holy Spirit and sin will prevent the believer from being filled with the Spirit.

Do not quench the Holy Spirit (1 Thess. 5:19). The context of this passage relates to ministry. The believer is exhorted to pray without ceasing (5:17), be thankful (5:18), and not despise prophetic utterances (5:20). When believers pour cold water on the fire of ministry they quench the Spirit. The Spirit's ministry is not to be hindered; Christians also should not hinder others in their ministry for God.

Walk by the Spirit (Gal. 5:16). Walk means to conduct one's life. Rather than living in the sphere or under the domination of the old nature, believers are exhorted to conduct their lives in the sphere of the Holy Spirit.

Other conditions that are sometimes added to the above are: confession of sin (1 John 1:9) and dedication of the believer to God (Rom. 6:13; 12:1-2). However, it can be argued that these elements are subordinate factors within the three conditions discussed above.

RESULT

Although there no doubt are numerous consequences of being filled with the Spirit, probably most of them would be bound up in the statement of Galatians 5:22-24. The result of being filled with the Spirit will be to produce the fruit of the Spirit. In contrast to the deeds of the flesh produced by a walk according to the flesh (Gal. 5:19-21), the filling of the Spirit produces "love, joy, peace, patience, kindness, goodness, faithfulness, gentleness, and self-control" (vv. 22-23). Additionally, believers will be receptive to the teaching ministry of the Holy Spirit (1 Cor. 2:9-13; John 16:12-15); will exhibit joy, unity, and thankfulness in the assembly (Eph. 5:19-20); will be unified and discerning in ministry (1 Thess. 5:17-22); and will show dedication to God and nonconformity to the world (Rom. 12:1-2).

NOTES ON PNEUMATOLOGY

1. One example of serious error regarding the Holy Spirit is the view that the Trinity consists of Father, Mother (the Holy Spirit), and Son. One advocate of this position is Lois Roden of Waco, Texas. See a report by Mary Barrineau, "She Preaches Holy Spirit Is a Woman," in the *Florida Times-Union,* November 29, 1980.

2. Emery H. Bancroft, *Christian Theology* (Grand Rapids: Zondervan, 1976), p, 157.

3. Ibid.

4. Charles C. Ryrie, *The Holy Spirit* (Chicago: Moody, 1965), p. 11. This clear and concise study is probably the best work on the Holy Spirit for the beginning theologian.

5. William F. Arndt and F. Wilbur Gingrich, *A Greek-English Lexicon of the New Testament and Other Early Christian Literature,* revised by F. Wilbur Gingrich and Frederick W. Danker (Chicago: U. of Chicago, 1979), p. 866.

6. The phrase, "just as He will," *kathos bouletai,* stands in the emphatic position in the Greek text drawing attention to the fact that the Holy Spirit does *just as He wills.*

7. Arndt and Gingrich, *Greek-English Lexicon,* p. 146.

8. *Allos,* translated "another," stresses the idea of "another of the same kind" in contrast to *heteros* which means "another of a different kind."

9. Arndt and Gingrich, *Greek-English Lexicon,* p. 249.

10. Ryrie, *The Holy Spirit,* p. 13.

11. Rene Pache, *The Person and Work of the Holy Spirit* (Chicago: Moody, 1954), p. 14.

12. These statements are tautalogical, repetitious of an idea.

13. This chart is adapted from the information in John F. Walvoord, *The Holy Spirit* (Grand Rapids: Zondervan, 1958), pp. 10-12.

14. Keil remarks, *"raqeph* in the Piel is applied to the hovering and brooding of a bird over its young, to warm them, and develop their vital powers (Deut. 32:11). In such a way as this the Spirit of God moved upon the deep, which had received at its creation the germs of all life, to fill them with vital energy by His breath of life." C. F. Keil and F. Delitzsch, *Biblical Commentary on the Old Testament,* 25 vols. (Reprint. Grand Rapids: Eerdmans, 1968), 1:49.

15. There is a problem in the interpretation of this passage in that it is not entirely clear whether *pneuma* refers to the Holy Spirit or whether it is a reference to the human spirit of Christ. Although either is possible, most scholars argue in favor of the Holy Spirit.

16. There is an abnormal emphasis on experience today among Christians. Although Christianity is experiential it should also be recognized that the Holy Spirit will never lead a believer into an "experience" that is contrary to the Word of God. A spiritual experience is only valid insofar as it agrees with the Word of God. See *Faith Misguided: Exposing the Dangers of Mysticism* by Arthur L. Johnson (Chicago: Moody, 1988).

17. The NASB translation is "By His breath." The Hebrew word *ruach* may be translated "Spirit," "breath," or "wind." Some passages like Job 26:13 are more difficult to settle, although the context usually determines which option is meant.

18. Lewis Sperry Chafer, *Systematic Theology*, 8 vols. (Dallas: Dallas Seminary, 1948), 6:33.

19. Ibid., 6:45-46.

20. Walvoord, *The Holy Spirit*, p. 14.

21. J. Oliver Buswell, Jr., *A Systematic Theology of the Christian Religion*, 2 vols. (Grand Rapids: Zondervan, 1962), 1:119.

22. Arndt and Gingrich, *Greek-English Lexicon*, p. 109.

23. Ibid., p. 796.

24. Ryrie, *The Holy Spirit*, p. 33.

25. See Ryrie's helpful discussion on this on p. 33 in *The Holy Spirit*.

26. B. B. Warfield, *The Inspiration and Authority of the Bible* (Reprint. Philadelphia: Presbyterian and Reformed, 1970), p. 133.

27. Leon Wood, *The Holy Spirit in the Old Testament* (Grand Rapids: Zondervan, 1976), pp. 122-23; cf. G. Vos, *Biblical Theology* (Grand Rapids: Eerdmans, 1948), pp. 83-85.

28. Wood, *Holy Spirit in the Old Testament*, p. 123.

29. Ibid.

30. There is a question of how to understand *ruach* in v. 12. The NASB translated it "mind" and relates it to David's mind. KJV and NKJV translate it "by the Spirit," while the NIV translates it "all the Spirit had put in his mind."

31. Ryrie, *The Holy Spirit*, pp. 41-42.

32. Wood, *Holy Spirit in the Old Testament*, p. 41.

33. Walvoord, *The Holy Spirit*, p. 72.

34. There is a problem regarding the word "strives," *yadon*. Some suggest it means "to rule" or "to abide." Nonetheless, "the thought is that God will not forever bear the consequences of man's sin" (Harold Stigers, *Commentary on Genesis* [Grand Rapids: Zondervan, 1975], p. 98).

35. I. Howard Marshall, *The Gospel of Luke: A Commentary on the Greek Text* (Grand Rapids: Eerdmans, 1978), p. 70.

36. Ibid., p. 71.

37. Franz Hesse, *Xrio* in *Theological Dictionary of the New Testament*, 10 vols., edited by Gerhard Kittel and Gerhard Friedrich (Grand Rapids: Eerdmans, 1974), 9:501.

38. A. T. Robertson, *Word Pictures in the New Testament*, 6 vols. (Nashville: Broadman, 1930), 2:48.

39. Ibid., 1:255.

40. This is a problem passage inasmuch as *pneuma* may refer to Christ's human spirit or to the Holy Spirit. However, if His human spirit was intended one would expect the author to have said *His* spirit. The conclusion is not entirely clear.

41. See F. F. Bruce, *The Epistle to the Hebrews* (Grand Rapids: Eerdmans, 1964), p. 205.

42. J. Dwight Pentecost, *The Divine Comforter* (Chicago: Moody, 1963), p. 97.

43. It is difficult to determine the meaning of "Spirit of holiness." Some suggest it refers to Christ's deity or to His spiritual nature, but others to the Holy Spirit.

44. Pentecost, *Divine Comforter,* p. 100.

45. The interrogative particle *meti* is used in questions that expect a negative answer. Cf. Arndt and Gingrich, *Greek-English Lexicon,* p. 520.

46. See J. Dwight Pentecost, *The Words and Works of Jesus Christ* (Grand Rapids: Zondervan, 1981), p. 207.

47. A no less notable person than R. A. Torrey confused the baptizing work of the Spirit with the filling of the Spirit. See R. A. Torrey, *The Baptism with the Holy Spirit* (New York: Revell, 1895).

48. See Merrill F. Unger, *The Baptism and Gifts of the Holy Spirit* (Chicago: Moody, 1974). This is a comprehensive, biblical study of the subject and it is highly recommended.

49. Arndt and Gingrich, *Greek-English Lexicon,* pp. 192-93.

50. The phrase, "having also believed," "is called by grammarians the 'coincident' aorist participle because it denotes an action coincident in time with that of the main verb" (F. F. Bruce, *The Epistle to the Ephesians* [London: Pickering & Inglis, 1961], p. 36).

51. R. Schippers, "Seal," in Colin Brown, ed., *New International Dictionary of New Testament Theology,* 4 vols. (Grand Rapids: Zondervan, 1986), 3:497-99; see also previous discussion under "Representations of the Spirit."

52. Cf. Ephesians 1:13; 4:30. The passive Greek form *esphragisthete* emphasizes that God does the sealing of the believer.

53. William McRae, *The Dynamics of Spiritual Gifts* (Grand Rapids: Zondervan, 1976), p. 18.

54. Charles C. Ryrie, *The Holy Spirit* (Chicago: Moody, 1965), pp. 83-84.

55. McRae, *Dynamics of Spiritual Gifts,* p. 21.

56. Pentecost, *Divine Comforter,* p. 178; cf. Walvoord, *The Holy Spirit,* p. 176.

57. See B. B. Warfield, *Counterfeit Miracles* (Carlisle, Pa.: Banner of Truth, 1918); John F. MacArthur, Jr., *The Charismatics* (Grand Rapids: Zondervan, 1978), pp. 73-84.

58. William McRae, *The Dynamics of Spiritual Gifts* (Grand Rapids: Zondervan, 1976), pp. 72-73.

59. Fritz Rienecker, *A Linguistic Key to the Greek New Testament,* edited by Cleon Rogers (Grand Rapids: Zondervan, 1980), p. 429.

60. McRae, *Dynamics of Spiritual Gifts,* p. 69.

61. Ryrie, *The Holy Spirit,* pp. 86-87.

62. It is speculative to suggest that the tongues of Corinthians are angelic languages on the basis of 1 Corinthians 13:1. In that text Paul did not say there actually were angelic languages, nor did he define the gift of tongues as angelic tongues. Instead Paul was supposing a hypothetical situation to emphasize the importance of love.

63. Leslie B. Flynn, *19 Gifts of the Spirit* (Wheaton: Victor, 1974), p. 57.

64. See McRae, pp. 56-57, and Flynn, pp. 57-61.

65. Pentecost, *Divine Comforter,* p. 173.
66. Ibid.
67. Rienecker, *Linguistic Key to the Greek New Testament*, p. 430.
68. A. T. Robertson and Alfred Plummer, *A Critical and Exegetical Commentary on the First Epistle of St. Paul to the Corinthians* in *The International Critical Commentary* (Edinburgh: Clark, 1914), p. 281.
69. McRae, *Dynamics of Spiritual Gifts*, p. 66.
70. See Arthur T. Pierson, *George Müller of Bristol* (Old Tappan, N.J.: Revell, 1971); and Dr. and Mrs. Howard Taylor, *Hudson Taylor's Spiritual Secret* (Chicago: Moody, n.d.).
71. Pentecost, *Divine Comforter, p. 174.*
72. W. E. Vine, *The Epistle to the Romans* (Grand Rapids: Zondervan, 1948), p. 180.
73. McRae, *Dynamics of Spiritual Gifts*, pp. 49-50.
74 H. H. Esser, "Mercy," in Colin Brown, ed., *New International Dictionary of New Testament Theology* (Grand Rapids: Zondervan, 1976), 2:594.
75. Rienecker, *Linguistic Key to the Greek New Testament*, p. 376.
76. Charles Hodge, *First Corinthians,* pp. 245-46.
77. McRae, *Dynamics of Spiritual Gifts*, p. 65.
78. Hodge, *First Corinthians*, p. 246.
79. McRae, *Dynamics of Spiritual Gifts*, p. 66.
80. Rienecker, *Linguistic Key to the Greek New Testament*, p. 538.
81. Pentecost, *Divine Comforter*, p. 154.
82. See discussion by Lewis Sperry Chafer in his classic work, *He That Is Spiritual* (Grand Rapids: Zondervan, 1918), pp. 82-172, in which he discusses these aspects in considerable detail.

FOR FURTHER STUDY ON PNEUMATOLOGY

THE PERSONALITY OF THE SPIRIT

* Emery H. Bancroft. *Christian Theology*, 2d rev. ed. Grand Rapids: Zondervan, 1976. Pp. 157-59.
* Rene Pache. *The Person and Work of the Holy Spirit.* Chicago: Moody, 1954. Pp. 11-13.
* J. Dwight Pentecost. *The Divine Comforter.* Chicago: Moody, 1963. Pp. 11-20.
* Charles C. Ryrie. *The Holy Spirit.* Chicago: Moody, 1965. Pp. 11-16.
** John F. Walvoord. *The Holy Spirit.* Grand Rapids: Zondervan, 1958. Pp. 5-7.

THE DEITY OF THE SPIRIT

** Lewis Sperry Chafer. *Systematic Theology*, 8 vols. Dallas: Dallas Seminary, 1948. 6:22-46.
* Millard J. Erickson. *Christian Theology*, 3 vols. Grand Rapids: Baker, 1985. 2:857-59.
* Arthur L. Johnson. *Faith Misguided: Exposing the Dangers of Mysticism.* Chicago: Moody, 1988.

* Rene Pache. *The Person and Work of the Holy Spirit.* Chicago: Moody, 1954. Pp. 14-19.
* Charles C. Ryrie. *The Holy Spirit.* Chicago: Moody, 1965. Pp. 17-22.
** John F. Walvoord. *The Holy Spirit.* Grand Rapids: Zondervan, 1958. Pp. 8-17.

REPRESENTATIONS OF THE SPIRIT

** F. E. Marsh. *Emblems of the Holy Spirit.* New York: Alliance, 1911.
* J. Robertson McQuilkin. *Understanding and Applying the Bible.* Chicago: Moody, 1983. Pp. 221-26.
** A. Berkeley Mickelsen. *Interpreting the Bible.* Grand Rapids: Eerdmans, 1963. Pp. 236-64.
* Rene Pache. *The Person and Work of the Holy Spirit.* Chicago: Moody, 1954. Pp. 20-25.
** Bernard Ramm. *Protestant Biblical Interpretation.* 3rd rev. ed. Grand Rapids: Baker, 1970. Pp. 215-40.
* Charles C. Ryrie. *The Holy Spirit.* Chicago: Moody, 1965. Pp. 23-25. This succinct explanation is especially helpful in defining a type and contrasting it with an ordinary illustration.
* T. Norton Sterrett. *How to Understand Your Bible.* Downers Grove, Ill.: InterVarsity, 1974. Pp. 107-14. This is a most useful book in the beginning study of hermeneutics and is highly recommended.
** John F. Walvoord. *The Holy Spirit.* Grand Rapids: Zondervan, 1958. Pp. 18-25.

THE BAPTIZING WORK OF THE SPIRIT

** Lewis Sperry Chafer. *Systematic Theology*, 8 vols. Dallas: Dallas Seminary, 1948. 6:138-61.
* W. A. Criswell. *The Baptism, Filling and Gifts of the Holy Spirit.* Grand Rapids: Zondervan, 1973. Pp. 7-25.
* Rene Pache. *The Person and Work of the Holy Spirit.* Chicago: Moody, 1954. Pp. 70-79.
* J. Dwight Pentecost. *The Divine Comforter.* Chicago: Moody, 1963. Pp. 136-43.
* Charles C. Ryrie. *The Holy Spirit.* Chicago: Moody, 1965. Pp. 74-79.
** Merrill F. Unger. *The Baptism and Gifts of the Holy Spirit.* Chicago: Moody, 1974.
** John F. Walvoord. *The Holy Spirit.* Grand Rapids: Zondervan, 1958. Pp. 138-50.

GIFTS OF THE SPIRIT

* W. A. Criswell. *The Baptism, Filling and Gifts of the Holy Spirit.* Grand Rapids: Zondervan, 1973. Pp. 40-127.
** Thomas R. Edgar. *Miraculous Gifts.* Neptune, N.J.: Loizeaux, 1983. This is unquestionably one of the finest, well-researched works on the subject.
* Leslie B. Flynn. *19 Gifts of the Spirit.* Wheaton: Victor, 1974.
** John F. MacArthur, Jr. *The Charismatics.* Grand Rapids: Zondervan, 1978. A serious treatment on a vital subject.
* William McRae. *The Dynamics of Spiritual Gifts.* Grand Rapids: Zondervan, 1976. This may well be the most helpful book on the subject.
* J. Dwight Pentecost. *The Divine Comforter.* Chicago: Moody, 1963. Pp. 165-92.
* Charles C. Ryrie. *The Holy Spirit.* Chicago: Moody, 1965. Pp. 83-92.

** Robert L. Thomas. *Understand Spiritual Gifts.* Chicago: Moody, 1978. This is probably the most complete, thoroughly researched work on spiritual gifts.

THE FILLING OF THE SPIRIT

* Lewis Sperry Chafer. *He That Is Spiritual.* Grand Rapids: Zondervan, 1918.

* David Ewert. *The Holy Spirit in the New Testament.* Scottdale, Pa.: Herald, 1983. Pp. 232-38.

* William Fitch. *The Ministry of the Holy Spirit.* Grand Rapids: Zondervan, 1974. Pp. 183-92.

* Rene Pache. *The Person and Work of the Holy Spirit.* Chicago: Moody, 1954. Pp. 114-36.

* J. Dwight Pentecost. *The Divine Comforter.* Chicago: Moody, 1963. Pp. 154-64.

* Charles C. Ryrie. *The Holy Spirit.* Chicago: Moody, 1965. Pp. 93-103.

* J. Oswald Sanders. *The Holy Spirit and His Gifts.* Grand Rapids: Zondervan, 1940. Pp. 137-44.

** John F. Walvoord. *The Holy Spirit.* Grand Rapids: Zondervan, 1958. Pp. 189-224.

22

ANGELOLOGY:
DOCTRINES OF ANGELS, SATAN, AND DEMONS

DOCTRINE OF ANGELS

DEFINITION OF ANGELS

There are a number of different words used in Scripture to define angelic beings.

Angel. The Hebrew word *malak* simply means "messenger"; it may refer to a human messenger (1 Kings 19:2) or a divine messenger (Gen. 28:12). The basic meaning of the word is "one who is sent." As a divine messenger an angel is a "heavenly being charged by God with some commission."[1] The word is found 103 times in the Old Testament. The Greek word *angelos* occurs 175 times in the New Testament; however, of men it is used only 6 times. The word *angelos* is similar to the Hebrew *malak*; it also means "messenger . . . who speaks and acts in the place of the one who has sent him."[2]

Sons of God. Angels are called "sons of God" in that in their unfallen estate they are God's sons by His creation (Job 1:6; 38:7).[3]

Holy ones. Angels are also referred to as "holy ones" (Ps. 89:5, 7) in the sense that they are "set apart" by God and for God as attendants to His holiness.

Host. Angels are referred to as the "host," which can be understood to denote the armies of heaven (Ps. 89:6, 8; 1 Sam. 17:45). The phrases used to describe the angels in this manner are "host of heaven" (1 Sam. 1:11), and as the millions of heavenly beings that surround God they are called "hosts" in the phrase "Lord of hosts" (Isa. 31:4).

EXISTENCE OF ANGELS

The existence of angels is uniformly presented in Scripture. Thirty-four books of the Bible make reference to angels (seventeen in the Old Testament; seventeen in the New Testament). Critical to the belief in angels is the relationship of angels to Christ. Christ was helped by angels following His temptation (Matt. 4:11); He referred to the resurrected state as comparable to angels (Matt. 22:29-30); He taught that angels would regather the nation Israel at the time of His return (Matt. 25:31-32, 41). The existence of angels is tied to the reliability of the testimony of Christ.

NATURE AND ATTRIBUTES OF ANGELS

Angels are spirit beings. Although angels may reveal themselves to mankind in the form of human bodies (Gen. 18:3) they nonetheless are called "spirits" (Heb. 1:14), suggesting they do not have corporeal bodies. Hence, they do not function as human beings in terms of marriage (Mark 12:25) nor are they subject to death (Luke 20:36).

Angels are created beings. The psalmist calls upon all nature to praise God for His creation. Along with the celestial bodies the Lord created the angels by His word (Ps. 148:2-5). Job was reminded that the angels sang praise to God when they were created (Job 38:6-7). Christ created the angels that they might ultimately give praise to Him (Col. 1:16).

Angels were created simultaneously and innumerable in number. The statement of creation in Colossians 1:16 points to the creation of angels as a singular act; the act of creating angels does not continue.[4] Because the angels are incapable of reproducing (Matt. 22:30), their number remains static. The number of their creation is "myriads" (Heb. 12:22). Although the term *myraids* (Gk. *muriasin*) literally means ten thousand, here it denotes "countless thousands" (cf. Rev. 5:11).[5] The repetition of myriads in Revelation 5:11 suggests the number of angels is countless.

Angels are a higher order than man. Mankind, including our incarnate Lord, is "lower than the angels" (Heb. 2:7). Angels are not subject to the limitations of man, especially since they are incapable of death (Luke 20:36). Angels have greater wisdom than man (2 Sam. 14:20), yet it is limited (Matt. 24:36). Angels have greater power than man (Matt. 28:2; Acts 5:19; 2 Pet. 2:11), yet they are limited in power (Dan. 10:13).[6]

Angels, however, have limitations compared to man, particularly in future relationships. Angels are not created in the image of God, therefore, they do not share man's glorious destiny of redemption in Christ. At the consummation of the age, redeemed man will be exalted above angels (1 Cor. 6:3).

CLASSIFICATION OF ANGELS

Angels who are governmental rulers. Ephesians 6:12 refers to "ranking of fallen angels": *rulers* are "those who are first or high in rank"; *powers* are "those invested with authority"; *world-forces of this darkness* "expresses the power or authority which they exercise over the world"; *spiritual forces of wickedness* describes the wicked spirits, "expressing their character and nature."[7] Daniel 10:13 refers to the "prince of the kingdom of Persia" opposing Michael. This was not the king of Persia but rather a fallen angel under Satan's control; he was a demon "of high rank, assigned by the chief of demons, Satan, to Persia as his special area of activity"[8] (cf. Rev. 12:7).

Angels who are highest ranking. Michael is called the *archangel* in Jude 9 and the great prince in Daniel 12:1. Michael is the only angel designated archangel, and may possibly be the only one of this rank. The mission of the archangel is protector of Israel. (He is called "Michael your prince" in Dan. 10:21.) There were *chief princes* (Dan. 10:13), of whom Michael was one, as the highest ranking angels of God. *Ruling angels* (Eph. 3:10) are also mentioned, but no further details are given.

Angels who are prominent individuals. (1) Michael (Dan. 10:13; 12:1; Jude 9). The name *Michael* means "who is like God?" and identifies the only one classified as an archangel in Scripture. Michael is the defender of Israel who will wage war on behalf of Israel against Satan and his hordes in the Tribulation (Rev. 12:7-9). Michael also disputed with Satan about the body of Moses, but Michael refrained from judgment, leaving that to God (Jude 9). Jehovah's Witnesses and some Christians identify Michael as Christ; this view, however, would suggest Christ has less authority than Satan, which is untenable.

(2) Gabriel (Dan. 9:21; Luke 1:26). His name means "man of God" or "God is strong." "Gabriel seems to be God's special messenger of His kingdom program in each of the four times he appears in the Bible record . . . . He reveals and interprets God's purpose and program concerning Messiah and His kingdom to the prophets and people of Israel."[9] In a highly significant passage, Gabriel explained the events of the seventy weeks for Israel (Dan. 9:21-27). In Luke 1:26-27 Gabriel told Mary that the One born to her would be great and rule on the throne of David. In Daniel 8:15-16 Gabriel explained to Daniel the succeeding kingdoms of Medo-Persia and Greece as well as the untimely death of Alexander the Great. Gabriel also announced the birth of John the Baptist to Zacharias (Luke 1:11-20).

(3) Lucifer (Isa. 14:12) means "shining one" or "star of the morning." He may have been the wisest and most beautiful of all God's created beings who was originally placed in a position of authority over the cherubim surrounding the throne of God.[10] (See aditional discussion under "Origin and Nature of Satan.")

Angels who are divine attendants. (1) *Cherubim* are "of the highest order or class, created with indescribable powers and beauty . . . . Their main purpose and activity might be summarized in this way: they are proclaimers and protectors of God's glorious presence, His sovereignty, and His holiness."[11] They stood guard at the gate of the Garden of Eden, preventing sinful man from entering (Gen. 3:24); were the golden figures covering the mercy seat above the ark in the Holy of Holies (Exod. 25:17-22); and attended the glory of God in Ezekiel's vision (Ezek. 1). Cherubim had an extraordinary appearance with four faces—that of a man, lion, ox, and eagle. They had four wings and feet like a calf, gleaming like burnished bronze. In Ezekiel 1 they attended the glory of God preparatory for judgment.

(2) *Seraphim*, meaning "burning ones," are pictured surrounding the throne of God in Isaiah 6:2. They are described as each having six wings. In their threefold proclamation, "holy, holy, holy" (Isa. 6:3), it means "to recognize God as extremely, perfectly holy. Therefore, they praise and proclaim the perfect holiness of God. The seraphim also express the holiness of God in that they proclaim that man must be cleansed of sin's moral defilement before he can stand before God and serve Him."[12]

MINISTRY OF ANGELS

Ministry to God. The cherubim have a ministry to God in defending the holiness of God; Seraphim have a ministry to God in surrounding the throne of God as they attend to His holiness.

Ministry to Christ. Angels have a significant ministry to Christ from prior to His birth until His Second Advent. The fact that angels have this important ministry to Christ also emphasizes His deity; just as the angelic beings surround the throne of the Father so the angels attend to God the Son.

(1) Angels predicted His birth (Luke 1:26-38). Gabriel came to Mary explaining that her child would be called "Son of the Most High," who would also rule on the throne of David, His father, having an eternal kingdom.

(2) Angels protected Him in infancy (Matt. 2:13). An angel warned Joseph of Herod's intention and told Joseph to flee to Egypt until the death of Herod. An angel also instructed Joseph when it was safe to return to the land of Israel (Matt. 2:20).

(3) Angels ministered to Him after the temptation (Matt. 4:11). The ministry probably included encouragement following the exhaustion of forty days of temptation, as well as supplying him with food as an angel did to Elijah (1 Kings 19:5-7).

(4) Angels strengthened Him at Gethsemane (Luke 22:43). Just as Christ had a spiritual battle with Satan at His temptation, so Christ had a spiritual battle at Gethsemane concerning the cross. Angels strengthened Him as He wrestled in prayer in anticipation of His crucifixion.

(5) Angels announced His resurrection (Matt. 28:5-7; Mark 16:6-7; Luke 24:4-7; John 20:12-13). The angels invited the women to enter the empty tomb to see the empty wrappings that they might be certain of the resurrection and proclaim it to the world. The angels reminded the women of Jesus' earlier promise that He would rise on the third day.

(6) Angels attended His ascension (Acts 1:10). As angels surround the throne of the Father, so angels attended the triumphal ascension of the Son into glory and reminded the onlookers of Jesus' future triumphant return.

(7) Angels will attend His Second Coming (Matt. 25:31). Angels will prepare the world for the return of the Son by regathering Israel to the land preparatory for their Messiah's return and rule (Matt. 24:31). As God the Son returns to earth He will be attended by a host of angels, adding to the splendor and glory of His triumphal return (Matt. 25:31).

Ministry to believers. Angels are termed "ministering spirits" in Hebrews 1:14. The Greek term for *ministering* "*(leitourgika)* does not convey the idea of slavery, but of official functioning. They have been duly commissioned and sent forth with the responsibility of aiding believers."[13] The following responsibilities are carried out in angels' ministry to believers.

(1) Physical protection. David experienced physical protection by the angel when he was forced to flee to the Philistines (Ps. 34:7). Angels may frustrate the plans of the enemies of God's people (Ps. 35:4-5). Angels protect from physical harm those that seek refuge in the Lord (Ps. 91:11-13). They released the apostles from prison (Acts 5:19) and Peter from prison (Acts 12:7-11). They will protect the 144,000 in the Tribulation (Rev. 7:1-14).

(2) Physical provision. An angel brought physical nourishment for Elijah when he was weakened from a lengthy journey (1 Kings 19:5-7).

(3) Encouragement. During the storm at sea an angel encouraged Paul, reminding him he would arrive safely at Rome to bear witness for Christ (Acts 27:23-25).

(4) Direction. An angel directed Philip to witness to the Ethiopian eunuch (Acts 8:26); an angel arranged the meeting of Cornelius and Peter that brought the Gentiles into acceptance in the believing community (Acts 10:3, 22).

(5) Assist in answers to prayer. There seems to be a relationship between the prayer for Peter's release from prison and the angel's releasing him (Acts 12:1-11). Similarly, Daniel's prayer was explained by the angel (Dan. 9:20-27; cf. 10:10–12:13).

(6) Carry believers home. Luke 16:22 describes the death of Lazarus and the angels carrying him to Abraham's bosom. This may be the way God causes all His dying saints to be "absent from the body . . . at home with the Lord."

Relationship to unbelievers. Angels have been and will be involved in meting out judgment on unbelievers. Angels announced the coming destruction of Sodom because of those people's sin (Gen. 19:12-13); prior to the climactic bowl judgments angels will announce the destruction of the world powers along with those that worshiped the beast (Rev. 14:4, 7, 8-9, 15, 17-18). Angels are seen judging the people of Jerusalem for their idolatry (Ezek. 9:1-11); an angel struck Herod Agrippa I for his blasphemy so that he died (Acts 12:23). Angels will also be instrumental in judgment at the end of the age when they cast unbelievers into the furnace of fire (Matt. 13:39-42); angels will sound the trumpet judgments during the Tribulation (Rev. 8:2-12; 9:1, 13; 11:15); angels pour out the bowl judgments upon the earth (Rev. 16:2-17).

Doctrine of Satan

EXISTENCE OF SATAN

The primary witness to the reality and existence of Satan is not experience or sensational stories but the testimony of Scripture. Both the Old Testament and New Testament affirm the reality and existence of Satan. When Genesis 3 discusses the serpent, it is recognized that the serpent was Satan and that the judgment pronounced (Gen. 3:15) must be a reference to him. Satan is specifically mentioned in Job 2:1 as he came to accuse Job before God. In 1 Chronicles 21:2 Satan led David to take a census of the Israelites. In Zechariah 3:1-2 Satan is seen accusing the nation before God.

Although Satan is not so-named in Isaiah 14:12-17 and Ezekiel 28:11-19, these passages are understood with good reason to refer to his original state and subsequent fall.

The New Testament evidence for Satan's existence is extensive. Every New Testament writer and nineteen of the books make reference to him (cf. Matt. 4:10; 12:26; Mark 1:13; 3:23, 26; 4:15; Luke 11:18; 22:3; John 13:27, etc.). Christ Himself makes reference to Satan twenty-five times. The fact of Satan's existence finds ultimate support in the veracity of Christ's words.

Aside from prefall terms like *Lucifer* or *cherub*, there are many names for Satan in both Testaments that cumulatively establish his existence and evil character.

PERSONALITY OF SATAN

Satan exhibits attributes of personality. Scripture mentions three major features of personality when discussing Satan. Satan reflects *intellect* in that he schemes and is crafty in his work (Eph. 6:11). His work of deception[14] indicates his ability to think and plan a course of action that will be successful in deceiving people (Rev. 12:9). His knowledge and facility with Scripture (in deception) further illustrates his intellect (Matt. 4:5-6). Satan's *emotion* is seen in his desire to exalt himself above the rule of God (Isa.

NAMES OF SATAN

Name	Meaning	Citation
Satan	Adversary	Matthew 4:10
Devil	Slanderer	Matthew 4:1
Evil one	Intrinsically evil	John 17:15
Great red dragon	Destructive creature	Revelation 12:3, 7, 9
Serpent of old	Deceiver in Eden	Revelation 12:9
Abaddon	Destruction	Revelation 9:11
Apollyon	Destroyer	Revelation 9:11
Adversary	Opponent	1 Peter 5:8
Beelzebul	Lord of the fly (Baalzebub)	Matthew 12:24
Belial	Worthless (Beliar)	2 Corinthians 6:15
God of this world	Controls philosophy of world	2 Corinthians 4:4
Ruler of this world	Rules in world system	John 12:31
Prince of the power of the air	Control of unbelievers	Ephesians 2:2
Enemy	Opponent	Matthew 13:28
Tempter	Solicits people to sin	Matthew 4:3
Murderer	Leads people to eternal death	John 8:44
Liar	Perverts the truth	John 8:44
Accuser	Opposes believers before God	Revelation 12:10

14:12-17); note the "I will's"). Satan desires to trap new converts through their conceit (1 Tim. 3:6). Recognizing he has only a short time on earth, Satan vents great wrath (Gk. *thumon*), "burning anger" (Rev. 12:12). Satan demonstrated his *will* in attempting to entice Christ to sin (Matt. 4:3). Satan's will is most clearly reflected in his wish to be like God (Isa. 14:13-14).

Satan exhibits actions of personality. Satan speaks (Job 1:9-10), tempts Christ (Matt. 4:3), plans (Eph. 6:11), and accuses believers (Rev. 12:10).

Above all, Satan is deceptive, scheming to defeat Christians. His intent and opposition to believers is graphically portrayed in 1 Peter 5:8. In his opposition he is as ferocious as a lion, continually walking about with the intent of devouring someone. He continually brings legal accusations against Christians (Rev. 12:9-10). He schemes (Gk. *methodeia*) against Christians to make them fall (Eph. 6:11).

All of these elements demonstrate that Satan is a person.

ORIGIN AND NATURE OF SATAN

Satan's original state. Ezekiel 28:12-15 describes Satan prior to his fall.[15] He enjoyed an exalted position in the presence of God; the brilliance of heaven was his surrounding (28:13). He was called the "anointed . . . covering cherub" who enjoyed the position of highest honor before God (28:14, 16). Isaiah refers to this supreme angel as "star of the morning (KJV *Lucifer*; NIV *morning star*), son of the dawn" (14:12). After he became God's chief adversary (Heb. *Satan*) he is never again called by any of these honorable titles. But in his prefall splendor he was filled with wisdom and beauty, and he was blameless (Ezek. 28:12, 15).

Satan's fall. Satan's fall is described in both Ezekiel 28 and Isaiah 14. Because of his sin Satan was cast from the presence of God (Ezek. 28:16). The reason for Satan's downfall was his pride; his heart was lifted up because of his beauty, and his wisdom became corrupt (28:17). The statement indicates Satan must have had extraordinarily high rank that led to his pride. Isaiah 14:12-14 further describes the sin that led to his downfall. Five "I will's" emphasize his sin (14:13-14). He desired to enter the very presence of God and establish his throne on God's throne above the other angels. He wanted to be like the "Most High." For that reason God thrust him down out of heaven.

Satan's moral responsibility. Satan is a morally responsible person, accountable to God (Job 1:7). He does not have freedom in an unrestricted sense but is subordinate to and restricted by God.

JUDGMENT OF SATAN

Satan fell from his original exalted position. As the anointed cherub Satan led a host of angels, possibly one-third of all the angels, from heaven in his fall (Ezek. 28:16-17; Rev. 12:4).

Satan's ultimate defeat was pronounced in Eden. God informed Satan that he would have a minor victory ("you shall bruise him on the heel"), but Christ would have a major victory through the cross ("He shall bruise you on the head" Gen. 3:15).

Satan was rendered powerless through the cross. Christ partook of humanity, and through His substitutionary death He defeated Satan, rendering him impotent in the believer's life. Satan had the power of death over people but that power was broken through Christ (Heb. 2:14).

Satan will be cast out of heaven during the Tribulation. The casting out of heaven (Rev. 12:13) is an act of judgment and probably refers to the stellar heavens, also known as the second heaven (not the presence of God).

Satan will be bound in the pit for 1,000 years. At the triumphant return of Christ, Satan is bound for 1,000 years and shut up in the abyss, no longer able to deceive anyone on earth for the duration of the Millennium (Rev. 20:2-3).

Satan will finally be cast into the lake of fire. At the end of the Millennium Satan is released whereupon he deceives many people, leads a rebellion against God, is defeated and finally cast into the lake of fire for eternity (Rev. 20:7-10).

DOCTRINE OF DEMONS

ORIGIN OF DEMONS

There are a number of theories about the origin of demons. For the Christian each one must be tested by the insights of the Bible.

Spirits of deceased evil people. This was the view of Philo, Josephus, some early Christian writers, and ancient Greeks. This theory is proved false by Scripture because evil people are in Hades after death (Luke 16:23).

Spirits of a pre-Adamic race. This theory is based on the "gap theory" of an original creation of Genesis 1:1, rebellion and a fall of that originally created race between Genesis 1:1 and 1:2, and the resultant chaos. Genesis 1:3 describes the recreation. The original creation of humanity that fell is now the spirits of demons. The problem with this view is that it depends on a creation of humanity prior to Genesis 1 and 2, and there is no bibical warrant for such a view.[16] Furthermore, Romans 5:12 makes it clear that it was through Adam, not some pre-Adamic creature, that the conditions of sin and death began in the cosmos.

Offspring of angels and women. This theory is based on the suggestion that the "sons of God" in Genesis 6:2 were angels who came to earth, had intercourse with the "daughters of men," and produced a resultant offspring, the Nephilim (Gen. 6:4), who were demons. This theory has several problems. The suggestion that sons of God refers to angels can be challenged; this was not an unnatural sexual union for the phrase "took wives for themselves" refers to a marriage relationship, never to an act of illicit sexual relationship.[17] In addition, there is no indication that Nephilim were demons; rather, they were probably "heroes" or "fierce warriors."[18]

Fallen but unconfined angels. This view, which is preferable, is held by Hodge, Strong, Morgan, Gaebelein, Unger, and others. It teaches that when Lucifer rebelled against God he fell from his place of prominence and led with him a host of lower-ranking angels. Lucifer, now called Satan, is the "ruler of demons" (Matt. 12:24). Matthew 25:41 also refers to "the devil and his angels," which would refer to demons; similarly, Revelation 12:7 mentions "the dragon and his angels."

Scripture indicates there are two groups of fallen angels. One group is the demons who are free and active in the world. Other fallen angels are bound in confinement. Some are mentioned as being confined to *tartarus*, (translated "hell" in 2 Pet. 2:4); they are confined because of some enormous sin (some relate this to Genesis 6 in suggesting the "sons of God" were angels). Jude 6 may refer to the same confinement. Another group of fallen angels are kept confined in the pit (Luke 8:31; Rev. 9:2). They were "apparently too depraved and harmful to be allowed to roam upon the earth."[19] Revelation 9 indicates these demons will be released from confinement during the Tribulation to afflict people who do not have the seal of God on their foreheads (Rev. 9:3-11).

CLASSIFICATIONS OF ANGELS[20]

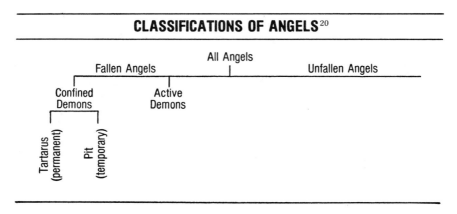

CHARACTERISTICS OF DEMONS

Demons are spirit beings. They are beings called spirits, that is, ones without fleshly bodies (Matt. 8:16; Luke 10:17, 20).

Demons are localized but not omnipresent. They can be in only one place at one time. The demons indwelt the two men of the Gadarenes, and when they were expelled they indwelt the swine. In each case they were localized (Matt. 8:28-34; cf. Acts 16:16).

Demons are intelligent but not omniscient. Demons were aware of the identity of Jesus (Mark 1:24); they were also aware of their ultimate destiny (Matt. 8:29). Paul refers to "doctrines of demons" (1 Tim. 4:1), indicating that they propagate their false teaching through their emissaries. They are not, however, omniscient or they would be like God; only God is omniscient.

Demons are powerful but not omnipotent. Because of the indwelling demons the man of the Gerasenes could break shackles and chains; no one was able to bind him beause of his unusual strength (Mark 5:3-4). The demon in the boy sought to have the boy commit suicide by throwing him into fire and water (Mark 9:22). Demon possession impaired a man's speech (Matt. 9:32) and kept a girl in cruel slavery (Matt. 15:22), yet demons are limited in their power; they cannot do the work of God (John 10:21).

ACTIVITY OF DEMONS

Demons inflict disease. Luke 13:11 testifies a woman had a crippling sickness "caused by a spirit"; Luke 13:16 further declares that "Satan has bound for eighteen long years" this woman in her suffering. Sometimes there is a correlation between mental illness, sickness, and demonic activity; however, it is not always possible to identify the distinction and anyone attempting such a diagnosis should be cautious. Affliction by Satan or demons can come only as God permits (Job 1:12; 2:6; cf. 2 Cor. 12:7-10).

Demons influence the mind. Satan initially deceived Eve into sinning by perverting the truth and changing Eve's thinking about God (Gen. 3:1-5). Satan and his demons continue to influence the thinking of people through blinding their minds (2 Cor. 4:4). This passage indicates Satan inhibits the ability to think or reason.[21] Even though this passage refers to unbelievers, Satan can also influence the thinking of believers (2 Cor. 11:3); he can lead believers away from "the simplicity and purity of devotion to Christ." Satan can thus lead the believer away from a singleminded devotion to Christ. James 3:15 indicates earthly wisdom is demonic and leads to jealousy and strife.

The solution to demonic influence of the mind is to bring the thought process into subjection to Christ (2 Cor. 10:5). A similar exhortation is given in Philippians 4:6-8. The mind will be guarded when the believer entrusts every matter to God in prayer and meditates on the things that are true, honorable, right, and pure.

Demons deceive people. Paul was fearful of the fledgling Thessalonian church, that Satan may have enticed them to sin amid their suffering and persecution (1 Thess. 3:5). Although the Thessalonians had received the gospel with joy, their hope could be sidetracked through the onslaught of Satan.

Through his emissaries Satan also works in unbelievers; Paul refers to the prince of the power of the air "working in the sons of disobedience" (Eph. 2:2). The context indicates Satan deceives the unbelievers into living according to the lusts of the flesh and desires of the flesh and mind. Matthew 13:19 further indicates Satan's deception in that he snatches the Word away when unbelievers hear it, thwarting their understanding.

Demons deceive nations. Demons will eventually gather the nations of the world together in rebellion against Christ. Demons deceive the nations through performing signs in order to incite them in warfare against the returning Messiah (Rev. 16:14).

DEMON POSSESSION

Definition. Charles Ryrie defines demon possession as

> A demon residing in a person, exerting direct control and influence over that person, with certain derangement of mind and/or body. Demon possession is to be distinguished from demon influence or demon activity in relation to a person. The work of the demon in the latter is from the outside; in demon possession it is from within. By this definition a Christian cannot be possessed by a demon since he is indwelt by the Holy Spirit. However, a believer can be the target of demonic activity to such an extent that he may give the appearance of demon possession.[22]

Fact of demon possession. There was a great outbreak of demon activity and demon possession during Christ's sojourn on earth, no doubt in opposition to His Messiahship. The gospels abound with accounts of demon possessed people (Matt. 4:24; 8:16, 28, 33; 12:22; 15:22; Mark 1:32; 5:15, 16, 18; Luke 8:36; John 10:21). Leaders in the early church such as Justin Martyr and Tertullian make reference to demon possession as does the *Shepherd of Hermas.*

Nature of demon possession.[23] Demon possession evidences itself by a change in moral character and spiritual disposition. Frequently a different voice, a different educational level, or even a foreign language will reflect a difference in the affected person's personality. The demons speaking through the man immediately recognized who Christ was (Mark 1:23-24), which meant he had supernatural knowledge and intellectual power. Another symptom of demon possession was exhibited by the man in the country of the Gerasenes with his supernatural physical strength and ability to break shackles and chains (Mark 5:3-4).

JUDGMENT OF DEMONS

Through the cross the power of demons has been conquered. Christ conquered Satan and his demons at the cross and made a public display of them—as a victor displaying the spoils of war (Col. 2:15).

At the return of Christ the demons will be cast into the lake of fire. Demons are associated with judgment against Satan (Matt. 25:41; Rev. 12:9), and therefore will be cast into the lake of fire with Satan (Rev. 19:19-21).

Notes on Angelology

1. Gerhard von Rad, *"Mal'āk* in the Old Testament," in Gerhard Kittel, ed., *Theological Dictionary of the New Tesament,* 10 vols. (Grand Rapids: Eerdmans, 1964), 1:76-77.

2. H. Bietenhard, "Angel," in Colin Brown, ed., *New International Dictionary of New Testament Theology,* 4 vols. (Grand Rapids: Zondervan, 1975), 1:101.

3. Roy Zuck, "Job," in *The Bible Knowledge Commentary,* 2 vols. (Wheaton: Victor, 1985), 1:719.

4. The aorist *ektisthe* views "the whole of creative activity is summed up in Christ including the angels of heaven and everything on earth." A. T. Robertson, *Word Pictures in the New Testament,* 6 vols. (Nashville: Broadman, 1930), 4:478.

5. William F. Arndt and F. Wilbur Gingrich, *Greek-English Lexicon of the New Testament and Other Early Christian Literature,* revised by F. Wilbur Gingrich and Frederick W. Danker (Chicago: U. of Chicago, 1979), p. 529.

6. Henry C. Thiessen, *Lectures in Systematic Theology,* revised by Vernon D. Doerksen (Grand Rapids: Eerdmans, 1979), pp. 135-36.

7. Charles Hodge, *A Commentary on the Epistle to the Ephesians* (Reprint. London: Banner of Truth, 1964), pp. 378-79.

8. Leon Wood, *A Commentary on Daniel* (Grand Rapids: Zondervan, 1973), p. 272.

9. C. Fred Dickason, *Angels: Elect and Evil* (Chicago: Moody, 1975), p. 70.

10. J. Dwight Pentecost, *Your Adversary the Devil* (Grand Rapids: Zondervan, 1969), p. 20.

11. Dickason, *Angels: Elect and Evil,* pp. 61, 63.

12. Ibid., p. 66.

13. Homer A. Kent, Jr., *The Epistle to the Hebrews* (Grand Rapids: Baker, 1972), p. 46.

14. The present participle *planon* indicates the habitual action of something that is characteristic of the person.

15. There is considerable discussion concerning the interpretation of this passage; however, the text must pass beyond the king of Tyre since expressions such as "perfect in beauty," "you were in Eden," "anointed cherub," "you were on the holy mountain of God," and "you were blameless" are hardly descriptive of that heathen king. These statements must be understood as referring to Satan as a high ranking angel prior to his fall.

16. This view also depends on a gap of time between Genesis 1:1 and 1:2 which is not supported by the Hebrew grammar, cf. Weston W. Fields, *Unformed and Unfilled* (Nutley, N.J.: Presbyterian & Reformed, 1976).

17. C. F. Keil and F. Delitzsch, *Biblical Commentary on the Old Testament,* 25 vols. (Reprint. Grand Rapids: Eerdmans, 1968), 1:131.

18. Milton C. Fisher, *"Nepîlîm,"* in *Theological Wordbook of the Old Testament,* 2 vols. (Chicago: Moody, 1980), 2:587.

19. Merrill F. Unger, *Demons in the World Today* (Wheaton: Tyndale House, 1971), p. 16.

20. This chart is adapted from Charles C. Ryrie, *A Survey of Bible Doctrine* (Chicago: Moody, 1972), p. 97.

21. Fritz Rienecker, *A Linguistic Key to the Greek New Testament,* edited by Cleon Rogers (Grand Rapids: Zondervan, 1980), p. 463.

22. Charles C. Ryrie, *Study-Graph: Bible Doctrine II* (Chicago: Moody, 1965).

23. See Merrill F. Unger, *Demons in the World Today,* pp. 102-8.

For Further Study on Angelology

HOLY ANGELS

** H. Bietenhard. "Angel." In Colin Brown, ed., *New International Dictionary of New Testament Theology*, 4 vols. Grand Rapids: Zondervan, 1975. 1:101-4. Articles on "Gabriel" and "Michael" are also included as well as an extensive bibliography.

 * G. W. Bromiley. "Angel." In Walter A. Elwell, ed., *Evangelical Dictionary of Theology*. Grand Rapids: Baker, 1985. Pp. 46-47.

** Lewis Sperry Chafer. *Systematic Theology*, 8 vols. Dallas: Dallas Seminary, 1947. 2:3-32.

** C. Fred Dickason. *Angels: Elect and Evil*. Chicago: Moody, 1975, pp. 9-111. This is probably the most valuable book on the subject and ought to be consulted by the serious student.

 * G. B. Funderburk. "Angel." In Merrill C. Tenney, ed., *Zondervan Pictorial Encyclopedia of the Bible*, 5 vols. Grand Rapids: Zondervan, 1975. 1:160-66. See additional articles such as "Gabriel," "Michael," "Lucifer," "Host," and so forth.

 * Henry C. Thiessen. *Lectures in Systematic Theology*. Revised by Vernon D. Doerksen. Grand Rapids: Eerdmans, 1979. Pp. 133-48.

 * Merrill F. Unger. *Unger's Bible Dictionary*. Chicago: Moody, 1961. P. 52.

SATAN

 * Emery H. Bancroft. *Christian Theology*. Grand Rapids: Zondervan, 1976. Pp. 320-40.

** Donald Grey Barnhouse. *The Invisible War*. Grand Rapids: Zondervan, 1965.

** Lewis Sperry Chafer. *Systematic Theology*, 8 vols. Dallas: Dallas Seminary, 1947. 1:33-112.

** C. Fred Dickason. *Angels: Elect and Evil*. Chicago: Moody, 1975. Pp. 115-49; 210-21.

 * D. Edmond Hiebert. "Satan." In Merrill C. Tenney, ed., *Zondervan Pictorial Encyclopedia of the Bible*, 5 vols. Grand Rapids: Zondervan, 1975. 5:282-86.

** J. Dwight Pentecost. *Your Adversary the Devil*. Grand Rapids: Zondervan, 1969.

 * J. Oswald Sanders. *Satan Is No Myth*. Chicago: Moody, 1975.

 * Merrill F. Unger. "Satan." In Walter A. Elwell, ed., *Evangelical Dictionary of Theology*. Grand Rapids: Baker, 1985. Pp. 972-73.

DEMONS

** Donald Grey Barnhouse. *The Invisible War*. Grand Rapids: Zondervan, 1965.

** Lewis Sperry Chafer. *Systematic Theology*, 8 vols. Dallas: Dallas Seminary, 1947. 2:113-121.

** C. Fred Dickason. *Angels: Elect and Evil*. Chicago: Moody, 1975. Pp. 150-221.

_____. *Demon Possession and the Christian: A New Perspective*. Chicago: Moody, 1987.

 * J. Dwight Pentecost. *Your Adversary the Devil*. Grand Rapids: Zondervan, 1969.

 * J. Oswald Sanders. *Satan Is No Myth*. Chicago: Moody, 1975.

 * Merrill F. Unger. *Demons in the World Today*. Wheaton: Tyndale, 1971.

** _____. *Biblical Demonology*. Wheaton: Scripture, 1952.

23

ANTHROPOLOGY AND HAMARTIOLOGY: DOCTRINES OF MAN AND SIN

DOCTRINE OF MAN

The study of man is called *anthropology* from the Greek words *anthropos*, meaning "man," and *logos*, meaning "word" or "discourse," hence, anthropology is a discourse about man. The term *anthropology* can be the study of the doctrine of man from a biblical standpoint or it can refer to the study of man in his cultural environment. The former procedure will occupy this study.

ORIGIN OF MAN

There are a variety of views by Christians and non-Christians concerning the origin of man. Non-Christians commonly hold to atheistic or humanistic evolution; some Christians argue for a mediating view suggesting God began the process but did it through evolution, hence, they hold to theistic evolution. Other Christians argue for some kind of creation, either divine fiat (act of God) or some form of "developing creation."

Atheistic evolution. The evolutionary theory begun by Charles Darwin and refined by others is an attempt to explain the origin of matter and life apart from God. The origin of man, animals, and plant life is all explained apart from any supernatural process. "All that is needed, according to naturalistic evolution, is atoms in motion. A combination of atoms, motion, time, and chance has fashioned what we currently have."[1]

The tenets of evolution, as spelled out in Darwin's *The Origin of Species*, are: "(1) Variation results in some offspring being superior to their parents. (2) A struggle for existence eliminates the weaker, less fit varieties. (3) A process of natural selection is constantly at work by which the fittest survive. (4) Through heredity, new and better qualities produced by variation are passed on and gradually accumulated. (5) New species come into existence by this method, after the passage of sufficient time."[2]

The implications of atheistic evolution are significant. If there is no God who has created the world then man is not accountable to God concerning any moral structure; in fact, if atheistic evolution is true then there are no moral absolutes to which man must adhere.

Theistic evolution. "Theistic evolution is the teaching that plants, animals, and man gradually evolved from lower forms, but that God supervised the process."[3] Theistic evolutionists generally accept the findings of science and attempt to harmonize the evolutionary hypothesis with the Bible. Ironically, theistic evolution is rejected by both strict evolutionists and biblicists alike. Humanistic evolutionists have sharp words of criticism for theistic evolutionists and do not take them seriously in scientific matters.[4]

There are several serious problems facing the theistic evolutionist.[5] If the human race has evolved then Adam was not a historical person and the analogy between Christ and Adam in Romans 5:12-21 breaks down. Furthermore, the theistic evolutionist must take a poetic or allegorical approach in interpreting Genesis 1:1–2:4 for which there is no warrant. Further, the suggestion that humanity is derived from a non-human ancestor cannot be reconciled with the explicit statement of man's creation in Genesis 2:7.

Progressive creationism. This theory (also called the day-age theory) is based in part on Psalm 90:4 and 2 Peter 3:8 in rejecting a literal six-day creation. The days of creation are not to be understood as days of twenty-four hours but as ages. Traditionally, the day-age theory held that the days were equivalent to geological ages. However, this posed several problems: the fossil record did not demonstrate this, and the creation of plants bearing seeds prior to the creation of land animals posed a problem in that some seeds depended on insects for pollination and fertilization.[6]

Progressive creationism is a more serious attempt to reconcile the Bible with science. Regarding science, progressive creationism harmonizes the antiquity of the earth according to the teaching of science; at the same time, progressive creationists acknowledge the direct creation of man and general species in consideration of Genesis 1-2. They, however, allow for "intrakind" development (microevolution) within species while rejecting "interkind" development (macroevolution).[7]

Several problems face the progressive creationist. Exodus 20:10-11 draws an analogy between a person working six days and resting on the seventh and God creating six days and resting on the seventh. The analogy demands twenty-four hour days. Furthermore, this theory would mean there was death before the Fall because it involves a long period of time. Genesis, however, indicates there was no death until Adam sinned.

Gap theory. The gap theory places a lengthy period of time between Genesis 1:1 and 1:2, basically as an accommodation to science. In that way gap theorists can hold to the antiquity of the earth yet understand the words of Genesis 1 and 2 literally, adhering to twenty-four hour days of creation. The gap theory teaches that there was an original creation (some place the gap prior to v. 1; others place it between 1:1 and 1:2) and as a result of Lucifer's rebellion and fall, the earth *became* chaos. The phrase "formless and void" (Gen. 1:2) describes the chaotic earth that God judged. Millions of years took place between Genesis 1:1 and 1:2, in agreement with scientific evaluation concerning the age of the earth.

The problems of the gap theory have been well documented.[8] The grammar of Genesis 1:1-2 does not allow for a gap. Verse one is an independent clause. Verse two is composed of three circumstantial clauses, explaining the condition of the earth when God began to create, and it is connected to verse 3.[9] There is no break between verses 1 and 2. The gap theory also depends on "formless and void" meaning evil or the result of a judgment; however, its usages in Job 26:7 and Isaiah 45:18 do not suggest this. Gap theorists also draw a distinction between the Hebrew verb *bara* (Gen. 1:1), suggesting it means creation ex nihilo (out of nothing), whereas *asa* (Gen. 1:7, 16, 25, etc.) means a refashioning. A careful study of these two verbs reveals they are used interchangeably; *asa* does not mean to refashion.[10]

The gap theory is not built on exegesis but is rather an attempt to reconcile the Bible with the views of science.

Literal twenty-four-hour days. The view that God created in twenty-four hour days is also called *fiat creation*—God created directly and instantaneously. Literal creationists hold to a recent earth, approximately 10,000 years old. Geological formations can be explained through the Noahic flood.[11] All forms of evolution are rejected by fiat creationists.

The basis for the twenty-four-hour creation days is the biblical account of Genesis 1 and 2. (1) God created man directly (Gen. 1:27; 2:7; 5:1; Deut. 4:32). Genesis 1:27 is the general statement, while 2:7 provides additional detail concerning how God created man. The statement in 2:7 also explains God's manner of creating—He created man out of the dust of the ground. Christ affirmed the same truth (Matt. 19:4).

(2) God created the male and female genders (Gen. 1:27). According to this account man and woman were both created directly by God; they did not evolve from lower forms of life. God gave them their gender by creating them male and female. These statements would disallow any form of evolution.

(3) God created in six twenty-four-hour days. There are several indicators in the creation account to validate this thesis. (a) The Hebrew word day (*yom*) with a numeral always designates a twenty-four-hour day.[12] (b) The phrase "evening and morning" (Gen. 1:5, 8, 13, 19, 23, 31) emphasizes a twenty-four-hour day. To suggest any form of a day-age concept involves

denying the normal meaning of these words. (c) Exodus 20:9-11 emphasizes a twenty-four hour creation by analogy to the command for man to
labor in six days and rest on the seventh day even as God did.

(4) God created man as a unique being. If man evolved, he is only a
higher form of animal, without moral sensibility or accountability. Scripture,
however, presents man as a moral creature, accountable to God. Man also
is a soul and thus eternal (Gen. 2:7); moreover, he is made in the image of
God (Gen. 1:26), hardly a statement applicable to one who is the product of
any form of evolution.

MATERIAL PART OF MAN

Structure of the body. Scripture makes a distinction between the material (body) and the nonmaterial (soul/spirit) (cf. 2 Cor. 5:1; 1 Thess. 5:23).
Genesis 2:7 indicates the body of man was formed from the dust of the
ground. There is a definite play on words: "The Lord God formed man
(*adam*) of dust from the ground (*adamah*)" (Gen. 2:7). The very name
Adam was to remind man of his origin: he is of the earth. A chemical analysis of the human body reveals that man's components are those of the earth:
calcium, iron, potassium, and so forth. Moreover, at death the body again
unites with the dust from which it had its origin (Gen. 3:19; Ps. 104:29;
Eccles. 12:7).

Views concerning the purpose of the body. (1) The body is the prison
house of the soul. This was the view of the Greek philosophers who placed
a great dichotomy between the body and soul. The soul was nonmaterial
and good; the body was material and evil. In this view, therefore, the body
was depreciated. However, it is unbiblical to place this kind of dichotomy
between the material and nonmaterial. The Bible does not refer to the body
as intrinsically evil. In fact, the Song of Solomon in its entirety focuses on
the value of the human body and the bliss of married love and sexual
expression. Divine revelation makes it clear that "man is . . . a unity—one
being—and the material and immaterial can be separated only by physical
death."[13]

(2) The body is the only part of man that is important. This view is
called *hedonism* and represents the opposite of the preceding view. Hedo-
nists suggest a person should seek to please the body by doing what he
enjoys doing. This philosophy is a denial of the soul. The testimony of Jesus
Christ invalidates this view inasmuch as Christ spoke of the enormous value
of the soul as distinct from the body (Matt. 10:28; 16:26). Other Scriptures
also affirm the existence of the soul (2 Cor. 5:8; Eccles. 12:7).

(3) The body is the partner of the soul. The body is the means of glorifying God since it is the temple of God (1 Cor. 6:19). The body is not to be the
master so that the believer caters to it in self-indulgence, nor is it to be an
enemy that needs to be punished. The body is to be submitted to God

(Rom. 12:1) in order that Christ may be glorified in that body (Phil. 1:20). Ultimately, the believer will be rewarded for deeds done in the body (2 Cor. 5:10).

NONMATERIAL PART OF MAN

Scriptural account. When God created man He created him in His own image (Gen. 1:26-27). The question is: What is the image of God in man? The image of God in man cannot be physical because God is spirit (John 4:24) and does not have a body. The image, then, must be nonmaterial and would involve the following major elements.

(1) Personality. Man has a self-consciousness and a self-determination that enables him to make choices, lifting him above the realm of animals. This factor is important because it renders man capable of redemption. But this facet involves many natural elements; personality reveals man's ability to exercise dominion over the world (Gen. 1:28) and to develop the earth (Gen. 2:15). All aspects of man's intellect would come under this category.

(2) Spiritual being.

> God is a Spirit, the human soul is a spirit. The essential attributes of a spirit are reason, conscience, and will. A spirit is a rational, moral, and therefore also, a free agent. In making man after his own image, therefore, God endowed him with those attributes which belong to his own nature as a spirit. Man is thereby distinguished from all other inhabitants of this world, and raised immeasurably above them. He belongs to the same order of being as God Himself, and is therefore capable of communion with his Maker. . . . it is also the necessary condition of our capacity to know God, and therefore the foundation of our religious nature. If we were not like God, we could not know Him. We should be as the beasts which perish.[14]

(3) Moral nature. Man was created in "original righteousness" also referred to as "knowledge, righteousness, and holiness."[15] This original righteousness and holiness was lost through the fall but is restored in Christ. Ephesians 4:24 emphasizes that the new self of the believer is "in the likeness of God (and) has been created in righteousness and holiness." Colossians 3:10 declares that the new self is "being renewed to a true knowledge according to the image of the One who created him," a reference to Genesis 1:26.

Origin of the nonmaterial part of man. (1) Theory of preexistence. This view, which advocates that the human soul has existed previously, has its roots in non-Christian philosophy; it is taught in Hinduism and was also held by Plato, Philo, and Origen. This theory teaches that in a previous existence men were angelic spirits, and as punishment and discipline for sin, they were sent to indwell human bodies. There are a number of problems with this view: there is no clear statement of Scripture to support this view (although the idea may have been presented in John 9:2); no one has any recollection of such an existence; the doctrine of sin is not related to Adam's sin in Genesis 3 but to sin in an angelic sphere.

(2) Creation theory. This theory teaches that each human soul is an immediate and individual creation by God; the body alone is propagated by the parents. This view is held by Roman Catholics and many Reformed Christians, among them Charles Hodge.[16] There are two reasons for this view: it maintains the purity of Christ—with this view Christ could not inherit a sinful nature from His mother; a distinction is made between a mortal body and an immortal soul—parents may propagate a mortal body but only God can produce an immortal soul. The problems with this view are: it necessitates an individual fall by each person because God can create only perfection; it does not account for the problem of why all men sin.

(3) Traducian theory. This view, ably defended by William G. T. Shedd,[17] affirms that the soul as well as the body is generated by the parents. "Man is a species, and the idea of a species implies the propagation of the entire individual out of it. . . . Individuals are not propagated in parts."[18] The problems with this view are: how can parents pass on the soul, which is nonmaterial?; and Christ must have partaken of the sinful nature of Mary if traducianism is true.

The strengths of traducianism are as follows. It explains the depravity of man. If the parents pass on the nonmaterial nature then it explains the propagation of the sin nature and the tendency, from birth, of every human being to sin. The sin nature cannot be explained if God creates each soul directly. Traducianism also explains the heredity factor—the intellect, personality, and emotional similarities of children and their parents. If creationism were correct the similarities should not be as prevalent and noticeable. The Scripture seems to affirm the traducian position (Ps. 51:5; Rom. 5:12; Heb. 7:10).

Composition of the nonmaterial part of man. While most will acknowledge that man has a nonmaterial constitution, what is the nature of the nonmaterial part of man? Are the soul and the spirit distinct, or are they the same? Generally, the Eastern church believed that man was trichotomous —consisting of three parts—body, soul, and spirit. Originally, the Greek and Alexandrian church Fathers held this view, including men like Origen and Clement of Alexandria. The Western church, on the other hand, generally held to the dichotomous position: man is body and soul. Men like Augustine and Anselm held to this view.

(1) Dichotomous view. Dichotomy comes from Greek *dicha*, "two," and *temno*, "to cut." Hence, man is a two-part being, consisting of body and soul. The nonmaterial part of man is the soul and spirit, which are of the same substance; however, they have a different function. The support for the dichotomous view is:[19] (a) Genesis 2:7 affirms only two parts. God

formed man from the dust of the ground, breathed life into him, and he became a living soul (cf. Job 27:3). (b) The words soul and spirit may be used interchangeably. Compare Genesis 41:8 with Psalm 42:6, and Hebrews 12:23 with Revelation 6:9. (c) Body and soul (or spirit) together are mentioned as constituting the entire person (cf. Matt. 10:28; 1 Cor. 5:3; 3 John 2).

(2) Trichotomous view. Trichotomy comes from Greek *tricha*, "three," and *temno*, "to cut." Hence, man is a three-part being, consisting of body, soul, and spirit. The soul and spirit are said to be different both in function and in substance. The body is seen as world-conscious, the soul as self-conscious, and the spirit as God-conscious. The soul is seen as a lower power consisting of man's imagination, memory, and understanding; the spirit is a higher power, consisting of reason, conscience, and will.[20] The support for the trichotomous view is: (a) Paul seems to emphasize the three-part view in desiring the sanctification of the entire person (1 Thess. 5:23). (b) Hebrews 4:12 implies a distinction between soul and spirit. (c) 1 Corinthians 2:14–3:4 suggests a threefold classification: natural (fleshly), carnal (soulish), and spiritual (spiritual).[21]

(3) Multi-faceted view.[22] Although soul and spirit are common terms used to describe the nonmaterial nature of man, there are a number of additional terms that describe man's non-physical nature. Hence, man's nonmaterial nature can be understood as multi-faceted.

There are at least four terms used to describe man's nonmaterial nature. *Heart:* The heart describes the intellectual (Matt. 15:19-20) as well as the volitional part of man (Rom. 10:9-10; Heb. 4:7). *Conscience:* God has placed within man a conscience as a witness. The conscience is affected by the Fall and may be seared and unreliable (1 Tim. 4:2); nonetheless, it can convict the unbeliever (Rom. 2:15). In the believer it may be weak and overly scrupulous (1 Cor. 8:7, 10, 12). *Mind:* The unbeliever's mind is depraved (Rom. 1:28), blinded by Satan (2 Cor. 4:4), and darkened and futile (Eph. 4:17-18). In the believer there is a renewed mind (Rom. 12:2) that enables him to love God (Matt. 22:37). *Will:* The unbeliever has a will that desires to follow the dictates of the flesh (Eph. 2:2-3), whereas the believer has the ability to desire to do God's will (Rom. 6:12-13). At conversion, the believer is given a new nature that enables him to love God with all his heart, mind, and will.[23]

FALL OF MAN

Genesis 3 does not describe the origin of sin, but it does describe the entrance of sin into the realm of humanity. Genesis 3 describes a historical event; Adam and Eve were historical people who sinned against God in time and space. The historicity of this event is essential if an analogy is to be seen in Romans 5:12-21. If Adam was not a real creature who brought sin

VARIOUS VIEWS OF MAN'S COMPOSITION

Viewpoints	Analysis	
	Material	Non-material
Dichotomy	Body	Soul
		Spirit
Trichotomy	Body	Soul
		Spirit
Multi-faceted	Body	Soul
		Spirit
		Heart
		Conscience
		Mind
		Will

into the human race at one point in history, then there is no point to Jesus' redeeming humanity at another point in history. Christ's own testimony, however, confirms Genesis 3 as a historical event (Matt. 19:3-5).

The test. During their life in the garden, God tested Adam and Eve regarding their obedience. They were free to eat of the fruit from any tree in the garden except the tree of knowledge of good and evil (Gen. 2:16-17). The test was simple: it was to determine whether or not they would believe God and obey Him. Disobedience, however, was highly consequential—it meant death, both physical and spiritual death. God's purpose in the test was to give Adam and Eve a knowledge of sin through obedience by not eating the fruit of the tree of knowledge. They came to a knowledge of good and evil, but they attained the knowledge in the wrong manner.[24]

The temptation. The avenue through which the temptation came to man and woman was the serpent (Gen. 3:1). However, the temptation must be seen as coming through Satan; the devil inspired Cain to kill his brother (John 8:44). The devil is called the serpent of old (Rev. 12:9; 20:2), and the allusion in Romans 16:20 indicates that the judgment of Genesis 3:15 refers to Satan, not simply the serpent. The serpent was crafty (Gen. 3:1), hence, Satan would be crafty in conducting his test. His strategy can be summarized in three phases.

(1) Satan raised doubt concerning God's Word (Gen. 3:1).[25] The temptation created suspicion about the goodness of God; it raised a question whether God was dealing wisely and fairly with Adam and Eve. Eve succumbed to the temptation in that she exaggerated God's prohibition by her response to Satan (Gen. 3:3). God had said nothing about touching the fruit.

(2) Satan lied by saying they would not die (Gen. 3:4). Satan made a categorical denial of God's earlier statement; Satan said, "You surely shall not die!"[26]

(3) Satan told a partial truth (Gen. 3:5). Satan told them they would be like God, knowing good and evil if they ate the fruit. It was true they would know good and evil, but Satan did not tell them the rest—he did not tell them about the pain, suffering, and death that would occur through their sin. The test was in three areas, the lust of the flesh, the lust of the eyes, and the boastful pride of life (1 John 2:16; cf. Matt. 4:1-11).

The results of the sin. (1) Judgment on the serpent (Gen. 3:14). The serpent had earlier been a noble creature; as a result of the judgment it was altered in form and shape. Because the serpent exalted itself it would now be forced to crawl on its belly and eat the dust of the earth as it crawled along.

(2) Judgment on Satan (Gen. 3:15). Genesis 3:15 must be understood as addressed not to the serpent, but to Satan. There would be enmity between Satan's seed (unbelievers and possibly demons) and the woman's seed (believers, but specifically Christ). "He shall bruise you on the head" indicates Christ delivered a death blow to Satan at the cross (Col. 2:14-15; Heb. 2:14). Christ would have a major victory. "You shall bruise Him on the heel" suggests Satan would have a minor victory in the fact that Christ died; nonetheless, that death became Satan's own defeat.

(3) Judgment on the woman (Gen. 3:16). The woman would experience pain in childbirth. The pain (Heb. *yizabon*) in childbirth is similarly used of Adam's toil (Gen. 3:17). Both would suffer in their respective roles. The desire of the woman would be toward her husband. This is a difficult phrase and may mean (a) sexual desire (Song of Sol. 7:10), (b) desire for security under her husband's authority, or (c) desire to rule over her husband (cf. Gen. 4:7).[27] A final aspect of the judgment upon the woman was that the husband would rule over her.

(4) Judgment on the man (Gen. 3:17-19). The first judgment was against the ground. No longer would the earth spontaneously produce its fruit but only through hard toil by the man. The second judgment on the man was death. Adam had been made from the elements of the ground. The death process would return the man to the dust from which his body had been taken.

(5) Judgment on the human race (Rom. 5:12). The result of Adam's sin was passed on to the entire human race. All humanity now became subject to death.

(6) Judgment on creation (Gen. 3:17-18). All animal and plant life would be affected by the sin of Adam. Animal life and nature would resist the man. Animals would become wild and ferocious; plant life would produce weeds to hinder productivity. All creation would groan with the effect of the Fall and anxiously long for the day of restoration (Rom. 8:19-21).

DOCTRINE OF SIN

DEFINITION OF SIN

Sin is a transgression of the law of God. The Greek word *parabasis* means "overstepping, transgression."[28] God gave the Mosaic law to heighten man's understanding of His standard and the seriousness of transgressing that standard (Rom. 4:15). Thereafter, when God said, "You shall not bear false witness," a lie was seen to be what it is: an overstepping or transgression of the law of God (cf. Rom. 2:23; 5:14; Gal. 3:19).

Sin is a failure to conform to the standard of God. The Greek word *hamartia* means "miss the mark," "every departure from the way of righteousness."[29] Hence, it means that all people have missed the mark of God's standard and continue to fall short of that standard (Rom. 3:23). This involves both sins of commission as well as omission. Failure to do what is right is also sin (Rom. 14:23).

Sin is a principle within man. Sin is not only an act but also a principle that dwells in man.[30] Paul refers to the struggle with the sin principle within (Rom. 7:14, 17-25); all people have this sin nature (Gal. 3:22). Hebrews 3:13 refers to it "as the power that deceives men and leads them to destruction."[31] Jesus also refers to sin as a "condition or characteristic quality"[32] (John 9:41; 15:24; 19:11).

Sin is rebellion against God. Another Greek word for sin is *anomia*, which means "lawlessness" (1 John 3:4) and can be described as a "frame of mind."[33] It denotes lawless deeds (Titus 2:14) and is a sign of the last days, meaning "without law or restraint" (Matt. 24:12).

Sin is wrongful acts toward God and man. Romans 1:18 refers to "ungodliness and unrighteousness of men." Ungodliness refers to man's failure to obey God and keep the commandments related to Him (Exod. 20:1-11); unrighteousness is seen in man's failure to live righteously toward his fellow man (Exod. 20:12-17).

ORIGINAL SIN

Definition. Original sin may be defined as "the sinful state and condition in which men are born."[34] It is so designated because: (1) "it is derived from the original root of the human race (Adam), (2) it is present in the life of every individual from the time of his birth, and (3) it is the inward root of all the actual sins that defile the life of man."[35] Simply stated it refers to "the corruption of our whole nature."[36]

Results. First, man is totally depraved. "Total depravity does not mean that everyone is as thoroughly depraved in his actions as he could possibly be, nor that everyone will indulge in every form of sin, nor that a person cannot appreciate and even do acts of goodness; but it does mean that the corruption of sin extends to all men and to all parts of all men so that there is nothing within the natural man that can give him merit in God's sight."[37]

Second, man has an innate sin nature. "The sin nature is the capacity to do all those things (good or bad) that can in no way commend us to God."[38] Every part of man is affected: intellect (2 Cor. 4:4); conscience (1 Tim. 4:2); will (Rom. 1:28); heart (Eph. 4:18); and the total being (Rom. 1:18–3:20).[39]

IMPUTATION OF SIN

The word *imputation* comes from the Latin word *imputare*, meaning "to reckon," "to charge to one's account,"[40] and relates to the problem of how sin is charged to every person. The basic Scripture is Romans 5:12, which teaches that sin entered the world through Adam. The interpretation of that verse determines one's view of imputation. Historically, there have been four major views of how sin is imputed to the human race.

Pelagian view. Pelagius was a British monk born about A.D. 370 who taught his strange doctrines at Rome in A.D. 409. Modern Unitarians continue his basic scheme of doctrine. Pelagius taught that God created every soul directly (he despised the traducian theory), and that every soul therefore was innocent and unstained. No created soul had any direct relation to the sin of Adam; the only significance of Adam's sin upon humanity was the bad example. Pelagius, therefore, did not view Romans 5:12 as affecting all humanity; it did not. No sin of Adam was imputed to the human race; only those acts of sin that people themselves committed were imputed to them. Moreover, man did not die because he sinned but because of the law of nature. Adam would have died even if he had not sinned. Pelagius and his doctrines were condemned at the Council of Carthage in A.D. 418.[41]

Pelagius's teaching ran contrary to the Scriptures on a number of points. He taught that man did not die because of sin, yet Scripture affirms the opposite (Ezek. 18:20; Rom. 6:23). Pelagius taught that man did not have a natural tendency toward sin, but Scripture affirms the opposite (Rom. 3:9-18). If the Pelagian view is followed out logically, then each person born free of the sin of Adam would require an individual "fall," or there would be some perfect people.

Arminian view. Jacobus Arminius (1560-1609) was a Dutch theologian. The Arminian view is similar to semi-Pelagianism and is representative in the Methodist church, Wesleyans, Pentecostals, and others. In thought similar to Pelagianism, Arminius taught that man was not considered guilty because of Adam's sin. When people would voluntarily and purposefully choose to sin even though they had power to live righteously—then, and only then, would God impute sin to them and count them guilty. Although man does not possess original righteousness because of Adam's sin, "God bestows upon each individual from the first dawn of consciousness a special influence of the Holy Spirit, which is sufficient to counteract the effect of the inherited depravity and to make obedience possible, provided the human will cooperates, which it still has power to do."[42] Thus Arminius recognized an effect from Adam's sin but not in the sense of total depravity; through divine enablement man could still make righteous choices. Romans 5:12 is not understood as all humanity suffering the effect of Adam's sin and death; but rather because of the individual agreement with Adam's act is sin imputed to the individual.

Federal view. The federal view was originally propounded by Cocceius (1603-1669) and became a standard of belief in Reformed theology. It was taught by men like Charles Hodge; J. Oliver Buswell, Jr.; and Louis Berkhof. This view is called the federal view because Adam is seen as the federal head or representative of the entire human race. God entered into a covenant of works with Adam whereby He promised to bless Adam and thereby the entire human race with eternal life if Adam obeyed. Disobedience would bring suffering to the entire human race. As a result of Adam's sin, since he was the representative of the human race, his sin plunged the entire human race into suffering and death. Through the one sin of Adam, sin and death are imputed to all humanity because all humanity was represented in Adam. Charles Hodge defines the view: "in virtue of the union, federal and natural, between Adam and his posterity, his sin, although not their act, is so imputed to them that it is the judicial ground of the penalty threatened against him coming also upon them."[43]

Augustinian view. This view is named after Augustine (A.D. 354-430) and has been more recently held by Calvin, Luther, Shedd, and Strong. This view teaches that the statement "all sinned" in Romans 5:12 suggests that all humanity was a participant in Adam's sin. Just as Levi (although not yet born) paid tithes to Melchizedek through Abraham in that Levi was "seminally present" in Abraham (Heb. 7:9-10), in a similar way, all humanity was "seminally present" in Adam when Adam sinned and therefore all humanity participated in the sin. Therefore, the sin of Adam and the resultant death is charged to all humanity because all humanity is guilty. God holds all humanity guilty because all humanity *is* guilty.

VIEWS OF THE IMPUTATION OF SIN

Views	Romans 5:12	Adam	Humanity	Modern Adherents
Pelagian View	People incur death when they sin after Adam's example.	Sin affected Adam alone.	No one affected by Adam's sin.	Unitarians
Arminian View	All people consent to Adam's sin—then sin is imputed.	Adam sinned and partially affected humanity.	Depravity is not total; people received corrupt nature from Adam but not guilt or culpability.	Methodists Wesleyans Pentecostals Holiness groups
Federal View	Sin is imputed to humanity because of Adam's sin.	Adam alone sinned but human race affected.	Depravity is total; sin and guilt are imputed.	Presbyterians Others holding to Covenant theology.
Augustin- ian View	Sin is imputed to humanity because of Adam's sin.	Humanity sinned in Adam.	Depravity is total; sin and guilt are imputed.	Reformers Later Calvinists

THE CHRISTIAN AND SIN

The conflict. The Christian's conflict with sin, according to 1 John 2:16, arises from three areas. (1) The world. The *world* (Gk. *kosmos*) denotes "that which is hostile to God, i.e., lost in sin, wholly at odds with anything divine, ruined and depraved."[44] Believers are warned not to love the world nor the things in the world (1 John 2:15). This statement indicates there is both a material element as well as a philosophy to be shunned. John further indicates that the world lures the Christian to sin through the lust of the flesh, the lust of the eyes, and the boastful pride of life (1 John 2:16). This world lies under the control of Satan (1 John 5:19) and manifests itself in foolishness (1 Cor. 3:19), immorality (1 Cor. 5:10), and hostility toward God (James 4:4). The Christian is to reckon that he has been crucified with regard to the world (Gal. 6:14).

(2) The flesh. The *flesh* (Gk. *sarx*) "is the willing instrument of sin, and is subject to sin to such a degree that wherever flesh is, all forms of sin are likewise present, and no good thing can live in the *sarx*."[45] The term *flesh*

may be used in a material sense; however, it is frequently given a nonmaterial meaning to refer to "the old nature of the flesh . . . that capacity which all men have to serve and please self . . . the capacity to leave God out of one's life."[46] The flesh as a capacity for sin is described in Paul's Christian experience in Romans 7:17-20. It involves lust and controls the mind (Eph. 2:3); it governs the life of the non-Christian (Rom. 8:5-6). The solution to the dilemma of Romans 7:25 is the power of the Holy Spirit (Rom. 8:2ff) and a renewed mind (Rom. 12:1) that reckons the flesh crucified (Rom. 6:6).

(3) The devil. The devil is a real, personal being who opposes the Christian and seeks to make him ineffective in his Christian life. He is a formidable enemy of the Christian since he is intent on devouring Christians (1 Pet. 5:8); hence, the Christian is called on to resist the devil (James 4:7). This can be accomplished through putting on the armor for a spiritual battle (Eph. 6:10-17).

The provision. God has made ample provision for the Christian to keep him from the path of sin. (1) The Word of God. God has given the Christian a "God-breathed" Bible that is profitable for "training in righteousness" that the believer may be "equipped for every good work" (2 Tim. 3:16-17). It is this Word that can keep the believer from a life of sin (Ps. 119:9-16); it is this Word that cleanses the believer (Eph. 5:26), sanctifies the believer (John 17:17), and aids in answer to prayer (John 15:7).

(2) The intercession of Christ. Christ is the believer's advocate or defense attorney when the believer commits sin (1 John 2:1). Because Christ continually lives His intercession is effective (Heb. 7:25). John 17 reveals the nature of Christ's intercession for Christians: He prays for their security (17:11), concerning their joy (17:13), for their protection from Satan (17:15), for their being set apart in the truth (17:17), and that they might ultimately be with Christ (17:25).

(3) Indwelling of the Holy Spirit. The Holy Spirit's ministry in the believer's life is crucial regarding a life of separation from sin. The Spirit's ministry involves indwelling (Rom. 8:9), anointing (1 John 2:20; 4:4), sealing (Eph. 1:13, 4:30), empowering (Acts 1:8), filling (Eph. 5:18), and enabling the believer to live constantly by the Spirit (Gal. 5:16).

Notes on Anthropology and Hamartiology

1. Millard J. Erickson, *Christian Theology*, 3 vols. (Grand Rapids: Baker, 1984), 2:478.

2. S. Maxwell Coder and George F. Howe, *The Bible, Science, and Creation* (Chicago: Moody, 1965), pp. 60-61.

3. C. Richard Culp, *Remember Thy Creator* (Grand Rapids: Baker, 1975), p. 148.

4. Compare the comment by a humanistic evolutionist: "Another type of evolutionary theory hardly deserves to be mentioned in a scientific paper. This is the mystical approach, which hides its insufficient understanding of the facts behind such empty words as creative evolution, emergent evolution, holism, and psycho-Lamarchism. . . . The biologist does not receive any constructive help from such ideas and is forced to ignore them." R. B. Goldschmidt, "Evolution, as Viewed by One Geneticist," *American Scientist* 40 (January 1952): 85, quoted by John C. Whitcomb, Jr., and Henry M. Morris, *The Genesis Flood* (Grand Rapids: Baker, 1961), p. 443.

5. Compare P. P. T. Pun, "Evolution," in Walter A. Elwell, ed., *Evangelical Dictionary of Theology* (Grand Rapids: Baker, 984), pp. 390-91. Pun concludes: "Theistic evolutionists also give too much credence to the as yet poorly formulated theory of organic evolution. In their efforts to reconcile the naturalistic and theistic approaches to the origin of life they have inadvertently put themselves into the inconsistent position of denying the miracles of creation while maintaining the supernatural nature of the Christian message."

6. Ibid.

7. Erickson, *Christian Theology*, 2:482. Erickson contrasts progressive creationism with the other views: "Progressive creationism agrees with fiat creationism in maintaining that the entirety of man's nature was specially created. It disagrees, however, in holding that there was a certain amount of development in creation after God's original direct act. It agrees with naturalistic evolution, deistic evolution, and theistic evolution in seeing development within the creation, but insists that there were several *de novo* acts of creation within this overall process. And although it agrees with theistic evolution that man is the result of a special act of creation by God, it goes beyond that view by insisting that this special creative act encompassed man's entire nature, both physical and spiritual."

8. Weston W. Fields, *Unformed and Unfilled* (Nutley, N.J.: Presbyterian & Reformed, 1976); and Edward J. Young, *Studies in Genesis One* (Nutley, N.J.: Presbyterian & Reformed, 1976).

9. Bruce K. Waltke, *Creation and Chaos* (Portland: Western Conservative Baptist Seminary, 1974), p. 31.

10. Fields, *Unformed and Unfilled*, pp. 51-74.

11. The work of Whitcomb and Morris, *The Genesis Flood*, remains a hallmark for study on this subject.

12. Bruce K. Waltke, unpublished class notes, Dallas Theological Seminary.

13. Lewis Sperry Chafer, *Systematic Theology*, 8 vols. (Dallas: Dallas Seminary, 1947), 2:146.

14. Charles Hodge, *Systematic Theology*, 3 vols. (Reprint. London: Clarke, 1960), 2:96-97.

15. Louis Berkhof, *Systematic Theology* (Grand Rapids: Eerdmans, 1938), p. 204; and Hodge, *Systematic Theology*, 2:99.

16. Hodge provides a capable defense, *Systematic Theology*, 2:70-76.

17. Wm. G. T. Shedd, *Dogmatic Theology*, 3 vols. (Reprint. Nashville: Nelson, 1980), 2:19-94.

18. Ibid., 2:19.

19. See the helpful discussion in A. H. Strong, *Systematic Theology* (Valley Forge, Pa.: Judson, 1907), pp. 483-84.

20. Henry C. Thiessen, *Lectures in Systematic Theology*, edited by Vernon Doerksen (Grand Rapids: Eerdmans, 1979), p. 161.

21. Ibid.

22. Charles C. Ryrie, *Survey of Bible Doctrine* (Chicago: Moody, 1972), pp. 104-7.

23. J. Dwight Pentecost, *Designed to Be Like Him* (Chicago: Moody, 1972), pp. 42-84.

24. C. F. Keil and F. Delitzsch, *Biblical Commentary on the Old Testament*, 25 vols. (Reprint. Grand Rapids: Eerdmans, 1968), 1:84-86.

25. Ibid., 1:94. *'Ap kî* (Heb.) literally means "Indeed, really!" "*'Ap kî* is an interrogative expressing surprise (as in 1 Sam. 23:3; 2 Sam. 4:11): 'Is it *really* the fact that God has prohibited you from eating of *all* the trees of the garden?' "

26. The construction is an infinitive absolute: "You will by no means die!" "The Infinitive Absolute expresses emphasis when it immediately precedes the finite verb." J. Weingreen, *A Practical Grammar for Classical Hebrew* (Oxford: Clarendon, 1959), p. 79.

27. The word desire (*shuq*) occurs only three times in the Old Testament (Gen. 3:16, 4:7; S. of S. 7:10). In Genesis 4:17 it refers to sin's desire for mastery over man; in Song of Solomon 7:10 it refers to sexual desire. The word means "to have a violent craving for a thing," Keil and Delitzsch, *Biblical Commentary on the Old Testament*, 1:103.

28. William F. Arndt and F. Wilbur Gingrich, *A Greek-English Lexicon of the New Testament and Other Early Christian Literature*, 2d ed., revised by F. Wilbur Gingrich and Frederick W. Danker (Chicago: U. of Chicago, 1979), p. 611.

29. Ibid., p. 43.

30. Ibid.

31. Ibid.

32. Ibid.

33. Ibid., p. 71.

34. Berkhof, *Systematic Theology*, p. 244.

35. Ibid.

36. Hodge, *Systematic Theology*, 2:227.

37. Ryrie, *Survey of Bible Doctrine*, p. 111.

38. Ibid.

39. Ibid.

40. R. K. Johnston, "Imputation," in Walter A. Elwell, ed., *Evangelical Dictionary of Theology* (Grand Rapids: Baker, 1984), p. 555.

41. See the helpful discussion of Pelagius's doctrine as well as a critique of it in A. H. Strong, *Systematic Theology*, pp. 597-601. A helpful survey of his life and teachings is also given by B. L. Shelley, "Pelagius, Pelagianism," in *Evangelical Dictionary of Theology*, pp. 833-34.

42. Strong, *Systematic Theology*, p. 601.

43. Hodge, *Systematic Theology*, 2:192-93.

44. Arndt and Gingrich, *Greek-English Lexicon*, p. 446.

45. Ibid., p. 744.

46. Charles C. Ryrie, *Balancing the Christian Life* (Chicago: Moody, 1969), pp. 34-35; see also J. Dwight Pentecost, *Designed to Be Like Him* (Chicago: Moody, 1966), pp. 85-93, 208-14.

FOR FURTHER STUDY ON ANTHROPOLOGY AND HAMARTIOLOGY

ORIGIN OF MAN

** G. Richard Culp. *Remember Thy Creator.* Grand Rapids: Baker, 1975.

** Helena Curtis. *Biology*, 3rd ed. New York: Worth, 1979. This is a standard text on evolution.

** Millard J. Erickson. *Christian Theology*, 3 vols. Grand Rapids: Baker, 1984. 2:473-93. A most helpful overview of the different views.

** Weston W. Fields. *Unformed and Unfilled.* Nutley, N.J.: Presbyterian and Reformed, 1976. Detailed refutation of the gap theory and defense of the young earth.

** R. Laird Harris. *Man: God's Eternal Creation.* Chicago: Moody, 1971. Pp. 7-71.

* Henry M. Morris. *Evolution and the Modern Christian.* Grand Rapids: Baker, 1967.

* P. T. T. Pun. "Evolution." In Walter A. Elwell, ed., *Evangelical Dictionary of Theology.* Grand Rapids: Baker, 1984. Pp. 388-92. A helpful survey of the different views.

* Henry C. Thiessen. *Lectures in Systematic Theology.* Revised by Vernon D. Doerksen. Grand Rapids: Eerdmans, 1979. Pp. 151-54.

* John C. Whitcomb, Jr. *The Early Earth.* Grand Rapids: Baker, 1972.

** _____, and Henry M. Morris. *The Genesis Flood.* Grand Rapids: Baker, 1961. A most valuable work in refuting evolution and arguing for the young earth.

** Davis A. Young. *Christianity and the Age of the Earth.* Grand Rapids: Zondervan, 1982.

THE NATURE OF MAN

* Emery H. Bancroft. *Christian Theology.* Grand Rapids: Zondervan, 1976. Pp. 186-97.

* Louis Berkhof. *Summary of Christian Doctrine.* Grand Rapids: Eerdmans, 1938. Pp. 67-73.

** _____. *Systematic Theology.* Grand Rapids: Eerdmans, 1941. Pp. 191-210.

** Lewis Sperry Chafer. *Systematic Theology*, 8 vols. Dallas: Dallas Seminary, 1947. 2:160-99.

** Millard J. Erickson, ed. *Man's Need and God's Gift.* Grand Rapids: Baker, 1976. Pp. 37-98.

** _____. *Christian Theology*, 3 vols. Grand Rapids: Baker, 1984. 2:495-539.

** Charles Hodge. *Systematic Theology*, 3 vols. Reprint. London: Clarke, 1960. 2:42-76.

* H. D. McDonald. *The Christian View of Man.* Westchester, Ill.: Crossway, 1981. Pp. 68-79.

* Charles C. Ryrie. *A Survey of Bible Doctrine.* Chicago: Moody, 1972. Pp. 104-7.

** Wm. G. T. Shedd. *Dogmatic Theology*, 3 vols. Reprint. Nashville: Nelson, 1980. 2:3-94.

** A. H. Strong. *Systematic Theology.* Valley Forge, Pa.: Judson, 1907. Pp. 483-513.

* Henry C. Thiessen. *Lectures in Systematic Theology.* Revised by Vernon D. Doerksen. Grand Rapids: Eerdmans, 1977. Pp. 158-67.

THE FALL OF MAN

* Emery H. Bancroft. *Christian Theology.* Grand Rapids: Zondervan, 1976. Pp. 197-207.

** Louis Berkhof. *Systematic Theology.* Grand Rapids: Eerdmans, 1941. Pp. 219-25.

** J. Oliver Buswell, Jr. *A Systematic Theology of the Christian Religion*. Grand Rapids: Zondervan, 1962. Pp. 255-320.

** Lewis Sperry Chafer. *Systematic Theology*, 8 vols. Dallas: Dallas Seminary, 1947. 2:200-23.

* William Evans. *The Great Doctrines of the Bible*. Chicago: Moody, 1949. Pp. 129-34.

* B. A. Demarest. "Fall of Man." In Walter A. Elwell, ed., *Evangelical Dictionary of Theology*. Grand Rapids: Baker, 1984. Pp. 403-5.

* A. A. Hodge. *Outlines of Theology*. Reprint. Grand Rapids: Zondervan, 1972. Pp. 315-24.

** Wm. G. T. Shedd. *Dogmatic Theology*, 3 vols. Reprint. Nashville: Nelson, 1980. 2:115-67.

* Henry C. Thiessen. *Lectures in Systematic Theology*, revised by Vernon D. Doerksen. Grand Rapids: Eerdmans, 1977. Pp. 168-84.

* Merrill F. Unger. *Unger's Bible Dictionary*. Chicago: Moody, 1961. Pp. 342-43.

SIN

* Louis Berkhof. *Systematic Theology*. Grand Rapids: Eerdmans, 1941. Pp. 227-43.

** Millard J. Erickson. *Christian Theology*, 3 vols. Grand Rapids: Baker, 1984. 2:631-39.

** Charles Hodge. *Systematic Theology*, 3 vols. Reprint. London: Clarke, 1960. 2:192-256.

* H. D. McDonald. *The Christian View of Man*. Westchester, Ill.: Crossway, 1981. Pp. 57-67.

** Wm. G. T. Shedd. *Dogmatic Theology*, 3 vols. Reprint. Nashville: Nelson, 1980. 2:168-257.

* B. L. Shelley. "Pelagius, Pelagianism." In Walter A. Elwell, ed., *Evangelical Dictionary of Theology*. Grand Rapids: Baker, 1984. Pp. 833-34. See also article on *imputation*, Pp. 554-55.

** A. H. Strong. *Systematic Theology*. Valley Forge, Pa.: Judson, 1907. Pp. 597-637.

* Henry C. Thiessen. *Lectures in Systematic Theology*, revised by Vernon D. Doerksen. Grand Rapids: Eerdmans, 1979. Pp. 185-95.

* Merrill F. Unger. *Unger's Bible Dictionary*. Chicago: Moody, 1961. Pp. 520-21, 1028-29.

24

SOTERIOLOGY: DOCTRINE OF SALVATION

FALSE THEORIES ON THE ATONEMENT

The death of Christ is highly significant in Christian doctrine but the understanding of His death has been reflected in widely divergent views. The following are the principal views regarding the death of Christ.

RANSOM TO SATAN THEORY

This theory was developed by Origen (A.D. 185-254), and it advocated that Satan held people captive as a victor in war. This theory, which was also held by Augustine, advocated that because Satan held people captive, a ransom had to be paid, not to God, but to Satan.

In response to this view it should be noted that God's holiness, not Satan's, was offended, and payment had to be made to God to avert His wrath. Furthermore, Satan did not have the power to free man, God alone had the power.

This theory is false because it makes Satan the benefactor of Christ's death. This view has too high a view of Satan; the cross was a judgment of Satan, not a ransom to Satan.

RECAPITULATION THEORY

The recapitulation theory, advanced by Irenaeus (A.D. 130-200?), taught that Christ went through all the phases of Adam's life and experience, including the experience of sin. In this way, Christ was able to succeed wherein Adam failed.

The element of truth is that Christ is known as the Last Adam (1 Cor. 15:45), however, Christ had no personal encounter with sin whatsoever (1

John 3:5; John 8:46). The theory is incomplete in that it neglects the atonement; it is the death of Christ that saves, not His life.

COMMERCIAL THEORY

The commercial theory was set forth by Anselm (A.D. 1033-1109), who taught that through sin, God was robbed of the honor that was due Him. This necessitated a resolution that could be achieved either through punishing sinners or through satisfaction. God chose to resolve the matter through satisfaction by the gift of His Son. Through His death Christ brought honor to God, and received a reward, which He passed on to sinners. The gift was forgiveness for the sinner and eternal life for those who live by the gospel.

Although this view changed the focus from payment to Satan to a proper emphasis on payment to God, there are nonetheless problems with this view. It emphasizes God's mercy at the expense of other attributes of God, namely, justice or holiness. It also neglects the obedience of the life of Christ, and in addition, it ignores the vicarious suffering of Christ. Rather than emphasizing Christ died for the penalty of sin, this view embraces the Roman Catholic concept of penance, "so much satisfaction for so much violation."

MORAL INFLUENCE THEORY

Abelard (A.D. 1079-1142) first advocated this theory that has since been taught by modern liberals such as Horace Bushnell and others of a more "moderate" liberal stance. The moral influence view was originally a reaction to the commercial theory of Anselm. This view taught that the death of Christ was not necessary as an expiation for sin, rather, through the death of Christ, God demonstrated His love for humanity in such a way that sinners' hearts would be softened and brought to repentance.

The weaknesses of the moral influence view are obvious. The basis for the death of Christ is His love rather than His holiness; this view also teaches that somehow the moving of people's emotions will lead them to repentance. Scripture affirms that the death of Christ was substitutionary (Matt. 20:28), and thereby the sinner is justified before a holy God, not merely influenced by a demonstration of love.

ACCIDENT THEORY

A more recent view, the accident theory, was advocated by Albert Schweitzer (1875-1965), who taught that Christ became enamored with His messiahship. This theory saw Him preaching the coming kingdom and being mistakenly crushed in the process. Schweitzer saw no value to others in the death of Christ

The deficiency of Schweitzer's view centers on the suggestion that Christ's death was a mistake. Scripture does not present it in that way. On numerous occasions Jesus predicted His death (Matt. 16:21; 17:22; 20:17-19; 26:1-5); Christ's death was in the plan of God (Acts 2:23). Moreover, His death had infinite value as a substitutionary atonement (Isa. 53:4-6).

EXAMPLE (MARTYR) THEORY

In reaction to the Reformers the example theory was first advocated by the Socinians in the sixteenth century and more recently by Unitarians. This view, which is a more liberal view than the moral influence view, suggests the death of Christ was unnecessary in atoning for sin; sin did not need to be punished. There was no relationship between the salvation of sinners and Christ's death. Rather, Christ was an example of obedience and it was that example of obedience to the point of death that ought to inspire people to reform and live as Christ lived.

The weaknesses of this view are multiple. Christ is viewed only as a man in this theory; atonement is unnecessary yet Scripture emphasizes the need for atonement (Rom. 3:24). This view emphasizes Christ as an example for unbelievers, but 1 Peter 2:21 teaches that Christ's example was for believers, not unbelievers.

GOVERNMENTAL THEORY

Grotius (1583-1645) taught the governmental theory as a reaction to the example theory of Socinius. The governmental theory served as a compromise between the example theory and the view of the Reformers. Grotius taught that God forgives sinners without requiring an equivalent payment. Grotius reasoned that Christ upheld the principle of government in God's law by making a token payment for sin through His death. God accepted the token payment of Christ, set aside the requirement of the law, and was able to forgive sinners because the principle of His government had been upheld.

Among the problems with this view are the following. God is subject to change—He threatens but does not carry out (and in fact changes) the sentence. According to this view God forgives sin without payment for sin. Scripture, however, teaches the necessity of propitiating God (Rom. 3:24; 1 John 2:2)—the wrath of God must be assuaged. Also, substitutionary atonement must be made for sin (2 Cor. 5:21; 1 Peter 2:24).

CORRECT MEANING OF THE ATONEMENT

Although there are some points of merit in the previously discussed views concerning the death of Christ, the views are incomplete or deficient

THEORIES OF THE ATONEMENT [1]

Theory	Original Exponent	Main Idea	Weakness	Recent Exponents
Ransom to Satan	Origen (A.D. 184-254)	Ransom paid to Satan because people held captive by him.	God's holiness offended through sin; cross was judgment on Satan, not ransom to Satan.	No known current advocates.
Recapitulation	Irenaeus (A.D. 130-200)	Christ experienced all Adam did, including sin.	Contradicts Christ's sinlessness. (1 John 3:5)	None known.
Commercial (Satisfaction)	Anselm (1033-1109)	Sin robbed God of honor; Christ's death honored God enabling Him to forgive sinners.	Elevates God's honor above other attributes; ignores vicarious atonement.	None known.
Moral Influence	Abelard (1079-1142)	Christ's death unnecessary to atone for sin; His death softens sinners hearts to cause them to repent.	Basis of Christ's death is God's love, not holiness. Atonement viewed as unnecessary.	Friedrich Schleiermacher Albrecht Ritschl Horace Bushnell
Example	Socinus (1539-1604)	Christ's death unnecessary to atone for sin; His death was example of obedience to inspire reform.	Views Christ only as a man; atonement viewed as unnecessary.	Thomas Altizer Unitarians
Governmental	Grotius (1583-1645)	Christ upheld government in God's law; His death was a token payment; enables God to set law aside and forgive people.	God is subject to change; His law is set aside; God forgives without payment for sin.	Daniel Whitby Samuel Clarke Richard Watson J. McLeod Campbell H. R. Mackintosh
Accident	A. Schweitzer (1875-1965)	Christ became enamored with a Messiah complex and was mistakenly crushed under it in the process.	Views Christ's death as a mistake; denies substitutionary atonement.	None known.

in their evaluation of His death. The foundational meaning of the death of Christ is its substitutionary character. He died in place of sinners that He might purchase their freedom, reconcile them to God, and thereby satisfy the righteous demands of a holy God. The following terms explain the meaning of Christ's death.

SUBSTITUTION

The death of Christ was substitutionary—He died in the stead of sinners and in their place. This is also described as *vicarious* from the Latin word *vicarius* meaning "one in place of another." The death of Christ "is vicarious in the sense that Christ is the Substitute who bears the punishment rightly due sinners, their guilt being imputed to Him in such a way that He representatively bore their punishment."[2] There are many passages that emphasize Christ's substitutionary atonement in the place of mankind. Christ was a substitute in being made sin for others (2 Cor. 5:21); He bore the sins of others in His body on the cross (1 Pet. 2:24); He suffered once to bear the sins of others (Heb. 9:28); He experienced horrible suffering, scourging, and death in place of sinners (Isa. 53:4-6).

There are two Greek prepositions that emphasize the substitutionary nature of Jesus' death. The preposition *anti*, translated "for," means Christ died "instead of" sinners (Matt. 20:28; Mark 10:45). The preposition *huper*, also translated "for," means Christ died "in behalf of" or "in place of" sinners (Gal. 3:13; 1 Tim. 2:6; 2 Cor. 5:21; 1 Pet. 3:18). Philemon 13 shows that *huper* must mean "in place of."

The doctrine of substitution is important in that through Christ's death the righteous demands of God have been met; it was a legal transaction in which Christ dealt with the sin problem for the human race. He became the substitute for humanity's sin.

REDEMPTION

The word *redemption* comes from the Greek word *agorazo* and means "to purchase in the marketplace." Frequently it had to do with the sale of slaves in the marketplace. The word is used to describe the believer being purchased out of the slavemarket of sin and set free from sin's bondage. The purchase price for the believer's freedom and release from sin was the death of Jesus Christ (1 Cor. 6:20; 7:23; Rev. 5:9; 14:3, 4).

Because the believer has been bought by Christ, he belongs to Christ and is Christ's slave. "The redeemed are paradoxically slaves, the slaves of God, for they were bought with a price. . . . Believers are not brought by Christ into a liberty of selfish ease. Rather, since they have been bought by God at terrible cost, they have become God's slaves, to do His will."[3]

A second word related to the believer's redemption is *exagorazo*, which teaches that Christ redeemed believers from the curse and bondage of the law that only condemned and could not save. Believers have been purchased in the slave market (*-agorazo*) and removed from (*ex-*) the slave market altogether. Christ set believers free from bondage to the law and from its condemnation (Gal. 3:13; 4:5). "A curse rests on everyone who does not fulfill the law; Christ died in such a way as to bear or be a curse; we who should have been accursed now go free . . . (moreover, this is) a legally based freedom."[4]

A third term that is used to explain redemption is *lutroo* which means "to obtain release by the payment of a price."[5] The idea of being set free by payment of a ransom is prevalent in this word (Luke 24:21). Believers have been redeemed by the precious blood of Christ (1 Pet. 1:18) to be a special possession for God (Titus 2:14).

Redemption is viewed *sinward*; mankind was in bondage to sin and in need of release from bondage and slavery to sin.

RECONCILIATION

The emphasis of *reconciliation* is that of making peace with God. Man who was estranged from God is brought into communion with God. Sin had created a barrier between man and God and rendered man hostile toward God (Isa. 59:1-2; Col. 1:21, 22; Ja. 4:4). Through Christ that enmity and the wrath of God was removed (Rom. 5:10). Reconciliation may thus be defined as "God removing the barrier of sin, producing peace and enabling man to be saved." There are two parts to reconciliation. The *objective* aspect of reconciliation is that in which man is reconciled to God prior to faith and man is rendered savable (2 Cor. 5:18*a*, 19*a*). This is *provisional* reconciliation. The *subjective* aspect of reconciliation is that in which man is reconciled to God when he believes (2 Cor. 5:18*b*, 19*b*). This is *experimental* reconciliation.

The word *reconciliation* comes from the Greek word *katalasso*, which means "to effect a change, to reconcile."[6] God is the one who initiated this change or reconciliation; He moved to reconcile sinful man to Himself (2 Cor. 5:18, 19). On the other hand, man is the object of reconciliation. It was man who had moved out of fellowship with God; therefore, man needed to be restored. This reconciliation has been provided for the whole world, but it is effective only when it is received by personal faith.[7]

Reconciliation is *manward*: man was the one that had moved out of fellowship because of sin, and man needed to be reconciled to renew the fellowship.

PROPITIATION

Propitiation means that the death of Christ fully satisfied all the righteous demands of God toward the sinner. Because God is holy and righteous He cannot overlook sin; through the work of Jesus Christ God is fully satisfied that His righteous standard has been met. Through union with Christ the believer can now be accepted by God and be spared from the wrath of God.

The Old Testament word *kaphar* means "to cover"; it involved a ritual covering for sin (Lev. 4:35; 10:17). The Greek verb *hilaskomai*, meaning "to propitiate," occurs twice in the New Testament. In Luke 18:13 the repentant tax collector prayed for God to be propitiated, or that God would provide a covering for sin. In Hebrews 2:17 it declares that Christ has made propitiation for sin. The word also occurs three times in the noun form *(hilasmos* —1 John 2:2; 4:10; and *hilasterion*—Rom. 3:25).

Propitiation is related to several concepts. (1) The wrath of God. Because God is holy, His wrath is directed toward sin and must be assuaged to spare man from eternal destruction. (2) God provides the remedy. God provides the solution to sin by sending Christ as a satisfaction for sin. (3) Christ's death assuages the wrath of God. The gift of Christ satisfied the holiness of God and averted His wrath.

Propitiation is *Godward*; God is propitiated—His holiness is vindicated and satisfied by the death of Christ.

FORGIVENESS

Forgiveness is the legal act of God whereby He removes the charges that were held against the sinner because proper satisfaction or atonement for those sins has been made. There are several Greek words used to describe forgiveness. One is *charizomai*, which is related to the word *grace* and means "to forgive out of grace."[8] It is used of cancellation of a debt (Col. 2:13). The context emphasizes that our debts were nailed to the cross, with Christ's atonement freely forgiving the sins that were charged against us.

The most common word for forgiveness is *aphiemi*, which means "to let go, release" or "send away." The noun form is used in Ephesians 1:7 where it stresses the believer's sins have been forgiven or sent away because of the riches of God's grace as revealed in the death of Christ. Forgiveness forever solves the problem of sin in the believer's life—all sins past, present, and future (Col. 2:13). This is distinct from the daily cleansing from sin that is necessary to maintain fellowship with God (1 John 1:9).

Forgiveness is *manward*; man had sinned and needed to have his sins dealt with and removed.

JUSTIFICATION

Whereas forgiveness is the negative side of salvation, justification is the positive side. To justify is to declare righteous the one who has faith in Jesus Christ. It is a forensic (legal) act of God whereby He declares the believing sinner righteous on the basis of the blood of Christ. The major emphasis of justification is positive and involves two main aspects. It involves the pardon and removal of all sins and the end of separation from God (Acts 13:39; Rom. 4:6-7; 5:9-11; 2 Cor. 5:19). It also involves the bestowal of righteousness upon the believing person and "a title to all the blessings promised to the just."[9]

Justification is a gift given through the grace of God (Rom. 3:24) and takes place the moment the individual has faith in Christ (Rom. 4:2; 5:1). The ground of justification is the death of Christ (Rom. 5:9), apart from any works (Rom. 4:5). The means of justification is faith (Rom. 5:1). Through justification God maintains His integrity and His standard, yet is able to enter into fellowship with sinners because they have the very righteousness of Christ imputed to them.

Justification is *manward*; man had sinned and broken God's standard. Man was in need of receiving the righteousness of God to enter into fellowship with Him.

EXTENT OF THE ATONEMENT

A debate of long standing is over the issue of the extent of the atonement: *for whom did Christ die?* Some suggest Christ died only for the elect, whereas others emphasize that the death of Christ was universal—He died for everyone even though not everyone will be saved.

LIMITED ATONEMENT

A term that is preferred to "limited atonement" is *definite* or *particular* redemption, suggesting that the atonement of Christ is limited to a definite or particular number of people. The defense for particular redemption is as follows.

There are a number of passages that emphasize Christ died for a particular group of people and not for everyone. As the Good Shepherd, Christ laid down His life for the sheep (John 10:15); not everyone is included in this flock. Christ gave His life for the church (Acts 20:28; Eph. 5:25); He died for the elect (Rom. 8:32-33). Therefore, the objects of God's love are particular; He does not love everyone with the same love (cf. Rom. 1:7; 8:29; 9:13;

Col. 3:12; 1 Thess. 1:4; 2 Thess. 2:13). "Since the objects of the Father's love are particular, definite, and limited, so are the objects of Christ's death."[10] This truth is also reflected in verses such as 1 John 4:10, and Romans 5:8 and 8:32.

If Christ actually made an atonement for sin then the objects of that atonement must be a particular group. Otherwise the atonement's effect is weakened because not everyone is saved for whom Christ made atonement.

Other arguments advanced for limited atonement include the following. If God is sovereign (Eph. 1:11) then His plan cannot be frustrated, but if Christ died for all people and all people are not saved then God's plan *is* frustrated. If Christ died for all people then redemption has been made for all and all are justified. That thinking logically leads to universalism (everyone will be saved). In passages stating that Christ died for the world it means He died for "people from every tribe and nation—not only the Jews."[11] Similarly, when the word "all" is used (2 Cor. 5:15) it means all classes of people but not every person.

UNLIMITED ATONEMENT

The doctrine of unlimited atonement, as understood by evangelicals, means that Christ died for every person but His death is effective only in those who believe the gospel. The arguments for unlimited atonement are as follows.

(1) If the statements of the New Testament are taken at face value, then it is evident they teach Christ died for everyone.

(2) Limited atonement is not based on exegesis of the texts of Scripture but more on the logical premise that if Christ died for everyone and everyone is not saved, then God's plan is thwarted.

(3) The *world*, as John describes it, is "God-hating, Christ-rejecting, and Satan-dominated. Yet that is the world for which Christ died"[12] (cf. John 1:29; 3:16; 17; 4:42; 1 John 4:14). These passages emphasize a universal atonement.

(4) The word *whosoever* is used more than 110 times in the New Testament and always with an unrestricted meaning[13] (cf. John 3:16; Acts 2:21; 10:43; Rom. 10:13; Rev. 22:17).

(5) The word *all*, or an equivalent term, is used to denote everyone. Christ died for the ungodly—everyone is ungodly (Rom. 5:6); Christ died for all, suggesting everyone (2 Cor. 5:14-15; 1 Tim. 2:6; 4:10; Tit. 2:11; Heb. 2:9; 2 Pet. 3:9).

(6) Second Peter 2:1 indicates Christ died for the false teachers who were "denying the Master who bought them." The context indicates these are heretics doomed to destruction, yet it is said of them "the Master bought them." This militates against the limited atonement view.

(7) "The Bible teaches that Christ died for 'sinners' (1 Tim. 1:15; Rom. 5:6-8). The word 'sinners' nowhere means 'church' or 'the elect,' but simply all of lost mankind."[14]

PROCESS OF SALVATION

GOD'S SIDE

Work of the Father. While there is human responsibility in salvation, there is first a divine side to salvation in which God sovereignly acts to secure the sinner's salvation.

(1) Election. The question concerning election is not whether or not one understands it but whether or not the Bible teaches it. If, indeed, the Bible teaches election (or any other doctrine), then one is obligated to believe it. The doctrine of election includes a number of areas: Israel is elect (Deut. 7:6); angels are elect (1 Tim. 5:21); the Levitical priests were elect (Deut. 18:5); Jeremiah the prophet was elect (Jer. 1:5); and believers are elect (Eph. 1:4).

What is election? Election may be defined as "that eternal act of God whereby He, in His sovereign good pleasure, and on account of no foreseen merit in them, chooses a certain number of men to be the recipients of special grace and of eternal salvation."[15] One of the principal passages concerning election is Ephesians 1:4 in the statement "He chose us." The verb "chose" is the Greek *eklego*, which means "to call out" from among the people. The word means that God selected some individuals from out of the masses. Moreover, the word is always used in the middle voice meaning God chose *for Himself.* This describes the purpose of the choosing—God chose believers to be in fellowship with Him and to reflect His grace through their living a redeemed life.

Several characteristics are to be noted in election: it took place in eternity past (Eph. 1:4); it is an act of a sovereign God, and it is according to His sovereign will (Rom. 9:11; 2 Tim. 1:9); it is an expression of the love of God (Eph. 1:4); it is not conditioned on man in any way (2 Tim. 1:9; Rom. 9:11); it reflects the justice of God; there can be no charge of injustice against God in election (Rom. 9:14, 20).

(2) Predestination. The word *predestination* comes from the Greek *proorizo*, which means "to mark out beforehand," and occurs six times in the New Testament (Acts 4:28; Rom. 8:29-30; 1 Cor. 2:7; Eph. 1:5, 11). The English word *horizon* is derived from *proorizo*. God by His sovereign choice marked believers off in eternity past. Several characteristics of predestination can be seen: it includes all events—not just individual salvation (Acts 4:28); it determined our status as adopted sons of God (Eph. 1:5); it assures our ultimate glorification (Rom. 8:29-30); it is for the purpose of extolling

the grace of God (Eph. 1:6); it secures our eternal inheritance (Eph. 1:11); and it is according to the free choice of God and according to His will (Eph. 1:5, 11).

Election and predestination do not, however, take away man's responsibility. Even though election and predestination are clearly taught in Scripture, man is still held accountable for his choices. Scripture never suggests that man is lost because he is not elect or has not been predestined; the emphasis of Scripture is that man is lost because he refuses to believe the gospel.

(3) Adoption. The word *adoption* (Gk. *huiothesia*) means "placing as a son" and describes the rights and privileges as well as the new position of the believer in Christ. The word is taken from Roman custom where, in a legal ceremony, the adopted son was given all the rights of a natural-born son. In this rite, four things happened. "[a] The adopted person lost all rights in his old family, and gained all the rights of a fully legitimate son in his new family. [b] He became heir to his new father's estate. [c] The old life of the adopted person was completely wiped out. For instance, legally all debts were cancelled; they were wiped out as if they had never been. [d] In the eyes of the law the adopted person was literally and absolutely the son of his new father."[16]

Paul employs this Roman background to describe the Christian's new status in Christ. In adoption the believer is released from slavery into freedom and maturity in Christ (Rom. 8:15). In adoption the believer is released from bondage under the law into a new status as a son (Gal. 4:5). In adoption the believer enjoys a new relationship wherein he may address God as "Abba! Father!" (Rom. 8:15; Gal. 4:6), an intimate term of address used by a child in addressing its father. Ephesians 1:5 indicates the act of adoption is connected with predestination, having taken place in eternity past but realized when the person believes in Jesus Christ.

Work of Christ. In discussing the process of salvation, the work of Christ is supreme in achieving man's salvation. Primarily, it involves the death of Christ as a substitutionary atonement for sin in securing man's release from the penalty and bondage of sin and meeting the righteous demand of a holy God.

Another important aspect of salvation, not previously mentioned, is sanctification. The word *sanctification* (Gk. *hagiasmos*) means "to set apart." The same root word is found in the English words *saint, holy,* and *holiness.* Sanctification and its related terms are used in a variety of ways in both the Old Testament and the New Testament. With respect to the New Testament believer, however, there are primarily three aspects of sanctification.

(1) Positional sanctification. This is the believer's position or standing before God, based on the death of Christ. In positional sanctification the

believer is accounted holy before God; he is declared a saint. Paul frequently began his letters by addressing the believers as saints (Rom. 1:7; note, the supplied word "as" hinders the statement by Paul; it simply reads, "to all who are beloved of God in Rome, called saints." Compare 1 Cor. 1:2; 2 Cor. 1:1; and Eph. 1:1). It is noteworthy that so carnal a group as the church at Corinth is addressed as "those who have been sanctified in Christ Jesus" (1 Cor. 1:2). This positional sanctification is achieved through the once-for-all death of Christ (Heb. 10:10, 14, 29).

(2) Experiential Sanctification. Although the believer's positional sanctification is secure, his experiential sancitification may fluctuate because it relates to his daily life and experience. Paul's prayer is that believers should be sanctified entirely in their experience (1 Thess. 5:23); Peter commands believers to be sanctified or holy (1 Peter 1:16). This experiential sanctification grows as the believer dedicates his life to God (Rom. 6:13; 12:1-2) and is nourished by the Word of God (Ps. 119:9-16). Clearly, additional factors enter into experiential sanctification.

(3) Ultimate Sanctification. This aspect of sanctification is future and anticipates the final transformation of the believer into the likeness of Christ. At that time all believers will be presented to the Lord without any blemish (Eph. 5:26-27).

Work of the Holy Spirit. The work of the Holy Spirit in salvation involves the convicting ministry to the unbeliever, regenerating the person to give him spiritual life, indwelling the believer, baptizing the believer into union with Christ and other Christians, and sealing the believer. (See expanded discussion in chap. 21, "Pneumatology: Doctrine of the Holy Spirit.")

MAN'S SIDE

The issue of the terms of salvation is important because the purity of the gospel is at stake. What are the terms of salvation? Is salvation something in addition to faith? The issue is critical because Paul pronounced anathema on anyone who preached a gospel contrary to what he had preached (Gal. 1:8-9).

Erroneous views. There are a number of false views of the human condition(s) for salvation. These views add conditions to man's response of faith and thereby nullify the grace of God and corrupt the purity of the gospel. Some of the false views are as follows.[17]

(1) Repent and believe. Repentance shoula not be understood as a separate condition for believing in Christ. If repentance is cited as a condition of salvation in terms of feeling sorry for one's sins, then it is a wrong usage of the term. It should not be understood as a separate step in salvation. Acts 20:21 indicates that repentance and faith should not be seen as separate items in response to the gospel but together they signify belief in

Christ. To believe in Christ is to change one's mind about Christ and trust Him alone for salvation.

(2) Believe and be baptized. This suggestion is taken from a misunderstanding of Acts 2:38. Peter did not suggest that baptism is necessary for the forgiveness of sins, rather, he was calling for members of that generation which was guilty of having crucified Christ to separate themselves from a generation under the judgment of God. That separation was to be publicly signified through baptism. Moreover, the baptism signified that the people *had* received the forgiveness of sins.[18]

A second passage sometimes cited to suggest that baptism is necessary for salvation is Mark 16:16. The phrase "He who has believed and has been baptized shall be saved" is not the same as saying baptism is necessary to salvation; this is seen in the last half of the verse, which omits the reference to baptism. Condemnation comes from refusal to believe, not from a failure to be baptized. Additionally, it is tenuous to argue the point from Mark 16:16 because some of the oldest New Testament manuscripts do not contain Mark 16:9-20.

(3) Believe and confess Christ. The condition of publicly confessing Christ for salvation is sometimes added to faith on the basis of Romans 10:9. This passage, however, is not establishing an additional condition for salvation. Rather, to confess Jesus as Lord means to acknowledge His deity. That was and always will be a critical issue in terms of salvation. The one who believes in Christ as Savior must of necessity acknowledge His deity. That is the meaning of Romans 10:9.

(4) Believe and surrender. The issue here is whether or not one can become a Christian simply by believing the gospel, or whether or not one must surrender to Christ as the Lord of one's life. Part of the answer lies in a misunderstanding of Romans 10:9. Confession of Christ as Lord identifies Christ as deity; the issue is not concerning His Lordship. In addition, if surrendering one's life to Christ as Lord is necessary for salvation, then there could be no carnal Christians, yet Paul makes it clear that the Corinthians whom he speaks of as being "in Christ" were indeed carnal (1 Cor. 3:1). Lordship is based on application of the knowledge of Scripture, and the knowledge of Scripture comes with spiritual maturity, which in turn *follows* salvation. Lordship is important, but it cannot be a condition for salvation; that is adding to the gospel.

A further problem in this view relates to a misunderstanding of the term *disciple.* When Jesus called men to follow Him as disciples (cf. Luke 14:25-35), He was not calling them to salvation. It was a call to follow Him as a learner, which is the meaning of disciple. Discipleship always follows salvation; it is never a part of it, otherwise grace is no longer grace. Furthermore, if discipleship is a condition of salvation, then so is baptism, because being baptized is part of becoming a disciple (Matt. 28:19, 20).[19]

Biblical view. Many passages of Scripture affirm that man's only responsibility in salvation is believing the gospel (John 1:12; 3:16, 18, 36; 5:24; 11:25-26; 12:44; 20:31; Acts 16:31; 1 John 5:13, and so forth). But what is faith? What does it mean to believe the gospel? Faith may be succinctly defined as "confiding trust."[20] John's use of the word *faith* is similar to Paul's use in describing faith as believing "into Christ." For John, faith "is an activity which takes men right out of themselves and makes them one with Christ."[21]

Saving faith, however, is not mere intellectual assent to a doctrine; it involves more than that. Saving faith involves at least three elements.

(1) Knowledge. This involves the *intellect* and emphasizes that there are certain basic truths that must be believed for salvation. Jesus claimed to be God; belief in His deity became the central issue in salvation (Rom. 10:9-10). Unless a person believed that Jesus was all He claimed to be he would die in his sins (John 8:24). Saving faith, then, involves believing the basic truths fundamental to man's salvation: man's sinfulness, Christ's atoning sacrifice, and His bodily resurrection. John wrote down the claims of Christ in order that people might believe these truths about Christ to be saved (John 20:30, 31).

(2) Conviction. Conviction involves the *emotions.* This element emphasizes that the person has not only an intellectual awareness of the truths but that there is an inner conviction (cf. John 16:8-11) of their truthfulness.

(3) Trust. As a result of knowledge about Christ and a conviction that these things are true there must also be a settled trust, a moving of the *will*—a decision must be made as an act of the will. The "heart" frequently denotes the will, and that is Paul's emphasis in the statement, "believe in your heart" (Rom. 10:9).

The Grace of God

Although much has already been said about the grace of God, sharper focus on this glorious truth is needed.

COMMON GRACE

Definition of common grace. If God is sovereign and man is depraved in his sinful estate, then God must move to bring about reconciliation between man and God. Differing categories are given to grace, but for this work the categories of common and efficacious grace will be used. Common grace is broader in scope, aimed at all mankind. In concise terms common grace may be defined as "the unmerited favor of God toward all men displayed in His general care for them."[22] An expanded definition of common grace is "(a) those general operations of the Holy Spirit whereby He, without renewing the heart, exercises such a moral influence on man through His general or special revelation, that sin is restrained, order is maintained in social life, and civil righteousness is promoted; or, (b) those general blessings, such as rain and sunshine, food and drink, clothing and shelter, which God imparts to all men indiscriminately where and in what measure it seems good to Him."[23]

Explanation of common grace. (1) General blessings to all mankind. The designation "common" stresses that all mankind is the recipient of God's common grace. *Material provisions* are one aspect of common grace. Jesus commanded His followers to love their enemies because God exhibits His love toward all people (Matt. 5:45). God gives sunshine and rainfall to the atheistic farmer that enables him to harvest his crop just as He provides for the Christian farmer. Paul reminded the unbelievers at Lystra that God had given them "rains from heaven and fruitful seasons" (Acts 14:17), an exhibition of God's common grace.

In Psalm 145:8-9 the psalmist exults: "The Lord is gracious and merciful; slow to anger and great in lovingkindness. The Lord is good to all, and His mercies are over all His works." God's grace and mercy are particularly exhibited in His delay and *withholding of judgment.* That God does not immediately judge man is an evidence of His grace. The reason is to enable man to come to repentance (Rom. 2:4).

God has provided *spiritual provisions* for all mankind. First Timothy 4:10 refers to Christ as "the Savior of all men, especially of believers." This verse does not teach universalism, but it indicates spiritual provision has been made for everyone. If Christ is God then His death had infinite value in which He is potentially the Savior of all men and actually the Savior of those who believe. God's common grace extends to all men inasmuch as that provision has been made for everyone through the death of Christ.

(2) Restraining of sin. God's restraint of sin is an extension of common grace, and it functions through at least four channels. *Through Direct Actions:* Although Laban had cheated Jacob considerably, God restrained the deceit of Laban (Gen. 31:7). When Satan challenged God concerning Job's loyalty, God put a limitation on what Satan could do to Job (Job 1:12; 2:6). *Through the Holy Spirit:* In Genesis 6:3 God said, "My Spirit shall not strive with man forever." This text infers that the Holy Spirit does centend with and restrain man's sinful behavior. *Through the prophets:* The ministry of the prophets was to call the people back to obedience and adherence of the Mosaic law. In that ministry the prophets served as a restraint on sin (cf. Isa. 1:16-20). *Through human government:* In Romans 13:1-4 Paul establishes that governments are ordained by God (v. 1), and they are established as a restraint to evil.

In this present age there is a restraining force against evil mentioned in 2 Thessalonians 2:6-7. In this case the restraining force is withholding the manifestation of "the lawless one." When the Restrainer is removed, then the lawless one will be revealed. It is significant that the phrase, "what restrains" (neuter gender) in v. 6 shifts to the masculine gender, "he who now restrains" in v. 7. Moreover, the Restrainer must be strong enough to hold back the forces of Satan, leaving the suggestion that the Restrainer is the Holy Spirit.[24]

(3) Convicting of sin. In the accompanying diagram, the work of convicting has a narrower focus than the material provisions of common grace. It is still classified as a narrower aspect of common grace because it is not effective in everyone who encounters it.[25] The convicting work of the Holy Spirit is set forth in John 16:8-11. He "will convict the world concerning sin, and righteousness, and judgment" (v.8). The word *convict* (Gk. *elegchein*) is a legal term that means "to cross-examine for the purpose of convincing or refuting an opponent (the word being specially used of legal proceedings)."[26]

> It involves the conceptions of authoritative examination, of unquestionable proof, of decisive judgment, of punitive power. Whatever the final issue may be, he who "convicts" another places the truth of the case in dispute in a clear light before him, so that it must be seen and acknowledged as truth. He who then rejects the conclusion which this exposition involves, rejects it with his eyes open and at his peril. Truth seen as truth carries with it condemnation to all who refuse to welcome it.[27]

This convicting work of the Holy Spirit is threefold. It concerns *sin* (16:9) in the refusal of people to believe in Christ (John 16:9). The sin is specifically the unbelief of the people in spite of Christ's revelation concerning Himself through His words and works. It concerns *righteousness* in the conviction of the world whereby Christ is vindicated through His death, resurrection, and ascension (John 16:10). The fact that Christ arose and ascended to the Father demonstrated that He was indeed the Righteous One. It concerns *judgment* in the conviction of the world because Satan was judged at the cross (John 16:11). Satan rules by means of sin and death, yet Christ triumphed over both and defeated Satan. If the ruler has been judged then his followers will be judged also. The Holy Spirit will convict the world of these truths.

Necessity of common grace. It is preliminary to efficacious grace. Before a person can be saved there must be a witness from God; that witness comes first through a knowledge of God. God reveals Himself to people through the avenue of common grace. When people participate in the material blessings of God (Matt. 5:45) it ought to make them reflect on the goodness of God. Additionally, God has revealed something of Himself in nature: His "eternal power and divine nature" are clearly seen by all (Rom. 1:20). All people have an awareness of their accountability to a righteous God, all the while having been participants of His blessings toward them. With that awareness in mankind, the Holy Spirit convicts persons of the righteousness of Jesus Christ who offers the solution to mankind's dilemma (John 16:8-11). A person cannot receive the efficacious grace of God for salvation without having received and recognized the work of God in common grace. Common grace thus is preparatory for efficacious grace; it brings man to a realization of his sin and of the righteousness of Jesus Christ.

EFFICACIOUS GRACE

Definition of efficacious grace. Efficacious grace is narrower in scope than common grace and as the name indicates, it is *efficacious*, that is *effective*, in those to whom it is given. All who are the recipients of efficacious grace respond to it and become believers. Efficacious grace is also called special grace in contrast to common grace.

A concise definition of efficacious grace is "the work of the Holy Spirit which effectively moves men to believe in Jesus Christ as Saviour."[28] A further definition is that "Special grace is irresistible. . . . by changing the heart it makes man perfectly willing to accept Jesus Christ unto salvation and to yield obedience to the will of God."[29] An important emphasis in this definition is that efficacious grace renders the person *willing* to believe in Jesus Christ; in other words, the individual willingly believes. He does not come against his will. Walvoord's definition has a similar emphasis: "[efficacious grace is] the instantaneous work of God empowerng the human will and inclining the human heart to faith in Christ."[30] Efficacious grace is based on the "called" passages of Scripture (cf. Rom. 1:1, 6-7; 8:28; 1 Cor. 1:1-2, 24, 26; Eph. 1:18; 4:1, 4; 2 Tim. 1:9). This calling denotes the effective invitation of God whereby He woos the person through the power of the Holy Spirit and renders the individual willing to respond to the gospel.

Explanation of efficacious grace. Eight observations about efficacious grace help give it precise meaning.

First, not everyone is called; efficacious grace is not dispensed to everyone. It is limited to the elect. Conversely, all the elect are the recipients of efficacious grace. In Romans 1:5-6 Paul emphasizes that from among the broad spectrum of Gentiles, the select group making up the church in Rome were called. Not all the Gentiles were called; only those who constituted the church at Rome had been called by the special grace of God. This narrow focus is also seen in 1 Corinthians 1:24-28. From the broad sector of Jews and Gentiles who either found Christ a stumblingblock or foolishness, God called *some* Jews and *some* Gentiles to whom Christ represented the power of God. Note the emphasis on called or chosen (same root word as called) in this passage (vv. 24, 26-28).

Second, it is effective because it is never successfully rejected. It is irresistible. This is not to suggest that some would refuse to come but are forced and therefore come into the kingdom struggling. As already mentioned, it means God moves upon the sinner's will to make him willing to come. As a result, he comes of his volition and does not resist the efficacious grace of God. First Corinthians 1:23-24 emphasizes that the gospel is foolishness to unbelievers, but it is the power of God and it is effective in believers.

The other side of efficacious grace is the need to believe. Thirdly, then, it does not operate contrary to man's will. Man is still responsible to believe the gospel in order to be saved, and he cannot be saved apart from believing (Acts 16:31). Jesus admonished the unbelieving Jews, "You are unwilling to come to Me, that you may have life" (John 5:40; cf. Matt. 23:37). This was a deliberate refusal and an unwillingness to believe in Christ.

Next, efficacious grace involves the drawing power of God. John 6:44 states, "No one can come to Me, unless the Father who sent Me draws him." "Those who come to Christ are here described as being drawn to him by the Father . . . the divine initiative in the salvation of believers is emphasized. The responsibility of men and women in the matter of coming to Christ is not overlooked (cf. John 5:40); but none at all would come unless divinely persuaded and enabled to do so."[31]

Fifth, the work of the Holy Spirit is involved in efficacious grace. Preliminary to a person responding to special grace, the Holy Spirit must convict the person of their sin of unbelief and of the righteousness of Christ (John 16:8-11; see previous discussion). The Holy Spirit is also the one who effects efficacious grace in the person as He regenerates the person (Titus 3:5).

Sixth, efficacious grace must involve the Word of God. In response to the gift of efficacious grace the person responds in faith, but faith must have content and a knowledge of truth to be believed. Efficacious grace, therefore, is not given apart from biblical truth. "Faith comes from hearing, and hearing by the word of Christ" (Rom. 10:17). The Word of God is living and is applied to the heart of the believer by the Holy Spirit (Heb. 4:12). Peter reminds the believers that they have been born again "through the living and abiding word of God" (1 Pet. 1:23). Both these texts from Hebrews and 1 Peter emphasize that the Word of God is *living* and instrumental in effecting the new birth. Efficacious grace and the application of the living Word of God are vital in bringing salvation to the person.

Seventh, the application of efficacious grace is toward individuals, not to groups, nor to the church as a whole. Jacob is an example of individual election and the recipient of efficacious grace (Rom. 9:11-13). God passed over Esau and chose Jacob to reveal His grace. Just as justification must be on an individual basis and not corporate (such as the entire church being elected as a distinct entity), so election through the application of efficacious grace must be individual. In Romans 8:30 the very ones God called (efficacious grace) were the very ones God justified. It is necessary for consistent interpretation to recognize the calling (efficacious grace) and the justification as applied similarly (i.e., individual, not corporate).

Finally, efficacious grace is from eternity. While the application of efficacious grace takes place in time, its plan was determined in eternity. Romans 9:11 emphasizes that God's plan and *resolve* (Gk. *prothesis*) alone determined the object of His grace in eternity past. Before Jacob and Esau had done anything good or bad, God chose Jacob and passed over Esau to reveal His grace; it was not in accord with human works but as a result of the eternal counsel of the sovereign God. Similarly, Romans 8:30 teaches that the application of efficacious grace is as a result of having predestined certain ones to be the objects of that grace. God called by efficacious grace the ones whom He had previously predestined.

Defense of efficacious grace. The necessity of efficacious grace becomes apparent as four factors are considered.

First, it is necessary because of sin. Ephesians 2:1 states the condition of the unsaved person: "And you were dead in your trespasses and sins."[32] If the unbeliever is *dead* then he cannot make the initial response to God. God must make the first move. Hence, God through His grace calls the one who is dead in trespasses and sin.

Also, it is effective because God cannot fail. In the sequence involving those whom God calls in Romans 8:29-30, none are lost. The same ones God foreknows He also predestines, calls, justifies, and glorifies. God loses none in the process. The text is clear in emphasizing, "whom He called, these He also justified." The very ones God called by His grace were also justified, indicating that the efficacious grace was effective in every person whom God called.

Next, efficacious grace is fair because God is always just. In the discussion of God's sovereign call following the discussion of God calling Jacob and passing over Esau, Paul asks the question that would be on the lips of many, "What shall we say then? There is no injustice with God, is there?" (Rom. 9:14). Paul answers with the strongest possible negative statement: "May it never be!"[33] Although the finite human mind cannot comprehend God's sovereign dealing, nonetheless, God is just in all His actions.

Lastly, this grace is fair because man must believe. The fact that God gives efficacious grace does not nullify man's responsibility to believe. Numerous Scriptures emphasize the necessity of believing (cf. John 3:16, 18, 36; 5:24). John 3:18, 36 in particular emhasize that man is lost because he willfully refuses to believe the gospel, not because he does not receive efficacious grace.

Objections to efficacious grace. First, responsibility is unnecessary. It appears that if man is dead in sin and God must demonstrate efficacious grace in order to save an individual, then human responsibility is unnecessary. The problem, however, relates to human inability to comprehend fully God's work and man's response in salvation. Although it is true that God must initiate the action and that man cannot be saved apart from God's efficacious grace, these truths do not absolve man from his responsibility. The solution is found in recognizing that this is one of many antinomies (paradoxes) in Scripture.[34] The numerous passages of Scripture commanding people to believe are sufficient evidence in showing that man is indeed responsible (cf. John 3:18, 36; 6:37; Acts 16:31, etc.).

Second, it is unjust. Romans 9:14 indicates that man cannot suggest there is injustice with God. Man may not comprehend the working of God but nonetheless, God is just. One further point should be noted. God does not owe anyone anything. If He chooses to display His grace to some and not to others it is not unfair since He owes nothing to anyone; moreover, *all people* have volitionally turned their backs on God. If He decides not to display His grace to all it is not unfair since all have rejected Him as an act of the will (Rom. 3:11-12). Ryrie's conclusion on this difficult subject is worth noting.

> God does not bestow His efficacious grace whimsically and without purpose. His purpose is not only to enlighten, regenerate, and bring a sinner into fellowship with Himself but it is primarily that through this operation He may bring glory to Himself. His purpose is that sinners who have been the recipients of efficacious grace may also "show forth the excellencies of him" who called them "out of the darkness into his marvellous light" (1 Peter 2:9-10, ASV). God is glorified through the display of His efficacious grace in the redeemed life.[35]

REGENERATION

DEFINITION OF REGENERATION

The word *regeneration* (Gk. *paliggenesia*) appears only twice in the New Testament. Once is is used eschatologically, "of the renewing of the world in the time of the Messiah" (Matt. 19:28),[36] the second usage is "of the rebirth of a redeemed person" (Titus 3:5).[37] Regeneration should be distinguished from conversion.

> Conversion refers to the response of the human being to God's offer of salvation and approach to man. Regeneration is the other side of conversion. It is God's doing. In regeneration the soul is passive; in conversion, it is active. Regeneration may be defined as the communication of divine life to the soul . . . as the impartation of a new nature . . . or heart . . . and the production of a new creation.[38]

Succinctly stated, *to regenerate* means "to impart life." Regeneration is the act whereby God imparts life to the one who believes.

SCRIPTURES CONCERNING REGENERATION

Two basic passages of Scripture discuss regeneration as it pertains to the impartation of new life to a believer. John 3:3 (although not using the word *regeneration*) refers to regeneration as a "new birth." The Greek word translated "new" is *anothen* and may be translated "from above." In other words, the second birth is a birth from above, from God. The new birth is a spiritual birth in contrast to the first birth which is a physical birth. In the spiritual birth the Holy Spirit regenerates the person; He is the *means* of regeneration. In John 3:5 the phrase "is born" is passive,[39] indicating it is a work done *upon* man, not *by* man. Man does not bring about regeneration; the Holy Spirit produces it. Titus 3:5 is the other passage where regeneration is explained. In this passage regeneration is linked to two things: washing and renewing by the Holy Spirit. It is noteworthy that in both John 3:5 and Titus 3:5 two elements are mentioned: water and the Holy Spirit. It is possible to understand water as symbolic of God's Word (cf. Eph. 5:26).[40] Others link water and the Holy Spirit to cleansing as in Ezekiel 36:25-27. In this case the water would refer to the cleansing that comes through repentance.[41] A contrast between the first and second births can be seen in the following chart.[42]

CONTRASTS OF THE TWO BIRTHS

	The First Birth	The Second Birth
Origin	Of sinful parents	Of God
Means	Of corruptible seed	Of incorruptible seed
Nature	Of the flesh—carnal	Of the Spirit—spiritual
Realm	Satan's slave	Christ's free man
Position	An object of divine wrath	An object of divine love

EXPLANATION OF REGENERATION

It is instantaneous. Just as a child is born at a specific moment in the physical birth, so the spiritual birth occurs instantaneously when the Holy Spirit imparts new life.[43]

It is not the result of human experience. In other words, it is not something the person does but something that is done to the person. Experience may *result* from regeneration, but experience as such is not a cause of regeneration.

It is not based on human effort. John 1:13 indicates the new birth is not effected by the will of man. Regeneration is an act of God, not a cooperative effort between God and man.[44] That is not to say, however, that faith is unnecessary in salvation. It may be suggested that although regeneration and faith are *distinct*, they occur simultaneously.[45] The two are set side by side in John 1:12-13. In John 1:12, at the moment of receiving Christ (believing), the person becomes a child of God; in John 1:13 it indicates that at that very moment the persons have been born of God. Surely there is a mystery here that surpasses human comprehension.

RESULT OF REGENERATION

A new nature. The result of regeneration is the impartation of a "divine nature" (2 Pet. 1:4). The believer has received a "new self" (Eph. 4:24), a capacity for righteous living. He is a "new creature" (2 Cor. 5:17).

A new life. The believer has received a new mind (1 Cor. 2:16) that he might know God; a new heart (Rom. 5:5) that he may love God (1 John 4:9); and a new will (Rom. 6:13) that he may obey God.[46]

ETERNAL SECURITY

There are two distinct views concerning the eternal security of the believer. The Arminian says that man has received his salvation as an act of his will and he may forfeit his salvation as an act of the will—or through specific sins. The Calvinist says that the true believer will persevere in his faith. This doctrine is sometimes called "perseverance of the saints," which is not a proper title since it places the emphasis on man's ability to persevere rather than on God's ability to keep the believer. A better title might be "perseverance of the Lord."

This doctrine does not suggest that the believer will never backslide or sin. It means, however, that when a person has genuinely believed in Christ as His Savior from sin he is forever secured by God by His keeping power.

The basis for the security of salvation does not rest with man, but with God. The security of the believer is based on the work of the Father, the Son, and the Holy Spirit.

SECURING WORK OF THE FATHER

Believers are secure because the Father has chosen them to salvation from eternity past (Eph. 1:4). The Father predestined believers to come to the status of sonship in Christ (Eph. 1:5). The Father has the power to keep believers secure in their salvation (Rom. 8:28-30). The ones the Father foreknew, predestined, called, and justified are the same ones He brings to glorification in the future. None are lost in the process. The Father's love for believers also guarantees their security (Rom. 5:7-10).

SECURING WORK OF THE SON

The Son has redeemed the believer (Eph. 1:7), removed the wrath of God from the believer (Rom. 3:25), justified the believer (Rom. 5:1), provided forgiveness (Col. 2:13), and sanctified the believer (1 Cor. 1:2). Moreover, Christ prays for believers to be with Him (John 17:24); He continues to be their Advocate at God's bar of justice (1 John 2:1); and He continues to make intercession as the believer's High Priest (Heb. 7:25). If a believer could be lost it would imply Christ is ineffective in His work as the believer's Mediator.

SECURING WORK OF THE HOLY SPIRIT

The Holy Spirit has regenerated the believer, giving him life (Tit. 3:5); the Holy Spirit indwells the believer forever (John 14:17); He has sealed the believer for the day of redemption (Eph. 4:30), the sealing being a down payment, guaranteeing our future inheritance; the believer is baptized into union with Christ and into the body of believers (1 Cor. 12:13).

For a believer to lose his salvation would demand a reversal and an undoing of all the preceding works of the Father, Son, and Spirit. The key issue in the discussion of the believer's security concerns the issue of who does the saving. If man is responsible for securing his salvation, then he can be lost; if God secures the person's salvation, then the person is forever secure.

The eternal security of the believer by the grace of God is the completion and crowning glory of God's plan of salvation.

NOTES ON SOTERIOLOGY

1. This chart is adapted from Charles M. Horne, *Salvation* (Chicago: Moody, 1971), p. 32.
2. Louis Berkhof, *Systematic Theology* (Grand Rapids: Eerdmans, 1941), p. 392.
3. Leon Morris, *The Apostolic Preaching of the Cross*, 3rd ed.(Grand Rapids: Eerdmans, 1965), p. 54. This book is a most important work on the subject with a serious, biblical discussion of the key terms related to salvation. The serious student should not neglect the study of this work by Morris.
4. Ibid., pp. 56, 58.
5. Fritz Rienecker, *A Linguistic Key to the Greek New Testament*, Cleon Rogers, ed. (Grand Rapids: Zondervan, 1980), p. 655.

6. Ibid., p. 470.

7. John F. Walvoord, *Jesus Christ Our Lord* (Chicago: Moody, 1969), p. 182.

8. Rienecker, *Linguistic Key to the Greek New Testament*, p. 574.

9. J. I. Packer, "Justification," in Walter A. Elwell, ed., *Evangelical Dictionary of Theology* (Grand Rapids: Baker, 1984), p. 594.

10. Edwin H. Palmer, *The Five Points of Calvinism* (Grand Rapids: Guardian, 1972), p. 44.

11. Ibid., p. 45.

12. Elwell, "Atonement, Extent of," in *Evangelical Dictionary of Theology*, p. 99.

13. Lewis Sperry Chafer, *Systematic Theology*, 8 vols. (Dallas: Dallas Seminary, 1947), 3:204.

14. Elwell, *Evangelical Dictionary of Theology*, p. 99.

15. Berkhof, *Systematic Theology*, p. 114.

16. William Barclay, *The Letter to the Romans* (Edinburgh: Saint Andrew, 1957), pp. 110-11.

17. See Charles C. Ryrie, *A Survey of Bible Doctrine* (Chicago: Moody, 1972), pp. 134-39 for a helpful discussion of the erroneous views.

18. The preposition *for* in the phrase "for the forgiveness of your sins" translates the Greek preposition *eis*, which may also be translated "because of," meaning those people were to be baptized as a public witness that their sins had been forgiven.

19. See the important work by G. Michael Cocoris, *Lordship Salvation: Is It Biblical?* (Dallas: Redencion Viva, 1983). See also G. Michael Cocoris, *Evangelism: A Biblical Approach* (Chicago: Moody, 1984); and Charles C. Ryrie, *Balancing the Christian Life* (Chicago: Moody, 1969), pp. 169-81.

20. William G. T. Shedd, *Commentary on Romans* (Reprint. Grand Rapids: Baker, 1980), p. 76.

21. Leon Morris, *The Gospel According to John* (Grand Rapids: Eerdmans, 1971), p. 336. See Morris's helpful note on believing as used in John's gospel, pp. 335-37.

22. Charles C. Ryrie, *The Holy Spirit* (Chicago: Moody, 1965), p. 55. See also Ryrie's *The Grace of God* (Chicago: Moody, 1963), for a comprehensive discussion of grace.

23. Berkhof, *Systematic Theology*, p. 436.

24. See the excellent discussion by D. Edmond Hiebert, *The Thessalonian Epistles* (Chicago: Moody, 1971), pp. 312-14.

25. See Ryrie's discussion in *The Holy Spirit*, pp. 58-59.

26. Leon Morris, *The Gospel According to John* (Grand Rapids: Eerdmans, 1971), p. 697.

27. B. F. Westcott, *The Gospel According to St. John* (Reprint. Grand Rapids: Eerdmans, 1967), p. 228.

28. Ryrie, *The Holy Spirit*, p. 61.

29. Berkhof, *Systematic Theology*, p. 436.

30. John F. Walvoord, *The Holy Spirit* (Grand Rapids: Zondervan, 1958), p. 122.

31. F. F. Bruce, *The Gospel of John* (Grand Rapids: Eerdmans, 1983), p. 156.

32. The word "were" (Gk. *ontas*) is a present participle (a better translation would be "being") that stresses their state of existence. They are in a state of being dead in sin.

33. *Me genoito* (Gk.) "expresses the abhorrence of an inference which may be falsely drawn from the argument." Fritz Rienecker, *Linguistic Key to the Greek New Testament*, p. 354.

34. Antinomy comes from the Greek *anti,* meaning "against," and *nomos,* meaning "law," hence, something that is contrary to law or contrary to human reason. The student is encouraged to study Ken Boa, *God, I Don't Understand* (Wheaton: Victor, 1975) for a most helpful discussion of antinomies. An awareness of antinomies in Scripture will help resolve many tensions and also help avoid giving undue emphasis on one side or the other in an antinomy.

35. Ryrie, *The Holy Spirit,* p. 63.

36. William F. Arndt and F. Wilbur Gingrich, *Greek-English Lexicon of the New Testament and Other Early Christian Literature,* revised by F. Wilbur Gingrich and Frederick W. Danker (Chicago: U. of Chicago, 1979), p. 606.

37. Ibid.

38. Millard J. Erickson, *Christian Theology,* 3 vols. (Grand Rapids: Baker, 1985), 3:942.

39. *Egennethe* (Gk.) is in the passive voice and might roughly be translated "has been made to be born."

40. Homer A. Kent, Jr., *The Pastoral Epistles* (Chicago: Moody, 1958), p. 242.

41. See discussion of several variant views by S. Lewis Johnson, "Born of Water and Spirit," in *Believers Bible Bulletin* (Dallas; January 31, 1983), pp. 3-4.

42. Horne, *Salvation,* p. 51.

43. The Greek aorist tense in John 1:13 and 3:5 would indicate the new birth is an instantaneous act.

44. Walvoord, *The Holy Spirit,* p. 133.

45. Ryrie, *The Holy Spirit,* pp. 64-65.

46. See J. Dwight Pentecost, *Designed to Be Like Him* (Chicago: Moody, 1966). This is a most helpful work in explaining what has happened in the new birth. Pentecost has separate chapters on the new mind, new heart, and new will.

FOR FURTHER STUDY ON SOTERIOLOGY

FALSE THEORIES ON THE ATONEMENT

** Louis Berkhof. *Systematic Theology.* Grand Rapids: Eerdmans, 1941. Pp. 384-91.

** Millard J. Erickson. *Christian Theology,* 3 vols. Grand Rapids: Baker, 1984. 2:781-800.

* Charles M. Horne. *Salvation.* Chicago: Moody, 1971. Pp. 24-36.

* Leon Morris. "Atonement, Theories of." In Walter A. Elwell, ed., *Evangelical Dictionary of Theology.* Grand Rapids: Baker, 1984. Pp. 100-102.

** A. H. Strong. *Systematic Theology.* Valley Forge, Pa.: Judson, 1907. Pp. 728-71.

* Henry C. Thiessen. *Lectures in Systematic Theology,* revised by Vernon D. Doerksen. Grand Rapids: Eerdmans, 1979. Pp. 231-35.

** John F. Walvoord. *Jesus Christ Our Lord.* Chicago: Moody, 1969. Pp. 157-63.

* Merrill F. Unger. *Unger's Bible Dictionary.* Chicago: Moody, 1961. Pp. 106-8.

CORRECT MEANING OF THE ATONEMENT

* Walter A. Elwell, ed. *Evangelical Dictionary of Theology.* Grand Rapids: Baker, 1984.

** Millard J. Erickson. *Christian Theology,* 3 vols. Grand Rapids: Baker, 1984. 2:802-19.

* Charles M. Horne. *Salvation.* Chicago: Moody, 1971. Pp. 33-41, 70-74.

* Lawrence O. Richards. *Expository Dictionary of Bible Words.* Grand Rapids: Zondervan, 1985.

** Leon Morris. *The Atonement: Its Meaning and Significance.* Downers Grove, Ill.: InterVarsity, 1983.

** _____. *The Apostolic Preaching of the Cross*, 3rd ed. Grand Rapids: Eerdmans, 1965. This work is invaluable in the study of this subject.

** Wm. G. T. Shedd. *Dogmatic Theology*, 3 vols. Reprint. Nashville: Nelson, 1980. 2:378-552.

* Merrill F. Unger. *The New Unger's Bible Dictionary.* Chicago: Moody, 1988.

EXTENT OF THE ATONEMENT

Limited atonement.

* Walter A. Elwell. "Atonement, Extent of." In *Evangelical Dictionary of Theology.* Grand Rapids: Baker, 1984. Pp. 98-99. He discusses both points of view.

** R. B. Kuiper. *For Whom Did Christ Die?* Grand Rapids: Baker, 1959.

* Edwin H. Palmer. *The Five Points of Calvinism.* Grand Rapids: Guardian, 1972. Pp. 41-55.

** Robert A. Peterson. *Calvin's Doctrine of the Atonement.* Phillipsburg, N.J.: Presbyterian & Reformed, 1983.

** Benjamin B. Warfield. *The Plan of Salvation*, rev. ed. Grand Rapids: Eerdmans, 1977.

Unlimited atonement.

** Lewis Sperry Chafer. *Systematic Theology*, 8 vols. Dallas: Dallas Seminary, 1947. 3:183-205.

** Robert P. Lightner. *The Death Christ Died.* Des Plaines, Ill.: Regular Baptist, 1967.

** A. H. Strong. *Systematic Theology.* Valley Forge, Pa.: Judson, 1907. Pp. 771-73.

* John F. Walvoord. *Jesus Christ Our Lord.* Chicago: Moody, 1969. Pp. 186-88.

PROCESS OF SALVATION

** Louis Berkhof. *Systematic Theology.* Grand Rapids: Eerdmans, 1941. Pp. 109-25.

* Lewis Sperry Chafer. *Major Bible Themes*, edited by John F. Walvoord. Grand Rapids: Zondervan, 1974. Pp. 230-35.

** Loraine Boettner. *The Reformed Doctrine of Predestination.* Philadelphia: Presbyterian & Reformed, 1966.

* Gordon H. Clark. *Biblical Predestination.* Phillipsburg, N.J.: Presbyterian & Reformed, 1969.

* Walter A. Elwell, ed. *Evangelical Dictionary of Theology.* Grand Rapids: Baker, 1984. See the articles entitled "Election," "Predestination," and "Adoption."

** Millard J. Erickson. *Christian Theology*, 3 vols. Grand Rapids: Baker, 1984. 2:825-41.

** J. Oliver Buswell, Jr. *A Systematic Theology of the Christian Religion*, 2 vols. Grand Rapids: Zondervan, 1962. 2:133-56.

* Charles C. Ryrie. *A Survey of Bible Doctrine.* Chicago: Moody, 1972. Pp. 115-18, 129-30.

* Henry C. Thiessen. *Lectures in Systematic Theology*, revised by Vernon D. Doerksen. Grand Rapids: Eerdmans, 1977. Pp. 257-63, 281-82.

** Louis Berkhof. *Systematic Theology.* Grand Rapids: Eerdmans, 1941. Pp. 527-44.

** J. Oliver Buswell, Jr. *A Systematic Theology of the Christian Religion*, 2 vols. Grand Rapids: Zondervan, 1962. 2:196-211.

* Lewis Sperry Chafer. *Major Bible Themes*, edited by John F. Walvoord. Grand Rapids: Zondervan, 1974. Pp. 202-11.

** ————. *Systematic Theology*, 8 vols. Dallas: Dallas Seminary, 1947. 7:274-84.

* Lawrence O. Richards. *Expository Dictionary of Bible Words*. Grand Rapids: Zondervan, 1985. Pp. 542-43.

* Henry C. Thiessen. *Lectures in Systematic Theology*, revised by Vernon D. Doerksen. Grand Rapids: Eerdmans, 1977. Pp. 283-89.

THE GRACE OF GOD

** Louis Berkhof. *Systematic Theology*. Grand Rapids: Eerdmans, 1941. Pp. 454-64.

* ————. *Summary of Christian Doctrine*. Grand Rapids: Eerdmans, 1938. Pp. 125-26.

* P. E. Hughes. "Grace." In Walter A. Elwell, ed., *Evangelical Dictionary of Theology*. Grand Rapids: Baker, 1984. P. 480.

* Charles C. Ryrie. *The Holy Spirit*. Chicago: Moody, 1965. Pp. 61-63.

** John F. Walvoord. *The Holy Spirit*. Grand Rapids: Zondervan, 1958. Pp. 119-27.

REGENERATION

** Louis Berkhof. *Systematic Theology.* Grand Rapids: Eerdmans, 1941. Pp. 465-79.

* Sinclair B. Ferguson. *Know Your Christian Life*. Downers Grove, Ill.: InterVarsity, 1981. Pp. 42-54.

* Charles M. Horne. *Salvation*. Chicago: Moody, 1971. Pp. 50-55.

* Edwin H. Palmer. *The Holy Spirit*, rev. ed. Philadelphia: Presbyterian & Reformed, 1958. Pp. 77-86.

* J. Dwight Pentecost. *The Divine Comforter.* Chicago: Moody, 1963. Pp. 120-35.

* Charles C. Ryrie. *The Holy Spirit*. Chicago: Moody, 1965. Pp. 64-66.

** John F. Walvoord. *The Holy Spirit.* Grand Rapids: Zondervan, 1958. Pp. 128-37.

ETERNAL SECURITY

** Louis Berkhof. *Systematic Theology*. Grand Rapids: Eerdmans, 1941. Pp. 545-49.

** G. C. Berkouwer. *Studies in Dogmatics, Faith and Perseverance*. Grand Rapids: Eerdmans, 1958.

** Lewis Sperry Chafer. *Major Bible Themes*, edited by John F. Walvoord. Grand Rapids: Zondervan, 1974. Pp. 220-29.

* ————. *Salvation*. Grand Rapids: Zondervan, 1945. Pp. 70-98.

* ————. *Systematic Theology*, 8 vols. Dallas: Dallas Seminary, 1947. 3:313-39.

** Robert G. Gromacki. *Salvation Is Forever.* Chicago: Moody, 1973.

* Charles M. Horne. *Salvation*. Chicago: Moody, 1971. Pp. 88-100.

** John Murray. *Redemption: Accomplished and Applied*. Grand Rapids: Eerdmans, 1955.

* Henry C. Thiessen. *Lectures in Systematic Theology.* Revised by Vernon D. Doerksen. Grand Rapids: Eerdmans, 1977. Pp. 290-95.

* Merrill F. Unger. *Unger's Bible Dictionary.* Chicago: Moody, 1961. Pp. 990-91.

25

ECCLESIOLOGY: DOCTRINE OF THE CHURCH

DEFINITION

MEANING OF THE CHURCH

The English word *church* is related to the Scottish word *kirk* and the German designation *kirche*, and all of these terms are derived from the Greek word *kuriakon*, the neuter adjective of *kurios* ("Lord"), meaning "belonging to the Lord."[1] The English word *church* also translates the Greek word *ekklesia*, which is derived from *ek*, meaning "out of," and *kaleo*, which means "to call," hence, the church is "a called out group." *Ekklesia* appears 114 times in the New Testament, 3 times in the gospels, and 111 times in the epistles. In the gospels it appears only in Matthew 16:18 and 18:17 (twice). The latter two occurrences are probably used in a nontechnical sense of a Jewish congregation. Thus in a technical sense, *ekklesia* is used only once in the gospels, and in that passage it is a prophetic reference to the church. This helps establish the fact that the church began after the ascension as recorded in the book of Acts and is a particularly Pauline doctrine.

The word *ekklesia*, however, does not indicate the nature of the called out group; it can be used in a technical sense of the New Testament church, or it can be used in a nontechnical sense of any kind of group. For example, in Acts 7:38 it refers to the congregation of the people of Israel as the *ekklesia* (it is translated "congregation"). In Acts 19:32 it refers to the mob at Ephesus that was angry at Paul (here it is translated "assembly"). Most often, however, the word is used in a technical sense to designate the New Testament church, a group of called-out believers in Jesus Christ.

ASPECTS OF THE CHURCH

The local church. The most common use of the word *church* in the New Testament is to designate a group of believers that is identified as a local assembly or congregation. Thus there was a church in Jerusalem (Acts 8:1; 11:22), in Asia Minor (Acts 16:5), in Rome (Rom. 16:5), in Corinth (1 Cor. 1:2; 2 Cor. 1:1), in Galatia (Gal. 1:2), in Thessalonica (1 Thess. 1:1), and in the home of Philemon (Philem. 2).

These early believers did not have special buildings in which to meet; instead, they met in homes (Rom. 16:5; Philem. 2). The early believers came together for worship (1 Cor. 11:18), fellowship (Acts 2:45-46; 4:31), instruction (Acts 2:42; 11:26; 1 Cor. 4:17), and for ministry such as sending out missionaries (Acts 13:2; 15:3). The result was that people were continually being saved (Acts 2:47).

The universal church. While the local church views the church as a group of believers gathered together in a particular locality, the universal church views "all those who, in this age, have been born of the Spirit of God and have by that same Spirit been baptized into the Body of Christ (1 Cor. 12:13; 1 Pet. 1:3, 22-25)."[2] It was this corporate group of believers that Christ promised to build (Matt. 16:18); it was this Body for whom Christ died (Eph. 5:25), and He is the head over it, giving it direction (Eph. 1:22-23; Col. 1:18). In Ephesians 1:23 the church is referred to as "His body." This cannot refer to a local assembly but must depict instead the universal body of believers (cf. Col. 1:18). A particular emphasis of the universal church is its unity, whether Jews or Gentiles, all together compose one body, in a unity produced by the Holy Spirit (Gal. 3:28; Eph. 4:4).

The universal church is sometimes referred to as the invisible church and the local church as the visible church[3] (although some deny this equation). Men like Augustine, Luther, and Calvin all taught this distinction, which upheld the invisible church as emphasizing the perfect, true, spiritual nature of the church, whereas the visible church recognized the local assembly of believers with its imperfections and even unbelievers having membership in a local church. The term *invisible* is also used to indicate that its exact membership cannot be known. In reality, the members are entirely visible![4]

FORMATION OF THE CHURCH

When did the church begin? Although some would suggest the church existed in the Old Testament,[5] an examination of the New Testament indicates the church is a peculiar New Testament entity that had not previously existed. In Matthew 16:18 Jesus declared, "I will build my church," indicating the building of the church was future. This point is important. It emphasizes that the church was not yet in existence when Jesus spoke these words. He was making a prediction concerning His future building of the church.

First Corinthians 12:13 identifies the manner in which the church is being built—it is the work of the Holy Spirit in baptizing believers into the one Body of Christ. At the moment of regeneration, the Holy Spirit places believers into union with Christ. Ephesians 1:22-23 identifies the church as the Body of Christ, stressing this union with Christ that all believers are brought into at the moment of conversion.

In Acts 1:5 Jesus stated, "You shall be baptized with the Holy Spirit not many days from now." This indicates the work of the Holy Spirit in placing believers into union with Christ had not yet begun—but it was anticipated imminently. The context clarifies the event and indicates it began at Pentecost with the descent of the Holy Spirit (Acts 2:1-4). When Peter reported what had happened in Cornelius's house in Caesarea he indicated to the Jews in Jerusalem that the Holy Spirit fell on the Gentiles just as He had on the Jews "at the beginning" (Acts 11:15). This latter phrase identifies the beginning point of the baptizing work of the Holy Spirit and thus identifies the beginning of the formation of the New Testament church. The church began at Pentecost (Acts 2).

FIGURES OF THE CHURCH

When Jesus stated, "I will build my church" (Matt. 16:18), He was not referring to the local church, but to the universal church, the aggregate number of believers in the present age. A number of figures are used in Scripture to describe or illustrate the church as one living organism.

Body. A metaphor illustrating the unity and universality of the church is the word *body.* As the head has authority over the physical body and gives direction to it, so Christ is the head of the church, having authority over it and giving it direction (Eph. 1:22-23; Col. 1:18). The illustration of the body also emphasizes the unity of all believers in the church age because the church reconciles Jews and Gentiles into one body. There is no distinction; they are one in Christ (1 Cor. 12:13; Eph. 2:16; 4:4). Moreover, Christ nourishes the church by giving gifted leaders to the church that it might grow to maturity and be built up as one body in Christ (Eph. 4:12, 16; Col. 2:19). The participation in the elements of the Lord's Supper illustrates the oneness of the church as Christ's Body (1 Cor. 10:16-17).

Bride. The picture of the church as the bride of Christ is seen in Ephesians 5:23 where an analogy is drawn that compares the husband and wife relationship in marriage to Christ and His bride the church. The illustration is apt because it reveals the magnitude of Christ's love for the church (Eph. 5:2, 25). A second emphasis of the illustration is the exalted position of the bride.[6] As in the Oriental wedding custom, at the engagement (betrothal) the bride receives the promise of future blessing with her husband. Similarly, the church today is an espoused bride, awaiting her husband's return from glory. The second stage of the Oriental marriage was the wedding itself, when the husband came to take the bride to be with him. In an analogous figure, the church awaits the return of Christ, when she will be espoused to her husband (John 14:1-3; 1 Thess. 4:16-17). In Oriental weddings, the wedding feast followed; similarly the church, as Christ's bride, awaits the husband's return (Rev. 19:7-9) and the glory of the millennial kingdom to follow.

Building. Paul has emphasized that Jews and Gentiles alike are one in Christ because God abolished the wall that separated Jew and Gentile (Eph. 2:11-18). Now Paul describes the oneness of the church under the figure of a building. The church, a union of Jews and Gentiles, is built upon the "foundation of the apostles and prophets" (Eph. 2:20). "The apostles" are collectively one of the foundational gifts, designed to equip the believers (Eph. 4:12) and bring the church to maturity (Eph. 4:13).

In the figure of the building, Jesus Christ is the cornerstone (Eph. 2:20; cf. 1 Cor. 3:11), which may refer to the "primary foundationstone at the angle of the structure by which the architect fixes a standard for the bearings of the walls and cross-walls throughout."[7] In Christ the whole building, the church, is being "fitted together" (Gk. *sunarmologoumene*;[8] Eph. 2:21), emphasizing Christ's work of constructing His church. As a building "grows" when under construction, so the church, as a living organism, is growing as new believers are added to the "building" (cf. 1 Pet. 2:5).

Priesthood. In 1 Peter 2:5 the apostle combines the figures of a building and a priesthood, stating, "You also, as living stones, are being built up as a spiritual house for a holy priesthood." The statement is reminiscent of Exodus 19:5-6 where God declared that Israel was "a kingdom of priests."[9] In the nation Israel, however, only those of the tribe of Levi could serve as priests, whereas in the church, every believer is a priest. Peter indicates all believers are priests for the purpose of offering spiritual sacrifices instead animal sacrifices.

The uniqueness of the New Testament priesthood is further seen in 1 Peter 2:9 where Peter refers to a "royal priesthood." Church age believers are both kings and priests (cf. Rev. 1:6). In the Old Testament it was impossible to combine both offices for one could only be either of the Levitical line or the kingly line, the line of Judah. The entire church functions as a priesthood, whereas in Israel only the Levitical line had that privilege. All church age believers have access to God through Christ, the church's High Priest; in Israel individual believers could approach God only through the Levitical priests. All church age believers may approach God boldly at any time (Heb. 4:14-16), whereas Israelites could approach God only during the particular offerings (Lev. 1-7).[10] These contrasts indicate that while both Israel and the church are called a priesthood, Israel and the church are distinct entities.

Flock. A beautiful, tender image depicting the relationship of believers to the Lord is found in John 10:16 where the church is called a flock (cf. Acts 20:28; 1 Pet. 5:3). Israel had a relationship to the Lord as sheep to a shepherd (Psalm 23) and was called a flock (Ps. 80:1; Jer. 13:17), but in the Old Testament that figure was restricted to Israel. The uniqueness about the church being a flock and Christ the Shepherd is that this flock is composed of both Jews and Gentiles. Jesus declared, "I have other sheep [Gentiles], which are not of this fold [Jews]; I must bring them also, and they shall hear My voice; and they shall become one flock [the church composed of Jews and Gentiles] with one Shepherd" (John 10:16).

The image emphasizes that members of the church as the sheep of Christ belong to Him. Jesus emphasizes that the flock is "My sheep" (John 10:26, 27) and that they are secure in His hand. Moreover, the sheep respond to the Shepherd's voice—there is intimacy for the Shepherd knows His sheep individually, and they recognize His voice and respond to Him.

Branches. In John 15 Jesus describes the close relationship church age believers enjoy with Him as being one of branches related to a vine. Jesus is the true vine (John 15:1), while the Father is the farmer who tills the land in order that the branches may bear fruit (John 15:1). Church age believers are the branches that draw their life from the vine because they are "in Him" (John 15:4, 5). The branches receive their life-giving nourishment in their attachment to the vine; as they remain in the vine, they are able to grow and bear fruit.

This relationship describes both union and communion of church age believers with Christ.[11] Christ's exhortation to the church is to "abide in me." "Abide" (Gk. *meno*) means essentially "to remain," "stay," or "live." In this context it means to *remain* or *continue* in the realm in which one finds himself.[12] The exhortation to abide in Christ is an exhortation to continue believing in Him (cf. 1 John 2:22, 24, 28).[13]

The purpose of the branches abiding in the vine is to produce fruit. Every branch that does not bear fruit he "lifts up"[14] that it may bear fruit. The ones who continue with Christ will bear fruit (John 15:5). To enhance the fruit-bearing process the branches are pruned that they may bear more fruit (John 15:2). "The figure of the vine thus demonstrates the vital relationship between the members of the church and Christ."[15]

DISTINCTIVES OF THE CHURCH

In relation to Israel. The church is a separate entity from Israel and remains distinct from Israel. The evidence for this is as follows. Israel always means the physical descendants of Jacob. A simple concordance study of the usage of the term *Israel* will demonstrate this. In all sixty-six occurrences in the New Testament the term refers to Jews.[16] The term *new Israel* as an identification for the church is not accurate; Israel always means Jewish people.

Paul retains a distinction between Israel and the church. In warning believers not to offend others, he mentions Jews, Greeks (Gentiles), and the church (1 Cor. 10:32). After the church was established, Israel continued to be recognized as a people distinct from Gentiles and from the church (Acts 3:12; 4:8, 10; 5:21, 31, 35; 21:19).[17]

In relation to the kingdom. Some Christians believe that the church is synonymous with the kingdom and that the church inaugurates the kingdom. This is a misunderstanding of the word *kingdom*, which means "royal dominion; a designation both of the power (Ezra 4:5) and the form of government, and especially in later writers, of the territory and the rule, the kingship and the kingdom."[18] Hence, the basic meaning of kingdom involves three things: a ruler, a people who are ruled, and a territory over which they are ruled.

There are two basic forms of the kingdom.[19] (1) The universal kingdom. This form of the kingdom exists throughout all times (Lam. 5:19), includes all in time and space (Pss. 103:19; 139:7-10), and involves the divine control of history (Isa. 44:26–45:4). The universal kingdom is God's sovereign rule from eternity to eternity.

(2) The mediatorial kingdom. This is "(a) the rule of God through a divinely chosen representative who not only speaks and acts for God but also represents the people before God; (b) a rule which has especial reference to the earth; and (c) having as its mediatorial ruler one who is always a member of the human race."[20] Thus, God dispensed His will on earth through divinely appointed mediators: Adam, Noah, Abraham, Moses, and others. But these mediators all anticipated the final mediator, Messiah, who would come to rule on earth at the end of the age. Gabriel promised Mary concerning her Son: "The Lord God will give Him the throne of His father David; and He will reign over the house of Jacob forever; and His kingdom will have no end" (Luke 1:32-33). This is the promised future kingdom (2 Sam. 7:12-16) over which Messiah will rule. The church is not the kingdom. The church exists in this present age, whereas the kingdom, which is future, will be inaugurated at the Second Coming of Christ.

There are several distinctions between the church and the kingdom. The terms *church* and *kingdom* are never used interchangeably in Scripture.[21] Of the 114 occurrences of the word *church* (Gk. *ekklesia*), it is never equated with the kingdom.[22] Jesus came to offer the kingdom to the Jewish nation, hence, the proclamation, "the kingdom of heaven is at hand" (Matt. 4:17). When the kingdom was rejected, it was held in abeyance, to be introduced at His Second Advent (Matt. 13). Jesus announced He would build His church after the offer of the kingdom was rejected (Matt. 16:18).

FUNCTIONS OF THE LOCAL CHURCH

What constitutes a local church? When is it actually a church? Does a group of people meeting together to listen to tapes by Christian leaders constitute a church? Does a group gathering to hear different Bible conference speakers each week constitute a church?

Several important features identify a biblical, New Testament local church.

Worship.[23] There are several New Testament Greek words designating worship. *Proskuneo*, which means "to bow down" or "prostrate," is used many times in the gospels, but in the epistles only in 1 Corinthians 14:24-25 in connection with an unbeliever. The physical act of bowing should reflect the inner attitude of the heart—submission to God. *Latreuo* has a basic meaning of "priestly service," hence, Paul served God through preaching (Rom. 1:9). Rather than bringing a dead animal in worship, the New Testament believer offers God a living body, set apart to God in an act of worship (Rom. 12:1). *Sebomai* means "to reverence or fear God" (1 Tim. 2:10; 5:4; 2 Pet. 1:3; 3:11).

True worship must be of a spiritual nature or realm, and it must be in accordance with truth as God has revealed it (John 4:24). It involves the decisive presentation of the believer's entire being to God (Rom. 12:1-2).

Whereas Old Testament believers met on the Sabbath for worship, the book of Acts traces the transition wherein Christians began to worship on Sunday, the first day of the week, in commemoration of Christ's resurrection (John 20:1, 19, 26). They observed the ordinance of the Lord's Supper on the first day of the week (Acts 20:7) and took up offerings on the first day of the week (1 Cor. 16:2). Hymn singing was also a part of corporate worship in the early church (1 Cor. 14:26; Eph. 5:19; Col. 3:16).

Instruction. Instruction was a vital element in the life of the early church. God gave the Scriptures for the purpose of teaching people and bringing them to maturity (2 Tim. 3:16-17). Teaching is the antidote to false doctrine (1 Tim. 1:3); it produces love among believers (1 Tim. 1:5); it provides spiritual nourishment (1 Tim. 4:6); godliness (1 Tim. 4:6-16); submission (1 Tim. 5:17; 6:2); and a proper focus on life (1 Tim. 6:17). Paul instructed Timothy to teach others in order to reproduce himself (2 Tim. 2:2; cf. 1 Tim. 4:14, 16; 6:20).

At the very outset, the church devoted itself to the apostles' teaching (Acts 2:42) and then proceeded to fill the city with Christian doctrine (Acts 5:28). Paul commended the church at Rome for adhering to the teachings it had received. During his missionary journeys Paul taught the churches

(Acts 18:11), which teaching was done both publicly and in the homes (Acts 20:20). In fact, the book of Acts concludes with Paul teaching those that came to him at Rome (Acts 28:31). The importance of teaching as a major function of the church can hardly be overstated.

Fellowship. The word *fellowship* (Gk. *koinonia*) means "sharing" and emphasizes the unity and oneness of the church. Fellowship takes place in a variety of ways. The early church met together for the fellowship of breaking bread and prayer (Acts 2:42). The breaking of bread consisted of eating a fellowship meal, called the love feast, which was followed by the Lord's Supper. The early church placed great emphasis on the fellowship of prayer (cf. Acts 4:24-31; 12:5, 12; Phil. 1:3-4). Fellowship may also involve material means in helping spread the gospel (Rom. 15:26; 2 Cor. 9:13; Phil. 1:5) or sharing rejection through identification with Christ (Phil 3:10).

Fellowship also emphasizes the fact that believers belong together. Paul stresses this through his use of "one another." Because of their fellowship in Christ, Paul instructs that believers are to accept one another (Rom. 15:7), love one another (Eph. 4:2, 15, 16; 5:2), refrain from judging one another (Rom. 14:3, 13), build up one another (Rom. 14:19), be unified (Rom. 15:5), and admonish one another (Rom. 15:14). This relationship with one another is important in keeping the unity of the faith for which Christ prayed (John 17) and Paul pleaded (Phil. 2:1-4).

Ministry. The local church is also involved in ministry (see Purpose of the Church for additional discussion). This involves evangelism toward unbelievers in the world (Acts 8:4; 11:19, 20; 16:31; 17:12) and a variety of ministries toward believers in the church fellowship. It involves the exercise of spiritual gifts in ministering to one another (Rom. 12:3-8; 1 Cor. 12; Eph. 4:8-13) and, by that token, serving others (Rom. 12:7), giving to the needs of others (Rom. 12:8), showing mercy (Rom. 12:8), and helping others (1 Cor. 12:28). Ministry also involves the exercise of church discipline. It is necessary to exercise church discipline (exclusion from fellowship) because of immorality (1 Cor. 5:1-13) and false doctrine (2 Thess. 3:14; 2 John 10). Galatians 6:1-2 provides an important principle in the exercise of church discipline. Ministry must also involve the care for the needy in the church, particularly widows (James 1:27). First Timothy 5:1-8 provides details on the importance of the care for widows.

Organization. Once a church was formed, elders and deacons were appointed to oversee the ministry of the church (Acts 14:23; Titus 1:5). (See "Leaders of the Church" for expanded discussion.)

Ordinances. The church practiced the ordinances of baptism and the Lord's Supper (Acts 2:41; 1 Cor. 11:23-24). (See "Ordinances of the Church" for further discussion.)

LEADERS OF THE CHURCH

Hebrews 13:17 identifies leaders in the local church that care for the spiritual welfare of the people; believers are to be in submission to those in authority over them. Several offices denoting the leaders are mentioned in Scripture.

ELDERS

Designations. There are two basic terms that identify the office of elder.

(1) Presbyters. The first term is *elder* (Gk. *presbuteros*), which identifies someone who is older as a Christian. It may be used in a literal sense for an older man (1 Tim. 5:1) or an older woman (1 Tim. 5:2). It may also be used in a figurative sense for leaders, such as members of the Sanhedrin (Acts 4:5) or church leaders (Acts 14:23; 15:2, 4, 6).

Presbuteros also stresses the dignity and maturity of the office. Elders have authority to distribute money (Acts 11:30); they have authority to make decisions concerning what constitutes orthodox doctrine (Acts 15:2, 4, 6, 22; 16:2); they receive reports about missionary work (Acts 20:17; 21:18); they are to be respected (1 Tim. 5:17), yet they are not to be dictators (1 Pet. 5:1-3); they are to visit the sick and pray for them, offering counsel and encouragement[24] (James 5:14).

(2) Overseers. The second term related to the office of elder is *overseer* ("bishop" in KJV; Gk. *episkopos*). This term means "to watch over" like a shepherd. It stresses the work or function of the elder. It is his duty to nurture and feed the flock of God entrusted to him (cf. Acts 20:28; 1 Tim. 3:2; Tit. 1:7). A comparison of Acts 20:17, 28 and Titus 1:5, 7 reveals that *elder* and *overseer* are used interchangeably, denoting the same office. The important distinction is that *presbuteros* stresses the dignity of the office while *episkopos* emphasizes the work.

Qualifications. The qualifications of elders are set forth in 1 Timothy 3:1-7 and Titus 1:5-9. Elders are to be typified by the following fifteen characteristics. Above reproach: he is one who "can't be censored"; there is nothing in his life for which to accuse him. Husband of one wife: it does not mean "one at a time" (polygamy was unknown among Greeks and Romans); he has not been divorced and remarried.[25] Temperate: he is sober in judgment. Prudent: he is discreet, sound-minded. Respectable: he is well-balanced, not abrasive. Hospitable: he loves and hosts strangers. Able to teach: he discerns and communicates sound doctrine. Not addicted to wine: he does not linger at the table drinking wine. Not pugnacious: he is not a fighter. Gentle: he is reasonable. Uncontentious: he avoids fighting. No lover of money: he is not greedy or irresponsible concerning money. Managing his own household: he attends to his own family so that they are believers and are orderly. Not a new convert: he is not a neophyte. Good reputation with unbelievers: he is respected in the community at large.

Duties. The duties of the elder involve shepherding the flock (Acts 20:28), teaching (1 Tim. 3:2), ruling or general leadership (1 Tim. 5:17), and guarding against error (Tit. 1:9).

Number. A plurality of elders is mentioned frequently (Acts 14:23; Phil. 1:1; Tit. 1:5).

DEACONS

Designation. The word *deacon* (Gk. *diakonos*) is the common word that means "minister" or "servant" and is used many times in the New Testament in a nontechnical sense (Matt. 20:26; Mark 9:35).

Office. Whereas it is not clearly stated, it appears that the origin of the office began in Acts 6:1-6 where seven men were selected to care for the material needs of widows in the congregation. That allowed the apostles to devote their time to prayer and ministry of the Word. This indicates the function of deacons is to be subordinate and auxiliary to the elders; while the elders teach the congregation, the deacons care for the material needs of the congregation. The term "double-tongued" suggests the deacons have house to house contact (cf. 1 Tim. 3:8).

Qualifications. The qualifications of deacons are given in 1 Timothy 3:8-13. Deacons are to be typified by the following eight characteristics. Men of dignity: they are serious, worthy of the respect of others. Not double tongued: they do not spread conflicting stories in the congregation. Not addicted to much wine: they show moderation in the use of food and drink. Not fond of sordid (or dishonest) gain: they are not greedy for money and do not use their position for financial gain. Holding to the mystery of the faith: they practice what they proclaim. Tested: they have been observed and found to be approved. One wife: they have not been divorced and remarried. Good managers of their households: they are qualified to manage church affairs because they can manage their own home affairs.

DEACONESSES

A debatable question is the office of deaconess. There are two passages under consideration for the office. Romans 16:1 refers to Phoebe as a "servant" (Gk. *diakonon*) of the church. *Diakonon* could be translated deaconess. The question is whether the term is used in a technical sense of a church office or in a nontechnical sense of the Christian ideal of servanthood. Although it is difficult to give a firm answer to the question, it appears Paul is using the term in a nontechnical sense, consistent with his informal greetings at the end of the letter (cf. 1 Cor. 16:15). Paul uses the term in a nontechnical way in other passages (Eph. 3:7; Col. 1:25; 1 Tim. 4:6).

A second passage is 1 Timothy 3:11, which mentions "women" (Gk. *gunaikas*). The question is whether *women* refers to the deacons' wives or whether it refers to a separate office of deaconess. The context would suggest an unnatural break if this refers to deaconesses; deacons would then be referred to in verses 8-10 and 12-13, which appears somewhat awkward. Homer A. Kent, Jr., on the other hand, argues strongly for 3:11 referring to the office of deaconess.[26] First Timothy 5:9-16 refers to the ministry of women in the church. It does not state, however, if this is the ministry of deaconesses.

GOVERNMENT OF THE CHURCH

The church as the Body of Christ is a living organism, analogous to the human body with the head giving it direction, even as Christ is the Head of the church, giving it direction. Nonetheless, there is also organization that governs the functioning of the church. Historically, three different types of church government have emerged.

TYPES OF CHURCH GOVERNMENT

Episcopal. The name *episcopal* comes from the Greek word *episkopos*, meaning "overseer" (the word is also translated "bishop" in the KJV), and identifies churches governed by the authority of bishops. Different denominations are identified by episcopal government, the simplest form being the Methodist church. More complex structure is found in the Episcopal (Anglican) church. The most complex episcopal structure is found in the Roman Catholic church, with the ultimate authority vested in the bishop of Rome, the pope.[27] The Lutheran church also follows the episcopal form.

In the episcopal form of church government the authority rests with the bishops who oversee not one church, but a group of churches. Inherent in the office of bishop is the power to ordain ministers or priests. Roman Catholics suggest this authority is derived through apostolic succession from the original apostles. They claim this authority on the basis of Matthew 16:18-19. Others, such as the Methodists, do not acknowledge authority through apostolic succession.

This form of government arose in the second century, but adherents would claim biblical support from the position of James in the church of Jerusalem, as well as the position and authority of Timothy and Titus.

Presbyterian. The name *presbyterian* comes from the Greek word *presbuteros*, meaning "elder," and suggests the dignity, maturity, and age of the church leaders. Presbyterian (sometimes termed *federal*) designates a church government that is governed by elders as in the Presbyterian and Reformed churches. In contrast to the congregational form of government, the presbyterian form emphasizes representative rule by the elders who are appointed or elected by the people. The session, which is made up of elected ruling elders (the teaching elder presiding over it), governs the local church. Above the session is the presbytery, including all ordained ministers or teaching elders as well as one ruling elder from each local congregation in a district.[28] "Above the presbytery is the synod, and over the synod is the general assembly, the highest court. Both of these bodies are also equally divided between ministers and laymen or ruling elders."[29] The pastor serves as one of the elders.

The biblical support for this is the frequent mention of elders in the New Testament: there were elders in Jerusalem (Acts 11:30; 15:2, 4) and in Ephesus (Acts 20:17); elders were appointed in every church (Acts 14:23; Titus. 1:5); elders were responsible to feed the flock (1 Pet. 5:1, 2); there were also elders who ruled (1 Tim. 5:17).

Congregational. In congregational church government the authority rests not with a representative individual but with the entire local congregation. Two things are stressed in a congregational governed church: autonomy and democracy.[30] A congregational church is autonomous in that no authority outside of the local church has any power over the local church. In addition, congregational churches are democratic in their government; all the members of the local congregation make the decisions that guide and govern the church. This is particularly argued from the standpoint of the priesthood of all believers. Baptists, Evangelical Free, Congregational, some Lutherans, and some independent churches follow the congregational form of church government.

The biblical support for congregational church government is that the congregation was involved in electing the deacons (Acts 6:3-5) and elders (Acts 14:23)[31]; the entire church sent out Barnabas (Acts 11:22) and Titus (2 Cor. 8:19) and received Paul and Barnabas (Acts 14:27; 15:4); the entire church was involved in the decisions concerning circumcision (Acts 15:25); discipline was carried out by the entire church (1 Cor. 5:12; 2 Cor. 2:6-7; 2 Thess. 3:14); all believers are responsible for correct doctrine by testing the spirits (1 John 4:1), which they are able to do since they have the anointing (1 John 2:20).

EVALUATION OF CHURCH GOVERNMENT

In evaluating the three forms of church government, the *episcopal* form is based partly on the authority of the apostles, which really does not have a counterpart in the New Testament church beyond the apostolic era. Christ had given a unique authority to the Twelve (Luke 9:1) that cannot be claimed by any person or group, nor is there a biblical basis for any form of apostolic succession. The authority Jesus gave to Peter (Matt. 16:18-19) was given to all the apostles (Matt. 18:18; John 20:23) but to no successive group. The episcopal form of church government can be seen in the second century but not in the first.

FORMS OF CHURCH GOVERNMENT

Form	Adherents	Authority	Basis
Episcopal	Roman Catholic Orthodox Episcopal Lutheran Methodist	Bishops	Acts 6:6; 14:23 Galatians 1:19; 2:9
Presbyterian	Presbyterian Reformed	Elders	Acts 20:17 1 Tim. 5:17 Titus 1:5
Congregational	Congregational Baptist Mennonite Evangelical Free	Congregation	Acts 15:12, 22-25 Colossians 1:18 1 Peter 2:9

The *presbyterian* form of church government has strong support for its view of the plurality of the elders; there are many New Testament examples. The New Testament, however, reveals no organization beyond the local church.

The *congregational* form of church government finds biblical support for all the people being involved in the decision-making of the church. It can safely be said that elements of both the presbyterian and congregational forms of church government find support in Scripture.

ORDINANCES OF THE CHURCH

Protestants have historically recognized two ordinances, baptism and the Lord's Supper, whereas Roman Catholics have held to seven sacraments: baptism, the eucharist (Lord's Supper), confirmation, penance, extreme unction, holy orders, and marriage. There is a difference of opinion regarding terminology. Catholics (and some Protestants) prefer the term *sacrament*, which comes from the Latin *sacramentum*, meaning "a thing set apart as sacred." The term *sacramentum* in the Latin Vulgate was also used to translate the Greek word *musterion* (Eph. 5:32) and "came to be used for anything that had a secret or mysterious significance. Augustine called it 'the visible form of an invisible grace.' "[32] Sacrament was later defined as an "outward and visible sign of an inward and spiritual grace."[33] It is for this reason that many Protestants have preferred the term *ordinance*, which does not have the connotation of conveying grace. An ordinance might simply be defined as "an outward rite prescribed by Christ to be performed by His church."[34]

LORD'S SUPPER

Christ instituted the Lord's Supper on the eve of His crucifixion, commanding that His followers continue to observe it until His return (Matt. 26:26-29; Mark 14:22-25; Luke 22:14-23). This was a new covenant or testament in contrast with the old Mosaic covenant. To enact the covenant, death was necessary because death provided forgiveness of sins. Paul also rehearsed the ordinance for the Corinthian church (1 Cor. 11:23-32). Of course, the issue at hand is, what is the meaning of the Lord's Supper? There have been four distinct views in Christendom concerning its meaning.

Transubstantiation. The Roman Catholic view concerning the Lord's Supper is called *transubstantiation*, meaning "a change of substance." The Roman Catholic church teaches that a miracle takes place at the eucharist (the Mass) in which the elements of the bread and wine are actually changed into the literal body and blood of Christ, although the sensory characteristics (which the Catholics call "accidents") of the elements—touch, taste, smell—may remain the same. The Creed of Pope Pius IV stated: "I profess that in the Mass is offered to God a true, proper, and propitiatory sacrifice for the living and the dead; . . . there is truly, really, and substantially, the body and blood, together with the soul and divinity, of our Lord Jesus Christ; and that there is a conversion of the whole substance of the bread into the body, and of the whole substance of the wine into the blood."[35] As the priest consecrates the elements, their substance is changed from bread and wine to the body, blood, soul, and divinity of Christ. Thus in Catholic teaching, the participant actually partakes of the body of Christ. The Catholic church claims that this is the teaching of John 6:32-58.

John O'Brien, a Roman Catholic, has stated, "The Mass with its colorful vestments and vivid ceremonies is a dramatic re-enactment in an unbloody manner of the sacrifice of Christ on Calvary."[36] A contemporary Roman Catholic theologian equates it with salvation, stating, "In his body and blood, then, Jesus himself is offered. He presents himself as a gift for salvation."[37]

There are several serious problems with this view. (1) It views the work of Christ as unfinished, the sacrifice of Christ continuing in the Mass. Yet Christ declared His work completed (John 19:30) as did also the writer of Hebrews (Heb. 10:10-14). (2) Christ's human body would have to be omnipresent if this teaching were true; however, Christ's human body is localized in heaven (Acts 7:56). (3) In instituting the Supper, Christ used a common figure of speech—the metaphor ("This is my body . . . my blood")—in referring to the bread and cup. He was physically present yet distinct from the elements when He referred to them as His body and blood. Similarly, in the John 6 passage, Jesus used a powerful metaphor ("eat my flesh . . . drink my blood") to vividly picture a saving faith-relationship to Himself. To insist that these expressions are literal language is to do violence to fundamental hermeneutical principles. (4) It was forbidden for Jews to drink blood (Lev. 17:10-16), yet this is what Jesus would be asking them to do if transubstantiation was what He intended.

Consubstantiation. The Lutheran view is referred to as *consubstantiation*, meaning Jesus' body and blood are actually present in the elements but the bread and wine remain such; they do not change into literal body and blood as taught in Roman Catholic doctrine. To emphasize the presence of Christ in the elements, Lutherans use the terms "in, with, and under" to express the actual presence of the body and blood of Christ. Martin Luther illustrated the point by stating that as heat penetrated an iron bar when placed in the fire, the bar nonetheless remained iron.[38]

Lutherans also differ from the Roman Catholic view in rejecting the notion of the perpetual sacrifice of Christ in the eucharist. Luther insisted, however, "that by partaking of the sacrament one experiences a real benefit—forgiveness of sin and confirmation of faith. This benefit is due, however, not to the elements in the sacrament, but to one's reception of the Word by faith."[39]

The problem with the Lutheran view of the eucharist is the failure to recognize Jesus' statement, "This is My body" as a figure of speech.

Reformed view. The Reformed view is also called the Calvinist view because its adherents are from the Reformed churches (and others) who follow Calvin's teaching on the subject. Adherents to this view reject the notion of the literal presence of Christ in any sense and in this are similar to adherents of the memorial view. This view, however, does emphasize the "present spiritual work of Christ." Calvin taught that Christ is "present and enjoyed in His entire person, both body and blood. He emphasizes the mystical communion of believers with the entire person of the Redeemer. . . . the body and blood of Christ, though absent and locally present only in heaven, communicate a life-giving influence to the believer."[40] Because of the mystical presence of Christ in the elements, grace is communicated to the participant in the elements; moreover, it is a grace that is similar to that received through the Word and in fact, it adds to the effectiveness of the Word.[41]

A problem with this view is that there is no explicit statement or inference from Scripture suggesting that grace is imparted to the participant.

Memorial view. The memorial view is also referred to as the Zwinglian view because the Swiss reformer Ulrich Zwingli (1484-1531) is considered a clear exponent of this view in contrast to other current views of his time. In contrast to the Calvinist view, Zwingli taught that there was no real presence of Christ but only a spiritual fellowship with Christ by those who partake in faith. Essential to the memorial view is the notion that the bread and cup are figurative only; they are a memorial to the death of Christ. While Zwingli acknowledged a spiritual presence of Christ for those who partake in faith, Anabaptists rejected the idea of Christ being present in the Lord's Supper any more than He would be present anywhere else. The memorial view emphasizes that the participants demonstrate faith in the death of Christ through this symbolic activity.

The memorial view has much to commend it in the Scriptures. An examination of the passages reveals the significance of the Lord's Supper. It is a memorial to His death (1 Cor. 11:24, 25): the recurring statement, "in remembrance of Me," makes this clear, the bread symbolizing His perfect body offered in sin-bearing sacrifice (1 Pet. 2:24) and the wine His blood shed for forgiveness of sins (Eph. 1:7). It is a proclamation of the death of Christ while waiting for His coming (1 Cor. 11:26): it involves a looking back to the historical event of the cross and an anticipating of His return in the future (Matt. 26:29). It is a communion of believers with each other (1 Cor. 10:17): they eat and drink the same symbolic elements, focusing on their common faith in Christ.

VIEWS ON THE LORD'S SUPPER

View	Christ and the Elements	Significance
Transubstantiation (Roman Catholic)	Bread and wine literally change to body and blood of Christ.	Recipient partakes of Christ, who is being sacrificed in the Mass to atone for sins.
Consubstantiation (Lutheran)	Bread and wine contain the body and blood of Christ but do not literally change. Christ is actually present "in, with, and under" the elements.	Recipient receives forgiveness of sins and confirmation of one's faith through partaking of the elements, but they must be received through faith.
Reformed (Presbyterian, Reformed)	Christ is not literally present in the elements but there is a spiritual presence of Christ.	Recipient receives grace through partaking of the elements.
Memorial (Baptist, Mennonite)	Christ is not present physically or spiritually.	Recipient commemorates the death of Christ.

BAPTISM

Meaning. New Testament baptism had its origin in the command of Christ to make disciples and baptize them (Matt. 28:19). In the origination of this ordinance there is a particular order established; the first act was to make disciples, then those disciples were to be baptized. This is the pattern that is carried out in the book of Acts. Peter commanded that his hearers should first repent, then be baptized (Acts 2:38). Only those who heard the gospel, understood and responded to it through faith and repentance, could be baptized. The result was that the people received the Word, then were baptized (Acts 2:41). Those who responded to Philip's message first believed, then were baptized (Acts 8:12), similarly with the Ethiopian (Acts 8:38), with Paul (Acts 9:18), the Caesarean Gentiles (Acts 10:48), Lydia (Acts 16:14-15), the Philippian jailer (Acts 16:32-33), and Crispus (Acts 18:8). All of these references indicate that baptism follows belief; repentance and faith precede the ordinance of baptism.

Baptism means identification. In New Testament baptism it involves identification with Christ in His death and resurrection. Being baptized in the name of Christ (Acts 2:38) stresses association with Christ in the rite. Although Romans 6:4-5 refers to Spirit baptism and not water baptism, the passage nonetheless illustrates the meaning of water baptism. It is a public declaration that the believer has been united to Christ by faith in His death and resurrection.

Views of baptism.[42] (1) Means of saving grace (baptismal regeneration). In this view baptism "is a means by which God imparts saving grace; it results in the remission of sins. By either awakening or strengthening faith, baptism effects the washing of regeneration."[43] The Roman Catholic view is that faith is not necessary; the rite itself, properly performed, is sufficient. The Lutheran view is that faith is a prerequisite. Infants should be baptized and may possess unconscious faith or faith of the parents.

(2) Sign and seal of the covenant. This is the view of Reformed and Presbyterian churches. The sacraments of baptism and the Lord's Supper are "signs and seals of an inward and invisible thing by means whereof God works in us by the power of the Holy Spirit. . . . Like circumcision in the Old Testament, baptism makes us sure of God's promises. . . . The act of baptism is both the means of initiation into the covenant and a sign of salvation."[44]

(3) Symbol of our salvation. The view of Baptists and others is that baptism is only an outward sign of an inward change. It serves as a public testimony of faith in Christ. "It does not produce any spiritual change in the one baptized. . . . Baptism conveys no direct spiritual benefit or blessing."[45] Moreover, it is to be conducted only with believers. Hence, this third view is the only view that holds only believers should be baptized. The first two views state that, along with adult converts, children (infants) should or may be baptized.

Mode. There are differences of long standing concerning the mode of baptism. Part of the problem is that the word *baptism* is actually an untranslated word, having been incorporated into English through transliteration of the Greek word *baptisma* (verb, *baptizo*). There are three modes of baptism being practiced today: sprinkling, pouring, and immersion. The defense for each of the modes is as follows.[46]

(1) Pouring or affusion. Historically, pouring was applied by the one baptizing pouring water three times over the head of the one being baptized —once for each member of the Trinity. It is argued that pouring best illustrates the work of the Holy Spirit bestowed on the person (Acts 2:17-18). Phrases such as "went down into the water" (Acts 8:38) and "coming up out of the water" (Mark 1:10), it is claimed, can relate to pouring just as well as immersion. The *Didache*, written early in the second century, stated, "But concerning baptism, thus shall ye baptize. Having first recited all these things, baptize in the name of the Father and of the Son and of the Holy Spirit in living (running) water. But if thou has not living water, then baptize in other water; and if thou art not able in cold, then in warm. But if thou hast neither, then pour water on the head thrice in the name of the Father and of the Son and of the Holy Spirit."[47] The inference is that although the early church employed immersion, it allowed for pouring. It appears that both of these modes were in existence as early as the second century.

Further support for the pouring mode is claimed from early pictorial illustrations showing the baptismal candidate standing in the water with the minister pouring water on his head. And finally, in the household baptisms of Cornelius (Acts 10:48) and the Philippian jailer (Acts 16:33) it would appear more likely that pouring rather than immersion was employed.

(2) Sprinkling or aspersion. In the early centuries sprinkling was reserved for the sick or those too weak to receive public baptism by immersion or pouring. Sprinkling was not accepted in general usage until the thirteenth century. Two precedents are often cited in support of sprinkling. In the Old Testament, Levites were cleansed when water was sprinkled on them (Num. 8:5-7; 19:8-13). Hebrews 9:10 refers to these ritual cleansings as "baptisms" (translated "washings" in the NASB). In the third century, Cyprian declared that it was not the amount of water nor the method of baptism that cleansed from sin; rather, where the faith of the recipient was genuine, sprinkling was as effective as another mode.

(3) Immersion. It is generally acknowleged that the early church immersed the people coming for baptism. A lexical study of *baptizo* indicates it means to "dip, immerse."[48] Oepke indicates *baptizo* means "to immerse" and shows how the word has been used: "to sink a ship," "to sink (in the mud)," "to drown," and "to perish."[49] This basic meaning accords with the emphasis of Scripture: Jesus was baptized by John "in the Jordan" and He came up "out of the water" (Mark 1:9-10; cf. Acts 8:38). On the other hand, the Greek has words for *sprinkle* and *pour* that are not used for baptism.

The many pools in Jerusalem would have been used for immersion and would likely have been used to immerse a large group like the 3,000 on the day of Pentecost (Acts 2:41). It is also known that proselytes to Judaism were self-immersed, and immersion was also the mode practiced by the early church. Immersion best illustrates the truth of death and resurrection with Christ in Romans 6.

Infant baptism. Infant baptism, which is practiced by Roman Catholics, Anglicans, Presbyterians, Methodists, and Lutherans, is defended on several grounds. It is related to covenant theology. As infants in the nation Israel were circumcised and thereby brought into the believing community, so infant baptism is the counterpart of circumcision, which brings the infants into the Christian community. It is related to household salvation (cf. Acts 16:15, 31, 33-34; 18:8). Some understand the statement, "when she and her household had been baptized" (Acts 16:15) to mean infants were baptized.[50]

PURPOSE OF THE CHURCH

Two overriding purposes of the church can be delineated: gathered, ministering to the body, and scattered, ministering to the world.[51] It is important to distinguish these two purposes. On the one hand, the church gathers as a body of believers wherein believers minister to one another; on the other hand, the church is to minister the gospel to unbelievers in the world. These two purposes must be kept distinct: the church ministers to both believers and unbelievers. There are a number of functions in each of these two major areas. (Also see the discussion under Function of the Local Church.)

GATHERED: MINISTERING TO THE BODY

The purpose for the church gathered is for the church to come to maturity (Eph. 4:13). Many activities are noted in the gathered church to accomplish this end.

Teaching. The word *teaching* (Gk. *didache*) is synonymous with the word doctrine. Teaching is an important factor in edification, and it made up a vital part of the New Testament church. Members of the early church steadfastly devoted[52] themselves to the teaching of the apostles (Acts 2:42). They taught the doctrine of the resurrection of Christ (Acts 4:2); they taught continually, as they had opportunity (Acts 5:21, 25), to the extent that the entire city of Jerusalem was saturated with the teaching about Christ and His atonement (Acts 5:28). The heart of their message was that Jesus was indeed the Messiah (Acts 5:42; 17:3). Teaching the new believers resulted in their maturity (Acts 11:26; 15:35).

The goal of Paul's teaching was to present a believer mature in Christ (Col. 1:28); hence, teaching was to be an ongoing practice to succeeding generations (2 Tim. 2:2). Failure to do so or failure to respond to teaching resulted in spiritual babyhood (Heb. 5:12). A simple concordance study will reveal the importance of teaching as a New Testament emphasis.

Fellowship. In addition to teaching, the New Testament church utilized other spiritual gifts in ministering to the Body. This relationship within the Body of Christ is seen in the term "one another" (cf. Rom. 12:5, 10, 16; 13:8; 14:13, 19; 15:5, 7, 14). This also emphasizes the importance of fellowship with the church gathered. The gathered church had fellowship in suffering (Acts 4:23; 5:41), fellowship in unity (Acts 2:46; 4:31; Phil. 2:1-4), fellowship in ministry (Acts 4:31), fellowship in prayer (Acts 2:14, 42; 4:31; 12:5, 12; 13:3; 16:25), fellowship in the Lord's Supper (Acts 2:14), as well as fellowship around meals (Acts 2:46). Interestingly, this fellowship was daily (Acts 2:46). This fellowship also demanded supporting widows, orphans, and the needy in one's own family (1 Tim. 5:8; James 1:27).

Worship. Worship is an integral part of the church gathered. Many of the things already mentioned are a reflection of worship (e.g., the Lord's Supper). From the start, prayer was an important aspect of worship by the gathered church. When fellow believers were in need, the church prayed (Acts 12:5, 12). Scripture reading also had a central part in the church gathered (Acts 4:24-26; 1 Tim. 4:13; 2 Tim. 3:15-17). This no doubt followed the pattern of synagogue worship in which the reading and exposition of Scripture was emphasized.[53] Singing was a vital part of the early church as a sincere expression of worship (Acts 16:25; 1 Cor. 14:26; Eph. 5:19; Col. 3:16).

SCATTERED: MINISTERING TO THE WORLD

The New Testament church did not attempt to carry out its evangelism within the confines of a building but rather out in the world. The foundational command for evangelism in the world is Matthew 28:18-20. The work of the church in the world is to make disciples (learners), baptize them, and bring them into the fellowship of believers. The ministry of evangelism was not carried on by a select few but by ordinary believers as well (Acts 8:4). The central message the early church proclaimed was Christ (Acts 8:5, 12, 35; 9:20; 11:20)· moreover, they took their message beyond the Jewish boundary, crossing previously rigid cultural barriers (Acts 10:34-43; 11:20; 14:1). The result was that many people became believers (Acts 2:41; 4:4; 5:14; 6:1; 8:12; 10:48; 11:24; 13:48; 14:1, 21).

The question concerning the nature of the gospel has long been debated. However, the New Testament has little to say about social responsibility in the world. Galatians 6:10 stresses helping fellow believers; believers are also to "do good to all men." In examining Paul's message in Acts, the emphasis is on believing that Jesus is the Christ (Acts 16:31). Thus, Paul delineates the essence of the gospel in 1 Corinthians 15:1-4—it is believing in the death and resurrection of Christ.

NOTES ON ECCLESIOLOGY

1. Robert L. Saucy, *The Church in God's Program* (Chicago: Moody, 1972), p. 11.

2. Henry C. Thiessen, *Lectures in Systematic Theology*, revised by Vernon D. Doerksen (Grand Rapids: Eerdmans, 1979), p. 307.

3. Millard J. Erickson, *Christian Theology*, 3 vols. (Grand Rapids: Baker, 1985), 3:1043-48; cf. Douglas Kelly et al., eds., *The Westminster Confession of Faith*, 2nd ed. (Greenwood, S.C.: Attic, 1981), p. 44.

4. Saucy, *The Church in God's Program*, p. 17.

5. This argument is based on the use of *ekklesia* in the Septuagint, the Greek translation of the Old Testament. However, as has already been shown, *ekklesia* may be used in a nontechnical sense or to denote any particular gathering of people. Thus it may be used to identify Israel in the Old Testament. That is not adequate evidence, however, to equate the New Testament church with Israel. In its New Testament usage the church is distinct from Israel.

6. Earl D. Radmacher, *What the Church Is All About: A Biblical and Historical Study* (Chicago: Moody, 1978), pp. 256-65.

7. A. T. Robertson, *Word Pictures in the New Testament*, 6 vols. (Nashville: Broadman, 1931), 4:528-29.

8. "In construction terms it represents the whole of the elaborate process by which stones are fitted together: the preparation of the surfaces, including the cutting, rubbing, and testing; the preparation of the dowels and the dowel holes, and finally the fitting of the dowels w. molten lead" Fritz Rienecker, *Linguistic Key to the Greek New Testament*, edited by Cleon Rogers (Grand Rapids: Zondervan, 1980), p. 527.

9. "While these descriptions of the church [1 Pet. 2:9] are similar to those used of Israel in the Old Testament, this in no way indicates that the church supplants Israel and assumes the national blessings promised to Israel (and to be fulfilled in the Millennium). Peter just used similar terms to point up similar truths." Roger M. Raymer, "1 Peter" in John F. Walvoord and Roy B. Zuck, eds., *The Bible Knowledge Commentary*, 2 vols. (Wheaton: Victor, 1983), 2:845-46.

10. See the helpful contrast in Saucy, *The Church in God's Program*, pp. 39-40.

11. James E. Rosscup, *Abiding in Christ: Studies in John 15* (Grand Rapids: Zondervan, 1973), pp. 16-19.

12. William F. Arndt and F. Wilbur Gingrich, *A Greek-English Lexicon of the New Testament and Other Early Christian Literature*, revised by F. Wilbur Gingrich and Frederick W. Danker (Chicago: U. of Chicago, 1979), p. 505.

13. Homer A. Kent, Jr., *Light in the Darkness: Studies in the Gospel of John* (Grand Rapids: Baker, 1974), p. 183.

14. The word translated "takes away" in John 15:2 may well be translated "lifts up," a translation justified by both definition and culture. The word *airei* may legitimately be translated "lift up." Cf. usages in Arndt and Gingrich, *Greek-English Lexicon*, p. 24. The traveler to Israel will notice the vineyards have stones measuring perhaps five inches in height placed under the vines, lifting them off the ground to enable them to bear fruit.

15. Saucy, *The Church in God's Program*, pp. 55-56.

16. Donald K. Campbell, "Galatians" in *The Bible Knowledge Commentary*, 2:611. The one disputable passage is Galatians 6:16 where it reads, "And those who will walk by this rule, peace and mercy be upon them, and upon the Israel of God." "The phrase is not to be taken as an explanation of the preceding but as a separate entity or

group. His thoughts turn to his own brethren after the flesh and he pauses to specify those who were once Israelites according to the flesh but now are the Israel of God" (Rienecker, *Linguistic Key to the Greek New Testament*, p. 520).

17. Charles C. Ryrie, *Basic Theology* (Wheaton: Victor, 1987), p. 399.

18. Hermann Cremer, *Biblico-Theological Lexicon of New Testament Greek* (Edinburgh: Clark, 1895), p. 132.

19. See Alva J. McClain, *The Greatness of the Kingdom* (Chicago: Moody, 1968), pp. 23ff. This book is a most important treatment on the subject. For an exhaustive study see George N. H. Peters, *The Theocratic Kingdom*, 3 vols. (Reprint. Grand Rapids: Kregel, 1957).

20. McClain, *Greatness of the Kingdom*, p. 41.

21. See Saucy, *The Church in God's Program*, pp. 84-85; Emery H. Bancroft, *Christian Theology*, 2d ed. (Grand Rapids: Zondervan, 1976), pp. 284-88; and Radmacher, *What the Church Is All About*, pp. 166-76 on distinctions between the church and the kingdom.

22. Radmacher, *What the Church Is All About*, p. 168.

23. See the helpful summaries in Saucy, *The Church in God's Program*, pp. 166-90; and Ryrie, *Basic Theology*, pp. 428-32.

24. See the valuable discussion concerning the word *sick* (Gk. *asthenei*) which means "to be weak" and stressed one who is weary morally and spiritually. Cf. J. Ronald Blue, "James" in *The Bible Knowledge Commentary*, 2:834-35.

25. See the important discussion by Homer A. Kent, Jr., *The Pastoral Epistles*, rev. ed. (Chicago: Moody, 1982), pp. 122-26. Kent discusses the variant views and concludes Paul is prohibiting remarriage after divorce. The argument on divorce usually centers on the exceptive clause of Matt. 19:9. For a careful, biblical study of the entire subject of divorce see J. Carl Laney, *The Divorce Myth* (Minneapolis: Bethany, 1981). Perhaps the most important book that has been recently written on the subject is William A. Heth and Gordon J. Wenham, *Jesus and Divorce: The Problem with the Evangelical Consensus* (Nashville: Nelson, 1984). They conclude that the common suggestion that Jesus allowed the "innocent party" to remarry after divorce is a recent view first espoused by Erasmus and is biblically deficient and erroneous. No study of the subject will be complete without consulting this important work.

26. Kent, *The Pastoral Epistles*, pp. 135-37.

27. Erickson, *Christian Theology*, 3:1070.

28. Saucy, *The Church in God's Program*, p. 112.

29. Ibid.

30. Erickson, *Christian Theology*, 3:1078-79.

31. The word *appointed* (Gk. *cheirotonesantes*) is particularly interesting; it means to "choose; elect by raising hands." Arndt and Gingrich, *A Greek-English Lexicon*, p. 881.

32. Saucy, *The Church in God's Program*, p. 191.

33. R. S. Wallace, "Sacrament" in Walter A. Elwell, ed., *Evangelical Dictionary of Theology* (Grand Rapids: Baker, 1984), p. 965.

34. Charles C. Ryrie, *A Survey of Bible Doctrine* (Chicago: Moody, 1972), p. 149.

35. Loraine Boettner, *Roman Catholicism* (Philadelphia: Presbyterian and Reformed, 1965), pp. 168-69.

36. Ibid., p. 114.

37. Alois Stoger, "Eucharist," in J. B. Bauer, ed., *Encyclopedia of Biblical Theology* (New York: Crossroad, 1981), p. 234.

38. Erickson, *Christian Theology*, 3:1117.

39. Ibid., p. 1118.

40. Louis Berkhof, *Systematic Theology* (Grand Rapids: Eerdmans, 1941), p. 653.

41. Ibid., p. 654.

42. For a summary of these views see Erickson, *Christian Theology*, 3:1090ff.

43. Ibid., 3:1090.

44. Ibid., 3:1093.

45. Ibid., 3:1096.

46. See the summaries of the three views in Ryrie, *Basic Theology*, p. 424; and G. W. Bromiley, A. T. Robertson, T. M. Lindsay, and W. H. T. Dau, "Baptism" in Geoffrey W. Bromiley, ed., *The International Standard Bible Encyclopedia*, 4 vols. (Grand Rapids: Eerdmans, 1988), 1:410-26.

47. J. B. Lightfoot, orig. ed.; J. R. Harmer, ed. & comp., *The Apostolic Fathers* (Reprint. Grand Rapids: Baker, 1956), p. 126.

48. Arndt and Gingrich, *Greek-English Lexicon*, p. 131.

49. Albrecht Oepke, *"Baptizo"* in Gerhard Kittel, trans. & ed., and Geoffrey W. Bromiley, trans., *Theological Dictionary of the New Testament*, 10 vols. (Grand Rapids: Eerdmans, 1964), 1:530.

50. Lenski states, "Now 'her house,' as here used, is the regular term for the members of one's immediate family. Thus any children Lydia may have had would be included (in baptism). . . . the point at issue is in regard to children up to the age of discretion and not only 'infants.' . . . The apostles and their assistants baptized entire households and by baptism received them into the Christian church." R. C. H. Lenski, *The Interpretation of the Acts of the Apostles* (Minneapolis: Augsburg, 1961), p. 660. Cf. David John Williams, *Acts: A Good News Commentary* (San Francisco: Harper, 1985), p. 185; and William Neil, "The Acts of the Apostles" in *The New Century Bible Commentary* (Grand Rapids: Eerdmans, 1981), p. 143.

51. See Gene A. Getz, *Sharpening the Focus of the Church* (Chicago: Moody, 1974), pp. 40-50, 75-83, 269-316.

52. The Greek present participle *proskarterountes* stresses that they were continually doing this.

53. Bruce M. Metzger, *The New Testament: Its Background, Growth, and Content* (Nashville: Abingdon, 1965), pp. 56-60.

FOR FURTHER STUDY ON ECCLESIOLOGY

FORMS OF CHURCH GOVERNMENT

** Louis Berkhof. *Systematic Theology.* Grand Rapids: Eerdmans, 1941. Pp. 579-84.

** Millard J. Erickson. *Christian Theology*, 3 vols. Grand Rapids: Baker, 1985. 3:1069-87.

* G. W. Kirby. "Church, The." In Merrill C. Tenney, ed., *The Zondervan Pictorial Encyclopedia of the Bible*, 5 vols. Grand Rapids: Zondervan, 1975. 1:845-55.

* L. Morris. "Church Government." In Walter A. Elwell, ed., *Evangelical Dictionary of Theology*. Grand Rapids: Baker, 1984. Pp. 238-41.

* Robert L. Saucy. *The Church In God's Program.* Chicago: Moody, 1972. Pp. 105-19.
** A. H. Strong. *Systematic Theology.* Valley Forge, Pa.: Judson, 1907. Pp. 903-14.

ORDINANCES OF THE CHURCH

* G. W. Bromiley. "Baptism," "Baptism, Believers'," and "Baptism, Infant." In Walter A. Elwell, ed., *Evangelical Dictionary of Theology.* Grand Rapids: Baker, 1984. Pp. 112-17. See also articles entitled "Lord's Supper, Views of," and "Sacrament."

* —————, et al. "Baptism." In G. W. Bromiley, ed., *The International Standard Bible Encyclopedia*, 4 vols. Revised. Grand Rapids: Eerdmans, 1988. 1:410-26.

** Millard J. Erickson. *Christian Theology*, 3 vols. Grand Rapids: Baker, 1985. 3:1189-27.

* Charles C. Ryrie. *Basic Theology.* Wheaton: Victor, 1986. Pp. 393-436.

** Robert L. Saucy. *The Church in God's Program.* Chicago: Moody, 1972. Pp. 191-234.

** A. H. Strong. *Systematic Theology.* Valley Forge, Pa.: Judson, 1907. Pp. 930-80.

* Henry C. Thiessen. *Lectures in Systematic Theology*, revised by Vernon D. Doerksen. Grand Rapids: Eerdmans, 1977. Pp. 319-25.

26

ESCHATOLOGY:
DOCTRINE OF LAST THINGS

The relatively recent study of last things has frequently divided believers over the years. Differing systems of interpretations (such as premillennialism, postmillennialism, and amillennialism) have affected other areas of theology in addition to eschatology. There are, however, many areas of commonality among believers in the study of last things. Christians have been in agreement over the explanation of death, the believer's immediate presence with the Lord, the hope of Christ's return, the resurrection, judgment, and the eternal state. An explanation of the areas of commonality is stated below with a discussion of areas of controversy following.

COMMON FACTORS IN ESCHATOLOGY

DEATH

Death is a reality for every member of the human race (Heb. 9:27). When the Bible speaks of death, it refers to the physical death of the body, not the soul. The body may die, but the soul, the life-principle of man, lives on (Matt. 10:28; Luke 12:4-5). There are instances in which the Bible uses the Greek word *psuche* (soul-life) in describing death (John 12:25; 13:37-38), but even passages like these denote the death of the body, not the death of the immaterial nature of man. Death may be thus defined as the end of physical life through the separation of soul and body (cf. James 2:26).[1]

Because the body was made from the elements of the dust, at death the body returns to the dust (Gen. 3:19). Physical death results because of sin. Through the sin of Adam in the garden, death spread to the entire human race; no one is exempted (Rom. 5:12). Death is the "wages" of sin (Rom. 6:23; 1 Cor. 15:56).

Death, however, should not be understood as annihilation. Life continues on for believer and unbeliever alike after the death of the body. Luke 16:19-31 graphically describes the continued existence of both Lazarus and the rich man after death. Lazarus, the poor beggar, continued in eternal bliss, described as "Abraham's bosom" (Luke 16:22), while the rich man was in eternal torment in Hades (Luke 16:23). For the believer, death means to "be absent from the body and to be at home with the Lord" (2 Cor. 5:8). Paul desired death so that he might "be with Christit" (Phil. 1:23).

HEAVEN

All orthodox Christian theologians agree on the existence of two eternal destinies for all angels and human beings: heaven and hell.

The word *heaven* in the Old Testament (Heb. *shamayim*) means "high, lofty,"[2] whereas the New Testament Greek *ouranos* simply means "heaven," probably coming from a root meaning "to cover" or "encompass."[3] Simply stated, the word means "that which is above."[4]

The word *heaven* is used in three ways in the Bible.[5]

The atmospheric heaven. Heaven may be used to describe the troposphere—the space surrounding the earth and extending to a height of about six miles. It is from the atmospheric heaven that the earth receives dew (Deut. 33:13), frost (Job 38:29), rain and snow (Isa. 55:10), wind (Job 26:13), and thunder (1 Sam. 2:10). The clouds are in the atmospheric heaven (Ps. 147:8), and the birds fly in it (Gen. 1:20). Since the necessities for life on earth—dew, rain, snow, wind—come from "heaven," it is a reminder that they are the gracious gift of God[6] (cf. Matt. 5:45).

The celestial heaven. Heaven is also used to describe the celestial realm—the realm of sun, moon, stars, and planets. God created the universe (Gen. 1:1; Ps. 33:6), placing these lights in the heaven (Gen. 1:14).

The dwelling place of God. This is probably what Paul referred to as the "third heaven" (2 Cor. 12:2). John (Rev. 4:1ff.) was taken up to God's heaven. This heaven is a specific place where God dwells, as salutation of Jesus' model prayer indicates ("Our Father who art in heaven" Matt. 6:9). It is in heaven that God sits enthroned (Ps. 2:4; Isa. 66:1); from heaven God renders judgment (Gen. 19:24; Josh. 10:11); but God's blessings also come from heaven (Exod. 16:4). From heaven God looks down upon His people (Deut. 26:15); from heaven He hears their prayer (Ps. 20:6); He comes down from heaven (Ps. 144:5). It is also in heaven that God's sovereign plan is established (Ps. 119:89).

The Bible speaks about the occupants of heaven. In the Old Testament the believer looked forward to the future reign of Messiah. For the Jews there were but two ages, the present age and the "age to come"—which was Messiah's reign on earth. The prophets had much to say about Messiah's future reign (cf. Isa. 9:6-7; 11:1-16; 25:1–27:13). Although little is said specifically about heaven in the Old Testament, the Old Testament saints went to heaven upon death. A commonly occurring phrase in the Old Testament, "and he was gathered to his people" (cf. Gen. 25:8) suggests immortality.[7] Old Testament believers did not wait until the ascension of Christ before they could enter God's presence. This is seen in Matthew 17:1-8 inasmuch as Moses and Elijah came from God's presence at the transfiguration of Christ. In this present church age, believers immediately go to God's presence in heaven upon death (Luke 23:43; 2 Cor. 5:8; Phil. 1:23; 1 Thess. 4:14).

The New Jerusalem. Of considerable importance in the discussion of heaven is the *New Jerusalem* of Revelation 21-22. Although some suggest this passage refers to the millennium, it should be regarded as the eternal state because the chronology of Revelation 20 suggests this.

In Revelation 21, the final eternal abode for believers is described as "a new heaven and a new earth" (21:1). The old heaven and old earth are renovated by fire (2 Pet. 3:10) because they were the domain of angelic and human rebellion against God. The redeemed believers of all ages will live in the New Jerusalem. Although the New Jerusalem is the home Christ has gone to prepare (John 14:2), it is also the heaven of the eternal state.

An important aspect of heaven will be the intimate, personal fellowship of believers with God (Rev. 20:3-4).[8] Earth's sorrows will disappear in heaven; every single tear will be wiped away.

Beauty of the New Jerusalem. Its brilliance (Rev. 21:9-11). Heaven reflects the brilliant glory of God because of His presence. The glory of the New Jerusalem (Rev. 21:11) denotes the Shekinah glory of God illuminating the city. Glory "refers to the shining radiance which comes from the presence and glory of God."[9]

Its walls and gates (Rev. 21:12-13). The high wall surrounding the city suggests security.

Its foundation stones (Rev. 21:14). The foundation stones, with the names of the apostles—who are the foundation of the church—suggest the church is also in the New Jerusalem.

Its measurement (Rev. 21:15-18). The New Jerusalem measures 1,500 miles long, wide, and high, possibly in the shape of a cone or pyramid, with God's throne at the top.

Its adornment (Rev. 21:19-21). It is adorned with brilliant, costly stones, further reflecting the Shekinah glory of God.

Its availability (Rev. 21:22). No longer is there a mediatorial priesthood because every inhabitant has immediate access to God.

Its light (Rev. 21:23). The city is illumined by the Shekinah glory, requiring no celestial lights.

Its purpose (Rev. 21:24-26). The ultimate purpose of the eternal abiding place of believers is to bring glory to their Lord who has provided for their redemption.

HELL

There are several terms in the Hebrew and Greek used to describe eternal punishment.

Sheol. In the Old Testament the word *sheol* occurs sixty-five times and is translated by words like "grave," "hell," "pit," and "sheol." A study of the occurrences indicates *sheol* is used in a variety of ways. It may refer to the grave (Job 17:13; Ps. 16:10; Isa. 38:10). It may refer to the place of the dead—where both good and bad people go upon death (Gen. 37:35; 42:38; 44:29, 31; Num. 16:33; Job 14:13; Ps. 55:15; Prov. 9:18). Believers will be rescued from sheol (Ps. 16:9-11; 17:15; 49:15). The wicked go to sheol upon death (Job 21:13; 24:19; Ps. 9:17; 31:17; 49:14; 55:15).

The dominant focus of the Old Testament seems to be on the place where the bodies of people go, not where their souls exist. Other words are used extensively in the Old Testament to emphasize that focus. The terms *grave* (Heb. *qeber*), used seventy-one times to describe the grave, *pit* (Heb. *bor*), and *earth below* (Heb. *erets tahtit*) all emphasize where the *body* goes upon death.[10] Thus, the Old Testament "gives us a picture of a typical Palestinian tomb, dark, dusty, with mingled bones and where 'this poor lisping stammering tongue lies silent in the grave.' All the souls of men do not go to one place. But all people go to the grave. As to the destiny of the souls of men in the intermediate state, the OT says little."[11]

Hades. The New Testament term used to describe the afterlife is *hades* and is equivalent to the Hebrew term *sheol.* In the Septuagint, the Greek translation of the Old Testament, the word *sheol* is almost always translated by *hades.* Hades was originally a proper noun, the name of the god of the nether world who ruled over the dead.[12]

In the intertestamental period there developed a two-compartment theory (probably an influence from Persian Zoroastrianism[13]), which taught that sheol and hades had two compartments, a place of bliss for the righteous and a place of torment for the wicked. The righteous were waiting for the resurrection of Christ who then delivered them from hades into God's presence. This argument was based on Ephesians 4:9-10 and 1 Peter 3:19. However, it is doubtful that this is what these passages teach.[14] Moreover, Moses' and Elijah's appearance at Christ's transfiguration suggests they were already in God's presence (Matt. 17:3), not in some intermediate holding place.

The word *hades* is probably used in two different ways. It is used to describe a *place* when referring to punishment and simply the *state* of death where all must go upon termination of life.[15] Of the ten occurrences[16] of hades in the New Testament, it is used as a place of punishment three times (Matt. 11:23; Luke 10:15; 16:23) and as the state of death, which both believers and unbelievers enter, seven times (Matt. 16:18; Acts 2:27, 31; Rev. 1:18; 6:8; 20:13, 14).

Gehenna. This term, occurring twelve times in the New Testament, is a designation for eternal punishment taken from the Hebrew *ge hinnom*, referring to the Valley of Hinnom that runs on the south and east sides of Jerusalem. The worship of Molech in which infants were sacrificed in fire to the god Molech also occurred in the Valley of Hinnom (2 Kings 16:3; 17:7; 21:6). Jeremiah announced the Valley of Hinnom would be the place of God's judgment (Jer. 7:32; 19:6). The valley also became the place where refuse and dead bodies of animals and criminals were burned. As a result, gehenna became synonymous with eternal punishment, the fire of hell. It describes the punishment connected with the final judgment, a punishment that has eternal duration, not annihilation (Matt. 23:15, 33; 25:41, 46).

Tartaroo. This term occurs only in 2 Peter 2:4. Tartarus is "the name in classical mythology for the subterranean abyss in which rebellious gods and other such beings as the Titans were punished. The word was, however, taken over into Hellenistic Judaism and used in the book of Enoch (Enoch 20:2) in connection with fallen angels."[17]

Abyss. The abyss (Gk. *abussos*), meaning "bottomless" and translated "pit" or "abyss," is the prison for demons (Luke 8:31; Rev. 9:1, 2, 11). Satan is the king over the demons in the abyss (Rev. 9:11) and releases the demons upon the earth during the Tribulation (Rev. 9:1ff.). At the Second Advent of Christ, Satan will be bound and confined to the abyss for a thousand years (Rev. 20:1-3).

Other terms. Other terms such as "unquenchable fire" (Matt. 3:12; Mark 9:43, 48), "furnace of fire" (Matt. 13:42, 50), "outer darkness" (Matt. 8:12; 22:13; 25:30), "eternal fire" (Matt. 25:41), "the lake that burns with fire and brimstone" (Rev. 21:8), and "lake of fire" (Rev. 19:20; 20:10, 14, 15) are used to describe eternal punishment. Unbelievers will be cast into the lake of fire at the great white throne judgment (Rev. 20:11-15) and there they will live in torment for eternity.

THE RETURN OF CHRIST

Although differing over details, the return of Christ is a doctrine that evangelicals hold in common. It is a prominent doctrine in the Scriptures, being mentioned more than three hundred times in the New Testament, with entire chapters being given to the discussion of Christ's return (Matt. 13, 24, 25; Mark 13; Luke 21) and even the majority of some books (1 and 2 Thess; Rev.).[18]

Christ taught that His return would be a literal, physical event; He would return in just the same way as the disciples had seen Him depart

(Acts 1:11). He also taught that His return would be a comfort to His followers because He would be returning to take them to be with Him in His Father's home (John 14:1-3). The time of His return, however, would be unknown, therefore people should be prepared for His coming (Matt. 24:36, 42; 25:1-13). During His absence, His people should be faithful stewards (Matt. 24:45-51), faithfully serving Him to receive His commendation and rewards upon His return (Matt. 25:14-30).

The return of Christ should be a joyous anticipation for believers because He will bring them to heaven, their true place of citizenship, transforming their mortal bodies into immortal bodies like His very own (Phil. 3:20-21; 1 John 3:2). This hope is a comfort, not only for living believers, but also for those who have departed, because they will rise from the dead, receiving new, immortal bodies (1 Thess. 4:13-18). Therefore, believers should be anticipating His coming as a happy event (Titus 2:13) and as the final stage of their salvation (Heb. 9:27). The New Testament concludes with John's rejoinder, "Amen, Come, Lord Jesus" (Rev. 22:20). But the New Testament also emphasizes that this doctrine has a present effect. Because believers will see Him who is pure, they should purify themselves (1 John 3:3). Moreover, because the end of this age will mean the destruction of this present earth and the introduction of a new heaven and a new earth, Peter emphasizes, "what sort of people ought you to be in holy conduct and godliness" (2 Pet. 3:11).

RESURRECTION OF THE DEAD

The return of Christ has an important implication for the believer because it means the hope of bodily[19] resurrection. The resurrection hope is taught in both the Old and New Testaments and is foundational to the Christian faith. David spoke of awakening in God's presence (Ps. 17:15). Korah expressed the hope that God would rescue him from the power of death and receive him to His presence (Ps. 49:15). Asaph had faith that God would guide him throughout life and when life was over, God would receive him to heaven (Ps. 73:24-25). Isaiah provides a clear statement of the resurrection hope: "Your dead will live; their corpses will rise. You who lie in the dust, awake and shout for joy. For your dew is as the dew of the dawn. And the earth will give birth to the departed spirits" (Isa. 26:19). Daniel also clearly describes the future resurrection as all people will be resurrected from the dust of the earth, some to enter into everlasting life, others to judgment and everlasting condemnation (Dan. 12:1-2).

The New Testament provides added revelation concerning the resurrection. In His debate with the Sadducees, Jesus rebuked them for their mistaken notion in denying the resurrection. They neither understood the Scriptures (for the Old Testament taught the resurrection) nor the power of God (for He is able to raise the dead) (Matt. 22:29; cf. Mark 12:24-27; Luke

20:34-38). In John 5:28-29 Jesus spoke words reminiscent of Daniel 12:2 when He explained that the dead would hear the voice of Christ and come forth, some to a resurrection life, others to a resurrection judgment (John 5:28-29). Christ also promised eternal life to those believing in Him; they had the assurance that He would raise them from the dead (John 6:39-40, 44, 54). At the raising of Lazarus Jesus declared, "I am the resurrection, and the life; he who believes in Me shall live even if he dies, and every one who lives and believes in Me shall never die" (John 11:25-26).

In his detailed defense and explanation of the resurrection in 1 Corinthians 15, Paul cites the resurrection as foundational to the Christian faith. If the resurrection is not true then Christ has not been resurrected, faith is useless, and the sin problem remains unsolved (1 Cor. 15:17). The resurrection is also explained in connection with the return of Christ (1 Thess. 4:16).

The doctrine of the resurrection was also at the heart of New Testament preaching (Acts 2:31; 4:2, 33; 17:18, 32; 23:6, 8; 24:15, 21; 26:23). Paul reminded Timothy to remember the resurrection of Christ (2 Tim. 2:8) and exhorted him to correct false teaching about the resurrection (2 Tim. 2:18). The New Testament climaxes with the announcement of the resurrection of the righteous, describing it as "the first resurrection" (Rev. 20:4-5).

THE JUDGMENTS

From the beginning Christians have recognized that this age will terminate with judgment at the return of Christ. Because God is holy, He must judge all that is unholy or He would no longer be holy. Judgment is a necessary expression of God's own character.[20] However, God's judgment will be fair and according to truth (Rom. 2:2).

Some think that the only judgment there will be is the present judgment. It is true that God has judged in this present age. At some point in the past God judged Lucifer and the fallen angels (2 Pet. 2:4; Jude 6). God judged the people with the Flood in the days of Noah (Gen. 6-7); He judged the people at the tower of Babel (Gen. 11:1-9); He judged the northern kingdom of Israel by sending her into captivity in Assyria (2 Kings 17:1-6); He judged the southern kingdom of Judah through the captivity in Babylon (2 Kings 25:1-12); He judged the church in the deaths of Ananias and Sapphira (Acts 5:1-11). Paul stressed the judgment takes place in the present age when he declared, "The wrath of God is revealed from heaven against all ungodliness" (Rom. 1:18). However, this is not the final judgment. The Scriptures indicate there will be a future judgment connected with the return of Christ.

As the Son of God, Jesus has the authority to render judgment (John 5:27-29). Jesus announced a future judgment connected with His return when He said people would be judged according to their deeds (Matt. 16:27). He also declared that the knowledge (or lack of it) that people had would affect the judgment. Those who had greater knowledge would receive greater judgment (Matt. 11:24).

All people, without exception, will die and come under the judgment of God (Heb. 9:27).

John the apostle described a final day when, before the great white throne, the books will be opened and unbelievers will be judged (Rev. 20:11-15). The records of the unbelievers will render them guilty before God and unworthy of eternal life. All the unbelieving dead, whether in the sea or on the earth, will be judged in the presence of God in that day. The destiny of unbelievers will be the lake of fire (Rev. 20:15).

Believers will also be judged because Paul declares, "We shall all stand before the judgment seat of God" (Rom. 14:10; cf. 2 Cor. 5:10). There believers will be recompensed for their deeds, whether good or worthless. The lives of believers will be reflected in this judgment (1 Cor. 3:12-15). Some will have no rewards; their works will be burned up because their motives were wrong (1 Cor. 3:14-15; 4:5). Others will have lived qualitative lives and will be rewarded accordingly (1 Cor. 3:12-13). The parables of the talents (Matt. 25:14-30) and the parable of money (Luke 19:11-27) both teach the importance of faithful stewardship in connection with the final judgment.

The eternal fire of hell has been prepared for the devil and his angels (Matt. 25:41). At the end of the age God will also judge Satan and his demons when, together with the beast and the false prophet, the devil is cast into the lake of fire (Rev. 20:10).

THE ETERNAL STATE

Evangelicals agree that the souls of all men will live forever in resurrected bodies in either heaven or hell.

Unbelievers will continue in an eternal state of torment. The expression "weeping and gnashing of teeth" (Matt. 8:12; 13:42, 50; 22:13; 24:51; 25:30; Luke 13:28) suggests both suffering and despair,[21] implying a continued existence of suffering. In Matthew 25:46 the terms "punishment" and "life" are modified by the same word "eternal," hence if life is eternal, then of necessity so is punishment. Annihilation is denied in this verse; punishment continues for an endless duration. The account of Lazarus and the rich man in Luke 16:19-31 also stresses the eternal existence of punishment. The phrase "being in torment" emphasizes the rich man's continued state of suffering (Luke 16:23).[22] One of the words for hell is Gehenna, the word being related to the Hinnom Valley which lay along the southern side of Jerusalem. The bodies of criminals and refuse were thrown into the Valley of Hinnom where they burned constantly,[23] making the term Gehenna an apt one for emphasizing eternal suffering in hell. (See again the discussion of this under "Hell" earlier in this chap..)

At the end of the age the devil, the beast, and the false prophet will be thrown into the lake of fire where "they will be tormented day and night forever and ever" (Rev. 20:10).

While there is not much said about it, it appears there will be degrees of punishment in hell. This is generally acknowledged from Luke 12:47-48 where the slave who did not know his master's will and did not do it will receive few floggings, whereas the slave who knew his master's will but did not do it will receive many lashes. Some also use Revelation 20:12 to suggest degrees of suffering, but this text probably stresses that the works of unbelievers will be deficient and will condemn them.

Finally, hell may be seen as "(a) a total absence of the favor of God; (b) an endless disturbance of life as a result of the complete domination of sin; (c) positive pains and sufferings in body and soul; and (d) such subjective punishments as pangs of conscience, anguish, despair, weeping, and gnashing of teeth, Matt. 8:12; 13:50; Mark 9:43-44, 47-48; Luke 16:23, 28; Rev. 14:10; 21:8."[24]

Believers will enjoy an eternal fellowship in Christ's company (John 14:2). The eternal dwelling places in the Father's house are taken from the imagery of Jewish family life. When a son married, he added an apartment to his father's house, and the son and his bride took up residence in the father's household.[25] Believers will enjoy that same family fellowship in the Father's household in heaven.

Heaven is also pictured as a banqueting scene (Matt. 8:11), emphasizing the fellowship, relaxation, joy, and happiness in Christ's presence.

Believers' eternal dwelling place will be the new heaven and the new earth (Isa. 65:17). John describes the new heaven and new earth in great detail (Rev. 21:1–22:5). Many would place the new heaven and the new earth as following the renovation of the heavens and the new earth, after Satan and man rebel against God (2 Pet. 3:10). This does not suggest the annihilation of the original heavens and earth, but a transition in which the heavens and earth are sanctified.[26]

Hebrews 12:22-24 describes the inhabitants of the New Jerusalem: angels, New Testament believers (identified as "church of the first-born"), God, Old Testament believers (identified as "spirits of righteous men made perfect"), and Jesus. The New Jerusalem is pictured as a holy city, coming down out of heaven; many understand that the New Jerusalem will hover over the earth. It is a literal city because it has measurements (Rev. 21:16). The brilliance of the Shekinah of God will illuminate the city (Rev. 21:9-11). The city itself will be secure (21:12-13); it measures fifteen hundred miles long, wide, and high with the throne of God at the top (21:15-18). The foundation stones are adorned with various kinds of precious stones (21:19-21).

Above all, the blessing of the New Jerusalem will be that God will dwell in fellowship with man.[27] There will be no need for a priest; believers will have direct access to God (21:22). Sorrow and the things that caused sorrow will be removed in the New Jerusalem (21:4,5). But Christ will be central there, and believers will serve Him and enjoy His fellowship for all eternity (22:3-5).

CONTROVERSIAL FACTORS IN ESCHATOLOGY

In conservative theology there are three major views concerning last things: amillennialism, postmillennialism, and premillennialism. The word *millennium* comes from the Latin *mille*, meaning "thousand," and relates to the statement in Revelation 20:4, "They came to life and reigned with Christ for a thousand years." Should this statement be understood literally or symbolically? The answer determines in part one's doctrine of last things.

AMILLENNIALISM

Introduction. This discussion on amillennial eschatology will concentrate on the view of Reformed eschatology, inasmuch as it is the prevalent conservative position that holds to amillennialism. While liberal theologians hold to a form of amillennialism, they are for the most part unconcerned with eschatology, albeit under more radical forms and designations. (These are discussed later in Part 5, "Contemporary Theology.")

The *a-* in *amillennialism* negates the term; hence, *amillennialism* means there will not be a literal, future millennium. Amillennialists do not deny the literal return of Christ, but they reject a literal thousand-year reign of Christ on the earth. According to amillennialism, the kingdom of God is present in the church age, and at the consummation of the present age, the eternal state is inaugurated without any intervening millennium.[28] For this reason some amillennialists suggest a term such as *realized millennialism* to indicate that they do not deny a millennium but believe it is fulfilled entirely in the present age.[29]

According to amillennialists, Revelation 20:4-6 refers to "the present reign of the souls of deceased believers with Christ in heaven" while the kingdom of God "is now present in the world as the victorious Christ is ruling his people by his Word and Spirit, though they also look forward to a future, glorious, and perfect kingdom on the new earth in the life to come."[30]

Some amillennialists interpret the book of Revelation according to *progressive parallelism*, wherein the Revelation consists of seven sections running parallel to each other, each depicting the church and the world from the time of Christ's first advent to His second coming: chapters 1-3 relate to events of the first century but have present application; chapters 4-7 describe the church suffering trial and persecution; chapters 8-11 envision the church avenged, protected, and victorious; chapters 12-14 describe the birth of Christ and opposition by Satan; chapters 15-16 describe God's wrath on the unrepentant; chapters 17-19 depict the final fall of the forces of secularism and godlessness; chapters 20-22 describe the final doom of the enemies of Christ and the final triumph of Christ and the church.[31]

Second coming of Christ. Amillennialists understand the second coming of Christ as a *single event*; in contrast, dispensationalists understand Christ's coming in two phases. Amillennialists teach that certain events must take place prior to the second coming; hence, the return of Christ cannot be termed "imminent" (meaning that Christ can come at any moment).[32] The signs prior to the second coming of Christ are the following: (1) The calling of the Gentiles (Matt. 24:14; Mark 13:10; Rom. 11:25), in which the nations will be evangelized. Some among these will believe and constitute the "fulness of the Gentiles." (2) The conversion of Israel. "All Israel" in Romans 11:26 does not mean national Israel but rather the elect number of Israelites. (3) Great apostasy and the Great Tribulation (Matt. 24:9-12, 21-24; Mark 13:9-22; Luke 21:22-24). These events had a partial fulfillment in the destruction of Jerusalem but will also have a future fulfillment. (4) The revelation of Antichrist. There have been elements of Antichrist during Paul's day and in the papal system of Rome, but Antichrist's identity will eventually be fulfilled in an eschatological person. (5) Signs and wonders. There will be wars, false prophets, astonishing satanic miracles, and signs in the heavens.

Christ will return at the "day of consummation"—the end of the world; no one, however, knows the time of His coming. The manner of His coming will be personal, physical, and visible (Acts 1:11); it is not to be equated with the coming of the Holy Spirit at Pentecost. Unlike premillennarians who teach that Christ's second coming is to establish His earthly kingdom, amillennialists teach that the purpose of Christ's return is for "introducing the future age, the eternal state of things."[33] This will be accomplished by the resurrection of the dead and the final judgment.

Resurrection of the dead. The amillennial understanding says that the Bible teaches a *bodily* resurrection at the end of the age (1 Cor. 15:35-49). The body of a resurrected believer "will be in a fundamental sense identical with the present body."[34]

With respect to the time of the resurrection, the resurrection of believers and unbelievers occurs at the same time.[35] This is implied by passages such as Daniel 12:2; John 5:28, 29; Acts 24:15; Revelation 20:13-15. Daniel 12:2 mentions the godly and the wicked in the same statement, as does John 5:28-29. The term "hour" in John 5:28 could not be used to denote a thousand-year distinction between two resurrections. In Acts 24:15 Paul uses the singular term "resurrection" to describe the resurrection of the just and the unjust. Revelation 20:11-15 must refer to all the dead, not simply unbelievers, because the term "death and Hades gave up the dead which were in them" must refer to all people.

This resurrection of believers and unbelievers occurs at the second coming of Christ (1 Cor. 15:23; Phil. 3:20-21; 1 Thess. 4:16), and is also designated "the last day" or the "day of the Lord." It is at the end of the age and at the advent of the eternal state.

Final judgment. The final judgment according to amillennialists is at the end of the age and is associated with the second coming of Christ, the resurrection of all people, and the inauguration of the eternal state. It will be a general judgment "for the very purpose of judging the living and consigning each individual to his eternal destiny."[36] Three distinct purposes for the final judgment may be delineated:[37] (1) "to display the sovereignty of God and the glory of God in the revelation of the final destiny of each person"; (2) "to reveal the degree of reward and the degree of punishment which each one shall receive"; (3) "to execute God's judgment on each person. God will now assign to each person the place where he will spend eternity."

The details of this judgment should be noted. Because the resurrection is a general resurrection, the *time* of the final judgment is at the end of the age (2 Pet. 3:7). The *judge* will be Christ. Because He is the One through whom people have been saved, it is fitting that unbelievers will face Him as Judge (John 5:22; Acts 17:31; 2 Tim. 4:8). Christ will, however, be assisted in judgment by angels (Matt. 13:41-43) and saints (Matt. 19:28;1 Cor. 6:2-3).[38] The *objects* of judgment will be angels (1 Cor. 6:2-3) and all people (Matt. 25:32; Rom. 2:5-6; 2 Cor. 5:10[39]), which includes both believers and unbelievers.

The *content* of judgment will involve a person's "deeds, words, and thoughts."[40] The judgment of a person's deeds is evident from Matthew 25:35-40; careless words will be judged (Matt. 12:36); thoughts will be exposed (1 Cor. 4:5). Even a believer's sins will be revealed, but they will be manifest as forgiven sins, covered by the blood of Christ.[41]

The *standard* of judgment will be the revelation of God. Those that received the revelation of the Old Testament will be judged according to that revelation; those that received the revelation of New Testament truth will be judged accordingly (Matt. 11:20-22); those who received neither Old Testament nor New Testament truth will be judged according to the light they received.[42] As a result, there will be levels of suffering for the lost (Luke 12:47-48). Believers, however, will be justified on the basis of their relationship to Jesus Christ (John 3:18, 36; 5:24), but will be rewarded variably for faithfulness (Luke 19:12-19; 1 Cor. 3:10-15).

Eternal state. Amillennialists teach that both believers and unbelievers will continue in conscious existence in eternity. Unbelievers will continue in conscious existence in hell, sometimes called gehenna (cf. Matt. 25:30, 46; Luke 16:19-31). Because the same term is used to describe the future

VIEWS CONCERNING LAST THINGS

Categories	Amillennialism	Postmillennialism	Historic Premillennialism	Dispensational Premillennialism
Second Coming of Christ	Single event; no distinction between rapture and second coming. Introduces eternal state.	Single event; no distinction between rapture and second coming; Christ returns after Millennium.	Rapture and second coming simultaneous; Christ returns to reign on earth.	Second coming in two phases: rapture for church; second coming to earth 7 years later.
Resurrection	General resurrection of believers and unbelievers at second coming of Christ.	General resurrection of believers and unbelievers at second coming of Christ.	Resurrection of believers at beginning of Millennium. Resurrection of unbelievers at end of Millennium.	Distinction in resurrections: 1. Church at rapture. 2. Old Testament/Tribulation saints at second coming. 3. Unbelievers at end of Millennium.
Judgments	General judgment of all people.	General judgment of all people.	Judgment at second coming. Judgment at end of Tribulation.	Distinction in judgment: 1. Believers works at rapture; 2. Jews/Gentiles at end of Tribulation. 3. Unbelievers at end of Millennium.
Tribulation	Tribulation is experienced in this present age.	Tribulation is experienced in this present age.	Posttrib view: church goes through the future Tribulation.	Pretrib view: church is raptured prior to Tribulation.
Millennium	No literal Millennium on earth after second coming. Kingdom present in church age.	Present age blends into Millennium because of progress of gospel.	Millennium is both present and future. Christ is reigning in heaven. Millennium not necessarily 1,000 years.	At second coming Christ inaugurates literal 1,000-year Millennium on earth.
Israel and the Church	Church is the new Israel. No distinction between Israel and church.	Church is the new Israel. No distinction between Israel and church.	Some distinction between Israel and church. Future for Israel but church is spiritual Israel.	Complete distinction between Israel and church. Distinct program for each.
Adherents	L. Berkhof O. T. Allis G. C. Berkhouwer	Charles Hodge B. B. Warfield W. G. T. Shedd A. H. Strong	G. E. Ladd A. Reese M. J. Erickson	L. S. Chafer J. D. Pentecost C. C. Ryrie J. F. Walvoord

existence of both believers and unbelievers ("eternal," Matt. 25:46), the suffering of unbelievers will be *eternal*, just as believers will enjoy heaven for all eternity.

The end of the age will issue in "the regeneration" (Matt. 19:28), in which there will be a "renewal of the present creation."[43] This will be the place the Scripture refers to as heaven—the eternal abode of believers with the triune God. Heaven is not simply a mental disposition, but an actual place (John 14:1) where believers will enjoy fulness of life. "They will see God in Jesus Christ face to face, will find full satisfaction in Him, will rejoice in Him, and will glorify Him."[44] Because believers will have bodies in their resurrected state, there will be recognition of others and social interaction.

POSTMILLENNIALISM

Introduction. The postmillennial view was particularly popular in the nineteenth century and was the view held by the major theologians of the late nineteenth and early twentieth centuries, among them Charles Hodge, William G. T. Shedd, B. B. Warfield, A. A. Hodge, A. H. Strong, and others. The occasion for this view is noteworthy, inasmuch as it followed a period of optimism and progress in science, culture, and the standard of living in general. It was also prior to World Wars I and II. Postmillennialism declined considerably following the world wars because the conflagrations militated against the optimism of the doctrine.

Postmillennialism may be defined as "that view of the last things which holds that the Kingdom of God is now being extended in the world through the preaching of the Gospel and the saving work of the Holy Spirit in the hearts of individuals, that the world eventually is to be Christianized, and that the return of Christ is to occur at the close of a long period of righteousness and peace commonly called the 'Millennium.' "[45]

The term *post*millennialism means that Christ will return *after* the Millennium. The present age will develop morally and spiritually until it issues in the millennial age, with Christ returning to earth at the conclusion of the Millennium.

The Millennium.[46] Postmillennialism adopts an optimistic view with respect to this present age, envisioning a golden age of progress in the church age that affects every dimension of life: economic, social, cultural, and political. Postmillennialism envisions a church triumphant, spreading the gospel to the ends of the earth with the result that "evil in all its many forms eventually will be reduced to negligible proportions, that Christian principles will be the rule, not the exception, and that Christ will return to a truly Christianized world."[47]

(1) Nature of the Millennium. The millennial age will be similar to the present age in many respects: there will be marriage and childbirth; sin will be present although greatly reduced because of the spread of the gospel;

and Christian principles and standards of conduct will be the norm rather than the exception. The present age will gradually give way to the Millennium as a result of the progress of the gospel, but life will continue in its present form. Christ will return at the conclusion of the Millennium.

(2) Progress of the gospel. There are passages of Scripture that seem to emphasize the conversion of a vast number of people. Zechariah 9:10 refers to Christ's kingdom as being "from sea to sea," Numbers 14:21 emphasizes "all the earth will be filled with the glory of the Lord." Isaiah 49:6 refers to Christ being a "light of the nations." Psalms 2:8; 47:2-8; 72:7-11; 86:9; 110:1 seem to refer to the same truth. Because Christ died for the world, it must be concluded that a vast majority of the people will ultimately be saved (but this is not suggesting a doctrine of universalism).

The reason for the Christianizing of the world is the progress of the gospel. Revelation 19:11-21 depicts Christ returning to a world that has seen obedience to and fulfillment of the Great Commission (Matt. 28:18-20); the gospel has been carried to the ends of the earth and Christ, through His servants, is victorious in the world. Revelation 19:11-21 "is a picture of the whole period between the first and the second advents, seen from the point of view of heaven. It is the period of advancing victory of the Son of God over the world, emphasizing, in harmony with its place at the end of the book, the completeness of the victory."[48]

(3) Progress in the world. Postmillennialists say that there has been progress materially and spiritually in the world, suggesting the world is getting better. Whereas in the Roman era there were more slaves than free people, today slavery is virtually eliminated, as are other forms of oppression, particularly of women and children. Since World War II the United States has given over 160 billion dollars in foreign aid,[49] which does not include many other forms of charitable giving, such as to local churches. In contrast to the pre-Reformation days, the Bible is available in most languages today, with the result that ninety-eight percent of the world's people have the Bible in their own language. Christian radio and television reach into countless homes with the gospel; Bible institutes, colleges, and seminaries are training more people than ever before. The result is that there are now nearly one billion nominal adherents to Christianity.

Great progress can also be observed in transportation with the advent of the automobile and the airplane. Advances in education and scientific achievements, as well as in health care, can be cited. All this suggests the progress and ultimate triumph of the gospel and the inauguration of the Millennium. The Millennium, however, should not be understood as a literal thousand years but rather symbolic. The Millennium may, in fact, be longer than one thousand years.

Second coming of Christ. In contrast to premillennialism, which states that Christ returns *prior* to the Millennium, postmillennialism states that

Christ returns *following* the Millennium. In contrast to premillennialism and amillennialism, which both state that Christ returns to a world that is getting progressively more sinful, postmillennialism teaches that Christ returns to a world that is getting better. Modern missions and the great revivals of George Whitefield and Jonathan Edwards are precursors to the second coming of Christ.[50] Passages such as Daniel 2:44-45; Matthew 13:31,32; 24:14; and Colossians 1:23 suggest the progress of the gospel prior to Christ's return.

Christ's return will be a literal, visible return (Acts 1:11; 1 Thess. 4:16; Rev. 1:7). The time of His coming, however, is unknown.

Resurrection of the dead. Postmillennialists are in general agreement with amillennialists concerning the resurrection. There will be a general resurrection of both believers and unbelievers (Dan. 12:2; Matt. 25:31, 32; John 5:28, 29; Acts 24:15; Rev. 20:12-13) that will take place in conjunction with the return of Christ (1 Cor. 15:23, 24; 1 Thess. 4:16).[51]

Final judgment. Postmillennialists are also in general agreement with amillennialists concerning the final judgment. At the second coming of Christ there will be a general resurrection and a general judgment of all people (Matt. 13:37-43; 25:32), as well as of angels (2 Pet. 2:4). There will be a judgment concerning the deeds done in the body and people will be judged according to the light they have received (Luke 12:47-48). Those who heard the gospel will be judged according to their attitude toward Christ.[52]

The eternal state. The judgment by Christ, as postmillennialists teach, will result in the eternal disposition of the righteous to eternal life and the wicked to everlasting punishment. The final disposition of both believer and unbeliever will be unalterable as well as endless. For believers it will be "the fulness and perfection of holy life, in communion with God and with sanctified spirits."[53] There will, however, be degrees of reward in conjunction with the faithfulness exhibited (Luke 19:17, 19; 1 Cor. 3:14, 15).

The believer will spend eternity in heaven, identified as this world in renovated form.[54] The wicked will spend eternity in endless punishment (Matt. 25:31-33, 41, 46).[55]

"HISTORIC" PREMILLENNIALISM

Introduction. The term *premillennialism* means that Christ will return before the Millennium to establish His earthly reign of one thousand years. There are, however, two distinct forms of premillennialism, one known as "historic" premillennialism (or nondispensational premillennialism), while the other is known as dispensational premillennialism. Prominent spokesmen for historic premillennialism have been George E. Ladd and J. Barton Payne.

The hermeneutical system of historic premillennialism distinguishes it from dispensational premillennialism. In historic premillennialism a distinction between Israel and the church is not maintained nor is a consistently literal interpretive method demanded.[56] Ladd suggests that in its setting, Isaiah 53 is not a prophecy of Messiah yet is seen as such in the New Testament, therefore, the "literal hermeneutic does not work."[57] Furthermore, "the New Testament applies Old Testament prophecies to the New Testament church and in so doing identifies the church as spiritual Israel."[58] An example of this is Romans 9:25-26, which cites Hosea 1:9,10; 2:23. In the Old Testament citation it refers to Israel, whereas in the New Testament citation it has reference to the church. Other examples of this "spiritualizing hermeneutic" are Romans 2:28-29; 4:11, 16 and Galatians 3:7, 29. The application of the New Covenant of Jeremiah 31:33-34 to the church in Hebrews 8 is a further example. Ladd concludes that "Paul sees the church as spiritual Israel."[59]

The aforementioned interpretive method and conclusions are similar to amillennialism as Ladd suggests.[60] A distinction, however, between historic premillennialism and amillennialism is the recognition of a literal future for national Israel, which the former acknowledges and the latter denies. Romans 11:26 states, "and thus all Israel shall be saved"—a reference to national Israel. From this statement it is clear there is a future for national Israel. However, the details concerning a future national Israel remain unclear. It is not even clear if Israel's future conversion is in relation to the Millennium.[61]

The Tribulation. Since the pretribulation rapture is connected to a clear distinction regarding God's program for Israel and His program for the church, and since historic premillennialism does not accept that distinction, historic premillennialism teaches that the church will go through the Tribulation. George Ladd argues that this was the belief of the early church[62] and further argues that the Greek terms related to the coming of Christ (*parousia, apokalypse,* and *epiphany*) do not distinguish between two different comings as taught by pretribulation rapturists.[63] Upon examination of the key passages used by pretribulation rapturists, Ladd concludes the pretribulation rapture is not clearly taught in the New Testament. He states: "Nowhere does the Word of God affirm that the Rapture and the Resurrection of believers will precede the Tribulation."[64]

Arguments that the church will be on earth during the Tribulation may be summarized as follows. (1) Posttribulationism is the historic view held by the early church; pretribulationism is recent.[65] (2) Although the church is on earth during the Tribulation, it will experience suffering and trial but not the wrath of God; that is reserved for unbelievers. (3) There is no separate resurrection of church age saints and Old Testament believers; all are resurrected at the same time—immediately prior to the establishment of Christ's kingdom.[66] (4) The hope of the New Testament writers was not a secret rapture, but the second advent of Christ. All statements referring to Christ's return relate to one coming, not a secret coming for the church prior to the Tribulation and subsequent to the Tribulation a visible coming to rule. [67] (5) The church includes the saved of all ages, and because Scripture indicates believers will be on earth during the Tribulation (e.g. Rev. 7:14), it means the church will not be raptured prior to the Tribulation.

The second coming. Historic premillennialism says that according to Revelation 19:6-10, at the second coming of Christ, the marriage feast of the Lamb will take place—"the union of Christ with his bride, the church."[68] This is further described in metaphorical language (Matt. 25:1-13; 2 Cor. 11:2). Christ conquers His enemies at His triumphant return, consigning the beast and the false prophet to the lake of fire (Rev. 19:20). The devil is also bound in the bottomless pit for a thousand years (Rev. 20:2-3), and at the end of the thousand years the devil is also consigned to the lake of fire (Rev. 20:10).

The "first resurrection" describes a bodily resurrection of the saints of all ages (Rev. 20:4-5); there will not be a separate resurrection of the church age saints and the Old Testament saints. The believing dead from all ages will be resurrected at the return of Christ; the unbelieving dead will be raised at the end of the Millennium.

The Millennium. Christ's reign does not begin at some future event—He is reigning now from heaven.[69] Christ is presently sitting at the right hand of God, reigning as Messianic King. "The New Testament does not make the reign of Christ one that is limited to Israel in the Millennium; it is a spiritual reign in heaven which has already been inaugurated."[70] Philippians 2:5-10 establishes that Christ is presently enthroned and ruling (cf. 1 Cor. 15:24; 1 Tim. 6:15). Acts 2:34-35 (which quotes Psalm 110:2) indicates that the throne of David has been transferred from Jerusalem to heaven.[71] Thus the rule of Christ does not simply belong to a future millennial age but to the present age as well.

According to 1 Corinthians 15:23-26 the triumph of Christ's kingdom can be seen in three stages:[72] (1) the resurrection of Christ is the first stage followed by an indefinite interval; (2) the *parousia* of Christ and the resurrection of believers followed by an undefined interval is the second stage; (3) "the end," when Christ completes the subjugation of His enemies, is the final stage.

Thus Christ's Messianic kingdom is disclosed in history, not simply in the Millennium;[73] in fact, "Christ began His Messianic reign as his resurrection-ascension; but his present reign is invisible . . . the order of the Age to Come will involve a new heaven and a new earth, and will be so different from the present order that we can speak of it as *beyond history.*"[74]

DISPENSATIONAL PREMILLENNIALISM

Introduction. Dispensational premillennialism[75] can be identified through two basic features: (1) a distinction is made between God's program for Israel and His program for the church; (2) a consistently literal interpretation of the Scriptures is maintained. Dispensational premillennialists believe that the church will be raptured (1 Thess. 4:13-18) prior to the Tribulation period; God will judge unbelieving Gentiles and disobedient Israel during the Tribulation (Rev. 6-19). At the end of the Tribulation Christ will return with the church and establish the millennial kingdom on earth. Following the thousand-year reign, Satan will be freed once more, whereupon he and his followers will be cast into the lake of fire (Rev. 20:7-10). The eternal state will follow.

The church from the beginning was premillennial in belief. The *Didache* (c. A.D. 100), Clement of Rome (A.D. 96 or 97), the *Shepherd of Hermas* (A.D. 140-150), Ignatius of Antioch (A.D. 50-115?), Papias (A.D. 80-163), Justin Martyr (b. c. A.D. 100), Irenaeus (d. A.D. 200), Tertullian (A.D. 150-225), and other sources indicate that the early church believed in the return of Jesus Christ to personally establish His earthly kingdom.[76]

Interpretation. There are two basic features that identify dispensational premillennialism. (1) Literal hermeneutic. Literal interpretation refers to "normal" interpretation—understanding words and statements in their normal, customary way.[77] Because prophecies concerning Christ's first coming were fulfilled literally, it makes good sense to expect the prophecies concerning His second coming to be interpreted literally. Furthermore, if prophecy can be spiritualized, all objectivity is lost. Dispensational premillennialists emphasize consistency in interpretation by interpreting prophecy literally. In this premillennialists criticize conservative amillennialists and postmillennialists for changing their methodology in hermeneutics by interpreting literally except in the case of prophecy.

(2) Distinction between Israel and the church. The term *Israel* always refers to the physical posterity of Jacob; nowhere does it refer to the church.[78] Although nondispensationalists frequently refer to the church as the "new Israel," there is no biblical warrant for doing so. Many passages indicate Israel was still regarded as a distinct entity after the birth of the church (Rom. 9:6; 1 Cor. 10:32). Israel was given unconditional promises (covenants) in the Old Testament that must be fulfilled with Israel in the millennial kingdom. The church, on the other hand, is a distinct New Testament entity born at Pentecost (1 Cor. 12:13) and not existing in the Old Testament, nor prophesied in the Old Testament (Eph. 3:9). It exists from

Pentecost (Acts 2) until the rapture (1 Thess. 4:13-18). Herein lies the reason for belief in the pretribulation rapture: the purpose of the Tribulation is to judge unbelieving Gentiles and to discipline disobedient Israel (Jer. 30:7); the church does not have purpose or place in the Tribulation.

Covenants. Although Revelation 20:4-6 confirms dispensational premillennialism, that is not the foundation of it; the foundation of dispensational premillennialism is found in the covenants of the Old Testament.[79] These covenants were *literal, unconditional*, and *eternal.* There are no conditions attached to the covenants and as such they unequivocally promise Israel a future land, a Messianic rule, and spiritual blessings. (1) The Abrahamic covenant. Described in Genesis 12:1-3, the Abrahamic covenant promised a *land* (v. l; cf. 13:14-17; further developed in the Palestinian covenant); numerous *descendants* involving a nation, dynasty, and a throne (v. 2; cf. 13:16; 17:2-6; further developed in the Davidic covenant); and *redemption* (v. 3; cf. 22:18; further developed in the New Covenant).

(2) The Palestinian covenant (Deut. 30:1-10). This covenant guarantees Israel's permanent right to the land. It is unconditional, as seen in the statements "God will," without corresponding obligations. This covenant promises the ultimate return of Israel to the land in repentance and faith (v. 2) in circumstances wherein God will prosper them (v. 3). This covenant will be fulfilled in the Millennium.

(3) The Davidic covenant (2 Sam. 7:12-16). The provisions of this covenant are summarized in v. 16 by the words "house," promising a dynasty in the lineage of David; "kingdom," referring to a people who are governed by a king; "throne," emphasizing the authority of the king's rule; "forever," emphasizing the eternal and unconditional nature of this promise to Israel. This covenant will be fulfilled when Christ returns to rule over believing Israel.

(4) The New Covenant (Jer. 31:31-34). This covenant provides the basis by which God will bless Israel in the future—Israel will enjoy forgiveness of sins through the meritorious death of Christ. The unconditional nature of this covenant is once more seen in the "I will" statements of vv. 33-34.

If these covenants are understood according to their normal meaning, then they call for a future blessing of believing, national Israel in the land under Messiah's rule. These covenants await a fulfillment in the Millennium.

The rapture. The term *rapture* comes from the Latin translation, meaning "caught up," in 1 Thessalonians 4:17. The rapture, which is distinguished from the second coming of Christ, is taught in John 14:1-3; 1 Corinthians 15:51-57; and 1 Thessalonians 4:13-18. Prior to the advent of the Tribulation, Christ will descend from heaven, catching up the church to be with Himself while the Tribulation is unleashed on an unrepentant and unbelieving world.

The pretribulation rapture is espoused for a number of reasons.[80] (1) The *nature* of the Tribulation. The seventieth week of Daniel—the Tribulation—is an outpouring of the wrath of God throughout the seven years (Rev. 6:16-17; 11:18; 14:19; 15:1; 16:1, 19); it is described as God's judgment (Rev. 14:7; 15:4; 16:5-7; 19:2) and God's punishment (Isa. 24:21-22). (2) The *scope* of the Tribulation. The whole earth will be involved (Isa. 24:1, 3, 4, 5, 6, 21; 34:2). It also involves God's chastisement of Israel (Jer. 30:7; Dan. 9:24). If this is the nature and scope of the Tribulation, it is inconceivable that the church will be on earth to experience the wrath of God. (3) The *purposes* of the Tribulation. The divine intentions of the Tribulation will be to judge people living on earth (Rev. 6:10; 11:10; 13:8, 12, 14; 14:6; 17:8) and to prepare Israel for her King (Ezek. 36:18-32; Mal. 4:5-6). Neither of these pertain to the church. (4) The *unity* of the Tribulation. The Tribulation is the seventieth week of Daniel; Daniel 9:24 makes it clear that it has reference to Israel. (5) The *exemption* of the Tribulation. The church is the bride of Christ, the object of Christ's love, not His wrath (Eph. 5:25). It would be a contradiction of the very relationship of Christ and the church for the church to go through the punishments of the Tribulation. Specific statements affirming the church will be kept from the Tribulation (cf. Rom. 5:9;[81] 1 Thess. 5:9; 2 Thess. 2:13; Rev. 3:10).[82] (6) The *sequel* of the Tribulation. The signs of Matthew 24 (and numerous other passages) were given to Israel concerning the second coming of Christ; no signs, however, were given to the church to anticipate the rapture (which means it will come suddenly, as pretribulationists have affirmed). "The church was told to live in the light of the imminent coming of the Lord to translate them in His presence (John 14:2-3; Acts 1:11; 1 Cor. 15:51-52; Phil. 3:20; Col. 3:4; 1 Thess. 1:10; 1 Tim. 6:14; James 5:8; 2 Pet. 3:3-4)."[83]

The tribulation. The Tribulation is the seventieth week of Daniel (Dan. 9:27), a week according to the prophet's terminology equaling seven years. It is the last of a seventy-week (490 years) prophecy regarding Israel's future (Dan. 9:24-27), which began in 444 B.C. Sixty-nine weeks (483 years) concluded with the death of Christ (Dan. 9:26). There is a gap between the sixty-ninth week (A.D. 33) and the seventieth week (the future Tribulation period).[84] As the seventieth week of Daniel, the Tribulation has particular reference to Israel (not the church), because Daniel was told, "Seventy weeks have been decreed for *your people*" (Dan. 9:24). When Jesus detailed the events of the Tribulation in Matthew 24-25, He explained to the disciples what would happen to the *nation Israel*, indicating the Tribulation has reference to Israel.

The Tribulation will begin with the signing of the covenant by the beast, who promises to protect Israel (Dan. 9:27). Technically, the rapture does not begin the Tribulation; there may be a brief period of time between the rapture of the church and the signing of the covenant. The Tribulation will involve the judgment of God upon an unbelieving world, as detailed in Revelation 6-19. The consecutive series of seals, trumpets, and bowl judgments of Revelation detail God's judgment upon unbelievers, climaxing in the triumphant return of Christ to earth with His bride, the church (Rev. 19:11-21).

A prophetic year was regarded as 360 days, with emphasis on the last half of the Tribulation period, called the Great Tribulation (Matt. 24:21) and referred to as 42 months (Rev. 11:2) or 1,260 days (Rev. 11:3).

The nature and purpose of the Tribulation is important in resolving the issue of the church's participation in it. (1) Nature of the Tribulation. It has already been shown that the Tribulation is a time of the outpouring of the wrath of God (1 Thess. 1:10; Rev. 6:16, 17; 11:18; 14:19; 15:1; 16:1, 19); it is a time of punishment (Isa. 24:20-21); a time of trouble (Jer. 30:7; Dan. 12:1); a time of great destruction (Joel 1:15; 1 Thess. 5:3); a time of desolation (Zeph. 1:14, 15); a time of judgment (Rev. 14:7; 16:5; 19:2). If the church is the object of Christ's love, how can it be present during the Tribulation?

(2) Source of the Tribulation. Posttribulationists suggest the Tribulation is a time of Satan's wrath, not God's. The emphasis of Scripture, however, is that the Tribulation is a time of God's wrath poured out in judgment upon an unbelieving world[85] (Isa. 24:1; 26:21; Zeph. 1:18; Rev. 6:16-17; 11:18; 16:19; 19:1-2, etc.).

(3) Purposes of the Tribulation.[86] The first purpose of the Tribulation is to bring about the conversion of Israel, which will be accomplished through God's disciplinary dealing with His people Israel (Jer. 30:7; Ezek. 20:37; Dan. 12:1; Zech. 13:8-9). The second purpose of the Tribulation is to judge unbelieving people and nations (Isa. 26:21; Jer. 25:32-33; 2 Thess. 2:12).

Judgment seat of Christ. The judgment seat of Christ is mentioned in Romans 14:10, 1 Corinthians 3:9-15, and 2 Corinthians 5:10. It does not denote a judgment concerning eternal destiny but rather rewarding church age believers for faithfulness. The term *judgment seat* (Gk. *bema*) is taken from the Grecian games where successful athletes were rewarded for victory in athletic contests. Paul used that figure to denote the giving of rewards to church age believers. The purpose of the judgment seat will be recompense for deeds done in the body, whether good or worthless (2 Cor. 5:10). The believer's works will be examined (1 Cor. 3:13) whether done by self-effort or whether done by God through the individual. If the believer's works do not endure, he is saved but receives no reward (1 Cor. 3:15); if the believer's works are genuine, he is rewarded (1 Cor. 9:25; 1 Thess. 2:19; 2 Tim. 4:8; 1 Pet. 5:4; James 1:12).

That the rewarding takes place prior to the Second Advent is seen in that the bride has already been rewarded when returning with Christ (Rev. 19:8).[87]

Marriage of the Lamb. Prior to the Second Advent, the marriage of Christ and the church takes place in heaven. When Christ returns with His bride in Revelation 19:7 the marriage has already taken place.[88] The marriage has reference to the church and takes place in heaven, whereas the marriage supper has reference to Israel and takes place on earth in the form of the millennial kingdom.[89]

Second coming of Christ. At the end of the Tribulation Christ will return physically to earth (Zech. 14:4) to render judgment and to inaugurate the millennial kingdom (Zech. 14:9-21; Matt. 25:31; Rev. 20:4). The Old Testament and Tribulation saints will be raised at that time to inherit the kingdom (Rev. 20:4). At the Second Advent Christ will judge Jews and Gentiles. The Jews will be judged on the basis of their preparedness for His return (Matt. 25:1-13) and their faithfulness as stewards of the Word of God (Matt. 25:14-30). The saved Jews will enter the millennial kingdom (Matt. 25:21), while the unsaved will be cast into outer darkness (Matt. 25:30). Unbelieving Gentiles will be judged in the Valley of Jehoshaphat (Kidron Valley; Zech. 14:4) regarding their treatment of the Jews (Joel 3:2; Matt. 25:40). A positive response would indicate their belief in Messiah; these will inherit the kingdom (Matt. 25:34), while the unbelieving will be turned away into everlasting punishment (Matt. 25:46).

Millennial kingdom. When Christ returns to earth He will establish Himself as King in Jerusalem, sitting on the throne of David (Luke 1:32-33). The unconditional covenants demand a literal, physical return of Christ to establish the kingdom. The Abrahamic covenant promised Israel a land, a posterity and ruler, and a spiritual blessing (Gen. 12:1-3); the Palestinian covenant promised Israel a restoration to the land and occupation of the land (Deut. 30:1-10); the Davidic covenant promised a ruler for the throne of David (2 Sam. 7:16); the New Covenant promised Israel forgiveness—the means whereby the nation could be blessed (Jer. 31:31-34). At the Second Advent these covenants will be fulfilled as Israel is regathered from the nations (Matt. 24:31), converted (Zech. 12:10-14), and restored to the land under the rulership of her Messiah.

The conditions during the Millennium will depict a perfect environment physically and spiritually. It will be a time of peace (Mic. 4:2-4; Isa. 32:17-18); joy (Isa. 61:7, 10); comfort (Isa. 40:1-2); and no poverty (Amos 9:13-15) or sickness (Isa. 35:5-6). Because only the believers will enter the Millennium, it will be a time of righteousness (Matt. 25:37; Ps. 24:3-4); obedience (Jer. 31:33); holiness (Isa. 35:8); truth (Isa. 65:16); and fulness of the Holy Spirit (Joel 2:28-29).

Christ will rule as king (Isa. 9:3-7; 11:1-10), with David as regent (Jer. 33:15, 17, 21; Amos 9:11); nobles and governors will also rule (Isa. 32:1; Matt. 19:28; Luke 19:17).

Jerusalem will be the center of the world and rule (Zech. 8:3), rising physically to reveal its prominence (Zech. 14:10). There will be topographical changes in Israel (Zech. 14:4, 8, 10).

At the end of the Millennium the unsaved dead of all ages are resurrected and judged at the great white throne. They will be condemned and cast into the lake of fire, their final abode (Rev. 20:11-15). The devil, the beast (the Antichrist), and the false prophet are also cast into the lake of fire (Rev. 20:10).

Eternal state. Following the Millennium, the heavens and the earth are judged (2 Pet. 3:10), because they were the domain of Satan's rebellion against God. The eternal state, the abode of all redeemed (Heb. 12:22-24), will be ushered in (Rev. 21-22).

NOTES ON ESCHATOLOGY

1. Louis Berkhof, *Systematic Theology* (Grand Rapids: Eerdmans, 1941), p. 668; and Millard J. Erickson, *Christian Theology*, 3 vols. (Grand Rapids: Baker, 1985), 3:1169.

2. Francis Brown, S. R. Driver, and Charles A. Briggs, *A Hebrew and English Lexicon of the Old Testament* (Oxford: Clarendon, 1968), p. 1029.

3. Joseph Henry Thayer, *A Greek-English Lexicon of the New Testament* (Grand Rapids: Zondervan, 1962), p. 464.

4. Wilbur M. Smith, *The Biblical Doctrine of Heaven* (Chicago: Moody, 1968), p. 27.

5. See the excellent article by Wilbur M. Smith, "Heaven" in Merrill C. Tenney, ed., *The Zondervan Pictorial Encyclopedia of the Bible*, 5 vols. (Grand Rapids: Zondervan, 1975), 3:60-64. See also his important work *The Biblical Doctrine of Heaven.* This is undoubtedly the most important book on the subject.

6. Smith, "Heaven," in *The Zondervan Pictorial Encyclopedia of the Bible,* 3:61.

7. Keil and Delitzsch have an important comment: "This expression ("gathered to his people"), which is synonymous with 'going to his fathers' (xv. 15), or 'being gathered to his fathers' (Judg. ii. 10), but is constantly distinguished from departing this life and being buried, denotes the reunion in Sheol with friends who have gone before, and therefore presupposes faith in the personal continuance of a man after death, as a presentiment which the promises of God had exalted in the case of the patriarchs into a firm assurance of faith (Heb. xi. 13)." Cf. C. F. Keil and F. Delitzsch, "The Pentateuch" in *Biblical Commentary on the Old Testament*, 25 vols. (Reprint. Grand Rapids: Eerdmans, 1968), 1:263.

8. The preposition translated "among" is *meta* and means "in company with someone; of close association" (William F. Arndt and F. Wilbur Gingrich, *A Greek-English Lexicon of the New Testament and Other Early Christian Literature*, 2nd ed., revised by Wilbur Gingrich and Frederick W. Danker [Chicago: U. of Chicago, 1979], p. 508). It was used to describe the relationship of Christ and the apostles. Cf. Mark 3:14; John 13:33; 14:9; 15:27; 16:4; 17:12, 24. *Meta* is used three times in this verse, stressing man's fellowship with God.

9. Fritz Rienecker, *A Linguistic Key to the Greek New Testament*, Cleon L. Rogers, Jr., ed. (Grand Rapids: Zondervan, 1980), p. 860.

10. R. Laird Harris, "Sheol," *Theological Wordbook of the Old Testament*, 2 vols., edited by R. Laird Harris, Gleason L. Archer, Jr., and Bruce K. Waltke (Chicago: Moody, 1980), 2:892-93.

11. Ibid., 2:893.

12. Hermann Cremer, *A Biblico-Theological Lexicon of New Testament Greek*, 4th ed. (Edinburgh: Clark, 1895), p. 67.

13. H. Buis, "Hades," in Merrill C. Tenney, ed., *The Zondervan Pictorial Encyclopedia of the Bible*, 5 vols. (Grand Rapids: Zondervan, 1975), 3:7.

14. Harris, *Theological Wordbook of the Old Testament*, 2:892.

15. Buis in *The Zondervan Pictorial Encyclopedia of the Bible*, 3:8.

16. The word does not occur in 1 Corinthians 15:55, as some suggest.

17. Rienecker, *Linguistic Key to the Greek New Testament*, p. 775.

18. Henry C. Thiessen, *Lectures in Systematic Theology*, revised by Vernon D. Doerksen (Grand Rapids: Eerdmans, 1979), p. 337.

19. Some who are identified as evangelicals deny the bodily resurrection. Donald Bloesch states, "The resurrection connotes not the resuscitation of the flesh but the renewal of the person. *Soma* can mean body in the earthly, physical sense (here it is identical with *sarx*), but it can also refer to 'the self' or 'breath,' and it is in this latter usage that we can speak of the resurrection of the body. The resurrection entails both soul and body, but it negates the 'flesh' " (Donald G. Bloesch, *Essentials of Evangelical Theology*, 2 vols. [San Francisco: Harper, 1982], 2:184). With its denial of a resurrected physical body of flesh, this statement appears out of harmony with Scripture. Jesus invited Thomas to put his hands in the scar on His side (John 20:27); Jesus ate fish with the disciples on the seashore (John 21:13). Jesus reminded the disciples that "a spirit does not have flesh and bones as you see that I have" (Luke 24:39). These statements indicate that Jesus' resurrected body was more than simply a "renewed self;" they indicate Jesus had a physical body of flesh. His statement in Luke 24 expressly declares that He had a body of flesh.

20. Thiessen, *Lectures in Systematic Theology*, p. 383.

21. D. A. Carson, "Matthew," in Frank E. Gaebelein, ed., *The Expositor's Bible Commentary*, 12 vols. (Grand Rapids: Zondervan, 1984), 8:203.

22. The word translated "being" is the Greek present participle *huparchon*, stressing the condition and continued state of the torment.

23. R. E. Davies, "Gehenna" in *Zondervan Pictorial Encyclopedia of the Bible*, 2:671.

24. Berkhof, *Systematic Theology*, p. 736.

25. J. Dwight Pentecost, *The Words and Works of Jesus Christ* (Grand Rapids: Zondervan, 1981), p. 436.

26. Thiessen, *Lectures in Systematic Theology*, p. 398.

27. The continued emphasis of the preposition "among" in Revelation 21:3 is noteworthy: "The tabernacle of God is *among* men, and He shall dwell *among* them, and they shall be His peoples, and He Himself shall be *among* them." The preposition "among" is *meta*, meaning "in company with someone; in close association" (Arndt and Gingrich, *A Greek-English Lexicon of the New Testament and Other Early Christian Literature*, 2d ed., p. 508). The preposition is used to describe the fellowship of Christ and the disciples (Mark 3:14; John 13:33; 14:9; 15:27; 16:4; 17:12, 24).

28. Berkhof, *Systematic Theology*, p. 708.

29. Jay E. Adams, *The Time Is at Hand* (Philadelphia: Presbyterian & Reformed, 1970), pp. 7-11.

30. Anthony A. Hoekema, *The Bible and the Future* (Grand Rapids: Eerdmans, 1979), p. 174.

31. Anthony A. Hoekema, "Amillennialism," in Robert G. Clouse, ed., *The Meaning of the Millennium: Four Views* (Downers Grove, Ill.: InterVarsity, 1977), pp. 156-58; and William Hendriksen, *More Than Conquerors* (Grand Rapids: Baker, 1939).

32. The events that must take place prior to Christ's second advent are delineated by Berkhof in *Systematic Theology*, pp. 696-703.

33. Ibid., p. 707.

34. Ibid., p. 722.

35. Berkhof states: "All of these passages speak of the resurrection as a single event and do not contain the slightest indication that the resurrection of the righteous and that of the wicked will be separated by a period of a thousand years." Ibid., p. 724; and Hoekema, *The Bible and the Future*, pp. 240-43.

36. Berkhof, *Systematic Theology*, p. 728.

37. Hoekema, *The Bible and the Future*, p. 254.

38. Ibid., pp. 256-57.

39. No distinction is made between the judgment seat of Christ or the great white throne judgment in amillennialism.

40. Hoekema, *The Bible and the Future*, p. 258.

41. Ibid., p. 259.

42. Ibid., p. 259-60.

43. Berkhof, *Systematic Theology*, p. 737.

44. Ibid.

45. Loraine Boettner, *The Millennium* (Philadelphia: Presbyterian & Reformed, 1966), p. 14. See pp. 3-105 for the definitive, representative position of postmillennialism.

46. See Boettner, *The Millennium*, pp. 14-62, and "Postmillennialism," in *The Meaning of the Millennium*, pp. 117-41 for details.

47. Boettner, *The Millennium*, p. 14.

48. B. B. Warfield, *Biblical Doctrines* (New York: Oxford U., 1929), p. 648.

49. Boettner, "Postmillennialism," in *The Meaning of the Millennium*, p. 126.

50. A. H. Strong, *Systematic Theology* (Valley Forge, Pa.: Judson, 1907), pp. 1003, 1008.

51. See the discussion by Charles Hodge, *Systematic Theology*, 3 vols. (Reprint. London: Clarke, 1960), 3:838-44.

52. Ibid., 3:849-50.

53. Strong, *Systematic Theology*, p. 1030.

54. William G. T. Shedd, *Dogmatic Theology*, 3 vols. (Reprint. Nashville: Nelson, 1980), 2:665.

55. For a thorough biblical discussion of the doctrine of hell, see Shedd, *Dogmatic Theology*, 2:667-754. Shedd presents a convincing exegetical study of the eternal duration of the suffering in hell while also refuting the doctrine of annihilation.

56. George E. Ladd, "Historic Premillennialism," in *The Meaning of the Millennium*, pp. 19-27.

57. Ibid., p. 23.

58. Ibid.

59. Ibid., p. 25.

60. Ibid., p. 27.

61. Ibid., p. 28.

62. George E. Ladd, *The Blessed Hope* (Grand Rapids: Eerdmans, 1956), pp. 19-31.

63. Ibid., pp. 62-70.

64. Ibid., p. 88.

65. Ibid., pp. 19-31; Alexander Reese, *The Approaching Advent of Christ* (Reprint. Grand Rapids: Grand Rapids International, 1975), p. 19. The suggestions that posttribulationism was the view of the early church and that pretribulationism is a recent view have both been called into question. See Walvoord, *The Rapture Question* (Grand Rapids: Dunham, 1957), pp. 52-56, 135-39.

66. Reese, *The Approaching Advent of Christ*, pp. 34-94.

67. Ibid., pp. 125-66; Ladd, *The Blessed Hope*, pp. 61-70.

68. Ladd, "Historic Premillennialism," in *The Meaning of the Millennium*, p. 34.

69. Ibid., pp. 29-32.

70. Ibid., pp. 29-30.

71. Ibid., p. 31.

72. Ibid., pp. 38-39.

73. Ibid., p. 39. Ladd states: "The New Testament for the most part does not foresee the millennial kingdom...the New Testament nowhere expounds the theology of the Millennium."

74. Ibid., p. 39.

75. Dispensational premillennialism will hereafter frequently be referred to simply as *premillennialism*. It is safe to say that the vast majority of premillennialists are also dispensationalists; by Ladd's own admission, historic premillennialists are similar to amillennialists in their view of eschatology. It is, in fact, a serious question whether "historic premillennialism" is an apt designation for that eschatological position because it was not, we think, the position of the apostles and because it eliminates the dispensational elements that are historically integral to most premillennialism.

76. Charles C. Ryrie, *The Basis of the Premillennial Faith* (Neptune, N.J.: Loizeaux, 1953), pp. 17-26. This is an extremely valuable source in not only tracing the history of premillennialism but also explaining the hermeneutical principles and the biblical foundation of premillennialism in the unconditional covenants of the Old Testament.

77. See Charles C. Ryrie, *Dispensationalism Today* (Chicago: Moody, 1965), pp. 86-98; and Bernard Ramm, *Protestant Biblical Interpretation*, 3rd ed. (Grand Rapids: Baker, 1970), pp. 119-27.

78. The only passage that is somewhat debatable is Galatians 6:16. The Greek *kai* should probably be understood epexegetically as "even." Israel of God thus refers to believing Israelites who walk by faith and not as the legalistic Judaizers.

79. For a detailed discussion of these covenants see J. Dwight Pentecost, *Things to Come* (Grand Rapids: Zondervan, 1958), pp. 65-128; Ryrie, *The Basis of the Premillennial Faith*, pp. 48-125; John F. Walvoord, *The Millennial Kingdom* (Grand Rapids: Zondervan, 1959), pp. 139-220; and Charles L. Feinberg, *Millennialism: The Two Major Views*, 3d ed. (Chicago: Moody, 1980).

80. See Pentecost, *Things to Come*, pp. 193-218.

81. The statement "wrath" is emphatic in the Greek text, being at the end of the sentence, and additionally is definite by use of the article in *tes orges*. Both of these factors show that it is not just any wrath that is referred to, but a specific wrath—*the wrath* of the Tribulation. If God loved us while we were sinners He has promised to deliver us from *the wrath* to come.

82. For comprehensive studies of this subject see John F. Walvoord, *The Rapture Question*, rev. ed. (Grand Rapids: Zondervan, 1979); and Gerald B. Stanton, *Kept from the Hour* (Grand Rapids: Zondervan, 1956).

83. Pentecost, *Things to Come*, p. 203.

84. See Harold W. Hoehner, *Chronological Aspects of the Life of Christ* (Grand Rapids: Zondervan, 1977), pp. 115-39 where Hoehner discusses the seventieth week and establishes the necessity of a gap between the sixty-ninth and seventieth weeks. See also Alva J. McClain, *Daniel's Prophecy of the Seventy Weeks* (Grand Rapids: Zondervan, 1940).

85. Ibid., pp. 235-37.

86. Ibid., pp. 237-39.

87. The plural term "righteous acts" suggests the righteous deeds of the believer that have been rewarded.

88. The phrase translated "has come" in Revelation 19:7 is the Greek aorist form, *elthen*, indicating it has already taken place.

89. Pentecost, *Things to Come*, p. 227.

For Further Study on Eschatology

HEAVEN AND HELL

** Colin Brown, ed. *The New International Dictionary of New Testament Theology*, 4 vols. Grand Rapids: Zondervan, 1976. See the articles "Heaven," 2:184-96 and "Hell," 2:205-10.

* J. D. Douglas, ed. *The New Bible Dictionary.* Grand Rapids: Eerdmans, 1962. Pp. 510, 518-19.

* Walter A. Elwell, ed. *Evangelical Dictionary of Theology.* Grand Rapids: Baker, 1984. Consult the various articles on "Heaven," "Hell," "Hades," "Sheol," and "Gehenna."

** Millard J. Erickson. *Christian Theology*, 3 vols. Grand Rapids: Baker, 1985. 3:1225-41.

** R. Laird Harris. "Sheol." In *Theological Wordbook of the Old Testament*, 2 vols., edited by R. Laird Harris, Gleason L. Archer, Jr., and Bruce K. Waltke. Chicago: Moody, 1980. 2:892-93.

** Gerhard Kittel and Gerhard Friedrich, eds. *Theological Dictionary of the New Testament*, 10 vols. Translated by Geoffrey W. Bromiley. Grand Rapids: Eerdmans, 1964-1967. See the articles on "Hades," 1:146-49, and "Heaven," 5:497-536.

** Wilbur M. Smith. *The Biblical Doctrine of Heaven.* Chicago: Moody, 1968. This outstanding work ought to be consulted for a definitive discussion of heaven. An extensive bibliography is included.

** William G. T. Shedd. *Dogmatic Theology*, 3 vols. Reprint. Nashville: Nelson, 1980. 2:667-754.

* Merrill C. Tenney, ed. *The Zondervan Pictorial Encyclopedia of the Bible*, 5 vols. Grand Rapids: Zondervan, 1975. See the various articles on "Heaven," "Hell," "Hades," "Sheol," and "Gehenna."

* Merrill F. Unger. *Unger's Bible Dictionary.* Chicago: Moody, 1961. Pp. 462-64, 467.

LAST EVENTS

* Emery H. Bancroft. *Christian Theology*, 2d ed., revised by Ronald B. Mayers. Grand Rapids: Zondervan, 1976. Pp. 345-410.
** Louis Berkhof. *Systematic Theology*. Grand Rapids: Eerdmans, 1941. Pp. 661-738.
** J. Oliver Buswell, Jr. *Systematic Theology of the Christian Religion*, 2 vols. Grand Rapids: Zondervan, 1962. 2:285-538.
** Millard J. Erickson. *Christian Theology*, 3 vols. Grand Rapids: Baker, 1985. 3:1149-1247.
* Charles C. Ryrie. *Basic Theology*. Wheaton: Victor, 1986. Pp. 439-522.
* Henry C. Thiessen. *Lectures in Systematic Theology*, revised by Vernon D. Doerksen. Grand Rapids: Eerdmans, 1979. Pp. 331-99.

AMILLENNIALISM

** Oswald T. Allis. *Prophecy and the Church*. Philadelphia: Presbyterian and Reformed, 1945.
* Louis Berkhof. *Summary of Christian Doctrine*. Grand Rapids: Eerdmans, 1938. Pp. 181-98.
** ⸺. *Systematic Theology*. Grand Rapids: Eerdmans, 1938. Pp. 661-738.
** G. C. Berkouwer. *The Return of Christ*. Grand Rapids: Eerdmans, 1972.
* William E. Cox. *Amillennialism Today*. Phillipsburg, N.J.: Presbyterian & Reformed, 1966. Pp. 57-135.
* Anthony A. Hoekema. "Amillennialism." In Robert G. Clouse, ed., *The Meaning of the Millennium: Four Views*. Downers Grove, Ill.: InterVarsity, 1977. Pp. 155-87.
** ⸺. *The Bible and the Future*. Grand Rapids: Eerdmans, 1979.

POSTMILLENNIALISM

* Loraine Boettner. *The Millennium*. Philadelphia: Presbyterian & Reformed, 1966. Pp. 3-105.
* ⸺. "Postmillennialism." In Robert G. Clouse, ed., *The Meaning of the Millennium: Four Views*. Downers Grove, Ill.: InterVarsity, 1977. Pp. 47-54, 95-103, 117-41, 199-208.
** John Jefferson Davis. *Christ's Victorious Kingdom: Postmillennialism Reconsidered*. Grand Rapids: Baker, 1986. This is an important and recent work on postmillennialism.
** Charles Hodge. *Systematic Theology*. Reprint. London: Clarke, 1960. 3:771-880.
** William G. T. Shedd. *Dogmatic Theology*, 3 vols. Reprint. Nashville: Nelson, 1980. 2:641-754.
** A. H. Strong. *Systematic Theology*. Valley Forge, Pa.: Judson, 1907. Pp. 1003-56.

"HISTORIC" PREMILLENNIALISM

** Robert H. Gundry. *The Church and the Tribulation*. Grand Rapids: Zondervan, 1973. Gundry actually identifies himself as a dispensationalist. However, he holds to a post-tribulational rapture, a tenet of "historic premillennialism."

* George E. Ladd. *The Blessed Hope.* Grand Rapids: Zondervan, 1956.

** _____. *Crucial Questions About the Kingdom of God.* Grand Rapids: Eerdmans, 1952.

* _____. "Historic Premillennialism." In Robert G. Clouse, ed., *The Meaning of the Millennium: Four Views.* Downers Grove, Ill.: InterVarsity, 1977. Pp. 17-40.

** _____. *Jesus and the Kingdom.* New York: Harper, 1964.

* _____. *The Presence of the Future.* Grand Rapids: Eerdmans, 1974.

* Douglas J. Moo. "The Case for the Posttribulation Rapture Position." In *The Rapture: Pre-, Mid-, or Post- Tribulational?* Grand Rapids: Zondervan, 1984.

** J. Barton Payne. *Encyclopedia of Biblical Prophecy.* New York: Harper, 1973.

** Alexander Reese. *The Approaching Advent of Christ.* Reprint. Grand Rapids: Grand Rapids International, 1975.

DISPENSATIONAL PREMILLENNIALISM

** Charles L. Feinberg. *Millennialism: The Two Major Views.* Chicago: Moody, 1980.

* Rene Pache. *The Return of Jesus Christ.* Chicago: Moody, 1955.

** J. Dwight Pentecost. *Prophecy for Today.* Grand Rapids: Zondervan, 1961.

* _____. *Things to Come.* Grand Rapids: Zondervan, 1958. This is the most important work on the subject detailing the chronology of prophecy. This work also compares the differing interpretive positions: premillennialism, postmillennialism, amillennialism, pre-, mid-, post-, and partial rapture views. This is a comprehensive work that ought to be consulted by every serious student of prophecy.

* Charles C. Ryrie. *The Basis of the Premillennial Faith.* Neptune, N.J.: Loizeaux, 1953. This work is particularly important in establishing the foundations of premillennialism.

** Paul Lee Tan. *The Interpretation of Prophecy.* Rockville, Md.: Assurance, 1974. This work is significant in discussing the hermeneutical principles of premillennialism.

* John F. Walvoord. *Israel, the Nations, and the Church in Prophecy.* Grand Rapids: Zondervan, 1988. This is a valuable study delineating the distinctives of Israel, the nations, and the church, showing God's particular purpose for each. This volume is a compilation of three works that were previously published separately.

** _____. *The Millennial Kingdom.* Grand Rapids: Zondervan, 1959. This work discusses the different millennial views, tracing their historical developments and their hermeneutical systems.

* _____. *The Rapture Question*, rev. & enlarged ed. Grand Rapids: Zondervan, 1979. This work explains the biblical basis of the pretribulational view and also interacts with the other tribulational views.

PART 3:
HISTORICAL THEOLOGY

27

INTRODUCTION TO HISTORICAL THEOLOGY

DEFINITION OF HISTORICAL THEOLOGY

Historical theology is the unfolding of Christian theology throughout the centuries. It is cognizant of the development, growth, and changes of Christian theology. It examines the formation of the cardinal doctrines about God, Christ, the Holy Spirit, salvation, the church, and other areas to see how these doctrines have been formulated and how they have evolved.

PURPOSE OF HISTORICAL THEOLOGY

The purpose of historical theology is "to describe the historical origin of the dogma of the Church and to trace its subsequent changes and developments."[1] Historical theology attempts to understand the formation of the doctrines, their development and change—for better or worse. The direction of the church has influenced the direction of theology. Scholasticism, with its emphasis on reason, influenced theology away from the sovereignty of God; the Reformation, with its return to the centrality of the Bible, returned theology to an emphasis on grace; the Enlightenment directed theology toward an antisupernatural bias.

Historical theology delineates the theological movement throughout the centuries. It is important and helpful to see the doctrinal beginnings, how they have evolved, and how they have sometimes deviated from biblical truth.

DIVISIONS OF HISTORICAL THEOLOGY

Four main divisions will be recognized in the development of historical theology: (1) ancient theology (1st Century-A.D. 590); (2) medieval theology (A.D. 590-1517); (3) reformation theology (1517-1750); (4) modern theology (1750-present).

DEVELOPMENT OF HISTORICAL THEOLOGY

IN THE ANCIENT CHURCH

The writings of the apostolic Fathers are significant because those men were close to the events of the life of Christ and the apostolic era. They addressed important issues such as the Trinity, the deity and eternality of Christ, and salvation. The apologists were another second-century group that defended Christianity against criticism and vigorously debated the Christian doctrines with philosophers and emperors. Aberrations of the Christian faith also appeared during this era. Jewish sects sought to retain the Mosaic law, Gnostics sought to tie Christianity to a philosophical system that proclaimed matter evil and spirit good, Marcionites tried to corrupt the canon, and Montanists corrupted the doctrines of the Holy Spirit and eschatology. Early in its history, Christianity was forced both on the defensive and offensive. Because of Marcion, the early church was forced to formulate its canon, affirming the twenty-seven books of the New Testament.

The doctrine of the Trinity was also challenged by Arius; his ongoing debate with Athanasius engulfed the Christian world. In A.D. 325 the Council of Nicea affirmed the historic view of the Trinity in which Christ was understood to be of the same substance as the Father.

The church struggled over the relationship of the two natures of Christ during the fourth and fifth centuries, declaring what was orthodox and what was heretical at Nicea in A.D. 325 and finally at Chalcedon in 451.

The conflict between Augustine and Pelagius raged when Pelagius taught that man was free of original sin and able to choose the good. Augustine, a great proponent of grace, emphasized that God's grace was necessary to rescue man from his state of total depravity. Yet Augustine himself taught the necessity of baptism to wash away sins committed beforehand. Baptismal regeneration and infant baptism quickly became part of the church's teaching.

IN THE MEDIEVAL CHURCH

The medieval period existed from A.D. 590 to 1517 when the Reformation began. The period from 500-1500 is frequently called the Dark Ages because of the ecclesiastical corruption. It was, in fact, this corruption that sparked the Protestant Reformation under Martin Luther.

Roman Catholic doctrine developed considerably during the medieval period: purgatory in 593; prayer to Mary, saints, and angels in 600; kissing the pope's foot in 709; canonization of dead saints in 995; celibacy of the priesthood in 1079; the rosary in 1090; transubstantiation and confessing sins to a priest in 1215; and the seven sacraments in 1439.

A number of controversies confronted the medieval church. The iconoclastic controversy emerged in which the use of images in worship became an integral part of the Western church. The filioque controversy (did the Father alone or the Father *and the Son* send the Spirit) split the Eastern and Western church. The predestination controversy resulted in rejection of Gottschalk's predestinarian view. The eucharist controversy led to the doctrine of transubstantiation. Controversial views over the atonement also emerged.

The medieval period developed scholasticism, which trained scholars to defend the faith from a rational viewpoint. One scholastic, Thomas Aquinas, became prominent in the formulation of Catholic doctrine.

Other doctrinal views emerged as the Roman Catholic church increasingly moved away from Augustinian doctrine. Man was viewed as cooperating with God both in salvation and sanctification. Works became an important part in salvation and sanctification, especially with the adoption of the seven sacraments. The authority of the papacy also emerged during this time, the pope being termed "vicar of Christ." Submission to the pope was essential in both religious and political matters.

IN REFORMATION THEOLOGY

Several individuals figure prominently in the reformation period. Martin Luther, a Roman Catholic priest, sparked the Reformation when he nailed the ninety-five theses opposing the Catholic church on the church door at Wittenberg, Germany, on October 31, 1517. Luther experienced a conversion based on grace through faith, and that truth became a motivation for him throughout his life. Luther stressed a return to the Scriptures as ultimate authority in the believer's life. This period marked a return to a study of the Scriptures, particularly with the publication of the Greek New Testament by Erasmus.

John Calvin, the Swiss reformer, emerged as pastor, writer, politician, and scientific interpreter of the Bible. Calvin's massive *Institutes of the Christian Religion* were to leave their imprint on Protestant theology for centuries to follow. Calvin emphasized the sovereignty of God; all events have been foreordained by God through the eternal decree of God.

Ulrich Zwingli, who generally followed Calvin's theology, influenced the Anabaptist movement, particularly in the Anabaptist view of the Lord's Supper, advocating the memorial view. In rejecting everything the Scriptures did not advocate, Zwingli carried the reformation further than Luther or Calvin.

The doctrine of the atonement became a major controversial issue during this time. Whereas Luther and Calvin stressed the substitutionary atonement of Christ, Socinus, the forerunner of Unitarianism, rejected it. Grotius taught that Christ's death was merely a "token payment" to God. Arminian theology also rejected the strict substitutionary atonement.

The Lord's Supper became an issue of division in the reformation period. Lutheran theology stressed consubstantiation, the view that Christ's presence surrounded the elements. Reformed theology emphasized that grace was transmitted to the recipient in partaking; Zwingli taught the memorial view, no grace was transmitted in partaking.

The Anabaptists dramatically influenced the doctrine of the church with their stress on believers' baptism, and their consequent rejection of infant baptism.

IN MODERN THEOLOGY

Modern theology was seriously affected by the Enlightenment and its after effects. The Enlightenment brought an emphasis on the centrality of man and reason. Eighteenth-century philosophers and theologians carried that concept further. Immanuel Kant stressed the importance of reason and the rejection of all outside that realm. Friedrich Schleiermacher rejected creeds and doctrines, emphasizing instead the importance of feeling in religion. George Hegel saw religion as a constant evolution with the synthesizing of two opposing views. These three men, in particular, left their mark on modern theology. At the root of modern theology lay man's reason, rejection of the supernatural, and a fallible Bible.

In 1919 modern theology took a new turn when Karl Barth, trained in liberal theology, rejected it but did not return completely to conservative theology. Neo-orthodoxy was born. Neo-orthodoxy stressed an experiential encounter with God through a "leap of faith." While neo-orthodox theologians differed widely in their views, none accepted an inspired Bible. Many rejected the historicity of Christ's bodily resurrection: the Bible was to be considered *geschichte* (story) rather than history. Many varied forms of modern theology have evolved from liberal and neo-orthodox theology.

NOTE ON HISTORICAL THEOLOGY

1. Louis Berkhof, *The History of Christian Doctrines* (Edinburgh: Banner of Truth, 1937), p. 20.

FOR FURTHER STUDY ON HISTORICAL THEOLOGY

** Louis Berkhof. *The History of Christian Doctrines*. Edinburgh: Banner of Truth, 1937. Pp. 15-34.

** Geoffrey W. Bromiley. *Historical Theology: An Introduction*. Grand Rapids: Eerdmans, 1978. Pp. xxi-xxix.

* _____. "History of Theology." *New Dictionary of Theology*, edited by Sinclair B. Ferguson, David F. Wright, and J. I. Packer. Downers Grove, Ill.: InterVarsity, 1988. Pp. 309-12.

** E. H. Klotsche. *The History of Christian Doctrine*, rev. ed. Grand Rapids: Baker, 1979. Pp. 1-16.

28
ANCIENT THEOLOGY

The study of the history of doctrine is similar to the study of church history, yet distinct in that a history of theology emphasizes the development of doctrine over the centuries, whereas church history emphasizes in greater detail the outward problems related to the development of the church.

APOSTOLIC FATHERS

The writings of the apostolic Fathers are important because they represent the writings of those who were still alive during the lifetime of the New Testament apostles. The writings of the apostolic Fathers are the following: *The First Epistle of Clement of Rome to the Corinthians*, written about A.D. 97; *The Second Epistle of Clement*, actually a homily rather than an epistle, and written about A.D. 150 by an unknown author rather than Clement. *The Epistles of Ignatius*, the bishop of Antioch, written about A.D. 110 to the churches of the Ephesians, Magnesians, Trallians, Romans, Philadelphians, Smyrnans, and to Polycarp, the bishop of Smyrna; *The Didache*, or "Teaching of the Twelve Apostles," written about A.D. 100; *The Epistle of Barnabas*, written sometime between A.D. 70 and 132; *The Shepherd of Hermas*, written about A.D. 140-145; *The Fragments of Papias*, bishop of Hierapolis, written about A.D. 125.

In studying the works of the apostolic Fathers it quickly becomes apparent that there is a considerable difference in quality from the New Testament writings, and that there is little new material offered. Moreover, instead of a doctrinal emphasis, there is a decided emphasis on ethics. The writings, however, are important in that "they witness to the canonicity and integrity of the New Testament books and form a doctrinal link between the New Testament and the more speculative writings of the apologetes which appeared during the second century."[1]

BIBLIOLOGY OF THE FATHERS

A common feature of the apostolic Fathers is the incorporation of the Scripture into the flow of their writings. They quote extensively from the Old Testament and New Testament, weaving the texts (including lengthy sections) into their writings.

They also recognize the authority of Scripture. Clement warns against sinful living, basing it on "the scripture saith" (*1 Clement, Cor.* 35, 46). Clement affirms the Scriptures to be true, given through the Holy Spirit, and that there was "nothing unrighteous or counterfeit" written in them (*Cor.* 45). He refers to the Old Testament as the "sacred scriptures" and "the oracles of God" (*Cor.* 53).

The apostolic Fathers were frequently allegorical in their interpretation. Referring to the Old Testament quotation, "Rejoice, thou barren that bearest not," it is interpreted as "our Church was barren, before that children were given unto her" (*2 Clement* 2).[2] *The Shepherd of Hermas* is another example. Ignatius exhorts the Trallians: "Recover yourselves in faith which is the flesh of the Lord, and in love which is the blood of Jesus Christ" (*Tral.* 8).

THEOLOGY PROPER OF THE FATHERS

Belief in the Trinity is affirmed; Clement sets forth the equality of the triune God in his statement: "For as God liveth, and the Lord Jesus Christ liveth, and the Holy Spirit, who are the faith and the hope of the elect" (*Cor.* 58). Clement acknowledged God as "Creator and Master of the universe" (*Cor.* 33).

CHRISTOLOGY OF THE FATHERS

Noteworthy truths about Christ are affirmed. Ignatius makes significant statements declaring the deity of Christ: he refers to Him as "Jesus Christ our God" (*Eph.* 1; *Rom.* 1); as indwelling the believer—"He Himself may be in us as our God" (*Eph.* 15, also *Mag.* 12); as being the " mind of the Father" (*Eph.* 3); as the "knowledge of God" (*Eph.* 17); as being "with the Father before the worlds" (*Mag.* 6); and as "the Son" (*Rom.* 1). Polycarp also refers to Jesus as "our Lord and God Jesus Christ" (*Phil.* 12). He is declared to be "sent forth from God" (Clement, *Cor.* 42). His humanity is affirmed in the words of John the Apostle (Polycarp, *Phil.* 7). His resurrection is acknowledged with some frequency (Clement, *Cor.* 24, 42; Ignatius, *Trallians* 9; *Phila.* 1). They affirm His high priesthood and His superiority to angels (Clement, *Cor.* 36, 61; Polycarp, *Phil.* 12).

SOTERIOLOGY OF THE FATHERS

The apostolic Fathers frequently mention that salvation was through the blood of Christ. Clement states: "Let us fix our eyes on the blood of Christ and understand how precious it is unto His Father, because being shed for our salvation it won for the whole world the grace of repentance" (*Cor.* 7; cf. *Cor.* 23, 49; *Barnabas* 5). Clement's statement also seems to suggest unlimited atonement. Ignatius indicates it is faith in the blood of Christ that procures salvation (*Smyrn.* 6). Repentance is also emphasized (*2 Clement* 13; 19).

A prominent emphasis, however, is the necessity of works in salvation. In a lengthy discussion Clement emphasizes the importance of obedience in procuring salvation, indicating Lot was saved because of his hospitality (*Cor.* 11) as was Rahab (*Cor.* 12). Salvation also involves doing the will of the Father, keeping the flesh pure, and guarding the commandments of the Lord (*2 Clement* 8). Love is also necessary for entrance into the kingdom (*2 Clement* 9) as is the necessity of bidding farewell to worldly enjoyments and refusing evil lusts (*2 Clement* 16). Practicing righteousness is also essential (*2 Clement* 19).

These statements indicate a commendable emphasis on a godly walk, but at the same time confuse the salvation message and detract from the free grace of God. This is one of many doctrinal errors that surfaced very early in the history of Christian thought.

ECCLESIOLOGY OF THE FATHERS

There is a clear development of the church offices of deacon, presbyter (elder), and bishop, with increasing authority granted to them. A predominant emphasis of the apostolic Fathers is that believers are to submit to the authority of the elders and bishops. Clement exhorts believers to be at peace with the elders (*Cor.* 54), submit to their authority, and receive chastisement from them (*Cor.* 57; 63). Polycarp teaches submission to elders and deacons (*Phil.* 5). Ignatius likens the believer's obedience to the bishop as Christ's obedience to the Father and as the apostles to Christ (*Mag.* 13). The leaders are to be accorded considerable honor. To the Trallians Ignatius writes: "Do nothing without the bishop; but be ye obedient also to the presbytery, as to the Apostles of Jesus Christ . . . let all men respect the deacons as Jesus Christ, even as they should respect the bishop as being a type of the Father and the presbyters as the council of God" (*Tral.* 2, 3). To the Philadelphians Ignatius states: "As many as are of God and of Jesus Christ, they are with the bishop" (*Phila.* 3). He further says: "Do ye all to follow your bishop, as Jesus Christ followed the Father, and the presbytery as the Apostles; and to the deacons pay respect, as to God's commandment. . . . Wheresoever the bishop shall appear, there let the people be; even as where Jesus may be, there is the universal Church" (*Smyrn.* 8).

The developing authority of the bishop is clearly seen in Ignatius's statements.

> Let no man do aught of things pertaining to the Church apart from the bishop. Let that be held a valid eucharist which is under the bishop or one to whom he shall have committed it. . . . It is not lawful apart from the bishop either to baptize or to hold a love-feast; but whatsoever he shall approve, this is well-pleasing also to God; that everything which ye do may be sure and valid. . . . It is good to recognize God and the bishop. He that honoureth the bishop is honoured of God. (*Smyrn.* 8; 9.)

The Lord's Supper is referred to as "the medicine of immortality and the antidote that we should not die but live for ever in Jesus Christ" (*Eph.* 20). The *Didache* gives instruction concerning the prayers before and after the Lord's Supper (9; 10). Instruction is also given concerning baptism and fasting (7; 8).

ESCHATOLOGY OF THE FATHERS

There is not a great deal of information concerning last things. *Second Clement* refers to the kingdom of God coming at God's appearing (12; 17); people will be amazed when the kingdom of this world is received by Christ (17). Distinction is also made between the kingdom and life eternal (5); it is in the kingdom that believers will be crowned for contending bravely (7). At Christ's appearing those who have lived ungodly lives will be judged and punished in unquenchable fire (17).

Barnabas exhorts believers on the basis of the imminent return of Christ (21). Papias acknowledges a millennial kingdom in this statement.

> The blessing thus foretold belongs undoubtedly to the times of the Kingdom, when the righteous shall rise from the dead and reign, when too creation renewed and freed from bondage shall produce a wealth of food of all kinds from the dew of heaven and from the fatness of the earth . . . how the Lord used to teach concerning those times, and to say, The days will come, in which vines shall grow, each having ten thousand shoots, and on each shoot ten thousand branches, and on each branch again ten thousand twigs, and on each twig ten thousand clusters, and on each cluster ten thousand grapes, and each grape when pressed shall yield five-and-twenty measures of wine. . . . and all the animals, using these fruits which are products of the soil, shall become in their turn peaceable and harmonious, obedient to man in all subjection. (*Frag. Pap.* 14.)

ANCIENT APOLOGISTS

Because of a general misunderstanding of Christianity and the slander that resulted, there arose prominent Gentile Christians who wrote "apologies" in defense of Christianity. These early Christian writers became known as Apologists. Their task was threefold.[3] (1) They defended Christianity against the false charges of atheism, cannibalism, incest, indolence, and other anti-social behavior. (2) They took the offensive, charging the Jews with misunderstanding the typological and shadowy nature of the Old Testament in anticipating Christ. They also attacked paganism, its immorality, as well as the immorality of the pagan deities, particularly in comparison with the revelation of God in the New Testament. (3) They were also constructive, arguing for the reality of the New Testament revelation through fulfilled prophecy and through miracles.

The major apologetical writings and Apologists are the following:[4] *Epistle to Diognetus,* written by an unknown author about A.D. 150; Quadratus, bishop of Athens, wrote an apology, now lost, to emperor Hadrian about A.D. 125; Aristides, an Athenian philosopher wrote to either Hadrian or Antoninus Pius; Melito, bishop of Sardis, wrote an apology to Marcus Aurelius; Claudius Apollinaris, bishop of Hierapolis, also wrote an apology to Marcus Aurelius; Miltiades, an Athenian philosopher wrote against both Jews and pagans; Athenagoras defended Christians in an apology to Marcus Aurelius in about A.D. 177, refuting charges of atheism, cannibalism, and immorality; Theophilus of Antioch wrote three works defending belief in God and the hope of the resurrection, denouncing heathen beliefs and exposing the inferiority of heathen literature compared to the Old Testament; Tatian, an Assyrian, defended the reasonableness of Christianity against the "worthlessness of paganism"; and Justin Martyr, considered the greatest of the apologists, wrote two *Apologies* and the *Dialog with Trypho the Jew.* He was a converted philosopher and retained his philosophical bent in defending Christianity.

BIBLIOLOGY OF THE APOLOGISTS

The *Epistle to Diognetus* emphasizes the revelation of God; the Creator of the universe has revealed Himself to mankind: "The Invisible God Himself from heaven planted among men the truth and the holy teaching which surpasseth the wit of man, and fixed it firmly in their hearts" (*Diog.* 7). This statement contrasts the revelation of God to man with the speculative groping of philosophers. The epistle declares that God has revealed Himself through the Word (meaning Christ), a philosophical term (Gr. *logos*), meaning *word* or *discourse*; hence, Christ is the discourse of God to mankind. In this sense, particularly, the Apologists emphasize Christ as Teacher who communicates the revelation of God to mankind. The reader is exhorted, therefore, to "understand the discourses which the Word holds by the mouth" (*Diog.* 11).

THEOLOGY PROPER OF THE APOLOGISTS

The author of the *Epistle to Diognetus* declares at length the insignificance and futility of gods of wood and stone. He reminds his reader that these gods are made of stone just like the stone the people walk on; these gods rot and decay. In fact, the gods made of silver and gold have to be locked up at night and guarded (*Diog.* 2). God is referred to as the "Almighty Creator of the Universe, the Invisible God" (*Diog.* 7), and "the Master and Creator of the Universe, Who made all things and arranged them in order" (*Diog.* 8). Justin Martyr refers to God as "the most true God, the Father of righteousness and temperance and the other virtues, who is untouched by evil" (*1 Apol. Just.* 6).

Prior to His revelation people did not know what He was like; now they know Him to be "kindly and good and dispassionate and true, and He alone is good" (*Diog.* 8). While man was deserving of punishment and death, God was longsuffering and patient, therefore, He sent His Son as a ransom for sin (*Diog.* 9). In this God has demonstrated that He is a God of love (*Diog.* 10). The words of John 3:16 are prominent in this declaration.

Athenagoras provides a clear statement of monotheism and the Trinity. He states: "We acknowledge one God, who is uncreated, eternal, invisible, impassible, incomprehensible, illimitable. He is grasped only by mind and intelligence, and surrounded by light, beauty, spirit, and indescribable power. By him the universe was created through his Word, was set in order, and is held together. (I say 'his Word'), for we also think that God has a Son" (*Athen. Plea* 10). The Holy Spirit is referred to as "an effluence from God, flowing from him and returning like a ray of the sun" (Ibid.). Justin Martyr gives an interesting statement of the Trinity in saying the Son holds the second place and the prophetic Spirit the third rank (*1 Apolo. Just.* 13).

CHRISTOLOGY OF THE APOLOGISTS

As the Word, Christ has been sent forth from God to be rejected by His people but believed on by the Gentiles (*Diog.* 11). He is referred to as eternal in the statement, "This Word, Who was from the beginning . . . Who is eternal" (*Diog.* 11). Although Athenagoras describes Christ as "the first offspring of the Father," he nonetheless denies the Son was created. He says, "since God is eternal mind, he had his Word within himself from the beginning, being eternally wise" (*Athen.* 10; cf. *1 Apol. Just.* 21). Christ is further described as the Son of God but also as God's "Word in idea and in actuality . . . the Son of God is the mind and Word of the Father" (*Athen.* 10).

In His work, Christ is presented as "a ransom for us, the holy for the lawless, the guileless for the evil, the just for the unjust, the incorruptible for the corruptible, the immortal for the mortal" (*Diog.* 9). Through One Righteous Man people are justified (*Diog.* 9). The language of Romans 5 and 1 Peter 3:18 are clearly in view.

ECCLESIOLOGY OF THE APOLOGISTS

Justin Martyr suggests Isaiah 1:16-20 refers to Christian baptism, apparently suggesting that this rite produces the new birth (*1 Apol. Just.* 61). Justin also indicates the Eucharist is only for believers and states that the "food consecrated by the word of prayer which comes from him, from which our flesh and blood are nourished by transformation, is the flesh and blood of that incarnate Jesus" (66). The seeds of the Roman Catholic doctrine of transubstantiation are noticeable in this statement.

ANCIENT PERVERSIONS

RELATING TO MOSAIC LAW

It is readily understood how Jewish converts to Christianity would still cling to the Mosaic law, because this was even a problem with New Testament personalities like Peter. It was also the problem the church dealt with in Acts 15. Early in church history there were Jewish Christian sects that taught it was essential to adhere to the law for salvation.[5] The *Nazarenes* strictly observed the Mosaic law, enforcing the Sabbath, circumcision, and dietary laws, although they did not impose it on Gentiles. They acknowledged the virgin birth and deity of Jesus, recognizing His teachings as superior to Moses and the prophets. The Nazarenes used only the Hebrew edition of Matthew's gospel, but at the same time they recognized Paul's apostleship. The *Ebionites* denied the virgin birth and deity of Christ, teaching that He was the natural son of Mary and Joseph and as such, just a man, howbeit, a prophet. Paul's apostleship was rejected; they considered him an apostate from the law. The *Elkesaites* claimed an angel had given a book to Elkesai that taught that Christ was an angel born of human parents. Rejecting Christ's virgin birth, they taught He was the highest archangel. Insisting the law was still in force, they taught the necessity of Sabbath-keeping and circumcision. The epistles to the Colossians and First Timothy may refer to this heresy.

RELATING TO GNOSTIC PHILOSOPHY

The name *gnosticism* comes from the Greek word *gnosis*, meaning "knowledge," and stresses the character of this heresy. Gnosticism was a philosophical system built upon Greek philosophy that stressed matter was evil but spirit was good. This being the case, God could not have created the material world. In their philosophical system, therefore, the *Gnostics* constructed a series of emanations or aeons, beginning with the highest God who was entirely spirit. One of the intermediate beings in the chain was a demiurge, the God of the Old Testament whom they disliked. This demiurge "had enough of spirit in him to have creative power and enough of matter to create the material world."[6]

This philosophical system also affected the Gnostics' view of Jesus. There were two differing views: one view was that because matter was evil, Jesus could not have actually come in human form; He only appeared in human form and only appeared to suffer. The other view suggested that the divine Logos came upon the human Jesus and departed prior to the crucifixion. Salvation was also philosophical—it was knowing the truth, which was imparted only to the esoteric (those who are specially initiated). Sin and evil were associated with ignorance or lack of knowledge. A modern form of gnosticism is Christian Science.

RELATING TO MARCION'S CANON

Marcion, a man of great wealth, came to Rome about A.D. 139 and there attempted to influence the church. When he was unsuccessful he organized his own church with its peculiar doctrines. He followed some aspects of gnosticism but rejected its philosophical emphases. Marcion believed the book of Galatians was the foundational truth of the gospel, which had been corrupted by mingling the gospel with law. Hence, Marcion rejected all Scripture except ten of Paul's epistles and an edited version of Luke. He distinguished between the Creator God of the Old Testament, who had given the Old Testament law and whom Marcion considered evil, and the God of the New Testament, who revealed Himself in Christ. Christ, however, was not the Messiah of the Old Testament, nor did He come in a physical body, but He revealed the merciful God of the New Testament. This was in opposition to the Old Testament God whom Jesus rejected through His opposition to the law. For this reason the Jews crucified Jesus. He was not harmed, however, because He did not have a real body. Marcion proclaimed a salvation by faith, in contrast to the salvation through knowledge.

Marcion actually aided the church in that it was forced to determine the true canon of Scripture because of Marcion's selective canon.

RELATING TO MONTANIST TEACHING

In contrast to Gnosticism there arose the strict, ascetic teaching of Montanus of Phrygia in Asia Minor. At his baptism Montanus spoke in tongues, declaring that the age of the Holy Spirit had come and that the end of the world was near. The New Jerusalem was soon to come down out of heaven and inaugurate the millennial age. He and his disciples were the last prophets, bringing the revelation of God to the world. Two women, as his disciples, also were known as prophets giving new revelation. Montanus found refuge in the writings of John and taught that he (Montanus) was the mouthpiece through whom the Paraclete, the Holy Spirit, was revealing Himself to the world. While being generally orthodox in his docrine, Montanus taught "that the Holy Spirit continued to speak through prophets, and among these it included women."[7] Because it was the end of the age, the gifts of the Spirit were being manifested.

Montanus emphasized strict moral requirements of his followers and for that reason found a considerable following in Asia Minor. He emphasized fasting and dieting, prohibited a second marriage after the death of a mate, and encouraged celibacy as well as martyrdom.

Although the Council of Constantinople condemned Montanism in A.D. 381, the teaching enjoyed considerable popularity, even converting Tertullian to its teaching.

CANONIZATION AND CREEDS

RULE OF FAITH

With the advent of heretical groups and teachers, particularly Marcion, it became necessary to determine what was true doctrine and which books were inspired Scripture and which were not. Prior to the recognition of the New Testament canon the early Christians were forced to develop a "rule of faith" (Lat. *regula fidei*) to determine true doctrine and recognize and reject false doctrine. This was the earliest form of the Apostles' Creed. The earliest form of the Rule of Faith was the baptismal formula of Matthew 28:19, which confessed a triune God. The Roman symbol was probably an elaboration of the baptismal formula.

A brief statement of faith called the Old Roman Form, believed to have its origin with the apostles and brought to Rome by Peter, was in use by the middle of the second century A.D. The short form of the Old Roman Form reads: "I believe in God the Father Almighty, and in Jesus Christ His Only Son our Lord, who was born of the Holy Ghost and Virgin Mary; crucified under Pontius Pilate, and buried; the third day He rose from the dead; He ascended into heaven and sitteth at the right hand of the Father, from thence He shall come to judge the quick and the dead. And in the Holy Ghost; the holy Church; the forgiveness of sins; the resurrection of the body; the life everlasting."[8]

CANON OF THE NEW TESTAMENT

In the initial stages of recognizing a New Testament canon, Paul's letters were read in churches and recognized as authoritative. In opposition to Marcion and the Gnostics, Irenaeus recognized the four gospels. In approximately A.D. 175 the Muratorian Canon listed all New Testament books except Hebrews, James, 1 and 2 Peter, and 1 John. Writing in A.D. 367, Athanasius listed all the books of the New Testament. Widespread agreement on these twenty-seven books followed.

APOSTLES' CREED

The Apostles' Creed, the oldest form appearing approximately A.D. 340, was a further endeavor to affirm the true doctrines of Scripture and repudiate the false teachings of Marcion and others. Legend has it that each of the apostles contributed an article to the creed. It may well have had its origin in a concise statement such as Matthew 28:19. Other foundational Scripture statements could be Romans 10:9-10; 1 Corinthians 12:3; 15:4; and 1 Timothy 3:16.

The origin of the Apostles' Creed was in apostolic times with the preaching and teaching of the apostles. The term *Rule of Faith* has reference to the Apostles' Creed in its earliest form. The creed developed into two forms, one shorter, known as the Old Roman Form, and the longer creed, known as the Received Form. The Received Form reads: "I believe in God the Father Almighty; Maker of Heaven and Earth; and in Jesus Christ His only (begotten) Son our Lord; who was conceived by the Holy Ghost, born of the Virgin Mary; suffered under Pontius Pilate, was crucified, dead, and buried; He descended into hell; the third day He rose from the dead; He ascended into heaven; and sitteth at the right hand of God the Father Almighty; from thence He shall come to judge the quick and the dead. I believe in the Holy Ghost; the holy catholic Church; the communion of saints; the forgiveness of sins; the resurrection of the body; and the life everlasting. Amen."[9] The earliest form of the expanded creed first appeared about A.D. 650 but was in existence at least by A.D. 460.

The purpose of the Apostles' Creed was not to supplant Scripture but to corroborate the Scriptures and to protect the church from the infiltration of heretics. For example, the confession that God is Almighty and Maker of heaven and earth militates against Marcion's concept of an evil Creator God; the confession that Jesus was born of a virgin and died excludes the Gnostic and Docetic beliefs that Jesus was merely a phantom.

ANCIENT TRINITARIANISM

A major problem in formulating the doctrine of the Trinity related to the Old Testament monotheistic belief. How could the church recognize the belief that God is one and yet acknowledge the deity of Christ? In its beginnings the church had no clear concept of the Trinity, in fact, Christ was variously explained as the mind of God—an impersonal Logos who became personal at the incarnation. Others pictured Him as eternal with the Father yet subordinate to the Father. There was even less understanding concerning the Person of the Holy Spirit. Some understood Him to be subordinate to both the Father and the Son.

MONARCHIANISM

The two issues facing the church concerning the Trinity were maintaining the unity of God on the one hand and affirming the deity of Christ on the other hand. The first heresy connected with the Trinitarian controversy was Monarchianism of which there were two forms. The less influential form was *dynamic monarchiansim,* which stressed the unity of God at the expense of the person of Christ. This doctrine was advanced by Theodotus of Byzantium in A.D. 190 and later by Paul of Samosata, bishop of Antioch. He taught that the Logos was

> consubstantial with the Father, but was not a distinct Person in the Godhead. He could be identified with God, because He existed in Him just as human reason exists in man. He was merely an impersonal power, present in all men, but particularly operative in the man Jesus. By penetrating the humanity of Jesus progressively, as it did that of no other man, this divine power gradually deified it. And because the man Jesus was thus deified, He is worthy of divine honour, though He cannot be regarded as God in the strict sense of the word.[10]

It is clear that although this doctrinal view maintained the oneness of God, the distinctiveness of the three persons within the Godhead was lost.

A second form of monarchianism was *modalistic monarchianism,* the more popular of the two. It also sought to preserve the unity of God but additionally emphasized the deity of Christ. It was also called *patripassianism,* out of the belief that the Father was the one who became incarnate, suffered, and died. It was further known as *Sabellianism* after Sabellius, its proponent in the east.

The designation *modalistic* stressed the idea that God was one God who variously manifested Himself as Father, other times as the Son, and other times as the Holy Spirit. Even though modalistic monarchianists spoke of three persons, they nonetheless believed that there was but one essence of deity who variously manifested Himself in three different modes. Hence, the Father was born as the Son, the Father died on the cross and the Father also raised Himself from the dead. In fact, Praxeas, the probable originator of modalistic monarchianism, said the Father became His own Son.

ARIANISM

The most prominent name in the Trinitarian controversy is Arius, a presbyter of Alexandria. In opposition to modalistic monarchianism, Arius taught that only one who is called God is eternal and, in fact, is incomprehensible. To suggest that Christ is eternal would be to affirm two Gods. Arius taught that the Son had a beginning; there was a time when the Son did not exist. The Son was not of the "same substance" (Gk. *homoousios*) as the Father; the Son was created by the Father—also referred to (incorrectly) by Arius as being generated by the Father. Arius further taught that Christ was created prior to all other creation, He being the medium through which God later created. As such, Christ is the highest ranking of all created beings, however Christ is subject to change because He is not God.

Arius was opposed by the highly capable Athanasius of Alexandria. Athanasius stressed the oneness of God while maintaining three distinct Persons within the Godhead. He also propounded the eternal existence of the Son. Athanasius stands out in the history of the church as one of the brilliant defenders of orthodoxy.

COUNCIL OF NICEA

Because of the Arian controversy, the Council of Nicea met in A.D. 325 to deal with the problem. Three hundred bishops attended. The council rejected Arianism and any concessions to Arius and, with the approval of the emperor, adopted the following creed.

> We believe in one God, the Father Almighty, maker of all things visible and invisible, and in one Lord, Jesus Christ, the Son of God, the only-begotten of the Father, that is, of the substance [*ousias*] of the Father, God from God, light from light, true God from true God, begotten, not made, of one substance [*homoousion*] with the Father, through whom all things came to be, those things that are in heaven and those things that are on earth, who for us men and for our salvation came down and was made flesh, and was made man, suffered, rose the third day, ascended into the heavens, and will come to judge the living and the dead.

The designation *homoousion* stressed that Christ is not merely like the Father but He is of the identical substance as the Father. The terms "God from God" and "true God from true God" further stressed the deity of Christ. At the same time "begotten, not made" and "came down" stressed His eternality.

Following the council of Nicea controversy continued, with the center of controversy revolving around the term *homoousian*, a term to which many objected. The controversy shifted back and forth, with both Arius and Athanasius being banished at different times. The West favored Athanasius's view, whereas the East wanted a modified statement. In A.D. 381 Emperor Theodosius convened the Council of Constantinople and accepted the Nicene Creed, reaffirming the *homoousian* clause.

COUNCIL OF CONSTANTINOPLE

Good as it was, the Nicene Creed only affirmed "We believe in the Holy Ghost." There was no clear doctrinal formulation concerning the Person of the Holy Spirit. Arius, meanwhile, taught that the Holy Spirit was the first creation of the Son. Macedonius, bishop of Constantinople, taught that the Holy Spirit was a creature, like angels, subordinate to the Son. Athanasius emphasized that the Holy Spirit was also of the same substance (*homoousian*) as the Son and the Father. It was not until the Council of Constantinople in A.D. 381, however, that the matter was settled. The council adopted the following statement: "We believe in the Holy Ghost, the Lord, the Giver of Life, who proceedeth from the Father, who with the Father and the Son together is worshipped and glorified, who spake by the prophets." The statement emphasized that the Holy Spirit was not subordinate to the Son nor the Father but was of the same substance as Father and Son.

ANCIENT CHRISTOLOGY

BACKGROUND

The Trinitarian controversy was clearly also a Christological controversy. The discussion involved not only the true deity and genuine humanity of Christ, but also the relationship of His two natures. The pendulum swung back and forth: the Docetists denied Jesus' humanity; the Ebionites denied His deity; the Arians "reduced" His deity, while the Apollinarians "reduced" His humanity; the Nestorians denied the union of the two natures, while the Eutychians emphasized only one nature.

APOLLINARIANISM

Apollinaris (the Younger) was opposed to Arianism so that he taught an opposite extreme, which also proved heretical. Apollinaris taught "that the divine pre-existent Logos took the place of the 'spirit' in the man Jesus, so that Jesus had a human body and a human 'soul' but not a human 'spirit.' He held also that Christ had a body, but that the body was somehow so sublimated as to be scarcely a human body . . . Apollinaris reduced the human nature of Christ to something less than human."[11] Apollinaris believed the spirit of man was the seat of sin; therefore, to remove any possibility of sin from Christ, Apollinaris felt he had to deny the humanity of Jesus' spirit.

The problem with Apollinaris's view was that while retaining the deity of Christ, he denied the genuine humanity of Christ. In Apollinaris's teaching Jesus was less than man. In seeking the unity of the person of Christ, Apollinaris denied Jesus' humanity. Apollinaris was condemned at the Council of Constantinople in A.D. 381.

NESTORIANISM

Nestorius disliked the Chalcedon statement describing Mary as "mother of God." Although the statement also affirmed "as to his humanity," Nestorius resisted this statement that led to the worship of Mary. Instead of acknowledging two natures in one Person concerning Christ, Nestorius "denied the real union between the divine and the human natures in Christ . . . (and) virtually held to two natures and two persons."[12] Nestorius taught that while Christ suffered in His humanity, His deity was uninvolved (which was also the view of John of Damascus). The teaching was a denial of a real incarnation; instead of affirming Christ as God-man, He was viewed as two persons, God and man, with no union between them. Nestorius believed that because Mary was only the source of Jesus' humanity, He must be two distinct persons.

Nestorius sought to defend Christ's deity against Arianism and to resist Mariolotry. But he ultimately denied the unity of Christ. He was condemned at the Council of Ephesus in A.D. 431.

EUTYCHIANISM

In reaction to Nestorius, Eutyches (A.D. 380-456) founded the monophysite heresy, declaring that Christ had only one nature. "The divine nature was so modified and accommodated to the human nature that Christ was not really divine . . . At the same time the human nature was so modified and changed by assimilation to the divine nature that He was no longer genuinely human."[13]

The result of the Eutychian teaching was that Christ was neither human nor divine; Eutychians created a new third nature. In their teaching, Christ had only one nature that was neither human nor divine.

This view was condemned at the Council of Chalcedon in A.D. 451, but the view continued in the Coptic church in Egypt.

A variation of this view was later propagated under a new designation, the monothelite view, suggesting Christ had only one will. This teaching was condemned at Constantinople in A.D. 680.

PERVERSIONS OF THE DOCTRINE OF CHRIST [14]

Party	Time	Reference	Human Nature	Divine Nature
Docetists	Late 1st century	1 John 4:1-3	Denied	Affirmed
Ebionites	2nd century	Irenaeus	Affirmed	Denied
Arians	4th century	Condemned at Nicea, A.D. 325	Affirmed	Reduced
Apollinarians	4th century	Condemned at Constantinople, A.D. 381	Reduced	Affirmed
Nestorians	5th century	Condemned at Ephesus, A.D. 431	Affirmed	Affirmed [15]
Eutychians	5th century	Condemned at Chalcedon, A.D. 451	Reduced	Reduced [16]

ANCIENT ANTHROPOLOGY

SIN AND GRACE

Pelagius. Pelagius, a British monk, was a man quite unlike Augustine, having led a quiet, austere life and knowing nothing of the spiritual conflicts that Augustine experienced.

Pelagius first propounded his doctrine of man and salvation in Rome about A.D. 400. In 410 he came to Africa where he met Augustine, with whom he disagreed sharply. The conflicting issues involved original sin and freedom of the will. Pelagius taught that man is born neutral with the ability and freedom to choose good or evil; man is not born with original sin. Because God creates each soul individually at birth, each person is born free and neutral as Adam, and each has the capacity for good or evil; in fact, a sinless life is possible. Adam's sin did not affect the human race; it affected only himself. Hence, any person can choose good or evil at any given moment, having the capacity for good as well as evil. Pelagius explained the problem of sin in the world as being due to "wrong education" or "bad example."[17] God's grace was helpful in overcoming evil in life, but it was unnecessary for salvation because man could choose that of his own ability. Because man is not born inherently evil, Pelagius also rejected the necessity of infant baptism for salvation; infant baptism was merely a dedicatory rite.

Augustine. Augustine was born in A.D. 354 in North Africa. Although he had a Christian mother, he led a wild life that was restless and without peace. In his search for peace he became a disciple of the Manichaeans and later studied Neo-Platonic philosophy. Under the influence of Ambrose, bishop of Milan, Augustine was introduced to Christianity, but he experienced the "terrible power of sin and his own inability to overcome his sinful desires."[18] Upon reading Romans 13:14, Augustine experienced release from his burdens and was converted. He immediately began a diligent study of Paul's epistles, wherein he had experienced the grace of God.

Undoubtedly the greatest theologian between Paul and Luther, Augustine formulated the following doctrines.[19]

Man's original state prior to the Fall was one of natural perfection in which he enjoyed the image of God in wisdom, holiness, and immortality. Through the Fall man lost his privileged status with God. Love for God was exchanged with love for self; he passed into a state wherein he was unable not to sin (Lat. *non posse non peccare*). The will was entirely affected, now being inclined toward evil instead of neutral. Man was no longer free.

The fallen sinful nature and disposition was passed on to the entire human race. In the Augustinian doctrine of the imputation of sin, all humanity was "seminally present" in Adam. Therefore, when Adam sinned, each person of the entire human race to the end of time was judged guilty as having individually participated in the first sin. This was Augustine's understanding of Romans 5:12. Even infants were included in this depravity.

God's grace was absolutely essential in rescuing man from his state of total depravity. Because of the Fall, man's only freedom was freedom to sin; man was now incapable of doing right. To secure salvation, God extends His grace—which Augustine termed "irresistible grace." God's grace does not operate contrary to the nature of man, but "so changes the will that man voluntarily chooses that which is good. The will of man is renewed and thus restored to its true freedom. God can and does so operate on the will that man of his own free choice turns to virtue and holiness. In this way the grace of God becomes the source of all good in man."[20] This grace was even necessary for the ability to believe the gospel. "Grace is imparted to sinful man, not because he believes, but in order that he may believe; for faith itself is the gift of God."[21]

Conclusion. The distinction between Pelagius and Augustine was sharp. Pelagius believed man was born neutral, without a depraved will and without an inherent tendency toward evil. He believed man had the ability to choose to serve God without any need of God's grace. Augustine believed Adam's fall had affected the entire human race so that man was thoroughly

PELAGIAN AND AUGUSTINIAN VIEWS OF SIN

Comparisons	Pelagius	Augustine
Effect of Fall	Only Adam affected	All humanity affected
Original sin	No	Yes
Hereditary sin	No	Yes
Humans at birth	Born neutral	Born with fallen nature
Man's will	Free	Enslaved to sin
Fact of universal sin	Due to bad examples	Due to man's innate sinfulness: man is "not able not to sin"
Turning to God in salvation	Is possible independent of God's grace	Only possible through God's grace

corrupt, his will inclined toward evil. Only the intervention of God's grace could save man; man was not free to choose good. Salvation was not man cooperating with God, but man was entirely dependent on God's grace for salvation.[22]

Pelagius was ultimately accused of heresy at the Synod of Jerusalem, and Pelagianism was condemned as heresy in A.D. 416 at the Synods of Carthage and Mileve. The Council of Ephesus also condemned Pelagianism in A.D. 431.

Unfortunately semi-Pelagianism, which attempted to follow a mediating position, resulted. Followers of this new mediating theology stressed that both the grace of God and the free will of man were operative in salvation. Man could cooperate with God in salvation because his will was weakened but not fatally injured in the Fall. Semi-Pelagianism ultimately came to full fruition in the Roman Catholic church.

ANCIENT SOTERIOLOGY

ATONEMENT AND SALVATION

The apostolic Fathers taught the substitutionary atonement of Christ and adhered to the statements and phraseology of Scripture; they did not elaborate on the theme and provide a further explanation of the atonement. It is noteworthy, however, to consider their statements on the atonement. Clement refers to the blood of Christ as being precious to the Father "because being shed for our salvation it won for the whole world the grace of repentance" (*1 Cor.* 7). This statement seems to imply that man makes a saving contribution to his own salvation ("the grace of repentance" as distinct from what the blood achieved); it also implies unlimited atonement ("for the whole world"). Clement also refers to the blood of Christ providing redemption for all who believe (*1 Cor.* 12). Ignatius makes a similar statement (*Smyrn.* 6). Other similar statements indicate the concept of the blood of Christ was prominent for salvation. Polycarp refers to substitutionary atonement in stating that Christ "took up our sins in His own body upon the tree" (*Phil.* 8).

Athanasius taught Christ's substitutionary atonement as satisfying not the holiness or justice of God but rather the truth of God. Augustine taught that the death of Christ assuaged the wrath of God and reconciled man to God; however, Augustine's teaching on the atonement is not well formulated.

APPLICATION OF SALVATION

While the apostolic Fathers recognized the importance of the death of Christ in procuring salvation, they nonetheless stressed works as a part of salvation. Clement goes to great length in stressing the importance of obedience in salvation, citing Enoch, Noah, Abraham—even Lot. Rahab was saved "for her faith and hospitality" (*Clem. 1 Cor.* 12). Salvation is expressed in terms of a "path in holiness and righteousness" (48); baptism (*Clem. 2 Cor.* 6); doing the will of the Father, keeping the flesh pure, guarding the commandments of the Lord (8); loving one another (9); refusing evil lusts (16); and practicing righteousness (19). The cooperation of man with God in transacting salvation became increasingly prominent in the centuries that followed. The belief that baptism atones for sin became prominent and eventually so did the belief that the suffering of some Christians, such as martyrs, could atone for others.[23]

Men such as Pelagius deviated even further from the Scriptures, suggesting salvation could be attained by keeping the law. Gnostics taught salvation was attained through avoiding contamination with matter. Origen, the allegorist, taught that eventually all—even demons—would be saved, however, after undergoing educative punishment.[24]

ANCIENT ECCLESIOLOGY

BAPTISM

The *Teaching of the Twelve Apostles* requires that a person be baptized in the name of the triune God; prior to baptism, the one baptizing and the one being baptized should fast (*Did.* 7).

Very early in the Christian church, prominence was given to the rite of baptism so that many, in effect, taught baptismal regeneration. Justin Martyr taught that, to obtain the remission of sins, the name of the Father should be invoked over the one being baptized (*1 Apol.* 61). "After baptism, the Christian was supposed not to sin, and some sins, if indulged in after that rite had been administered, were regarded as unforgivable."[25] Although this concept was not as emphatic among the apostolic Fathers, it became increasingly so in the following centuries. Augustine, for instance, taught that original sin and sins committed before baptism were washed away through baptism.[26] For that reason he advocated baptism for infants. Augustine nonetheless emphasized the need for repentance and faith as the conditions whereby baptism might be received by adults. Irenaeus and Origen both acknowledged the validity of infant baptism, but Tertullian opposed it.

The mode of baptism was not expressly taught by the apostolic Fathers; however, the *Didache* permits affusion as an alternate mode. The general practice in the early church, nonetheless, was immersion.

LORD'S SUPPER

In writing to the Ephesians, Ignatius identifies the Lord's Supper as the "medicine of immortality and the antidote that we should not die but live for ever in Jesus Christ" (*Eph.* 20). The *Didache* gives instructions for observing the Lord's Supper, with prescribed prayers designated for use both prior and following it. Baptism was also a qualification for participation (*Did.* 9, 10). Justin Martyr teaches that "the food consecrated by the word of prayer which comes from him, from which our flesh and blood are nourished by transformation, is the flesh and blood of that incarnate Jesus" (*1 Apol.* 66). The beginnings of the Roman Catholic doctrine of transubstantiation can be seen in this statement.

Early Christians observed the *agape* (Gk.) or love feast prior to the Lord's Supper. This food was reckoned as a thank offering to God, blessed by the bishop and presented as a *thank offering* (Gk. *eucharist*) to God; hence, the meal came to be known as a thanksgiving or offering. With the advent of the priesthood, the priest assumed Christ's place in offering Christ's body and blood as a sacrifice for sins. The Roman Catholic Mass clearly has its beginnings in this ritual of the early church. Although recognizing the ordinance as a memorial, Augustine himself taught the elements became the body and blood of Christ.

ANCIENT ESCHATOLOGY

Papias, who wrote about A.D. 130-140, provided a rather developed statement concerning the millennial kingdom. Irenaeus indicates Papias spoke of "the Kingdom, when the righteous shall rise from the dead and reign, when too creation renewed and freed from bondage shall produce a wealth of food of all kinds" (*Frag.* 14). Papias refers to the Lord teaching that "vines shall grow, each having ten thousand shoots . . . a grain of wheat shall produce ten thousand heads . . . grass shall produce in similar proportions, and all the animals, using these fruits which are products of the soil, shall become in their turn peaceable and harmonious, obedient to man in all subjection" (Ibid.). Photius indicates that Papias and Irenaeus both taught "that the kingdom of heaven will consist in enjoyment of certain material foods" (*Frag.* 17). These statements give quite a clear affirmation of a literal millennial kingdom.

Of the early writers, Irenaeus gives perhaps the most sophisticated statements concerning the millennial kingdom. He distinguishes between the resurrections, teaching that the righteous will rise first to receive a newly created order and to reign. Judgment follows the reign. Irenaeus bases this belief on the Abrahamic covenant (Gen. 12:1-3) (*Against Heresies* 32). He also speaks of a New Covenant in which the inheritance of the land would be renewed in which "new produce of the vine is drunk" (33). He teaches that the just would rise to reign in a created order made new and set free, producing an abundance of food (33). Irenaeus quotes Isaiah 11 and 65 in referring to the millennial age. Irenaeus's use of Scripture appears considerably more sophisticated and systematized than that of his contemporaries.

George N. H. Peters identifies Justin Martyr, Tatian, Irenaeus, Tertullian, Hippolytus, and Apollinaris (as well as others) as second-century premillennialists.[27] Amillennialism can be related to the allegorical school of interpretation in Alexandria, Egypt, and men like Clement, Origen, and Dionysius. Augustine was probably the first explicit amillennialist, teaching that the present age was a conflict between the church and the world. The reason for Augustine opting for amillennialism is noteworthy: he observed that Christians holding to a millennial view saw the kingdom in carnal terms. As a result, Augustine abandoned a literal millennial view.

NOTES ON ANCIENT THEOLOGY

1. Louis Berkhof, *The History of Christian Doctrines* (Edinburgh: Banner of Truth, 1937), p. 39.

2. J. B. Lightfoot, ed. and trans., *The Apostolic Fathers* (Reprint. Grand Rapids: Baker, 1956), p. 44.

3. Berkhof, *History of Christian Doctrines,* pp. 56-57; and Earle E. Cairns, *Christianity Through the Centuries* (Grand Rapids: Zondervan, 1954), p. 114.

4. E. H. Klotsche, *The History of Christian Doctrine,* rev. ed. (Grand Rapids: Baker, 1979), pp. 23-25.

5. Berkhof, *History of Christian Doctrines,* pp. 44-45; and Klotsche, *History of Christian Doctrine,* pp. 28-29.

6. Cairns, *Christianity Through the Centuries,* p. 106.

7. Kenneth Scott Latourette, *A History of Christianity* (New York: Harper, 1953), p. 129.

8. Addison H. Leitch, "Apostles' Creed, The" in Merrill C. Tenney, ed., *The Zondervan Pictorial Encyclopedia of the Bible,* 5 vols. (Grand Rapids: Zondervan, 1975), 1:220.

9. James Orr, "Apostles' Creed, The" in James Orr, ed., *The International Standard Bible Encyclopaedia,* 5 vols. (Grand Rapids: Eerdmans, 1939) 1:204-5.

10. Berkhof, *History of Christian Doctrines,* p. 78.

11. J. Oliver Buswell, Jr., *A Systematic Theology of the Christian Religion,* 2 vols. (Grand Rapids: Zondervan, 1962), 2:49-50.

12. A. H. Strong, *Systematic Theology* (Valley Forge, Pa.: Judson, 1907), p. 671.

13. Buswell, *A Systematic Theology of the Christian Religion,* 2:51.

14. Ibid., 2:46.

15. Nestorians believed that Christ was two persons.

16. Eutychians taught that Christ had one mixed nature, neither fully human nor fully divine.

17. Berkhof, *History of Christian Doctrines,* p. 133.

18. Klotsche, *History of Christian Doctrine,* p. 88.

19. Ibid., pp. 89-93.

20. Berkhof, *History of Christian Doctrines,* p. 135.

21. William G. T. Shedd, *A History of Christian Doctrine,* 2 vols. (Reprint. Minneapolis: Klock & Klock, 1978), 2:50-92. See valuable and extended discussions of Augustine's doctrines of man and sin.

22. See Norman L. Geisler, "Augustine of Hippo" in Walter A. Elwell, ed., *Evangelical Dictionary of Theology* (Grand Rapids: Baker, 1984), pp. 105-7, for a concise summary of Augustine's theology.

23. Berkhof, *History of Christian Doctrines,* p. 205.

24. Latourette, *History of Christianity,* p. 151.

25. Ibid., p. 138.

26. Ibid., p. 179.

27. George N. H. Peters, *The Theocratic Kingdom,* 3 vols. (Grand Rapids: Kregel, 1952), 1:495-96.

FOR FURTHER STUDY ON ANCIENT THEOLOGY

APOSTOLIC FATHERS

* Louis Berkhof. *The History of Christian Doctrines.* Edinburgh: Banner of Truth, 1937 Pp. 37-42.

* Geoffrey W. Bromiley. *Historical Theology: An Introduction.* Grand Rapids: Eerdmans, 1978. Pp. 3-17.

* E. H. Klotsche. *The History of Christian Doctrine,* rev. ed. Grand Rapids: Baker, 1979. Pp. 17-22.

* Kenneth Scott Latourette. *A History of Christianity.* New York: Harper, 1953. Pp. 115-18, 131-33.
** J. B. Lightfoot, trans. and ed. *The Apostolic Fathers.* Reprint. Grand Rapids: Baker, 1956.
** Cyril C. Richardson, ed. *Early Christian Fathers.* New York: Macmillan, 1970.

ANCIENT APOLOGISTS

* Louis Berkhof. *The History of Christian Doctrines.* Edinburgh: Banner of Truth, 1937. Pp. 56-61.
* Geoffrey W. Bromiley. *Historical Theology: An Introduction.* Grand Rapids: Eerdmans, 1978. Pp. 18-26.
* Earle E. Cairns. *Christianity Through the Centuries.* Grand Rapids: Zondervan, 1954. Pp. 114-17.
* E. H. Klotsche. *The History of Christian Doctrine,* rev. ed. Grand Rapids: Baker, 1979. Pp. 23-27.
* Kenneth Scott Latourette. *A History of Christianity.* New York: Harper, 1953. Pp. 83-84.
** J. B. Lightfoot, trans. and ed. *The Apostolic Fathers.* Reprint. Grand Rapids: Baker, 1956. Pp. 245-59.
** Cyril C. Richardson, ed. *Early Christian Fathers.* New York: Macmillan, 1970. Pp. 205-397.

ANCIENT PERVERSIONS

* Louis Berkhof. *The History of Christian Doctrines.* Edinburgh: Banner of Truth, 1937. Pp. 43-55.
** Geoffrey W. Bromiley. *Historical Theology: An Introduction.* Grand Rapids: Eerdmans, 1978. Pp. 18-29.
* Walter A. Elwell, ed. *Evangelical Dictionary of Theology.* Grand Rapids: Baker, 1984.
* E. H. Klotsche. *The History of Christian Doctrine,* rev. ed. Grand Rapids: Baker, 1979. Pp. 28-39.
** William G. T. Shedd. *A History of Christian Doctrine,* 2 vols. Reprint. Minneapolis: Klock & Klock, 1978. Vol. 1.
* Merrill C. Tenney, ed. *The Zondervan Encyclopedia of the Bible,* 5 vols. Grand Rapids: Zondervan, 1977.

CANONIZATION AND CREEDS

** J. N. D. Kelly. *Early Christian Creeds.* Reprint. Chicago: Longman, 1981. Pp. 364-434.
.* E. H. Klotsche. *The History of Christian Doctrine.* Grand Rapids: Baker, 1979. Pp. 40-45.
* Addison H. Leitch, "Apostles' Creed, The." In Merrill C. Tenney, ed., *The Zondervan Pictorial Encyclopedia of the Bible*, 5 vols. Grand Rapids: Zondervan, 1975. 1:220-21.
** A. C. McGiffert. *The Apostles' Creed.* New York: Scribner's, 1902.
* J. L. Neve. *A History of Christian Thought,* 2 vols. Philadelphia: Muhlenburg, 1948. 1:61-68.
* James Orr. "Apostles' Creed, The." In James Orr, ed., *The International Standard Bible Encyclopaedia,* 5 vols. Grand Rapids: Eerdmans, 1939. 1:204-6.

** Philip Schaff. *The Creeds of Christendom*, 3 vols., 6th ed. New York: Scribner's, 1890. Vol. 1.

ANCIENT TRINITARIANISM

** Joseph Ayer, Jr. *A Source Book for Ancient Church History.* New York: Scribner's, 1913. Pp. 297-356.

* Louis Berkhof. *The History of Christian Doctrines.* Edinburgh: Banner of Truth, 1937. Pp. 83-93.

* G. W. Bromiley, rev. *The International Standard Bible Encyclopaedia*, 4 vols. Grand Rapids: Eerdmans, 1988.

* Walter A. Elwell, ed. *Evangelical Dictionary of Theology.* Grand Rapids: Baker, 1984.

* E. H. Klotsche. *The History of Christian Doctrine*, rev. ed. Grand Rapids: Baker, 1979. Pp. 58-70.

** Kenneth Scott Latourette. *A History of Christianity.* New York: Harper,, 1953. Pp. 142-69.

** A. T. Robertson, P. Schaff, and H. Wace, eds. *A Select Library of Nicene and Post-Nicene Fathers of the Christian Church*, 14 vols. New York: Scribner's, 1903. Vol. 4, *Select Writings and Letters of Athanasius, Bishop of Alexandria.*

** Philip Schaff. *Creeds of Christendom*, 3 vols., 6th ed. New York: Scribner's, 1890.

ANCIENT CHRISTOLOGY

* Louis Berkhof. *The History of Christian Doctrines.* Edinburgh: Banner of Truth, 1937. Pp. 101-13.

** J. Oliver Buswell, Jr. *A Systematic Theology of the Christian Religion*, 2 vols. Grand Rapids: Zondervan, 1962. 2:46-52.

* E. H. Klotsche. *The History of Christian Doctrine*, rev. ed.. Grand Rapids: Baker, 1979. Pp. 71-82.

** Kenneth Scott Latourette. *A History of Christianity.* New York: Harper, 1953. Pp. 165-73.

** R. Seeberg. *Text-Book of the History of Doctrines*, rev. ed. Philadelphia: United Lutheran, 1905. 1:243-88.

** William G. T. Shedd. *A History of Christian Doctrine*, 2 vols. Reprint. Minneapolis: Klock & Klock, 1978. 1:392-408.

* David F. Wells. *The Person of Christ.* Westchester, Ill.: Crossway, 1984. Pp. 98-109.

ANCIENT ANTHROPOLOGY

* Louis Berkhof. *The History of Christian Doctrines.* Edinburgh: Banner of Truth, 1937. Pp. 131-39.

* Geoffrey W. Bromiley. *Historical Theology: An Introduction.* Grand Rapids: Eerdmans. 1978. Pp. 109-23.

** William Cunningham. *Historical Theology*, 2 vols. Reprint. London: Banner of Truth, 1960. 1:321-58.

* Norman L. Geisler. "Augustine of Hippo." In Walter A. Elwell, ed., *Evangelical Dictionary of Theology.* Grand Rapids: Baker, 1984. Pp.105-7.

** _____, ed. *What Augustine Says.* Grand Rapids: Baker, 1982.

* E. H. Klotsche. *The History of Christian Doctrine,* rev. ed. Grand Rapids: Baker, 1979. Pp. 83-96.

* Kenneth Scott Latourette. *A History of Christianity.* New York: Harper,, 1953. Pp. 173-82.

** A. T. Robertson, P. Schaff, and H. Wace, eds. *A Select Library of Nicene and Post-Nicene Fathers of the Christian Church,* 14 vols. New York: Scribner's, 1903. Vol. 5, *Saint Augustine's Anti-Pelagian Works.*

* B. L. Shelley. "Pelagius, Pelagianism." In Walter A. Elwell, ed., *Evangelical Dictionary of Theology.* Grand Rapids: Baker, 1984. Pp. 833-34.

ANCIENT ECCLESIOLOGY

* Louis Berkhof. *The History of Christian Doctrines.* Edinburgh: Banner of Truth, 1937. Pp. 242-56.

** J. F. Bethune-Baker. *An Introduction to the Early History of Christian Doctrine.* London: Methuen. Pp. 376-92.

** Geoffrey W. Bromiley. *Historical Theology: An Introduction.* Grand Rapids: Eerdmans, 1978.

** G. Dix. *The Shape of the Liturgy.* Westminster: Dacre, 1945.

* E. H. Klotsche. *The History of Christian Doctrine,* rev. ed. Grand Rapids: Baker, 1979. Pp. 97-108.

* J. L. Neve. *A History of Christian Thought,* 2 vols. Philadelphia: Muhlenberg, 1946. 1:152-64.

* Kenneth Scott Latourette. *A History of Christianity.* New York: Harper, 1953. Pp. 193-205.

29

MEDIEVAL THEOLOGY

The medieval period can be understood as existing from A.D. 590, when Gregory I was inaugurated as bishop of Rome, until 1517, when Martin Luther sparked the Protestant Reformation. Gregory I was a serious student of Augustine and wrote prolifically, interpreting the doctrines of Augustine.

The era from A.D. 500-1500 is also often called the Dark Ages because of the corruption of the church during this period—a condition, in fact, that led to the Reformation under Martin Luther, who sought to cleanse the church and restore true doctrine to it.

Roman Catholic doctrine developed during the medieval period. In general, the church assumed a semi-Pelagian stance, depreciating the fall of man so that he was no longer considered spiritually dead but weakened; nonetheless, able to cooperate with God in salvation. Specifically, doctrines such as purgatory, prayers to Mary and the saints, sacrifice of the Mass, and transubstantiation were initiated during this period.

MEDIEVAL CONTROVERSIES

ICONOCLASTIC CONTROVERSY

The term *iconoclastic* comes from the word *icon* (from the Greek *eikon*, "to resemble"), signifying a religious picture or image, and *klan* (Gk., meaning "to break"). Hence, an iconoclast was one who advocated the destruction of images. Toward the end of the third century people in the church began the use and adoration of images[1], a practice that increased in the succeeding centuries. The Eastern branch of the church was particularly involved through the influence of heathen worship. The West also, however, became involved. Images and pictures of Mary, Christ, the apostles, and other saints were used increasingly to aid the illiterate people in their prayers. Although the church taught that the images were to be venerated but not worshiped, it is probable that the illiterate laypersons worshiped the images.

Basil the Great indicated that "the honor paid to the image passes on to the prototype"—an action that would surely encourage the use and worship of images. Proponents of images declared that "they beautify the Churches, awaken the memories of the past, and take the place of the Scriptures for the illiterate."[2] The issue climaxed in A.D. 726 when Emperor Leo forbade the use of images. Popes Gregory II and III, with John of Damascus, defended the use of images. John taught that images had sacramental value and dispensed grace. He also distinguished between worship of God and veneration of images. In A.D. 787, an ecumenical church council met in Nicea and approved the use of icons, stating that images of Christ and the saints should receive "affection and respectful reverence." Thereafter, image worship became an integral part of the church. In A.D. 843, the Eastern church abandoned the use of sculptured figures and confined its use of images to pictures.

FILIOQUE CONTROVERSY

The *filioque* (Gk., meaning "and Son") controversy relates to the question, "Who sent the Holy Spirit?" Was it the Father or the Father *and the Son*? Historically, this seemingly non-consequential point has marked the difference between the Eastern and Western churches. The Greek (Eastern) church taught the "single procession" of the Holy Spirit—only the Father was involved in sending the Spirit. On the basis of John 15:26, and the fact that the Son is of the same essence as the Father, the Roman (Western) church taught the "double procession" of the Holy Spirit—both the Father and the Son were responsible for sending the Holy Spirit. At the Council of Toledo in A.D. 589 the phrase "and the Son" was added to the Nicene Creed. The Eastern church refused to accept the doctrine and this was ultimately the issue that permanently split the Eastern and Western churches in 1054.

PREDESTINATION CONTROVERSY

The Roman Catholic church had proceeded on a semi-Pelagian course that led a monk named Gottschalk, in the ninth century, to attempt to return the church to the Augustinian doctrine of predestination. Gottschalk vigorously defended Augustinian doctrine, emphasizing that God had determined all things through His eternal decree. Gottschalk rejected the notion of election based on mere foreknowledge of man's spiritual responses. He taught a double predestination: an election to salvation for some and reprobation to eternal punishment for others. Others said that sin was not a part of God's predestination; God only predestined punishment for sin. Therefore, election to damnation could not be a fact. Gottschalk also emphasized salvation by grace rather than works.

Gottschalk was severely opposed because his teaching on the way of salvation left no room for sacraments and good works—nor for other aspects of medieval church doctrine. In A.D. 848, at the Synod of Mainz, Gottschalk was condemned, scourged, and imprisoned for life. He died in 869 without recanting.

LORD'S SUPPER CONTROVERSY

In A.D. 831 Radbertus, a monk in the monastery of Corbie, France, wrote a treatise entitled "On the Body and Blood of the Lord," in which he taught the doctrine of transubstantiation. Radbertus taught that when the priest uttered Christ's words of the consecration ("This is my body . . . this is my blood"), a miracle took place: the bread and wine changed to the literal body and blood of Christ. Although the outward phenomena, including color, form, and taste of the physical elements, remained the same, inwardly a miracle took place. Radbertus based his belief on John 6 ("I am the bread of life . . . eat the flesh of the Son of Man and drink His blood") and Christ's upper room statements, interpreted as literal language. He said that the value of this miracle, however, only applied to the believer who partook in faith; it was noneffective for the unbeliever.

This view was initially opposed but was officially adopted in the thirteenth century by the Roman Catholic church.

MEDIEVAL SCHOLASTICISM

Scholasticism is the term given to the monastic schools called *scholae* during the eleventh and twelfth centuries. It was there that scholars came to study in order to defend and explain the faith from a rational point of view. They did not endeavor to uncover new truth but sought to defend the doctrines of the church through reason. "Theology was to be treated from a philosophical point of view rather than from a Biblical viewpoint."[3]

Scholasticism became prominent in large part because of the translation in the twelfth century of the works of Aristotle. Scholastics followed the deductive logic of Aristotle in their approach to understanding biblical truth. There were three forms of scholasticism. Realism, which followed Plato, taught that universal ideas exist apart from individual objects. Anselm and Bonaventura were prominent realists. Moderate realists, who followed Aristotle, taught that universal ideas such as truth and goodness have an objective existence but are not separate from their existence in individual things. Abelard and Thomas Aquinas (who was the greatest of the scholastics) were representative of this view. Nominalism, which was a reaction against realism, taught that ideas have no existence outside the mind. Occam represented this view. Nominalists denied anything outside of human experience, hence, they denied the Trinity. The concept of nominalism was seen in later centuries in empiricism and pragmatism.

MEDIEVAL ANTHROPOLOGY

ANSELM

Anselm (1033-1109) taught the doctrine of original sin but emphasized that original could also be called "natural" because it did not refer to the origin of the human race. It referred only to the condition of the individual as a result of the Fall. Because all human nature was representative in Adam and Eve, their sin affected all humanity; it was henceforth propagated with a corrupted nature. Children are also affected because they partake of human nature. They sinned in Adam and are therefore polluted with sin and stand guilty.

Anselm taught that true freedom was lost as a result of the fall but the "voluntary faculty" was not destroyed. Man retains his will; but Anselm distinguished between freedom—which he rejected—and voluntary ability—which he acknowledged. Anselm rejected the notion that man has freedom with the sense of indifference, to choose either right or wrong; man's will is made for the purpose of choosing good.[4]

THOMAS AQUINAS

Thomas not only defined sin as something negative—the loss of original righteousness—but also something positive—the lust of the flesh. This sinful nature is propagated by the parents to their offspring. Aquinas taught that Adam's sin was transferred to all humanity because of the unity of the human race. He declared, "All who are born of Adam may be considered as one man; thus men derived from Adam are members of one body." The results of original sin are alienation of the human will from God, disorder of the powers of the soul, and liability to punishment.[5]

The scholastics, with whom Aquinas was identified, recognized capital sins as pride, covetousness, lust, anger, gluttony, envy, and sloth. These they divided into mortal sins, which constituted a willful transgression of the law of God and which separated man from God; venial sins, however, were considered only "a deviation from God without sufficient reflection or full consent of the will. They may be atoned for by temporal punishments."[6]

SINLESSNESS OF MARY

Because of the growing prominence of Mary, the church taught that Mary was without sin. The debated question, however, was whether Mary was conceived without sin, or whether she, too, was stained by original sin but then made immaculate in her prenatal state.[7] Radbertus first taught that Mary remained sinless in the womb and entered the world without the stain of sin. When the doctrine of the immaculate conception was first presented in 1140 it was opposed by Bernard of Clairvaux and Thomas Aquinas, but the belief gradually gained acceptance and was declared faithful dogma in 1854.

CONCLUSION

During the medieval period, the Roman Catholic view of anthropology emerged—man originally possessed a righteousness that was supernaturally endowed; he was not morally neutral. As a result of the Fall, man lost his supernatural righteousness, but he did not lose his natural abilities. The result was not total depravity but rather moral neutrality out of which man had the ability to cooperate with God in salvation (semi-Pelagianism).

MEDIEVAL SOTERIOLOGY

THE ATONEMENT

Anselm. Anselm taught that through sin man had robbed God of the honor that was due Him. God could elect either to punish sin or to provide satisfaction whereby His honor would be vindicated by providing the gift of His Son. He chose the latter and through His death Christ brought honor back to God. In turn Christ received a reward. He passes this on to sinners in the form of forgiveness.[8] (Further discussion of this viewpoint appears in the section on theories regarding the meaning of Christ's atonement in chap. 24, "Soteriology: Doctrine of Salvation.")

Abelard. In reaction to the Commercial Theory of Anselm, Abelard taught that God did not require the death of Christ to atone for sin. Instead, God revealed His love through the death of Christ. In Abelard's view, God freely pardons sinners because of His love revealed in Christ's death. His view was called the Moral Influence view.

Others. Bernard of Clairvaux rejected Abelard's theory stating that it was the blood of Christ, not His example, that procured believers' redemption. Peter Lombard combined the concepts of Anselm and Abelard, stating that Christ died for sinners. That death moves sinners to love God, and as a result they are released from sin.

Thomas Aquinas also reflected views of both Anselm and Abelard. He viewed Christ as the head of the human race who dispensed His perfection to the human race. Aquinas viewed Christ as "the teacher and pattern of the human race by His teachings, acts, and sufferings. These sufferings reveal more particularly the love of God and awaken a responsive love in the hearts of men."[9]

Conclusion. The medieval age contributed little to a further awareness of the doctrine of the atonement.

GOD'S GRACE

Although the medieval church gave verbal assent to Augustine, the doctrinal teachings were moving it increasingly in a direction of semi-Pelagianism. It was the general view that man's will was not destroyed through the Fall; he could cooperate with God in salvation. In general, however, the scholastics acknowledged the need for grace in salvation although grace was variously defined. Thomas Aquinas taught that grace is essential for salvation. He indicated that it is impossible for man to turn from a state of guilt or sin to righteousness apart from God's grace.[10] However, Aquinas distinguished between "free grace" and "sanctifying grace."[11] Included in free grace is knowledge (faith and understanding), demonstration (healing, miracles, predictive prophecy), and communication (tongues and interpretation). Sanctifying grace involves operative (prevenient) and cooperative (subsequent) grace. In cooperative grace Aquinas understood man to be cooperating with God in receiving God's grace.

Peter Lombard also distinguished between operating grace, which is wholly a work of God that enables man to turn to God in faith, and cooperating grace (which involves all subsequent grace), which requires man's cooperation with God for its reception. The inclination, even among the scholastics, was toward semi-Pelagianism.

FAITH AND WORKS

The scholastics categorized faith in two dimensions. *Fides informis* is a knowledge of church doctrine, while *fides informata* is the faith that produces works of love. It is only *fides informata* that results in salvation and justification. Moreover, religious life is centered not on faith, but on love and good works. That is because the scholastics' view of justification did not produce a new relationship with God but merely the capability for good works.[12]

JUSTIFICATION

The scholastics taught that justification is effected not as a judicial act of God but as a cooperative venture in which God dispenses sanctifying grace to the individual. Simultaneously, the individual turns to God in contrition and faith in an act of free will. However, in scholastic teaching, justification does not include security of salvation; that is unattainable.

MEDIEVAL ECCLESIOLOGY

THE SACRAMENTS

There was a twofold interest in the sacraments in the medieval church: to present salvation to the individual in a tangible form and to tie the salvation of the individual to the church.[13] The sacraments thus became visible signs of the communication of grace to the individual.

The number of sacraments had not been determined; some authorities had advocated six, others seven, still others twelve. Peter the Lombard was the first to delineate seven sacraments: baptism, Lord's Supper, confirmation, extreme unction, penance, ordination, and marriage. These seven sacraments were officially acknowledged at the Council of Florence in 1439.

SPIRITUAL EFFECTS OF MEDIEVAL SACRAMENTS[14]

Sacrament	Effect
Baptism	Regeneration; confers spiritual life
Confirmation	Strengthens spiritual life
Eucharist	Nourishes spiritual life
Penance	Restores spiritual life if lost through sin
Extreme unction	Heals the soul; sometimes the body
Holy orders	Creates rulers of the church
Matrimony	God's blessing on family; children produced; heaven filled with the elect

It becomes apparent that according to medieval theology salvation and sanctification are achieved through works rather than through the grace of God.

THE PAPACY[15]

During the scholastic period, and with the support of scholastics such as Thomas Aquinas and Bernard of Clairvaux, the papacy claimed spiritual and temporal supremacy over the entire world. This concept arose from the notion that Christ had given Peter authority over the other apostles, and that Peter had been the first bishop of Rome with the concomitant authority passing on to the future bishops of Rome.

Gratian taught that to disobey the pope is to disobey God. Thomas Aquinas taught that the pope, as bishop of Rome, is the supreme head who guarantees purity of morals and teaching in the church; the pope alone can teach what is to be believed. Pope Innocent III declared the pope to be the "vicar of Christ" on earth and was thereafter addressed as "holiness" or "most holy." Innocent III also taught that Melchizedek is a type of the pope. Because the pope has the keys to the kingdom and the power to bind and loose, anyone who does not submit to the pope's authority is declared a heretic. There is therefore no salvation outside the Roman Catholic church.

The pope's supremacy also passed to the state. Innocent III declared that the Lord gave Peter the entire earth that he might rule over it. Hence, all civil authority should be subject to the pope. The pope has authority to depose rulers, receive tribute, give away territory, punish objectors, and annul a country's legislation. Pope Gregory VII declared that he was accountable to God for the kingdoms of the world. In 1302 Pope Boniface VIII issued a papal bull stating that the pope has authority over two realms—he controls the spiritual sword as well as the temporal sword.

NATURE OF THE CHURCH

A concept identifying the church with the kingdom of God developed during the medieval period, deriving its support from two forged documents, the *Donation of Constantine* (written about the middle of the eighth century) and the *Decretals of Isidore* (written about the middle of the ninth century). The former was allegedly written by Constantine, willing his palace, the city of Rome, its districts, and the cities of Italy to the pope and his successors. All of life began to revolve around the church, and all that did not relate to the church was renounced and considered secular. But the church itself became secularized.[16] Because it was considered the kingdom of God, it became preoccupied with politics rather than the salvation of people.

In the Middle Ages the concept of the church developed the following elements.[17] (1) The visible nature of the church was emphasized; since Christ is visible in the incarnation, the church now continues Christ's incarnation. The popes, as visible successors of Peter, possess absolute authority. (2) There is a distinction between the teaching church (all the clergy with the pope at the head) and the hearing church (the faithful who honor the clergy). (3) The church is made up of body (those professing the true faith) and soul (those united to Christ by supernatural gifts and graces). (4) The church distributes the graces of Christ through the agency of the clergy. (5) The church is "an institution of salvation, a saving ark." It teaches the true faith, effects sanctification through the sacraments, and governs believers in accordance with ecclesiastical law.

Notes on Medieval Theology

1. E. H. Klotsche, *The History of Christian Doctrine*, rev. ed. (Grand Rapids: Baker, 1979), p. 118.
2. J. L. Neve, *A History of Christian Thought*, 2 vols. (Philadelphia: Muhlenberg, 1946), 1:177.
3. Earle E. Cairns, *Christianity Through the Centuries* (Grand Rapids: Zondervan, 1954), p. 251.
4. William G. T. Shedd, *A History of Christian Doctrine*, 2 vols. (Reprint. Minneapolis: Klock & Klock, 1978), 2:130.
5. Klotsche, *History of Christian Doctrine*, p. 143.
6. Neve, *History of Christian Thought*, 1:202.
7. Klotsche, *History of Christian Doctrine*, p. 143.
8. Louis Berkhof, *Systematic Theology* (Grand Rapids: Eerdmans, 1939), p. 385.
9. Louis Berkhof, *The History of Christian Doctrines* (London: Banner of Truth, 1937), p. 177.
10. Geoffrey W. Bromiley, *Historical Theology: An Introduction* (Grand Rapids: Eerdmans, 1978), p. 205.
11. Ibid., p. 206.
12. Klotsche, *History of Christian Doctrine*, p. 143.
13. Neve, *History of Christian Thought*, p. 203.
14. Klotsche, *History of Christian Doctrine*, p. 148.
15. See the excellent discussion by David S. Schaff, *The Middle Ages*, in Philip Schaff, *History of the Christian Church*, 8 vols. (New York: Scribner's, 1926), 5:1:772-80.
16. Berkhof, *History of Christian Doctrines*, p. 233.
17. Ibid., pp. 234-36.

For Further Study on Medieval Theology

MEDIEVAL CONTROVERSIES

** Geoffrey W. Bromiley. *Historical Theology: An Introduction.* Grand Rapids: Eerdmans, 1978.

** Hubert Cunliffe-Jones, ed. *A History of Christian Doctrine.* Philadelphia: Fortress, 1978.

** William Cunningham. *Historical Theology*, 2 vols. Reprint. London: Banner of Truth, 1960. 1:359-89.

* E. H. Klotsche. *The History of Christian Doctrine*, rev. ed. Grand Rapids: Baker, 1979. Pp. 116-26.

** Kenneth Scott Latourette. *A History of Christianity.* New York: Harper, 1953. Pp. 292-363.

* J. L. Neve. *A History of Christian Thought*, 2 vols. Philadephia: Muhlenberg, 1946. 2:176-80.

MEDIEVAL SCHOLASTICISM

* Louis Berkhof. *The History of Christian Doctrines*. Edinburgh: Banner of Truth, 1937. Pp. 171-81.
* Geoffrey W. Bromiley. *Historical Theology: An Introduction*. Grand Rapids: Eerdmans, 1978.
** William G. T. Shedd. *A History of Christian Doctrine*, 2 vols. Reprint. Minneapolis: Klock & Klock, 1978. 2:273-318.

MEDIEVAL ANTHROPOLOGY

* Louis Berkhof. *The History of Christian Doctrines*. Edinburgh: Banner of Truth, 1937. Pp. 140-46.
* Geoffrey W. Bromiley. *Historical Theology: An Introduction*. Grand Rapids: Eerdmans, 1978. Pp. 180-83, 204-5.
* E. H. Klotsche. *The History of Christian Doctrine*, rev. ed. Grand Rapids: Baker, 1979. Pp. 142-44.
** Heiko A. Oberman. *The Harvest of Medieval Theology*. Grand Rapids: Eerdmans, 1967. Pp. 120-45, 281-322.
** William G. T. Shedd. *A History of Christian Doctrine*, 2 vols. Reprint. Minneapolis: Klock & Klock, 1978. 2:111-51.

MEDIEVAL SOTERIOLOGY

* Louis Berkhof. *The History of Christian Doctrines*. Edinburgh: Banner of Truth, 1937. Pp. 211-16.
* Geoffrey W. Bromiley, *Historical Theology: An Introduction*. Grand Rapids: Eerdmans, 1978 Pp. 204-9.
** A. M. Fairweather, ed. *Nature and Grace*, and Thomas Aquinas, *Summa Theologica*. In *Library of Christian Classics*, edited by J. Baillie, J. T. McNeill, and H. P. Van Dusen. Philadelphia: Westminster, 1954.
* E. H. Klotsche. *The History of Christian Doctrine*, rev. ed. Grand Rapids: Baker, 1979. Pp. 144-46.
** A. C. McGiffert. *A History of Christian Thought*. New York: Scribner's, 1946. 2:185-312.
** Heiko A. Oberman. *The Harvest of Medieval Theology*. Grand Rapids: Eerdmans, 1967. Pp. 120-84.

MEDIEVAL ECCLESIOLOGY

* Louis Berkhof. *The History of Christian Doctrines*. Edinburgh: Banner of Truth, 1937. Pp. 227-41.
* E. H. Klotsche. *The History of Christian Doctrine*, rev. ed. Grand Rapids: Baker, 1979. Pp. 146-58.
* J. L. Neve. *A History of Christian Thought*, 2 vols. Philadelphia: Muhlenberg, 1946. 2:179-83, 198-206.
** Heiko A. Oberman. *The Harvest of Medieval Theology*. Grand Rapids: Eerdmans, 1967. Pp. 271-80, 412-22.
** David Schaff. *The Middle Ages*. In Philip Schaff, ed., *History of the Christian Church*, 8 vols. Grand Rapids: Eerdmans, 1960. 5:1:700-829.

30

REFORMATION THEOLOGY

REFORMATION ROOTS

The Reformation marked a major turning point in the doctrinal development of the church. For the preceding one thousand years the authority of the church had developed continuously until the tradition of the Roman Catholic church and the authority of the papacy determined what the people were to believe. The Reformation changed all that.

There were a number of factors that sparked the Protestant Reformation. One was the political factor. Islam had conquered Constantinople in 1453, causing the downfall of the Eastern church. Islam moved westward, threatening the power of the papacy and also influencing the papacy through its literature, which flowed into Europe. Additionally, the creation of national states and free cities in Europe challenged the political authority of Rome. The nationalistic spirit that arose through strong local political leaders encouraged the support of the Reformers.

A second factor was educational, evoked by the Renaissance. The *Renaissance* (Fr., meaning "rebirth") opened men's minds to the study of classical literature in addition to the Bible. Christian humanists were at the forefront of this educational movement, particularly Erasmus, who produced a Greek edition of the New Testament. Erasmus's work encouraged the study of the New Testament in the original language rather than in the Latin Vulgate. The advent of the printing press further enabled more people to study the Scriptures for themselves.

The Renaissance also brought an emphasis on the centrality of man, which, at least in some measure, coincided with the Reformers' call to individual faith and salvation.

There was also a social and economic factor encouraging the Reformation. With the end of the Middle Ages came a surge of economic development through the markets produced by the cities and also the colonies. A new middle class emerged that resisted the flow of money to Rome.

Undoubtedly, the religious factor was very significant. Having access to the New Testament, the Reformers and Christian humanists discovered a discrepancy between the church in the New Testament and the practices of the church of Rome. There was corruption from the priesthood to the papacy in the Roman church; simony enabled men to buy and sell church offices. Through the sale of indulgences a person could pay for sins beforehand and be assured of the forgiveness of sins. It was this practice in particular that angered Martin Luther and ultimately led to his break with the Roman church.

Men like Luther brought a return to the authority of the Scriptures—the Bible alone was the final authority on what was to be believed and practiced. With the renewed emphasis on biblical authority and study of the Scriptures came a new awareness of the doctrine of justification by faith, as well as other historic Christian doctrines. Luther in Germany and Zwingli and Calvin in Switzerland spread the teachings of Scripture from the pulpit and through voluminous writings. A new day had dawned. The knowledge of the Scriptures was again being propagated.

REFORMATION LEADERS

MARTIN LUTHER (1483-1546)

Martin Luther, the catalyst of the Protestant Reformation, was born of peasant parentage in Eisleben, Saxony, in 1483. The foundation of his theological thinking perhaps came when he was confronted by the need of divine revelation while a student at the University of Erfurt. Luther entered a Roman Catholic monastery, having promised St. Anne he would become a monk after he was spared during a violent thunderstorm. However, during a trip to Rome, Luther became disillusioned with the Roman Catholic church as he saw its corruption. He returned to Wittenberg where he received the doctor of theology degree and subsequently taught the Bible. Through the study of the Bible, and particularly Romans 1:17, Luther came to a knowledge of justification by faith alone. This formed the foundation of his theology and opposition to the Catholic church. On October 31, 1517, Luther nailed his Ninety-Five Theses on the door of the church at Wittenberg. These statements outlined his disagreements with the Catholic church. Luther stressed *sola scriptura*—the Scriptures alone are the authority for people—not the church and its councils.

Luther left an enormous theological legacy: he taught that only the sacraments of baptism and the Lord's Supper were legitimate; he wrote prolifically, challenging the Roman church and establishing his own catechisms; he provided the church with some of the great hymns, such as "A Mighty Fortress"; he established an educational system, teaching the people to read the Bible.

JOHN CALVIN (1509-1564)

John Calvin, the respected and influential theologian of the Reformation, was born in France in 1509. He began his studies at the University of Paris where he came under the influence of the humanists. Later, Calvin studied law at Orleans, with further studies at Bourges. In 1534 he identified himself with Protestantism and was forced to leave France. Calvin came to Basel, Switzerland, where at the young age of twenty-six he completed his magnum opus, *The Institutes of the Christian Religion*, an apologetic that defended Protestantism to the king of France. The work eventually underwent several revisions until it consisted of eighty chapters in four volumes.

After a brief interlude in Strasbourg, Calvin returned to Geneva, Switzerland, in 1541, to remain there the rest of his life. There, as pastor, Calvin spent his time preaching and lecturing daily. He also wrote commentaries on twenty-seven books of the Old Testament and on all the New Testament books except Revelation. Calvin's authority in Geneva was both ecclesiastical and political, prosecuting (and sometimes executing) people for heresy. The burning of Servetus for anti-Trinitarian heresy is viewed today as a serious blight on Calvin's career. However, in Calvin's day, at Geneva and at other places also, leaders and heretics alike knew that Servetus's kind of teaching was more serious an offense than murder and would likely incur capital punishment. Calvin unsuccessfully struggled in various ways to spare Servetus but at last sadly concurred with the judgment against him.

Calvin was called the first scientific interpreter of the Bible. He built a theology on the sovereignty of God that directed the Reformed church in Europe and Scotland.

ULRICH ZWINGLI (1484-1531)

While Calvin ministered to the French-speaking population of Switzerland, Ulrich Zwingli, born in 1484, served the German-speaking people of Switzerland. Zwingli studied at Berne, Vienna, and Basel, whereupon he entered the Roman Catholic priesthood from 1506-1518. It was during the latter days of this period that, while studying Erasmus's Greek New Testament, Zwingli was converted to Christ and to Reformation views. In 1519, while pastor of the great cathedral church in Zurich, Zwingli began both to preach expository sermons and to denounce Roman Catholic practices. In a public debate before the city council, Zwingli's views were adopted, causing the spread of Reformation theology and practice. Priests married, images were banned, the Mass abolished, and church property was confiscated for educational use.

Zwingli, adopting the memorial view of the Lord's Supper, caused Luther to break fellowship with him, even though they both agreed on salvation by faith. Zwingli was killed in 1531 in a war with a neighboring Roman

Catholic canton (province). Zwingli also left his imprint on the Anabaptists, having adopted some views that appeared more radical than those of Luther or Calvin.

REFORMATION BIBLIOLOGY

ACCORDING TO LUTHER

For Martin Luther, the Bible was the only infallible authority regarding faith and salvation. In coming to this view, Luther rejected the authority of the pope, the church councils, indulgences, and the Roman Catholic sacraments. Luther declared, "The Word of God shall establish articles of faith, and no one else, not even an angel." Moreover, the Scriptures were authoritative because they were the witness of the Holy Spirit. Luther referred to the Scriptures as "the Book given by God, the Holy Spirit, to his church" and in the preface of his commentary on Genesis he referred to Genesis as "Scripture of the Holy Spirit."[1]

In Scripture Luther was concerned with what pointed to Christ. Therefore, the book of James was termed a "strawy epistle," whereas he placed a preeminence on Romans, Galatians, and Ephesians because they were pure gospel and provided instruction about Christ. Luther also questioned the Solomonic authorship of Ecclesiastes and believed Esther should not be included in the Old Testament canon.

Luther provided helpful principles for the interpretation of Scripture. (1) The illumination of the Holy Spirit and not simply the letter of the law was important. (2) The historical circumstances were essential. (3) A distinction was to be recognized between the Old Testament, which was law, and the New Testament, which was gospel. (4) Scripture had one unifying element—Christ. (5) Literal interpretation was important; allegorical interpretation was "monkey tricks."[2]

ACCORDING TO ZWINGLI

Ulrich Zwingli acknowledged the infallibility of the Scriptures, terming them "the certainty of power," meaning "the certainty that the Word will do what it says."[3] He was converted through reading Erasmus's Greek New Testament, whereupon he disavowed the authority of the Roman Catholic church. Scripture alone was authoritative in matters of salvation.

Zwingli devoted himself to serious study of the Scriptures. After recognizing their authority, he began preaching exegetical sermons, beginning in Matthew. "His work as a reformer rested also on the principle . . . that all disputed matters must be decided by the Word of God. Zwingli always attempted to base his actions on biblical teaching and to meet opponents, whether Roman Catholic, Lutheran, or Anabaptist, with biblical arguments. No less than Luther, he wanted a theology and a church of the Word."[4]

An important thesis of Zwingli was the clarity of the Word of God and the ability of the common person to understand it. Zwingli declared that the Bible "is perfect in itself, and revealed for the welfare of man." Hence, there is no need for an ecclesiastical person, be it pope, priest, or church council, to interpret the Word of God. That is the ministry of the Holy Spirit. Furthermore, the Scriptures could be interpreted when approached in humility, prayer, and without prejudice. Amid these conditions, the Holy Spirit would enlighten the reader concerning the meaning.

ACCORDING TO CALVIN

John Calvin affirmed the Bible, not the church, as the final authority in religious matters. It was seen as the binding authority upon all people at all times. His adherence to inspiration was affirmed when he stated that it was the duty of people to accept "without any exception all that is delivered in the sacred Scriptures."

Calvin has been referred to as the "king of commentators," "the greatest exegete of the sixteenth century," and the "creator of genuine exegesis."[5] Others have referred to Calvin as the first of the scientific interpreters. Calvin produced sound exegetical commentaries on nearly all the books of Scripture, as well as an exposition of his theology in his *Institutes of the Christian Religion.* He enunciated the following important principles for biblical interpretation.[6] (1) The illumination of the Holy Spirit is necessary to prepare the interpretator of Scripture. (2) Allegorical interpretation is satanic, leading people away from the truth of Scripture, and therefore is to be rejected. (3) Scripture interprets Scripture. This involved a number of things for Calvin. It meant literal interpretation; it meant listening to Scripture and letting the author say what he will; it meant a study of the grammar of Scripture—meaning of words, the context, and comparing Scripture with Scripture on common subjects.

REFORMATION CHRISTOLOGY

Calvin and Zwingli followed the orthodox view of Christ—He is one Person with two distinct natures, with no intermingling of the two natures. In this, however, Luther took a different view. He held to a real presence of Christ in the Lord's Supper, teaching that the human nature of Christ takes on certain attributes of the divine nature, such as omniscience, omnipresence, and omnipotence.

The problem with this view is that it fails to maintain a proper distinction of the two natures of Christ.

REFORMATION ANTHROPOLOGY

VIEW OF THE REFORMERS

Luther and Calvin were in general agreement regarding the total depravity of man—his utter inability by himself to effect his own salvation. Both also acknowledged that because of man's total depravity the grace of God is necessary to redeem fallen man. Zwingli was also in agreement with this. Theodore Beza (1519-1605), Calvin's successor in Geneva, taught that Adam was the federal head of the human race, therefore, when Adam sinned as humanity's representative, the entire human race fell and became polluted. Henceforth, every child born into the world has been born in a depraved condition.

Because of man's condition of total depravity, Calvin disavowed the idea of a free will; that was forfeited through the Fall. He taught that the will is bound, unable to move in any direction except toward evil.[7] Yet Calvin taught that man is held responsible for his sin because he sins out of his own will and not by any outward compulsion. Moreover, although man's reason is impaired, man can discern between good and evil, therefore man is responsible for "not willing the good but the bad."[8]

The corollary doctrine of total depravity is predestination, which Luther, Calvin, and Zwingli all affirmed. Because man was unable to make a positive move toward God as a result of his depravity, it was necessary for God to predestine certain ones to salvation.

SOCINIAN VIEW

Faustus Socinus (1539-1604) followed Pelagian views in denying man's depravity. Socinus taught that man was not created in the image of God in the sense of moral perfection, but only in achieving dominion over lower creation.[9] Although Adam sinned, his sin did not have adverse effects on his posterity because man's moral nature is transmitted intact to his posterity.[10] People sin today, not because of indwelling hereditary sin, but because of bad examples. On the contrary, Socinus taught that all people are born with Adam's nature prior to the Fall and that people have the ability to avoid sinning.

ARMINIAN VIEW

Jacobus Arminius (1560-1609) was at first a strict Calvinist, having studied under Beza at Geneva. In a debate he felt his opponent had stronger arguments than he had and he changed his view, advocating universal grace and freedom of the will. His position was basically that of semi-Pelagianism in which he denied the doctrine of original sin, disputing the idea that the guilt of Adam's sin was imputed to his descendants. He suggested that only the pollution of Adam's sin was passed on to succeeding generations, but this pollution is only a weakness, it does not bring a person under the sentence of condemnation. Rather, it renders him incapable of attaining eternal life by his own effort. The fall of man did not or does not render man incapable of making an initial, positive move toward God.[11] This is achieved through God dispensing prevenient grace to all people to offset the effects of inherited depravity, thereby making man capable of cooperating with God in salvation.

REFORMATION SOTERIOLOGY

PREDESTINATION

Calvin taught the doctrine of salvation by grace, which salvation is rooted in the eternal decree of God. Because God is sovereign, all events that transpire have been ordained by Him; hence, Calvin also taught the doctrine of double predestination. He declared, "Predestination we call the eternal decree of God, by which he has determined in himself the destiny of every man. For they are not all created in the same condition, but eternal life is foreordained for some, and eternal damnation for others. Every man, therefore, being created for one or the other of these ends, we say, he is predestinated either to life or to death." The doctrine of predestination involves election to salvation and reprobation to eternal condemnation. Calvin emphasized the necessity of both. While election to salvation is entirely of God's grace, reprobation is just because it is due to sin and guilt.[12]

Luther also taught the necessity of the doctrine of predestination, basing it on man's depravity and inability; Zwingli based his belief in predestination on the providence of God.[13]

ATONEMENT

View of the Reformers. Although both Protestants and Roman Catholics recognized the value of Christ's atonement, the Roman Catholic church followed the teaching of Thomas Aquinas, whereas the Reformers, in general, followed Anselm's view of the atonement. Anselm, however, taught that God had been robbed of His honor by man's sin and Christ died to satisfy the honor of God. The Reformers taught that Christ died to satisfy the justice of God. Christ bore upon Himself the punishment due sin and thereby satisfied the justice of God. This work of Christ can be appropriated only by faith, which unites the believer to Christ; the believer thereby has Christ's righteousness imputed to him. Luther said Christ "has redeemed me with His precious blood and with His innocent suffering and death, in order that I may be His own, and live under Him in His kingdom." Calvin taught that Christ's death was a particular atonement—He died only for the elect.

Socinian view. Socinus repudiated the idea of the justice of God necessitating the death of Christ. He taught that God could pardon sinners at will—without the atonement of Christ. God pardons sinners on the basis of His mercy, not because of the death of Christ. All that God requires of the sinner is repentance and the desire to obey the law of God. Socinus taught that Christ's death was an example of obedience that should inspire others.

Socinus's view is seen historically as Pelagianism and more recently as Unitarianism.

Grotian view. Hugo Grotius (1583-1645) reacted against the Socinian teaching. In teaching the governmental theory, however, Grotius was at variance with the Reformers. Grotius insisted it was unnecessary for God to demand full payment for the violation of sin; rather, Christ's death was a token payment to God, who, in accepting Christ's death as a token payment, set aside the requirements of the law.

The New Testament teaches that Christ's death in itself did satisfy the requirments of the law. Grotius was clearly wrong.

REFORMATION VIEWS OF THE ATONEMENT

Person	Christ's Death	God's Work
Socinius	Unnecessary.	Pardons through His mercy, not through Christ's death.
Grotius	"Token payment"; full payment unnecessary.	Set aside requirements of the law.
Arminius	Not a strict equivalent for sin but a substitute for a penalty.	Pardons through Christ's death but sets aside claims of justice.
Luther	Substitutionary atonement for sin; appeased the wrath of God.	Imputes righteousness to the believer.
Calvin	Substitutionary atonement for sin; appeased the wrath of God.	Imputes righteousness to the believer.

Arminian view. Arminian theology was formed primarily by Curcellaeus and Limborch, who wrote to correct the errors of Socinianism. They viewed the death of Christ as analogous to Old Testament sacrificial offerings in which the death of the animal had as its purpose to deliver the guilty from punishment. Although the death of Christ was a sacrifice, a sacrifice was not payment of the debt nor was it satisfaction of justice for sin.[14] In the analogy of the Old Testament sacrificial offering, the Old Testament worshiper who fulfilled the requirement of the law in offering an animal received remission of sin. Similarly, although Christ did not endure the exact punishment due sinners, God promised to pardon sinners on the basis of Christ's death. He did so by waiving the claims of justice. In His death Christ did not suffer what man deserved, but rather Christ's death was a substitute for a penalty.

The death of Christ in the Arminian view is not a strict equivalent for sin nor a substituted penalty, but a substitute for a penalty.[15] A substituted penalty demands equivalent worth; a substitute for a penalty can be of inferior worth. Similarities to Grotius's governmental view, in which Christ did not make the full payment for sin, are apparent in the Arminian view.

FAITH AND WORKS

Lutheran view. The light of grace came to Martin Luther through reading Romans 1:17, sometime before 1517. Thereafter, in breaking with Roman Catholic doctrine, Luther came to a strong convinction that justification is by faith alone (Lat. *sola fide*). October 31, 1517, when Luther posted the Ninety-Five Theses on the door of the church in Wittenberg, may be seen as the actual beginning of the Reformation, with the affirmation of salvation by grace through faith instead of the synergistic view of the Roman Catholic church. As a result, Luther rejected the Catholic doctrines of penance, indulgences, and any other form of human merit as necessary for salvation. Luther came to the conclusion that only God's grace is the foundation and basis for man's salvation and justification. He taught that it is God's grace alone that forgives sins and imputes the righteousness of Christ to the one who believes.

Works, Luther taught, have no part in salvation. Good works are the result or fruit of salvation but never a part of salvation. He distinguished between the "works of the law," which are done in a state of unbelief and provide no part of salvation, and the "works of faith," which are the proof of justification. These genuinely good works are found in the Ten Commandments, as Luther stated: "Thus we have the Ten Commandments, a compend of divine doctrine, as to what we are to do in order that our whole life may be pleasing to God, . . . outside of the Ten Commandments no work or thing can be good or pleasing to God."

Calvinist view. John Calvin was in general agreement with Luther on the subject of justification by faith. Calvin also emphasized justification as a forensic (legal) act, whereby God declares the believing sinner righteous, an act made possible by the free grace of God. In contrast to Luther, however, Calvin began his doctrine of salvation with God's election of the sinner. Calvin understood election to salvation as unconditional for "If election were dependent on man's faith and good works, grace would not be free, and in fact would cease to be grace."[16]

In relation to James 2:20, Calvin taught that justification by works does not relate to imputed righteousness but rather, as Luther also taught, works that demonstrate the reality of justification. Thus Calvin taught a "double justification." "Primarily, justification is acceptance before God through the imputation of righteousness. This comes by faith alone. Secondarily and in consequence, however, justification is the declaration or manifestation before men of the righteousness of faith. This is justification by works."[17]

Calvin's doctrine of salvation produced a milestone in that he related justification to sanctification. While maintaining the distinctiveness of each, he related both to the act of salvation. Christ does not justify someone whom He does not also sanctify. Justification, according to Calvin, becomes the motivation to sanctification. Although justification is free, sanctification becomes the believer's response of gratitude.[18] Calvin remarked: "No one can embrace the grace of the gospel, but he must depart from the error of his former life, enter into the right way, and devote all his attention to the exercise of repentance."

Arminian view. In contrast to Calvin's doctrine of unconditional election, Arminians taught conditional election; that is, God elects to salvation those whom He knows will believe in Christ. But provision has been made for all humanity, because Christ died for everyone, not simply the elect. Although man is incapable of responding to God because of sin, God dispenses prevenient grace to all people, which enables them freely to choose to believe in Christ or reject Christ. However, the believer is capable of resisting the Holy Spirit, falling back into the world, and losing his salvation. Perseverence is essential to maintain eternal life.

REFORMATION ECCLESIOLOGY

LUTHERAN VIEW

Church. Through his break with Roman Catholicism, Martin Luther rejected the infallibility of the church, as well as the concept of a unique priesthood. He taught instead the priesthood of all believers. This was an important recovery of biblical truth. Luther taught that the church is "an assemblage of all Christian believers on earth." This is the true church, encompassing all believers who are united to Christ in faith. Luther used the term *Christian* to emphasize the universality of the church. While maintaining there is but one church, Luther distinguished between the visible church, observable through the ministry of the Word and the sacraments, and the invisible church, observable by the provision of salvation through the Holy Spirit and by mystical fellowship with Christ.

Baptism. Luther taught that the sacraments of baptism and Lord's Supper are vehicles that communicate the grace of God. They are not depen-

REFORMERS' VIEWS ON THE CHURCH AND ORDINANCES

View	Church	Baptism	Lord's Supper
Lutheran	All believers on earth constitute the one invisible church. Visible church observed through ministry of Word and sacraments.	Necessary for salvation. Effects salvation. Infant baptism necessary; God works faith in them.	"Consubstantiation"— Christ is bodily present "in, with, under" the elements.
Reformed	Universal church completed at Christ's return. Salvation possible outside the church.	Sign of believer's faith. Infant baptism necessary and sign of covenant.	Christ is spiritually present and mediates grace to participant.
Anabaptist	Church composed only of believers (infants not part of the church). Emphasized church purity through discipline.	Baptism only for believers. Infant baptism rejected.	Memorial only. Bread and cup symbolize Christ and His death. No grace is mediated.

dent on the person's faith or worth, but are dependent on God's promise. Hence, Luther later taught that unbelievers profit from the sacraments.

Luther's concept of baptism did not differ markedly from the Roman Catholic view; he retained much of the Roman ceremony connected with the rite. Luther taught that baptism is necessary to salvation and, in fact, produces regeneration in the person. Luther emphasized that baptism is an agreement between God and man in which God promises to forgive the sins of the person and continue to provide His grace while the person promises God a life of penitent gratitude.[19] Concerning baptism Luther stated: "it is most solemnly commanded that we must be baptized or we cannot be saved. . . . the Sacrament by which we are first received into the Christian Church."

Luther also upheld infant baptism, teaching that although infants are unable to exercise faith, God, through His prevenient grace, works faith in the unconscious child. He based the baptism of infants on the command to baptize all nations (Matt. 28:19).

Lord's Supper. Luther rejected the Roman Catholic doctrine of transubstantiation, which teaches that the elements actually turn into the body and blood of Christ. Luther sharply disagreed with Zwingli, affirming the real presence of Christ at the Lord's Supper. His view was known as consubstantiation, in which he taught that even though the elements are not altered, Christ is bodily present, "in, with, and under" the elements.

REFORMED VIEW

Church. Even in their common departure from the Roman Catholic church, there was yet a marked difference between Lutherans and Reformed churches over what was to be retained or rejected. "Lutheranism rejected only those features of the Catholic Church which seemed to it expressly forbidden in the Scriptures. The Reformed Churches went further and retained from the Catholic Church only what they believed to have warrant in the Scriptures."[20]

Whereas Luther emphasized that the church is observable through the ordinances and that salvation occurs through the visible church, the Reformed believers held that salvation is possible outside the scope of the visible church. They taught the Holy Spirit could work and save people "when, where, and how He pleases."[21] The Reformed believers also expanded the explanation of the invisible church: it is universal because no one can see the church in all places and at all times; it will not be completed until the Lord's return; it is impossible always to distinguish believers from unbelievers.

Baptism. Reformed believers taught that the sacraments are to be administered only to believers as signs of their faith. God does, however, communicate His grace through the sacraments.

Reformed adherents held that, although baptism is to be administered only to believers, infants should be baptized to indicate their inclusion in the covenant. It is a symbol of assurance to the parents that the child is included in the covenant, and because children thus come under the covenant, they have a right to baptism.[22]

Lord's Supper. John Calvin rejected Luther's notion of the actual presence of Christ at the Lord's Supper, but he also rejected Zwingli's idea that it was only a memorial. Calvin taught that the ordinance is for believers only and that Christ is spiritually present, mediating grace to the believing participant. Although Calvin taught that the believer partakes of Christ at the Lord's Supper, it is not through the material elements, but spiritually by faith. The unbeliever who would partake of the elements does not benefit from the Lord's Supper as does the believer.

ANABAPTIST VIEW

Church. The Anabaptist view of the church differed from the Roman Catholic view most sharply of any of the Reformers. The very name, Anabaptist, means to baptize again. The Anabaptists stressed that the church is

THEOLOGY OF THE REFORMERS

Doctrine	Luther	Calvin	Zwingli/Anabaptists
Scripture	Only infallible authority for faith and salvation. Scriptures point to Christ.	Bible, not church, is final authority. First scientific interpreter.	Z: Infallible authority—must determine all practice. Scripture will be fulfilled. Common people can understand.
Predestination	All events ordained by God. Taught double predestination.	Predestination necessary because of man's depravity.	Predestination based on providence of God.
Christ	In Lord's Supper, human nature takes on His divine characteristics, such as omnipresence.	Orthodox view; one Person with two natures, with no intermingling.	Orthodox view; one Person with two natures, with no intermingling.
Man and sin	Man is depraved and unable to free himself. Grace necessary because of sin.	Man is depraved and unable to free himself. Grace necessary because of sin.	Man is depraved and unable to free himself. Grace necessary because of sin.
Atonement	Christ died a substitutionary death for all.	Christ died a substitutionary death for all.	Christ died a substitutionary death for all.
Salvation	Justification by faith alone, not works.	Justification by faith as legal act of God, imputing righteousness to the believer. Unconditional election is basis.	Christ died a substitutionary death; paid for original and actual sins. Dependent on eternal election.
Church	Priesthood of all believers, composed of all believers on earth.	Salvation is possible outside of church. Church is visible and invisible.	A: Church composed only of believers; infants not involved. Church and state separate. Believers are pacifists.
Baptism	Communicates grace. Produces forgiveness of sin; necessary for salvation. Infants baptized.	Only for believers, but children baptized to show they are in covenant.	Z: Infants baptized. A: Believers only; infant baptism rejected.
Lord's Supper	Christ present in real sense. Unbelievers may profit.	Communicates grace. Believer partakes of Christ through faith.	Z: Memorial only. Bread is symbol of Christ, not His literal body.

composed only of believers; hence, because infants are incapable of believing, they are not a part of the church. In distinction to Luther and Calvin, the Anabaptists also maintained a sharp distinction between church and state. A corollary doctrine that evolved was nonresistance—the prohibition concerning bearing arms in war. Some also insisted that Anabaptists are prohibited from serving on a police force or assuming judicial responsibilities.

Anabaptists adopted a simple way of life in which they endeavored to live by the teachings of the Sermon on the Mount. Anabaptists were also committed to the purity of the church and diligently exercised church discipline (corporal punishment) against husbands who mistreated their wives. They also exercised church discipline for other reasons. It is a sad chapter in church history to note that not only Roman Catholics but also Lutherans and Calvinists persecuted Anabaptists to the point of death.[23]

Baptism. Anabaptists stressed that only believers are to be baptized; as a result they rejected infant baptism as invalid, necessitating the rebaptism of those who had become believers but who had received only infant baptism. In this the Anabaptists even departed from Zwingli, who advocated infant baptism. Baptism is to be administered only to those who consciously exhibit faith in Christ. The name "Anabaptist" (the prefix *ana* is Latin meaning "again") was derived from the adherents' demand for rebaptism of those who had been baptized as infants. Interestingly, the mode of baptism was not an issue with Anabaptists; some held to immersion while many held to affusion.

Lord's Supper. Luther's rupture with Zwingli over the issue of the Lord's Supper is well known. Whereas Luther accepted the presence of Christ surrounding the elements, and Reformed believers believed in the communication of grace in the elements, Zwingli taught that the Lord's Supper is simply a memorial commemorating the death of Christ. While Luther understood Christ's statement, "This is my body," to be literal language, Zwingli said that the bread simply symbolizes the body of Christ. Anabaptists followed the view of Zwingli regarding the Lord's Supper. Yet the Lord's Supper meant a great deal to the Anabaptists. This eating and drinking in brotherly fellowship gave them strength and encouragement and the certitude of belonging to a company of redeemed souls, and of being part of the "true body of Christ."[24] The Lord's Supper was seen as confirming the inner unity of the believers and providing the horizontal element of spiritual sharing and togetherness.[25]

Notes on Reformation Theology

1. E. H. Klotsche, *The History of Christian Doctrine*, rev. ed. (Grand Rapids: Baker, 1979), p. 170.

2. A. Berkeley Mickelsen, *Interpreting the Bible* (Grand Rapids: Eerdmans, 1963), p. 39.
3. Geoffrey W. Bromiley, *Historical Theology: An Introduction* (Grand Rapids: Eerdmans, 1978), p. 214.
4. Ibid., p. 214.
5. Philip Schaff, *History of the Christian Church*, 8 vols., 3rd ed. rev. (Reprint. Grand Rapids: Eerdmans, 1960), 8:524-25.
6. Bernard Ramm, *Protestant Biblical Interpretation*, 3rd rev. ed. (Grand Rapids: Baker, 1970), pp. 57-59.
7. A. Mitchell Hunter, *The Teaching of Calvin* (Westwood, N.J.: Revell, 1950), p. 121.
8. G. P. Fisher, *A History of Christian Doctrine*, edited by Hubert Cunliffe-Jones (Philadelphia: Fortress, 1978), pp. 391-92.
9. Louis Berkhof, *History of Christian Doctrines* (Edinburgh: Banner of Truth, 1937), p. 149.
10. Ibid.
11. Ibid., pp.150-51.
12. Schaff, *History of the Christian Church*, 8:551.
13. Ibid., 8:547.
14. Wm. G. T. Shedd, *A History of Christian Doctrine*, 2 vols. (Reprint. Minneapolis: Klock & Klock, 1978), 2:371.
15. Ibid., 2:371.
16. Philip Schaff, *The Creeds of Christendom with a History and Critical Notes*, 3 vols. (Reprint. Grand Rapids: Baker, 1977), 1:453.
17. Bromiley, *Historical Theology*, p. 236.
18. Ibid., p. 238.
19. E. G. Schwiebert, *Luther and His Times* (St. Louis: Concordia, 1950), p. 448.
20. Kenneth Scott Latourette, *A History of Christianity* (New York: Harper, 1953), p. 778.
21. Berkhof, *History of Christian Doctrines*, p. 238.
22. Ibid., pp. 250-51.
23. See C. Henry Smith, *The Story of the Mennonites* (Newton, Kans.: Mennonite, 1957).
24. Robert Friedmann, *The Theology of Anabaptism* (Scottdale, Pa.: Herald, 1973), p. 139.
25. Ibid., p. 140.

FOR FURTHER STUDY ON REFORMATION THEOLOGY

REFORMATION BIBLIOLOGY

* Geoffrey W. Bromiley. *Historical Theology: An Introduction.* Grand Rapids: Eerdmans, 1978. Pp. 210-17, 222-28.
* E. H. Klotsche. *The History of Christian Doctrine*, rev. ed. Grand Rapids: Baker, 1979. Pp. 169-70, 188, 230-31.
* Bernard Ramm. *Protestant Biblical Interpretation*, 3rd rev. ed. Grand Rapids: Baker, 1970. Pp. 51-59.

** Philip Schaff. *History of the Christian Church*, 8 vols. Reprint. Grand Rapids: Eerdmans, 1950. Vol. 8.

REFORMATION ANTHROPOLOGY

** Carl Bangs. *Arminius.* Nashville: Abingdon, 1971.

 * Louis Berkhof. *The History of Christian Doctrines.* Edinburgh: Banner of Truth, 1937. Pp. 147-51.

** William Cunningham. *Historical Theology*, 2 vols. Reprint. London: Banner of Truth, 1960. 2:371-513.

 * E. H. Klotsche. *The History of Christian Doctrine*, rev. ed. Grand Rapids: Baker, 1979. Pp. 174-76, 231-32.

** Martin Luther. *The Bondage of the Will.* Translated by J. I. Packer and A. R. Johnston. London: Clarke, 1957.

** Wm. G. T. Shedd. *A History of Christian Doctrines*, 2 vols. Reprint. Minneapolis: Klock & Klock, 1978. 2:111-196.

REFORMATION SOTERIOLOGY:

Meaning of atonement.

 * Louis Berkhof. *The History of Christian Doctrines.* Edinburgh: Banner of Truth, 1937. Pp. 182-89.

** William Cunningham. *Historical Theology*, 2 vols. Reprint. London: Banner of Truth, 1960. 2:237-370.

 * Walter A. Elwell, ed. *Evangelical Dictionary of Theology.* Grand Rapids: Baker, 1984.

** Wm. G. T. Shedd. *Dogmatic Theology*, 3 vols. Reprint. Nashville: Nelson, 1980. 2:378-489.

** _____. *A History of Christian Doctrine*, 2 vols. Reprint. Minneapolis: Klock & Klock, 1978. 2:333-86.

** A. H. Strong. *Systematic Theology.* Valley Forge, Pa.: Judson, 1907. Pp. 728-73.

Faith and works.

 * Louis Berkhof. *The History of Christian Doctrines.* Edinburgh: Banner of Truth, 1937. Pp. 217-24.

 * Geoffrey W. Bromiley. *Historical Theology: An Introduction.* Grand Rapids: Eerdmans, 1978. Pp. 229-32, 235-39, 242-45, 248-53.

** John Calvin. *Institutes of the Christian Religion.* Philadelphia: Presbyterian Board of Christian Education, n.d. 2 vols.

** H. T. Kerr. *A Compend of Luther's Theology.* Philadelphia: Westminster, 1943.

 * E. H. Klotsche. *The History of Christian Doctrine*, rev. ed. Grand Rapids: Baker, 1979. Pp. 176-78, 235-38.

REFORMATION ECCLESIOLOGY

 * Louis Berkhof. *The History of Christian Doctrines.* Edinburgh: Banner of Truth, 1937. Pp. 236-38, 245-56.

** Robert Friedmann. *The Theology of Anabaptism.* Scottdale, Pa.: Herald, 1973. Pp. 115-57.

** A. Mitchell Hunter. *The Teaching of Calvin*, rev. ed. Westwood, N.J.: Revell, 1950. Pp. 166-90.

* E. H. Klotsche. *The History of Christian Doctrine*, rev. ed. Grand Rapids: Baker, 1979. Pp. 180-84, 238-43.

** John T. McNeill. *The History and Character of Calvinism.* New York: Oxford U., 1957. This work is useful in discussing not only the teachings of Calvin but also those of Luther, Zwingli, and the Anabaptists.

** E. G. Schwiebert. *Luther and His Times.* St. Louis: Concordia, 1950. See the index for the topical discussions. This is a well researched work on the life of Luther.

31

MODERN THEOLOGY

Although it might seem strange to call developments of the seventeenth through the twentieth centuries "modern," from the perspective of comprehensive history that embraces millennia this caption does not seem so inappropriate. This is the sense for which the title of this chapter is given.

Because there is an obvious overlap between the doctrinal development in the modern church and contemporary (twentieth century) theology, this chapter will provide only a brief summary of the major theological views that surfaced following the Reformation. Many specific, distinctive theologies that developed in the church since the start of this century are discussed in greater detail in the chapters of Part 5 of this volume, "Contemporary Theology."

COVENANT THEOLOGY

Covenant theology was an outgrowth of the Reformation, particularly through the theological writings of men like Zwingli, Bullinger, Calvin, and Cocceius. Although these men did not teach what is today known as covenant theology, their theology laid the foundation for what would later be known as covenant theology. Johannes Wollebius (1586-1629), a Reformed theologian from Basel, and William Ames (1576-1633), a Puritan, both made important contributions to the development of covenant theology. Johannes Cocceius (1603-1669), a pupil of Ames, was responsible for systematizing covenant theology.

Covenant theology involves two primary features: the covenant of works and the covenant of grace. The covenant of works, although not mentioned specifically in the Old Testament, is implied. According to covenant theologians, God entered into a covenant with Adam prior to the Fall. In this covenant He promised eternal life for obedience during a probationary period and death if Adam disobeyed. In this test Adam stood as the federal head of all humanity; had he obeyed, he would have been confirmed in righteousness with the benefits passing to all humanity. Conversely, because he failed and fell, Adam's act of disobedience was transmitted to all humanity —all are born in sin and under sin's authority.

After the Fall God entered into another covenant with Adam (who was representing the human race) wherein God out of His abundant mercy promised eternal life to all who would believe in Jesus Christ. Essentially, the covenant of grace is based on the covenant of redemption, made in eternity past by the triune God in which the Father delegated the Son, who agreed to provide salvation for the world through His atoning death. The covenant of grace is understood as the application of the covenant of redemption and is thereby restricted to the elect.

LUTHERAN THEOLOGY

Following the establishment of Lutheranism in the sixteenth century, Lutheran theology was influenced by neo-Aristotelian thought, which had established a foothold in German universities. It was not at the expense of Lutheran doctrine, however.[1] A pietistic movement led by Philipp Jakob Spener (1635-1705), German pastor and royal chaplain, reacted to the scholastic methodology and called the people to individual, spiritual experience. In the eighteenth century, Christian Wolff (1679-1754), German mathematician and philosopher, led Lutheran theology into rationalism, claiming that nothing should be acknowledged without proof. He attempted to harmonize faith and reason, but the consequence was that reason became the final authority.[2]

Following the Reformation, a distinctive Luther theology developed. The foundation of it was the principle of *sola Scriptura*—the Bible alone is the reliable authority for Christians. It was this truth that led Luther to break with the Roman Catholic church in 1517, and it continued to be the foundational truth that led Lutheran theology into the 1600s.

The second important doctrine that was at the heart of Lutheran theology following the Reformation period was the manner of justification. As Luther, so also his followers taught that justification is based on the meritorious death of Christ, which death alone atoned for sins. The Augsburg Confession of 1530 explained justification as "to absolve a guilty man and pronounce him righteous, and to do so on account of someone else's righteousness, namely, Christ's."

The third important Lutheran doctrine that developed was *sola fide*, faith alone is the means whereby a person may appropriate salvation and God's justification.

REFORMED THEOLOGY

The designation *Reformed* distinguishes Calvinistic doctrine from Lutheran or Anabaptist theology.[3] The foundation of Reformed theology is found in John Calvin's *Institutes of the Christian Religion*, although there has been considerable diversity among the different adherents in the Reformed tradition. Some of the great catechisms and confessions of faith were the products of this era. The First Helvetic Confession (1536), composed by Johann Bullinger (1504-1575; Zwingli's successor) and others, represented the Reformed faith of all the cantons in Switzerland.[4] The Second Helvetic Confession (1566), also written by Bullinger and published in Latin, German, and French, had an even broader influence.[5] The Heidelberg Catechism (1563)[6] has had a wide influence down to the present day.

Calvin's *Institutes* also gained a foothold in Britain among the Puritans and the independent Presbyterians. Even some Anabaptists, known as Particular Baptists to indicate their adherence to particular redemption, followed Reformed theology. The Westminster Confession of Faith[7] became the doctrinal standard for British adherents of the Reformed faith.

Reformed theology also extended to the Netherlands, finding perhaps its greatest followers among the Dutch in more recent adherents such as Herman Bavinck (1895-1964) and Abraham Kuyper (1837-1920), the latter the founder of the Free University of Amsterdam and also prime minister of Holland. Following in the Reformed tradition were other twentieth-century men such as James Orr in Scotland and Benjamin B. Warfield, J. Gresham Machen, and Cornelius Van Til in America.

The heart of Reformed theology may be summarized in The Canons of the Synod of Dort[8] (1619), which responded to the Remonstrance—the doctrinal affirmation of James Arminius. Five positive statements that summarize Calvinism were set forth at the Synod of Dort: (1) total depravity of man; (2) unconditional election to salvation; (3) limited atonement (for the elect only); (4) irresistible grace; (5) perseverance of the saints.

LIBERAL THEOLOGY

The roots of liberal theology (also referred to as modernism) may be traced to Germany in the eighteenth century. Immanuel Kant (1724-1804) is normally considered the father of modern religious liberalism. Kant denied the proofs for the existence of God, maintaining that man could know God only through reason. This approach was the outcome of the Enlightenment, which viewed tradition and biblical authority with suspicion and acclaimed the merit of reason. Friedrich Schleiermacher (1768-1834) brought a new feature to theology through his emphasis on "feeling" in religion. Schleiermacher attempted to make theology compatible with the modern mind. He taught that religion cannot be identified with creeds but rather with expressions of feeling, be they art, literature, or other expressions. Schleiermacher defined religions as "the feeling of absolute dependence." Conversely, he identified sin as a selfish preoccupation with this world. George Hegel (1770-1831) carried liberal thought in another direction. Hegel brought the concept of evolution into history (and religion) when he taught that history is the meeting of opposing movements (thesis-antithesis) with the resultant blending of the two (synthesis). Many feel that it was Hegelian philosophy strongly influenced Ferdinand C. Baur (1792-1860) and Julius Wellhausen (1844-1918) in their critical studies of the Bible. Higher criticism was thus born, in which the traditional views concerning the authors of the biblical books are questioned.

The tenets of liberal theology include the following.[9] Emphasis on human reason and experience: religious beliefs must pass the tests of human reason and the findings of science; and Christianity must be adapted to the modern world. The Bible is not an infallible, authoritative book: it is a record of the experiences of others; and it has exemplary but not dogmatic value. There is no distinction between natural and supernatural: distinction between God and nature, man and animals, Christ and man is played down; the logical result of this view is pantheism.

Liberalism was an optimistic view of life that lost its influence as a result of World War I, and through the advent of a new approach to religious beliefs called Neo-orthodoxy.

NEO-ORTHODOX THEOLOGY

The term *neo-orthodoxy* means "new orthodoxy"; however, although it is new, it is not orthodox. Neo-orthodoxy was a reaction to the failure of liberalism. The advent of World War I demonstrated the theological error of liberalism with its denial of sin and its affirmation of the basic goodness of man. Karl Barth (1886-1968) sought to recover the truth when he abandoned his liberal training and gave himself to a serious study of the Scriptures. The publication of Barth's *Commentary on the Epistle to the Romans* in 1919 is considered the beginning of neo-orthodoxy, the break from liberalism. Neo-orthodoxy, however, has a wide divergence of theological opinions.

Søren Kierkegaard (1813-1855), Danish philosopher and theologian, brought an emphasis on experience to theology that was later developed by neo-orthodox theologians. Kierkegaard denounced the cold orthodoxy of his native people who gave verbal assent to creeds and were automatically considered Christians because they were members of the state church. Kierkegaard taught that life is not believing doctrines but involves experience and commitment. In contrast to the liberal emphasis on the immanence of

God, Kierkegaard taught the transcendence of God and that it is difficult for man to know God. Man must take a "leap of faith" to discover God. Kierkegaard's theology (also known as the "theology of despair") marked the birth of existentialism, an emphasis on personal experience as the standard of reality.

Karl Barth followed Kierkegaard in acknowledging a transcendent God and emphasizing a religion of experience. Barth taught that God could not be known objectively because He is transcendent; He must be known subjectively through experience. (Many of Barth's views will be discussed later in this chapter as well as in Part 5: Contemporary Theology.) Emil Brunner (1889-1966) was known for his emphasis on Christology—he denounced the liberal view of Christ and taught that a personal encounter is necessary for knowing God. From his teaching came the designation "crisis theology," because God meets man in a crisis. Reinhold Niebuhr (1892-1971), as pastor in working-class areas of Detroit, concentrated on social ethics. Rudolf Bultmann (1884-1976) denied the reliability of the Bible, suggesting it had been encrusted with the views of the church rather than factual teaching about God and Christ. His thinking has impacted many theologians so that the viewpoint known as Bultmannism has become synonymous with a particular form of Neo-orthodoxy.

The major tenets of neo-orthodoxy are the following.[10] The Bible is not revelation but a witness to revelation: it is not to be equated objectively with the Word of God; the revelation of God is not in words. Jesus Christ is the focal point of God's revelation: man meets God in an experiential encounter with Jesus Christ. The events of Scripture, such as Christ's resurrection, are termed *geschichte*, "story," in contrast to *historie*, "history." *Geschichte* refers to the transcendent, experiential truth of God that is unaffected by the truth or error that may characterize the earthbound particulars of *historie*. *Historie* is historically verifiable and, therefore, the lower level of Scripture in which errors can and have been discovered. *Geschichte* is historically unverifiable and, therefore, the higher level of Scripture in which errors cannot be discovered. It is unimportant, therefore, whether or not the stories of the Bible really took place in space and time; the fact that many Bible accounts are "myths" or "sagas" does not affect their higher meaning and validity. God is transcendent, the "wholly other." A sharp distinction exists between man and God; man can come to fellowship with God only through a "leap of faith."

CONCLUSION

This then is historical theology. It is for contemporary Christians to embrace the strengths and avoid the errors of past theologians. This can be done only by evaluating all doctrines in the light of the Word of God. For this cause the Bible was given to be profitable (2 Tim. 3:16-17).

THEOLOGICAL VIEWS IN THE MODERN CHURCH

Comparisons	Covenant	Lutheran	Reformed	Liberal	Neo-Orthodox
Adherents	J. Wollebius Wm. Ames J. Cocceius Modern adherents	M. Luther Lutheran theologians	J. Calvin A. Kuyper B. B. Warfield Modern Reformed theologians	I. Kant F. Schleiermacher G. Hegel Other liberals	K. Barth S. Kierkegaard R. Bultmann Other neo-orthodox theologians
Features	Covenant of works means life through obedience. Covenant of grace means life through faith.	Scripture alone. Faith alone. Believer justified through faith based on Christ's death.	Man's total depravity. Unconditional election. Limited atonement. Irresistible grace. Perseverance of saints.	Emphasis on human reason and experience. Bible fallible. Optimistic view of man.	Emphasis on experience. Bible fallible: only a witness to revelation. Events of Bible are "myth."

Notes on Modern Theology

1. J. F. Johnson, "Lutheran Tradition, The" in Walter A. Elwell, ed., *Evangelical Dictionary of Theology*, (Grand Rapids: Baker, 1984), p. 669.
2. Ibid.
3. See W. S. Reid, "Reformed Tradition, The" in *Evangelical Dictionary of Theology*, pp. 921-24 for a helpful summary article.
4. Philip Schaff, *The Creeds of Christendom*, 3 vols. (Reprint. Grand Rapids: Baker, 1977), 3:211-31.
5. Ibid., 3:233-306.
6. Ibid., 3:307-55.
7. Ibid., pp. 600-73.
8. Ibid., 3:550-97.
9. Bernard Ramm, *A Handbook of Contemporary Theology* (Grand Rapids: Eerdmans, 1966), p. 81; and R. V. Pierard, "Liberalism, Theological" in *Evangelical Dictionary of Theology*, pp. 631-32.
10. Ramm, *Handbook of Contemporary Theology*, pp. 89-92.

For Further Study on Modern Theology

* Walter A. Elwell, ed. *Evangelical Dictionary of Theology.* Grand Rapids: Baker, 1984.
** Eric W. Gritsch and Robert W. Jenson. *Lutheranism.* Philadelphia: Fortress, 1976.
** Warren F. Groff and Donald E. Miller. *The Shaping of Modern Christian Thought.* Cleveland: World, 1968.
* William E. Hordern. *A Layman's Guide to Protestant Theology*, rev. ed. London: Macmillan, 1968. Pp. 1-129.
** John T. McNeill. *The History and Character of Calvinism.* New York: Oxford U., 1957.
* Bernard Ramm. *A Handbook of Contemporary Theology.* Grand Rapids: Eerdmans, 1966.

PART 4:
DOGMATIC THEOLOGY

32

INTRODUCTION TO DOGMATIC THEOLOGY

DISTINCTION

Dogmatic theology is frequently confused with systematic theology and is often used as a synonym for systematic theology.[1] Although William G. T. Shedd wrote a three volume systematic theology which was entitled *Dogmatic Theology*, he used the terms *systematic* and *dogmatic* interchangeably.[2] Although the definition that follows will indicate the distinction between dogmatic theology and systematic theology, it appears that, in general, the designation *dogmatic theology* is more common in Germany and Holland, whereas systematic theology is the popular designation in Britain and America.[3]

DEFINITION

The word *dogma* comes from a Greek and Latin word meaning "that which is held as an opinion" and may also denote "a doctrine or body of doctrines of theology and religion formally stated and authoritatively proclaimed by a church."[4] Berkhof defines dogma as "a doctrine, derived from Scripture, officially defined by the Church, and declared to rest upon divine authority."[5] Historically, the church councils sought to resolve theological problems and to distinguish truth from error, hence, the church councils formulated doctrinal statements known as *dogma*.[6] Because the church had officially affirmed those dogmas, the statements were binding on Christians. It is important to see that from the beginning, the term *dogma* emphasized not only the statements from Scripture, but also the ecclesiastical, authoritative affirmation of that dogma.

The term *dogmatic theology* was probably first used by L. Reinhardt in 1659 as the title of a book. The word *dogma* or *dogmatics* came into vogue following the Reformation and was used to designate "those articles of faith which the church officially formulated," hence, the term indicated the dogmatic theology of the Roman Catholic church, the Reformed church, and others.[7]

In relation to his dogmatic theology, Shedd defines *dogma* as "1. It denotes a doctrinal proposition that has been derived exegetically from the Scriptures. 2. It denotes a decree or decision of the Church. The authority of the dogma, in the first case, is divine; in the latter, it is human."[8] This definition distinguishes dogmatic theology from systematic theology. A definition of systematic theology would not need to include a statement on the authority of the church. Many systematic theologies have been written without the official sanction or endorsement of a church or ecclesiastical body. Dogmatic theology discusses the same doctrines and normally in the same outline and manner as systematic theology, but from a particular theological stance and church identification.

Louis Berkhof explains the word *dogma* as referring to "those statements or formulations of doctrines which are regarded as established truths by the body of Christians which formulated them, and which are therefore clothed with authority."[9] Thus, down through the centuries, differing Christian groups—the church Fathers, the Roman Catholic church, and the Reformers—all affirmed their dogmas according to their understanding of Scripture. Karl Barth defines dogmas as "the doctrinal propositions acknowledged and confessed by the Church, which are deposited in the Church Symbols, with their relative authority."[10] This statement helps to understand the authority of the church in dogmas.

In relating the word *dogma* to dogmatic theology, Louis Berkhof provides what may be the best understanding of dogmatic theology: "Dogmatics deals with the doctrinal truth of Scripture in a systematic way, and more particularly with that truth as it is confessed by the Church."[11]

AUTHORITY

ROMAN CATHOLIC VIEW

Dogmatic theology in the Roman Catholic church, while acknowledging the authority of Scripture, also looks to tradition and official church decisions for the formulation of its dogma. In recent years, Roman Catholic theologians like Karl Rahner have argued for the necessity of experiencing dogma in life rather than simply acknowledging creedal statements.

PROTESTANT VIEW

Dogmatic theology written in the Protestant tradition, whether Calvinistic, Arminian, Covenant, or Dispensational, has the Scriptures, not the church, as its authority. In points of controversy the solution is sought in

Scripture, not in the decision of the church councils. Just as conservative theology rejected the authority of the church in formulating its doctrines, so in the last two centuries conservative theology has rejected rationalism as an authority.

The following categories of Calvinistic, Arminian, Covenant, Dispensational, and Catholic theologies are grouped under this section entitled "Dogmatic Theology." Each of these systems reflects the interpretation and theological views of a particular ecclesiastical body or Christ-professing movement.

Notes on Dogmatic Theology

1. F. H. Klooster, "Dogmatics" in Walter A. Elwell, ed., *Evangelical Dictionary of Theology* (Grand Rapids: Baker, 1984), p. 328.

2. William G. T. Shedd, *Dogmatic Theology*, 3 vols. (Reprint. Nashville: Nelson, 1980), 1:1f.

3. Hendrikus Berkhof, *Introduction to the Study of Dogmatics* (Grand Rapids: Eerdmans, 1985), p. 7; and Louis Berkhof, *Introduction to Systematic Theology* (Reprint. Grand Rapids: Baker, 1979), p. 17. Although Louis Berkhof prefers the designation *dogmatic theology*, for practical reasons he uses the expression *systematic theology* for his work.

4. *Webster's New Collegiate Dictionary* (Springfield, Mass.: Merriam, 1949), p. 245. The biblical and extra-biblical usage of the word may denote such ideas as "decree," "ordinance," "decision," or "command." It is used for Caesar's *decree* (Luke 2:1; Acts 17:7), the *commands* of Christ (Barnabas 1:6; 1 Mg. 13:1), or the Mosaic *law* (1 Macc. 1:3; Eph. 2:15; Col. 2:14). Compare William F. Arndt and F. Wilbur Gingrich, *A Greek-English Lexicon of the New Testament and Other Early Christian Literature* 2nd ed., revised by F. Wilbur Gingrich and Frederick W. Danker (Chicago: U. of Chicago, 1979), p. 201. These examples further indicate that the word is used to emphasize the beliefs of an individual or a group.

5. Louis Berkhof, *The History of Christian Doctrines* (Reprint. Edinburgh: Banner of Truth, 1969), pp. 18-19.

6. Hendrikus Berkhof, *Introduction to the Study of Dogmatics*, pp. 4-5.

7. T. W. J. Morrow, "Dogma" in *New Dictionary of Theology*, edited by Sinclair B. Ferguson, J. I. Packer, and David F. Wright (Downers Grove, Ill: InterVarsity, 1988), p. 203.

8. Shedd, *Dogmatic Theology*, 1:11.

9. Louis Berkhof, *Introduction to Systematic Theology*, p. 19.

10. Ibid, p. 20.

11. Ibid, p. 35.

For Further Study on Dogmatic Theology

** Hendrikus Berkhof. *Introduction to the Study of Dogmatics*. Grand Rapids: Eerdmans, 1985.

** Louis Berkhof. *Introduction to Systematic Theology*. Reprint. Grand Rapids: Baker, 1979.

* F. H. Klooster. "Dogmatics." In Walter A. Elwell, ed. *Evangelical Dictionary of Theology*. Grand Rapids: Baker, 1984. Pp. 328-29.

* T. W. J. Morrow. "Dogma." In *New Dictionary of Theology*, edited by Sinclair B. Ferguson, J. I. Packer, and David F. Wright. Downers Grove, Ill.: InterVarsity, 1988. Pp. 202-4.

33

CALVINISTIC THEOLOGY

To speak of Calvinism is to speak of the Reformed faith. The term *Reformed* is today basically synonymous with Calvinism and historically distinguishes the Calvinistic churches from the Lutheran and Anabaptist traditions.[1] The theology of Calvinism or the Reformed faith finds its roots in the writings of John Calvin, particularly as expressed in the *Institutes of the Christian Religion.* Calvin's theology centers on the sovereignty of God, the other doctrines being tied to that premise. The theology of Calvin is restated in the form of many confessional statements that have been adhered to over the centuries in Europe, Britain, and America.

HISTORICAL DEVELOPMENT OF CALVINISTIC THEOLOGY

JOHN CALVIN AND THE *INSTITUTES*

John Calvin (1509-1564) was born in Noyon, Picardy, sixty miles northeast of Paris. He began study for the priesthood at the University of Paris at the age of fourteen, but through a conflict with the bishop he eventually left to study law. He became proficient in Latin, Greek, and Hebrew. His conversion occurred through his contact with Protestants, probably in 1533 or 1534, but information is lacking concerning details. At that point Calvin rejected the "superstitions of the Papacy." He was persecuted for his faith, imprisoned, but subsequently freed. He found refuge in Basel, Switzerland, where he began his extensive writing ministry. In 1536 Calvin published the first edition of the *Institutes* (when he was only 26). The *Institutes* were originally written in Latin and later translated into French by Calvin. He constantly revised his writings, expanding the first edition of the *Institutes* from six chapters to eighty chapters in the fourth and final edition of 1559.[2]

It was in Geneva, Switzerland, where Calvin was befriended by Guillaume Farel (1489-1565), a Reformation leader, that Calvin further developed the *Institutes* and also became a leader in the Reformation. At Geneva he and Farel began teaching Reformation theology but were banished. Calvin went to Strasbourg for three years (1538-1541) as a pastor to French refugees. A change in the political scene in 1541 enabled him to return to Geneva to work with Farel. Calvin served as pastor as well as community leader, shaping a union of church and state. He imposed strict morals on the community but also developed the commerce of Geneva into a prosperous state. Calvin was also a prolific writer, writing commentaries on forty-nine books of the Bible, as well as pamphlets and the ever-expanding *Institutes.*

SPREAD OF CALVINISM

John Calvin's influence was felt throughout Europe as his doctrinal teachings spread quickly. The Heidelberg Catechism, written in 1563 by friends of Calvin, influenced the Reformed churches in Holland, Germany, and America. The Belgic Confession, written in 1561 by Guy de Bray, became the standard of belief in the Dutch Reformed church. The Synod of Dort met in 1618-1619, condemned Arminianism and the Remonstrants, and reaffirmed Calvinistic doctrine as expressed in the Heidelberg and Belgic Confessions.

During the period mentioned earlier, Calvinism was replacing Lutheranism as an influential force. Calvinism also spread to Scotland in the form of Presbyterianism. From Scotland Calvinism would ultimately affect English Puritanism. John Knox (1505-1572), who studied under Calvin in Geneva, was the Scottish leader of the Reformation. He returned to lead Scotland to an official rejection of the Pope's authority and adoption of a Calvinistic confession of faith. In England, Calvinism also prevailed since it was the theology behind the Thirty-Nine Articles (1563) of the Church of England. The Puritans became an important force for Calvinism in England. Building on the work of William Tyndale and John Knox, the Puritans sought to purify the Church of England.

Colonization of America brought Calvinism to the North American shores. The standards of the Westminster Confession became the doctrine of the Presbyterian churches.

Ultimately, Calvinism produced some of the outstanding scholars and Christian leaders both in Europe and America. In Europe, Abraham Kuyper became both prime minister and Calvinistic scholar; James Orr wrote in defense of Calvinism in Scotland, while America produced the likes of Charles and A. A. Hodge, William G. T. Shedd, J. Gresham Machen, Benjamin B. Warfield, Cornelius Van Til, and many others.

THE SYNOD OF DORT

In the Netherlands a conflict arose between the followers of Jacobus Arminius and the Calvinists. Calvinism was attacked for its teaching of predestination and reprobation as well as for other issues. The States General called a synod in 1618 to settle the issue, but the Arminians did not come as equals. Rather, the Remonstrants were summoned to present their doctrines, which were subsequently condemned. The synod reaffirmed the Heidelberg and Belgic Confessions. The following points were affirmed at Dort and are given here in synthesized form.[3]

Of divine predestination. All men sinned in Adam and lie under the curse, but God made provision for salvation through the death of Christ. The fact that some and not others receive the gift of faith stems from God's eternal decree of election and reprobation. Election is unconditional, not based on God's foreknowledge; before the foundation of the world and purely out of His grace and according to His sovereign good pleasure, God chose some to salvation. The non-elect are left to condemnation, yet God is not the author of sin.

Of the death of Christ. While the death of Christ is of infinite value and sufficient to save the whole world, His atoning death extends to the elect only.

Of the corruption of man and his conversion to God. Man was created in the image of God, but through the sin of Adam all mankind is corrupted. Sin has passed to the human race so that all people are born in sin and are children of wrath. But while man is incapable of saving himself, God accomplishes salvation for elect individuals through the operation of the Holy Spirit. Those whom He has chosen in eternity, He calls effectually in time. The faith that realizes salvation is itself a gift.

Of the perseverance of the saints. Whom God calls, He also delivers from the dominion and slavery of sin. Since God is faithful, He preserves those who believe to the end.

WESTMINSTER CONFESSION

The Westminster Confession arose out of the stormy political scene in England during the reign of Charles I. Charles met with resistance when he attempted to impose episcopacy on the Church of Scotland and to conform its services to the Church of England's Common Book of Prayer. A civil war erupted and Oliver Cromwell led the Puritan forces to victory. Charles I was beheaded in the process. In 1643 the English parliament commissioned the Westminster Assembly to develop the creed of the Church of England. The 121 English Puritan ministers met for 1,163 daily sessions from 1643 to

1649. The Westminster Confession of Faith, completed in 1646, affirmed a strong Calvinistic position and disavowed "the errors of Arminianism, Roman Catholicism, and sectarianism."[4]

The following points summarize the Westminster Confession of Faith:[5]

Scripture. The sixty-six books of the Old and New Testaments are recognized to provide "divine inspiration, authority, and sufficiency as an infallible rule of faith and practice." The traditions of Roman Catholicism, the Apocrypha, and humanism are to be rejected.

God. God, who is infinite in His being, exists as God the Father, God the Son, and God the Holy Spirit. He is absolutely sovereign, having from all eternity, by His own free will, ordained whatever comes to pass. The triune God has created the world out of nothing in the space of six days. God, in His providence, upholds all things by His sovereign authority.

Man. Man fell from original righteousness and became dead in sin, that sin and death being imputed to all mankind. God originally entered into a covenant of works with Adam, but when he sinned, God enacted the covenant of grace. In his sin man lost all ability to will anything spiritually good.

Christ. Jesus Christ is of one substance with the Father; became virgin born; as the God-Man became the Mediator, offering a perfect sacrifice. Christ purchased reconciliation for all those whom the Father has given Him.

Salvation. Through His Word and His Spirit, God effectually calls all those whom He has predestined to eternal life. He renews their spirit and draws them to Jesus Christ. Hence, salvation is entirely by grace. God justifies these believers, declaring them righteous; He adopts them as His children; and He sanctifies them. Saving faith is a gift of the Spirit of Christ. Repentance is a doctrine to be preached along with saving faith. Good works are the fruit of a true faith.

Perseverance. Those whom God has saved can neither totally nor finally fall away from grace but shall persevere to the end and be eternally saved.

Assurance. Only true believers will have assurance that they are in the state of grace; unbelievers will not have that assurance.

Worship. God is to be feared, loved, praised, called upon, trusted in, and served with all the heart, soul, and might. Worship is to be accorded the Father, Son, and Spirit and no one else. Prayer is to be offered to God. A lawful oath may be part of religious worship.

Civil duties. God has appointed those in authority, and believers ought to pray for them; believers may also be called on to serve as magistrates.

Divorce. Marriage is between one man and one woman. The innocent party may divorce when adultery or fornication has taken place.

Church. The catholic or universal church consists of the whole number of the elect; the visible church consists of those who confess their faith. All believers are united to Christ and are in a holy fellowship in the worship of

God. The sacraments are the seals of the covenant of grace. There is in every sacrament a spiritual relation or sacramental union. Baptism is a sacrament and also a sign and seal of the covenant of grace. Baptism is rightly administered by pouring or sprinkling water on the person. The Lord's Supper is spiritual nourishment and promotes growth in Christ. No remission of sins is made in communion; it is a commemoration. Christ has given authority to the church officers in which they enact church discipline. For the better government of the church there ought to be synods or councils.

Death and judgment. After death, bodies return to dust, but the soul immediately returns to God: the righteous are received into heaven; the wicked into hell. All authority has been given to Christ who will judge the world in righteousness.

FIVE POINTS OF CALVINISM

Calvin did not author the so-called "five points of Calvinism." They originated at the Synod of Dort (1619) and are also a result of affirming the distinctives of Calvinism over the centuries since. God as sovereign was central in the theology of Calvin, and that is reflected in the five points. The five points emphasize God in His sovereignty and grace but also man in his depravity and sin. The five points are popularly named: total depravity; unconditional election; limited atonement; irresistible grace; and perseverance of the saints. (Theologians have nicknamed these points "tulip," a popular acronym based on the first letters of the doctrines.)

These five concepts are arranged logically and are contingent upon one another. If man is totally depraved, then he is unable to make an initial response to God; God must call man to salvation through unconditional election. God also makes provision for those whom He calls to salvation by the death of Christ; He secures their salvation by the effectual call of the Holy Spirit and keeps them secure in order that they might receive the eternal life He has promised them. The accompanying table and the discussion that follows will give a more detailed explanation.

DOCTRINAL AFFIRMATIONS OF CALVINISTIC THEOLOGY

The following discussion will affirm the major tenets of Calvinism as it is generally taught today. There are also statements about John Calvin's doctrinal teachings. It is recognized, however, that Calvinism has undergone some modifications over the centuries. The views that are presented are those *generally* held by Calvinists today and are taken from Calvinistic works. (For further information see chap. 30, "Reformation Theology.") It is not the purpose here to study all aspects of Calvin's theology; for that the reader is referred to a work like Wilhelm Niesel, *The Theology of Calvinism.*

FIVE POINTS OF CALVINISM

Doctrine	Explanation
Total Depravity	As a result of Adam's fall, the entire human race is affected; all humanity is dead in trespasses and sin. Man is unable to save himself.
Unconditional Election	Because man is dead in sin, he is unable to initiate response to God; therefore, in eternity past God elected certain people to salvation. Election and predestination are unconditional; they are not based on man's response.
Limited Atonement	Because God determined that certain ones should be saved as a result of God's unconditional election, He determined that Christ should die for the elect. All whom God has elected and Christ died for will be saved.
Irresistible Grace	Those whom God elected and Christ died for, God draws to Himself through irresistible grace. God makes man willing to come to Him. When God calls, man responds.
Perseverence of the Saints	The precise ones God has elected and drawn to Himself through the Holy Spirit will persevere in faith. None whom God has elected will be lost; they are eternally secure.

The purpose of this study is simply to summarize the essential distinctives that set Calvinism apart from Arminianism and from other doctrinal systems.

SOVEREIGNTY OF GOD

Foundational to the entire system of Calvinism is the doctrine of the sovereignty of God. "Calvinism asserts that the sovereignty of God is supreme; that He has absolute and undisputable authority over all creation, that nothing can lie outside of or be viewed as not being subject to the sovereignty of His will, that He is not only the Creator and Upholder but the Disposer of all events from the beginning of time to its close."[6] Calvin himself taught that God's providence is manifested in three ways:[7] (1) God sustains all creation in its being—apart from Him it would be dissolved; (2) God daily bestows life and ability to all things as it pleases Him—apart from Him nothing could have life and existence; (3) God guides all things to their appointed end. Calvin further taught that even though God sustains and guides the whole world and every individual, His providential care is particularly focused on the church, where He manifests His divine purposes.[8] Calvin maintained, however, that divine sovereignty does not vitiate man's responsibility. God imbued man with reason and with a will, and people are held responsible for their decisions. On the other hand, man's responsibility does not dethrone God from His sovereignty. God does not simply wait to see what man's decision will be before He moves to action; rather, God subdues the actions and decisions of men to accomplish His purpose.[9] In a word, God is not governed by any circumstances outside of Himself, but only by His own good pleasure.[10] God thereby determines the result of all people, events, and things.

The result of God's sovereignty is that His purpose will be achieved. Nothing can thwart His plan; history will be worked out according to the predetermined will of God.

PREDESTINATION

Calvin defined predestination as follows: "Predestination we call the eternal decree of God, by which he hath determined in himself what he would have to become of every individual of mankind. . . . eternal life is foreordained for some, and eternal damnation for others. Every man, therefore, being created for one or the other of these ends, we say he is predestinated either to life or to death."[11]

Predestination has both a wider and a narrower aspect. In its wider aspect it emphasizes that God has foreordained whatever comes to pass, based on Ephesians 1:11. From eternity past God has determined the events of history. The narrower aspect of predestination is personal; it means that from eternity past God has elected (or chosen) some to salvation while allowing remaining members of humanity to go their own way. This latter doctrine is known as reprobation (Rom. 9:16-19).[12] Although they deserved nothing and had no merit in themselves, God chose some to salvation; God also passed over some, condemning them to eternal punishment for their sins. Calvin called this a "horrible" doctrine but insisted that the Scripture clearly teaches it and that the doctrine could not be avoided.[13]

The word *predestinate* (Gk. *prooridzo*) means "to mark out beforehand" (Eph. 1:5, 11; Rom. 8:29; Acts 4:28; 1 Cor. 2:7). On this basis Calvinists teach that God, in the act of predestination, elected certain ones to salvation. Election itself is based on the term *call* (Gk. *kaleo*), which means "to call out from among." It suggests the sovereign work of God in choosing some people for salvation out from among the masses of humanity. The many references to *call* in the New Testament emphasize God's sovereign call to salvation (e.g., Rom. 1:1; 8:28, 30; 9:11;1 Cor. 1:1, 2).

As indicated earlier, there are close relationships among the essential doctrines of the Calvinistic system. Calvinists insist that election and predestination are necessary because of man's fall. If man is dead in trespasses and sins (Eph. 2:1), then it is necessary for God to initiate salvation. If God had not marked out some to salvation, no one could have been saved. Man in his depraved state is utterly unable to make a move toward God.

TOTAL DEPRAVITY

Total depravity should first be defined negatively: it does *not* mean "(1) that depraved people cannot or do not perform actions that are good in either man's or God's sight. . . . (2) that fallen man has no conscience which judges between good and evil for him. . . . (3) that people indulge in every form of sin or in any sin to the greatest extent possible."[14]

The word *depravity* means that because of sin's corruption "there is nothing man can do to merit saving favor with God," while *total* means that depravity "has extended to all aspects of man's nature, to his entire being."[15] Calvin defined man's depraved estate as follows: "All men are conceived in sin, and born the children of wrath, indisposed to all saving good, propense to evil, dead in sin, and the slaves of sin; and without the regenerating grace of the Holy Spirit, they neither are willing nor able to return to God, to correct their depraved nature, or to dispose themselves to the correction of it."[16]

The Scriptures[17] emphasize the depravity of man by man's continual sinning (Gen. 6:5; Jer. 17:9; Rom. 3:10-18). The reason is that man is born a fallen creature with the pollution of sin (Ps. 51:5). Depravity also affirms the inability of man to do good (Matt. 7:17-18; John 15:4-5; 1 Cor. 12:3). Depravity further affirms man's inability to understand the good (Matt. 13:14; John 1:11; 8:43; Acts 16:14; 1 Cor. 1:18; 2:14; 2 Cor. 3:12-18; Eph. 4:18). Depravity also indicates man cannot desire the good (Matt. 7:18; John 3:3; 6:44; 8:43; 15:4-5; Eph. 2:1).

Total depravity indicates man's utter inability to do anything for his salvation. God must initiate the process if a person is to be saved.

UNCONDITIONAL ELECTION

Unconditional election is logically tied to the doctrine of the total depravity of man. If the Scriptures teach that man is totally depraved, dead in trespasses and sin, then man is unable to initiate a response toward God for salvation. God must act. Calvinism teaches that from eternity past, God has unconditionally elected certain ones to salvation regardless of any merit on their part. *Unconditional* emphasizes that election is not conditioned on God's foreknowledge that certain ones will believe in Christ. Election is not conditioned on man's ability or response. *Unconditional* emphasizes that God alone initiates the process.

There are six main features involved in election.[18] (1) Election is a sovereign, eternal decree of God (Rom. 8:29; Eph. 1:4, 5, 11). (2) Election is necessary because of man's fall and total depravity. It therefore reflects the grace of God, not human effort (Rom. 9:11). (3) Election is "in Christ." From eternity past God chose believers to be united to Christ (Rom. 8:29; Eph. 1:4, 5, 11). In election God effects salvation through sending the Savior and effectually calling certain ones to salvation. (4) Election involves the salvation of the elect and the provision for their salvation. God determined to predestine, call, justify, and glorify certain ones (Rom. 8:29-30). This was planned and effected in eternity past. (5) Election and reprobation are individual, personal, specific, and particular. The pronouns in Romans 8 and Ephesians 1 emphasize the individual nature of election. (6) The goal of election is the glory and praise of God (Eph. 1:6, 12). Everything is to ascribe glory and praise to God.

LIMITED ATONEMENT

This view, also referred to as particular atonement or particular redemption, states that "God purposed by the atonement to save only the elect and that consequently all the elect, and they alone, are saved."[19] Christ's death saves all it intended to save. Connection is again made with the preceding doctrine of unconditional election. If God has elected certain ones to salvation from eternity past, then it logically follows that He will also provide for the redemption of precisely those whom He has chosen.

The emphasis on particular atonement is seen in a number of passages (italics added): Christ "will save *His people* from their sins" (Matt. 1:21); the Good Shepherd "lays down His life for *the sheep*" (John 10:11); Christ prayed only for "those *whom Thou hast given* Me" (John 17:9); Christ purchased the *church of God* "with His own blood" (Acts 20:28); God sent His Son, delivering "Him up *for us* all" (Rom. 8:32); Christ "loved *the church* and gave Himself up *for her*" (Eph. 5:25). In each case the biblical passage suggests not everyone, but only the elect. Christ died for "His people," "His sheep," "the ones He prayed for," "the ones given Him by the Father," and "the church." In a passage like John 3:16 the word "world" does not mean everyone, but "the whole world in the sense of people from every tribe and nation—not just the Jews."[20] In passages like John 1:29; 1 John 2:2, and 1 Timothy 2:6 the references that seemingly suggest everyone should rather be understood in a restricted sense. At times the Bible uses "world" and "all" in a restricted sense.[21]

Many Calvinists emphasize that although the atonement is particular, Christ died only for the elect, yet the offer of the gospel is for everyone.[22] How both of these facts can be true is paradoxical—a mystery that cannot be explained; it is one of many "irreconcilable" opposites of Scripture. God's thoughts and ways are not man's thoughts and ways. He has always been faithful and true. Therefore we trust Him where our philosophical efforts to harmonize His mysteries are utterly confounded.

IRRESISTIBLE GRACE

Grace is the unmerited favor of God. Calvinists emphasize the necessity of God's grace in salvation. If man can do nothing to save himself, then God must act; God must provide grace in order that man might be saved. That is the work of irresistible grace, which is also referred to as special or efficacious (because it is effective) grace. Opponents of this doctrine might suggest that if grace is irresistible then God forces someone to come against his own will. That is not the idea of irresistible grace, according to Calvinists. It does not make someone come contrary to his will. Rather, irresistible grace makes the individual *willing* to come, as is seen in Berkhof's definition: "By changing the heart it makes man perfectly willing to accept Jesus Christ unto salvation and to yield obedience to the will of God."[23] Irresistible grace is the supernatural work of God wherein He works in the soul of the individual, changing the entire nature by the Holy Spirit's operation.[24]

In the logic of Calvinism, God, through His Spirit, draws precisely those whom God unconditionally elected from eternity past and Christ died for. Thus the purpose of God is accomplished. He elected certain ones, Christ died for those very ones, and now through the Holy Spirit, God dispenses His irresistible grace to them to make them willing to come. They do not want to resist.

The scriptural basis for irresistible grace is John 6:37, 44.[25] Jesus said that the precise ones whom the Father has given Him will come to Him; moreover, they do not come of themselves. They cannot come unless the Father supernaturally draws them to Christ. Jesus, as the Good Shepherd, brings all the sheep to Himself; none are left out (John 10:16). Paul also affirms that the ones Christ elected He also justified and will ultimately glorify (Rom. 8:28-30). None are lost in the process.

Irresistible grace does not remove man's responsibility to believe. Man must heed the call, "Believe in the Lord Jesus Christ, and you shall be saved" (Acts 16:31). But when man believes in Christ, it is God through irresistible grace who enables him to believe.

PERSEVERANCE OF THE SAINTS

This is the fifth and final factor of the five points of Calvinism. Again it should be observed that perseverance of the saints is logically connected with the preceding points. If man is totally depraved then he cannot respond to God; God must unconditionally elect man to salvation. For those who are elected, Christ has died to secure their salvation. God then irresistibly draws them to effect their salvation but also keeps them secure in that salvation to the end.

John Calvin taught the perseverance of the saints.

God, who is rich in mercy, from his immutable purpose of election, does not wholly take away his Holy Spirit from his own, even in lamentable falls; nor does he so permit them to glide down that they should fall from the grace of adoption and the state of justification; or commit the "sin unto death," or against the Holy Spirit; that, being deserted by him, they should cast themselves headlong into eternal destruction. So that not by their own merits or strength, but by the gratuitous mercy of God, they obtain it, that they neither *totally fall* from faith and grace, nor *finally continue* in their falls and perish.[26]

The doctrine of perseverance has often been expressed "once saved, always saved." Concisely defined, the perseverance of the saints means that believers "will persevere in trusting Christ as their Savior. . . . Thus they will always be saved."[27] Berkhof defines perseverance as "that continuous operation of the Holy Spirit in the believer, by which the work of divine grace that is begun in the heart, is continued and brought to completion."[28]

The doctrine is sometimes referred to as "eternal security," which emphasizes the certainty of the salvation of the elect. However, perseverance also has an important emphasis, namely, that the Christian perseveres in believing. Although the term *perseverance* seems to suggest that continuance in the faith depends on the believer, that is not the stress of the doctrine. Continuance in the faith is dependent on God.

Scriptural consideration for this doctrine is found in John 10:27-29 where Jesus emphasizes that He gives eternal life to the sheep and they cannot ever perish.[29] In Romans 8:29-30 Paul indicates that the ones God foreknew, He predestined, called, justified, and will ultimately glorify. None are lost in the process. Ephesians 1:3-14 also emphasizes this truth. God the Father planned the salvation of certain ones and marked them out for salvation (Eph. 1:3-6); God the Son secured their salvation by redeeming them through His blood (Eph. 1:7-12); God the Holy Spirit effected their salvation by sealing them—the sign of their eternal security (Eph. 1:13-14).

SUMMARY EVALUATION OF CALVINISTIC THEOLOGY

There are seven Calvinistic emphases that deserve specific evaluation.

(1) The emphasis on the sovereignty of God is scriptural (Ps. 135:6; Dan. 4:35; Eph. 1:11, etc.).

(2) Predestination and election are biblical concepts. The reason many reject these doctrines is that they suppose the doctrines exclude human responsibility. However, most Calvinists recognize the antinomy (the seeming contradiction of biblical teaching about both God's sovereignty and human responsibility), and they live with it as a divine paradox. There are differences among Calvinists on how these two contrasting ideas are interrelated. To be biblical in theology both concepts must be preserved to the

full extent of scriptural revelation. Human responsibility must not be sacrificed because of a myopic interpretation of the sovereign predestination and election of God.

(3) The doctrine of total depravity is consistent with Scripture (cf. Eph. 2:1). The Fall did not merely wound man; man died spiritually, thus affecting his mind, heart, and will. As a result of the Fall man is not disposed to seek God (Rom. 3:11).

(4) Unconditional election is both a logical necessity and a scriptural emphasis. Believers are chosen from before the foundation of the world (Eph. 1:4). The corollary doctrine of reprobation (that God decreed the non-elect to suffer eternally in hell) is not sustained by Scripture, at least in the clear way that positive election is. Although John Calvin taught reprobation, not all Calvinists agree on that point.

(5) The doctrine of limited atonement may well be the most controversial point of Calvinism—some Calvinists accept it, while moderate ones either categorically reject it or modify it. Many moderates say that Christ *actually* died only for the elect but *potentially* died for all. Strict Calvinists insist that limited atonement is a logical necessity in view of God's sovereignty. If Christ died for everyone and not everyone is saved, then God has been defeated; for His sovereign purpose to be accomplished, Christ died only for the elect, and precisely those, and only those, are saved. Although the doctrine may be defensible logically, it is difficult to sustain biblically. In limited atonement, Scriptures that indicate Christ died for the world (John 3:16) must be restricted to the elect; moreover, passages like 1 Timothy 2:6, 2 Peter 2:1, and 1 John 2:2 teach that Christ died for everyone.

(6) Irresistible grace is also a necessity if humanity is totally depraved. Correctly understood, irresistible grace does not teach that God brings people into the kingdom contrary to their wills, but rather He moves upon their wills to effect willingness to come to Christ for salvation.

(7) Perseverance of the saints (security of the believer) is a strong emphasis of Scripture. Since salvation is a result of grace, with the believer being chosen from the foundation of the world, being redeemed by Christ, and being sealed by the Spirit, loss of salvation is impossible.

NOTES ON CALVINISTIC THEOLOGY

1. W. S. Reid, "Reformed Tradition, The" in Walter A. Elwell, ed., *Evangelical Dictionary of Theology* (Grand Rapids: Baker, 1984), p. 921; and Harvie M. Conn, *Contemporary World Theology* (Nutley, N.J.: Presbyterian & Reformed, 1974), p. 141.

2. See the helpful summary of Calvin's teaching, as well as historical notations in Justo L. Gonzalez, *A History of Christian Thought*, 3 vols. (Nashville: Abingdon, 1975), 3:120-61.

3. See the summary of the Canons of Dort in Philip Schaff, *The Creeds of Christendom*, 3 vols., 6th ed. (Reprint. Grand Rapids: Baker, 1977), 1:519-23, and the full articles on 3:581-95.

4. J. M. Frame, "Westminster Confession of Faith," in *Evangelical Dictionary of Theology*, p. 1168.

5. Schaff, *Creeds of Christendom*, 1:766-82 and 3:600-73. See also *The Westminster Confession of Faith*, 2nd ed., edited by Douglas Kelly, Hugh McClure, and Philip B. Rollinson (Greenwood, S.C.: Attic, 1981).

6. Ben A. Warburton, *Calvinism* (Grand Rapids: Eerdmans, 1955), p. 64.

7. Wilhelm Niesel, *The Theology of Calvin* (Reprint. Grand Rapids: Baker, 1980), p. 70.

8. Ibid., p. 73.

9. Ibid., pp. 75-76.

10. A. Mitchell Hunter, *The Teaching of Calvin*, 2d ed. (Westwood, N.J.: Revell, 1950), p. 55.

11. John McClintock and James Strong, "Calvinism," in *Cyclopaedia of Biblical, Theological and Ecclesiastical Literature*, 12 vols. (Grand Rapids: Baker, 1970), 2:42.

12. W. S. Reid, "Predestination,' in *Evangelical Dictionary of Theology*, p. 870.

13. W. S. Reid, "Reprobation," ibid., p. 937.

14. Charles C. Ryrie, "Depravity, Total," ibid., p. 312. See also Edwin H. Palmer, *The Five Points of Calvinism* (Grand Rapids: Guardian, 1972), pp. 9-13.

15. Ryrie, "Depravity, Total," in *Evangelical Dictionary of Theology*, p. 312.

16. McClintock and Strong, "Calvinism," in *Cyclopaedia of Biblical, Theological and Ecclesiastical Literature*, 2:44.

17. See the discussion of biblical passages by Palmer, *Five Points of Calvinism*, pp. 13-19.

18. F. H. Klooster, "Elect, Election," in *Evangelical Dictionary of Theology*, pp. 348-49.

19. R. B. Kuiper, *For Whom Did Christ Die?* (Reprint. Grand Rapids: Baker, 1982), p. 62.

20. Palmer, *Five Points of Calvinism*, p. 45.

21. Ibid., p. 52.

22. Ibid., pp. 50-52.

23. Louis Berkhof, *Systematic Theology* (Grand Rapids: Eerdmans, 1941), p. 436.

24. Ibid., pp. 437.

25. Palmer, *Five Points of Calvinism*, pp. 60-66.

26. McClintock and Strong, "Calvinism," in *Cyclopaedia of Biblical, Theological and Ecclesiastical Literature*, 2:44.

27. Palmer, *Five Points of Calvinism*, p. 68.

28. Berkhof, *Systematic Theology*, p. 546.

29. The double negative *ou me* in the Greek text of John 10:28 is particularly emphatic: "They shall not never perish."

FOR FURTHER STUDY ON CALVINISTIC THEOLOGY

** Louis Berkhof. *Systematic Theology*. Grand Rapids: Eerdmans, 1941.

** A. Dakin. *Calvinism*. Reprint. Port Washington, N.Y.: Kennikat, 1972.

** A. Mitchell Hunter. *The Teaching of Calvin*, rev. ed. Westwood, N.J.: Revell, 1950.

* John McClintock and James Strong. "Calvinism." In *Cyclopaedia of Biblical, Theological and Ecclesiastical Literature*, 12 vols. Grand Rapids: Baker, 1970. 2:42-46.

** John T. McNeill. *The History and Character of Calvinism*. New York: Oxford U., 1957.

** Wilhelm Niesel. *The Theology of Calvin*. Reprint. Grand Rapids: Baker, 1980.

* Edwin H. Palmer. *The Five Points of Calvinism*. Grand Rapids: Guardian, 1972.

* W. S. Reid. "Calvinism." In Walter A. Elwell, ed., *Evangelical Dictionary of Theology*. Grand Rapids: Baker, 1984. Pp. 186-88.

** Cornelius Van Til. *The Case for Calvinism*. Philadelphia: Presbyterian and Reformed, 1963.

* Ben A. Warburton. *Calvinism*. Grand Rapids: Eerdmans, 1955.

34

ARMINIAN THEOLOGY

Arminianism is a term used to describe the theological views of Jacobus Arminius (1560-1609) and the movement that followed his teachings. The Arminian position was expressed in detail by followers of Arminius in the Remonstrance, a document produced in 1610, formally protesting the strict Calvinism in the Netherlands.

Major theological emphases of Arminianism are: conditional election based on the foreknowledge of God; God's grace can be resisted; Christ's atonement was universal; man has a free will and through prevenient grace can cooperate with God in salvation; the believer may lose his salvation. Although Arminianism is a product of a theological difference within the Reformed church, its theological views are held by diverse groups today. Methodism and Wesleyanism adhere to Arminian doctrine, as also do the Holiness movement, many charismatics, and others such as the Free Will Baptists.

HISTORICAL DEVELOPMENT OF ARMINIAN THEOLOGY

JACOBUS ARMINIUS

Jacobus Arminius was born in the Netherlands and studied at Marburg, Leiden, Geneva, and Basel. He served as pastor of a congregation in Amsterdam (1588-1603) and professor in the University of Leiden, the Netherlands, the last six years of his life.

Although Arminius began as a strict Calvinist (he had studied under Beza, (Calvin's son-in-law) in Geneva, in defending Calvinism against Koornheert, he believed his opponent more ably defended his views. This defeat led Arminius to reject Calvinism.

Arminius objected to Calvin's doctrines of predestination and reprobation and sought to modify Calvinism so that "God might not be considered the author of sin, nor man an automaton in the hands of God."[1] In developing this concept he wrote a treatise on Romans 9, advocating conditional election. A corollary doctrine he advocated was man's ability to initiate salvation and cooperate with God in salvation. In contrast to both Luther and Calvin, who taught that freedom of the will was forfeited at the Fall, Arminius believed that God granted everyone primary or prevenient grace, enabling anyone to respond to the call of the gospel. Arminius also argued against *supralapsarianism*—the Calvinistic view that God decreed the salvation and reprobation of certain people prior to the Fall. He believed that supralapsarianism made God the author of sin.

Arminius also taught an unlimited view of Christ's atonement—Christ suffered for everyone. Additionally, he emphasized that God's grace could be resisted. On the basis of 1 Peter 1:10, Arminius also taught that believers could be eternally lost.

SYNOD OF DORT

Arminius's views stirred up considerable controversy in Holland, even among his colleagues. Therefore Arminius appealed to the government to convene a synod to deal with the issue. Arminius died in 1609, nine years before the synod met. The Synod of Dort convened by the States-General on November 13, 1618, until May 9, 1619. Eighty-four members attended, fifty-eight being Dutch. With the president and first secretary being strict Calvinists, and the entire Dutch delegation orthodox in view, the fate of the Remonstrants was sealed. Simon Episcopius, the Arminian leader and Arminius's successor as professor at Leiden, and twelve other Arminians were summoned as defendants before the Synod. The five articles of the Remonstrants were rejected and five canons of Calvinism adopted, along with the Belgic Confession and the Heidelberg Catechism.[2]

Persecution followed the Synod's decision. Two hundred Arminian pastors lost their posts; the statesman John van Olden Barneveldt was beheaded; Hugo Grotius was condemned and imprisoned for life, but he escaped after two years. Many Arminians fled the country.

DUTCH LEADERS

After 1625 persecution waned, and the Remonstrants returned to Holland, establishing churches and schools permitted by a decree in 1630. A prominent theological school was established in Amsterdam with Simon Episcopius as professor of theology. Episcopius wrote a statement of faith in 1621, which was to have considerable influence in attracting Lutherans and other groups to Arminian views. (Some less orthodox were disappointed at this creedal statement because it was orthodox concerning the Trinity; Arminianism had been accused of Socinian views regarding the Trinity.)

CALVINISM AND ARMINIANISM CONTRASTED

Doctrine	Arminianism	Calvinism
Depravity	As a result of the Fall, man has inherited a corrupted nature. Prevenient grace has removed the guilt and condemnation of Adam's sin.	As a result of the Fall, man is totally depraved and dead in sin; he is unable to save himself. Because he is dead in sin, God must initiate salvation.
Imputation of Sin	God did not impute sin to the entire human race through Adam's sin, but all people inherit a corrupt nature as a result of Adam's fall.	Through Adam's transgression, sin was imputed—passed to the entire human race so that all people are born in sin.
Election	God elected those whom He knew would believe of their own free will. Election is conditional, based on man's response in faith.	God unconditionally, from eternity past, elected some to be saved. Election is not based on man's future response.
Atonement of Christ	Christ died for the entire human race, making all mankind saveable. His death is effective only in those who believe.	God determined that Christ would die for all those whom God elected. Since Christ did not die for everyone but only for those who were elected to be saved, His death is completely successful.
Grace	Through prevenient or preparatory grace, which is given to all people, man is able to cooperate with God and respond to Him in salvation. Prevenient grace reverses the effects of Adam's sin.	Common grace is extended to all mankind but is insufficient to save anyone. Through irresistible grace God drew to Himself those whom He had elected, making them willing to respond.
Will of Man	Prevenient grace is given to all people and is exercised on the entire person, giving man a free will.	Depravity extends to all of man, including his will. Without irresistible grace man's will remains bound, unable to respond to God on its own ability.
Perseverance	Believers may turn from grace and lose their salvation.	Believers will persevere in the faith. Believers are secure in their salvation; none will be lost.
Sovereignty of God	God limits His control in accordance with man's freedom and response. His decrees are related to His foreknowledge of what man's response will be.	God's sovereignty is absolute and unconditional. He has determined all things according to the good pleasure of His will. His foreknowledge originates in advanced planning, not in advanced information.

After the persecuted Arminians returned to Holland, their principles of toleration had an effect on the land, which thereafter became a land of much more religious toleration. Arminianism, however, gradually diminished so that its influence waned in Holland. Its effect, however, went beyond religious and geographic boundaries, preparing "the way for Rationalism, which prevailed to a great extent in the Established Churches of Holland, Geneva, and Germany."[3]

ENGLAND AND JOHN WESLEY

Arminian doctrine had been held in England before Arminius. The Articles of Religion, for example, were sufficiently ambiguous that they could be interpreted as either Arminian or Calvinistic.[4] Thomas Cranmer (1489-1556) published a work in 1543 entitled *A Necessary Doctrine and Erudition for Any Christian Man*, which was Arminian in substance. Cambridge University, although Calvinistic in doctrine, felt the effects of Arminianism. Baro, a French refugee who was appointed professor of divinity at Cambridge in 1574, taught that "God predestined all men to eternal life, but on condition of their faith and perseverance."[5] Arminian publications followed: John Playfere, professor at Cambridge, wrote *An Appeal to the Gospel for the True Doctrine of Predestination* (1608), and Samuel Hoard published *God's Love to Mankind Manifested by Disproving His Absolute Decree for Their Damnation* in 1633.

Following the civil war Charles II, who despised the Presbyterians, reinstituted Arminian doctrine in the Church of England. It was dominant there for some fifty years. It should be noted, however, that the Arminianism in England differed from the Arminianism in Holland. English Arminianism neglected the doctrine of grace and emphasized the example theory concerning Christ's atonement. Arminianism in England moved toward Pelagianism, and it remained for John Wesley to revive the true teachings of Arminius.[6]

John Wesley (1703-1791), one of nineteen children, was tutored early in life by a devout mother, Susanna. Trained at Oxford, Wesley had a "religious conversion" in 1725, whereupon he initiated a methodical study of the Bible called "The Holy Club." This was later termed *Methodist* because of its strict method in studying the Bible. Wesley ultimately became the founder of the Methodist denomination. Having been impressed by the faith of the Moravians in his journey to America, Wesley, upon returning to England, met another Moravian, Peter Bohler, who led Wesley to faith in Christ alone for his salvation. This marked the true conversion of John Wesley, and he preached a new message: salvation by faith alone. This was an unusual message in the Church of England with its emphasis on the sacraments. Together with another former member of the Holy Club, George Whitefield, Wesley began an extensive evangelistic preaching ministry, traveling more than 250,000 miles and preaching 40,000 sermons. The Wesleyan revival brought back the doctrines of Arminianism to England.

Doctrinal Affirmations of Arminian Theology

Arminian doctrine is found in widely diversified groups today: Lutherans, Methodists, Episcopalians, Anglicans, Pentecostalists, Free Will Baptists, and most charismatic and holiness believers. The doctrinal views that will be presented here are generally representative of Arminianism (especially as held by Wesleyans), but because of the diversity of the denominations and groups holding to the general tenets of Arminianism, what is true in particular of one will not necessarily be true of all.

Not all the doctrines that are fundamental to the Christian faith will be discussed, but only those which particularly set Arminianism apart as distinctive.

THE REMONSTRANCE

In 1610 a group of Jacobus Arminius's followers outlined their opposition to Calvinism in five doctrinal articles collectively called the "Remonstrance." The five points of the Remonstrance emphasized: (1) conditional predestination based on the foreknowledge of God; (2) Christ's death was universal; He died for everyone, but His death was effective only for believers; (3) saving faith is impossible apart from the regeneration of the Holy Spirit; (4) God's grace can be resisted; and (5) although God supplies grace so that believers may persevere, the Scriptures are not clear that a believer could never be lost. The five articles of the 1610 Remonstance are reprinted in the following paragraphs.[7]

Article One: Election based on foreknowledge.

That God, by an eternal, unchangeable purpose in Jesus Christ his son, before the foundation of the world, hath determined, out of the fallen, sinful race of men, to save in Christ, for Christ's sake, and through Christ, those who, through the grace of the Holy Ghost, shall believe on this his Son Jesus, and shall persevere in this faith and obedience of faith, through this grace, even to the end; and, on the other hand, to leave the incorrigible and unbelieving in sin and under wrath, and to condemn them as alienate from Christ, according to the word of the gospel in John iii. 36: "He that believeth on the Son hath everlasting life: and he that believeth not the Son shall not see life; but the wrath of God abideth on him," and according to other passages of Scripture also.

Article Two: Unlimited atonement.

That, agreeably thereto, Jesus Christ, the Saviour of the world, died for all men and for every man, so that he has obtained for them all, by his death on the cross, redemption and the forgiveness of sins; yet that no one actually enjoys this forgiveness of sins except the believer, according to the word of the Gospel of John iii. 16: "God so loved the world that he gave his only-begotten Son, that whosoever believeth in him should not perish, but have everlasting life." And in the First Epistle of John ii.2: "And he is the propitiation for our sins; and not for ours only, but also for the sins of the whole world."

Article Three: Natural inability.

That man has not saving grace of himself, nor of the energy of his free will, inasmuch as he, in the state of apostasy and sin, can of and by himself neither think, will, nor do any thing that is truly good (such as saving Faith eminently is); but that it is needful that he be born again of God in Christ, through his Holy Spirit, and renewed in understanding, inclination, or will, and all his powers, in order that he may rightly understand, think, will, and effect what is truly good, according to the Word of Christ, John xv. 5: "Without me ye can do nothing."

Article Four: Prevenient grace.

That this grace of God is the beginning, continuance, and accomplishment of all good, even to this extent, that the regenerate man himself, without prevenient or assisting, awakening, following and co-operative grace, can neither think, will, nor do good, nor withstand any temptations to evil; so that all good deeds or movements, that can be conceived, must be ascribed to the grace of God in Christ. But as respects the mode of the operation of this grace, it is not irresistible, inasmuch as it is written concerning many, that they have resisted the Holy Ghost. Acts vii., and elsewhere in many places.

Article Five: Conditional perseverance.

That those who are incorporated into Christ by a true faith, and have thereby become partakers of his life-giving Spirit, have thereby full power to strive against Satan, sin, the world, and their own flesh, and to win the victory; it being well understood that it is ever through the assisting grace of the Holy Ghost; and that Jesus Christ assists them through his Spirit in all temptations, extends to them his hand, and if only they are ready for the conflict, and desire his help, and are not inactive, keeps them from falling, so that they, by no craft or power of Satan, can be misled nor plucked out of Christ's hands, according to the Word of Christ, John x. 28: "Neither shall any man pluck them out of my hand." But whether they are capable, through negligence, of forsaking again the first beginnings of their life in Christ, of again returning to this present evil world, of turning away from the holy doctrine which was delivered them, of losing a good conscience, of becoming devoid of grace, that must be more particularly determined out of the Holy Scripture, before we ourselves can teach it with the full persuasion of our minds.

ORIGINAL SIN

Arminians teach the doctrine of original sin; it affects the entire being of man; man is destitute of all positive good, and apart from God's grace,

ARMINIAN DOCTRINE (THE REMONSTRANCE)

Doctrine	Explanation
Election Based on Knowledge	God elected those whom He knew would of their own free will believe in Christ and persevere in the faith.
Unlimited Atonement	In His atonement, Christ provided redemption for all mankind, making all mankind saveable. Christ's atonement becomes effective only in those who believe.
Natural Inability	Man cannot save himself; the Holy Spirit must effect the new birth.
Prevenient Grace	Preparatory work of the Holy Spirit enables the believer to respond to the gospel and cooperate with God in salvation.
Conditional Perseverence	Believers have been empowered to live a victorious life, but they are capable of turning from grace and losing their salvation.

man commits evil continually. Through Adam's sin, sin and death entered the world. The penalty of death came upon all mankind because of a state of the human heart (not imputation).[8] In addition, all people inherited a corrupted human nature as offsprings of Adam. This is not to suggest a legal imputation of sin, however. The Apology of the Remonstrants declares, "There is no ground for the assertion that the sin of Adam was imputed to his posterity in the sense that God actually judged the posterity of Adam to be guilty of and chargeable with the same sin and crime that Adam had committed."[9]

There was a distinction between Arminius's position and that of John Wesley. "Arminius regarded the ability bestowed upon our depraved nature which enabled it to co-operate with God, as flowing from the justice of God, without which man could not be held accountable for his sins." Wesley, however, taught that the ability to cooperate with God is through the "free gift of prevenient grace, given to all men as a first benefit of the universal atonement made by Christ for all men."[10] Arminians thus teach, according to Romans 5:16, that the free gift of the grace of Christ removed the condemnation and guilt from mankind so that no one is condemned eternally because of original sin or its consequences. "Man is not now condemned for the depravity of his own nature, although that depravity is of the essence of sin; its culpability we maintain, was removed by the free gift in Christ. Man is condemned solely for his own transgressions."[11]

Thus while Arminianism recognizes original sin and depravity, it also teaches that the effects of original sin are erased and reversed in everyone through the grace of God, enabling the sinner to respond actively to God, or cooperate with God in salvation. No one is condemned because of imputed sin from Adam or because of a depraved nature, but only because of individual sins.

ELECTION AND PREDESTINATION

Arminius related the doctrine of predestination (God appointing certain people to salvation) to the foreknowledge of God. God knew who would choose Him and those are the ones God predestined. He also related his doctrine of predestination to those whom God knew would not only believe but also persevere. Concerning the election of individuals Arminius states, "(the) decree rests upon the foreknowledge of God, by which he has known from eternity which persons should believe according to such an administration of the means serving to repentance and faith through his preceding grace and which should persevere through subsequent grace, and also who should not believe and persevere."[12]

Arminianism includes all mankind in its definition of predestination, which may be defined as "the gracious purpose of God to save mankind from utter ruin. It is not an arbitrary, indiscriminate act of God intended to secure the salvation of so many and no more. It includes provisionally, all men in its scope, and is conditioned solely on faith in Jesus Christ."[13]

Arminians have always regarded election to eternal life as conditional upon faith in Christ.[14] It is not an arbitrary choice of God; instead it is based on man's faith response to the gospel.

PREVENIENT GRACE

Prevenient grace is the 'preparing" grace of God that is dispensed to all,[15] enabling a person to respond to the invitation of the gospel. Prevenient grace may be defined as "that grace which 'goes before' or prepares the soul for entrance into the initial state of salvation. It is the preparatory grace of the Holy Spirit exercised toward man helpless in sin. As it respects the guilty, it may be considered mercy; as it respects the impotent, it is enabling power. It may be defined, therefore, as that manifestation of the divine influence which precedes the full regenerate life."[16]

This leads to a belief in synergism, "working together" or a "cooperative action" between man and God with regard to salvation. Because God dispenses prevenient grace, the effects of Adam's sin are reversed, enabling the person to respond in faith to the gospel. Man may accept or reject the gospel and the grace of God of his own free will. "Through this awakening from original sin, one becomes open to the grace freely offered in Jesus Christ. Restoration to close and uncorrupted relationship with God is thereby made possible."[17]

The Arminian system of grace may be summarized as follows: "(1) the inability of man as totally depraved; (2) the state of nature as in some sense a state of grace through the unconditional benefit of the atonement; (3) the continuity of grace as excluding the Calvinistic distinction between common and efficacious grace; (4) synergism, or the co-operation of grace and free will; and (5) the power of man to finally resist the grace of God freely bestowed upon him."[18]

FREE WILL

It becomes apparent that there is a relationship between prevenient grace and free will. Wiley cites four propositions in relating prevenient grace to freedom of the will.

> (1) Prevenient grace is exercised upon the natural man, or man in his condition subsequent to the fall. This grace is exercised upon his entire being, and not upon any particular element or power of his being. . . . (2) Prevenient grace has to do with man as a free and responsible agent. The fall did not efface the natural image of God in man, nor destroy any of the powers of his being. It did not destroy the power of thought which belongs to the intellect, nor the power of affection which pertains to the feelings. So, also, it did not destroy the power of volition which belongs to the will. (3) Prevenient grace has to do further, with the person as enslaved by sin. . . . This slavery is not absolute, for the soul is conscious of its bondage and rebels against it. . . . Thus grace is needed . . . to awaken the soul to the truth . . . and to move upon the affections by enlisting the heart upon the side of truth. (4) The continuous co-operation of the human will with the originating grace of the Spirit, merges prevenient grace directly into saving grace . . . Arminianism maintains that through the prevenient grace of the Spirit, unconditionally bestowed upon all men, the power and responsibility of free agency exist from the first dawn of the moral life.[19]

In summation, Arminianism teaches that the fall of man did not destroy the power of the choice. Prevenient grace thus moves the person to see his spiritual need, enabling him to choose salvation. But grace, Wiley emphasizes, is prominent in the transaction.

TERMS OF SALVATION

Saving faith involves four things: "(1) an awareness of sin; (2) a turning toward God through the prevenient grace of the Holy Spirit, who convicts and woos; (3) repentance and confession that sin has separated from the grace of God and kept the new covenant from being joined; and (4) personal appropriation of the new birth in Jesus Christ."[20]

Human responsibility in salvation involves knowledge of sin, turning from sin, turning toward God, and faith in Christ. John Wesley emphasized repentance and belief as constituting "saving faith." When Wesley preached, his message was "repent and believe."[21] Repentance has the idea of change. Wesley called it a "change of heart from all sin to all holiness." To repent means that sin must be forsaken; change has taken place. Repentance, therefore, involves action; moreover, repentance, according to Wesley, comes before faith.[22] Wesley says, "We must repent before we can believe the gospel. We must be cut off from dependency upon ourselves before we can truly depend on Christ. We must cast away all confidence in our own righteousness, or we cannot have a true confidence in his. Till we are delivered from trusting in anything that we do, we cannot thoroughly trust in what he has done and suffered."[23]

Wesley defined saving faith in three terms: (1) to put one's trust in the mercy and forgiveness of God; (2) to receive assurance in the believer's life, for instance, that Jesus is the Son of God; (3) to express reliance upon Christ, turning one's life over to Christ as Lord. For Wesley, belief is ultimately expressed in obedience.[24] This is in agreement with Arminians today who also emphasize the importance of works as a condition of salvation.[25]

MEANING OF THE ATONEMENT

Arminians generally hold to the governmental view of the death of Christ, which, as taught by Grotius, teaches that Christ did not die a substitutionary death for sinners. Christ suffered to satisfy the justice or government of God. Instead of dying for mankind, Christ made a "token payment" that satisfied the government of God. God therefore sets aside the requirement of the law and forgives sinners on the basis that His government has been upheld and honored. (See further discussion in chap. 24, "Soteriology: Doctrine of Salvation," and also in H. Orton Wiley, *Christian Theology*, 3 vols. [Kansas City, Mo.: Beacon Hill, 1952], 2:270-300.)

EXTENT OF THE ATONEMENT

Arminians teach that the atonement of Christ was universal. "This does not mean that all mankind will be unconditionally saved, but that the sacrificial offering of Christ so far satisfied the claims of the divine law as to make salvation a possibility for all."[26] The provision of Christ in His atonement is for everyone; it is sufficient for everyone to be saved (although not all are). The Scriptures emphasize universal provision (John 3:16-17; Rom. 5:8, 18; 2 Cor. 5:14-15; 1 Tim. 2:4; 4:10; Heb. 2:9; 10:29; 2 Pet. 2:1; 1 John 2:2; 4:14). Since Christ made provision for all, the proclamation of the gospel is to all (Matt. 28:19; Mark 16:15; Luke 24:47).

Arminians also teach that the benefit of the atonement includes the following.

(1) The continued existence of the race. It is hardly conceivable that the race would have been allowed to multiply in its sin and depravity, had no provision been made for its salvation. . . . (2) The restoration of all men to a state of salvability. The atonement provided for all men unconditionally, the free gift of grace. This included the restoration of the Holy Spirit to the race as the Spirit of enlightenment, striving and conviction. Thus man is not only given the capacity for a proper probation, but is granted the gracious aid of the Holy Spirit. . . . (3) The salvation of those who die in infancy. We must regard the atonement as accomplishing the actual salvation of those who die in infancy.[27]

SALVATION MAY BE LOST

Arminians have adhered to the doctrine that believers can lose their salvation. Although Arminius himself did not clearly state that believers could be lost, his conclusions pointed in that direction. Arminius taught that man is saved by grace but not apart from his free will. The will remains free. Arminius emphasized that the free will had to concur in perseverance, otherwise the believer could be lost. "It is unavoidable that the free will should concur in preserving the grace bestowed, assisted, however, by subsequent grace, and it always remains within the power of the free will to reject the grace bestowed and to refuse subsequent grace, because grace is not an omnipotent action of God which cannot be resisted by man's free will."[28]

John Wesley also taught that the believer may "make shipwreck of faith and a good conscience, that he may fall, not only foully, but finally, so as to perish forever."[29] The basis for losing one's salvation is found in passages like Luke 13:14; Colossians 1:29; 2 Timothy 2:5; Hebrews 6:4-6; and 1 Peter 1:10.

SUMMARY EVALUATION OF ARMINIAN THEOLOGY

Arminianism stresses a number of important features. The emphasis on man's responsibility is surely a biblical factor: man must believe to be saved (John 3:16; Acts 16:31, etc.). If man refuses to believe, he is lost (John 5:40; 7:17). Arminianism's emphasis on the universality of the atonement is also biblical (1 Tim. 4:10; 2 Pet. 2:1; 1 John 2:2).

Several features within Arminianism should be evaluated. (1) Arminianism denies the imputation of sin; no one is condemned eternally because of original sin. Man is condemned because of his own sins. This appears at variance with Romans 5:12-21.

(2) Though variously interpreted, Arminians generally teach that the effects of the Fall were erased through prevenient grace bestowed on all men, enabling individuals to cooperate with God in salvation. There is, however, no clear indication of this kind of prevenient grace in Scripture.

(3) Arminians teach that the Fall did not destroy man's free will; furthermore, they teach that prevenient grace moves upon the heart of the unbeliever, enabling him to cooperate with God in salvation by an act of the will. While it is true that man must bear responsibility in responding to the gospel (John 5:40), man's will has been affected because of the Fall (Rom. 3:11-12; Eph. 2:1); man needs God's grace in order to be saved (Eph. 2:8; Acts 13:48; 16:14).

(4) Arminians relate predestination to God's foreknowledge of man's actions. They stress that God knew beforehand who would believe, and He elected those. In Arminianism, election and predestination are conditioned by faith. The word *foreknowledge* (Gk. *prognosis*), however, is basically equivalent to election (cf. Rom. 11:2; 1 Pet. 1:20). The data of God's foreknowledge originates in advanced *planning*, not in advanced *information*.

(5) Arminianism stresses human participation and responsibility in salvation: recognition of sin, turning from sin, repentance, confession, and faith. For Arminianism, repentance involves change of actions, forsaking sins, whereas the biblical word *repentance* (Gk. *metanoia*) means "change of mind." Although the stress on human responsibilities is significant, if it involves multiple conditions for salvation, this stress becomes a serious matter because the purity of salvation-by-grace-alone is then at stake. The sole condition of salvation stressed in scores of Scriptures is faith in Christ (John 3:16, 36; Acts 16:31; Rom. 10:9, etc.).

(6) Arminianism teaches that believers may lose their salvation because the human will remains free and so may rescind its earlier faith in Christ by choosing sin. Frequently this view is based on controversial passages like Hebrews 6:4-6 and 2 Peter 2:20-22. The clear emphasis of Scripture, however, is that the believer has eternal life as a present possession (John 3:16; 1 John 5:11-13) and is kept secure by Christ (John 10:28) because of what He has done (Rom. 5:1; 8:1).

NOTES ON ARMINIAN THEOLOGY

1. Earle E. Cairns, *Christianity Through the Centuries* (Grand Rapids: Zondervan, 1954), p. 351.
2. Philip Schaff, *The Creeds of Christendom*, 3 vols., 4th ed. (Reprint. Grand Rapids: Baker, 1977), 1:513-14. The canons of the Synod of Dort are given on 3:550-97.
3. Ibid., 1:516.
4. John McClintock and James Strong, *Cyclopaedia of Biblical, Theological and Ecclesiastical Literature*, 12 vols. (Grand Rapids: Baker, 1970), 1:416-17.
5. Schaff, *Creeds of Christendom*, 1:659.
6. McClintock and Strong, *Cyclopaedia of Biblical Literature*, 1:417.

7. Philip Schaff, *The Creeds of Christendom*, 3:545-49. Schaff also provides parallel Dutch and Latin texts, the Dutch text taken from the first edition of 1612, and the Latin edition from the 1616 edition. The English translation was made for Schaff's edition of *The Creeds of Christendom*.

8. H. Orton Wiley, *Christian Theology*, 3 vols. (Kansas City, Mo.: Beacon Hill, 1952) 2:97-98.

9. Ibid., 2:107-8.

10. Ibid., 2:108.

11. Ibid., 2:135.

12. Carl Bangs, *Arminius* (Nashville: Abingdon, 1971), p. 352.

13. Wiley, *Christian Theology*, 2:337.

14. Ibid., 2:341.

15. Steve Harper, *John Wesley's Message for Today* (Grand Rapids: Zondervan, 1983), p. 42.

16. Wiley, *Christian Theology*, 2:346.

17. Paul A. Mickey, *Essentials of Wesleyan Theology* (Grand Rapids: Zondervan, 1980), p. 86.

18. Wiley, *Christian Theology*, 2:353.

19. Ibid., 2:356-7.

20. Mickey, *Essentials of Wesleyan Theology*, p. 133.

21. Harper, *John Wesley's Message for Today*, p. 50.

22. Ibid., pp. 51-53.

23. Ibid., p. 53.

24. Ibid., pp. 55-57. See also excerpts from Wesley's writings on repentance and faith in Robert W. Burtner and Robert E. Chiles, *John Wesley's Theology* (Nashville: Abingdon, 1982), pp. 151-62.

25. Wiley, *Christian Theology*, 2:373.

26. Ibid., 2:295.

27. Ibid., 2:297.

28. Bangs, *Arminius*, p. 216.

29. Richard S. Taylor, "Historical and Modern Significance of Wesleyan Theology," in *A Contemporary Wesleyan Theology: Biblical, Systematic and Practical*, 2 vols., edited by Charles W. Carter, R. Duane Thompson, and Charles R. Wilson (Grand Rapids: Zondervan [Asbury], 1983), 1:63.

FOR FURTHER STUDY ON ARMINIAN THEOLOGY

** Carl Bangs. *Arminius*. Nashville: Abingdon, 1971.

** Robert W. Burtner and Robert E. Chiles, eds. *John Wesley's Theology*. Nashville: Abingdon, 1982.

** Charles W. Carter, ed. *A Contemporary Wesleyan Theology*. Grand Rapids: Asbury, 1983.

* J. K. Grider, "Arminianism." In Walter A. Elwell, ed., *Evangelical Dictionary of Theology*. Grand Rapids: Baker, 1984. Pp. 79-81.

* Steve Harper. *John Wesley's Message for Today*. Grand Rapids: Zondervan, 1983.

** A. W. Harrison. *Arminianism*. London: Duckworth, 1937.

** Thomas A. Langford. *Practical Divinity: Theology in the Wesleyan Tradition*. Nashville: Abingdon, 1983.

* Paul A. Mickey. *Essentials of Wesleyan Theology*. Grand Rapids: Zondervan, 1980. United Methodist.

** H. Orton Wiley. *Christian Theology*, 3 vols. Kansas City, Mo.: Beacon Hill, 1952. One of the most complete and important works spelling out the distinctives of Arminian theology and written from a Nazarene viewpoint.

* Mildred Bangs Wynkoop. *Foundations of Wesleyan-Arminian Theology*. Kansas City, Mo.: Beacon Hill, 1967.

35

COVENANT THEOLOGY

Covenant theology is a system of interpreting the Scriptures on the basis of two covenants: the covenant of works and the covenant of grace. Some covenant theologians specify three covenants: works, redemption, and grace. Covenant theology teaches that God initially made a covenant of works with Adam, promising eternal life for obedience and death for disobedience. Adam failed, and death entered the human race. God, however, moved to resolve man's dilemma by entering into a covenant of grace through which the problem of sin and death would be overcome. Christ is the ultimate mediator of God's covenant of grace.

HISTORICAL BACKGROUND OF COVENANT THEOLOGY

JOHANN BULLINGER

Johann Heinrich Bullinger (1504-1575) followed Ulrich Zwingli as leader of the Reformation in Zurich. Like the other Reformers, Bullinger held to the authority of the Scriptures and preached biblical doctrine that was also published. He wrote extensively, his works numbering 150 volumes. He was an influential leader in the Reformed church, second only to Calvin in authority.

Bullinger was the sole author of the Second Helvetic Confession of 1566, which Confession gave a clear statement of the Reformed faith.[1] He also played a part in the development of covenant theology, teaching federal representation in salvation in the *Compendium of the Christian Religion.*

JOHANNES WOLLEBIUS[2]

Johannes Wollebius (1586-1629), who taught New Testament studies in Basel, Switzerland, published a *Compendium of Christian Theology* in 1626 in which he espoused Reformed theology. Wollebius taught that God made a covenant of works with Adam in which God ruled over man before the Fall. Wollebius defined the covenant of works as it has usually been defined: "the promise of eternal life for obedience and the threat of death for disobedience." Wollebius understood the two trees in the garden as sacraments of the covenant of works.

Wollebius also taught a covenant of grace, made through God's mercy after the Fall. The covenant of grace, which extends across all ages after the Fall, is mediated by Christ. Wollebius referred to two administrations, the Old Testament and the New Testament. The Old Testament covered three ages: Adam to Abraham, Abraham to Moses, and Moses to Christ. The new administration is the period after Christ's coming. Wollebius emphasized five distinctions between the two administrations of the Old and New Testaments. The sacraments of the covenant of works are circumcision and the Passover ceremony in the Old Testament and baptism and the Lord's Supper in the New Testament.

WILLIAM AMES[3]

William Ames (1576-1633) was a learned, highly regarded Puritan theologian in England and Holland. He vigorously opposed Arminianism, involving himself in the Synod of Dort. Ames, like Wollebius, taught a covenant of works established before the Fall. Ames, however, held that the covenant of works, which was universal in scope, continued after the Fall. Its fulfillment was dependent upon man's obedience to God. Some theologians would place the continuation of the covenant idea under the covenant of law rather than suggesting it belongs to the covenant of works.

Ames taught a covenant of grace made after the Fall, but he preferred to call it a testament because it was related to the death of Christ. Ames saw God as the lone participant in the covenant of grace. He taught a universal sufficiency in the covenant but an application that is limited to those for whom God intended it. Ames also understood the covenant of grace to extend across all ages after the Fall. Ames taught that the covenant of grace spanned two administrations, the Old Testament and the New Testament; the Old Testament covered two ages—before Moses and after Moses; the New Testament also covers two ages—from Christ to the end of the world, and the end itself. The end will achieve the purpose of the covenant: God's glory and man's salvation. The sign of the covenant of grace is baptism, hence, infants should be baptized.

JOHANNES COCCEIUS

Johannes Cocceius (1603-1669), who taught at Bremen, Franeker, and Leiden, was a leader in the development of covenant theology. It came to a clear expression through his writings. Cocceius emphasized a biblical, exegetical theology, in which he recognized the need for a theology derived from the Scriptures themselves, just as the Reformers had practiced it.

Cocceius taught that God entered into a covenant of works with Adam.[4] This covenant enabled Adam to enjoy communion and friendship with God. Cocceius taught that Adam represented the entire human race in the covenant of works. If Adam obeyed God, he would come to a knowledge and sense of his own good; if he disobeyed, he would rush headlong into evil, or death. The tree of life was the "sacrament of the heavenly city and of eternal life" according to Cocceius. Because Christ is life, the tree of life signified the Son of God. Through his sin, Adam became guilty, fell from God's fellowship, from hope of eternal life, from spiritual grace, from uprightness, from authority over creatures, and from physical life.

Cocceius taught a universalistic basis for the covenant of grace.[5] God resolved to show His inexpressible mercy and "to employ an ineffable kindness and longsuffering towards the entire human race." But this had to be through a mediator who alone could atone for sin. Christ's death was "a guarantee which was already effective from the start, even before the Son, in view of this merit of his in the future, had fulfilled his vow by completing the work of redemption. Although the Son had not yet plucked out the guilt of sin, it was no longer reckoned unto them." This became a point of controversy for Cocceius. Cocceius also distinguished a "twofold time," the first was in the Old Testament "in expectation of Christ," whereas in the New Testament it was "in faith in Christ revealed." But Cocceius emphasized that in both Old Testament and New Testament eras, people were always saved by grace.

HERMANN WITSIUS

Hermann Witsius (1636-1708) gave further clarification to covenant theology. He defined the covenant of works as "the agreement between God and Adam created in God's image to be the head and prince of the whole human race, by which God was promising him eternal life and felicity, should he obey all the precepts most perfectly, adding the threat of death, should he sin even in the least detail; while Adam was accepting this condition."[6] The definition incorporates much of covenant theology: Adam as the representative head of the human race, and the covenant of works with the promise of eternal life upon obedience and the threat of death for disobedience.

Witsius also explained the results of the covenant and the solution provided by God.

> (1) The precepts of the covenant . . . bind one and all in whatever state to perfect performance of duty; (2) the life eternal promised by the covenant cannot be obtained on any other condition than that of perfect obedience achieved

in every detail; (3) no disobedience escapes God's lash and always the punishment of sin is death. These axioms however do not exclude the sponsor who meets the pledge in man's place by paying the penalty and fulfilling the condition.[7]

Thus, while man was under the sentence of death, God was also providing a solution.

The new covenant of grace displayed the unsearchable riches of God's wisdom "much more clearly than if everything had fallen out happily for man in accordance with the former covenant."[8] Witsius decribed this as a covenant ratified between God and Christ, with the promise being made to Christ Himself (Gal. 3:17).

WESTMINSTER CONFESSION

One of the earliest statements of covenant theology can be found in the Westminster Confession of 1647. This statement reads as follows:[9]

1. The distance between God and His creation is so great, that, although reasoning creatures owe Him obedience as their creator, they nonetheless could never realize any blessedness or reward from Him without His willingly condescending to them. And so it pleased God to provide for man by means of covenants.

2. The first covenant made with man was a covenant of works. In it life was promised to Adam and through him to his descendants, on the condition of perfect, personal obedience.

3. By his fall, man made himself incapable of life under that covenant, and so the Lord made a second, the covenant of grace. In it He freely offers sinners life and salvation through Jesus Christ. In order to be saved He requires faith in Jesus and promises to give His Holy Spirit to everyone who is ordained to life so that they may be willing and able to believe.

4. This covenant of grace is frequently identified in Scripture as a testament, in reference to the death of Jesus Christ, the testator, and to the everlasting inheritance and everything included in that legacy.

5. This covenant was administered differently in the time of the law and in the time of the gospel. Under the law it was administered by promises, prophecies, sacrifices, circumcision, the paschal lamb, and other types and ordinances given to the Jewish people, all foreshadowing Christ. For that time the covenant administered under the law through the operation of the Spirit was sufficient and effective in instructing the elect and building up their faith in the promised Messiah, by Whom they had full remission of their sins and eternal salvation. This administration is called the Old Testament.

6. Under the gospel Christ Himself, the substance of God's grace, was revealed. The ordinances of this New Testament are the preaching of the word and the administration of the sacraments of baptism and the Lord's supper. Although these are fewer in number and are administered with more simplicity

and less outward glory, yet they are available to all nations, Jews and Gentiles, and in them the spiritual power of the covenant of grace is more fully developed. There are not then two essentially different covenants of grace, but one and the same covenant under different dispensations.

DOCTRINAL AFFIRMATIONS OF COVENANT THEOLOGY

COVENANT OF WORKS

Definition. This covenant is variously called the covenant of life because it reflects the reward for obedience; it is also termed the covenant of works because works are the condition connected with the promise. The covenant of works may be defined as follows: God entered into a covenant with Adam as the federal head (representative) of the human race in which God promised to bless Adam with eternal life if he would obey; if he disobeyed God, Adam would be judged with death.[10]

Scriptural basis. Although there is no specific mention of a covenant in the early chapters of Genesis, the existence of a covenant is implicit. A covenant involves an agreement between two parties, in this case, between God and Adam in Genesis 2:16-17, where God laid down the terms of the covenant.[11] The covenant principle is also suggested in Leviticus 18:5; Ezekiel 20:11, 13, 20; Luke 10:28; Romans 7:10; 10:5; and Galatians 3:12 because these passages suggest the law was intended to give life.[12]

Features. (1) The promise. The promise of the covenant of works was that if Adam obeyed the command of God he would not die; this is suggested from the negative statement of Genesis 2:17, "in the day that you eat from it you shall surely die." In other words, if Adam did not eat of the fruit, he would live. This promise to Adam is consistent with other passages that emphasize the covenant, or law, that man was placed under by God. The promise for obedience was not the mere continuation of mortal life because that was already his possession. "The life thus promised included the happy, holy, and immortal existence of the soul and body,"[13] namely eternal life. This was "life raised to its highest development of perennial bliss and glory."[14]

(2) Condition. The condition God placed on Adam was perfect obedience. This is the condition for acceptance mentioned elsewhere in the Bible (cf. Gal. 3:10; James 2:10). Adam was instructed not to eat the fruit of the tree of the knowledge of good and evil (Gen. 2:17); that was the condition. The test was whether man would obey God or follow his own judgment.[15]

(3) Penalty. Punishment for disobedience to the covenant of works is stated in the term "die" (Gen. 2:17).[16] The term should be understood as comprehensive, including all penal evil. Death stands as the opposite of all that Adam was promised in life; Adam stood to forfeit physical, spiritual, and eternal life. "The life promised . . . includes all that is involved in the

happy, holy, and immortal existence of the soul and body; and therefore death must include not only all the miseries of this life and the dissolution of the body, but also all that is meant by spiritual and eternal death."[17]

(4) Present status of the covenant of works. This can be answered in a twofold manner. In one sense the covenant of works is not abrogated. God still demands perfect obedience of men, just as He did of Adam (Lev. 18:5; Rom. 10:5; Gal. 3:12); furthermore, the curse of death is evidence that the covenant is not abrogated. However, the covenant can be viewed as abrogated in the sense that its obligations are met in Christ.[18] Some covenant theologians are very emphatic that the covenant of works is no longer in force.[19]

COVENANT OF REDEMPTION

Covenant theologians view the covenants differently. Some refer only to the covenants of works and grace, whereas others refer to the covenants of works, redemption, and grace. The covenant of redemption and the covenant of grace should not, however, be understood as distinct covenants, but "two modes or phases of the one evangelical covenant of mercy."[20]

Definition. The covenant of redemption was made between God the Father and God the Son in eternity past in which they "covenanted together for the redemption of the human race, the Father appointing the Son to be the mediator; the Second Adam, whose life would be given for the salvation of the world, and the Son accepting the commission, promising that he would do the work which the Father had given him to do and fulfill all righteousness by obeying the law of God."[21]

Scriptural basis. There are numerous Scripture passages that emphasize the eternal nature of the plan of salvation (Eph. 1:3-14; 3:11; 2 Thess. 2:13; 2 Tim. 1:9; James 2:5; 1 Pet. 1:2). Moreover, Christ referred to His coming as a commissioning (John 5:30, 43; 6:38-40; 17:4-12). Christ is also regarded as the representative of the human race, the head of a covenant (Rom. 5:12-21; 1 Cor. 15:22).[22]

In the eternal plan of God it was decreed that the Father would plan the redemption through election and predestination; the Son would provide redemption through His atoning death; the Holy Spirit would effect the plan through regenerating and sealing the believers (Eph. 1:3-14).

Features. The features of the covenant of redemption relate to the work assigned to the Son. To achieve the redemption of man, Christ had to take on humanity in a genuine incarnation (Rom. 8:3). As man's representative, Christ became the guarantee of a better covenant—one that could genuinely effect salvation (Heb. 7:22). Christ subjected Himself to the dictates of the law, perfectly fulfilling the requirements of the law so that He could redeem a humanity under bondage to the law (Gal. 4:4-5). Final release of bondage from enslavement to the law came through the atoning death of Christ (Gal. 3:13).

COVENANT OF GRACE

Definition. The covenant of grace is a covenant made by God with the elect in which He offers salvation to the elect sinner in Christ. (There are differing views among Reformed theologians regarding the covenanted party: some suggest it is "the sinner"; others suggest it is the "elect sinner in Christ.")[23]

Scriptural basis. The scriptural basis for the covenant of grace is the frequently repeated phrase, "I will be God to you and to your descendants after you" (Gen. 17:7; cf. Jer. 31:33; 32:38-40; Ezek. 34:23-31; 36:25-28; 37:26-27; 2 Cor. 6:16-18; Heb. 8:10).

Features.[24] (1) It is a gracious covenant. God provides His Son as a guarantee for our salvation; through His grace God enables man to meet the demands of the covenant responsibilities by the gift of the Holy Spirit. (2) It is a Trinitarian covenant. The origin of the covenant is in the elective love of the Father, the redemption by the Son, and the application of the Holy Spirit (Eph. 1:3-14). (3) It is eternal and an unbreakable covenant. This covenant is unchangeable; God will forever be faithful to the covenant He has promised and provided. (4) It is a particular covenant. It is not a universal covenant because it does not extend to everyone; only the elect are the objects of the covenant. (5) It is the same in all dispensations. The summary phrase, "I will be God to you," is a unifying phrase in both the Old Testament and the New Testament (Gen. 17:7; Exod. 19:5; 20:1; Deut. 29:13; 2 Sam. 7:14; Jer. 31:33; Heb. 8:10). This is further seen in that people are saved by the same gospel in all ages (Gal. 1:8-9).

CONCEPTS OF COVENANT THEOLOGY

Comparisons	Covenant of Works	Covenant of Redemption	Covenant of Grace
Persons	With Adam	With Father and Son	With mankind
Promise	Physical/eternal life confirmed	Salvation provided for mankind	Eternal life
Condition	Obedience	— — —	Faith
Warning	Physical death	— — —	Eternal death
Time	Eden before Fall	Eternity past	Eden after Fall

SUMMARY EVALUATION OF COVENANT THEOLOGY

There are four emphases in covenant theology that merit particular evaluation.

(1) The overriding emphasis of grace in covenant theology is a valid and important truth. Salvation by grace is to be cherished and guarded; it is that doctrine for which the Reformers fought. It is true in every age, Old Testament and New Testament, that believers are always saved by grace.

(2) The concept of the covenant of works may be correct because the basic tenets of the covenant are indicated in Scripture: God promised Adam life on the condition of obedience; He promised death for disobedience. There is no clear statement, however, that this interchange between God and Adam was actually a covenant.

(3) The covenant of redemption, that the triune God planned man's redemption and its application in eternity past, is an inference drawn, although the covenant is not specifically mentioned in Scripture.

(4) The covenant of grace has an important emphasis in stressing the concept of grace in salvation. Probably the overriding weakness of the idea of this covenant is that it is an oversimplification; whereas it observes an abiding similarity in God's relationship to humanity, it fails to account for emphatic differences in that relationship. The covenant of grace is said to cover the time from Adam to the end of the age, with no distinctions being made between the differing covenants and covenanted people throughout this period. Scriptures related to Israel (e.g., Ezek. 36:25-28)) are made to refer to the church. Other such areas of legitimate distinction need to be considered by covenant theologians.

NOTES ON COVENANT THEOLOGY

1. See Philip Schaff, *The Creeds of Christendom with a History and Critical Notes*, 3 vols., 4th ed. (Reprint. Grand Rapids: Baker, 1977), 3:831-909.
2. See the discussion by Geoffrey W Bromiley, *Historical Theology: An Introduction* (Grand Rapids: Eerdmans, 1978), pp. 306-14.
3. Ibid.
4. See the extended discussion of Cocceius's teaching on the covenant of works in Heinrich Heppe, *Reformed Dogmatics*, revised and edited by Ernst Bizer (Reprint. Grand Rapids: Baker, 1978), pp. 281-319.
5. Ibid., pp. 371-447. See Cocceius's teaching on the covenant of grace.
6. Ibid., p. 283.
7. Ibid., p. 318.
8. Ibid., p. 371

9. Douglas Kelly et al., eds., *The Westminster Confession of Faith: A New Edition*, 2d. ed. (Greenwood, S.C.: Attic, 1981), pp. 13-14.

10. See the definitions by Heidegger and Witsius in Heinrich Heppe, *Reformed Dogmatics*, p. 283.

11. Louis Berkhof, *Systematic Theology*, 4th ed. (Grand Rapids: Eerdmans, 1941), p. 213.

12. Ibid., p. 214, 216.

13. Charles Hodge, *Systematic Theology*, 3 vols. (Reprint. London: Clarke, 1960), 2:118.

14. Berkhof, *Systematic Theology*, p. 216.

15. Ibid., p. 217.

16. See Hodge, *Systematic Theology*, 2:120.

17. Ibid.

18. Berkhof, *Systematic Theology*, p. 218.

19. J. Oliver Buswell, Jr., *A Systematic Theology of the Christian Religion*, 2 vols. (Grand Rapids: Zondervan, 1962), 1:312-14.

20. William G. T. Shedd, *Dogmatic Theology*, 3 vols., 2d ed. (Reprint. Nashville: Nelson, 1980), 2:360.

21. M. E. Osterhaven, "Covenant Theology," in Walter A. Elwell, ed., *Evangelical Dictionary of Theology* (Grand Rapids: Baker, 1984), p. 280.

22. Berkhof, *Systematic Theology*, p. 266.

23. Ibid., p. 273.

24. Ibid., pp. 278-82.

For Further Study on Covenant Theology

** Louis Berkhof. *Systematic Theology* 4th ed. Grand Rapids: Eerdmans, 1941. Pp. 211-18, 262-301. This is one of the most helpful and complete treatments of the subject.

* _____. *Summary of Christian Doctrine.* Grand Rapids: Eerdmans, 1938. Pp. 70-71, 80-89.

* Geoffrey W. Bromiley. *Historical Theology: An Introduction.* Grand Rapids: Eerdmans, 1978. Pp. 305-14.

* J. Oliver Buswell, Jr. *A Systematic Theology of the Christian Religion* 2 vols. Grand Rapids: Zondervan, 1962. 1:307-20, 2:121-24.

** Daniel P. Fuller. *Gospel and Law: Contrast or Continuum?* Grand Rapids: Eerdmans, 1980. A critique of dispensationalism and a defense of covenant theology.

* Carl F. H. Henry, ed. *Basic Christian Doctrines.* New York: Holt, Rinehart, and Winston, 1962. Pp. 96-102, 117-23.

* A. A. Hodge. *Outlines of Theology.* Reprint. Grand Rapids: Zondervan, 1972. Pp. 309-14, 367-77.

** Charles Hodge. *Systematic Theology*, 3 vols. Reprint. London: Clarke, 1960. 2:117-22, 354-77.

** Heinrich Heppe. *Reformed Dogmatics.* Revised and edited by Ernst Bizer. Reprint. Grand Rapids: Baker, 1978. Pp. 281-319, 371-409.

* M. E. Osterhaven. "Covenant Theology." In Walter A. Elwell, ed., *Evangelical Dictionary of Theology.* Grand Rapids: Baker, 1984. Pp. 279-80. See other articles such as "Ames, William," and "Cocceius, Johannes."

36

DISPENSATIONAL THEOLOGY

Dispensationalism is a system of interpretation that seeks to establish a unity in the Scriptures through its central focus on the grace of God. Although dispensationalists recognize differing stewardships or dispensations whereby man was put under a trust by the Lord, they teach that response to God's revelation in each dispensation is by faith (salvation is *always* by grace through faith). Dispensationalists arrive at their system of interpretation through two primary principles: (1) maintaining a consistently literal method of interpretation, and (2) maintaining a distinction between Israel and the church.[1]

HISTORICAL DEVELOPMENT OF DISPENSATIONAL THEOLOGY

ANCIENT DEVELOPMENTS[2]

Even though dispensationalism in an organized format is relatively recent, nonetheless the foundations and initial developments of dispensationalism are ancient. The following statements from early church leaders reflect an awareness of distinguishing economies (dispensations) in the program of God.

Justin Martyr (A.D. 110-165). Justin in his *Dialogue with Trypho* recognizes several differing economies in the Old Testament. Justin acknowledges that prior to circumcision and the law, one can please God without being circumcised and without keeping the Sabbath. After God's revelation to Abraham, circumcision was necessary to please Him; after the giving of the law to Moses, it was necessary to keep the Sabbath and observe the sacrificial system.

Justin Martyr held the essence of dispensationalism in his recognition of differing economies in the Old Testament.

Irenaeus (A.D. 130-200). Irenaeus refers in his writings to four principal covenants given to the human race, particularly drawing a distinction between three covenants of the Old Testament and the gospel. This distinction is typical of dispensationalism.

Clement of Alexandria (A.D. 150-220). Clement identified four dispensations: Adamic, Noahic, Abrahamic, and Mosaic.

Augustine (A.D. 354-430). Augustine distinguishes between the "former dispensation" when sacrifices were offered and the present age when it is unsuitable to offer sacrifices. Augustine writes that while God Himself is unchanging, He enjoins one kind of offerings in the former period and a different kind of offering in the latter period. Augustine calls this "the changes of successive epochs." Augustine recognizes that worshipers approach God in a different manner in different ages.

Ryrie concludes, "It is not suggested nor should it be inferred that these early Church Fathers were dispensationalists in the modern sense of the word. But it is true that some of them enunciated principles which later developed into dispensationalism, and it may be rightly said that they held to primitive or early dispensational concepts."[3]

MODERN DEVELOPMENTS[4]

Pierre Poiret (1646-1719). This French mystic and philospher wrote a six volume systematic theology entitled *L'O Economie Divine.* In this modified Calvinistic and premillennial work, Poiret presented a seven-fold dispensational scheme as follows:

1. Infancy—to the Deluge
2. Childhood—to Moses
3. Adolescence—to the prophets (about the time of Solomon)
4. Youth—to the coming of Christ
5. Manhood—"some time after that" (early part of Christianity)
6. Old Age—"the time of man's decay" (latter part of Christianity)
7. Renovation of all things—the Millennium

Poiret thus recognizes differing dispensations culminating in a literal, thousand year period.

John Edwards (1637-1716). This pastor and author published two volumes entitled *A Compleat History or Survey of All the Dispensations* in which he endeavors to show God's providential dealings from creation to the end of the world. He outlines the dispensations as follows:

1. Innocency and Felicity (Adam created upright)
2. Sin and Misery (Adam fallen)
3. Reconciliation (Adam recovered: from Adam's redemption to the end of the world)

A. Patriarchal economy
  (1) Adamical (antediluvian)
  (2) Noahical
  (3) Abrahamic
B. Mosaical economy
C. Gentile economy (concurrent with A and B)
D. Christian (Evangelical) economy
  (1) Infancy, past (primitive) period
  (2) Childhood, present period
  (3) Manhood, future (millennium) period
  (4) Old age, closing (the loosing of Satan to the conflagration) period

Isaac Watts (1674-1748). This notable hymnwriter, also a theologian, was more precise in defining dispensationalism; he recognized the dispensations as conditional ages wherein God had certain expectations of men and made conditional promises and prohibitions to them. Watts defines dispensations as follows:

> The public dispensations of God towards men are those wise and holy constitutions of his will and government, revealed or some way manifested to them, in the several successive periods or ages of the world, wherein are contained the duties which he expects from men, and the blessings which he promises, or encourages them to expect from him, here and hereafter; together with the sins which he forbids, and the punishments which he threatens to inflict on such sinners, or the dispensations of God may be described more briefly, as the appointed moral rules of God's dealing with mankind, considered as reasonable creatures, and as accountable to him for their behaviour, both in this world and in that which is to come.[5]

Watts's dispensational outline is as follows:

1. The Dispensation of Innocency (the Religion of Adam at first)
2. The Adamical Dispensation of the Covenant of Grace (the Religion of Adam after his Fall)
3. The Noahical Dispensation (the Religion of Noah)
4. The Abrahamical Dispensation (the Religion of Abraham)
5. The Mosaical Dispensation (the Jewish Religion)
6. The Christian Dispensation

It is noteworthy that this outline is similar to the *Scofield Reference Bible* except for the omission of the Millennium that Watts did not consider a dispensation.

John Nelson Darby (1800-1882). This scholar, although an important figure in systematizing dispensationalism, did not originate the system. Darby was a brilliant man—he graduated from Trinity College in Dublin at age eighteen and was admitted to the bar at twenty-two. Upon conversion he left his law practice and was ordained in the Church of England. Through his ministry hundreds of Roman Catholics became Protestants. Darby eventually left the Church of England, seeking a more spiritual group. He settled in Plymouth, England, where he met with believers in a breaking-of-bread service. By 1840 eight hundred people were attending and, although he insisted they were not a denomination, others called them "Plymouth Brethren."

Darby was an indefatigable writer, amassing forty volumes of six hundred pages each. Moreover, the volumes reflect his awareness of biblical languages, philosophy, and church history. Darby's dispensational system is as follows:

1. Paradisaical state to the Flood
2. Noah
3. Abraham
4. Israel
   A. Under the law
   B. Under the priesthood
   C. Under the kings
5. Gentiles
6. The Spirit
7. The Millennium

Darby advanced the scheme of dispensationalism by noting that each dispensation places man under some condition; man has some responsibility before God. Darby also noted that each dispensation culminates in failure.

C. I. Scofield (1843-1921). This biblical scholar, also a lawyer, identifies seven dispensations: "These periods are marked off in Scripture by some change in God's method of dealing with mankind, or a portion of mankind, in respect to the two questions: of sin, and of man's responsibility. Each of the dispensations may be regarded as a new test of the natural man, and each ends in judgment—marking his utter failure in every dispensation."[6]

Scofield categorizes the dispensations this way.

1. Man Innocent (from creation to expulsion from Eden)
2. Man Under Conscience (from Eden to the Flood)
3. Man in Authority Over the Earth (Noah to Abraham)
4. Man Under Promise (Abraham to Moses)
5. Man Under Law (Moses to Christ)
6. Man Under Grace (death of Christ to the rapture)
7. Man Under the Personal Reign of Christ (millennial reign of Christ)

Scofield's early influence included two individuals who in turn became teachers of dispensational truth. James H. Brookes (1830-1897), a Presbyterian pastor from St. Louis and a popular conference speaker, and James M. Gray (1851-1935), who became president of Moody Bible Institute, made notable impact in their time.

Later, Scofield's scheme of dispensationalism was popularized in the *Scofield Reference Bible*, through which many people came to fuller knowledge of the Scriptures. A new edition under the chairmanship of E. Schuyler English was published in 1967 and included updated notes by outstanding dispensational scholars: Frank E. Gaebelein (Stony Brook School), William Culbertson (Moody Bible Institute), Charles L. Feinberg (Talbot Seminary), Allan A. Mac Rae (Faith Seminary), Clarence E. Mason (Philadelphia College of Bible), Alva J. Mc Clain (Grace Seminary), Wilbur M. Smith (Trinity Evangelical Divinity School), and John F. Walvoord (Dallas Seminary).

Others. The writings of Dallas Theological Seminary professors have promulgated dispensationalism in recent years. Charles Ryrie's *Dispensationalism Today* is undoubtedly the premier defense of dispensationalism. Other writings, such as J. Dwight Pentecost's *Things to Come* and the eschatological writings of John F. Walvoord (principally *The Millennial Kingdom* and the trilogy *Israel in Prophecy, The Church in Prophecy,* and *The Nations in Prophecy*) have ably set forth the dispensational position. Charles L. Feinberg's *Millennialism: Two Major Views* has equally defended this system. Lewis Sperry Chafer's august *Systematic Theology* sets forth dispensationalism in a comprehensive manner.

Among the schools that are avowedly dispensational are: Dallas Theological Seminary, Grace Theological Seminary, Talbot Theological Seminary, Western Conservative Baptist Seminary, Multnomah School of the Bible, Moody Bible Institute, Philadelphia College of the Bible, and many others.

DOCTRINAL AFFIRMATIONS OF DISPENSATIONAL THEOLOGY

DEFINITION OF DISPENSATIONALISM

Etymology. A dispensation may be defined as "a distinguishable economy in the outworking of God's purpose."[7]

The English word *dispensation* comes from the Greek word *oikonomia,* which means "stewardship." This word is used in Luke 16:2, 3, 4; 1 Cor. 9:17; Eph. 1:10; 3:2, 9; Col. 1:25; 1 Tim. 1:4.

Several distinct examples of dispensations can be seen in Paul's usage. In Ephesians 1:10 Paul indicates that God planned a "stewardship" or "dispensation" in which all things would ultimately be summed up in Christ. Paul describes this future dispensation as "the fulness of the times," "the

REPRESENTATIVE DISPENSATIONAL SCHEMES*

Pierre Poiret 1646-1719	John Edwards 1639-1716	Isaac Watts 1674-1748	J. N. Darby 1800-1882	J. H. Brookes 1830-1897	James M. Gray 1851-1935	C. I. Scofield 1843-1921
Creation to the Deluge (Infancy)	Innocency	Innocency	Paradisaical State (to the Flood)	Eden	Edenic	Innocency
	Adam Fallen Antediluvian	Adamical (after the Fall)		Antediluvian	Antediluvian	Conscience
Deluge to Moses (Childhood)	Noahical	Noahical	Noah	Patriarchal	Patriarchal	Human Government
	Abrahamic	Abrahamical	Abraham			Promise
Moses to Prophets (Adolescence)	Mosaical	Mosaical	Israel— under Law	Mosaic	Mosaic	Law
Prophets to Christ (Youth)			under Priesthood under Kings			
Manhood and Old Age	Christian	Christian	Gentiles	Messianic	Church	Grace
			Spirit	Holy Ghost		
Renovation of All Things			Millennium	Millennial	Millennial	Kingdom
					Fullness of times	
					Eternal	

*Charles C. Ryrie, **Dispensationalism Today** (Chicago: Moody, 1965), p. 84.

summing up of all things in Christ." That has not yet happened; it is the future dispensation of the millennial kingdom.

In Ephesians 3:2, 9 Paul refers to the stewardship or dispensation that has previously been a mystery. Paul is referring to the age in which Gentiles are fellow-heirs with Jews (v. 6); that, however, did not occur until Acts 2; hence, Paul distinguishes the church age as a separate dispensation in these verses. But in so doing, he contrasts it with the previous age, which was the Mosaic law. Paul, therefore, distinguishes three distinct dispensations in Ephesians 1 and 3.

Other statements also emphasize different ages or dispensations. John 1:17 declares, "The law was given through Moses; grace and truth were realized through Jesus Christ." John points out that the new era of Christ stands in contrast to the period of the Mosaic law. The dispensation under Moses is termed "law," whereas the age under Jesus Christ is called "grace."

Romans 6:14 declares, "You are not under law, but under grace." With the advent of Christ the believer has died and risen together with Him so that sin need not dominate the believer's life. The believer can enjoy a measure of victory in this dispensation that he could not have under the law.

Galatians 3:19-25 explains the duration of the law: it was "added" and was in force "until" Christ came. The purpose of the law was to shut up all people under sin and to point them to faith in Christ. Like the tutor whose work is over when the child reaches maturity, so the function of the law is over now that Christ has come (Gal. 3:25).

Features. "Dispensationalism views the world as a household run by God."[8] In this divine household God gives man certain responsibilities as administrator. If man obeys God within that economy (dispensation), God promises blessing; if man disobeys God, He promises judgment. Thus there are three aspects normally seen in a dispensation: (1) testing; (2) failure; (3) judgment. In each dispensation God has put man under a test, man fails, and there is judgment.

The basic concept of a dispensation is a stewardship. This is particularly seen in Luke 16:1-2. This parable illustrates the distinctives of a dispensation.[9]

There are two parties. One has the authority to delegate duties; the other has the responsibility to carry them out. In this parable, the wealthy man and the steward are the two parties.

There are specific responsibilities. In the parable, the steward fails in his duties, wasting his master's goods.

There is accountability. The steward is called upon to give an account of his faithfulness as a steward.

There is change. The master has a right to remove the steward from his place of privilege and responsibility (Luke 16:2).

A dispensationalist is simply one who recognizes that God deals differently with people in different ages or economies. Lewis Sperry Chafer used to say that if one does not bring a lamb to the altar in worshiping God, then he is a dispensationalist. One who worships on Sunday instead of Saturday is also a dispensationalist, because he recognizes the Sabbath was for Israel, not the church (Exod. 20:8-11).

Number. The number of dispensations is not as important as recognizing that there are dispensations. Different people divide the ages up differently. Many dispensationalists suggest there are the following seven.[10]

Innocence. This covers the time before Adam's fall (Gen. 1:28–3:6).

Conscience. Romans 2:15 indicates God dealt with man through his conscience prior to the law. Others refer to this age as "self-determination" or "moral responsibility." This covers the period from Genesis 4:1–8:14.

Government. This involves features of the Noahic Covenant: animals' fear of man, promise of no more floods, and protection of human life through the institution of capital punishment. This period covers Genesis 8:15–11:9.

Promise. This covers the period of the patriarchs, in which God ordained that they should respond by faith to His revelation. This covers the time from Genesis 11:10 to Exodus 18:27.

Mosaic law. The law was given as a constitution to the nation Israel and covers the period from Exodus 19:1 until Acts 1:26. The law was in force until the death of Christ and the descent of the Holy Spirit.

Grace. Although grace is evident in every age, it is uniquely so in the coming of Christ. Through the advent of Christ God made His grace known to all mankind. This covers the period from Acts 2:1 to Revelation 19:21.

Millennium. This covers the period described in Revelation 20:4-6 when Christ will return to earth to reign for a thousand years.

It should be noted that features from one dispensation may be incorporated into subsequent dispensations; thus, elements from the periods *conscience*, *government*, and *promise* continue on in subsequent dispensations.

HERMENEUTICS OF DISPENSATIONALISM

Literal interpretation. Dispensationalists follow a consistently literal method of interpretation, which extends to eschatological studies. Many conservative non-dispensationalists interpret the Bible literally with the exception of prophecy; dispensationalists apply the literal scheme of interpretation to all the disciplines of theology. Although the term *literal* may raise questions in some quarters, it should be understood as the normal, customary approach to any literature—the way all language is commonly understood. *Literal*, when describing hermeneutical approach, refers to interpretive method, *not* to the kind of language used in the interpreted literature. Literal *interpretation* recognizes both literal and figurative *language*. Dispensationalists insist on literal *interpretation* for prophetic Scriptures even though they abound with figurative *language*. One reason for this, besides consistency, is the demonstrable literalness of prophecies already fulfilled in Christ's first coming.[11] There is every reason to expect the fulfillment of the prophecies concerning Christ's second coming to be literal as well.

Dispensationalism builds on the fact that God has given unconditional promises to Israel, such promises as the Abrahamic Covenant (Gen. 12:1-3). In that one God promised a land and a physical posterity to Abraham, wherein He would bless the descendants of Abraham. Dispensationalists believe these promises will be fulfilled literally in the future with Israel. Nondispensationalists spiritualize the prophecies and relegate them to the church.

Church uniqueness. Dispensationalists emphasize that Israel always denotes the physical posterity of Jacob and is never to be confused with the church. A concordance study of the term *Israel* indicates it is always used to denote Jacob's physical descendants and is never used in a "spiritualized" sense to refer to the church.[12] Although nondispensationalists frequently refer to the church as "the new Israel," it is an unwarranted designation.

Dispensationalists teach that God has a distinct program for Israel and a distinct program for the church. The commands given to one are not the commands to the other; the promises to the one are not the promises to the other. God calls on Israel to keep the Sabbath (Exod. 20:8-11), but the church keeps the Lord's Day (1 Cor. 16:2). Israel is the wife of Yahweh (Hos. 3:1), but the church is the Body of Christ (Col. 1:27).

First Corinthians 10:32 is important in noting that a distinction is maintained between Israel and the church *after* the birth of the church (Acts 3:12; 4:8, 10; 5:21, 31; Rom. 10:1; 11:1-29). In Romans 11 Paul discusses extensively the future when Israel will be saved, emphasizing a distinctive future hope for Israel as a nation. The chapter sets Israel in contrast with the Gentiles—who are coming to faith until the fullness of the Gentiles, when Israel will be saved.[13]

Biblical unity. Dispensationalists emphasize that the unifying theme of the Bible is the glory of God. In contrast to covenant theology, which emphasizes salvation as the unifying theme, dispensationalists see salvation as man-centered and simply one aspect of God's glory. "Scripture is not man-centered as though salvation were the main theme, but it is God-centered because His glory is the center."[14] In every age or dispensation God has revealed His glory, which is the unifying theme of Scripture.

DISTINCTIVES OF DISPENSATIONALISM

Grace. Although dispensationalists emphasize that the present church age is an age of grace (John 1:17; Rom. 6:14), that emphasis is not to imply that grace did not exist in previous dispensations. The approach to God in salvation is always through grace, and grace was also manifested in the dispensation of law.[15] God chose Israel but passed over the Gentiles. He promised the people of Israel a land, peace, victory over enemies, and blessing. Despite Israel's repeated failure, God continued to deal with the nation in grace—the period of the judges and the monarch were a display of such grace. Amid Israel's failure God promised the nation a new covenant whereby He would forgive her sins. God provided divine enablement through the display of His grace and the ministry of the Spirit.

While God's grace is uniquely displayed in the present age through the advent of Jesus Christ, grace was also displayed under the law.

Salvation. Dispensationalists have sometimes been accused of teaching different ways of salvation in different dispensations. That is, however, a false charge. Dispensationalists teach that "The *basis* of salvation in every age is the death of Christ; the *requirement* for salvation in every age is faith; the *object* of faith in every age is God; the *content* of faith changes in the various dispensations."[16] God's revelation to man differs in different dispensations, but man's responsibility is to respond to God in faith according to the manner in which God has revealed Himself. Thus when God revealed Himself to Abraham and promised him a great posterity, Abraham believed God, and the Lord imputed righteousness to the patriarch (Gen. 15:6). Abraham would have known little about Christ, but he responded in faith to the revelation of God and was saved. Similarly, under the law God promised life through faith. Whereas the Israelite under the law knew about the importance of the blood sacrifice, his knowledge of a suffering Messiah was still limited—but he was saved by faith (Hab. 2:4). Dispensationalists thus emphasize that in every dispensation salvation is by God's grace through faith according to His revelation.

Church. Dispensationalism is nowhere more distinctive than in its doctrine of the church. Dispensationalists hold that the church is entirely distinct from Israel as an entity. This is argued from several points. (1) The church was a mystery, unknown in the Old Testament (Eph. 3:1-9; Col. 1:26). (2) The church is composed of Jews and Gentiles; the Gentiles being fellow-heirs with Jews without having to become Jewish proselytes—something that was not true in the Old Testament (Eph. 3:6). This issue was resolved in Acts 15 when the Judaizers attempted to put Gentiles under the law. (3) The church did not begin until Acts 2. It is the baptizing work of the Holy Spirit that unites believers with Christ and one another, making up the church (1 Cor. 12:13). That work was still future in Acts 1:5, but in Acts 11:15 it is clear that it began in Acts 2, establishing the birth of the church. Dispensationalists also believe that the church will conclude its existence upon the earth at the rapture, prior to the Tribulation (1 Thess. 4:16). (4) The church is consistently distinguished from Israel in the New Testament (1 Cor. 10:32).

Prophecy. Dispensationalists attempt to be consistent in literal interpretation; therefore, the Old Testament prophecies concerning Israel are taken seriously. Furthermore, those prophecies pertain to Israel, the descendants of Jacob, not the church. The unconditional covenants of the Old Testament were given to Israel: the Abrahamic Covenant (Gen. 12:1-3) promised Israel a land, a posterity, and blessing; the Palestinian Covenant (Deut. 30:1-10) promised Israel would return to the land; the Davidic Covenant (2 Sam. 7:12-16) promised Israel that Messiah would come from Judah and have a throne and a kingdom, ruling over Israel; the New Covenant (Jer. 31:31-34) promised Israel the spiritual means whereby the nation would enter into blessing and receive forgiveness.

If these covenants are understood literally and unconditionally, then Israel has a future that is distinct from the church. On this basis dispensationalists subscribe to a literal millennium for Israel, which Messiah will establish at His Second Advent (Rev. 19:11-19). But before Israel will enter into blessing the nation must repent and recognize Jesus as the Messiah; a major purpose of the Tribulation is to discipline Israel to bring the nation to faith in Messiah (Jer. 30:7; Ezek. 20:37-38; Dan. 9:24). The Tribulation, thus, will have no reference point for the church, which will be raptured prior to the Tribulation (Rom. 5:9; 1 Thess. 5:9; Rev. 3:10). The *purpose* of the Tribulation pertains to Israel, not the church. This is a major reason why dispensationalists hold to a pretribulation rapture.

EXTREME OF DISPENSATIONALISM

The movement of faithful Bible students who push the dispensational approach beyond the point where most other dispensationalists would stop is generally called ultradispensationalism.[17] The distinctive feature of ultradispensationalism is its view concerning the beginning of the church. In contrast to mainstream dispensationalism, which holds that the church began at Pentecost in Acts 2, ultradispensationalism believes the church began later—the moderate group suggesting Acts 9 or 13 and the more extreme group, Acts 28.

The extreme group follows E. W. Bullinger (1837-1913), a scholar of some renown; earlier dispensationalism, in fact, was sometimes called Bullingerism. Others in this group include Charles H. Welch of London, successor to E. W. Bullinger; A. E. Knoch; Vladimir M. Gelesnoff; and Otis Q. Sellers of Grand Rapids. Bullinger taught that the gospels and Acts were under the dispensation of law, with the church actually beginning at Paul's ministry after Acts 28:28. The New Testament books that set forth the revelation concerning this concept of the church are Ephesians, Philippians, and Colossians. Bullinger identified three periods in the New Testament: (1) the time of the gospels when the gospel was preached to the Jews only and authenticated by water baptism; (2) the transitional period in Acts and the corresponding earlier New Testament epistles when the offer still went to the Jews, offering them participation in the "bride church" and authenticated by two baptisms, water and Spirit; (3) the period of Jew and Gentile as one body in Christ and authenticated by Spirit baptism alone. Because the Gentile church is related to Christ through the Spirit, baptism and the Lord's Supper have no significance for the church. Those rites relate to the flesh, according to Bullinger.

The moderate group, holding that the church began in Acts 9 or Acts 13, is identified by J. C. O'Hair, Cornelius R. Stam, and Charles F. Baker, author of *A Dispensational Theology.* Grace Bible College of Grand Rapids is the ultradispensational school leading to ministries with Grace Gospel Fellowship and Worldwide Grace Testimony.

Stam taught that the church began in Acts 9, with the conversion of Paul. The "Body Church" could only begin with the beginning of Paul's ministry because Paul was the minister to the Gentiles. Because after that time there was no further offer of the kingdom to Israel, J. C. O'Hair taught that the church began in Acts 13:46 with the statement: "We are turning to the Gentiles." Because O'Hair's followers begin the church within the time frame of Acts, they observe the Lord's Supper but not water baptism.

SUMMARY EVALUATION OF DISPENSATIONAL THEOLOGY

There are at least nine considerations in evaluating dispensational theology.

(1) A strength of dispensationalism has been its attempt to recognize the differing economies or dispensations in biblical history. This feature has led to maintaining a clear distinction between God's programs for Israel and for the church.

(2) Hermeneutically, dispensationalism follows a *consistently* literal approach to Scripture. Other systems like covenant theology freely admit to fundamental hermeneutical changes within their interpretations of the Bible.

(3) Dispensationalism has a legitimate biblical basis in the idea of differing economies (Eph. 1:10; 3:2, 9; etc.). Exegetically, it can be shown that there are at least three differing dispensations: Old Testament, New Testament, and the kingdom. The important thing is not the number of dispensations, but the principle of differing economies or "house rules" within the history of God's interaction with people. Even a postmillennialist like Charles Hodge and an amillennialist like Louis Berkhof recognized differing dispensations, though neither man accepted classification as a dispensationalist.

(4) Another strength of dispensationalism is its focus on the glory of God rather than the salvation of man as the objective of all things. It centers on God, not man.

(5) "Mainline" dispensationalism avoids the excesses of ultradispensationalism. This subgroup within dispensationalism in its most radical form has limited applicable Scriptures to some of Paul's epistles. The extremists in its ranks reject both baptism and the Lord's Supper, whereas the moderates will observe the Lord's Supper. The primary fallacy of this movement is failure to recognize the birth of the church at Pentecost (Acts 2); instead, the church's origin is located, depending on which ultradispensational faction is consulted, in Acts 9, 13, or 28.

(6) A misunderstanding concerning the way of salvation has sometimes been fostered by dispensationalism. Some important dispensationalists have wrongly taught that man's responsibility to be saved has differed from one dispensation to another. Although it is true that the expression or form of man's trust in God has differed throughout the dispensations, yet in every age salvation has been by God's grace through man's faith.

(7) Dispensationalism has sometimes erred in stressing grace as restricted to the church age while ignoring or minimizing grace in other dispensations. God's grace has been displayed in every age.

(8) Dispensationalism has also at times projected a negative attitude toward God's law as though it were opposed to God's grace. God's law is present in one or several forms throughout every dispensation for healthy and necessary divine reasons.

(9) Dispensationalists have sometimes relegated certain passages of Scripture to other dispensations past or future, thus obscuring their usefulness to the church. The Sermon on the Mount (Matt. 5-7) is one example. Recent dispensationalists, however, have modified this practice and have recognized and taught the legitimate applications of every Scripture to God's people today.

NOTES ON DISPENSATIONAL THEOLOGY

1. The writer is indebted to Charles C. Ryrie, *Dispensationalism Today* (Chicago: Moody, 1965) for much of the material in this chapter. This work delineates the meaning and hermeneutics of dispensationalism, contrasting it with both covenant theology and ultradispensationalism.
2. Ibid., pp. 66-76.
3. Ibid., p. 70.
4. Ibid., pp. 71-76.
5. Ibid., p. 73.

6. C. I. Scofield, *Rightly Dividing the Word of Truth* (New York: Loizeaux, 1896), p. 12.

7. Ryrie, *Dispensationalism Today*, p. 29.

8. Ibid., p. 31.

9. Ibid., p. 26.

10. Ibid., pp. 57-64.

11. Ibid., pp. 86-98; see also Bernard Ramm, *Protestant Biblical Interpretation*, 3d ed. (Grand Rapids: Baker, 1970), pp. 119-27.

12 The singular passage that is referred to by nondispensationalists is Galatians 6:16 where it is suggested that "Israel of God" may refer to the church. However, the Greek word *kai* (and) is probably used epexegetically in this case, that is, peace and mercy come upon the true Israel of God—Israelites who walk by faith, not the Judaizers.

13. See Ryrie, *Dispensationalism Today*, pp. 132-55, for a helpful discussion noting the distinction of the church from Israel.

14. Ibid., p. 46.

15. Charles C. Ryrie, *The Grace of God* (Chicago: Moody, 1963), pp. 101-9.

16. Ryrie, *Dispensationalism Today*, p. 123.

17. Ibid., pp. 192-205; and G. R. Lewis, "Ultradispensationalism," in Walter A. Elwell, ed., *Evangelical Dictionary of Theology* (Grand Rapids: Baker, 1984), pp. 1120-21.

For Further Study on Dispensational Theology

** Donald K. Campbell, ed. *Walvoord: A Tribute.* Chicago: Moody, 1982. There are several valuable articles related to dispensationalism: "A Biblical Defense of Dispensationalism"; "God, Evil, and Dispensations"; and "Hermeneutics and Dispensationalism."

* Gordon R. Lewis. "Ultradispensationalism." In Walter A. Elwell, ed., *Evangelical Dictionary of Theology.* Grand Rapids: Baker, 1984. Pp. 1120-21.

* Charles C. Ryrie. *Dispensationalism Today.* Chicago: Moody, 1965.

* _____. "Dispensationalism." In Walter A. Elwell, ed., *Evangelical Dictionary of Theology.* Grand Rapids: Baker, 1984. Pp. 321-23.

* E. Schuyler English, ed. *The New Scofield Reference Bible.* New York: Oxford U., 1967. The study notes in this Bible are valuable in explaining modern dispensationalism, particularly because the additional eight writers of this revision represent the hallmark of modern dispensationalism.

* _____. *Rightly Dividing the Word of Truth.* New York: Loizeaux, 1896.

** Paul Lee Tan. *The Interpretation of Prophecy.* Rockville, Md.: Assurance, 1974. A valuable work in explaining the dispensational hermeneutical method.

** Stanley D. Toussaint and Charles H. Dyer, eds. *Essays in Honor of J. Dwight Pentecost.* Chicago: Moody, 1986. Here are important essays related to dispensationalism.

37

CATHOLIC THEOLOGY

Dogmatic Roman Catholic theology refers to the detailed system that was produced primarily by the popes, theologians, and councils of the medieval and Reformation eras. It is protected by such sanctions as *de fide* labels and papal infallibility, thereby differentiating it from the flux and uncertainty of much of *contemporary* Catholic theology (see chap. 44).

HISTORICAL DEVELOPMENT OF CATHOLIC THEOLOGY

Roman Catholicism is generally referred to as semi-Pelagian in its theological stance. Pelagius taught that each person was born with a free will and the ability to choose good as well as evil. He rejected the notion that man's will had been affected by the fall of Adam. Although Roman Catholicism differs from Pelagianism, it does acknowledge the cooperation of the human will with God's grace in salvation—this being possible because the sin of Adam left man in a weakened condition but not spiritually dead. Man may therefore initiate salvation.

Catholicism has not been static but instead developing and evolving. Although tradition is recognized as authoritative, earlier pronouncements may be countermanded by later official pronouncements,[1] reflecting the ongoing change within Catholicism. Two developing traditions within Catholicism may be isolated.[2] The mainstream tradition stressing the transcendence of God and the church as the authoritative, divinely sanctioned institution. This tradition is variously labeled "medievalism," "Romanism," "Vaticanism," "papalism," and "Jesuitism." A minority reform tradition stressing the immanence of God and the church as community is variously labeled "Gallicanism," "Jansenism," "liberal Catholicism," and "modernism." Recently, further reform was sought through the Vatican Council II, convened by Pope John XXIII in 1962. This ecumenical council, although retaining its adherence to Catholic distinctives, sought to reform and modernize the Roman Catholic church.

DOCTRINAL AFFIRMATIONS OF CATHOLIC THEOLOGY

AUTHORITY

Whereas Protestantism holds that authority for faith and practice rests solely with the sixty-six books of Scripture, Roman Catholicism teaches that authority rests with the apocryphal writings (extra-biblical books accepted as canonical by Catholics) and church tradition as declared by the church Fathers and the papal pronouncements—as well as with the Bible. This disagreement over authority marks a foundational difference between Roman Catholicism and Protestantism.

Roman Catholicism recognizes fifteen books as authoritative in addition to the sixty-six books of Scripture. These are known as the Apocrypha (meaning "hidden") and are First and Second Esdras, Tobit, Judith, additions to Esther, Wisdom of Solomon, Ecclesiasticus, Baruch, Letter of Jeremiah, Song of the Three Children, Susanna, Bell and the Dragon, Prayer of Manasseh, and First and Second Maccabees.

The Council of Trent in 1546 officially decreed the authority of tradition as well as Scripture in this statement.

> The holy, ecumenical and general Council of Trent . . . keeps this constantly in view, namely, that the purity of the Gospel may be preserved in the Church after the errors have been removed. . . . It also clearly perceives that these truths and rules are contained in the written books and unwritten traditions which have come down to us, having been received by the apostles from the mouth of Christ himself . . . Following, then, the example of the orthodox Fathers, it receives and venerates with the same piety and reverence all the books of both Old and New Testaments—for God is the author of both—together with all traditions concerning faith and morals, for they come from the mouth of Christ or are inspired by the Holy Spirit and have been preserved in continuous succession in the Catholic Church.[3]

The Council of Trent also decreed the Latin Vulgate as the standard Bible for reading and teaching. A further important decree of the council was that the Roman church is to be the interpreter of Scripture.

> Further it determines, in order to restrain irresponsible minds, that no one shall presume in matters of faith or morals pertaining to the edification of Christian doctrine to rely on his own conceptions to turn Scripture to his own meaning, contrary to the meaning that Holy Mother Church has held and holds—for it belongs to her to judge the true sense and interpretation of Holy Scripture—or to interpret the Scripture in a way contrary to the unanimous consensus of the Fathers.[4]

This is important to note. The Roman church declared it is the official interpreter of the faith; no one is to interpret Scriptures for himself in a way that is contrary to the Roman Catholic interpretation.

THE CHURCH

Roman Catholicism teaches that the Roman Catholic church was established by Christ through Peter as the first visible head. The authority was the authority that God gave to Christ and that Christ in turn gave to the church. Non-Catholics would establish the beginning of the Roman Catholic church in A.D. 590 with Gregory I "who consolidated the power of the bishopric in Rome and started that church on a new course."[5]

Through the history of Roman Catholicism, a major point of emphasis has been that union with the Roman Catholic church is essential to salvation. In the twelfth century the Albigenses, a reform movement that separated from the Catholic faith, was condemned by the Fourth Lateran Council in 1215: "There is only one universal Church of the faithful, outside which none will be saved."[6] This was reaffirmed by Pope Boniface VIII's Bull, *Unam Sanctam*, in 1302. In 1854 Pope Pius IX declared, "It is to be held as a matter of faith that no one can be saved outside the Apostolic Roman Church. It is the only ark of salvation and anyone who does not enter it must sink in the flood."[7]

The Roman church was also considered the repository of truth. In 1862 Pope Pius IX wrote: "The Church, by virtue of her divine institution has the duty of most conscientiously maintaining the treasure of divine faith unimpaired and complete and of watching with the utmost zeal over the salvation of souls."[8]

The First Vatican Council of 1870 pronounced that the Roman church was "the guardian and teacher of the revealed Word . . . the doctrine of faith . . . has been delivered as a divine deposit to the Spouse of Christ, to be faithfully kept and infallibly declared . . . that meaning of the sacred dogmas is perpetually to be retained which our Holy Mother the Church has once declared."[9]

Roman Catholicism teaches that just as Christ is divine, He also must have a church of similar (divine) qualities. "The Church has qualities which are both human and divine, just as Jesus Christ is both human and divine, having both a human nature and a divine nature possessed by His one divine person. The glorious attributes of the Church are not due to its being merely human, they are due to the divine qualities."[10] The divine qualities which the Catholic church possesses include authority, infallibility, and indefectibility.[11]

Vatican II supplanted the idea of the church as the means of salvation with "the church as a mystery or sacrament," and the conception of the church as a hierarchical institution was replaced by a view of the church as "the whole people of God."[12]

THE PAPACY

Following a dispute with the patriarch of Constantinople, Pope Leo IX in 1053 signed an official letter advocating the authority of the pope. By the time of Pope Gregory IX, bishops were required to take an oath of obedience to the pope, much as a vassal to his lord; in addition, the pope was crowned with the triple crown originally used by the deified rulers of Persia.[13] At the crowning, the officiating cardinal declared: "Receive the tiara adorned with three crowns, and know that thou art the Father of Princes and Kings, Ruler of the World, the Vicar of our Saviour Jesus Christ."[14] In 1299 Pope Boniface VIII declared, "It is altogether necessary to salvation for every human creature to be subject to the Roman Pontiff."[15]

A significant declaration concerning the primacy of the pope was given at the First Vatican Council in 1870. It declared that in order to preserve the unity of the church, Christ set Peter over the other apostles to preserve this unity. The constitution further states that

> Peter, the Prince and Chief of the Apostles, the pillar of faith and foundation of the Catholic Church, received the keys of the kingdom from our Lord Jesus Christ, the Saviour and Redeemer of mankind, and lives, presides, and judges, to this day and always, in his successors the Bishops of the Holy See of Rome which was founded by him and consecrated by his blood. Whence, whoever succeeds to Peter in this See, does by the institution of Christ himself obtain the primacy of Peter over the whole Church. . . . blessed Peter, abiding in the strength of the Rock that he received, has not given up the direction of the Church undertaken by him. . . . the Roman Pontiff possess the primacy over the whole world, and that the Roman Pontiff is the successor of Blessed Peter, Prince of the Apostles, and is true Vicar of Christ, and Head of the whole Church, and Father and Teacher of all Christians; and that full power was given to him in Blessed Peter to feed, rule, and govern the Universal Church by Jesus Christ our Lord.[16]

Several points are noteworthy. The Roman Catholic church declares the succession of popes to have the authority of Peter; that Peter continues to direct the church; that the pope is the representative of Christ on earth; it also emphasizes papal authority over the church. The Roman church pronounces anathema on anyone who would dispute these conclusions.[17]

Vatican I further emphasized that all were to submit to this doctrine "from which no one can deviate without loss of faith and of salvation."[18] It also defined papal infallibility as "the Roman Pontiff, when he speaks *ex cathedra*, that is, when in discharge of the office of Pastor and Doctor of all Christians, by virtue of his supreme apostolic authority he defines a doctrine regarding faith or morals to be held by the Universal Church . . . is possessed of that infallibility with which the Divine Redeemer willed that his Church should be endowed for defining doctrine regarding faith or morals."[19]

The Second Vatican Council, held 1962-65, upheld the subordination of the people to the teaching of the pope, even when he spoke informally: "This loyal submission of the will and intellect must be given, in a special way, to the authentic teaching authority of the Roman Pontiff, even when he does not speak ex cathedra in such wise, indeed, that his supreme teaching authority be acknowledged with respect, and sincere assent be given to decisions made by him."[20]

MARY

The position Mary occupies in the theology of the Roman Catholic church is the result of centuries of development. The first recognition of Mary as the "Mother of God" was granted her at the Council of Ephesus in A.D. 431. That council qualified the expression by declaring that Mary was the "mother of God according to the manhood" of Jesus. While the phrase was considered inappropriate when applied to any mortal, yet it was intended to refer only to the humanity of Christ. This is not the position of the Roman church today. Today Catholicism teaches:

> The principal mysteries concerning the motherhood of God, the immaculate conception, sinlessness, and virginity are gifts made to Mary in view of her vocation to be Mother of God. Her motherhood of the Word of God is not just an external bringing about of Christ's bodily existence. Mary was mother of the Redeemer in the full sense of being his assistant in the work of redemption. . . . The mystery which completes Mary's cooperation in the work of Christ is her role as Mediatrix of Grace. . . . All of the graces which God accords us on account of Christ's merits come to us directly or indirectly through Mary.[21]

The doctrines concerning Mary are a recent development. One of the early statements concerning Mary was Pope Siricius's letter to the bishop of Thessalonica in A.D. 392. That letter declared Mary's perpetual virginity.[22] It was not until the Council of Trent in 1547 that the Roman Church announced the sinlessness of Mary, enabling her to avoid venial sins.[23] The most significant doctrines concerning Mary have been promulgated in little more than the past one hundred years. In 1854 Pope Pius IX declared Mary to be free of any sin throughout her entire life. He states: "We, by the authority of our Lord Jesus Christ, of the blessed Apostles Peter and Paul, and by Our own authority declare, pronounce and define that the doctrine which holds that the Most Blessed Virgin Mary from the first moment of her conception was, by the singular grace and privilege of Almighty God, in view of the merits of Christ Jesus the Saviour of the human race, preserved immune from all stain of original sin, is revealed by God."[24]

Mary's role as the mediatrix of grace and the co-redemptrix of Christ is prominent in recent Catholic theology. Pope Leo XIII declares in his 1891 Encyclical *Octobri Mense*: "The eternal Son of God, when he wished to take the nature of man for the redemption and glorification of mankind, . . . did not do so without first having the *absolutely free consent of his chosen mother* who in a sense personified the whole human race, . . . so that, just as no one can attain to the supreme Father except through the Son, to a certain extent, no one can attain to the Son except through the Mother."[25] The encyclical further declares that since people tremble before the justice of God, an advocate and protector is needed where none will be refused. "Mary is such a one, Mary worthy of all praise; she is powerful, mother of the all-powerful God; . . . So God gave her to us. . . . We should place ourselves under her protection and loyalty, together with our plans and our deeds, our purity and our penance, our sorrows and joys and pleas and wishes. All that is ours we should entrust to her. . ."[26]

In 1892 Pope Leo XIII's Encyclical *Magnae Dei Matris* declared adherents of the Catholic faith to pray to Mary and receive help from her treasury of grace. He declares her exalted position: "she stands high above all the orders of angels and men and she alone is next to Christ."[27] In 1904 Pope Pius X declared that all who are joined to Christ "came from Mary's womb in the manner of a Body joined to its Head. So we may call ourselves in a spiritual and mystical way children of Mary, and she is the Mother of us all."[28] He further declares that because Mary shared the sufferings of Christ, God "promoted her to the high dignity of restorer of the lost world and thus the dispenser of all the goods which Jesus won for us by his death and at the price of his blood."[29] Thus in the eyes of the Catholic church Mary has become "the most powerful mediatrix and conciliator between the whole world and her only-begotten Son . . . (and) *the chief minister in the distribution of graces.*"[30]

Pope Pius XII declared in 1943 in his Encyclical *Mystici Corporis Christi* that Mary was immune from all sin; she offered her son on Golgotha to the Father; she obtained the outpouring of the Holy Spirit at Pentecost; she now provides motherly care for the church; and she now reigns in heaven with Christ.[31] In 1950 Pope Pius XII declared that Mary was preserved from corruption of the body in death; "she conquered death and was raised body and soul to the glory of heaven, where as Queen she shines refulgent at the right hand of her Son . . .We proclaim and define it to be a dogma revealed by God that the immaculate Mother of God, Mary ever Virgin, when the course of her earthly life was finished, was taken up body and soul into the glory of heaven."[32] Vatican II reaffirmed Mary's role in Catholic theology as previously taught.[33]

PURGATORY

Roman Catholicism describes purgatory as "a place or state in which are detained the souls of those who die in grace, in friendship with God, but with the blemish of venial sin or with temporal debt for sin unpaid. Here the soul is purged, cleansed, readied for eternal union with God in Heaven."[34]

The suffering in purgatory is twofold: physical pain and separation from God. The suffering in purgatory is necessary because the person has not made complete satisfaction for sins and is not ready to see God because of imperfection. Further, in forgiving baptized people, Christ chose to change the greater punishment to a lesser punishment (instead of abolishing sins entirely), "changing eternal suffering into temporal suffering,"[35] thereby requiring cleansing in purgatory.

The length of suffering in purgatory is determined by the person's degree of sinfulness. The time of suffering can be shortened through the prayers and good works of living adherents. This is based on 2 Maccabees 12:43-45, 56. The souls of the departed are purified by fire in purgatory, as suggested in 1 Corinthians 3:14-15, according to Catholic interpretation.

THE SACRAMENTS

The sacramental system of the Roman Catholic church was primarily the work of the Council of Trent in Catholicism's counter-reformation. Roman Catholics view the sacraments as conveyors of grace, in them "Jesus Christ does today in His Mystical Body what he once did physically upon earth."[36] Catholicism defines a sacrament as: "an outward sign instituted by Jesus Christ to give grace."[37] The nature and amount of grace received is dependent on the disposition of one's soul.[38] The sacraments are also viewed as an extension of the redeeming acts of Christ.[39]

The Roman Catholic church has fixed the number of sacraments as seven: baptism, confirmation, holy communion, confession, holy orders, matrimony, and anointing of the sick.

Baptism. "Baptism is the sacrament that frees man from original sin and from personal guilt, that makes him a member of Christ and his church."[40] The Council of Trent affirmed that (water) baptism is necessary for salvation, that baptism of infants is legitimate, that adult believer's baptism is unnecessary, that keeping the law is still essential—faith alone is inadequate.[41] The core of Roman Catholic teaching on baptism is that it is necessary for salvation and, in fact, produces salvation. It also unites the person with the church. Catholics also teach a "baptism of desire" for those who desire to be baptized by water but are prevented.

Confirmation. "The sacrament of confirmation completes the sacrament of baptism. If baptism is the sacrament of re-birth to a new and supernatural life, confirmation is the sacrament of maturity and coming of age."[42] Whereas the priest administers baptism, the bishop administers confirmation by laying his hands on the head of the person. In this act the person is said to receive the Holy Spirit, strengthening him to live up to his profession and tell what he believes. The bishop's power is equated with the apostles at Pentecost and at Samaria (Acts 8:14-17) in conveying the Holy Spirit.[43] Baptism alone makes the person an "infant Christian," whereas confirmation makes the person an "adult Christian."[44]

The Eucharist. Holy communion, or the Eucharist, is also called the Mass. This ritual is considered the ongoing sacrifice of Christ. The term *Mass* is also used to describe the entire service in which the priest participates in the sacrifice of the body and blood of Christ.[45]

As a sacrament, the Roman Catholic church teaches the actual presence of Christ in the communion elements. The moment the priest pronounces the words "This is my body . . . the cup of my blood," Jesus Christ is actually present under the accidents (appearance, taste, smell, and feel) of both bread and wine.[46] This is referred to as "a Real Presence, a real substantial presence of the God-Man in sacramental form with His true Body, Blood, Soul and Divinity. Jesus Christ is most profoundly, directly and intimately present."[47] This is termed the doctrine of transubstantiation, meaning the elements change in essence to Jesus Christ. From the moment of consecration onward, the wafer and wine, separately or together, are "the Lamb of God" to be adored and received for eternal life.

In this most important of Catholic sacraments, partaking involves receiving grace, because it involves receiving Christ based on John 6:53-58. Partaking of the Eucharist results in:[48] (1) forgiveness from venial sins; (2) strengthening against temptation (extinguishing the power of evil desire); and (3) promise of eternal glory and a glorious resurrection. Vatican II encouraged frequent or daily participation since it "increases union with Christ, nourishes the spiritual life more abundantly, strengthens the soul in virtue and gives the communicant a stronger pledge of eternal happiness."[49] (See also the discussion of transubstantiation in chap. 25, "Ecclesiology: Doctrine of the Church.")

In the Mass the sacrifice of Christ is perpetuated; for the Catholic worshiper it amounts to being present at the sacrifice of the cross on Calvary 2,000 years ago; it is the same sacrifice that Christ offered on Calvary.[50] The difference exists in that the first sacrifice was a bloody one, whereas the Mass is an unbloody sacrifice. The ongoing nature of Christ's sacrifice is also defended from the ongoing bloody and unbloody sacrifices of the Old Testament. Moreover, the Council of Trent taught that as a sacrifice of Christ, the Mass is offered for sins and punishments, being propitiatory for

the penitent but it is also for those "departed in Christ but not yet purified."[51] Vatican II affirmed the teachings of the Council of Trent on the
Mass.[52]

In the sacrifice of the Mass the baptized Catholic worshiper is considered united to Christ, and also offered up in sacrifice together with Christ. In
this ritual the worshiper reaffirms his conversion from sin that is real but not
yet complete and effects reconciliation with the Father.[53]

Confession (Penance). Roman Catholicism teaches that Christ forgives
sins through the priest at confession or penance. The outward sign that the
confessor has been forgiven is the statement of absolution by the priest. He
has the authority through Christ's statement in John 20:23. In this the priest
has the power to forgive or retain sins.[54] A good confession requires five
things: examination of conscience, sorrow for sins, a firm intention of
avoiding sins in the future, confession of sins, willingness to perform the
penance determined by the priest.[55]

The sacrament of penance is described in the Council of Florence in
1439:

> The fourth sacrament is penance, of which as it were the matter consists of
> the actions of the penitent which are in three parts. The first of these is contri-
> tion of heart, which consists of sorrow for sin committed and the intention not
> to sin in the future. The second is oral confession, whereby the sinner confess-
> es to the priest all the sins he remembers in their entirety. The third is satisfac-
> tion for sins according to the judgment of the priest, which is mainly achieved
> by prayer, fasting and almsdeeds. The form of this sacrament is the words of
> absolution spoken by the priest when he says: I absolve thee etc. . . . The minis-
> ter of this sacrament is the priest who has the authority either ordinary or by
> commission from his superior, to absolve. The effect of this sacrament is abso-
> lution from sins.[56]

Holy Orders. The sacrament of holy orders involves ordination to the
offices of bishop, priest, or deacon, conferring "on a man the spiritual power and grace to sanctify others."[57] "The Sacrament of Holy Orders confers
upon the soul of the man ordained a special indelible mark or character of
Jesus Christ which will remain for all eternity."[58] The deacon assists priests
in baptism, marriage, preaching, and other duties. "The priesthood confers
on a man the power to consecrate and offer the Body and Blood of Jesus
Christ and to remit or retain sins."[59] The priest must be ordained by a bishop. The bishop is a successor of the apostles and has the power to ordain
priests, perpetuating the priesthood of Christ. He also has special teaching
authority. As Christ was ordained the eternal High Priest, so the Catholic
priest stands in the tradition of Christ, as an "authorized mediator who offers a true sacrifice in acknowledgment of God's supreme dominion over
men and for the expiation of their sins. . . . The priest mediates from the

THE SEVEN ROMAN CATHOLIC SACRAMENTS

Sacrament	Procedure	Significance	Vatican II Emphasis
Baptism	Priest performs the rite on infants.	Produces rebirth, "infant Christian." Necessary for salvation. Frees one from original sin and guilt. Unites one to Christ and the church.	Baptism to receive greater emphasis. Convert to receive instruction beforehand. Illustrates commitment to Christ. Emphasizes unity of all members in Christ.
Confirmation	Bishop lays hands on person whereby they receive the Holy Spirit.	Necessary sequence after baptism. With baptism, part of the "Sacrament of initiation." Person receives the Holy Spirit, bringing one to maturity and dedication.	Endeavor to unite baptism and confirmation as one act of initiation. Separating the two sacraments suggests there are "degrees of membership in church."
Eucharist	Priest celebrates Mass. Upon pronouncing, "This is my body," bread and wine turn to body and blood of Christ.	Mass is ongoing sacrifice of Christ. Same as Calvary except Mass is unbloody. In Mass, Christ offers atonement for sin. Participant receives forgiveness from venial sins. Eating the bread is eating Christ.	Frequent participation encouraged to increase "union with Christ." Ceremony now involves lay people. Shorter, simpler ceremony; more use of Scripture.
Confession (Penance)	Three steps: 1. Sorrow for sin. 2. Oral confession to priest. 3. Absolution of sins by priest.	Having confessed all known sins to priest, and stated intention not to sin in the future, the adherent receives absolution from sins by priest.	New view of sin: distorted personal relationship and motives. Allows for general confession and absolution. General confession performed in service of singing, Scripture, prayer, sermon, self-examination, confession, absolution.

Holy Orders	Ordination to office: bishop, priest, deacon. As successor to the apostles, bishop ordains priest.	Confers on recipient power to sanctify others. Priest receives power to offer body and blood of Christ and to remit sins. Priest mediates between God and men as Christ mediated between God and men.	Greater involvement of lay people in ministry. Laypeople to develop/use gifts in church. Reduced distinction between priest and people. Priest considered "brother among brothers."
Marriage	Vows are exchanged in presence of a priest.	Sign of union of Christ and church. Indissoluble because marriage of Christ and the church is indissoluble.	Marriage is not just for procreation. Greater emphasis on love in marriage. Mass permitted at weddings with baptized non-Catholics.
Anointing the Sick	Bishop consecrates oil. Person near death anointed by priest.	Removes infirmity and obstacles left by sin, which prevent soul from glory. Prepares people for death by making them like the risen Christ. Prepares soul for eternity.	Broadened usage: changed from "extreme unction" to "anointing the sick." Used to strengthen/heal body and soul. Sick person shares in readings, prayers.

people to God."[60] The priest has power to forgive sins in God's name. The priest is permanently appointed a priest after the order of Melchizedek. He thus acts as Jesus Christ: in offering the Mass he says, "This is *My* body" (italics added). In forgiving sinners he says, "I absolve you from your sins."[61]

Matrimony. The sacrament of marriage is a sign of the union between Christ and the church. The Council of Florence declared in 1439: "A triple good attaches to matrimony. The first is the begetting of children and their education to the worship of God. The second is the faithfulness which each spouse owes to the other. The third is the indissolubility of marriage because it represents the indissoluble union of Christ and the Church."[62] The Roman Catholic church emphasizes the permanence of marriage; divorce is forbidden. It also rejects abortion or artificial birth control. Vatican II emphasized the necessity of developing love in marriage and that marriage does not exist solely for procreation.[63]

Anointing the Sick (Extreme Unction).

> [Extreme unction] is the complement and completion of penance. . . . extreme unction takes away the infirmity left by sin; it "removes that state which might be an obstacle to the clothing with glory of the resurrection"; and, as every sacrament makes us men in some respect like Christ, "so we become by extreme unction like the risen Christ because it will be given to the dying as a sign of the glory to come" . . . the holy anointing makes the man who stands at the threshold of eternity and loyally cooperates with the grace of the sacrament ready to enter directly upon the Beatific Vision.[64]

Traditionally, a sick person near death was anointed with oil blessed by the bishop; however, the Second Vatican Council declared the rite should more fittingly be called "anointing of the sick," because it should not be viewed as a sacrament "for those only who are at the point of death."[65]

SUMMARY EVALUATION OF CATHOLIC THEOLOGY

While Roman Catholic theology has a number of doctrines in common with conservative Protestant theology (Trinity, deity of Christ, etc.), there are many deviations from orthodox theology. A fundamental difference is the authority of tradition in addition to the authority of the Bible. In its outworking, tradition in a sense supersedes the authority of the Bible because tradition and church councils make decrees that countermand and/or add to the explicit teachings of Scripture. The recognition of the Apocrypha is a further deviation. The place of Mary in Roman Catholic theology removes Christ from His rightful place as sole mediator between God and men (1 Tim. 2:5). Also the entire system of sacraments is a genuine rejection of the true grace of God and salvation by grace. Salvation in Roman Catholic theology is not by grace through faith but a complex adherence to the sacraments and rituals as legislated by the church hierarchy.

Notes on Catholic Theology

1. F. S. Piggin, "Roman Catholicism," in Walter A. Elwell, ed., *Evangelical Dictionary of Theology* (Grand Rapids: Baker, 1984), p. 955.

2. Ibid.

3. Josef Neuner, S.J., and Heinrich Roos, S.J., *The Teaching of the Catholic Church*, edited by Karl Rahner, S.J. (Staten Island, N.Y.: Alba, 1967), p. 59.

4. Ibid., p. 61.

5. Loraine Boettner, *Roman Catholicism* (Philadelphia: Presbyterian & Reformed, 1962), p. 126; cf. A. M. Renwick, *The Story of the Church* (London: InterVarsity, 1958), p. 64.

6. Rahner, ed., *Teaching of the Catholic Church*, p. 203.

7. Ibid., p. 207.

8. Ibid.

9. Ibid., p. 210.

10. Robert J. Fox, *The Catholic Faith* (Huntington, Ind.: Our Sunday Visitor, 1983), pp. 156-57.

11. Ibid., p. 157.

12. Piggin, "Roman Catholicism," in *Evangelical Dictionary of Theology*, p. 956.

13. Ibid.

14. Quoted from *The National Catholic Almanac* in Boettner, *Roman Catholicism*, p. 127.

15. Kenneth Scott Latourette, *A History of Christianity* (New York: Harper, 1953), p. 487.

16. Ibid. p. 223-24.

17. Ibid., p. 224.

18. Rahner, *Teaching of the Catholic Church*, p. 225.

19. Ibid., p. 229.

20. Fox, *The Catholic Faith*, p. 164.

21. Rahner, ed., *Teaching of the Catholic Church*, pp. 181-82.

22. Ibid., p. 183.

23. Ibid., p. 184.

24. Ibid., p. 186.

25. Ibid., p. 187; italics added.

26. Ibid., p. 188.

27. Ibid., p. 189.

28. Ibid., p. 190.

29. Ibid., p. 191.

30. Ibid.; italics added.

31. Ibid., p. 193.
32. Ibid., pp. 195-96.
33. Walter M. Abbot, S.J., ed., *The Documents of Vatican II* (New York: Herder and Herder, 1966), pp. 85-96. See index for additional references.
34. George Brantl, ed., *Catholicism* (New York: Braziller, 1962), p. 232.
35. Ibid., p. 234.
36. Fox, *The Catholic Faith*, p. 181.
37. Ibid.
38. Ibid., p.182.
39. Ibid., p. 183.
40. Rahner, ed., *Teaching of the Catholic Church*, p. 265.
41. Ibid., pp. 269-71.
42. Ibid., p. 273.
43. Ibid., p. 275.
44. Fox, *The Catholic Faith*, p. 191.
45. T. P. Weber, "Mass," in *Evangelical Dictionary of Theology*, p. 697.
46. Fox, *The Catholic Faith*, p. 205.
47. Ibid., pp. 205-6.
48. Ibid., pp. 212-13.
49. Ibid., p. 213.
50. Ibid., p. 220.
51. Rahner, ed., *Teaching of the Catholic Church*, p. 297.
52. Abbott, *Documents of Vatican II*, p. 156.
53. Fox, *The Catholic Faith*, p. 226.
54. Ibid., p. 197.
55. Ibid., p. 199.
56. Rahner, ed., *Teaching of the Catholic Church*, pp. 307-8.
57. Fox, *The Catholic Faith*, p. 232.
58. Ibid.
59. Ibid., pp. 232-33.
60. Ibid., p. 234.
61. Ibid., p. 236.
62. Rahner, ed., *Teaching of the Catholic Church*, p. 354.
63. Abbott, ed., *Documents of Vatican II*, pp. 252-55.
64. Rahner, ed., *Teaching of the Catholic Church*, p. 331.
65. Abbott, ed., *Documents of Vatican II*, p. 161.

FOR FURTHER STUDY ON CATHOLIC THEOLOGY

** Walter M. Abbott, S.J., ed. *The Documents of Vatican II.* New York: Herder and Herder, 1966. This is a most important work in explaining the authoritative teaching of recent Roman Catholicism as interpreted today under the direction of current and recent popes (John XXIII, Paul VI, and John Paul II).

* Loraine Boettner. *Roman Catholicism.* Philadelphia: Presbyterian and Reformed, 1965. This is a valuable, well-documented critique of Roman Catholicism.

** George Brantl, ed. *Catholicism.* New York: Braziller, 1962.

* Robert J. Fox. *The Catholic Faith.* Huntington, Ind.: Our Sunday Visitor, 1983. Clearly written and includes the documents of Vatican II.

** Anthony D. Lee, O.P., ed. *Vatican II: The Theological Dimension.* Thomist Press, 1963.

* Bernard C. Pawley. *The Second Vatican Council: Studies by Eight Anglican Observers.* London: Oxford U., 1967.

* F. S. Piggin. "Roman Catholicism." In Walter A. Elwell, ed., *Evangelical Dictionary of Theology.* Grand Rapids: Baker, 1984. Pp. 955-58. See also additional articles under "Mass" and "Vatican Council II."

* Karl Rahner, S.J., ed. *The Teaching of the Catholic Church.* Staten Island, N.Y.: Alba, 1967. This volume cites the doctrinal teachings of the major Catholic councils throughout the centuries.

PART 5:
CONTEMPORARY THEOLOGY

38

INTRODUCTION TO
CONTEMPORARY THEOLOGY

Several contributing *philosophical influences* prepared the way for much that is present in current theological thought and movements.

THE RENAISSANCE

The term *Renaissance* means "new birth" and describes the intellectual awakening that took place in Europe after the Middle Ages. The period was also termed a "revival of learning." The dating of this era, while difficult to delineate precisely, can be generally identified as from 1350 to 1650. The Renaissance "substituted a modern secular individualistic view of life for the medieval religious corporate approach to life. . . . Emphasis was placed upon the glory of man instead of upon the glory of God."[1] Interest in man and the world rather than in God and heaven developed. With the new interest in man and his capabilities came the reliance upon human reason rather than divine revelation. Man was now the focus of the universe, not God.

With the Renaissance came a skepticism concerning the Bible and the supernatural. Philosophers such as Descartes, Spinoza, and Leibniz argued for the ability of human reason and science to comprehend the riddles of life. The writings of the secular humanists did a great deal to undermine faith in the Bible, miracles, and divine revelation. The "enlightened" philosophy of the secular humanists laid the foundation for religious liberalism with its denial of supernaturalism.

THE ENLIGHTENMENT

JOHN LOCKE

John Locke (1632-1704) introduced subjectivism by teaching that knowledge comes from experience. Locke taught that man has *sensations*, in which he becomes aware of his external surroundings, then through *re-flections,* man contemplates the meaning.[2] Thus Locke argued that man has nothing in his mind that is not first in his senses. Although Locke acknowledged some aspect of divine revelation he nonetheless rejected the tenets of the Christian faith that contradicted experimental reason.[3]

It became apparent that the underpinnings of theological liberalism —as well as neo-orthodoxy—built upon the rationalistic, experiential emphasis of John Locke.

GEORGE BERKELEY

George Berkeley (1685-1753) built upon the sense-orientation of Locke, stating that "to be is to be perceived." Berkeley declared that things are "exactly what they are experienced to be. The experienced qualities make up the essence of the object."[4] All knowledge, Berkeley taught, exists in the mind. In this he denied special revelation.

Berkeley was not an atheist; in fact, he attempted to use his system as an apologetic for belief in God. But in so doing he developed an anti-supernaturalism that extolled the power of human reason and experience while denying the validity of divine revelation and supernaturalism.

DAVID HUME

David Hume (1711-1776) was a Scottish skeptic who carried the ideas of Locke and Berkeley to their logical conclusion by denying spiritual realities. Hume attacked the miracles of the Bible, denying that it was possible to know objective truth.

The Age of Enlightenment brought agnosticism, skepticism, as well as an emphasis on rationalism and the scientific method as bases for proving all truth. All those factors contributed to the rejection of the Bible and the supernatural.

IDEALISM

Idealism was the philosophy that reality does not lie in the physical realm but in the mind. Behind all reality is a divine mind, moving the world toward good.

IMMANUEL KANT

Immanuel Kant (1724-1804) argued that one's concept of God must come from reason; he therefore attacked the proofs for the existence of God, denying their validity. According to Kant, knowledge cannot exist apart from experience that can be proved through testing. In this Kant combined rationalism (reliance upon human reason) and empiricism (proving things by the scientific method). With this innovative emphasis, Kant may be termed the "theoretical founder of religious liberalism."[5]

Kant's view of Christianity did not allow for the supernatural; he thought Jesus to be merely a good teacher with a high ethical ideal. Liberal theology later built on Kant's emphasis on Christianity as a system of ethics rather than a revelation from God.

GEORG W. F. HEGEL

Georg W. F. Hegel (1770-1831) was a German idealist who taught that "only the mind is real; everything else is the expression of mind . . . all reality (is) an expression of the Absolute, who is God. All that exists is the expression of divine mind, so that the real is rational and the rational is real."[6]

Hegel saw God at work in history in his concept of dialectic: a thesis giving rise to its antithesis, which results in a synthesis of the two diverse concepts. The process is unending, however, as the synthesis gives birth to a new thesis which again has its antithesis. Hence, Hegel did not view Christianity as a revealed religion but simply as a synthesis of developing religion and culture. According to Hegel, Christianity, with its belief in the incarnation of Christ, eventually evolved into a higher form of knowledge, namely, speculative philosophy.[7] As an idealist, Hegel understood the Christian doctrines as merely symbols. Terms like *Son of God* were not to be understood in a literal sense but only symbolically.

Liberal theology built extensively on the foundations of the Enlightenment and Idealist philosophers. Specifically, the documentary hypothesis (which questioned the historically-held authors of the first five books of Scripture) and similar higher critical methods have their roots in Hegel's methodology.

NOTES ON CONTEMPORARY THEOLOGY

1. Earle E. Cairns, *Christianity Through the Centuries*, 4th ed. (Grand Rapids: Zondervan, 1961), p. 284.
2. Warren C. Young, *A Christian Approach to Philosophy* (Grand Rapids: Baker, 1954), p. 107.
3. Bruce A. Demarest, *General Revelation: Historical Views and Contemporary Issues* (Grand Rapids: Zondervan, 1982), p. 81.
4. Young, *A Christian Approach to Philosophy*, p. 76.
5. Stanley N. Gundry and Alan F. Johnson, eds., *Tensions in Contemporary Theology* (Chicago: Moody, 1976), p. 18.

6. P. H. DeVries, "Hegel, George Wilhelm Friedrich" in Walter A. Elwell, ed., *Evangelical Dictionary of Theology* (Grand Rapids: Baker, 1984), p. 502.

7. Ibid., pp. 502-3.

FOR FURTHER STUDY ON CONTEMPORARY THEOLOGY

** Karl Barth. *Protestant Theology in the Nineteenth Century.* Valley Forge, Pa.: Judson, 1973.

** E. Cassirer. *The Philosophy of the Enlightenment.* Princeton: Princeton U., 1951.

* Walter E. Elwell, ed. *Evangelical Dictionary of Theology.* Grand Rapids: Baker, 1984. Pp. 355-57, 502-3, 536-37, 599-600.

* William E. Hordern. *A Layman's Guide to Protestant Theology.* London: Macmillan, 1968. Pp. 73-90.

* Bernard Ramm. "The Fortunes of Theology from Schleiermacher to Barth and Bultmann." In *Tensions in Contemporary Theology*, edited by Stanley N. Gundry and Alan F. Johnson. Chicago: Moody, 1976. Pp. 15-41.

** Warren C. Young. *A Christian Approach to Philosophy.* Grand Rapids: Baker, 1954.

39

LIBERAL THEOLOGY

Liberalism denotes that facet of theology that arose as a result of the rationalism and experimentalism of the philosphers and scientists. Liberalism places a premium on man's reason and the findings of science; whatever does not agree with reason and science is to be rejected. As a result, liberalism has rejected the historic doctrines of the Christian faith because they deal with miracles and the supernatural: the incarnation of Christ, the bodily resurrection of Christ, and so forth. Modernism is a general equivalent of liberalism, but it stresses the findings of science, attempting to reconcile science and the Bible as in the case of Harry Emerson Fosdick.[1]

STANDARD LIBERALISM

HISTORICAL DEVELOPMENT OF STANDARD LIBERALISM

Friedrich Schleiermacher (1763-1834). This German Protestant theologian reacted to the cold rationalism of the philosophers, attempting to defend Christianity on the basis of feeling. He developed a "theology of feeling" and thereby could be considered the father of neo-orthodoxy (he is also known as the father of modern religious liberalism). Schleiermacher emphasized that religion was not to be found in philosophical reasoning or in doctrinal affirmations (he rejected the historic doctrines of Christianity), rather, religion was to be found in feeling in which the person could experience God. He emphasized the subjective nature of religion, which emphasis was later to find full expression in neo-orthodoxy.

Schleiermacher emphasized an ethical religion, which he defined as "the feeling of absolute dependence" or "God-consciousness."[2] He did not regard sin as a moral violation of God's law; he defined sin as occurring "when man tries to live by himself, isolated from the universe and his fellow men."[3] Schleiermacher also rejected historic doctrines like the virgin birth, the substitutionary atonement, and the deity of Christ. They were unimportant. He taught that Christ was a redeemer only in the sense that He was the ideal example and source of God-consciousness that overcomes sin. The believer experiences regeneration (Jesus' God-consciousness) "by participating in the corporate life of the contemporary church rather than by merely believing in Christ's death and resurrection in history."[4]

Schleiermacher's theology had a dramatic effect on the issue of authority. "No external authority, whether it be Scripture, church, or historic creedal statement, takes precedence over the immediate experience of believers."[5] The roots of subjectivism (with its emphasis on experience rather than objective, doctrinal truth), principally observed in neo-orthodoxy, as well as the liberal rejection of the authority of Scripture, are found in the theology of Schleiermacher.

Albrecht Ritschl (1822-1889). This theologian, from German Protestantism like Schleiermacher, taught that religion must not be theoretical, but practical. He rejected both the philosophical speculations of the philosophers as well as the emphasis on experience by Schleiermacher, teaching instead the importance of ethical values. "It must begin with the question, 'What must I do to be saved?' but if that question means, 'How can I go to heaven when I die?' then it is a theoretical question. To be saved means to live a new life, to be saved from sin, selfishness, fear, and guilt."[6]

Ritschl rejected the traditional doctrines of original sin, the incarnation, the deity of Christ, substitutionary atonement of Christ, the bodily resurrection of Christ, miracles, and other cardinal doctrines. These doctrines were unimportant because they were not practical—they did not relate to moral issues. Ritschl evaluated everything in terms of judgments of fact (historical events) and judgments of value (implications for the individual). Thus one could speak of the Jesus of fact and the Christ of value.[7] The importance of the discussion is simply the value of Christ for the community of believers. This Christ is apprehended through faith—the historical realities of His person are unimportant. Doctrinal statements are unimportant because they do not help the person in his moral conduct; thus, the death of Christ was not a propitiatory death, but a moral example of loyalty to His calling, which ought to inspire others to a similar life.

It is evident that Ritschl laid the groundwork for the dichotomy of the later distinctions between *historie* (events of history) and *geschichte* (story or myth). With his emphasis on moral values he is seen as laying the foundation for the liberal "social gospel."[8]

Adolph Von Harnack (1851-1930). This German theologian was a follower of Ritschl who "believed that Christian beliefs were moulded by Greek thought which introduced into the Gospel much that was not of the true essence of the faith."[9] Von Harnack popularized Ritschl's views through the best seller *What Is Christianity?* published in 1901.

Von Harnack denied that Jesus ever claimed to be deity, denied the miracles, and said Paul had corrupted the simple religion of Jesus. He emphasized the need to get back to the religion *of* Jesus, not the religion *about* Jesus. Thus it was necessary to get to the central truth or kernel by removing the husk of culture that shrouded the truth. The seeds of Rudolf Bultmann's demythologizing are seen in von Harnack's approach.

Biblical criticism. (1) New Testament. F. C. Baur (1792-1860) rejected the historic Christian doctrines and developed a historical-critical method by applying Hegel's philosophy of thesis-antithesis-synthesis to the Scriptures. He looked for contradictory elements in the New Testament to support his theory. Thus, he contended there was a conflict between the theology of Peter (Jewish) and the theology of Paul (Gentile). Each New Testament book should be considered in the light of the Jewish-Gentile conflict in the early church, according to Baur.

David Strauss (1808-1874), a student of Baur, denied the historical accuracy of the biblical accounts, suggesting they were embellished by Jesus' followers. Thus, he viewed the Bible as filled with "myths," a concept derived from Hegel's philosophy. In reinterpreting the New Testament, Strauss taught that Jesus was a symbol of the Absolute Idea in the human race. Thus the true God-man was not Jesus an individual but the entire human race.[10]

(2) Old Testament. In the Old Testament criticism the theory of the documentary hypothesis suggests that the Pentateuch was a compilation of different documents written over a span of five centuries (rather than having been authored entirely by Moses).[11] Jean Astruc (1684-1766), a French physician, suggested that Moses copied from two different documents, one that used the name Elohim for God and the other that used Jehovah. Astruc's suggestion became the foundation of the documentary hypothesis. Eichhorn developed the suggestion by dividing up Genesis and part of Exodus; DeWette continued the work by applying Astruc's thesis to Deuteronomy. Others made contributions, and the final theory related the composition of the Pentateuch to an evolutionary pattern by Julius Wellhausen.

This higher critical approach did much to destroy the historically-held views concerning the authorship of the biblical books. The way was paved for dissecting all the books of the Bible and generally assigning late dates to their writings. In New Testament books like the pastoral epistles, for example, Pauline authorship was rejected.[12]

Horace Bushnell (1802-1876). This American clergyman was to America what Schleiermacher was to Europe. He came to be known as the "father of American theological liberalism." In contrast to the dramatic, momentary conversions that evangelists of his day advocated, Bushnell became influential in teaching that children may "grow into" Christianity over a period of time rather than through an instantaneous conversion. In espousing this philosophy, Bushnell rejected the doctrine of original sin. He suggested instead that the child was born good and would stay that way if correctly nurtured.

Bushnell rejected the doctrine of biblical inspiration (among others) and also advocated the example theory of the death of Christ.

Walter Rauschenbusch (1861-1918). This American Baptist clergyman taught a social gospel and came to be known as the "father of the social gospel." Rauschenbusch's theology was influenced by his tenure as pastor of the Second German Baptist Church in New York City where he viewed the adverse living conditions of the immigrants, labor exploitations, and governmental indifference to the suffering of the poor.[13] When he returned to teach at the Baptist Theological Seminary in Rochester, New York, he taught and wrote extensively, advocating a theology of social concern. He criticized the capitalistic system that was motivated by greed and advocated collective ownership of property (although he denied Marxism). For Rauschenbusch the gospel was not a message of personal salvation but rather the ethic of Jesus' love that would transform society through resolving social evils.

World War One. Because the liberal message was essentially optimistic, with its denial of the sinfulness of man and the progressive betterment of society, the First World War was devastating to its teaching. The advent of the war destroyed the myth that man is getting better and dealt a death blow to liberalism as it had been known. Liberalism would reappear, but in a different format.

Karl Barth had trained under Harnack but with the world war discovered he had no message to preach. His liberal message of optimism had nothing to say to people devastated by war. Barth returned to the Scriptures to search for a new message. He would lead the theological world into a new theology as a result of this crisis.

DOCTRINAL AFFIRMATIONS OF STANDARD LIBERALISM[14]

Bibliology. Liberals viewed the Bible as an ordinary book, not inspired in any special way. Higher critics analyzed the books of the Bible from a human standpoint, attempting to discover the human factors concerning authorship, dating, and underlying sources. They were unconcerned about traditional views of Pauline authorship, for example. Thus, the books of the Bible were generally late dated, and frequently the traditional views concerning authorship were rejected.

The evolutionary scheme was applied to religious development in the Bible so that instead of acknowledging Israel's religion as a divine revelation, it was simply viewed as a human development of religion. Thus the religion of Israel in the Old Testament was viewed as a "blood-thirsty religion," and in development it was viewed as inferior to the "higher ethics of Jesus." Thus the seeming conflict between the Old and New Testaments could be explained in the evolution of religion.

Theology proper. Liberalism emphasized the immanence of God, which taught that God is everywhere and in everything. The extreme result of God's immanence is pantheism (God *is* everything). In liberal doctrine, God was seen at work everywhere—He was at work in nature and in the evolutionary process. Hence, there was no need for miracles. Liberals thus refused to distinguish between the natural and the supernatural.

Anthropology. The authority of Scripture and divine revelation was rejected. Human reason was extolled above Scripture and traditional doctrines. The Bible had to be understood from a rational standpoint. If the Bible contained stories that were rationally unpalatable to human understanding, they were to be rejected. Hence, the miracles of the Bible were discarded.

Theology was to be practical; therefore, human reason was combined with religious experience to replace divine revelation and the authority of Scripture.

Whereas traditional Christianity had taught absolutes in truth and morals, liberalism taught that the world is an open system. For the liberal there were no absolutes; dogmatic assertions could not be made. Everything was subject to question—including the Bible and traditionally-held doctrines. Traditional theology was to be rejected because it was a fixed system, whereas the liberal acknowledged the constant possibility of change.

With the advent of the Age of Reason and modern science, liberals were intent on making Christianity palatable for the people. They sought to discard archaic terms and views in favor of those that were in harmony with human reason and modern science. Christianity was not to be looked upon as something old-fashioned or outdated, but liberal Christianity was to relate to the spirit of the age. This was particularly seen in the work of a man like Harry Emerson Fosdick.

Soteriology. In liberalism's attempt to be relevant, emphasis on personal salvation from eternal punishment was rejected—it was considered irrelevant. With its optimistic bent, liberalism determined to bring in the kingdom through human effort; thus, the social gospel became its message. The kingdom of God was not some future, supernatural age, but it was the here and now through application of the principles and ethics of Jesus.

It is important to note that not all liberals—at least not in beginning stage of liberalism—taught the social message. Early liberalism was theoretical. Reinhold Niebuhr, a prominent neo-orthodox theologian, saw the social injustices during his ministry in Detroit and became an outspoken critic of liberalism. The social gospel was largely an American phenomenon in the nineteenth and early twentieth centuries.

LIBERAL THEOLOGY

Theologian	Emphasis	View of Christian Doctrines
Schleiermacher	Emphasized feeling and experience: father of modern religious liberalism.	Rejected the Fall, original sin, Virgin birth, and substitutionary atonement. Sin is interest in the world; faith is feeling, not response to what God says.
Ritschl	Emphasized ethical and practical aspects; his teaching became the ground for the social gospel.	Rejected original sin, incarnation, deity, atonement, and resurrection of Christ. Denied miracles. Defined sin as selfishness.
Harnack	Taught that Paul corrupted the teaching of Jesus and Christianity. Taught "fatherhood of God and brotherhood of man."	Denied the deity of Christ and His substitutionary atonement. Taught that Paul corrupted the religion of Jesus.
Baur	Developed the historical-critical method. Emphasized the historical evolution of the New Testament.	Denied revelation, incarnation, and bodily resurrection of Christ. Taught Christianity was a conflict between Jewish (Peter) and Gentile (Paul) factions.
Bushnell	Children are born good and can be taught to grow into Christianity.	Opposed sudden conversions. Denied substitutionary atonement of Christ; His death was only an example.
Rauschenbusch	Emphasized the social gospel; Jesus' love would transform society.	Taught the gospel is social concern, collective ownership, and equal distribution of goods. Rejected substitutionary atonement of Christ, His second coming, and a literal hell.

SUMMARY EVALUATION OF STANDARD LIBERALISM

The result of liberalism's emphasis on human reason and the scientific method can be seen in its abandonment of historic Christian doctrines. The doctrines of total depravity and original sin were rejected; man was seen not as evil but as basically good. Man could be directed to do good through education. The deity of Jesus was rejected; Jesus was a good teacher and the ideal man. He was the model for others. The miracles of the Bible were denied because they were not in harmony with human reason and the findings of modern science.

NEO-LIBERALISM

HISTORICAL DEVELOPMENT OF NEO-LIBERALISM

The impact of World War I dealt a death blow to old line liberalism. Thereafter, a new liberalism, termed "realistic theology," was formed.

Harry Emerson Fosdick (1878-1969) was the "founding father" of the new liberalism. Educated at the liberal Union Theological Seminary in New York City, Fosdick became an immensely popular pulpiteer at Riverside Church in New York. He wrote more than thirty books, had a weekly radio program, and with his popular pastorate in New York, was neo-liberalism's most influential spokesman during his time.

Fosdick attacked both fundamentalists and liberals. He became embroiled in the liberal-fundamentalist controversy and in 1922 preached (and later published) on the topic "Shall the Fundamentalists Win?" In 1935 he preached his famous sermon in New York entitled, "The Church Must Go Beyond Modernism." He accused modernism of being too occupied with intellectualism, of being too sentimental, of watering down the concept of God, and of being too well harmonized with the modern world.[15] This marked a new direction for liberalism, and out of this challenge by Fosdick, neo-liberalism was born. Neo-liberalism rejected the idealistic philosophy and subjectivism of older liberalism; neo-liberalism was looking for God outside of man, not within man.[16]

Walter M. Horton was another of the pioneers who redirected liberalism. Although Horton determined to retain some of liberalism, yet he, along with other neo-liberals, did not display as optimistic a view of man. He recognized that man's alienation from God produces war and human suffering. John C. Bennett was typical of neo-liberals in taking sin more seriously. Bennett also rejected "skepticism, subjectivism, and arbitrariness" and emphasized the importance of a "decision of faith."[17] He saw the inadequacies of "self-sufficient religious humanism and a reductive naturalism" and opened the door for the possibility of revelation.[18] Despite this, Bennett repudiated the idea of a Christological theme in the Old Testament. He also readily accepted the tenets of higher criticism.

The worldwide organization that originally united theological liberals was the Federal Council of Churches in 1908. This organization was superseded by the World Council of Churches, organized in 1948, with major support from mainline Protestant denominations that held to theologically liberal views.

DOCTRINAL AFFIRMATIONS OF NEO-LIBERALISM

Bibliology. The Bible was taken more seriously in neo-liberalism, as is seen in the serious study by a man like C. H. Dodd (1884-1973). Nonetheless, the presuppositions of old liberalism—higher criticism and denial of inspiration—were equally shared by neo-liberals.

Anthropology. Neo-liberals retained the basic beliefs of older liberalism concerning the nature of man. They viewed man as basically good, not evil but rather "a good thing spoiled." Neo-liberals, however, were not optimistic about building a utopia on earth as the older liberals had been.

Hamartiology. Neo-liberals were more realistic about sin than older liberals. To solve the human dilemma, John C. Bennett proposed a recognition of the following: (1) "the concept of sin, which is often a wrong choice because of self-deception"; (2) "the presence of sin on every level of moral and spiritual growth"; (3) "the possibility of solving all the problems of humanity once and for all by a change in the institutions of society is an illusion"; and (4) "repentance is a continuous necessity."[19] Neo-liberals did not, however, acknowledge original sin and the total depravity of mankind.

Christology. Neo-liberals had a higher view of Christ than did old liberals. Neo-liberals spoke of the "divinity" of Christ (although they would have rejected an orthodox statement of His full, unblemished deity); however, they rejected the notion that reference to the divinity of Christ demands belief in the virgin birth. Without acknowledging the substitutionary atonement, neo-liberals placed greater credence in the death of Christ, asserting that through His death the church was born and individuals were infused with God's power.

SUMMARY EVALUATION OF NEO-LIBERALISM

In contrast to older liberalism, neo-liberals had a lower view of man and a higher view of God. They did not, however, return to orthodoxy; it is fair to say that neo-liberalism was reshaping of older liberalism. At its core, neo-liberalism retained the essence of old liberalism.

Notes on Liberal Theology

1. Van A. Harvey, *A Handbook of Theological Terms* (New York: Macmillan, 1964), pp. 153-54.

2. W. A. Hoffecker, "Schleiermacher, Friedrich Daniel Ernst," in Walter A. Elwell, ed., *Evangelical Dictionary of Theology* (Grand Rapids: Baker, 1984), p. 982.

3. William E. Hordern, *A Layman's Guide to Protestant Theology*, rev. ed. (London: Macmillan, 1968), p. 45.

4. Hoffecker, "Schleiermacher," in *Evangelical Dictionary of Theology*, p. 982.

5. Ibid., pp. 982-83.

6. Hordern, *Layman's Guide to Protestant Theology*, pp. 46-47.

7. Warren F. Groff and Donald E. Miller, *The Shaping of Modern Christian Thought* (Cleveland: World, 1968), pp. 99-100.

8. Robert Lightner, *Neo-Liberalism* (Nutley, N.J.: Craig, 1959), p. 23.

9. Ibid., pp. 22-23.

10. R. V. Pierard, "Strauss, David Friedrich," in *Evangelical Dictionary of Theology*, p. 1056.

11. See the helpful discussion by Gleason L. Archer, Jr., *A Survey of Old Testament Introduction* (Chicago: Moody, 1964), pp. 73-109.

12. An interesting postscript to this entire discussion is the publication of John A. T. Robinson's *Redating the New Testament* (Philadelphia: Westminster, 1976). While Robinson is hardly known for his conservative stance, he determined to do an independent study of the New Testament, setting aside his liberal training and presuppositions. Robinson concluded that all the New Testament books were written prior to A.D. 70!

13. Mark A. Noll, "Rauschenbusch, Walter," in *Evangelical Dictionary of Theology*, p. 912.

14. See the helpful discussions in William E. Hordern, *A Layman's Guide to Protestant Theology*, pp. 73-84; Van A. Harvey, *A Handbook of Theological Terms*, pp. 144-46; and Bernard Ramm, *A Handbook of Contemporary Theology* (Grand Rapids: Eerdmans, 1966), pp. 80-82.

15. Lightner, *Neo-Liberalism*, p. 36; and Hordern, *A Layman's Guide to Protestant Theology*, pp. 102-4.

16. Hordern, *Layman's Guide to Protestant Theology*, p. 105.

17. Harold E. Fey, ed., *How My Mind Was Changed* (Cleveland: World, 1961), p. 13.

18. Ibid., p. 14.

19. Lightner, *Neo-Liberalism*, p. 64.

For Further Study on Liberal Theology

STANDARD LIBERALISM

Its history.

** Bruce A. Demarest. *General Revelation: Historical Views and Contemporary Issues.* Grand Rapids: Zondervan, 1982. Pp. 93-114.

** L. Harold DeWolf. *The Case for Theology in Liberal Perspective*. Philadelphia: Westminster, 1959.

 * Walter A. Elwell, ed. *Evangelical Dictionary of Theology*. Grand Rapids: Baker, 1984. See also the bibliographies under the specific articles for individual works by and about liberal theologians.

** William C. Fletcher. *The Moderns*. Grand Rapids: Zondervan, 1962.

 * Alasdair I. C. Heron. *A Century of Protestant Theology*. Philadelphia: Westminster, 1980. Pp. 22-67.

 * Stanley N. Gundry and Alan F. Johnson, eds. *Tensions in Contemporary Theology*. Chicago: Moody, 1976. Pp. 15-34.

 * William E. Hordern. *A Layman's Guide to Protestant Theology*, rev. ed. London: Macmillan, 1968. Pp. 73-110.

Its methodology.

** W. K. Cauthen. *The Impact of American Religious Liberalism*. New York: Harper, 1962.

** F. H. Cleobury. *Liberal Christian Orthodoxy*. London: Clarke, 1963.

** L. Harold DeWolf. *The Case for Theology in Liberal Perspective*. Philadelphia: Westminster, 1959.

 * Walter A. Elwell, ed. *Evangelical Dictionary of Theology*. Grand Rapids: Baker, 1984. See individual articles such as "Higher Criticism," "Social Gospel," "Liberalism," and others.

 * Van A. Harvey. *A Handbook of Theological Terms*. New York: Macmillan, 1964. See individual articles such as "Biblical Criticism," "Liberalism," and "Modernism."

 * William E. Hordern. *A Layman's Guide to Protestant Theology*. London: Macmillan, 1968. Pp. 73-87.

NEO-LIBERALISM

 * John C. Bennett. *How I Changed My Mind*, edited by Harold E. Fey. Cleveland: Meridian, 1961. Pp. 11-24.

** W. K. Cauthen. *The Impact of American Religious Liberalism*. New York: Harper, 1962.

 * Walter A. Elwell, ed. *Evangelical Dictionary of Theology*. Grand Rapids: Baker, 1984. Pp. 424, 631-35.

 * William E. Hordern. *A Layman's Guide to Protestant Theology*. London: Macmillan, 1968. Pp. 73-87.

** L. Harold DeWolf. *The Case for Theology in Liberal Perspective*. Philadelphia: Westminster, 1959.

 * Robert P. Lightner. *Neo-Liberalism*. Nutley, N.J.: Craig, 1972.

** John Macquarrie. *Twentieth-Century Religious Thought*. London: SCM, 1963.

** Martin E. Marty and Dean G. Peerman, eds. *A Handbook of Christian Theologians*. Cleveland: World, 1965.

40

NEO-ORTHODOX THEOLOGY

INTRODUCTION

Neo-orthodoxy is also known as "dialectical theology" (to describe the contrasting divine-human relationships) or "crisis theology" (to indicate that a person comes to experience God through a crisis situation). The designation *neo-orthodoxy* suggests a "new orthodoxy," implying a return to orthodox Christian beliefs following nearly two centuries of liberalism. The designation *orthodoxy*, however, is a misnomer; while neo-orthodoxy takes the Bible more seriously than older liberalism, it nonetheless has retained the foundations of liberalism.

Quite broad in scope and diverse in beliefs, neo-orthodoxy had its beginnings following World War I. The birth of neo-orthodoxy, while owing something to the writings of Søren Kierkegaard, is generally linked to the publication of Karl Barth's commentary on Romans in 1919. Barth had been trained under liberal theologians in Germany but found that his liberal message had no relevance to a people ravaged by war. Barth returned to a serious consideration of the Scriptures. During this same time Emil Brunner, another early pioneer of neo-orthodoxy, began writing and teaching. While there were distinct differences between these two men, they were to lead European and American theology into neo-orthdoxy. Other notable exponents of neo-orthodoxy were Reinhold Niebuhr, Paul Tillich, and John A. T. Robinson. (See additional discussion, including the primary theological beliefs of neo-orthodoxy, in chap. 31, "Modern Theology.")

THEOLOGY OF SØREN KIERKEGAARD

HISTORICAL DEVELOPMENT OF KIERKEGAARD'S THEOLOGY

Søren Kierkegaard (1813-1855) was a Danish philosopher and founder of existentialism,[1] upon which neo-orthodoxy is built. Kierkegaard's background seems to have had a profound effect on his theological beliefs. Kierkegaard had a melancholic disposition, as did his father, who thought he had committed the sin against the Holy Spirit. Kierkegaard had many personal problems. He suffered physically from a crooked back and a limp, and psychologically from recurring depression. He became engaged, but even though he loved his fiancee, he broke the engagement because he did not want to burden her with his problems. Kierkegaard absorbed himself in writing but found himself ridiculed by the press. His writings were not readily accepted until 1930. In his moodiness he had difficulty associating with others. Kierkegaard studied for the ministry at the University of Copenhagen but was never formally ordained because he wanted freedom. Those traumatic background experiences affected Kierkegaard and his theology in some ways.

DOCTRINAL AFFIRMATIONS OF KIERKEGAARD'S THEOLOGY

Theology proper. In contrast to liberalism's emphasis on the immanence of God, Søren Kierkegaard emphasized a transcendence of God in which it becomes difficult to know God. (Barth later also emphasized God's transcendence.) Kierkegaard rejected the notion that God could be proved through the arguments for His existence; according to Kierkegaard, God is absolute and can be discovered only by giving Him absolute obedience apart from the knowledge of His actual existence. This encounter with God demands a "leap of faith" in one's despair; in one's despair God encounters the person. Hence, Kierkegaard's theology was also known as the "theology of despair." In this subjective encounter with God, Kierkegaard opposed Hegel's objective theory of knowledge.

Christology. While liberalism relegated Christ to being the founder of a religion and a teacher of ethics, Kierkegaard asserted that knowing Christ means more than studying a past figure of history. Christ challenges people as one who is the truth; He encounters people in the present. This encounter cannot be explained through studying the Christ of history. Rather, to encounter Christ in the present, the one who reads of the disciples' encounter with Christ must also make the same leap of faith as they did.[2]

Soteriology. Kierkegaard decried the dead formalism of Denmark's state church with its cold recitation of creeds. To be a Dane and to be a Christian was synonymous in Kierkegaard's day, yet there was no spiritual life evident. Kierkegaard reacted sharply against this cold orthodoxy; it led him to emphasize the subjective nature of salvation. He said that a knowledge of doctrine is unimportant; experience is the important thing. Faith for Kierkegaard is not believing doctrines but rather a commitment of one's life. Salvation is a "leap of faith" which the mind or reason can not penetrate. It is a leap of faith into the dark unknown, hoping God will be there. It means taking life seriously, which in turn will result in one's despair—then God will meet him. In Kierkegaard's concept of salvation man does not become a Christian; he strives to be one but never arrives.

Søren Kierkegaard deemphasized the importance of the historicity of Christ and the biblical events. In his zeal for a subjective encounter with Christ he ignored the objective truths based on historical events. The legitimacy of an "encounter" with Christ is directly related to the historicity of His Person. If the events of the life of Christ are not historically genuine, any experience is invalid. Kierkegaard also reflected his rejection of historical events in his discussion about a "dark leap of faith into the unknown." But, contrary to Kierkegaard, the historical events concerning the life of Christ are true—it is not a dark leap of faith, nor is it unknown. Christianity is based on historical facts. Kierkegaard's denunciation of cold, dead orthodoxy, of course, has merit. Doctrinal statements should be affirmed because they are believed internally. A knowledge of Christ is both: *objective*—based on historical events, and *subjective*—experienced internally by the believer.

THEOLOGY OF KARL BARTH

HISTORICAL DEVELOPMENT OF BARTH'S THEOLOGY

Karl Barth was born on May 10, 1886, in Basel, Switzerland, the son of a Swiss Reformed minister. At eighteen Barth began his theological studies in Germany, ultimately studying at Bern, Berlin, Tübingen, and Marburg under such renowned liberal theologians as Adolph von Harnack and Wilhelm Herrmann. Despite the opposition of his father, Barth was attracted to the teaching of Harnack and became particularly interested in Schleiermacher's theology of experience.

Barth began his pastoral ministry in Switzerland in 1909, serving the Reformed Church in Safenwil from 1911 to 1921. Several noteworthy things happened during that time. First, Barth discovered that his training in liberalism had trained him to preach in accord with reason and experience, but it was not an authoritative word from God. World War I further complicated the problem; Barth realized the shallow nature of the liberal message was unable to minister to people in a time of adversity. Those events drove Barth to a new study of the Bible as well as a study of the Reformers, including Calvin's *Institutes*. Barth began studying Romans and in 1919 published his celebrated commentary. It proved to be a bombshell. In it Barth made God, not man, the focal point. Barth deprived man of all self-righteousness and self-reliance and exalted the grace of God in Christ. Barth sought to make his theology God-centered rather than man-centered. Liberals quickly rejected Barth's innovative commentary, but Barth received acclaim from many, including Emil Brunner.

In 1921 Barth was invited to serve as professor of Reformed theology at the University of Göttingen. There Barth lectured not only on the Reformed tradition, but also gave Bible book expositions. From 1925 to 1930 Barth taught at Münster where he also began to write his momentous twelve-volume *Church Dogmatics.* Barth taught at Bonn from 1930 to 1935, but when he refused to take a loyalty oath to Hitler, he was forced to flee from Germany. He returned to Basel, assuming the chair of theology at the university, where he taught until his retirement in 1962.

DOCTRINAL AFFIRMATIONS OF BARTH'S THEOLOGY

Bibliology. Although Karl Barth returned to a study of the Bible he did not equate the Bible with the Word of God. Barth rejected the notion of an infallible written Word, terming the concept a "paper-pope." To Barth the Bible is not the objective Word of God but rather a *witness* to the Word. The writers of Scripture simply related their experiences concerning the revelation of God. In reading their account a person can also experience the revelation of God; at that moment the Scripture becomes the Word of God to that person.

Barth categorized the Word of God into three realms. (1) The "Revealed Word" is God revealing Himself by speaking to the apostles and prophets. (2) The "Written Word" is the deposit of revelation made by man. Because man wrote the Bible it cannot be equated with the Word of God. (3) The "Preached Word" is the proclamation of the Word, and when the grace of God breaks through to the individual, then the Bible *becomes* the Word of God.

Barth took the Bible seriously; he wrote his voluminous *Dogmatics* using the Bible, rather than liberal philosophy, as the foundation. However, he did not believe that truths can be stated in doctrinal propositions; truths are encountered through God's revealing Himself in Christ.

Barth rejected the validity of general revelation in nature, stating that general revelation in nature is unable to reveal God to man. To Barth the event of revelation is Jesus Christ, although the Triune God is the entire subject of revelation.[3] God the Father through His eternal decree decided to reveal Himself in Christ; the Son executed the decree; the Holy Spirit consummates God's revelation by enabling man to behold it. Revelation continues today in the sense that revelation is the coming of the Word of God to man—and God comes to man in that Word. Furthermore, it can be termed *revelation* only if it is recognized and received by man. However, Barth ruled out any idea of progressive revelation. Revelation is possible only through the reconciliation in Christ,[4] and although the revelation of God occurred in Christ, it continues on when individuals experience the Word of God revealed.

Theology proper. Barth was influenced by John Calvin as well as other Reformers; hence, Barth stressed the sovereignty (as well as the transcendence) of God. God is wholly other, and man can only know God through His self-disclosure to man. But although Barth used Calvin's terminology, he ascribed different meanings to the terms. In explaining election, Barth emphasized the election of Christ rather than the election of man. Jesus Christ is both the subject as the elector and the object as the elected. (This is an example of dialectic theology in which topics are stated in contrasting statements.) Barth stated that in Christ all individuals are elect, yet he rejected the notion of universalism. God, in His grace, elected Christ, and through Him man is elected and reconciled to God. This includes those who do not believe in Christ but who are also determined to hear and believe.[5]

Christology. Barth emphasized the centrality of Jesus Christ in his theology. Christ must be the beginning point and the center of theology. Without Christ there is no revelation, according to Barth. For Barth the gospel begins with the eternal decree—the election of Jesus Christ. Barth taught that predestination is the election of Jesus Christ. Moreover, Christ is both the electing God and the elected man. The election of Christ means the election of the community. In his discussion of double election, Barth taught that God and Christ were reprobate by taking upon themselves the consequences that sinful man deserved. At the same time mankind is elected and wins salvation and participation in God's glory. Barth referred to the elected community as Israel that resists her election and as the church that is the ground of election. He finally dealt with the election of the individual, the "other"—the many from whom no one is excluded. It is this conclusion, in which Barth refused to refer to the non-elect as essentially different from the elect, that has brought charges of universalism—the belief that all humanity will eventually be saved. Because Christ has borne the sins of all humanity, all humanity can no longer be rejected. Barth even argued for Judas's election. Barth did not deny the charges that his doctrine of election led to universalism.

SUMMARY EVALUATION OF BARTH'S THEOLOGY

Several positive things can be said about Karl Barth's theology. He rejected his liberal training and recognized the need for a return to a study of the Bible apart from philosophy or liberal speculation. Barth also had a high view of God, emphasizing His sovereignty and transcendence. His emphasis upon the centrality of Christ in all the Scriptures is certainly valuable.

Some defects in Barth's theology are worthy of note. He denied the inspiration and inerrancy of the Bible and retained the liberal views concerning higher criticism. He also denied the possibility of stating propositional truths. Moreover, he declared that the Bible is not the Word of God until it *becomes* that for the individual; in other words, Barth emphasized subjectivity in his approach to the Bible. Barth also rejected general revelation, which Scripture nevertheless affirms (Ps. 19:1-6; Rom. 1:18-21). Barth also confused revelation with illumination. His view on sovereignty and election was not in the tradition of the Reformers nor in keeping with Scripture; in fact, his view leads to universalism.

THEOLOGY OF EMIL BRUNNER

HISTORICAL DEVELOPMENT OF BRUNNER'S THEOLOGY

Emil Brunner (1889-1966), along with Karl Barth and Rudolf Bultmann, was a pioneer in the neo-orthodox movement. Brunner was born near Zurich, Switzerland, where he also studied. He studied at Berlin and Union Seminary in New York as well. From 1924 he served as professor of theology in Zurich. Brunner was a prolific writer, completing 396 books and articles, of which 23 books were translated into English. He became a highly popular theologian, lecturing widely on the Continent, Great Britain, America, and Japan.

Brunner was a pioneer, having abandoned liberalism as well as having rejected orthodoxy. As a dialectical theologian, he, like Barth, built on the method of Kierkegaard.

DOCTRINAL AFFIRMATIONS OF BRUNNER'S THEOLOGY

Bibliology. Emil Brunner disagreed with Karl Barth by acknowledging the validity of general revelation; in fact, revelation continues in history and experience, which Brunner described as the Scriptures, the faith of the church, and the inner witness of the Holy Spirit. God's revelation, therefore, continues to encounter people.[6]

Brunner was in agreement with Barth that God does not reveal Himself objectively in the Bible but in the subjective encounter with Christ. But Brunner declared the necessity of both subject-object for communion with God. In this Brunner followed the Jewish theologian, Martin Buber (1878-1965), who popularized the I-Thou relationship. Brunner taught that God cannot be known in objective, doctrinal statements as taught by fundamentalists and Roman Catholics but only through a subjective, personal encounter—the I-Thou relationship. In this communion God does not reveal Himself in truths or propositions but in His Person.

Anthropology and hamartiology. Brunner dealt considerably with humanity and sin because sin determines man's relationship to God and society. Brunner rejected the total depravity of man, the inherited sin nature, and the historicity of Genesis 3. Adam was not an historical person; instead, mankind should see itself in Genesis 3.

In describing sin, Brunner declared that man is a sinner because he chooses to sin, not because of the inherited sin nature. Man is called to live in fellowship with God and others; failure to do so is self-centeredness, which was Brunner's definition of sin. This could be overcome only through a personal encounter with Christ. In his Christology, Brunner held to the Chalcedon statement of Jesus' true humanity and deity. Brunner emphasized the incarnation and resurrection of Christ in his teaching. Brunner believed God gave man the freedom to respond to His grace as revealed in Christ.

SUMMARY EVALUATION OF BRUNNER'S THEOLOGY

Emil Brunner separated himself from liberalism by rejecting its false view of Jesus, its belief in the goodness of man, and its optimism concerning establishment of the kingdom. Brunner also brought a new, biblical return to a declaration of man's sinfulness and the need for faith and responsible Christian conduct. He focused on the historic Christological doctrines of the incarnation and the resurrection.

Brunner's weaknesses involved his denial of the verbal, plenary inspiration of the Scriptures; he also denied the historicity of Adam and Genesis 3. While Brunner was strong in his affirmation of Christological doctrine, he denied the virgin birth. Brunner also denied the reality of hell.

THEOLOGY OF REINHOLD NIEBUHR

HISTORICAL DEVELOPMENT OF NIEBUHR'S THEOLOGY

Reinhold Niebuhr (1892-1971) was born in Missouri, the son of a German immigrant Lutheran pastor. Niebuhr attended the denomination's Lutheran seminary, followed by studies at Yale Divinity School. He was bored by scholarship and sought relevance in life. This desire was to provide the new theological direction that he was destined to pave.

Niebuhr served his only pastorate in Detroit from 1915 to 1928. That tenure was to shape him theologically. During that pastorate Niebuhr observed the social injustices of the working class, and he became embroiled in the conflict between labor and management. Niebuhr saw the poverty and difficult working conditions of the people and openly attacked the policies of Henry Ford, whom he saw as representative of the oppressive, capitalistic system.

Somewhat similar to Karl Barth's experience in Switzerland, Niebuhr came to reject his theologically liberal background when he saw its error. Liberalism's teaching of the innate goodness of man, with the coming utopian state, did not match the conditions as Niebuhr observed them. Although man had advanced technologically, he was also being exploited through technology. Niebuhr's solution was to adopt "socialism and pacifism for life in society, a new 'Christian realism' for theology."[7] With the advent of World War II, Niebuhr abandoned pacifism and socialism although he remained active in social causes.

From 1928 to 1960 he taught at Union Theological Seminary in New York City as professor of Christian ethics, emphasizing political and social affairs.

DOCTRINAL AFFIRMATIONS OF NIEBUHR'S THEOLOGY

Reinhold Niebuhr's theology was shaped by his experience during his pastoral work in Detroit. His main concern involved social justice and the cause of man; other doctrines were significant only as they related to man's need and social justice. In that sense "Niebuhr would say that sin was more social than spiritual, and that the evangelistic appeal should be with a view to converting society, not individuals. The Sermon on the Mount should be the law and code for business life today."[8]

Even though referring to sin and making biblical applications to social problems and injustices, Niebuhr nonetheless termed the creation account, as well as the Fall, "myth." Yet Niebuhr saw in the creation account a picture of humanity, where sin is real. Sin begins with man's fear of change, decay, and death; to alleviate the fear, man seeks security through the power exhibited in science and technology. Sin occurs through man's misuse of power in destroying others.[9]

Niebuhr rejected the historic view of sin; he referred to original sin as a perverse inclination in each human act.[10]

SUMMARY EVALUATION OF NIEBUHR'S THEOLOGY

Reinhold Niebuhr was not as conservative or biblical as Karl Barth and Emil Brunner. Although Niebuhr reacted against the optimism of liberalism and decried the social injustices as rooted in sin, he nonetheless redefined sin. He did not derive his concept of sin from the Scriptures; he rejected the doctrines of original sin as well as the historicity and fall of Adam.

THEOLOGY OF PAUL TILLICH

HISTORICAL DEVELOPMENT OF TILLICH'S THEOLOGY

Paul Tillich (1886-1965) was born in Prussia, the son of a Lutheran pastor who reared Tillich in traditional beliefs. Tillich's mother, however, encouraged openness. His love for nature in his rural setting remained with him throughout his life. As a young man his family moved to Berlin. He later

SOME NEO-ORTHODOX VIEWPOINTS

Theologian	Emphasis	Doctrine
Søren Kierkegaard	Knowledge unimportant. Subjective experience is important. Salvation is a commitment to God in a blind "leap of faith" amid one's despair.	Emphasized transcendence of God; God cannot be known through "proofs." Christ of history is unimportant; one must experience Him in the present. Historicity of biblical events is unimportant.
Karl Barth	Theology must be God-centered, not man-centered. Built on Kierkegaard's subjective emphasis. Man encounters God in reduplicating the experiences of the biblical writers.	Rejected general revelation. Bible is important but he rejected inspiration; Bible is a witness to revelation. Revelation takes place when man receives it. Christ-centered; Christ is the revelation of God and all mankind is elect in Christ.
Emil Brunner	God cannot be known through objective doctrine but through a subjective encounter with Christ. Emphasized a high Christology. God is known personally in an I-Thou relationship.	Allows for general revelation. Rejected inspiration of Scripture and reality of hell. Rejected inherited sin and Adam as historical. Man sins because of choice, not inherited nature. Sin is self-centeredness. Held to incarnation, deity, and resurrection of Christ.
Reinhold Niebuhr	Sin is basically social; society needs to be transformed from capitalistic greed. Man's need of social justice must be advocated.	Rejected liberal view of man's goodness. Rejected historic view of sin and historicity of Adam. Sin is social injustice and fear. Creation account is myth. Traditional theology useful only as it relates to modern man's need.

studied at Berlin, Tübingen, and Halle, receiving the doctor of philosophy degree at Breslau; he was ordained a Lutheran pastor in 1912. Tillich served Germany as a chaplain during World War I. In 1924 he began to teach theology at Marburg, where he also came under the influence of Martin Heidegger's existentialism. Because of his open opposition to Hitler in the 1930s, Tillich was fired from the University of Frankfurt faculty in 1933. He emigrated to the United States, where he taught at Union Seminary in New York, at Harvard, and at the University of Chicago. He wrote a three volume *Systematic Theology*, as well as numerous other volumes.

Tillich has frequently been termed "the theologian's theologian"; his writings are not easy reading. His theology was considered liberal in Germany but neo-orthodox in America. It can be appropriately named *dialectic theology*.[11] Tillich claimed to stand on the boundary between liberalism and neo-orthodoxy.[12] In the spectrum of neo-orthodoxy, he would represent the radical arm, whereas Karl Barth would represent the conservative wing.

DOCTRINAL AFFIRMATIONS OF TILLICH'S THEOLOGY

Theology Proper. Paul Tillich approached an understanding of God philosophically rather than theologically. Thus, traditional terms such as *God* are merely religious symbols. Tillich did not view God as a personal being but rather as "Being" itself. God is the Ground or Power of Being. He is "above everything belonging to finite being. . . . All finite beings exist. But God simply *is*."[13] Thus Tillich said, "It is as atheistic to affirm the existence of God as it is to deny it. . . . God is being-itself, not *a* being."[14]

Hamartiology. Sin is described as estrangement from one's true self or from the ground of our being. The Fall was not an historical event; "It is a non-temporal transition from essence to existence. It is a 'fall' and it is tragic, since it results in the situation where man is estranged from his essential being."[15] The essential character of sin for Tillich is disruption of the essential unity with God. "In existence man is estranged from the ground of his being, from other beings, and from himself."[16]

Soteriology. Salvation is not expressed in traditional terms; for Tillich salvation is found in the New Being which is "ultimate concern" for the kind of life seen in Christ because Christ evidenced real concern. Ultimate concern is understood as a primary concern over everything else; it relates to "being" or "non-being." Man is aware of his finiteness and "non-being," which results in anxiety. He looks in hope to Christ (not used in the orthodox sense), who will rescue him from his estrangement.

Christology. Jesus Christ is not described nor understood in traditional terms, nor is Christ understood as an historical person. Christ is "a symbol of the 'New Being' in which every force of estrangement trying to dissolve his unity with God has been dissolved."[17] Thus Tillich rejected belief in the incarnation and the resurrection of Christ.

SUMMARY EVALUATION OF TILLICH'S THEOLOGY

Paul Tillich was more of a philosopher than a theologian; he dealt with ideas and concepts rather than the historical events of Scripture. For this reason, Tillich gave too much credence to human reason. More to the point, his approach to the interpretation of the Scriptures is a modern kind of allegorism. He attached new meanings to biblical words. He denied the personality of God in referring to Him as the "Ultimate Ground of existence." Personal sin and rebellion against God was rejected, as was the historical event of the Fall in Eden. Man's sin is lack of concern. Salvation is not in the historical person of Christ, but in a symbol; Jesus Christ is not the historical person of the Scriptures in Tillich's theology. Salvation is not through atonement for sin but through ultimate concern.

Tillich's approach to the Scriptures did violence to all the major, historically-held doctrines of the Christian faith.

THEOLOGY OF JOHN A. T. ROBINSON[18]

HISTORICAL DEVELOPMENT OF ROBINSON'S THEOLOGY

John A. T. Robinson (b. 1919), bishop of Woolwich, England, is probably noted as the popularizer of Paul Tillich's theology. Most will acknowledge that Tillich's theology is difficult reading; Robinson has popularized it. Robinson has recorded his religious thoughts in his popular book *Honest to God.*

DOCTRINAL AFFIRMATIONS OF ROBINSON'S THEOLOGY

In agreement with Rudolf Bultmann, Robinson repudiates the idea of God "up there." He believes the concept of a localized God is objectionable in a scientific age. He also advocates rejection of this traditional language about God. Because Robinson rejects the traditional arguments for the existence of God and the idea of God as sovereign, he seeks to discover "that ultimate reality."[19] Thus Robinson rejects the view of God as a self-existent entity and suggests the term *God* is interchangeable with the word *universe.*[20] Robinson also rejects God's transcendence and self-existence.

Robinson's theology is rooted in three mentors: from Bultmann he suggests the need to demythologize the Scriptures in order to make them palatable for modern men and women; from Dietrich Bonhoeffer he adopts the concept of religionless Christianity; from Tillich he views God as the "Ground of our being," with man's objective being "ultimate concern."[21] He also reflects the language of process theology by suggesting a panentheistic view of God: "the belief that the Being of God includes and penetrates the whole universe, so that every part of it exists in him, but (as against pantheism) that his Being is more than, and is not exhausted by, the universe."[22]

SUMMARY EVALUATION OF ROBINSON'S THEOLOGY

John A. T. Robinson's concept of God is much the same as Paul Tillich's. Robinson rejects the doctrine of a personal God as well as a transcendent God. He identifies God with the universe. Calling for a secularization of Christianity, Robinson seeks to make the old terminology commensurate with modern thought. Thus, even prayer is rejected in favor of social involvement. Robinson's doctrine of Christ is also unorthodox. In rejecting the incarnation, he suggests that Jesus never claimed to be God. For Robinson, salvation "is the life of 'the man for others,' the love whereby we are brought completely into one with the Ground of our being."[23]

Robinson's radical theology has little to commend itself to the historic Christian faith. His theology does violence to the normal meaning of words and to the historic tenets of hermeneutics.

NOTES ON NEO-ORTHODOX THEOLOGY

1. *Existentialism* "is a term used by neo-orthodoxy to designate the place of personal commitment in an act of faith. Existential faith believes with inward passion; it is concerned with the relation between the self and the object of belief; it chooses from within the center of moral freedom. Cheap faith believes too easily; it does not count the cost." (E. J. Carnell, "Existential, Existentialism" in Everett F. Harrison, ed., *Baker's Dictionary of Theology* [Grand Rapids: Baker, 1960], p. 205.)

2. Alasdair I. C. Heron, *A Century of Protestant Theology* (Philadelphia: Westminster, 1980), p. 49.

3. Karl Barth, *Church Dogmatics*, 4 vols. in 13 books (Edinburgh: Clark, 1936), 1:1:334ff.

4. See the explanation in Geoffrey W. Bromiley, *Introduction to the Theology of Karl Barth* (Grand Rapids: Eerdmans, 1979), pp. 175-243.

5. Barth, *Church Dogmatics*, 2:2:457ff.

6. R. D. Linder, "Brunner, Heinrich Emil," in Walter A. Elwell, ed., *Evangelical Dictionary of Theology* (Grand Rapids: Baker, 1984), pp. 176-77.

7. Mark A. Noll, "Niebuhr, Reinhold," in *Evangelical Dictionary of Theology*, p. 777.

8. Charles C. Ryrie, *Neo-Orthodoxy: What It Is and What It Does* (Chicago: Moody, 1956), p. 31.

9. Theodore Minnema, "Reinhold Niebuhr," in Philip Edgcumbe Hughes, ed., *Creative Minds in Contemporary Theology* (Grand Rapids: Eerdmans, 1969), pp. 384-86.

10. Ibid., p. 387.

11. *Dialectic theology* is actually a broad term that can be applied to a great many theologians, beginning with the neo-orthodox era. Ramm defines dialectic theology:

> It did not believe in the direct sort of assertions about man and God made by the older orthodox theologians and the more recent religious liberals. It believed that the divine-human relationship was one of tension. It had an existential dimension. The only kind of logic adequate for the situation is the logic of dialectic, with its Yes and No, with its assertion and counter-assertion. Thus a

theological truth was not adequately met until it was formulated paradoxically by way of proposition and the counter-proposition. (Bernard Ramm, *A Handbook of Contemporary Theology* [Grand Rapids: Eerdmans, 1966], pp. 35-36.)

Tillich applied the concept of dialectics to all of life, and thus his theology may be called dialectical theology. Compare Vernon C. Grounds, "Pacesetters for the Radical Theologians of the Sixties and Seventies," in *Tensions in Contemporary Theology*, edited by Stanley N. Gundry and Alan F. Johnson (Chicago: Moody, 1978), pp. 85-91.

12. William E. Hordern, *A Layman's Guide to Protestant Theology*, rev. ed. (London: Macmillan, 1968), p. 171.

13. Kenneth Hamilton, "Paul Tillich," in Philip Edgcumbe Hughes, ed., *Creative Minds in Contemporary Theology*, rev. ed. (Grand Rapids: Eerdmans, 1969), p. 455.

14. Ibid.

15. Ibid., p. 458.

16. Ibid.

17. Harvie M. Conn, *Contemporary World Theology*, rev. ed. (Nutley, N.J.: Presbyterian and Reformed, 1974), p. 89.

18. John A. T. Robinson could also be categorized under "Worldly Christianity" with Bonhoeffer, or under "God-is-dead (Secular) Theology."

19. Harold B. Kuhn, "Secular Theology" in *Tensions in Contemporary Theology*, p. 175.

20. Ibid.

21. Ibid., p. 176.

22. Ibid., p. 177.

23. Henlee H. Barnette, *The New Theology and Morality* (Philadelphia: Westminster, 1967), p. 36.

FOR FURTHER STUDY ON NEO-ORTHODOX THEOLOGY

SØREN KIERKEGAARD

* D. B. Eller. "Kierkeggard, Søren." In Walter A. Elwell, ed., *Evangelical Dictionary of Theology.* Grand Rapids: Baker, 1984. Pp. 605-6.

** Warren F. Groff and Donald E. Miller. *The Shaping of Modern Christian Thought.* Cleveland: World, 1968. Pp. 82-98, 210-25, 368-90.

* William E. Hordern. *A Layman's Guide to Protestant Theology,* rev. ed. London: Macmillan, 1968. Pp. 113-18.

** Søren Kierkegaard. *Christian Discourses.* London: Oxford U., 1940.

KARL BARTH

** Karl Barth. *Church Dogmatics*, 4 vols. in 13 books. Edinburgh: Clark, 1936.

** _____. *Evangelical Theology: An Introduction.* Grand Rapids: Eerdmans, 1963.

** Geoffrey W. Bromiley. *Introduction to the Theology of Karl Barth.* Grand Rapids: Eerdmans, 1979.

* Herbert Hartwell. *The Theology of Karl Barth: An Introduction.* Philadelphia: Westminster, 1964.

* Robert L. Reymond. *Barth's Soteriology.* Philadelphia: Presbyterian & Reformed, 1967.
* Charles C. Ryrie. *Neo-Orthodoxy: What It Is and What It Does.* Chicago: Moody, 1956. Pp. 17-27.
* R. V. Schnucker. "Barth, Karl." In Walter A. Elwell., ed., *Evangelical Dictionary of Theology*. Grand Rapids: Baker, 1984. Pp. 126-27.

EMIL BRUNNER

* Emil Brunner. *The Scandal of Christianity.* Richmond, Va.: Knox, 1951.
* _____. *The Theology of Crisis.* New York: Scribner, 1929.
* William E. Hordern. *A Layman's Guide to Protestant Theology,* rev. ed.. London: Macmillan, 1968. Pp. 118-29.
* R. D. Linder. "Brunner, Heinrich Emil." In Walter A. Elwell, ed., *Evangelical Dictionary of Theology*. Grand Rapids: Baker, 1984. Pp. 175-77.
* Charles C. Ryrie. *Neo-Orthodoxy: What It Is and What It Does.* Chicago: Moody, 1956. Pp. 28-30.
* Paul G. Schrotenboer. "Emil Brunner." In Philip Edgcumbe Hughes, ed., *Creative Minds in Contemporary Theology.* Grand Rapids: Eerdmans, 1969. Pp. 99-130.

REINHOLD NIEBUHR

* William E. Hordern. *A Layman's Guide to Protestant Theology,* rev. ed.. London: Macmillan, 1968. Pp. 150-69.
* Theodore Minnema. "Reinhold Niebuhr." In Philip Edgcumbe Hughes, ed., *Creative Minds in Contemporary Theology.* Grand Rapids: Eerdmans, 1969. Pp. 377-406.
** Reinhold Niebuhr. *Moral Man and Immoral Society.* New York: Scribner, 1932.
** _____. *The Nature and Destiny of Man*, 2 vols. New York: Scribner, 1946.
* Mark A. Noll. "Niebuhr, Reinhold." In Walter A. Elwell, ed., *Evangelical Dictionary of Theology.* Grand Rapids: Baker, 1984. Pp. 776-77.
* Charles C. Ryrie. *Neo-Orthodoxy: What It Is and What It Does.* Chicago: Moody, 1956. Pp. 31-34.

PAUL TILLICH

* Harvie M. Conn. *Contemporary World Theology.* Nutley, N.J.: Presbyterian & Reformed, 1974. Pp. 87-92.
* C. J. Curtis. *Contemporary Protestant Thought.* New York: Bruce, 1970. Pp. 150-57.
* David H. Freeman. *Tillich.* Philadelphia: Presbyterian & Reformed, 1962.
* Stanley N. Gundry and Alan F. Johnson, eds. *Tensions in Contemporary Theology.* Chicago: Moody, 1976. Pp. 82-96.
** Kenneth Hamilton. *The System and the Gospel: A Critique of Paul Tillich.* Grand Rapids: Eerdmans, 1963.
* J. D. Spiceland. "Tillich, Paul." In Walter A. Elwell, ed., *Evangelical Dictionary of Theology.* Grand Rapids: Baker, 1984. Pp. 1093-94.
** Paul Tillich. *Systematic Theology*, 3 vols. Chicago: U. of Chicago, 1951-63.

JOHN A. T. ROBINSON

* Henlee H. Barnette. *The New Theology and Morality.* Philadelphia: Westminster, 1967. Pp. 35-38.

* Harvie M. Conn. *Contemporary World Theology.* Nutley, N.J.: Presbyterian & Reformed, 1974. Pp. 46-52.

** David L. Edwards, ed. *The Honest-to-God Debate.* Philadelphia: Westminster, 1963.

* Stanley N. Gundry and Alan F. Johnson, eds. *Tensions in Contemporary Theology.* Chicago: Moody, 1976. Pp. 174-80.

** John A. T. Robinson. *Christian Morals Today.* Philadelphia: Westminster, 1964.

** ————. *Honest to God.* Philadelphia: Westminster, 1963.

41

RADICAL THEOLOGIES

A number of contemporary theologies contain essential factors that are startling and radical contrasts from traditional Christianity.

FORM CRITICISM: RUDOLPH BULTMANN

HISTORICAL DEVELOPMENT OF BULTMANN'S THEOLOGY

Rudolf Bultmann (1884-1976) was the son of an evangelical Lutheran minister. He pursued his theological studies at Tübingen, Berlin, and Marburg, where he became professor of New Testament in 1921 and remained until 1951. It was at Marburg that he became interested in dialectical theology. Although he had studied under liberals like Hermann Gunkel and Adolph Harnack, he too, like Karl Barth, was influenced by Søren Kierkegaard toward dialectical theology. He was particularly influenced by the philosopher Martin Heidegger, who served at Marburg from 1922 to 1928. Bultmann applied Heidegger's philosophy to the New Testament, with the outcome being a radical criticism of the text. Bultmann developed what is known as "form criticism,"[1] an attempt to discover the literary forms and sources the writer of Scripture was using. He concluded that the gospel records are a collection of myths "which portrayed truths about man's existence rather than told about actual historical events."[2] In order to understand the New Testament books it is necessary to "demythologize" them, that is, strip them of the myth with which the early church had cloaked the gospel writings.

DOCTRINAL AFFIRMATIONS OF BULTMANN'S THEOLOGY

At the heart of Rudolf Bultmann's theology is form criticism. Bultmann rejected the thesis that the New Testament writings are complete and authentic works of individual writers. He believed the gospels were the product of the early church, which had embellished the original records about the life of Christ. The gospel writers thus were seen by Bultmann, Martin Debelius, and others not as writers per se, but primarily as collectors of fragmentary writings and as editors who pieced the writings together. Thus, the conclusion of one form critic is, "We do not have the story of Jesus, we only have stories about Jesus."[3] It remains, therefore, the work of the critic to discover the original forms of the New Testament writings. Moreover, the Bible is not treated as a supernatural book but like any other writing.

The process of uncovering the original statements of Jesus is to "demythologize" the Scripture, that is, to peel off the layers of editorial embellishments by the early church. For example, the early church thought of the universe as three tiered: heaven above, earth, and hell below. Within these levels of existence were supernatural beings: God, angels, Satan, and demons. But this is all mythological statement—the words have symbolic meanings that need to be interpreted.

Recognizing that the New Testament is enshrouded with myth, Bultmann saw, nonetheless, a *kerygma*, a gospel proclamation that expresses the "true intent of the biblical writers behind their mythological pattern of thought."[4] In neo-orthodox fashion, he suggested that God meets the individual through the preached word.[5]

The result of Bultmann's methodology is skepticism. He concludes, "I do indeed think that we can now know almost nothing concerning the life and personality of Jesus, since the early Christian sources show no interest in either, are moreover fragmentary and legendary; and other sources about Jesus do not exist."[6]

SUMMARY EVALUATION OF BULTMANN'S THEOLOGY

Rudolf Bultmann's form criticism is a subjective methodology that approaches the Scriptures like an ordinary book. It is, first of all, a denial of the inspiration of Scripture. Form critics approach the Bible like any other piece of literature, dissecting it from a purely subjective standpoint. Demythologization builds upon form criticism and further extends the subjective approach to the Scriptures. The underlying premise is that Scripture is filled with myth and must be eliminated because it does not correspond to the modern scientific mind.

One might ask, in light of Bultmann's views, What is the benefit of proclaiming a gospel without historical validity? If the true Jesus cannot truly be known, as Bultmann suggests, what is the benefit of proclaiming the gospel? The true Christian faith is anchored to history and has historical validity; Bultmann's gospel is a proclamation of myth that offers little hope.

WORLDLY CHRISTIANITY: DIETRICH BONHOEFFER

HISTORICAL DEVELOPMENT OF BONHOEFFER'S THEOLOGY

Dietrich Bonhoeffer (1906-1945), the son of a Berlin neurologist, studied at the University of Tübingen and the University of Berlin, where he received the doctor of theology degree at the age of twenty-one. He completed a second dissertation in 1930, the same year he also began studies at Union Theological Seminary in New York City for one year. Upon returning to Germany, Bonhoeffer was greatly inspired by Karl Barth during a seminar by the famed neo-orthodox teacher. In 1931 he became chaplain in a high school and later lecturer at the University of Berlin. When Adolph Hitler became chancellor of Germany in 1933, Bonhoeffer was outspoken in his opposition to Naziism and its views of Aryan (Germanic) supremacy (Bonhoeffer's twin sister had a Jewish husband). After going to England in 1933, Bonhoeffer returned home to join the Confessing church by leading a seminary that was eventually closed by the Nazis in 1937. Bonhoeffer was also forbidden to speak publicly or write. Although he went to Union Seminary briefly in 1939, he returned to Germany almost immediately to join the struggle against the Nazis. Bonhoeffer himself had been involved in the planning to overthrow Hitler in 1938. In 1941 his books were banned, and in 1943 he was arrested and imprisoned. It was there that he wrote *Letters and Papers from Prison*, his most popular work. When evidence surfaced that he was involved in the bomb plot against Hitler in 1944, Bonhoeffer was hanged in 1945.

DOCTRINAL AFFIRMATIONS OF BONHOEFFER'S THEOLOGY

Christology. Dietrich Bonhoeffer was heavily indebted to Karl Barth for his theology, although Bonhoeffer was an independent thinker. For Bonhoeffer "religion" was unacceptable; all that matters is a personal encounter with Christ. He spoke of Jesus as "being there for others" and the one who is "haveable, graspable within his Word within the Church."

Bonhoeffer saw Christ active in a secularized life. "Christ is not exiled from our irreligious world but is present in it. He confronts people, not in the old process of repentance, faith, conversion, regeneration and sanctification, but in new ways through their 'godless' attitudes."[7] This is an example of Bonhoeffer's extreme terminology, which has caused considerable debate.

Ecclesiology. His forceful *Letters and Papers from Prison* express Bonhoeffer's emphasis on sacrifice and discipline: "The church is the church only when it exists for others. To make a start, it should give away all its property to those in need. The clergy must live solely on the free-will offerings of their congregations, or possibly engage in some secular calling. The church must share in the secular problems of ordinary human life, not dominating, but helping and serving."[8]

Religionless Christianity. A much debated question is what Bonhoeffer meant by his enigmatic statements on religionless Christianity. Some have understood this in a positive sense, suggesting a worldly discipleship in which life is lived responsibly "under the aspect of God as the ultimate reality."[9] This would mean living a disciplined life in this world as a disciple of Christ. However, the radical theologians of the 1960s also gained their impetus from Bonhoeffer's statements about religionless Christianity. Some, therefore, have understood Bonhoeffer as teaching that the "mature man" who has come of age must learn to live independent of God. Bonhoeffer rejected the notion of the "sacred" and "secular"; he saw the need for serving Christ in the world and not only in the "sacred" realm. Further, with the advent of science, man can learn to solve his own problems whereas previously he relied on God.

In seeing man's independence of God, Bonhoeffer declared, "Man has learnt to deal with himself in all questions of importance without recourse to the 'working hypothesis' called 'God.' "[10] Bonhoeffer did not deny the usefulness of this independence from God.

Certainly, Bonhoeffer made dualistic statements that have been difficult to understand, particularly because his untimely death terminated any possibility of later explanations or systematization.

SUMMARY EVALUATION OF BONHOEFFER'S THEOLOGY

A major problem in evaluating the writings of Dietrich Bonhoeffer is that he died before his writings could be developed more fully. Certainly many statements are enigmatic. Bonhoeffer was heavily indebted to Barth and followed dialectic theology, as is evident in many of Bonhoeffer's "contradictory" statements. However one evaluates his statements, one thing is true: the secular "God is dead" theologians found their roots in Bonhoeffer's writings that emphasized man's independence of God. At the very least, his statements about man's maturity in independence from God militate against the scriptural call to turn to God in faith, realizing one's weakness (e.g., 2 Cor. 12:9-10).

GOD-IS-DEAD THEOLOGY: FOUR VIEWPOINTS

HISTORICAL DEVELOPMENT OF GOD-IS-DEAD THEOLOGY

Many, no doubt, have considered the "God-is-dead" theology as a joke. It should be noted, however, that these theologians were serious in their statements. The roots of the God is dead theology go back to Friedrich Nietzsche (1844-1900). Thomas Altizer (b. 1927), like Nietzsche, maintained "that all of reality undergoes constant destruction and re-creation through an irresistible, ongoing dialectic. Thus, they deny all forms of traditional ontology and allow for no sovereign and unconditioned Being but only a 'God' who at some point in the dialectic wills His own self-annihilation."[11] It is also fair to say that the God-is-dead theologians borrowed from both Rudolf Bultmann and Dietrich Bonhoeffer. From Bultmann they concluded the Bible is mythological; from Bonhoeffer they concluded man must learn to live without God.

DOCTRINAL AFFIRMATIONS OF GOD-IS-DEAD THEOLOGY

To understand the God-is-dead theology the viewpoints of four main authors must be considered.

Theology of Gabriel Vahanian. Gabriel Vahanian studied at the Sorbonne and at Princeton. He also taught at Princeton and later at Syracuse University. He has written several works, including *The Death of God: The Culture of Our Post-Christian Era.* Vahanian sees our society as post-Christian; Christianity has been eclipsed by the modern, scientific age. "God is no longer necessary; he is irrelevant; he is dead."[12] Like other God-is-dead theologians, Vahanian observes a Christian culture in which God is no longer transcendent; the concept of God has merged with man. He sees this through the terms used to express the name of God (Co-Pilot, etc.). Although Vahanian did not himself believe God is dead, he urged a form of Christianity that was secular.

Theology of Paul Van Buren. Paul Van Buren (b. 1924) has served on the faculties of Episcopal Theological Seminary in Austin, Texas, and Temple University, Philadelphia. He came to Temple (once a religious university but now secular) to "ask the questions about religion more clearly as it arises in our society than it does in a professional religious context."[13]

Van Buren takes his starting point from Dietrich Bonhoeffer who declared, "Honesty demands that we recognize that we must live in the world as if there were no God. . . . We stand continually in the presence of the God who makes us live in the world without the God-hypothesis."[14] Whether or not Bonhoeffer intended to be understood in this way, nonetheless the God-is-dead theologians built on him as well as on Nietzsche.[15] Van Buren wrote *The Secular Meaning of the Gospel* and *Post Mortem Dei,* in which he suggests that because the Bible is myth, it is impossible and meaningless to speak of God. Secular man must instead find meaning in Jesus and the "Easter event," which event does not mean the resurrection, but rather a new, contagious freedom to love.

Theology of William Hamilton. William Hamilton (b. 1924) is a Baptist minister who has taught systematic theology at Colgate Rochester Divinity School, Rochester, New York. The books espousing his views include *The*

Christian Man, *The New Essence of Christianity*, and *Radical Theology and the Death of God* (with Altizer).

Hamilton rejects the traditional, orthodox view of God, but sees the death of God as a cultural event occurring in the last two hundred years. Man, therefore, must adapt himself to the death of God, not expecting any help from God; rather, solutions to life's problems are found in the secular world. "God is no longer necessary to deliver man from restlessness, despair, or self-righteousness; indeed, there is no God to do so."[16] The reason man can do without God is the rise in technology and modern science.[17] What is left of Christianity is an ethic derived largely from Jesus of Nazareth—but without God.[18] According to Hamilton, today's "Christian" must turn away from historic theology and religion and turn to the world.[19]

Theology of Thomas J. J. Altizer. Thomas J. J. Altizer, an Episcopalian, has taught at Emory University in Atlanta. He has written many books concerning his radical theology, notably *The Gospel of Christian Atheism* (Westminster).

Altizer rejects traditional, orthodox Christianity, citing Philippians 2:6-8 as his basis for suggesting that God died in history when Christ died on the cross. Altizer builds on Nietzsche's premise of the death of God when he states: "We shall understand the death of God as an historical event: God has died in *our* time, in *our* history, in *our* existence."[20]

Altizer, however, is difficult to understand because he speaks in poetic and dialectic language. It appears that Altizer stresses that God's transcendence no longer exists because of the death of Christ. God died as a transcendent God when Christ died; thus one should will the continuing death of God in order that He might become fully immanent with the world and in history. Altizer sees a union of the divine and the human as a result.[21]

SUMMARY EVALUATION OF GOD-IS-DEAD THEOLOGY

Although there are shades of difference between the God-is-dead theologians, in general, the following points will apply to most of them. They built on the philosophical systems of Kant and Ritschl, both of whom denied that one could demonstrably prove the existence of God. They also borrowed from Nietzsche, who proclaimed, "God is dead." Biblically, they begin with a Bultmannian approach in suggesting the Bible is myth; the accounts of Scripture are not to be taken seriously. Thus, as Vahanian, they see Jesus only as a human, not as God. They do not take the Bible seriously in its assertions about God, Jesus Christ, man, and the world. Because they ignore a biblical sense of sin, they ignore the biblical solution through Christ's atonement. The solution and the essence of "Christianity" is secularization—entering into the problems of the world, trying to solve them through the advantages of science and technology, but without any regard for God. Their "gospel" is man-centered rather than God-centered.

PROCESS THEOLOGY: SIX VIEWPOINTS

HISTORICAL DEVELOPMENT OF PROCESS THEOLOGY

One aspect of secular theology is the question of "God talk"—suggesting that it is not possible to talk intelligently about God in the old forms; talk about God must take on secular forms. This discussion is continued in process theology: Is it possible to talk intelligently about God? Like God-is-dead theology, process theology does not approach its study about God from a biblical perspective but from a philosophical one. Special revelation does not enter the picture. Process theology goes back to Hegel, who taught that the universe is incomplete, always changing. "Reality is a constant movement of the dialectic of thesis, antithesis, and synthesis. The syntheses of the Hegelian system of process are stages of creative evolution, and never final, static, unchanging perfections."[22] It is on this premise that process theology is built.

Alfred North Whitehead, philosopher and mathematician, is generally considered the father of process theology.

DOCTRINAL AFFIRMATIONS OF PROCESS THEOLOGY

Theology of Alfred North Whitehead. Alfred North Whitehead (1861-1947) began with the premise that reality is not static but dynamic and in process.[23] This includes God who also is composed of changing activities. Whitehead's concept of God in process arose out of his study of mathematics, which observed "the general activity of the flux of the world." Whitehead emphasized that "process is the rule of the world." Everything that is real is in the constant cycle of "becoming"; everything is undergoing transition. This concept of transition includes God, who is also in the process of "becoming." Whitehead suggested that there are two sides to God; He is "bipolar." His primordial nature, which relates only to eternal objects, and His consequent nature (His immanence), which relates to the world. In His consequent nature God is continually in the process of saving and preserving the world, but never arriving. Thus Whitehead also terms God "dipolar," a combination of eternal and temporal, of infinite and finite, of abstract concepts and of concrete materialization in the real world.[24]

For Whitehead, God is an impersonal force, the controlling force behind evolution, and also changing with nature. Neither is God omnipotent, but co-creator with man in shaping the future. God, "as actual entity included the world consequently within himself, and suffers and grows along with it through the creativity which he and the world possess."[25]

Theology of Charles Hartshorne. Like Alfred North Whitehead, Charles Hartshorne (b. 1896) rejected the traditional concept of God.[26] God is only a "Director" of the world, working in cooperation with the world, mutually dependent with the world. From a rationalistic and logical viewpoint, Hartshorne argued for the existence of a "necessary Being." As an impersonal Being, God is viewed as a "series of entities" which is the cause of the world. In agreement with Whitehead, Hartshorne "argues that God does not have an unchanging essence, but that he is also continually developing and completing himself by his own advancing experience of and participation in the universal process and the lives and sufferings of human beings."[27] Hartshorne's thesis and his conclusion base his concept of God on "natural theology" and thereby reject supernaturalism.

Theology of John Cobb. Although he remains within process theology, John Cobb (b. 1925) differs from Alfred North Whitehead in rejecting the notion of God's "bipolar thesis." Cobb sees God as a unity and a living Person rather than an actual entity as Whitehead suggested. Yet Cobb emphasizes a return to "natural theology" (like Whitehead's) for a proper understanding of God. The doctrine of "panentheism" (all things happen within God) are evident in Cobb's suggestion that "God is in the world and the world is in and from God."[28] This is an attempt to unite theism and pantheism. Evil in the world is explained not on the basis of Genesis 3 but on account of the evolutionary process that explains the rise of life and values that gave rise to freedom, self-consciousness, and reason.[29] The result is a basic optimism about humanity that is reminiscent of older liberalism.

Theology of Nelson Pike. Nelson Pike, also a part of the process theology movement, argues against Thomas Aquinas's belief in God's timelessness.[30] For Pike, timelessness would eliminate God's foreknowledge because there is no future for a timeless God. God cannot act in time, only in eternity, even though the world was created in time. Timelessness would eliminate God's personality because personality demands response. If God is timeless, then He cannot respond because He is immutable. Worship and prayer demand that God be moved by the suppliant, but if He is timeless He cannot be moved. Timelessness would nullify the incarnation because the incarnation demands change. Furthermore, argues Pike, the Bible speaks about God changing His mind.[31]

Theology of Schubert M. Ogden.[32] Schubert M. Ogden (b. 1928) also follows the thesis of process theology, but he sees the need for a process God from a Bultmannian background. That is, man must have an understanding for his own existence in the world. Ogden builds on Charles Hartshorne in his view of a dipolar God. God is relative. As "I" am related to my body, so God is related to the world; the world is the body of God. Therefore, God participates in the world through "sympathetic participation." God is absolute in that He is included in all beings and is related to every entity in the universe. Within this relatedness God is constantly subject to change.

Theology of Norman Pittenger.[33] Norman Pittenger (b. 1905) brings process theology to bear on the doctrine of Christ. Although Pittenger refers to the deity of Christ, he describes it not in terms of the essence of Christ's deity, but rather, the divine activity of God in Christ. The deity of Christ is the act of God in Christ; He is God's action among men.

Pittenger also follows process theology in his adherence to panentheism: "the being of God includes and penetrates the whole universe, so that every part of it exists in him, but (as against pantheism) that his being is more than, and not exhausted by, the universe."[34] God is active in the world, providing self-realization for each creature. As God acts in the world, each occasion is the incarnation of "God."

SUMMARY EVALUATION OF PROCESS THEOLOGY

The concept of God in process theology is not derived from revelation as given in the Scriptures, but from mathematical and scientific hypotheses (Alfred North Whitehead) and rationalistic speculation (Charles Hartshorne). The personality and sovereignty of God is denied; He is seen only as a "force," and a changing one at that. The supernatural and miraculous is abandoned in process theology. In evaluating process theology's use of biblical terms, Carl F. H. Henry has stated: "Creation becomes evolution, redemption becomes relationship, and resurrection becomes renewal. The supernatural is abandoned, miracles vanish, and the living God of the Bible is submerged in immanental motifs."[35] Process theology is based on the Kantian principle of reason rather than revelation. Process theology does violence to the immutability of God (Mal. 3:6; James 1:17) because it suggests God Himself is subject to change. Any biblical concept of sin and atonement for sin is also ignored.

NOTES ON RADICAL THEOLOGIES

1. For a summary explanation of the method of form criticism, see Stephen H. Travis, "Form Criticism," in I. Howard Marshall, ed., *New Testament Interpretation: Essays on Principles and Methods* (Grand Rapids: Eerdmans, 1977), pp. 153-64.
2. Grant R. Osborne, *The Resurrection Narratives: A Redactional Study* (Grand Rapids: Baker, 1984), p. 26.
3. Harvie M. Conn, *Contemporary World Theology*, rev. ed. (Nutley, N.J.: Presbyterian & Reformed, 1974), p. 28.
4. Robert D. Knudsen, "Rudolf Bultmann," in Philip Edgcumbe Hughes, ed., *Creative Minds in Contemporary Theology*, rev. ed. (Grand Rapids: Eerdmans, 1969), p. 135.
5. Rudolf Bultmann, *Jesus Christ and Mythology* (New York: Scribner, 1958), pp. 78-79.

6. Rudolf Bultmann, *Jesus and the Word* (New York: Scribner, 1958), p. 8.

7. David F. Wells, *The Search for Salvation* (Downers Grove, Ill.: InterVarsity, 1978), p. 103.

8. Dietrich Bonhoeffer, *Letters and Papers from Prison* (New York: Macmillan, 1972), p. 382.

9. Harold B. Kuhn, "Secular Theology," in *Tensions in Contemporary Theology*, edited by Stanley N. Gundry and Alan F. Johnson (Chicago: Moody, 1976), p. 173.

10. Vernon C. Grounds, "Radical Theologians of the Sixties and Seventies," in *Tensions in Contemporary Theology*, p. 72.

11. Harold B. Kuhn, "Secular Theology," in *Tensions in Contemporary Theology*, pp. 161-62.

12. Henlee H. Barnette, *The New Theology and Morality* (Philadelphia: Westminster, 1967), p. 11.

13. Ibid.

14. Ibid., p.15.

15. For this reason one could readily categorize Dietrich Bonhoeffer among the God-is-dead theologians. Bonhoeffer may not have intended the extreme conclusion to which those theologians arrived, but they nonetheless believed their ideas to be derivations of his system.

16. Kuhn, "Secular Theology," in *Tensions in Contemporary Theology*, p. 166.

17. Thomas Altizer and William Hamilton, *Radical Theology and the Death of God* (Indianapolis: Bobbs-Merrill, 1966), p. 33.

18. Ibid., pp. 33-34.

19. Harold B. Kuhn, "Secular Theology," in *Tensions in Contemporary Theology*, p. 167.

20. Altizer and Hamilton, *Radical Theology and the Death of God*, p. 95.

21. See William E. Hordern, *A Layman's Guide to Protestant Theology*, rev. ed. (London: Macmillan, 1968), pp. 240-41; and Stanley N. Gundry, "Death of God Theology," in Walter A. Elwell, ed., *Evangelical Dictionary of Theology* (Grand Rapids: Baker, 1984), p. 302.

22. C. J. Curtis, *Contemporary Protestant Thought* (New York: Bruce, 1970), p. 65.

23. See the helpful discussion by Norman L. Geisler, "Process Theology," in *Tensions in Contemporary Theology*, pp. 239-50.

24. Ibid., p. 250.

25. D. W. Diehl, "Process Theology," in *Evangelical Dictionary of Theology*, p. 882.

26. See the summary of similarities and differences between Whitehead and Hartshorne in Geisler, "Process Theology," pp. 250-57.

27. Alasdair I. C. Heron, *A Century of Protestant Theology* (Philadelphia: Westminster, 1980), p. 147.

28. Stanley T. Sutphin, *Options in Contemporary Theology* (Washington: U. Press of America, 1977), p. 79.

29. Ibid., pp. 89-90.

30. Geisler, "Process Theology," pp. 258-60.

31. Ibid., pp. 271-74. See the rebuttal to Pike.

32. Ibid., pp. 206-64. Geisler summarizes in a helpful way.

33. Ibid., pp. 265-67.

34. Ibid., p. 265.

35. Harvie M. Conn, *Contemporary World Theology*, rev. ed. (Nutley, N.J.: Presbyterian and Reformed, 1974), p. 85.

FOR FURTHER STUDY ON RADICAL THEOLOGIES

FORM CRITICISM

* G. C. Berkouwer. *A Half Century of Theology.* Grand Rapids: Eerdmans, 1977. Pp. 51-74.

** Rudolf Bultmann. *Theology of the New Testament,* 2 vols. New York: Charles Scribner's Sons, 1951-55.

** Rudolf Bultmann. *Form Criticism: Two Essays on New Testament Research.* New York: Harper, 1962.

* Harvie M. Conn. *Contemporary World Theology.* Nutley, N.J.: Presbyterian and Reformed, 1974. Pp. 26-38.

* Stanley N. Gundry and Alan F. Johnson, eds. *Tensions in Contemporary Theology.* Chicago: Moody, 1976. Pp. 46-56.

* Robert D. Knudsen. "Rudolf Bultmann." In Philip Edgcumbe Hughes, ed., *Creative Minds in Contemporary Theology*, rev. ed. Grand Rapids: Eerdmans, 1969. Pp. 131-62.

* Robert L. Reymond. *Bultmann's Demythologized Kerygma.* Philadelphia: Presbyterian and Reformed, 1967.

** Robert C. Roberts. *Rudolf Bultmann's Theology: A Critical Interpretation.* Grand Rapids: Eerdmans, 1976.

* _____. "Bultmann, Rudolf." In Walter A. Elwell, ed., *Evangelical Dictionary of Theology.* Grand Rapids: Baker, 1984. P. 180. See also articles under "Demythologization," "Existentialism," and "New Hermeneutic."

WORLDLY CHRISTIANITY

** Dietrich Bonhoeffer. *Letters and Papers from Prison.* New York: Macmillan, 1971.

** _____. *No Rusty Swords.* New York: Harper, 1965.

* C. J. Curtis. *Contemporary Protestant Thought.* New York: Bruce, 1970. Pp. 21-50.

** Andre Dumas. *Dietrich Bonhoeffer Theologian of Reality.* New York: Macmillan, 1971.

* Warren F. Groff and Donald E. Miller. *The Shaping of Modern Christian Thought.* Cleveland: World, 1968. Pp. 276-88.

* Stanley N. Gundry and Alan F. Johnson, eds. *Tensions in Contemporary Theology.* Chicago: Moody, 1976. Pp. 66-81, 170-74.

* William E. Hordern. *A Layman's Guide to Protestant Theology*, rev. ed. London: Macmillan, 1968. Pp. 210-29.

** Philip Edgcumbe Hughes, ed. *Creative Minds in Contemporary Theology*, rev. ed. Grand Rapids: Eerdmans, 1969. Pp. 479-515.

* R. Zerner. "Bonhoeffer, Dietrich." In Walter A. Elwell, ed., *Evangelical Dictionary of Theology.* Grand Rapids: Baker, 1984. Pp. 168-69.

GOD-IS-DEAD THEOLOGY

** Thomas Altizer and William Hamilton, eds. *Radical Theology and the Death of God.* Indianapolis: Bobbs-Merrill, 1966.

* Henlee H. Barnette. *The New Theology and Morality.* Philadelphia: Westminster, 1967. Pp. 9-30.

* Harvie M. Conn. *Contemporary World Theology.* Nutley, N.J.: Presbyterian and Reformed, 1974. Pp. 46-52.

* C. J. Curtis. *Contemporary Protestant Thought.* New York: Bruce, 1970. Pp. 85-96.

* Stanley N. Gundry. "Death of God Theology." In Walter A. Elwell, ed. *Evangelical Dictionary of Theology.* Grand Rapids: Baker, 1984. Pp. 301-2.

* William E. Hordern. *A Layman's Guide to Protestant Theology*, rev. ed.. London: Macmillan, 1968. Pp. 235-47.

* Harold B. Kuhn. "Secular Theology." In *Tensions in Contemporary Theology*, edited by Stanley N. Gundry and Alan F. Johnson. Chicago: Moody, 1976. Pp. 161-70.

** Paul M. Van Buren. *The Secular Meaning of the Gospel.* London: SCM, 1963.

* James M. Wall, ed. *Theologians in Transition.* New York: Crossroad, 1981. Pp. 67-73, 151-60.

PROCESS THEOLOGY

* James E. Caraway. *God as Dynamic Actuality: A Preliminary Study of the Process Theologies of John B. Cobb, Jr., and Schubert M. Ogden.* Washington: U. Press of America, 1978.

* Harvie M. Conn. *Contemporary World Theology*, rev. ed. Nutley, N.J.: Presbyterian and Reformed, 1974. Pp. 81-86.

** C. J. Curtis. *Contemporary Protestant Thought.* New York: Bruce, 1970. Pp. 51-84.

* D. W. Diehl. "Process Theology." In Walter A. Elwell, ed., *Evangelical Dictionary of Theology.* Grand Rapids: Baker, 1984. Pp. 880-85.

** Norman L. Geisler. "Process Theology." In *Tensions in Contemporary Theology*, edited by Stanley N. Gundry and Alan F. Johnson. Chicago: Moody, 1976. Pp. 237-84.

** Charles Hartshorne. *A Natural Theology for Our Time.* LaSalle, Ill.: Open Court, 1967.

* Alasdair I. C. Heron. *A Century of Protestant Theology.* Philadelphia: Westminster, 1980. Pp. 144-50.

** William Robert Miller. *Contemporary American Protestant Thought, 1900-1970.* Indianapolis: Bobbs-Merrill, 1973. Pp. 309-33, 450-68.

** Stanley T. Sutphin. *Options in Contemporary Theology.* Washington: U. Press of America, 1977. Pp. 69-102.

** Alfred North Whitehead. *Religion in the Making.* New York: Macmillan, 1926.

42

HISTORICIST THEOLOGIES

Two contemporary theologies emphasize the importance of biblical history as the revelation of God.

SALVATION HISTORY: OSCAR CULLMANN

HISTORICAL DEVELOPMENT OF CULLMANN'S THEOLOGY

Oscar Cullmann (b. 1902) is identified with the term *Heilsgeschichte*, meaning "salvation history" or "holy history." J. C. K. von Hofmann initiated usage of the term, and Cullmann further developed its usage.[1] *Heilsgeschichte* views the historical events of God's saving acts in history rather than focusing on a philosophy of religion. Salvation history does, however, acknowledge the critical approach to Scripture as advocated by older liberals and more recently, neo-orthodox writers. Although salvation history proponents view the Bible as the record of God's saving acts in history, they do not acknowledge the infallibility of the Bible, nor do they develop a systematized theology from the Bible. The importance of Scripture is that it is a record of God's dealings in history. In borrowing from neo-orthodoxy, salvation history proponents emphasize that the benefits of God's saving acts are personally appropriated by faith in Christ.

Oscar Cullmann studied at the University of Strasbourg, where he later taught Greek and ancient church history. Being invited to the University of Basel, he served as professor of church history and New Testament, enhancing the scholarship and reputation of the prestigious school. There he was also influenced by Karl Barth in his Christological approach to the New Testament. Cullmann's more conservative stance is seen in his opposition to some of the radical features of Rudolf Bultmann's form criticism and demythologization. Cullmann also was less dependent upon existentialism and emphasized exegesis to a greater extent.[2]

DOCTRINAL AFFIRMATIONS OF CULLMANN'S THEOLOGY

The main features of salvation history can be summarized as follows.[3] Great emphasis is placed on God's revealing Himself in the events of history. Cullmann rejected Bultmann's idea of church-enshrouded myths; the events of Scripture are historical, occurring in time, according to Cullmann. Scripture itself, however, is not infallible; it is only the vehicle explaining God's events of holy history. The important element is "holy history," not the words of Scripture. The culmination of salvation history is the coming of Jesus as the Messiah. The eschatological age has begun with the incarnation of Christ, but its completion is still future.[4] Eschatology is redefined by Cullmann. All New Testament events and the events of church history are defined as eschatological.[5] In concert with neo-orthodoxy, salvation history adherents insist on the necessity of a subjective encounter for a knowledge of the meaning of the revelation.[6]

SUMMARY EVALUATION OF CULLMANN'S THEOLOGY

There are a number of things that are commendable about Oscar Cullmann's approach. His emphasis on the historicity of the events of Scripture is crucial to the Christian message. Cullmann affirms that "one can assuredly possess authentic Christian faith only if one believes the historical fact that Jesus regarded himself as Messiah"[7]—a central truth to Christianity. Cullmann also stresses the centrality and historicity of Jesus Christ.[8] Nonetheless, he accepts as historical only those accounts that are verifiable. Other stories, such as the Adam story and events of eschatology, he identifies as myth.[9] In this Cullmann continues to follow the Bultmannian method of form criticism, dissecting the Scriptures as he sees fit. The salvation history school also follows Barth in identifying revelation as a subjective experience. Salvation history makes the spiritual encounter the focal point of revelation.[10]

THEOLOGY OF RESURRECTION: WOLFHART PANNENBERG

HISTORICAL DEVELOPMENT OF PANNENBERG'S THEOLOGY

Wolfhart Pannenberg (b. 1928), professor of systematic theology at the University of Munich, represents a break with the past and a new emphasis in German theology. In his attempt to divorce himself from Rudolf Bultmann's existential emphasis, Pannenberg has rooted his theology in history, particularly the resurrection of Jesus Christ, which he regards as central to Christianity. For this reason, Pannenberg's theology may be termed the "theology of history" or "theology of resurrection."

DOCTRINAL AFFIRMATIONS OF PANNENBERG'S THEOLOGY

Pannenberg emphasizes the necessity of the historicity of events of Scripture for a valid faith. In this he rejects Karl Barth's dichotomy between *historie* and *geschichte*. It is impossible to proclaim the gospel without having it rooted in history. Pannenberg understands all history to be revelation. Revelation comes through the events of history on a horizontal level, not on a vertical level from God. Thus Pannenberg investigates the life of Christ from a historical perspective and not in terms of direct revelation from God.[11] Revelation through history comes from all events of history, not just from Scripture or from God. No distinction is made between natural or special revelation. Revelation through history can be understood by anyone who comes to it by faith. Spiritual blindness does not enter into the question; thus, Pannenberg ignores the question of original sin.[12] The climax of revelation is in the past—the resurrection of Christ. In contrast with Bultmann, Pannenberg does not understand the resurrection as myth but as a historical event.[13]

SUMMARY EVALUATION OF PANNENBERG'S THEOLOGY

Although Wolfhart Pannenberg has emphasized the necessity of the historicity of the resurrection of Christ, defects in his theology may be noted.[14] Pannenberg does not identify man in his fallen estate in need of divine grace, but rather he understands natural man as capable of understanding revelation in history. In this assessment, Pannenberg rejects Barth's claim that "the truth of Christianity enters into the hearts of Christians only by a miracle of grace."[15] Pannenberg does not identify the Bible with revelation. He follows the theses of historical criticism by suggesting the virgin birth of Christ is a myth. Pannenberg ascribes error to the Bible, suggesting there are inaccuracies in the resurrection accounts. He suggests Jesus was in error regarding His resurrection, thinking it "would coincide with the end of the world and the general resurrection of all believers."[16] Pannenberg makes history the authority rather than Scripture, and the individual must submit to the interpreter of history rather than to the Scriptures.

Despite Pannenberg's emphasis on history, he has not followed historic orthodoxy because he rejects the Bible as God's revelation to mankind. He has, in fact, substituted history for the Bible as his authority.

NOTES ON HISTORICIST THEOLOGIES

1. See Bernard Ramm, *A Handbook of Contemporary Theology* (Grand Rapids: Eerdmans, 1966), pp. 55-56, for a concise discussion of the term. Another source is Van A. Harvey, *A Handbook of Theological Terms* (New York: Macmillan, 1964), pp. 113-14.
2. Harvie M. Conn, *Contemporary World Theology*, rev. ed. (Nutley, N.J.: Presbyterian and Reformed, 1974), p. 40.
3. Ibid., pp. 41-42.
4. David H. Wallace, "Oscar Cullmann," in Philip Edgcumbe Hughes, ed., *Creative Minds in Contemporary Theology*, rev. ed. (Grand Rapids: Eerdmans, 1969), p. 169.
5. Ibid.
6. Carl F. H. Henry, *Frontiers in Modern Theology* (Chicago: Moody, 1965), p. 46.
7. Ibid., p. 51.
8. Oscar Cullmann, *The Christology of the New Testament*, rev. ed. (Philadelphia: Westminster, 1963).
9. Henry, *Frontiers in Modern Theology*, pp. 51-52.
10. Ibid., p. 46.
11. David P. Scaer, "Theology of Hope," in *Tensions in Contemporary Theology*, edited by Stanley N. Gundry and Alan F. Johnson (Chicago: Moody, 1976), p. 219.
12. Ibid.
13. Wolfhart Pannenberg, *Faith and Reality* (Philadelphia: Westminster, 1977), pp. 68-77.
14. Conn, *Contemporary World Theology*, rev. ed., pp. 70-72.
15. Henry, *Frontiers in Modern Theology*, p. 74.
16. Conn, *Contemporary World Theology*, rev. ed., p. 71.

FOR FURTHER STUDY ON HISTORICIST THEOLOGIES

SALVATION HISTORY

* Harvie M. Conn. *Contemporary World Theology*, rev. ed. Nutley, N.J.: Presbyterian and Reformed, 1974. Pp. 39-45.
** Oscar Cullmann. *Christ and Time.* Philadelphia: Westminster, 1951.
** _____. *The Christology of the New Testament.* Philadelphia: Westminster, 1959.
* Carl F. H. Henry. *Frontiers in Modern Theology.* Chicago: Moody, 1965.
** I. Howard Marshall. *The Origins of New Testament Christology.* Downers Grove, Ill.: InterVarsity, 1977.
* Bernard Ramm. *A Handbook of Contemporary Theology.* Grand Rapids: Eerdmans, 1966. Pp. 55-56.
* David H. Wallace. "Oscar Cullmann." In Philip Edgcumbe Hughes, ed., *Creative Minds in Contemporary Theology*, rev. ed. Grand Rapids: Eerdmans, 1969. Pp. 163-202.

THEOLOGY OF RESURRECTION

* G. C. Berkouwer. *A Half Century of Theology*. Grand Rapids: Eerdmans, 1977. Pp. 159-78.

* Harvie M. Conn. *Contemporary World Theology*, rev. ed. Nutley, N.J.: Presbyterian and Reformed, 1974. Pp. 66-72.

** Allan D. Galloway. *Wolfhart Pannenberg*. London: Allen and Unwin, 1973.

* Stanley N. Gundry and Alan F. Johnson, eds. *Tensions in Contemporary Theology*. Chicago: Moody, 1976. Pp. 219-25.

* Carl F. H. Henry. *Frontiers in Modern Theology*. Chicago: Moody, 1965.

** Wolfhart Pannenberg. *Basic Questions in Theology*. Philadelphia: Fortress, 1970-73. Vols. 1-3.

** _____. *Faith and Reality*. Philadelphia: Westminster, 1977.

* Klaas Runia. *The Present-Day Christological Debate*. Downers Grove, Ill.: InterVarsity, 1984. Pp. 33-38.

43

SOCIALIST THEOLOGIES

There are at least two recent theological viewpoints that emphasize what some view as revolutionary social aspects of the Christian faith.

THEOLOGY OF HOPE: JÜRGEN MOLTMANN

HISTORICAL DEVELOPMENT OF MOLTMANN'S THEOLOGY

Jürgen Moltmann (b. 1926) came to prominence in the 1960s. At the University of Tübingen, Moltmann met the Marxist philosopher, Ernst Bloch, who influenced him to a great extent in the development of his theology. During those years there was a Christian-Marxist dialogue at Tübingen that affected the thinking of some of the young men. It was out of this interaction with Marxist philosophy that Moltmann wrote his *Theology of Hope*, published in the United States in 1967. The book was the result of a biblical study that focused on the Christian's hope of the future. These theses were further clarified in *Religion, Revolution, and the Future* in 1969.

"For Moltmann, the hermeneutical principle is eschatology, and hope is the major theme of the Bible."[1] But Moltmann understands the church as shaping the future and providing hope through social interaction, particularly on behalf of the poor in society.

DOCTRINAL AFFIRMATIONS OF MOLTMANN'S THEOLOGY

Moltmann's theology may be summarized as follows.[2] God is part of the process of time, moving toward the future. Hence, God is not absolute, but He is on the way to the future, where His promises will be fulfilled. Future is the essential nature of God. The resurrection of Jesus Christ as a historical event is unimportant. The importance of Christ's resurrection is eschatological and should be viewed from the future because it gives a hope of a general resurrection in the future. Instead of looking from the empty tomb to the future, Moltmann suggests looking to the future—that legitimizes the resurrection of Christ. Man also is to be viewed from the standpoint of the future. "Man can be understood only with reference to a restless, constantly unfolding history in relation to the future of God."[3] The solution is for man to associate himself with God "who discloses Himself wherever humanity is despised and brutalized. Moltmann calls this the theology of the cross. Man shares in this theology of the cross by accepting life's challenges as future moments breaking into the present."[4] Man must actively participate in society to effect change. "Race, class, status, and national churches" must be eliminated.[5] The church has the ability to shape the future and must preach to effect that change in society.[6] The church must look beyond "personal" salvation and challenge all barriers and structures between different people.[7] The church is God's instrument to bring out that change and reconciliation between rich and poor, between races and artificial structures. Revolution can be one of the means the churches use to effect change.

SUMMARY EVALUATION OF MOLTMANN'S THEOLOGY

Jürgen Moltmann, by his emphasis on the future, denies the normal understanding of history. He rejects the significance of the historicity of Christ's resurrection. In aligning history with eschatology he denies the true meaning of history and historical events. In his concept of God, Moltmann denies the immutability of God (Mal. 3:6) and suggests God is not absolute but "moving to the future."

In his concept of effecting change in society, Moltmann's influence from Marxism and the "Christian-Marxism" of Ernst Bloch is evident. Much of liberation theology undoubtedly has its roots in Moltmann's theology of revolution and social change. Such change is not achieved through individual salvation but through the church confronting society concerning injustices.

Moltmann's hope for the future is also tied to optimistic humanism as well as the philosophy of Hegel, in which he sees the past (thesis) as chaos, the future (antithesis) as hope, necessitating the present (synthesis) work to effect change. In summary, Moltmann is more indebted to Karl Marx for his theology than to the teachings of Scripture

LIBERATION THEOLOGY: FIVE VIEWPOINTS

HISTORICAL DEVELOPMENT OF LIBERATION THEOLOGY[8]

Liberation theology is a theological movement that has attempted to unite theology with the social/economic concerns of the poor and oppressed people, particularly in Central and South America. The movement, however, is even broader in scope, including blacks (which may be separately called "black theology"), feminists (which may be separately called "feminist theology"), and others.

There are four factors that have contributed to the rise of liberation theology. (1) The movement has borrowed from the philosophical theses of Immanuel Kant (who emphasized the priority of human reason apart from divine revelation), Georg W. F. Hegel (who saw the transformation of society through thesis-antithesis-synthesis), and particularly Karl Marx (through overcoming class distinctions and barriers). Although Roman Catholicism is strong in many of the Latin American countries, nonetheless the people have been severely oppressed, making them open to Marxist-socialist ideology.

(2) The movement has also been influenced by Jürgen Moltmann's theology of hope, which advocates revolution as one means to achieve hope for the future. Moltmann has himself built his theological views on Karl Marx.

(3) The movement is principally Roman Catholic in Latin America. Following the Second Vatican Council, with its liberalizing trends and greater freedom afforded the people, many priests turned to liberation theology as the solution to Latin American problems.

(4) The movement has been principally Latin American because those people have been oppressed through wealthy landowners and dictators; the dichotomy between rich and poor has been enormous. Theologians relate the oppression of the people to the beginning days of the colonization of South America.[9]

It should be noted that within the scope of liberation theology there are some that genuinely attempt to link Christian theology with a socialist, political endeavor; others, however, disavow Christian theology. For them it is entirely a political movement. In a brief summarization it is impossible to distinguish and discuss the various theologians and their viewpoints. The discussion must remain general. The reader is referred to additional sources for further research regarding specific theologians with their particular emphases.

The following are representative liberation theologians. The listing is by no means exhaustive; however, the message, in many instances, is similar. Although some theologians give a certain credence to the Scriptures, the emphasis of liberation theology usually has political overtones that calls for rescuing the oppressed people from their physical deprivation.

DOCTRINAL AFFIRMATIONS OF LIBERATION THEOLOGY

Theology of James H. Cone. James H. Cone (b. 1938), professor of theology at Union Theological Seminary in New York City, is perhaps the leading exponent of black liberation theology. He has written *A Black Theology of Liberation* in which he identifies Christian theology with liberation theology, defining it as "a rational study of the being of God in the world in light of the existential situation of an oppressed community, relating the forces of liberation to the essence of the gospel, which is Jesus Christ."[10] Cone identifies liberation with the gospel of Christ; the gospel is helping the oppressed. Biblically, Cone bases his theology of liberation on God's deliverance of Israel from oppression and what He did within the community of the oppressed within Israel.[11] Cone concludes, "The consistent theme in Israelite prophecy is Yahweh's concern for the lack of social, economic, and political justice for those who are poor and unwanted in the society. Yahweh, according to Hebrew prophecy, will not tolerate injustice against the poor; through his activity the poor will be vindicated. Again, God reveals himself as the God of liberation for the oppressed."[12] According to Cone, Jesus did not come to bring spiritual liberation but to liberate the oppressed.[13] The resurrection of Christ means "that all oppressed peoples become his people. . . . The resurrection-event means that God's liberating work is not only for the house of Israel but for all who are enslaved by principalities and powers. . . . It is hope which focuses on the future in order to make men refuse to tolerate present inequities . . . to see also the contradiction of any earthly injustice."[14]

Theology of Gustavo Gutierrez. Gustavo Gutierrez (b. 1928), professor of theology in Lima, Peru, has written *A Theology of Liberation: History, Politics and Salvation* that has been called the Magna Carta of liberation theology.[15] In his approach to theology, Gutierrez does not see theology as a systematization of timeless truths, but in concert with others, "Theology is a dynamic, ongoing exercise involving contemporary insights into knowledge, man, and history. . . . It means the discovery and the formation of theological truth out of a given historical situation through personal participation in the Latin American class struggle for a new socialist society."[16] Gutierrez claims liberation theology is "based on the Gospel and experiences of men and women committed to the process of liberation in the oppressed and exploited land of Latin America. It is a theological reflection born of the experience of shared efforts to abolish the current unjust situation and to build a different society, freer and more human."[17] The way that this is accomplished is through the participation of the individual in fighting the oppressors. Christ is seen as God's gift for liberating them.

Theology of Jose Miguez Bonino. Jose Miguez Bonino, a Methodist professor of theology in Buenos Aires, Argentina, has written *Doing Theology in a Revolutionary Situation* in which he supports Marxist socialism as the proper way to transform the world. "Class struggle is a fact of life and Christians are called to participate in this struggle by identifying with the oppressed."[18]

Interestingly, Miguez Bonino has criticized both the right and left in the theological spectrum, aligning himself in a central position. He has criticized the fundamentalists for their lack of social involvement, and he has criticized the liberals for their neglect of the message of faith and conversion.[19] Miguez Bonino draws three conclusions:[20] (1) Christians are responsible for their governments and therefore must work to create conditions where people will be more receptive to the gospel. This involves removing the barriers that create misery and oppression. (2) The church must serve the world through love, which means participating in the world's problems. (3) The church must participate in the "work of Christ" by creating "peace and order, justice and liberty, dignity and community."

Theology of Juan Luis Segundo. Juan Luis Segundo (b. 1925), a Uruguayan Jesuit priest, is a prolific writer who basically follows the theology of Pierre Teilhard de Chardin. In *The Liberation of Theology* he indicates Christians have committed themselves to a radical reinterpretation of their faith, not only as individuals, but within the structure of the church. In following Teilhard, he suggests theology is not to be viewed as an academic subject but in a revolutionary spirit that endeavors to change the world. He states: "There is no such thing as Christian theology or a Christian interpretation of the gospel message in the absence of a prior political commitment. Only the latter makes the former possible at all."[21] This work also outlines Segundo's hermeneutical methodology, which is constantly dictated, he suggests, by changes in society, necessitating constant change in the way one interprets the Bible. In fact, one should view with suspicion the prevailing interpretation of the Bible. One's ideology becomes crucial in interpretation; one cannot interpret the Bible without first having an ideological commitment.[22] "Here he sees a strong similarity between a faith, such as Christianity, and an ideology, such as Marxism."[23]

Theology of Jose Portirio Miranda.[24] Jose Portirio Miranda, an ex-Jesuit priest, has written a volatile book entitled *Marx and the Bible: A Critique of the Philosophy of Oppression.* Although Miranda has made his research an independent study of other liberation theologians, even reflecting independence of Jürgen Moltmann, his conclusions are much the same. Miranda seeks for "Christian social action" among the poor of Mexico. Following a study of Karl Marx's writings he concludes: "The essential meaning of the Bible's message has been eluding us Christians and our organizations. The Bible, especially Exodus and the prophets, is the revelation of the Transcendent God, the Liberator of the oppressed who fights against the oppressors in their behalf."[25] This is in basic agreement with other liberation theologians who use the Exodus account as a biblical basis for resistance against the prevailing government. Miranda also sees the central thesis of the Bible as social justice, the salvation of the poor. The only thing God wants is justice between people. In his study of Marx, Miranda finds a relationship between Karl Marx and the apostle Paul: "Both believe that man can cease being selfish, merciless, and self-serving and can find his greatest fullness in loving his neighbor."[26] One critic has suggested Miranda has made "Marx nothing less than a prophet beholden to biblical tradition."[27]

SUMMARY EVALUATION OF LIBERATION THEOLOGY

The evaluation of liberation theology is a *general* one; it is clear there are diverse voices in the movement, some further to the left, others that are more moderate. Conservative Christians have serious reservations about liberation theology for the following reasons.

(1) Liberation theologians give secondary meaning to the ordinary meaning of the Scriptures. James Cone, for example, suggests the resurrection of Christ means the liberation of all people, relating it to physical deliverance from oppression. The historic significance of the resurrection as release from sin is ignored (cf. 1 Cor. 15).

(2) The matter of man's sinfulness, and his need of a spiritual Savior to atone for sin is ignored in liberation theology. Liberation from sin is ignored; liberation is normally seen as essentially political. In fact, liberation theologians view themselves as liberating their unjust oppressors from sin by overthrowing them. The greatest sin is not the violation of God's standard but social injustice.

(3) Hope for liberation theologians is not based on the biblical concept of eternal life through Jesus Christ, but hope is related to Jürgen Moltmann's view of realizing the future hope in the present through helping to shape the future (often through revolutionary means).

(4) For liberation theologians like Gustavo Gutierrez theology is not the objective revelation of God given in propositional truths (as it has been historically understood), but theology is in flux, changing, and related to the changing of society. It is a "Christian coating" of Marxist socialism.

(5) Liberation theology stands in violation of the injunction of Scripture concerning submission to government as outlined in Romans 13.

(6) The interpretive methodology of liberation might seriously be called into question, as in the case of Juan Luis Segundo who does not begin with an inductive study of the Scriptures (allowing them to speak for themselves), but allows his political ideology to interpret the Scriptures.

(7) It is a false assumption of liberation theology, as Peter Wagner points out, to suggest that people will respond more readily to the gospel if they enjoy a more affluent environment.[28] Jose Porfirio Miranda relates Karl Marx to the apostle Paul, suggesting Marxist principles will lead people to love one another—all without the acknowledgment of sin and salvation through Christ.

In summation, liberation theology does not approach the concepts of God, Christ, man, sin, and salvation from an orthodox, biblical viewpoint, but reinterprets them in a political context.

NOTES ON SOCIALIST THEOLOGIES

1. David P. Scaer, "Theology of Hope" in *Tensions in Contemporary Theology*, edited by Stanley N. Gundry and Alan F. Johnson (Chicago: Moody, 1976), p. 210.
2. For a summary of Moltmann's theology see Scaer, "Theology of Hope" pp. 212-18; and Harvie M. Conn, *Contemporary World Theology* (Nutley, N.J.: Presbyterian and Reformed, 1973), pp. 59-65.
3. Scaer, "Theology of Hope" in *Tensions in Contemporary Theology*, p. 212.
4. Ibid., p. 213.
5. Jürgen Moltmann, *The Experiment Hope* (Philadelphia: Fortress, 1975), p. 117.
6. Conn, *Contemporary World Theology*, p. 62.
7. S. M. Smith, "Hope, Theology of" in Walter A. Elwell, ed., *Evangelical Dictionary of Theology*, (Grand Rapids: Baker, 1984), p. 533.
8. For helpful summaries see D. D. Webster, "Liberation Theology" pp. 635-38; and V. Cruz, "Black Theology" in *Evangelical Dictionary of Theology*, pp. 158-61. Also see Harvie M Conn, "Theologies of Liberation: An Overview" and "Theologies of Liberation: Toward a Common View" in *Tensions in Contemporary Theology*, expanded edition, 1979, pp. 327-434.
9. Dean William Ferm, *Contemporary American Theologies* (New York: Seabury, 1981), p. 59.
10. James H. Cone, *A Black Theology of Liberation* (Philadelphia: Lippincott, 1970), pp. 17-18.
11. Ibid., p. 18.
12. Ibid., p. 19.
13. Ibid., pp. 19-20.
14. Ibid., p. 21.
15. Ferm, *Contemporary American Theologies*, p. 64.
16. Webster, "Liberation Theology" in *Evangelical Dictionary of Theology*, p. 635.
17. Gustavo Gutierrez, *A Theology of Liberation* (Maryknoll, N.Y.: Orbis, 1971), p. ix.
18. Ferm, *Contemporary American Theologies*, p. 68.
19. C. Peter Wagner, *Latin American Theology* (Grand Rapids: Eerdmans, 1970), pp. 27-28.
20. Ibid., pp. 28-30.
21. Juan Luis Segundo, *Liberation of Theology* (Maryknoll, N.Y.: Orbis, 1976), p. 94.
22. Harvie M. Conn, "Theologies of Liberation: An Overview" in *Tensions in Contemporary Theology*, p. 367.
23. Ibid.
24. Ibid., pp. 364-66.

25. Ibid., pp. 364-65.

26. Ibid., p. 365.

27. Ibid., p. 366.

28. Peter Wagner, *Latin American Theology*, p. 29.

FOR FURTHER STUDY ON SOCIALIST THEOLOGIES

THEOLOGY OF HOPE

* Harvie M. Conn. *Contemporary World Theology*, rev. ed. Nutley, N.J.: Presbyterian and Reformed, 1974. Pp. 59-65.

* Stanley N. Gundry and Alan F. Johnson, eds. *Tensions in Contemporary Theology*. Chicago: Moody, 1976. Pp. 209-18.

** Jürgen Moltmann. *Experiences of God.* Philadelphia: Fortress, 1980.

** _____. *Religion, Revolution and the Future.* New York: Scribner's, 1969.

** _____. *The Theology of Hope.* New York: Harper, 1967.

* _____. "Toward a Political Hermeneutics of the Gospel." In *New Theology*, no. 6, edited by Martin E. Marty and Dean G. Peerman. New York: Macmillan, 1969. Pp. 66-90.

* S. M. Smith. "Hope, Theology of." In Walter A. Elwell, ed., *Evangelical Dictionary of Theology.* Grand Rapids: Baker, 1984. Pp. 532-34.

LIBERATION THEOLOGY

* Carl E. Armerding, ed. *Evangelicals and Liberation.* Nutley, N.J.: Presbyterian and Reformed, 1977.

** Calvin E. Bruce and William R. Jones, eds. *Black Theology II.* Cranbury, N.J.: Associated U., 1978.

* Harvie M. Conn. "Theologies of Liberation: An Overview" and "Theologies of Liberation." In *Tensions in Contemporary Theology*, edited by Stanley N. Gundry and Alan F. Johnson. Chicago: Moody, 1976. Pp. 327-434. These are two excellent articles giving the history and philosophy of the movement.

** James M. Cone. *A Black Theology of Liberation.* Philadelphia: Lippincott, 1970.

** Dean William Ferm. *Contemporary American Theologies: A Critical Survey.* New York: Seabury, 1981. This work deals with black, South American, and feminist theological perspectives.

** Gustavo Gutierrez. *A Theology of Liberation.* Maryknoll, N.Y.: Orbis, 1971.

** Jose Miguez-Bonino. *Christians and Marxists: The Mutual Challenge to Revolution.* Grand Rapids: Eerdmans, 1976.

* Emilio A. Núñez. *Liberation Theology.* Chicago: Moody, 1985.

* C. Peter Wagner. *Latin American Theology: Radical or Evangelical?* Grand Rapids: Eerdmans, 1970.

* D. D. Webster. "Liberation Theology." In Walter A. Elwell, ed., *Evangelical Dictionary of Theology.* Grand Rapids: Baker, 1984. Pp. 635-38.

44

CATHOLIC THEOLOGY

HISTORICAL DEVELOPMENT OF CONTEMPORARY CATHOLICISM

Contemporary Roman Catholicism must be evaluated from the standpoint of the Second Vatican Council, convened in 1962 by Pope John XXIII, and concluded in 1965 by Pope Paul VI.[1] Prior to the council there were changes in the offing, but those changes did not crystalize until the council. One question that struck at the heart of Roman Catholicism involved the authority of the church. Men like Hans Küng, Edward Schillebeeckx, and more recently Charles Curran, have dissented from the traditional teaching that Rome is infallible in its *ex cathedra* pronouncements. This reaction is not entirely new, however. In the nineteenth century Roman Catholics began calling for the separation of church and state but were severely chastized by Pope Pius IX. Early in the twentieth century Alfred Loisy contradicted Rome in his position on inspiration and was relieved of his teaching post. Although Pope Pius X attacked Catholic liberals and dissidents in an encyclical in 1910, the tide could not be stopped. Undoubtedly, these earlier developments paved the way for the Second Vatican Council, which sought to modernize the Catholic faith and bring it in step with the twentieth century.

One negative effect of Vatican II can be seen in Archbishop Marcel Lefebvre's denunciation of Vatican II, which said antichrists had taken over the Vatican. While having abandoned the Catholic church, Lefebvre continues to ordain bishops and hold to the old Catholic traditions as the true Catholic faith. It appears some traditional-minded Roman Catholics have also been affected. A survey reported that 1963 church attendance was seventy-one percent, whereas in 1974 it was down to fifty percent. In the same period, those not going to church at all had doubled.[2]

DOCTRINAL AFFIRMATIONS OF CONTEMPORARY CATHOLICISM

BY RADICAL THEOLOGIANS

Hans Küng. Undoubtedly, the Tübingen professor Hans Küng (b. 1928) has been one of the most influential and outspoken critics of Rome. He has sought for further changes than those forthcoming at Vatican II. He has suggested, for example, that there is little distinction between the Catholic and Calvinist view of justification. In 1968 he published *Apostolic Succession* in which he suggests prophets, teachers, and other gifted individuals can claim succession just as well as apostles. Further questioning concerning papal authority in *Infallible?* led to Küng's removal as an official Catholic teacher. In actuality, Küng has not only departed from historic Catholicism, but he has aligned himself with much of modern liberalism. He has, for instance, abandoned a belief in the infallibility of the Scriptures, suggesting some of the stories are unreliable, thereby following historical criticism. His view of Christ abandons any form of orthodoxy: he suggests Jesus did not assume any titles of Messiahship, but that these were later attributed to him by the church. The title "Son of God" had nothing to do with the nature of Jesus' person.[3]

Karl Rahner.[4] German-born Karl Rahner (1904-1984) has been a prominent Catholic theologian, particularly regarding Vatican II. He has taught at Innsbruck and Münster. In his theology, Rahner develops a transcendental Thomism (Thomism refers to the theological and philosophical system of Thomas Aquinas); as a result, he concludes that because the absolute being of God stands behind all human knowledge, a human being is by nature of his intellect predisposed to the knowledge of God.[5]

Rahner develops this anthropocentric theology, which states that God has given every man the potential to receive divine grace, the "supernatural existential." It is a human characteristic to be able to hear God. This includes atheists and people of other religions. The implication of this is that man may relate to God internally, not externally through the church, eliminating the necessity of being connected to the church. For Rahner, Christ fulfills human potentiality in His obedience. Rahner perceives Christ as the pinnacle of human evolution.[6]

Edward Schillebeeckx. Edward Schillebeeckx (b. 1919) has been a Dutch Roman Catholic theologian who has provided some consternation for the Roman church through his deviations from prescribed Catholic doctrine. In the matter of revelation, Schillebeeckx emphasizes that revelation is not only in word but also in reality.[7] In the Eucharist for example, by the act of partaking, the participant comes into contact with the revelation-in-word as well as the revelation-in-reality. The reality of partaking is possible only through the illumination of the Holy Spirit, the "light of faith." Thus the development of doctrine has its final meaning in the inner witness of the Holy Spirit.

Schillebeeckx has also done extensive study concerning the historical Jesus. In employing historical critical methodology, he has, in his conclusions, particularly emphasized a human Jesus. Jesus' ministry was carried out by His unique relationship to God. Although he has suggested a trinitarian view, it is doubtful that Schillebeeckx holds to the historic, orthodox view of Christ and the Trinity.[8]

BY VATICAN COUNCIL II

Vatican II,[9] also termed the Twenty-first Ecumenical Church Council, was convened by Pope John XXIII in October 1962, and reconvened for several separate sessions by Pope Paul VI from September 1963 until its conclusion in 1965.

The council was called to meet the impact of the technological age and its emphasis on materialism and weakened spiritual values. The Roman Catholic church sought to renew itself and to minister mercy to the suffering and poor in a world with its inequitable distribution of wealth. The church sought unity among Christians, reaching out to Protestants and Eastern Orthodox Christians. Vatican II also sought a biblical emphasis in its decisions, rather than abstract theological affirmations.

Revelation. Vatican II sought to resolve the long standing tension between the authority of the Scriptures and the authority of tradition. In its statement on divine revelation, Vatican II affirmed that both Scripture and tradition were the revelation of God and could not therefore be contradictory, especially because both were given by the Holy Spirit. Together, Scripture and tradition form "one sacred deposit of the Word of God." To ensure reconcilation of the two, interpretation should concentrate on the revelation that both the Scriptures and tradition give.

Vatican II emphasized that revelation is not merely a set of doctrines, but revelation is in a Person. Neo-orthodox theologian Søren Kierkegaard appears to have influenced Vatican II theologians on this point.

Inerrancy. On the issue of inerrancy the Second Vatican Council affirmed, "The books of Scripture must be acknowledged as teaching firmly, faithfully, and without error that truth which God wanted put into the sacred writings for the sake of our salvation."[10] In this definition the new Catholic emphasis aligns itself with liberal Protestantism in allowing for "error in the Bible where this does not affect its essential message" or for "incidental misstatements."[11]

Ecumenism. Through the Decree on Ecumenism, Vatican II reached out to non-Catholic Christians with the hope that "there may be one visible church of God, a Church truly universal and sent forth to the whole world."[12]

No longer calling for a return to the Roman Catholic church as the true church, Vatican II recognized non-Catholics as legitimate Christian communities. Non-Catholic Christians were now referred to as "separated brethren," and Vatican II allowed for Catholics to engage in public worship together with Protestants.

Vatican II indicated that both Protestants and Catholics alike were responsible for the division at the Reformation. With conciliatory language the council sought for unity with non-Catholics. This was further encouraged by the appointment of a permanent Secretariat for Promoting Christian Unity.

Papacy. Vatican I (1869-1870) had decreed that the pope was infallible when speaking *ex cathedra*, that is, with the authority of his office as pastor of all Christians, according to the authority given him as a successor of the apostle Peter. Vatican II reaffirmed this doctrine but modified the absolutism of the papacy by giving authority to the bishops under the auspices of the pope. Under the principle of collegiality, the bishops were affirmed in their authority, together with the pope, as a college of bishops over the church. This action, with its shared authority, mollified some elements in the church.

Mary. Vatican II sought to emphasize Mary as a "fellow member of the Church and not as some kind of semidivine being exalted above the Church."[13] Nonetheless, Mary is to be venerated above all the saints because of her sublime dignity as the mother of God and mother of the church. Vatican II also affirmed Mary as entirely holy and free from sin from the time of conception. At every point in Christ's life, Mary stood at His side, cooperating with Him in restoring life to souls, which function Mary continued after she was taken up into heaven. The council also recommended devotion to Mary, the mother of God.[14]

Sacraments. There were indeed noticable changes by Vatican II in some forms of the seven Catholic sacraments. Instead of facing the altar with his back to the people, the priest now faces the people; instead of Latin liturgy, the Mass is now in the language of the people. Laymen may now assist the priest, and women may also serve as lectors at the Mass.[15] "The general objectives were to make the liturgy more *simple*, more *participatory*, more *intelligible*, and more *dynamic*. The rites were simplified by eliminating repetitions, bows, kisses, signs of the cross and genuflections . . . Much emphasis was placed on making it participatory by assigning many responses to the people and above all by putting the liturgy in the vernacular so that they could understand what was being said."[16]

(1) Baptism. Much greater emphasis would now be placed on baptism, emphasizing the unity of the members with Christ in His death and resurrection. The catechumenate, a class in which the baptismal candidate is prepared through instruction and examination, was revived.

(2) Confirmation. Although originally formulated and decreed as a separate sacrament in the Middle Ages, confirmation is today sometimes regarded as part of the baptism ritual. As a result, it is common for the priest to administer both sacraments at the same time, particularly where adult converts are involved.

(3) Eucharist. Vatican II designed the Eucharist to involve the people. The ceremony was to be simplified and shorter, enabling the people to understand it. People were to become involved as readers and presenting offerings. More Scripture was to be employed. Catholics were now encouraged to pray with Protestants and occasionally worship with them, which had previously been forbidden.

(4) Penance. With the decline of the use of confession, Vatican II reformed the rite of penance, which included general confession and general absolution. In private confession the priest was encouraged to be more flexibile, less legalistic, reminding the penitent of God's love.[17]

(5) Anointing the sick. The term *extreme unction* was dropped in favor of *anointing the sick*, which reflected a "shift away from viewing it mainly as the final act of the Church assisting the soul as it enters eternity and toward seeing it as a means of strengthening and healing both body and soul."[18] Through Vatican II's reform, this sacrament stresses the involvement of the individual. Instead of anointing a sick person near death, the ritual now is designed to involve the sick person in readings and prayer.[19]

(6) Marriage. The traditional Catholic view of marriage was that its primary reasons are the procreation and the education of children; the expression of love was only a secondary reason. Vatican II erased these distinctions, placing greater importance on love in marriage. Vatican II also permitted Mass to be said in the ceremony when a Catholic marries a baptized non-Catholic.[20] Divorce continues to be forbidden.

(7) Holy orders. Prior to Vatican II the ministry was considered almost entirely the work of the clergy. Vatican II sought to involve laypersons in the ministry through educating them to recognize their gifts and use them. The priest was now viewed as a "brother among brothers." All adherents are to be regarded as equals; laypersons now can assume an active role in the ministry of the church (although the clergy retains its unique ministry).[21]

BY CHARISMATIC/EVANGELICAL CATHOLICS[22]

The charismatic movement has affected many different groups, and the Roman Catholic church is no exception. Some trace the beginnings of the Catholic involvement in the charismatic movement to the *cursillo*, an intense, emotional weekend of prayer practiced by Spanish-speaking people. At Duquesne University in Pittsburgh, two professors, who had been to Protestant Pentecostal meetings and the *cursillo*, organized a weekend retreat in February 1967 when the group had the Pentecostal experience. Similar experiences followed at Notre Dame and Michigan State in the spring of the same year. In 1969 the church gave cautious approval, and the movement swelled. In 1973 there were an estimated 50,000 Catholic Pentecostals in the United States and Canada; by 1984 there were some 5,700 prayer groups in the United States, with 250,000 people attending charismatic prayer meetings weekly and another 250,000 involved in other ways. There have been an estimated eight to ten million Catholics involved in the movement since 1967.

Although the Catholic charismatic movement has drawn priests into it, it is predominantly a laymen's movement. It has separate headquarters in South Bend, Indiana, a magazine and publishing house, and annual conventions, usually at Notre Dame University.

The evangelical Catholic movement has coincided with the charismatic movement in the Catholic church. With the emphasis on a personal, experiential religion, some Catholics began to meet in groups for Bible study and prayer. They began to witness concerning their faith. Groups began to meet as communities to "discern life in Christ together" and to share in one another's financial needs. Many reports of healings occurred. Evangelical revivals have become a popular form of evangelism in black Catholic churches. Without question, the Bible and the personalization of faith has become noticeable in parts of the Catholic church since Vatican II.

SUMMARY EVALUATION OF CONTEMPORARY CATHOLICISM

OBSERVATIONS[23]

The Second Vatican Council has set the stage for new directions in Roman Catholic theology. There has been a greater movement toward involvement of the people and, to some extent, a breakdown of the distinction between priest and people. Hence revelation is seen as being mediated through the religious perceptions of the people in addition to the Bible and Roman Catholic tradition. Some authority has been removed from the hierarchy because it now receives its mandate from the people and becomes responsible to the people. Thus there is a decided movement to the conception that the church should be self-governing and self-taught.

The 1960s began a trend toward secularization with Catholics leaving their isolation in their institutions and becoming more involved in secular life and culture. While supporting the institution, John Courtney Murray advocated living and adapting to a pluralistic society. Daniel Berrigan, by contrast, supported the use of violence to overthrow a corrupt society.

Existentialism has also affected Roman Catholicism and has helped move Catholicism away from its previous rationalism. This is observable in the new Dutch catechism that begins with man rather than with God. Neo-orthodoxy is evident in man's approach to Christ through an existential encounter. The existential encounter has also been applied to the sacraments; man may encounter God through the sacraments.

In summary, it is observable that since Vatican II the Roman Catholic church has become more broad-minded, reaching out to Protestants as "separated brethren." The Bible is no longer the closed book it used to be. Catholic theology has also shifted from a God-centered approach to a man-centered approach; the emphasis has moved from evaluating the world from God's perspective to experiencing the world from man's perspective.

EVALUATIONS

Hans Küng, employing historical criticism, has rejected the deity of Jesus Christ, suggesting Christ never claimed Messiahship for Himself. By the same methodology Küng has also rejected the inspiration of the Scriptures.

Rahner's view of man does not properly take into account man's fallen condition in sin because Rahner perceives every person as being disposed to the knowledge of God. Rahner's view of Christ is also defective. He views Christ with admiration but only from the standpoint of His obedience as a human being and as the pinnacle of evolution. Obviously, Rahner does not teach Christ's two natures as the God-Man.

Edward Schillebeeckx emphasizes existentialism by relating it to the Eucharist—at the same time confusing the illuminating ministry of the Holy Spirit with the reception of the elements of the Eucharist. Schillebeeckx appears to deny the union of the two natures of Christ, fully human and fully divine in the one God-Man.

Vatican II has dramatically redirected the Roman Catholic church by countermanding many of the emphases of Vatican I. Vatican II has sought to personalize the Catholic faith and make the faith more meaningful through use of the language of the people and through their involvement. There has been a greater emphasis on the Bible, which has resulted in prayer and study groups, evangelism, and charismatic groups. As a result of Vatican II, the Roman Catholic church is an amalgam, some local churches remaining pre-council traditionalists, others becoming progressive and contemporary, and still others confused and seeking identity.

NOTES ON CATHOLIC THEOLOGY

1. See also the discussion "Catholic Theology," chapter 37.
2. Jay P. Dolan, *The American Catholic Experience* (Garden City, N.Y.: Image, 1985), p. 433. By the late seventies, church attendance was apparently on the increase once again.

3. Klaas Runia, *The Present-Day Christological Debate* (Downers Grove, Ill.: InterVarsity, 1984), p. 59.

4. See the summary by W. Corduan, "Rahner, Karl," in Walter A. Elwell, ed., *Evangelical Dictionary of Theology* (Grand Rapids: Baker, 1984), pp. 906-7.

5. Ibid., p. 906.

6. Ibid. For another fine summary of Rahner's theology see Robert Kress, *A Rahner Handbook* (Atlanta: Knox, 1982), pp. 36-41.

7. Peter Toon, *The Development of Doctrine in the Church* (Grand Rapids: Eerdmans, 1979), pp. 96-99.

8. Runia, *Present-Day Christological Debate*, pp. 53-58.

9. For discussions of the *developments* of Vatican II in contemporary Roman Catholicism see: F. S. Piggin, "Roman Catholicism," and C. T. McIntire, "Vatican Council II," in *Evangelical Dictionary of Theology*, pp. 955-59, 1135-37; and David F. Wells, "Recent Roman Catholic Theology," in *Tensions in Contemporary Theology* edited by Stanley N. Gundry and Alan F. Johnson (Chicago: Moody, 1979), pp. 287-384. For discussions of the *documents* of Vatican II, see: Walter M. Abbott, S.J., ed., *The Documents of Vatican II* (New York: Herder and Herder, 1966); and Thomas Bokenkotter, *Essential Catholicism* (Garden City, N.Y.: Image, 1986).

10. Quoted in Bokenkotter, *Essential Catholicism*, p. 32.

11. Ibid.

12. Ibid., p. 100.

13. Ibid., p. 133.

14. Ibid., pp. 133-34.

15. Ibid., p. 161.

16. Ibid., p. 168.

17. Ibid., pp. 232-33.

18. Ibid., p. 245.

19. Ibid.

20. Ibid., p. 250.

21. Ibid., pp. 256-57.

22. See the helpful summary in Dolan, *The American Catholic Experience*, pp. 431-33.

23. See Wells, "Recent Roman Catholic Theology," in *Tensions in Contemporary Theology*, pp. 292ff.

FOR FURTHER STUDY ON CATHOLIC THEOLOGY

** Walter M. Abbott, ed. *The Documents of Vatican II.* New York: Herder and Herder, 1966.

** G. C. Berkouwer. *The Second Vatican Council and the New Catholicism.* Grand Rapids: Eerdmans, 1965.

** Thomas Bokenkotter. *Essential Catholicism.* Garden City, N.Y.: Image, 1986.

* Walter A. Elwell, ed. *Evangelical Dictionary of Theology.* Grand Rapids: Baker, 1984. See articles such as "Vatican Council II"; "Küng, Hans"; "Rahner, Karl"; "Roman Catholicism"; and others.

* Deane William Ferm. *Contemporary American Theologies: A Critical Survey.* New York: Seabury, 1981. Pp. 112-34.

** George A. Lindbeck. *The Future of Roman Catholic Theology: Vatican II—Catalyst for Change.* Philadelphia: Fortress, 1970.

** Robert Kress. *A Rahner Handbook.* Atlanta: Knox, 1982.

* Klaas Runia. *The Present-Day Christological Debate.* Downers Grove, Ill.: InterVarsity, 1984. Pp. 47-65.

** E. Schillebeeckx. *Revelation and Theology.* New York: Sheed & Ward, 1967.

* Peter Toon. *The Development of Doctrine in the Church.* Grand Rapids: Eerdmans, 1979. Pp. 89-103.

* David F. Wells. "Recent Roman Catholic Theology." In *Tensions in Contemporary Theology* edited by Stanley N. Gundry and Alan F. Johnson. Chicago: Moody, 1976. Pp. 287-324.

45

CONSERVATIVE THEOLOGY

There are at least three terms that identify biblical Christianity today: *conservative*, *evangelical*, and *fundamentalist*. Without question, these terms mean different things to different people. *Conservative* is a general term that identifies a person or organization that stands opposed to liberal Christianity and holds to the historic doctrines of the Christian faith. The other two terms demand more lengthy explanations.

EVANGELICALISM

Evangelical is a biblical term, derived from the Greek *euangelion*, meaning "the good news," hence, an evangelical is one who heralds the good news of Jesus Christ.[1] The term must be understood in its context, however. In Europe, an evangelical is not necessarily one who holds to conservative doctrines because there the term has become synonymous with Protestant.[2] However, in America the term is understood to denote one who holds to the historic doctrines of the faith. Evangelical is frequently preferred to the term *fundamentalist* because the former is usually considered a more irenic term whereas the latter is frequently identified with separatism and legalism. Although about fifty million Americans were identified as evangelicals in the 1970s and 1980s, probably no more than 10 percent of these identify themselves as separatist fundamentalists.[3]

HISTORICAL DEVELOPMENT OF EVANGELICALISM

Evangelicalism is linked historically to the reform movements throughout church history, particularly the Reformation, but also the evangelical awakenings of the eighteenth century. In the nineteenth and twentieth centuries evangelicalism has tended to retreat at the onslaught of liberalism. In recent years evangelicalism has become more prominent through its colleges and seminaries, writings, and the media.

George Marsden has identified four stages of evangelicalism.[4] The first stage was from the 1870s to the end of World War I, which period saw theological liberals emerge within evangelical denominations. The Holiness-Pentecostal groups also emerged during this time, as well as revivalists, and premillennialists with their emphasis on eschatology. The second stage was from 1919 to 1926 when modernists were attacked within the major denominations. Evangelicals were within the mainstream of Protestantism during this time. The third stage was from 1926 to about the 1940s when evangelicals (fundamentalists) were viewed as sectarian, working largely outside of the main denominations through independent schools and missions. Evangelicals shifted from the North to the South in the United States during this time. The fourth stage was from the 1940s to the present, with a new evangelicalism emerging out of the original fundamentalist tradition. Two new movements surfaced: evangelicalism and separatistic fundamentalism. More numerous among the two groups at the present are evangelicals, who do not wish to refer to themselves as fundamentalists but are conservative theologically.

Several important groups have emerged as voices for evangelicalism. Founded in 1941, the National Association of Evangelicals was organized to defend orthodoxy in opposition to liberalism, yet these evangelicals did not want to be known as reactionary or negative as the American Council of Christian Churches, their fundamentalist counterpart. In 1949 the Evangelical Theological Society was formed to promote scholarship within evangelicalism. Only one doctrinal proposition, affirming the inerrancy of Scripture, binds these evangelicals together.

DOCTRINAL AFFIRMATIONS OF EVANGELICALISM

The foundational doctrine of evangelicalism is the inerrancy of Scripture as found, for example, in the doctrinal statement of the Evangelical Theological Society: "The Bible alone, and the Bible in its entirety, is the Word of God written and is therefore inerrant in the autographs." Evangelicals generally hold to verbal plenary inspiration (Matt. 5:18) rather than conceptual or mechanical inspiration.

Evangelicals believe in a triune, sovereign God, coexisting as the Father, Son, and Holy Spirit. In particular, the deity of the Son and the personality of the Holy Spirit are affirmed.

Evangelicals also teach that man was originally created innocent (Col. 3:10), but through Adam's transgression sin entered the human race and is passed on to succeeding generations (Rom. 5:12). Because of the Fall man is totally depraved and corrupted, requiring the grace of God to act in providing redemption. Jesus Christ paid this redemption price for the entire human race as a sufficient substitute (Matt. 20:28; 2 Cor. 5:21; 1 Tim. 2:6). Through His atoning death Christ satisfied the justice of a holy God and thereby reconciled man to God (2 Cor. 5:19). To affirm the reality of redemption, Christ rose bodily from the grave (Matt. 28:6), a harbinger of good things for believers who will follow in His train (1 Cor. 15:20-23). Christ ascended bodily into heaven (Acts 1:9) and will return again in His physical person (Acts 1:11).

Evangelicals are divided concerning the nature of end-time events, premillennialists believing Christ will establish a literal kingdom on earth for a thousand years, whereas amillennialists believe Christ's return will usher in the eternal state.

Salvation by grace through faith and not works is an important doctrine in evangelicalism (Eph. 2:8-9). Through faith alone, the believer is declared righteous (Rom. 5:1) and reconciled to God (2 Cor. 5:19). Because the name *evangelical* implies "good news," evangelicals believe strongly in evangelism, the necessity of telling the message of salvation by grace through faith (Matt. 28:18-20; Luke 24:47; Acts 1:8).

SUMMARY EVALUATION OF EVANGELICALISM

Through the evangelical organizations mentioned earlier, and through other evangelical institutions such as colleges and seminaries, there has been a resurgence of theological scholarship, a development of more influential leadership, and a greater public affirmation of the historic Christian faith.

FUNDAMENTALISM

The word *fundamentalist* was first used in 1920 by Curtis Lee Laws, Baptist editor of the *Watchman-Examiner*, to identify someone who stood for the historic doctrines of the Christian faith in contrast to modern religious liberals who rejected doctrines such as the inspiration of Scripture, the deity of Christ, and the genuineness of miracles.

Marsden defines fundamentalism as: "1. an evangelical Protestant; 2. an anti-modernist, meaning that one subscribes to the fundamentals of traditional supernaturalistic biblical Christianity; and 3. militant in this anti-modernism or in opposition to certain aspects of secularization. A fundamentalist, then, is a militantly anti-modernistic evangelical."[5]

HISTORICAL DEVELOPMENT OF FUNDAMENTALISM

Historically, fundamentalism has been used to identify one holding to the five fundamentals of the faith adopted by the General Assembly of the Presbyterian Church in the U.S.A. in 1910. The five fundamentals were the miracles of Christ, the virgin birth of Christ, the substitutionary atonement of Christ, the bodily resurrection of Christ, and the inspiration of Scripture.[6]

Fundamentalism has stood for the historic fundamentals of Christianity, particularly as developed in *The Fundamentals*. These were initially issued as twelve booklets edited by R. A. Torrey and A. C. Dixon. More than three million copies have been distributed to pastors and others. The series responded to liberalism's higher criticism; denied evolution; affirmed the Mosaic authorship of the Pentateuch; supported the unity of Isaiah; defended inspiration, the virgin birth, deity, and atonement of Christ; and addressed many other issues. Writers included the conservative giants of the faith: W. H. Griffith Thomas, J. Orr, A. C. Gaebelein, B. B. Warfield, C. I. Scofield, H. C. G. Moule, A. T. Pierson, C. R. Erdman, and many others.[7]

The early proponents of fundamentalism argued cogently, howbeit vigorously, for the historic tenets of the Christian faith. This was seen in *The Fundamentals* as well as works like *Christianity and Liberalism* and *The Christian Faith in the Modern World* by J. Gresham Machen (1881-1937). Machen was an early vocal leader of fundamentalism, leading a group of former Princeton Seminary professors to form Westminster Theological Seminary when they were unable to prevent a doctrinal change at Princeton in 1929. Westminster stood as a conservative counterpart to Princeton, which had all but abandoned its historic conservative position. In 1936 Machen, along with Carl McIntyre and J. Oliver Buswell, helped form the Presbyterian Church of America. Machen and others had been expelled from the denomination for forming an independent mission board.[8] The outstanding pulpiteer Clarence Macartney joined Machen in his endeavors. Later Carl McIntyre organized the Bible Presbyterian Church and Faith Theological Seminary over the issue of premillennialism. In 1930 the Independent Fundamental Churches of America (a fellowship of independent churches) was formed.

Fundamentalist Baptists also fought liberalism in the North. This resulted in new Baptist denominations: the General Association of Regular Baptists in 1932 and the Conservative Baptist Association of America in 1947. In 1919 William B. Riley, founder of Northwestern College in Minneapolis, helped establish the World's Christian Fundamentals Association with an emphasis on premillennialism and the second coming of Christ. Meanwhile, T. T. Shields, pastor of Jarvis Street Baptist Church in Toronto, Canada, founded the Toronto Baptist Seminary. In the South, J. Frank Norris, pastor of the First Baptist Church of Fort Worth, founded the Baptist Bible Seminary. Together these men also founded the Bible Baptist Union to "encourage individual Baptist churches to secede from the parent denomination and unite as a separatist body to narass the Northern Baptist Convention."[9]

DOCTRINAL AFFIRMATIONS OF FUNDAMENTALISM

Fundamentalist doctrine is centered on the five fundamentals, although the doctrine can be delineated in much greater detail. Fundamentalists affirm verbal plenary inspiration as well as the inerrancy of the Scriptures (2 Tim. 3:16; 2 Pet. 1:21). Historically, this in turn has meant a denial of the following: the documentary hypothesis of the Pentateuch, deutero- or trito-Isaiah, the late date of Daniel, higher criticism, and other more recent developments. Fundamentalism has also taught the necessity of believing in the virgin birth of Christ (Isa. 7:14; Matt. 1:18-25; Luke 1:35).

Fundamentalists believe in the reliability of the Scriptures in affirming the miracles of Christ: He walked on water (not on a sandbar); He stilled the storm, cast out demons, gave sight to the blind, and raised the dead. The accounts of Christ's works are to be understood literally.

Important to fundamentalist doctrine is the substitutionary atonement of Christ (Mark 10:45; Gal. 3:13). Christ did not merely die as an example or as a martyr; He died as a substitute, the Righteous One in the place of sinners (2 Cor. 5:21; 1 Pet. 2:24).

Equally important is the fundamentalist doctrine of the bodily resurrection of Christ from the dead. When Christ arose it was not merely His spirit or His teachings that lived on; He rose bodily from the grave as affirmed by the fact that He could eat (John 21:9-12) and could be touched (John 20:27-28) and seen (Luke 24:34; 1 Cor. 15:3-8; 1 John 1:1). Fundamentalists also believe in the literal return of Jesus Christ from heaven (Zech. 14:4; Matt. 25:31).

Included in some restatements of the five fundamentals is the deity of Christ, a doctrine that is at the heart of fundamentalism (John 1:1; Col. 2:9; Heb. 1:8-10).

Regarding man's origin, fundamentalists have affirmed that God directly created individual species of all living things including man (Gen. 1:12, 24, etc.), and have rejected evolution in any form.

Fundamentalists have taught: the literalness of hell (Luke 16:19-31) and the reality of Satan and demons; man's need for spiritual salvation through believing the gospel (Acts 16:31) and the inadequacy of the social gospel; and the separation not only from sin and worldliness, but from liberals and others who deny the fundamentals of the Christian faith.

SUMMARY EVALUATION OF FUNDAMENTALISM

In the early years of this century, fundamentalism had a good record in defending orthodoxy. The intellectual giants of orthodoxy as well as the prominent preachers of that day stood for the historic Christian faith. These leaders defended the doctrines that have been believed by devout Christians throughout the centuries. Later in the twentieth century the emphasis shifted to some extent. Separation became as important a doctrine as the historic fundamentals. The harsh spirit of fundamentalism did not always properly adorn the gospel of Christ, and although the statements may or may not have been correct, the attitude in which it was presented was not always favorable, especially when it involved negative statements against fellow believers.

NEO-EVANGELICALISM

HISTORICAL DEVELOPMENT OF NEO-EVANGELICALISM

The term *neo-evangelical* was coined by Dr. Harold John Ockenga, pastor of the Park Street Congregational Church in Boston, in a convocation address given at Fuller Theological Seminary in California in 1948. Ockenga explained neo-evangelicalism's position:

> The new evangelicalism breaks with . . . three movements. The new evangelicalism breaks first with neo-orthodoxy because it (evangelicalism) accepts the authority of the Bible . . . He (the evangelical) breaks with the modernist . . . in reference to his embrace of the full orthodox system of doctrine against that which the modernist has accepted. He breaks with the fundamentalist on the fact that he believes that the Biblical teaching, the Bible doctrine and ethics, must apply to the social scene, that there must be an application of this to society as much as there is an application of it to the individual man.[10]

Neo-evangelicalism arose as a reaction, particularly expressed in its dissatisfaction with fundamentalism. Carl F. H. Henry (b. 1913), a prominent evangelical theologian and founder of *Christianity Today*, suggested fundamentalism had shifted "from classic fundamentalism as a theology to fundamentalism as a negative reactionary spirit."[11] Henry believed fundamentalism was misrepresenting biblical Christianity through narrow thinking by concentrating on only part of the biblical message; showing a lack of scholarship; having a preoccupation with fighting modernism; and exhibiting a harsh, unloving, and contentious spirit. Henry emphasized the need for social responsibility.

Even though all the adherents within the movement do not share the same views, there has been a tendency toward toleration of liberals. They have been called "fringe friends," whereas fundamentalists would call them heretics.

Advocates of neo-evangelicalism have been men like Harold Ockenga, Carl F. H. Henry, E. J. Carnell, Billy Graham, and Bernard Ramm. Fuller

Theological Seminary has been the leading institution for the movement. *Christianity Today* has been regarded as its publishing voice.

DOCTRINAL AFFIRMATIONS OF NEO-EVANGELICALISM

Social responsibility. Neo-evangelicals believed fundamentalists had neglected the social implications of the gospel. Therefore neo-evangelicals sought to respond to social problems. They accused fundamentalists of being preoccupied with personal salvation from sin because of their belief in man's sinfulness and the soon return of Christ.[12] Neo-evangelicals "were not advocating a social gospel; personal regeneration was still a necessity for individual salvation. A social application of the evangelical gospel was their concern."[13]

Separation. The issue of separation usually goes back to J. Gresham Machen at Princeton Seminary, who left the seminary to help form Westminster Seminary and also left the Presbyterian Church, U.S.A. because of liberalism. For this Machen stands as an example of a separatist. Neo-evangelicals have tended to be critical of Machen and others who have separated from churches, denominations, or mission organizations because of liberalism. E. J. Carnell was most critical of Machen, charging him with dishonoring the doctrine of the church through his separatism.

Ronald H. Nash has argued against separatism because (1) it "has tended to foster divisive attitudes within orthodoxy"; (2) it "has exalted minor doctrines unduly and made them tests of fellowship"; (3) it "has failed or refused to communicate with those with whom it disagrees."[14]

Inerrancy. There is some diversity of opinion among neo-evangelicals regarding inerrancy and critical methodology. Richard Quebedeaux identifies neo-evangelicalism as committed to historical criticism. This is because it recognizes the Scriptures as not merely the product of God, but also the product of man. The Scriptures bear the marks of cultural conditioning. "The old concepts of infallibility and inerrancy are being reinterpreted to the point that a number of evangelical scholars are saying that the *teaching* of Scripture (i.e., matters of faith and practice) rather than the text itself is without error."[15] It should be recognized, however, that while some neo-evangelicals deny biblical inerrancy, others affirm it. Harold Ockenga was one such neo-evangelical.

Science. The relationship of modern science to the Bible differentiates neo-evangelicalism from fundamentalism. Concerning the Genesis record, fundamentalists have traditionally argued for the gap theory, which allowed for the expanse of time suggested by science, or recent creationism. The neo-evangelical view of science has perhaps been best expressed by Bernard Ramm (b. 1916) in *The Christian View of Science and Scripture.* Ramm suggests the harmony of modern science and the Bible, positing a figure of four to five billion years for the age of the universe. While Ramm refers to himself as a progressive creationist, he also suggests that belief in evolution is not anti-Christian. He states that because some Protestants and Catholics believe in evolution, "This is strong evidence that evolution is not metaphysically incompatible with Christianity."[16] E. J. Carnell argued for "threshold evolution," which allows for "a wide and varied change within the 'kinds' originally created by God."[17]

SUMMARY EVALUATION OF NEO-EVANGELICALISM

Social responsibility. With all the emphasis neo-evangelicalism gives to social responsibility it is noteworthy that Scripture has very little to say about the Christian's social responsibility to unbelievers. Galatians 6:10 is one of the few passages that has application to the issue and then only in a secondary sense. (Some, of course, would make applications from the social emphases of the prophets. The issue is not entirely the same, however, because Israel was a theocratic nation.)

Separation. Neo-evangelicals have tended to ignore the teachings of Scripture on the issue of separation. The Bible has much to say on the subject (cf. Rom. 12:2; 16:17; 2 Cor. 6:14-18; Titus 3:10; James 4:4; 2 John 9-11). Although the application of these passages is not always easy, it does have many serious ramifications. At the very least, the Christian should ask if it is possible to cooperate in any way, religiously, with those who deny fundamental doctrines such as the deity of Christ or His substitutionary atonement.

Inerrancy. The issue of critical methodology is under serious discussion, and many conservatives question whether, in fact, historical, source, form, or redaction criticism can be employed without sacrificing inerrancy or the divine element in inspiration. Too much is based on unverifiable assumptions in the critical methodologies. Neo-evangelicals also distinguish between inspiration and inerrancy.[18] Nash argues against inerrancy in the original writings, suggesting it is only an assumption.[19] This is a serious problem because if the Bible is God-breathed (2 Tim. 3:16), how can it contain error?[20]

Science. A problem in attempting to reconcile the Bible with science is science's state of flux. What was believed to be scientifically true several decades ago may be rejected today. Those who have attempted to reconcile science and the Bible in the past have sometimes later been embarrassed. Further, the Bible is frequently interpreted in the light of science, in which case science becomes the authority rather than the Bible. This is true in some of the arguments for progressive creationism or for a localized Flood. Men like Henry M. Morris have written extensively, refuting the possibility of evolution from both a scientific and biblical viewpoint.

NEO-FUNDAMENTALISM

HISTORICAL DEVELOPMENT OF NEO-FUNDAMENTALISM

Over the years the mood of fundamentalism has changed, which has led some to designate the modern fundamentalist movement as *neo-fundamentalism*.[21] Whereas historic fundamentalism emphasized separatism from apostasy, later fundamentalism stressed "secondary separation,"—avoidance of other conservatives who associated with liberals.

DOCTRINAL AFFIRMATIONS OF NEO-FUNDAMENTALISM

These fundamentalists shunned Billy Graham, not because he was a liberal but because he talked to liberals. Billy Graham was accused of destroying Scriptural mass evangelism through his "spirit of inclusivism."[22]

The neo-evangelical label on people, schools, or organizations meant disassociation; thus, neo-fundamentalists refused to cooperate with Billy Graham in his evangelistic campaigns, rejected the journal *Christianity Today*, and excoriated schools like Moody Bible Institute and Dallas Theological Seminary for inviting certain evangelical speakers.[23]

Other writers have identified the neo-fundamentalist movement with fundamentalist leaders like Jerry Falwell, Tim La Haye, Hal Lindsey, and Pat Robertson.[24] These leaders have spoken out publicly,

> offering an answer for what many regarded as a supreme social, economic, moral, and religious crisis in America. They identified a new and more pervasive enemy, secular humanism, which they believed was responsible for eroding churches, schools, universities, the government, and above all families. They fought all enemies which they considered to be offspring of secular humanism—evolutionism, political and theological liberalism, loose personal morality, sexual perversion, socialism, communism, and any lessening of the absolute, inerrant authority of the Bible.[25]

The Moral Majority, with its political action, is also seen as a further aspect of neo-fundamentalism.

SUMMARY EVALUATION OF NEO-FUNDAMENTALISM

Neo-fundamentalism may be identified as the modern movement that, while holding to the historic fundamental doctrines of Scripture, has evolved into a movement with different emphases and perspectives. Neo-fundamentalism has remained true to the historic doctrines of the Christian faith, steadfastly defending those doctrines in pulpits and classrooms. However, although historic fundamentalism has fielded intellectual giants like Robert Dick Wilson, W. H. Griffith Thomas, Bishop J. C. Ryle, J. Gresham

Machen, and many others, neo-fundamentalism has tended to reject intellectualism and seminary training.

This anti-intellectualism has resulted in aberrations of orthodoxy, particularly seen in the "King James only" movement. Even though early fundamentalists certainly believed in the inspiration of the autographs, some neo-fundamentalists have tended to go further and actually advocate the inspiration of the King James Version, even including it in their doctrinal statements.

Neo-fundamentalism has also tended toward legalism, adding explicit statements regarding behavior to doctrinal statements.

In addition, neo-fundamentalism has also advocated secondary separationism, calling for avoidance of other Christians who do not follow the same rigid standards. In advocating this attitude, neo-fundamentalism has tended toward divisiveness, splitting of churches, and fostering of ill will among genuine Christians. This is an unfortunate commentary on those who otherwise hold to correct doctrine. Ultimately, sound doctrine should issue in life-changing behavior, the relational expression of which must be love (John 13:34-35; 1 John 2:10,11; 3:14). Love is the Christian's duty even when engaged in conflict with heresy or immorality. The biblical admonitions to love need to be taken seriously, especially where alleged compromise is not in the realm of doctrines central to the faith.

CONCLUDING OBSERVATIONS

In concluding this chapter that refers to distasteful and embarrassing features of contemporary fellowships of the true church, two positive observations need to be stressed. First, evangelicals and fundamentalists believe, teach, and defend the historic doctrines of the Christian faith as found in the Holy Bible. The section in this volume called "Part 2: Systematic Theology" is written from an evangelical standpoint, and the reader is referred to it for a presentation of particular doctrines from the conservative position.

Second, out of the evangelical-fundamentalist endeavor have come many heartening developments: a strong emphasis in missions, both through denominations as well as through independent foreign missions; the resurgence of evangelistic campaigns (most notably those of Billy Graham); the multiplication and growth of Bible institutes, Christian colleges, and seminaries; and the prospering of evangelical publications. The current results of all this in the United States alone has been that some fifty million people identify themselves at least nominally as born again, and that the glorious gospel of Christ has received a greater public awareness and more respectful hearing than ever before.

NOTES ON CONSERVATIVE THEOLOGY

1. Some have opted for the term *evangelical* over *fundamentalist* on two bases: the former is a biblical term, and the latter has a negative connotation. Compare J. I. Packer, *"Fundamentalism" and the Word of God* (London: InterVarsity, 1958).

2. R. V. Pierard, "Evangelicalism," in Walter A. Elwell, ed., *Evangelical Dictionary of Theology* (Grand Rapids: Baker, 1984), p. 380.

3. George M. Marsden, "Fundamentalism," in *New Dictionary of Theology*, edited by Sinclair B. Ferguson, David F. Wright, and J. I. Packer (Downers Grove, Ill.: InterVarsity, 1988), p. 266.

4. George M. Marsden, "From Fundamentalism to Evangelicalism: A Historical Analysis," in *The Evangelicals: What They Believe, Who They Are, Where They Are Changing*, edited by David F. Wells and John D. Woodbridge (Nashville: Abingdon, 1975), pp. 124-33.

5. Marsden, "Fundamentalism," in *New Dictionary of Theology*, pp. 266-68. Bernard Ramm offers a rather harsh definition of fundamentalists:

   > 1) As to attitude. . . . A Fundamentalist is a person with orthodox convictions who defends them with an anti-intellectual, anti-scholarly, anti-cultural belligerency. 2) As to separation. The Fundamentalist asserts that the leadership of traditional denominations has fallen into the hands of men who are liberal or neo-orthodox in theological persuasion, and he must take a strong stand against such leadership. This stand demands severance from such denominations and affiliation with denominations that demand and obtain purity of doctrine. . . . 3) As to Scripture. . . . A Fundamentalist . . . equates revelation with the words of Scripture, and accepts the verbal inspiration and inerrancy of the Scriptures. Involved in this is also a repudiation of higher criticism of both the Old and New Testaments. Thus a Fundamentalist is a person who holds with obscurantism to the verbal inspiration and inerrancy of the Holy Scriptures. 4) As to eschatology. . . . A Fundamentalist has been defined as one who is in essential agreement with Scofield's eschatology of dispensationalism and premillennialism. (Bernard Ramm, *A Handbook of Contemporary Theology* [Grand Rapids: Eerdmans, 1966], pp. 53-54.)

6. C. T. McIntire, "Fundamentalism," in Walter A. Elwell, ed., *Evangelical Dictionary of Theology*, p. 433. Compare Wells and Woodbridge, eds., *The Evangelicals*, p. 30; and Louis Gasper, *The Fundamentalist Movement 1930-1956* (Grand Rapids: Baker, 1963). Others have identified the five fundamentals as "an inerrant Bible, the Virgin Birth, the deity of Christ, the substitutionary Atonement, the physical Resurrection and the physical Second Coming." (Earle E. Cairns, *Christianity Through the Centuries* [Grand Rapids: Zondervan, 1954], p. 481.)

7. The twelve booklets were later issued in four volumes and subsequently revised and reissued as *The Fundamentals For Today*, 2 vols., by Kregel Publications in 1958 under the editorship of Charles L. Feinberg.

8. Gasper, *The Fundamentalist Movement 1930-1956*, p. 16.

9. Ibid., p. 17.

10 Quoted in Ronald H. Nash, *The New Evangelicalism* (Grand Rapids: Zondervan, 1963), p. 14.

11. Harvie M. Conn, *Contemporary World Theology*, rev. ed. (Nutley, N.J.: Presbyterian and Reformed, 1974), p. 126. See Carl F. H. Henry, *Evangelical Responsibility in Contemporary Theology* (Grand Rapids: Eerdmans, 1957), pp. 32-47 for a summary of Henry's dissatisfaction.

12. Millard Erickson, *The New Evangelical Theology* (Westwood, N.J.: Revell, 1968), p. 32.

13. Ibid., p. 33.

14. Nash, *The New Evangelicalism*, pp. 91-93.

15. Richard Quebedeaux, *The Young Evangelicals* (New York: Harper, 1974), pp. 37-38.

16. Bernard Ramm, *The Christian View of Science and Scripture* (Grand Rapids: Eerdmans, 1954), p. 204.

17. Edward John Carnell, *An Introduction to Christian Apologetics* (Grand Rapid: Eerdmans, 1948), p. 238.

18. Nash, *The New Evangelicalism*, pp. 75-77.

19. Ibid., p. 76.

20. See the helpful treatment by Charles C. Ryrie, *What You Should Know About Inerrancy* (Chicago: Moody, 1981).

21. Conn, *Contemporary World Theology*, pp. 119-24.

22. George W. Dollar, *A History of Fundamentalism in America* (Greenville, S.C.: Bob Jones U., 1973), p. 194.

23. Compare George W. Dollar, *The Fight For Fundamentalism: American Fundamentalism, 1973-1983* (Sarasota, Fla.: George W. Dollar, 1983).

24. C. T. McIntire, "Fundamentalism," in *Evangelical Dictionary of Theology*, p. 435.

25. Ibid.

FOR FURTHER STUDY ON CONSERVATIVE THEOLOGY

EVANGELICALISM, FUNDAMENTALISM, NEO-FUNDAMENTALISM

 * Harvie M. Conn. *Contemporary World Theology*, rev. ed. Nutley, N.J.: Presbyterian and Reformed, 1974. Pp. 112-24.

** George W. Dollar. *A History of Fundamentalism in America.* Greenville, S.C.: Bob Jones U., 1973.

** Charles L. Feinberg, ed. *The Fundamentals For Today*, 2 vols. Grand Rapids: Kregel, 1958.

** Louis Gasper. *The Fundamentalist Movement 1930-1956.* Reprint. Grand Rapids: Baker, 1981.

 * George M. Marsden. "Fundamentalism." In *New Dictionary of Theology*, edited by Sinclair B. Ferguson, David F. Wright, and J. I. Packer. Downers Grove, Ill.: InterVarsity, 1988. Pp. 267-68.

*·C. T. McIntire. "Fundamentalism." In Walter A. Elwell, ed., *Evangelical Dictionary of Theology.* Grand Rapids: Baker, 1984. Pp. 433-35.

 * R. V. Pierard. "Evangelicalism." In Walter A. Elwell, ed., *Evangelical Dictionary of Theology.* Grand Rapids: Baker, 1984. Pp. 379-82.

** Bernard Ramm. *The Evangelical Heritage: A Study in Historical Theology.* Grand Rapids: Baker, 1981.

* Ian S. Rennie. "Evangelical Theology." In *New Dictionary of Theology,* edited by Sinclair B. Ferguson, David F. Wright, and J. I. Packer. Downers Grove, Ill.: InterVarsity, 1988. Pp. 239-40.

** Ernest R. Sandeen. *The Roots of Fundamentalism: British and American Millennarianism, 1800-1930.* Grand Rapids: Baker, 1970.

** R. A. Torrey, A. C. Dixon, et al., eds. *The Fundamentals,* 4 vols. Reprint. Grand Rapids: Baker, 1980.

** David F. Wells and John D. Woodbridge, eds. *The Evangelicals: What They Believe, Who They Are, Where They Are Changing.* Nashville: Abingdon, 1975.

NEO-EVANGELICALISM

** Edward J. Carnell. *The Case for Orthodox Theology.* Philadelphia: Westminster, 1959.

* Harvie Conn. *Contemporary World Theology.* Nutley, N.J.: Presbyterian and Reformed, 1974. Pp. 125-40.

** Millard Erickson. *The New Evangelical Theology.* Westwood, N.J.: Revell, 1968.

** Carl F. H. Henry. *Evangelical Responsibility in Contemporary Theology.* Grand Rapids: Eerdmans, 1957.

** Robert P. Lightner. *Neo-Evangelicalism Today.* Schaumburg, Ill.: Regular Baptist, 1979.

** Ronald H. Nash. *The New Evangelicalism.* Grand Rapids: Zondervan, 1963.

* R. V. Pierard. "Evangelicalism." In Walter A. Elwell, ed., *Evangelical Dictionary of Theology.* Grand Rapids: Baker, 1984. Pp. 379-82. There is a brief but insightful discussion of neo-evangelicalism within this article.

** Richard Quebedeaux. *The Young Evangelicals.* New York: Harper, 1974.

* Charles Woodbridge. *The New Evangelicalism.* Greenville, S.C.: Bob Jones U., 1969.

EPILOGUE

Throughout the course of this sizable volume, the reader has been introduced to five important categories of theology: biblical, systematic, historical, dogmatic, and contemporary. These "faces" of theology have been explained and demonstrated in the hope that the completed book will serve as a ready reference manual, faithfully adhering to the Scriptures as its authoritative standard.

In reflecting on the development and history of biblical doctrine, one truth predominates: the grace of God. In looking back at the theology of the Old Testament with the beginning promise of God in Genesis 3:15, in seeing the unfolding of God's revelation in the centuries following, the story is always the same: man is sinful, turning away from God, while God continually manifests Himself in grace. In the New Testament the attentive believer is deeply moved by the climax of God's work in salvation, redemption, and sanctification. God, through Christ, has achieved and provided for man what man never could attain by himself. Man has been reconciled to God.

Even though the theological truths of Scripture have been presented on the pages of this book in as great detail as purpose and space have allowed, it must be said that there is still much about God that remains incomprehensible This is certainly true of the incarnation, when God became flesh and dwelt among us. Who can fully understand that the eternal God, creator of the boundless heavens, was born on earth as a baby, grew into manhood, thus becoming a bondservant, humbling Himself to the extent of dying on a cross? That God should so love man that He would leave Heaven's glories, suffer humiliation, scorn, ridicule, and death ought to evoke a worshipful response. Perhaps the greatest tragedy would be if one would be able to delineate orthodox doctrine without having entered into personal fellowship with the One to whom the doctrines testify. It is conceivable that a reader has ventured this far in this volume without personally knowing the reality of new life in Christ. To properly know doctrine should mean an appropriate change in one's life (2 Tim. 3:16-17).

There is no greater blessing than the gift of God's Son, and there is no greater sin than the willful scorning of the gift of God's grace. The epitome of God's revelation to man is Jesus Christ. To attain true knowledge is to live in experiential fellowship with Him. He came to satiate our spiritual hunger (John 6:35) and to slake our spiritual thirst (John 7:37-38). He came to give us life. The person who trusts Him and His atoning sacrifice will never die (John 11:26) but may enjoy the privilege of unbroken fellowship, peace, and calm amid a turbulent world. "He who has the Son has the life" (1 John 5:12).

Dear reader, may you experience the greatest theological truth that can be known: "God has given us eternal life, and this life is in His Son" (1 John 5:11). No human effort can contribute to or attain this; it is a gift received through trusting in the everliving Christ. Believe in Him who alone is able to rescue you and give you the hope of eternal bliss with Him (John 3:16, 36; Acts 16:31). Then live in harmony with His Word and will, growing in experiential fellowship with Him (Gal. 2:20; 5:24; 6:14; Phil. 1:21; 3:7-10).

Praise be "to Him who loves us, and released us from our sins by His blood. . . . Worthy is the Lamb that was slain to receive power and riches and wisdom and might and honor and glory and blessing. . . . To Him who sits on the throne, and to the Lamb, be blessing and honor and glory and dominion forever and ever" (Rev. 1:5; 5:12-13).

GLOSSARY

A

ABRAHAMIC COVENANT. An unconditional covenant (binding on God alone) in which God promised to give the physical descendants of Abraham a land, a posterity issuing in Messiah, and spiritual blessings (Gen. 12:1-3). *See* Covenant.

ACCIDENT THEORY. Formulated by Albert Schweitzer, this theory taught that Christ became enamored with His messiahship and was mistakenly crushed to death in the process.

ADONAI. A Hebrew name for God meaning "Lord" or "Master" and stressing the lordship or authority of God.

ADOPTION. The believer's "placing as a son," emphasizing the believer's rights and privileges in his new position in Christ.

AGNOSTIC. Derived from the Greek components *gnostos*, meaning "knowledge," with the *a-* prefix negating the statement; hence, "one who does not know if God exists."

AMILLENNIALISM. The teaching that there will be no literal millennium following Christ's return to earth.

AMYRALDIANISM. A variation of the lapsarian views in which the order of decrees is: create man, permit the Fall, provide redemption in Christ for all, elect some to salvation, and send the Spirit to effect salvation This view allows for unlimited atonement.

ANGEL. A messenger that may be human or divine. As a divine messenger an angel is sent from God with a specific commission.

ANTHROPOLOGICAL ARGUMENT. Comes from the Greek word *anthropos*, meaning "man." Because man is a moral being possessing conscience, intellect, emotion, and will, God must have created man with his moral nature.

ANTICHRIST. A term referring to anyone who denies that Jesus has come in genuine humanity. It is a popular (though not biblical) term used to describe the final world ruler whom Scripture calls the Beast (Rev. 13:1).

APOLLINARIS (THE YOUNGER) (b. A.D. 310). Taught the deity of Christ but denied the true humanity of Christ, stating that Jesus had a human body and soul but not a human spirit; bishop of Laodicea; heretic.

APOSTLE. The word may be used in two senses: (1) as an office, it denotes one who followed Christ throughout His ministry; hence, it is limited to the Twelve and, in a special way, to Paul; (2) as a gift, it may be used in a general sense as "one who is sent from." In all likelihood the gift was restricted to the twelve and to Paul.

APOSTLES' CREED. A brief summary Trinitarian and Christological belief probably from sometime before A.D. 250 designed to protect the church from heresy.

AQUINAS, THOMAS (1224-1274). A prominent Roman Catholic theologian of the thirteenth century who stressed the necessity of reason in faith.

ARIANISM. The belief founded by Arius that denied the eternality of Christ, stating that Christ had been created by the Father. Arius was condemned by the Council of Nicea in A.D. 325.

ARMINIANISM. A doctrinal system formed by Jacobus Arminius (1560-1609) as a reaction to Calvinism in the Netherlands. These beliefs were later affirmed in the five points of the Remonstrance: (1) conditional election based on God's foreknowledge; (2) unlimited atonement; (3) although man has a free will he cannot save himself; (4) prevenient grace, which enables man to cooperate with God in salvation; (5) conditional perseverance—believers can be lost.

ATHANASIUS (A.D. 296-373). The great defender of the deity of Christ against the heretical teaching of Arius.

ATHEIST. Derived from the Greek components *theos*, meaning "God," with the *a-* prefix negating the statement; hence, "one who does not believe in God."

ATONEMENT, LIMITED. Also called "definite" or "particular," this view emphasizes that Christ died only for the elect.

ATONEMENT, UNLIMITED. The view that Christ died for everyone but that His death is effective only in those who believe the gospel.

ATTRIBUTES OF GOD. The distinguishing characteristics of God that set Him apart and through which He reveals Himself to mankind.

ATTRIBUTES, ABSOLUTE and NON-ABSOLUTE (RELATIVE). Absolute attributes (e.g., spirituality, self-existence, immutability) describe the perfections of God that He has in Himself, independent of anyone or anything else. Relative attributes (e.g., eternity, omnipresence, infinity) are so named because they are related to time and space.

ATTRIBUTES, INCOMMUNICABLE and COMMUNICABLE. Incommunicable attributes are those found only with God (e.g., eternity, omnipresence, immutability). Communicable attributes are those which, at least in some degree, are also found in man (e.g., wisdom, justice, truth).

ATTRIBUTES, NON-MORAL (NATURAL) and MORAL. Non-moral or natural attributes are those perfections of God that do not involve principles of right or wrong (e.g., infinity, omnipotence, omnipresence). Moral attributes involve principles of right or wrong (e.g., holiness, righteousness, truth).

ATTRIBUTES, INTRANSITIVE (IMMANENT) and TRANSITIVE. Intransitive attributes, like incommunicable attributes, are those found only in God, unrelated to man (e.g., self-existence, life), while transitive attributes, like communicable attributes, are those which relate to man (e.g., truth, mercy).

AUGUSTINE (A.D. 354-430). Augustine is sometimes called the greatest theologian between Paul and Martin Luther. Augustine stressed the total depravity of man and the grace of God.

AUGUSTINIAN VIEW. Named after Augustine, this view teaches that all mankind participated in Adam's sin since each person was seminally present in Adam (cf. Heb. 7:9). All human beings, therefore, are charged individually with sin and death.

B

BAPTISM OF THE SPIRIT. The work of the Holy Spirit in placing the believer into union with Christ as the Head and with other believers as the Body of Christ.

BARTH, KARL (1886-1968). A German theologian who rejected his liberal training and returned to a study of the Bible. He published his Romans commentary in 1919, considered the beginning of neo-orthodoxy. Barth taught that the Bible becomes the Word of God only as the reader enters the experience of the biblical writers. He denied general revelation but was perhaps the most conservative of neo-orthodox theologians.

BIBLE. The English word comes from the Greek word *biblion*, meaning "book" or "roll." The Greek word is derived from *byblos*, the papyrus plant from which the writing materials for ancient manuscripts were made. Eventually *biblia* came to signify all the books of the Old and New Testaments.

BIBLICAL THEOLOGY. The term can be used in several ways. (1) It is used to describe the modern movement within liberalism that emphasized the exegetical study of the Scriptures while retaining the liberal methodology. (2) It is used to describe an exegetical methodology that considers the historical circumstances and development of a doctrine. In Old Testament biblical theology, consideration is usually given to different periods of doctrinal development and to the unifying theme, whereas New Testament biblical theology considers the theology of the individual writers.

BONHOEFFER, DIETRICH (1906-1945). Bonhoeffer, a German theologian, rejected the idea of "sacred" and "secular," emphasizing the need for "worldly discipleship." It is not entirely clear what Bonhoeffer meant about religionless Christianity, but the radical theologians carried his ideas to an extreme end. Despite his controversial theology, Bonhoeffer must be admired for the fearless commitment of his doctrine and practice of Christian discipleship. He was imprisoned and eventually executed for his opposition to the Nazi regime.

BRUNNER, EMIL (1889-1966). A pioneer in neo-orthodoxy, Brunner emphasized the subjective encounter in meeting God while denying the inspiration of Scripture and the historicity of Adam. In accepting general revelation, he disagreed with Barth.

BULTMANN, RUDOLF (1884-1976). Developed "form criticism," the attempt to discover the literary forms and sources in Scripture. Bultmann stressed the need to "demythologize" the Scripture—to strip away the layers of myth with which the early church had embellished Scripture.

C

CALVIN, JOHN (1509-1564). A Swiss Reformer who stressed man's depravity and the necessity of God's grace and predestination in salvation. He became a prolific commentator and the church's first scientific interpreter.

CALVINISM. A doctrinal system expressed in the following five points formulated by John Calvin. (1) total depravity of man; (2) unconditional election; (3) limited atonement; (4) irresistible grace; (5) perseverance of the saints. The sovereignty of God is central in Calvinism.

CANONICITY. A term used relative to the sixty-six books of the Bible, indicating they have passed the tests used to determine their inspiration and inclusion in the body of sacred Scripture.

CHURCH. Means "a called-out group." The term may refer to a local church (e.g., 1 Thess. 1:1) or the universal church, all who have believed from Pentecost until the Rapture. The universal church is also called Christ's Body (Eph. 1:22-23).

COMMERCIAL THEORY. A theory of Christ's atonement formulated by Anselm of Canterbury (1033-1109). It taught that God was robbed of His honor through sin. Through His death Christ restored God's honor and received a reward, which He passed on to sinners.

CONGREGATIONAL. A form of church government in which the authority is vested in the congregation as in Baptist, Evangelical Free, and independent churches.

CONSUBSTANTIATION. The Lutheran view of the Lord's Supper, which teaches that the body and blood of Christ are present in the elements but the elements do not change.

CONTEMPORARY THEOLOGY. As used in this volume, the study of the doctrines of Christian groups as they have developed within the twentieth century.

COSMOLOGICAL ARGUMENT. The argument affirming the existence of God. Cosmological comes from the Greek word *kosmos*, meaning "world." Because the world exists, it must have a maker (God), because something does not come from nothing.

COVENANT. A covenant is an agreement between two parties. A bilateral (conditional) covenant is an agreement that is binding on both parties for its fulfillment (e.g., Mosaic). A unilateral (unconditional) covenant, although an agreement between two parties, is binding only on the party making the covenant (e.g., Abrahamic, Palestinian, Davidic, New).

COVENANT THEOLOGY. A system of theology teaching that God entered into a covenant of works with Adam, who failed, whereupon God entered into a covenant of grace, promising eternal life to those who believe. Covenant theology affirms there is one people of God called true Israel, the church (in contrast to dispensationalism, which teaches there are two people of God, called Israel and the church).

CREATIONISM, IMMEDIATE. The view that God's work in creation was without use of secondary causes or processes. The earth, theuniverse, and man himself were brought into being instantaneously by the Creator. The term *creationism* is also used in Christian anthropology. It refers to the view that the origin of each human being's soul is by direct divine creation rather than by generation of the parents. *See* Traducian Theory.

CREATIONISM, MEDIATE or PROGRESSIVE. The view that God created the world, the universe, and man himself over a long period of time and through secondary causes that could have included evolution. It is somewhat like theistic evolution.

CRITICISM, FORM. A method of Scripture analysis that builds on source criticism in attempting to understand the collection and editing of the materials used to make up the books of the Bible.

CRITICISM, HIGHER. A method of Scripture analysis concerned with the matter of dating and authorship of biblical books through studying the underlying sources used in the writing of Scripture.

CRITICISM, HISTORICAL. A method of Scripture analysis that seeks to discover what actually happened in the biblical narrative by studying the narrative, extra-biblical materials, and the possibility of miracles actually happening. An element of skepticism is inherent in this methodology.

CRITICISM, LOWER. A method of Scripture analysis that is concerned with the text of Scripture through the study of variant readings of the manuscripts.

CRITICISM, REDACTION. A method of Scripture analysis that builds on form criticism in attempting to understand the work of a final editor in theologically shaping a book of Scripture according to his theological views.

CRITICISM, SOURCE. An analytical attempt to discover the underlying sources used in writing the gospels.

CULLMANN, OSCAR (b. 1902). A historicist theologian who viewed the importance of Scripture to be its "holy history" or "salvation history" (*heilsgeschichte*), not its propositions nor its words.

D

DAVIDIC COVENANT. An unconditional covenant in which God promised David he would have: (1) a *house*—a continuing dynasty; (2) a *kingdom*—Messiah would one day rule; (3) a *throne*; (4) an *eternal rule.*

DAY OF THE LORD. A term that can be used: (1) of any judgment of God in history; (2) of God's judgment in the Tribulation period; (3) of the blessings in the millennial kingdom; (4) of the entire period from the beginning of the Tribulation to the end of the millennium.

DEACON. A New Testament church office denoting someone who has spiritual maturity (1 Tim. 3:8-13) and who cares for the material needs of the needy in the congregation (Acts 6:1-6).

DECREE(S) OF GOD. Stressing the sovereignty of God, the decree (all aspects of God's plan named as a unity) or decrees (all aspects of God's plan named as a plurality) of God states that God, apart from any decision of man, has planned and appointed everything that happens.

DEISM. The belief that although God exists, He is an impersonal God, uninterested and uninvolved in the world.

DEMONS. Angels who fell with Lucifer when he rebelled against God.

DEPRAVITY. A term used to refer to the corruption of sin extending to all people and affecting the entire person–his intellect, emotions, and will– so that nothing in the person can commend him to God.

DEVIL. The highest ranking angel Lucifer, who fell from prominence and is now the "slanderer" who accuses believers before God. *See also* Satan.

DIALECTICAL THEOLOGY. Another term for neo-orthodoxy in which truth is sought through paradoxical statements. In modern times this was first formulated by Søren Kierkegaard. Examples of the paradoxical statements are the transcendence and immanence of God, Christ as God and man, God as a God of wrath and mercy. It is in the crisis of facing the contradictions that a person is saved, where *yes* and *no* meet.

DICHOTOMOUS. The view of man's nature that says he consists of two parts: body and soul.

DICTATION THEORY. The theory that God dictated the actual words of Scripture to the writers, who wrote them down in a passive, mechanical fashion.

DISPENSATIONALISM. A system of theology recognizing different stewardships of man under God. Dispensationalism was popularized by C. I. Scofield, with later refinements. Dispensationalism is distinguished by: (1) consistent literal interpretation; (2) clear distinction between Israel and the church; (3) the glory of God as God's ultimate purpose in the world.

DOCETISTS. An early Christian sect that affirmed the deity of Christ while denying His humanity.

DOGMATIC THEOLOGY. As used in this volume, the study of the doctrines of Christian groups throughout church history, as they have been systematized within exclusive hermeneutical boundaries.

E

EBIONITES. A sect in the early Christian church that denied the virgin birth and deity of Christ, teaching instead that Christ was only a human prophet.

ELDER. A New Testament church office, denoting someone who is older and spiritually mature (1 Tim. 3:1-7) and who provides spiritual leadership in the local assembly.

ELECTION. Comes from a compound Greek verb *eklego* meaning "from" (*ek*) and "to gather, pick out" (*lego*) and describes God's sovereign act of choosing some individuals for salvation.

ELOHIM. A Hebrew name for God that emphasizes His strength, power, and superiority over all other so-called gods.

EPISCOPAL. A form of church government in which the authority is vested in bishops as in the Methodist, Episcopal, and Roman Catholic churches.

EUTYCHIANISM. A view formulated by Eutyches (c. A.D. 378-454) that taught that Christ had only one nature, not truly divine or truly human.

EVOLUTION, ATHEISTIC. An anti-supernatural approach to biological life origins, teaching that all life has evolved from a single cell through natural processes and chance over billions of years into the highly developed forms we see today.

EVOLUTION, THEISTIC. A theological system that teaches that God guided the process as plants, animals, and the human race have gradually evolved from lower forms of life over millions of years.

EX NIHILO. Means creation "out of nothing." It refers to God's creating the world without any pre-existing materials.

EXAMPLE THEORY. A theory of the atonement that teaches Christ's death was an example of obedience rather than a substitution for sin.

EXEGESIS. A word derived from the Greek term *exegesis* meaning "to draw out" or "to explain"; hence, the explaining of a passage of Scripture.

EXISTENTIALISM. A neo-orthodox expression emphasizing the spiritual encounter of man with God; it stresses the personal experience or commitment in contrast to simply believing facts or creeds.

F

FALL OF MAN. The historic event described in Genesis 3 in which Adam disobeyed God with the result that sin and death entered the human race (Rom. 5:12).

FEDERAL VIEW. The view that Adam is the federal head or representative of the human race. The entire human race is charged with sin, not because all mankind participated in the first sin, but because Adam was the representative of the human race.

FILIOQUE CONTROVERSY. The *filioque* (meaning "and son") controversy relates to the question "who sent the Holy Spirit?" The Eastern Church taught that only the Father sent the Spirit, while the Western Church taught that both the Father and the Son sent the Spirit. The issue permanently split the two wings of the church in A.D. 1054.

FORGIVENESS. The legal act of God in removing the charges against the sinner because atonement for the sins has been made.

FUNDAMENTALISM. A conservative system of theology which, historically, has held to five major tenets of the faith: (1) miracles of Christ; (2) virgin birth of Christ; (3) substitutionary atonement of Christ; (4) bodily resurrection of Christ; (5) inspiration of Scripture. Fundamentalism stood opposed to liberalism and modernism. In recent decades fundamentalism split into evangelical and separatist fundamentalist camps.

G

GAP THEORY. The theory that there was an original creation and fall causing the created world to become chaotic through God's judgment. A gap of perhaps millions of years followed (between Gen. 1:1 and 1:2), whereupon God refashioned the earth in literal twenty-four hour days.

GENERATION OF CHRIST. The miraculous act of the Holy Spirit who came upon Mary supernaturally (Luke 1:31, 35), caused her pregnancy that produced the sinless humanity of Christ.

GIFTS, SPIRITUAL. The "grace gifts" that are sovereignly given to believers by the Holy Spirit at the moment of salvation as a special ability for service to God and to others, particularly believers.

GNOSTICISM. A second century dualistic heresy that stressed the importance of philosophical knowledge (Gk. *gnosis*) for salvation. Gnosticism taught that a series of emanations of deity come forth in which a lower God, the God of the Old Testament, created the material world and was in conflict with the higher, supreme God, who could not have association with the evil, material world.

GOVERNMENTAL THEORY. A theory of the atonement formulated by Grotius, teaching that through His death, Christ made a token payment to God, who set aside the requirement of the law, forgiving sinners because His government had been upheld.

GRACE, COMMON. God's unmerited favor to all mankind in providing sunshine, rainfall, food, and clothing. It may also denote God's withholding judgment and restraining sin.

GRACE, EFFICACIOUS (IRRESISTIBLE, SPECIAL). God's sovereign work in effectively calling some to salvation. None of those whom God calls can reject His call; hence, it is also termed *irresistible grace*.

H

HISTORICAL THEOLOGY. As used in this volume, the study of the doctrines of the Christian religion as they were progressively debated, modified, and articulated by individuals and groups throughout the centuries since the end of the apostolic era.

HISTORY OF RELIGIONS. A view that saw the Bible as the product of a religious evolutionary process, the Hebrew faith and Christianity developing not as a result of divine revelation, but from a source common to other religions.

HISTORY, THEOLOGY OF. Developed by Wolfhart Pannenberg, this doctrinal system stressed the necessity of the historical events of Scripture, particularly the resurrection of Christ. The source of authority is history rather than Scripture.

HOPE, THEOLOGY OF. A theology developed by Jürgen Moltmann. Influenced by Marxism, Moltmann taught a theology of revolution and social change by the church's confronting society's injustices. Liberation theology has its roots in Moltmann's theology.

HYPOSTATIC UNION. A theological expression that refers to the dual nature of Christ. God the Son took to Himself a human nature, and He remains forever true God and true man—two natures in one Person forever. The two natures remain distinct without any intermingling; but they nevertheless compose one Person, Christ the God-Man.

I

ICONOCLAST. Someone advocating the destruction of images.

ILLUMINATION. The ministry of the Holy Spirit in enlightening the believer, enabling the believer to understand the Word of God.

IMMANENCE. The contrast to transcendence. God condescends to enter into personal fellowship and live with those who have repented of their sins and trusted His Son for their salvation.

IMMENSITY OF GOD. God's quality of transcendent greatness and supremacy in relation to the smaller size of angelic and human individuals. This quality is developed further by (but is not identical to) the term *omnipresence. See* Omnipresence.

IMMINENT. Means "ready to take place" or "impending." Generally used in theology for the view that the rapture can occur at any time; no prophecy remains to be fulfilled before the rapture.

IMMUTABILITY OF GOD. God cannot and does not change.

IMPECCABILITY. The view that Christ could not have sinned.

IMPUTATION. Means "to place on one's account" whether as a charge or a credit. The three biblical concepts of imputation are: the sin of Adam is *charged* to all humanity; the sin of all humanity is *charged* to Christ; Christ's righteousness is *credited* to all who believe on Him.

INCARNATION. Meaning "in flesh," the incarnation defines the act wherein the eternal God the Son took to Himself an additional nature, humanity, through the virgin birth. By that act Christ did not cease to be God but remains forever fully God and fully man—two natures in one Person.

INERRANCY. The teaching that since the Scriptures are given by God, they are free from error in all their contents, including doctrinal, historical, scientific, geographical, and other branches of knowledge.

INFRALAPSARIANISM. This term (also called *sublapsarianism*) comes from the Latin words *infra*, "below" and *lapsus*, "fall," hence, it is the view that God decreed election after the Fall. The order of the decree is: create man, permit the Fall, elect some to eternal life, provide Christ to redeem the elect, send the Spirit to save the elect, and sanctify all the redeemed. This view teaches limited atonement.

INSPIRATION. The act of the Holy Spirit in which He superintended the writers of Scripture so that, while writing according to their own styles and personalities, they produced God's Word written, authoritative, trustworthy, and free from error in the original writings. The English word *inspiration* is the KJV translation of the Greek term *theopneustos*, meaning "God breathed" (2 Tim. 3:16).

INSPIRATION, CONCEPTUAL. The view that the concepts or ideas of the biblical writers are inspired but not the words of Scripture. God gave the concepts to the writers who wrote in their own words; hence, there may be errors in Scripture.

INSPIRATION, DYNAMIC. The view that the Holy Spirit motivated the writers of Scripture, yet they had freedom in writing, allowing the possibility of error. This view is sometimes equated with the *partial inspiration* theory.

INSPIRATION, NATURAL. The view that there is nothing supernatural about the Bible; the writers wrote the Scriptures with human insight and skill as other authors would produce other fine books.

INSPIRATION, PARTIAL. Means that parts of the Bible are inspired, but not necessarily all the Bible. Revelatory matters pertaining to faith and practice are inspired, but non-revelatory matters such as history and science may be in error.

INSPIRATION, VERBAL PLENARY. The view that the inspiration of Scripture extends to the actual words (verbal) and to every part of the entire (plenary) Bible. In past usage verbal plenary inspiration was equated with *inerrancy*.

J

JUDGMENT SEAT OF CHRIST. The place or occasion for the divine evaluation of the faithfulness of Christians' lives resulting in the giving or withholding of rewards (2 Cor. 5:10). The judgment seat occurs in the heavenlies while the Tribulation is taking place on earth.

JUSTIFICATION. Comes from a Greek concept meaning "to declare righteous." It is a legal act wherein God pronounces that the believing sinner has been credited with all the virtues of Jesus Christ. Whereas forgiveness is the negative aspect of salvation meaning the subtraction of human sin, justification is the positive aspect meaning the addition of divine righteousness.

K

KENOSIS. The word, taken from the Greek term *kenoō* in Philippians 2:7, means "emptied." The emptying of Christ was not setting aside His deity but the humiliation of taking on human form and nature to fulfil the service of God.

KIERKEGAARD, SØREN (1813-1855). Danish philosopher and founder of existentialism who emphasized an experiential encounter with God through a "leap of faith." Kierkegaard provided the foundation of neo-orthodoxy on which men like Barth and Bultmann would build.

KINGDOM. The normal use of the term *kingdom* denotes a dominion or physical sphere of rule involving a ruler, a people who are ruled, and a physical territory where the rule takes place. *See also* Theocratic.

KÜNG, HANS (b. 1928). A Roman Catholic theologian who denies the deity of Christ and embraces liberalism; questions papal authority.

L

LAW. Usually a designation of the law that God gave to Moses. The law can be divided into: (1) civil law, which legislated the social responsibilities with their neighbors; (2) ceremonial law, which legislated Israel's worship life; (3) moral law, found principally in the Ten Commandments, which identified God's timeless standards of right and wrong.

LIBERALISM. An antisupernatural approach to Christianity and the Bible that arose because of rationalism. Liberalism denied the miraculous element of the Scriptures, stressing the importance of reason; whatever disagreed with reason and science was rejected.

LIBERATION THEOLOGY. A system of theology influenced by Jürgen Moltmann and Marxism, and emphasizing social concerns, particularly in Latin America where people have been oppressed. Liberation theology includes black theology, which is similar in emphasis.

LOGOS. The most usual Greek term for "word" or "reason." It is used in the prologue of John's gospel (1:1, 14), in other places of John's writings, and in early Christian literature as a name for Jesus Christ, who is the personal expression of the thoughts of God to man.

LORD. The covenant name for God in His relationship with Israel (Ex. 6:2-3). *Lord* translates the Hebrew letters YHWH, which should probably be read Yahweh. The name YHWH is probably derived from the Hebrew verb "to be," suggesting God is the eternally existing One.

LUTHER, MARTIN (1483-1546). The most prominent leader of the Protestant Reformation, who was excommunicated from the Roman Catholic church because of his persistent efforts to change some of the church's doctrines and customs. He taught that the Bible alone, apart from church tradition, had authority to declare what was to be believed. In salvation Luther stressed justification by faith alone, apart from the works of law.

M

MARCION. A second-century heretic who rejected all Scripture except ten of Paul's epistles and part of Luke. He distinguished between the Old Testament creator God, whom Marcion considered evil, and the God of the New Testament, who revealed Himself in Christ.

MARRIAGE OF CHRIST. An event involving the wedding of the church to Christ that takes place in heaven prior to Christ's return to earth.

MARRIAGE SUPPER. A celebration on earth by repentant Israel in honor of the marriage of Christ and His millennial kingdom.

MARTYR THEORY. *See* Example Theory.

MEDIATOR. An agent who mediates between two parties. Christ mediated salvation between God and the human race (1 Tim. 2:5). Human leaders such as Abraham and Moses mediated God's will to the people.

MESSIAH. Taken from the Hebrew word *meshiach*, meaning "anointed," and equivalent to the Greek word *christos* (also meaning "anointed"). It is a title of Jesus, designating Him as the Anointed One of God.

MILLENNIUM. The word *millennium* is derived from the Latin words *mille* meaning "a thousand," and *annus* meaning "year"; hence, a period of "one thousand years." Although the concept of the millennium has its foundation in the unconditional covenants of the Old Testament, Revelation 20:4-6 specifically mentions that Christ will reign on earth for a thousand years following His return to earth.

MODALISM. The anti-trinitarian view that states there is only one person in the Godhead, variously manifested in the form or *mode* as Father, Son, or Holy Spirit. Also called *Sabellianism* and *Modalistic Monarchianism.*

MONARCHIANISM, DYNAMIC. Belief in the absolute unity of the Godhead thereby denying the deity of the Son and the Spirit. This view teaches that the logos isan impersonal power present in all men but particularly in the man Jesus, who was an extraordinary human but not deity.

MONARCHIANISM, MODALISTIC. An anti-trinitarian view that is also called *Modalism* and *Sabellianism. See* Modalism.

MONTANUS. An second-century thinker who taught that the end of the world was near and that he was the spokesman through whom the Holy Spirit was now speaking, giving new revelations. His doctrines were rejected by orthodox leaders.

MORAL INFLUENCE. A view of Christ's atonement in which Peter Abelard (1079-1142) denied the substitutionary atonement of Christ. Abelard taught that Christ's death demonstrated God's love, thus influencing sinners to repentance.

N

NEO-EVANGELICALISM. A movement within evangelical Christianity originally led by Harold J. Ockenga, Carl F. H. Henry, and others. It emphasizes social responsibility while rejecting the fundamentalists' separatism. Some neo-evangelicals deny inerrancy.

NEO-LIBERALISM. Following liberalism's failure with the advent of World War I, neo-liberalism rejected the optimism of liberalism and generally held to a higher view of the Bible and Christ, taking a more serious view of sin. Nonetheless, Harry Emerson Fosdick and other neo-liberals who followed maintained the essential beliefs of liberalism.

NEO-ORTHODOXY. Means "new orthodoxy." Most historians say that neo-orthodoxy began in 1919 with the writing of Karl Barth's commentary on Romans. Neo-orthodoxy sought a return to a serious study of the Bible because of liberalism's failure. Neo-orthodoxy stresses an experiential encounter with God and retains many of liberalism's beliefs.

NESTORIANISM. The view taught by Nestorius (d. A.D. 451) that acknowledged the human and divine natures of Christ, but denied the union of the two natures, teaching Christ was two persons.

NEW COVENANT. An unconditional covenant in which God promised to provide for forgiveness of sin (Jer. 31:31-34). The death of Christ is the foundation of forgiveness, and its ultimate fulfillment will be in the future millennial kingdom.

NICEA, COUNCIL OF. The first ecumenical council, which met in A.D. 325 to resolve the Arian controversy. The council upheld the deity of Christ, affirming Him to be "true God from true God."

NIEBUHR, REINHOLD (1892-1971). Rejecting his liberal background, Niebuhr was mainly involved in social justice for the working class in Detroit. He rejected the historic view of sin and was less conservative than Karl Barth and Emil Brunner.

NOAHIC COVENANT. An agreement God entered into with Noah wherein God gave directives for the transmission, provision, and protection of the human race. Man was to procreate to fill the earth; he was allowed to be carnivorous, and the death penalty was imposed for murder.

O

OMNIPOTENCE. That quality of deity that means God is all powerful and can do anything that is consistent with His nature.

OMNIPRESENCE. That attribute of deity that means God is everywhere present in His totality at the same time.

OMNISCIENCE. That characteristic of God that means He knows all things actual and possible whether past, present, or future.

ONTOLOGICAL ARGUMENT. The argument for the existence of God that since man can conceive of the idea of God, therefore God must exist.

P

PALESTINIAN COVENANT. An unconditional covenant in which God promised to restore the repentant nation Israel to the land that was unconditionally given to her (Deut.30:1-10).

PANENTHEISM. Whereas pantheism says that God and the cosmos are coextensive, panentheism claims that God is greater than all things and contains all things within (*en*) Himself.

PANTHEISM. Derived from the Greek words *pan*, meaning "all," and *theos*, meaning "God," hence, one who believes that everything is God and God is in everything.

PARACLETE. A title meaning "one called alongside." It is used only by the apostle John to refer to the Holy Spirit (John 14-16; translated "Comforter" [KJV], "Helper" [NASB], and "Counselor" [NIV]), or to Jesus Christ (1 John 2:1; translated "Advocate" [KJV, NASB], and "one who speaks . . . in our defense" [NIV]).

PARTIAL RAPTURE. The view that not all believers but only those who are watching and waiting for Christ will be raptured.

PECCABILITY. The belief that Christ could have sinned, even though He never did.

PELAGIANISM. The view taught by Pelagius that every soul was created directly by God and therefore innocent. Man, therefore, had the ability to initiate salvation by himself.

PERSEVERANCE OF THE SAINTS. The Calvinistic doctrine of the believer's security. Those whom Christ chose and died for are eternally secure in their salvation; they can never fall away or be lost once they are saved.

PERSONALITY. The intellect, emotions, and will, which is characteristic of a personal being.

POLYTHEISM. Derived from the Greek words *poly*, meaning "many," and *theos*, meaning "God"; hence, "the belief in many gods."

POSTMILLENNIALISM. Popular in the nineteenth century, this view holds that the world will become progressively better with the ultimate triumph of the gospel. Christ will return after the millennium. It is presently being revived in "Christian Reconstructionism."

POSTTRIBULATIONISM. The belief that the church will be on earth during the Tribulation; it will not be raptured away.

PREDESTINE. Means "to mark out beforehand" and refers to God's determining in eternity past whatever comes to pass in history (Eph. 1:11); in salvation it means God marked out certain people to salvation in eternity past (Eph. 1:5)

PREMILLENNIALISM, DISPENSATIONAL. A form of premillennialism teaches that the church will be raptured before the Tribulation when God will again focus on Israel in His plan for the world. Christ will return at the end of the Tribulation to rescue Israel and establish the Millennium. Identified by: (1) a consistently literal interpretation and (2) a distinction between Israel and the church.

PREMILLENNIALISM, "HISTORIC." A form of premillennialism that is generally posttribulational. This view has many similarities to amillennialism in that Israel and the church are not seen as completely distinct at all times. The millennial kingdom is not restricted to a thousand years. It began in heaven at the first coming of Christ and continues at the second coming of Christ.

PRESBYTERIAN. A form of church government in which the authority is vested in elders as in Presbyterian and Reformed churches.

PRETRIBULATIONISM. The belief that Christ will rapture the church before the Tribulation.

PROCESS THEOLOGY. A theology identified with Alfred North Whitehead, John Cobb, Schubert Ogden, and Norman Pittenger. It teaches that God is impersonal and by applying the evolutionary concept suggests God is subject to change. The supernatural and miraculous is denied.

PROCESSION OF THE SPIRIT. The act of the Holy Spirit in proceeding forth on Pentecost at the direction of the Father and the Son.

PROPHET. A mediator or spokesman between God and men who received direct revelation from God, revealing God's will to man.

PROPITIATION. Comes from a Greek concept meaning "to appease or to atone" and stresses that the holiness of God was fully satisfied, His wrath appeased, and His righteous demands were met through the atoning death of Christ.

PROTEVANGELIUM. The first announcement of the gospel in the Scriptures (Gen. 3:15), declaring that God would send a Redeemer who would defeat Satan.

Q

Q. The designation taken from the German word *quelle*, meaning "source." It is the symbol for the hypothetical document that purportedly was a common source for writing the gospels.

R

RANSOM THEORY. The view, developed by Origen, that Christ's death was a ransom paid to Satan since he held mankind in bondage.

RAPTURE. Means "caught up" as in 1 Thess. 4:17, referring to Christ's return in the air (not to earth) and the sudden catching up of the church to be with Him.

RECAPITULATION THEORY. The view of redemption, taught by Irenaeus, that Christ redeemed man by experiencing all phases of Adam's life and experiences.

RECONCILIATION. Through sin man was alienated from God, but through Christ's death peace with God, and salvation itself, was made possible for all who believed in Jesus.

REDEMPTION. Comes from several Greek terms that cumulatively mean "to set free by the payment of a price." It emphasizes that through His death, Christ set the believer free from enslavement to sin.

REFORMED THEOLOGY. Distinguishes Calvinism from Lutheranism and Anabaptist theology. Reformed theology developed confessional statements espousing the Calvinistic position; it also embraced covenant theology, identifying one people of God (in contrast to dispensationalism which recognizes two people of God—Israel and the church).

REGENERATION. The work of the Holy Spirit in giving life to the believing sinner, effecting the new birth.

REMONSTRANCE. A doctrinal statement embodying the teachings of Jacobus Arminius. *See* Arminianism.

RENAISSANCE. The "new birth" of intellectualism, 1350-1650, which marked a trend toward secularism, rationalism, and skepticism, focusing attention on man rather than on God.

REVELATION. Means "unveiling" and describes the unveiling or disclosure of truth from God to mankind that man could not otherwise know.

REVELATION, GENERAL. The truths God has revealed about Himself to all mankind through nature, providential control, and conscience.

REVELATION, PROGRESSIVE. The piecemeal divine unveiling of truth throughout the ages until the completion of the Bible. God did not reveal truth about Himself all at once but revealed it in "many portions and many ways" (Heb. 1:1).

REVELATION, SPECIAL. The divine revealing of truth through Jesus Christ and through the Scriptures. In contrast to general revelation which is available to everyone, special revelation is available only to those who have access to biblical truth.

ROBINSON, JOHN A. T. (b. 1919). Current British theologian who has popularized Paul Tillich's theology in *Honest to God*, combining it with elements from Dietrich Bonhoeffer and Rudolf Bultmann

ROMAN CATHOLICISM. Semi-Pelagian theology, teaching the authority of church tradition, the authority of the Roman church as the repository of truth, and the authority of the papacy. The sacraments (of which there are seven) are essential in salvation, beginning with baptism.

S

SABELLIANISM. An anti-triniatrian view that is also called *Modalism* and *Modalistic Monarchianism*. It was named after a third-century theologian named Sabellius. Unitarianism is a modern form of this doctrine. *See* Modalism.

SACRAMENTS. The term *sacrament* usually refers to a formal religious act commanded by Christ that is sacred as a sign or symbol of spiritual reality. Protestants sometimes prefer the designation "ordinances." Protestants generally hold to two ordinances: baptism and the Lord's Supper. Some Protestant groups believe in additional sacraments such as footwashing, the holy kiss, and the *agape* (a fellowship meal connected with the Lord's Supper). Roman Catholicism holds to seven sacraments: baptism, confirmation, confession, holy communion, holy orders, matrimony, and anointing the sick.

SALVATION HISTORY. A school of religious interpretation within liberalism that emphasizes the activity of God in history. It retains the presuppositions of liberalism in emphasizing "holy history"—God's divine acts as recorded in a fallible book. The emphasis is on God's acts in history, not the words recording the events. This system allows for errors in the Bible.

SANCTIFICATION. Comes from a Greek verb meaning "to set apart." It is used in two ways: (1) the believer is positionally sanctified; he stands sanctified before God; (2) the believer grows in progressive sanctification in daily spiritual experience.

SATAN. Meaning "adversary," Satan is a literal creature who once was a highranking angel but fell from prominence as a result of His rebellion against God. He now is the leader of an innumerable host of fallen angels (demons) in his opposition to God and God's people. *See also* Devil.

SCHLEIERMACHER, FRIEDRICH (1763-1834). Termed the "father of modern religious liberalism," Schleiermacher stressed the importance of "feeling" and subjectivity in experiencing God. He rejected the historic doctrines of the virgin birth and the substitutionary atonement of Christ.

SCHOLASTICISM. A movement in monastic schools that sought to defend the faith through a rationalistic point of view in the eleventh and twelfth centuries. It stressed existing beliefs of the church rather than attempting to discover new truths.

SCRIPTURE. Comes from the Greek word *graphe*, meaning "writing." The Old Testament writings were categorized by the Jews into three groups: Law, Prophets, and Psalms (or Writings). These three categories denote the entire Old Testament Scriptures. The word *Scripture* includes the sixty-six books of the Old and New Testaments.

SEALING OF THE SPIRIT. The act of God in giving the Holy Spirit to the believer at salvation as a sign of God's ownership.

SECOND COMING OF CHRIST. Distinguished in dispensationalism from the rapture, the second coming refers to Christ's return to earth following the Tribulation, to establish the millennial kingdom.

SEMI-PELAGIANISM. The view stressing both the grace of God and the free will of man. Man is seen as contributing with God in salvation. This view is embodied in Roman Catholicism.

SIN. A transgression of the law of God; missing the mark of God's standard for all people, i.e. the holiness of God as seen in Jesus Christ.

SOCINUS (1539-1604). Denied the Trinity, deity of Christ, and the substitutionary atonement. Socinus also denied man's depravity, teaching that people have the ability to avoid sinning. Socinus was unitarian in belief.

SOTERIOLOGY. From the words *soterion*, meaning "salvation," and *logos*, meaning "word"; hence, the discourse or study of "the doctrine of salvation."

SOVEREIGN. With reference to God, it means that God is the supreme ruler and authority, that He ordains whatever comes to pass, and that His divine purpose is always accomplished.

SUBSTITUTION. The true meaning of Christ's death because He sacrifices Himself in the place of condemned sinners to satisfy God's holy and righteous judgments against sinners. False explanations about the atonement include ransom-to-Satan, recapitulation, commercial, moral influence, accident, governmental, and example theories.

SUPRALAPSARIANISM. This term comes from the Latin words *supra*, "above" and *lapsus*, "fall," hence, the view that God decreed election and reprobation prior to the Fall. The order of the decree is: elect some to eternal life, permit the Fall, give Christ to redeem the elect, give the Spirit to save the redeemed, and sanctify all the redeemed. This view teaches limited atonement.

SUZERAINTY-VASSAL TREATY. An agreement between the suzerain (king) and his vassals (people). The Mosaic law follows the pattern of an ancient suzerainty-vassal treaty in which God, the suzerain, tells His subjects what He, as king, has done for them and what He expects of them.

SYNOPTIC. A designation from the Greek, meaning "to see things together." It is applied to the gospels of Matthew, Mark, and Luke, because they record the life of Christ in a similar manner, often using identical wording.

SYNOPTIC PROBLEM. The discussion centering on whether Matthew, Mark, and Luke wrote their gospels independent of each other or whether they borrowed from each other (or from other sources).

SYSTEMATIC THEOLOGY. The gathering and systematizing of truth about God from any and every source. Some restrict the gathering of truth for systematic theology to the Bible alone, whereas others allow for information from outside sources such as the natural and psychological sciences.

T

TELEOLOGICAL ARGUMENT. Comes from the Greek *telos*, meaning "end." The argument that because there is order and harmony in the universe, an intelligent designer must have created such a universe.

THEOCRATIC. Means the "rule of God"; hence, *theocratic kingdom* defines a kingdom under God's rule. In His theocracy God rules the earth through different mediators (such as Abraham and Moses) at different times in history. The final form of the theocratic kingdom is the earthly rule of Jesus Christ in the Millennium.

THEOLOGY. Comes from the Greek words *theos*, meaning "God," and *logos*, meaning "word"; hence, a word or discussion about God. *Theol-*

ogy is normally taken in a broad sense to signify the entire scope of Christian docrines. Sometimes it is also used as a shortened form of *theology proper*, the expression used to signify the study of the Godhead.

THEOPHANY. A physical manifestation of God. Sometimes referred to as a Christophany, a theophany usually refers to an appearance of Christ in human form in the Old Testament (e.g., Gen. 18; Judg. 6).

TILLICH, PAUL (1886-1965). A theologian who represented the radical end of neo-orthodoxy, viewing God as impersonal "Being," sin as estrangement from one's true self, and salvation as "ultimate concern."

TRADUCIAN THEORY. The theory that the soul as well as the body is transmitted by the parents.

TRANSCENDENCE. A term describing the fact that God is separated from man and above man. God is transcendent in that He is holy and man is sinful; He is transcendent because He is infinite and man is finite. God is "wholly other" than man.

TRANSUBSTANTIATION. The Roman Catholic view of the Lord's Supper, which teaches that the elements are changed metaphysically into the body, blood, soul, and divinity of Jesus Christ while retaining the physical properties of bread and wine.

TRIBULATION. The future seven-year period described in Revelation 6-19. During this period God judges an unbelieving world and His disobedient people, Israel.

TRICHOTOMOUS. A description of the composition of man as three parts: body, soul, and spirit.

TRINITY. While there is one God, there are three eternally distinct and equal persons in the godhead, existing as Father, Son, and Holy Spirit. Each is distinct from the other, yet the three are united as one God. The term *Triunity* may best express the idea.

U

ULTRADISPENSATIONALISM. Following E. W. Bullinger (1837-1913) and, more recently, C. F. Baker, ultradispensationalism teaches that there are two churches: (1) the bride church, which is solely Jewish and exists only in the transitional period in Acts; (2) the body church which includes Gentiles and which began with Paul's ministry. For this reason, some ultradispensationalists observe the Lord's Supper only, whereas others reject both the Lord's Supper and water baptism.

V

VICARIOUS. Meaning "one in place of another," this term describes the death of Christ as substitutionary—in the place of sinners.

VIRGIN BIRTH. Technically not a birth at all, this expression refers to Mary's miraculous conception of Christ through the power of the Holy Spirit, without any male participation. Not to be confused with the "immaculate conception," which is the Roman Catholic teaching that Mary herself was conceived without sin.

W

WESLEY, JOHN (1703-1791). The founder of Methodism, Wesley preached extensively, leading England in a great revival while preaching Arminian doctrine.

WESTMINSTER CONFESSION. A statement of Calvinistic theology formulated at Westminster in London, England, in 1643-1646 by over 150 English and Scottish delegates.

WORLD. Translates the Greek word *kosmos*, which means "an orderly arrangement," but is frequently used to denote the human race in hostile rebellion against God.

Y

YAHWEH. The four Hebrew letters, sometimes called the *tetragrammaton*, which constituted the name of God often pronounced Yahweh or Jehovah. *See* Lord.

Z

ZWINGLI, ULRICH (1484-1531). A sixteenth-century Swiss Reformer who stressed the ability of common people to interpret the Bible for themselves. Taught the memorial view of the Lord's Supper.

INDEX OF PERSONS

INDEX OF SUBJECTS

INDEX OF SCRIPTURES

Moody Press, a ministry of Moody Bible Institute, is designed for education, evangelization, and edification. If we may assist you in knowing more about Christ and the Christian life, please write us without obligation: Moody Press, c/o MLM, Chicago, Illinois 60610.